BOOKMARKS

David A. Weiss

This is a work of historical fiction set in the period from 1864-1907. Although events involving historical persons are incorporated, the characters, as well as their experiences, are otherwise fictional and a product of the author's imagination. Quotations from historical figures are incorporated.

"Bookmarks," by David A. Weiss.
ISBN 978-1-63868-026-0 (softcover).

Library of Congress control number on file with publisher.

Published 2021 by Virtualbookworm.com Publishing, Inc., P.O. Box 9949, College Station, TX 77842.

Acknowledgements

I GRATEFULLY ACKNOWLEDGE ALL OF THE FOLLOWING: my dear friend of more than four decades, Dr. Jeffrey Berman, Distinguished Teaching Professor of English, University at Albany-SUNY, for his invaluable critique and suggestions; Linda Hoxie, a friend from my tennis group, and Adrienne Weiss, my wonderful daughter-in-law, both of whom proofread this work and provided many excellent and incisive suggestions; Lori Weiss, my wonderful daughter, for proofreading, an abundance of invaluable suggestions and design of the cover; and my treasured wife Joyce for her constant love and support.

Quite apart from the assistance that the foregoing persons provided, each is kind, compassionate and steadfast. They exhibit the utmost character and justifiably merit and enjoy my highest esteem.

Preface

BOOKMARKS, A CHARACTER STUDY of an introspective, mathematically and scientifically oriented Black Seminole, spans nearly half a century from the middle of the Civil War to the early years of the twentieth century. During that period the nation endured enormous challenges and change. Secession of the southern states, accompanied by horrific bloodshed, threatened to shred the nation's fiber. With the country still reeling, Reconstruction wrestled with the aftermath of the war, slavery and issues of civil rights. The advent of the Second Industrial Revolution transported the country's economy from its agrarian roots to one in which new methods of production, transportation and communication delivered a wide array of merchandise to the masses. During these same decades, the science of physics embarked on a new era. Albert Michelson calculated the speed of light with remarkable accuracy. Hendrik Lorentz developed a series of contractions (a.k.a. transformations) that led to Einstein's Theory of Relativity, fracturing the seemingly inviolate principles of Newtonian mechanics. Just as the voyage of Christopher Columbus had crushed the idea of a flat earth in favor of the counterintuitive concept of individuals standing everywhere on a massive ball hurtling through space, the evolution of modern physics not only demonstrated that mass and energy are interchangeable, but also revealed that time, length and mass are a function of relative velocity, rather than absolute quantities. The new physics opened doors that dramatically altered perceptions of the universe and continue to precipitate stunning discoveries today.

Although *Bookmarks* is a work of fiction, a historical novel, when relating events from history, I have endeavored to be accurate. Occasionally the main text, as well as the accompanying footnotes, contain scientific formulae and mathematical equations. Understanding these expressions is not a prerequisite to following the story. The reader can skim or even skip these expressions and still get the gist of what is transpiring. That said, the more curious are encouraged to take a few moments to grasp the science and mathematics they encounter. Much of it involves nothing more than basic principles of algebra and geometry. The foregoing applies even when the story touches upon the Special Theory of Relativity. Where calculus and/or differential equations are invoked, the discussions are brief and, for the most part, include non-mathematical narrative sufficient to provide a general understanding of the relevant mathematical principles.

Mican Reinbow, the protagonist of *Bookmarks*, is a fictional character in no way based on any real person. His actions, words and thoughts are fictional. I have, however, endeavored to portray the settings and lifestyle of his environs in accordance with that which existed in the times and places he encounters. His scientific observations and conclusions should be analyzed and judged in the context of the knowledge that existed at the time, to wit: the particular point between 1864 and 1907 that he makes them. Mican sometimes engages in dialogue with real historical figures (e.g., Thomas Edison and Charles Steinmetz). Insofar as these figures voice substantive thoughts about science, philosophy or other subjects, in an effort to capture their views accurately, whenever possible, I have incorporated quotations from their writings and interviews.

The early chapters of *Bookmarks* suggest it might be a youthful adventure or coming-of-age story, but as Mican ages, increasing complexity demonstrates otherwise. Unlike certain of my earlier books, the goal is not to forge page-turning action. *Bookmarks* seeks to step into the shoes of a thoughtful and intelligent Black Seminole as he endeavors to find his way amidst the egregious conventions of America's post-Civil-War South.

While I have enjoyed writing all my novels, *Bookmarks* afforded me the unique opportunity to integrate aspects of history, philosophy, physics, mathematics, architecture, economics, theology, political science, social justice and law in a single work. Doing so engendered a challenge but one that was gratifying.

As the reader will quickly discover, Mican possesses an idiosyncratic personality with facets of compulsivity and perfectionism. This combination of traits, together with an extraordinary facility and fascination with numbers, shapes his behavior and ultimately, his life. His eccentricities are by no means so extreme to label him autistic, obsessive-compulsive, a savant or as manifesting Asperger's Syndrome. While he is not a gadfly—he is hardly hypercritical—Mican's analytical propensities can be annoying. His preoccupation with numbers can have the same effect. Rather than condemning his eccentricities, it is my hope that the reader will embrace his uniqueness, even view his oddities as endearing.

Certain characters in *Bookmarks* use the *n**** word. As a Caucasian who has enjoyed the benefits of white privilege, at no time should I use the execrable epithet. On an intellectual level I may be able to imagine the hurt the word imparts, but in no way can I experience the emotional pain it inflicts on a person of color. That said, I believe that specific characters in the novel would have used the word in the era and settings depicted. With the goal of authenticity and to underscore how hurtful and heinous the label can be, I have permitted my characters to utter the word.

Wonderful as America is, its history is hardly free from discrimination and injustice. *Bookmarks* explores a sampling of the nation's stains, particularly those from the 19th century. Echoes of sobs from the Trail of Tears[1] reverberate. Shadows of Jim Crow darken the landscape. Acknowledging these iniquities is not an indictment of America. Examined against the history of other nations and empires, the democratic experiment undertaken by America's forefathers has been a profound success. At its best, America has been a beacon to the rest of the world. But at its worst, America has exhibited shortcomings plaguing every society since the dawn of history. One could argue the inevitability of such failings. With human beings at the helm, utopia is a farfetched myth. Human foibles, among them power's corruptive nature, greed and ego, are ineluctable.

---

[1] *Trail of Tears,* history.com, original 9 Nov. 2009, updated 3 Jun. 2019, retrieved 21 Aug. 2019 <https://www.history.com/topics/active-american-history/trail-of-tears> stating: "At the beginning of the 1830s, nearly 125,000 Native Americans lived on millions of acres of land in Georgia, Tennessee, Alabama, North Carolina and Florida—land their ancestors had occupied for generations. By the end of the decade, very few natives remained anywhere in the southeastern United States. Working on behalf of white settlers who wanted to grow cotton on the Indians' land, the federal government forced them to leave their homelands and walk thousands of miles to a specially designated 'Indian Territory' across the Mississippi River. This difficult and sometimes deadly journey is known as the Trail of Tears." [Coveting the Indians' lands, some whites] "would do almost anything to get it. They stole livestock; burned and looted houses and towns; committed mass murder; and squatted on land that did not belong to them…By 1840, tens of thousands of Native Americans had been driven off their land in the southeastern states and forced to move across the Mississippi to Indian territory. The federal government promised that their new land would remain unmolested forever, but as the line of white settlement pushed westward, 'Indian Country' shrank and shrank. In 1907, Oklahoma became a state and Indian territory was gone for good."

David Weiss

The Declaration of Independence, a wonderful document, gloriously declared that "all men are created equal." History has manifested much of which the rhetoric promised. But the rhetoric fell short. Women were excluded from so-called universal equality. Even when the rhetoric was righteous on its face, its implementation failed to match its noble words. Slavery was blessed, not only in the South, but the North as well. Total it up, and from the nation's outset, a significant majority of the population, considerably more than fifty percent, was denied their so-called God-given, inalienable rights. Such denial inserted arduous mountains along the path that would lead the country from the Founding Fathers' embryonic experiment to the paradigm they envisioned.

Thirteen years after declaring independence, America adopted its governing document, the Constitution. Its Preamble commences as follows: "We the People of the United States, in Order to form a more perfect Union…" The fledgling nation, a conglomeration of states, often with different interests, was, understandably, far from perfect. If it had been, making it "more perfect" would have been a paradox—impossible. The language, nevertheless, merits respect. Striving for perfection is a worthy goal. That it is unattainable should never quell the effort. Unfortunately, like the days leading up to the Civil War, Americans remain bitterly divided on how to accomplish the country's aspirations. The "Grand Canyon" that separates right and left, conservative and liberal, is anything but grand. So wide is the divide that one side can't hear the other. Even if it could, deaf ears await.

The foregoing notwithstanding, Americans should strive for that perfect Union; America should continue to be a beacon to the world; and America should reach for the stars, both literally and figuratively. Whatever the future brings, Americans are blessed to live in a nation that embraces the values of freedom, integrity, compassion and equality. Though they will never be fully achieved, persistence can bring them closer.

David A. Weiss

Chapter I

IT WAS SUMMER, 1907, when I, Mican Reinbow, a Black Seminole, embarked on a journey north from my home in Fort Myers, Florida, the winter home of Thomas Edison, to Schenectady, New York, the place where the famous inventor had moved his Edison Electric Works. During the seven-plus years that had elapsed since the commencement of the 20th century, an exponential rate of change had overtaken the world. For thousands of years, progress had come at virtually imperceptible rates. With the great civilizations of ancient Egypt, Greece and Rome, advancements had emerged over spans of centuries. Following the Dark Ages, the Renaissance had launched a rebirth, accelerated progress in science and the arts, laying the foundation for the Industrial Revolution. Amidst the arrival of machines and factories, life changed in ways and at rates never seen. The locomotive, phonograph, light bulb, telegraph, photograph and many more altered the world. While some doubted that the rapid advancement could be sustained, the initial years of the 20th century belied their skepticism. If anything, the incredible rate of growth accelerated. The Wright Brothers, defying gravity, soared like birds over the banks of Kitty Hawk, North Carolina. Rumors abounded that Henry Ford, whose winter estate would later adjoin that of Edison, was about to introduce his Model T, a mass-produced automobile that would give common folks a share of the road. And Albert Einstein turned science on its head with his 1905 Theory of Relativity that, among other things, indicated mass and energy were different forms of the same thing ($E = mc^2$).

Roughly two decades had passed since I had first met Mr. Edison. Over the intervening years there were but a few occasions when I had enjoyed the privilege of spending time with him. With his hundreds of patents[2]—I had none—we were anything but equals. We ran in totally different circles. For that matter, I was not a member of any circle. Edison, on the other hand, was a celebrity, a member of the highest echelons of society. Both of us were enamored with science, but our interests differed. Edison was far more pragmatic than I. Where curiosity about the unknown was enough to sate my exploratory appetite, he demanded practical results. His many inventions and patents proved he got them. Apart from the fact that science intrigued us both and we had met several times, mentioning myself in the same breath as Edison is absurd. I had no significant accomplishments. Some viewed me as an unproductive hermit, not that I deemed myself as such.

But enough for now about my status, Edison and the state of science and innovation in 1907. Allow me to take you back nearly a half-century to the later stages of the Civil War. (The war has been known by several names, but since I knew it at the time as the "War of Secession," and the term "Civil War" only came into use years later, I will hereinafter refer to it as the "War of Secession.") The year was 1864. It is there I begin my tale and the events that took me from backwoods illiteracy into a world of scientific curiosity. As a matter of convenience, I will use the vernacular of my adulthood. Now and then, when my thoughts about motives and consequences differ from those that were contemporaneous with an event, I will include both. Draw your own conclusions. Scrutinize my objectivity or lack thereof.

It was the 11th of June 1864, when, alone in the one-room cabin occupied by my father and me, I heard a knock at the door. Twelve years of age and well prepared by my father, I peeked out the lone window in the cabin's front. A soldier clad in a blue uniform stood on the doorstep. Had it been a gray-suited Confederate Reb or other stranger, I would have slipped out through a small panel in the rear of the cabin and hidden in the woods. Even with what appeared to be a Union soldier, I exercised caution. "Who's there?" I said.

"Sergeant Thomas Wall of the United States Army."

I slid back the wooden slat that barred the door and opened it.

"You're Mican…Mican Reinbow?"

Conscious of his seeming irresolution, I nodded.

"I…I have some bad news." He briefly broke eye contact. "Your…your father was killed today."

I stood frozen, unable to say anything. I stared blankly at the soldier.

He stepped inside the cabin and put an arm over my shoulder.

---

[2] By the time Edison died in 1931, he had held 1093 patents. *Thomas Edison,* Wikipedia, 10 Jun. 2018 <https://en.wikipedia.org/wiki/Thomas_Edison>.

I bowed my head and shut my eyes, almost as if I were trying to escape the world and the horrible reality that was confronting me. Panic gripped me. My mother, of mixed race, predominantly Negro, had died when I was only three. I was all alone. In an instant, my world, the entire world, had become a scary place. Much as I wanted to shrivel up and cry, I couldn't. Catatonic, a statue, I remained motionless. The soldier, his arm still over my shoulder, was motionless as well. Whether he was providing me with some uninterrupted moments to digest the ineffable news or too unsure to react otherwise, I had no idea. I was sinking into a bottomless abyss.

Finally, the soldier said, "Your father was a very fine man."

The soothing words were a balm; yet a fruitless balm. Much as they were nice to hear, they drove me deeper into the abyss. Hope, denial, whatever…that the dreadful news might be a dream, abated.

"As I'm sure you know, your father was helping the North, the Union cause, fight the War of Secession. At Fort Myers, he was far and away our best scout. He knew these parts, every nook and cranny, better than anyone. With us soldiers coming from the North, we would have been lost without him. He was invaluable." The soldier patted my shoulder.

I opened my eyes, but my head remained bowed. Sun, slipping through the open portal of the cabin, reflected off the toes of the soldier's polished black boots. The luster stood in stark contrast to my gloom.

"We would like you to come to the fort.[3] The First Lieutenant, who asked me to convey his deepest condolences, promised we will help you."

I raised my head but said nothing. I didn't know what to say. No way did I want to leave our cabin, my home. But living alone, without my father, more than a mile from anyone, was inconceivable. I looked around the cabin. The one room, log structure, with dirt floor and limestone-mortar mixture filling the spaces between timbers, may have been unimpressive, but it was well constructed. More important, it was home and it was safe, at least it had been until moments earlier. I gazed

---

[3] *Battle of Fort Myers*, Wikipedia, 20 Aug. 2016 <https://en.wikipedia.org/wiki/Battle_of_Fort_Myers> stating: "Fort Myers had been abandoned after the Seminole Indian Wars and was re-occupied by Union soldiers in December 1863." Florida had seceded from the Union in February 1861, immediately following South Carolina's lead in January of that year. Within three months Florida had recruited 6,772 volunteers, the majority of whom "were small farmers who owned no slaves." *The Floridians: A Social History of Florida Revised 2015, Florida Under Civil Strife 1845-1865, Florida in the Civil War and Reconstruction*, Florida History Internet Center, 14 Feb. 2017 <http://floridahistory.org/civilwar.htm>.

at the fireplace, next to which lay logs of cedar, cypress, oak and palm, ready to burn and cook our meals. I mirrored the flameless ashes that lay within the brick framework. Like the sturdy woods whose remains they represented, my life had gone up in smoke.

"How 'bout it?"

"What?" I said, though I assumed the soldier was referring to his earlier offer.

"Will you come with me and stay at the fort?"

Reeling as I was from the news, any decision, let alone a major one, was all but impossible.

"It needn't be permanent. But at least for the time being."

I looked him in the eye.

"I'll help you get a few things together."

I shrugged, half-aware that I had acquiesced, though I had given neither a *yes* nor a *no*.

I ran my eyes over the entirety of the cabin. I had no idea what I should take. As far back as I could remember, I had never spent a night elsewhere. "Uh…what should I bring?"

"Your clothes…and whatever personal items you'd like."

I went to the shelf on the back wall that, along with the clothes I was wearing, was all I had. It included another pair of pants, a couple of shirts and some underwear and socks. Like our cooking utensils and some of our tools, my father had acquired the clothing by trading the pelts of animals, especially beaver, that he had hunted. I grabbed my knife, a six-inch blade with a handle nearly as long. "Can I take my fishing pole?" I pointed to the far corner of the cabin where the five-foot rod of cedar, a proud possession that I had hand-crafted, leaned against the wall.

"As long as you can carry it. If not, we'll come back for it." The soldier unfolded a couple of burlap bags that he had carried under his arm. We can put your clothes in these. He gestured toward the wall adjacent to the fireplace where various implements hung from pegs. "You won't need pots, pans, cooking utensils…tools, you name it. We've got plenty at the fort."

I went to the box that lay beneath my bed, a raised wooden platform, layered with dried palm leaves and topped with the fur of a bear. Ropes at either end and one in the middle held the coverings to the base. I slid the box out from under the bed and removed a tiny bag of stones, a collection of unusual specimens I had found in the woods and on the beaches nearby. While I assumed they were nothing more than ordinary rocks, I enjoyed collecting them. I pulled the drawstring at the top of the bag, making sure it was tightly closed. From the box, I also took a strip of wood and three pieces of rope. Out of the corner of my eye, I caught what seemed a puzzled look on the soldier's face. I said, "These are what I use to measure things."

"Measure things?"

I took the items to him, displaying first, the strip of wood. "It's a ruler, one foot long, with the inches marked off. I made it myself using my father's as a model."

"Very nice. You do good work." He eyed the pieces of rope. "Are they for measuring too?"

I held out the shortest. "This one's exactly three-feet, my yardstick. The other two are ten feet and fifty feet. I use them for measuring longer things."

The soldier nodded, though his face again showed puzzlement. "What else would you like to take?"

The exemplary dugout canoe that sat along the nearby shore of the Caloosahatchee, the one I had fashioned with the help and guidance of my father, came to mind. Lugging it was impossible. "I…I guess that's it," I said. I might have looked for other things, but with confusion and trepidations abounding, I chose the simple route. "This is just for now? I can come back to the cabin…"

"Sure." He smiled warmly. "You ready?"

I wasn't. But I wasn't ready to stay. "I…I guess."

He stuffed my things into the burlap bags. Together we carried my few items outside where his big stallion stood tethered to a stately royal palm, one my father had grown from a coconut. The soldier attached a leather strap with a loop in the middle and hooks at either end to the bags and draped the combination over his horse, affixing the loop to a clip at the rear of the saddle. He climbed up onto his horse. He pointed at the stirrup on the side where I stood with my fishing pole. "Put your foot in, and I'll pull you up."

I hesitated, looking back at the cabin. "Uh…just a minute." I laid my fishing pole down and hurried back to the structure, where I went inside. We generally left it unlocked. Still, I felt the need to bar the door. Why? I had no idea. Anyone could break in through the window. I grabbed the wooden slat and slid it through the three iron staples, two on the door and the third on the jamb. I took a last look around before slipping out the secret escape hatch in the rear. I circled around to the front where the soldier waited aboard his horse.

"All set?"

I nodded. I grabbed my fishing pole and, with the soldier's help, climbed onto the rear of the horse. I wrapped my free arm around the soldier's waist.

He jerked the reins, and the big stallion set us on our way. I glanced over my shoulder at the cabin. When would I be coming back? Would I? How would I manage without my father? The magnitude of my loss, the gravity of my circumstances, struck home. I began to cry. I struggled to suppress my sobbing, lest the soldier become aware of it. Likely he heard and felt my whimpering, but recognizing my need for private moments, gave no hint. I closed my eyes, unable to imagine how I would deal with the unknown facing me. Fear, the likes of which I could not recall, gripped me. I opened my eyes and leaned my head to the side, just enough that I could see the trail ahead. I knew it well, having traversed it countless times. Familiar though it was, I had no idea where I was headed.

Chapter II

I SLOWLY OPENED MY EYES, endeavoring to gain my bearings. Light angling through a window in the barracks where I had slept testified to morning's onset. The hay-stuffed rope bed on which I lay may have been superior to the makeshift cot I enjoyed at home, but I preferred the latter. It was mine. It was secure. It was where I belonged. I rolled over onto my back and stared upward at the rafters of the barracks' tiny alcove. I felt far from rested. For hours after the dark of night had arrived, I had tossed and turned, unable to sleep. Somewhere in the wee hours I had drifted off, a slumber that had lasted at most three hours. I climbed from bed and poked my head around the corner of the alcove.

A soldier dressed in a navy shirt and pants looked my way. "Good morning, Mican. Welcome to Fort Myers."

"Uh…thank you." I uttered the words so softly that they may have been inaudible to the soldier.

"I'm Private Jackson." He walked my way and shook my hand. "How 'bout we get you some grub?"

Not knowing the term, I shrugged. Living in the woods alone with my father, his vocabulary defined mine. Common words, particularly idioms and slang, were often unfamiliar.

"Are you hungry?"

The reference triggered a pang. I was famished. When I had arrived at the wilderness fort the evening before, I had no appetite. Enervated from the loss of my father, I had tried to escape the world. Despite encouragement, both from the sergeant who had brought me to the fort and another soldier, I had hardly eaten a bite. I had hardly spoken a word. "Uh…yes," I said halfheartedly, my reply not demonstrative of my hunger.

"Scrambled eggs, sausage and toast sound good?"

I nodded.

Private Jackson ushered me out of the barracks, across the way to the mess hall, a larger building with an array of picnic tables. He seated me at the end of one and a minute later returned with a mess kit filled with the promised items, along with a cup of orange juice. Tasty though the breakfast was, for the most part, I consumed it mindlessly. I said almost nothing. To his comments and questions, I responded with nods or at most a one or two-word answer.

"I'm really sorry about your father. He was a wonderful man."

The reference to my dad drew my interest. "You knew him?"

"Mostly by reputation. Around here, he was highly respected. Your father knew these parts better than anyone. The Everglades are a daunting maze. Most folks get lost in their winding marshlands. Your father, on the other hand, put bloodhounds to shame. Knew six ways to Sunday to get from here to there. One minute he'd be there in front of you, only to vanish in the next and sneak up from behind soon after." Private Jackson looked me in the eye. "My money says you're a chip off the old block."

Though presumably my face reflected confusion, with a second thought, the apparent compliment clicked.

"You know…like your dad. You probably know your way around these parts far better than most."

"Uh…pretty well."

"Pretty well?...Seems you're modest too. Once again, a chip off the old block."

This time the phrase needed no clarification.

"You look just like your dad, the spitting image." Private Jackson surveyed me up and down. "Muscular, you stand erect." He looked me in the eye. "High cheekbones, Roman nose and brilliant black hair. Ain't no doubt, Mican. You'll be strong and handsome, just like him."

The praise may have been a device to lift my spirits. No matter. The kudos to my father, ascription of the same to me, were welcome.

"Not to change the subject, but your English is good. I thought most Seminole-Negroes, what some refer to as Maroons,[4] speak in a unique patois, a mixture of Creole and English."[5]

---

[4] Maroons "were free blacks and fugitive slaves who forged a strategic alliance with Seminole Indians in Spanish Florida during the early 1800s." *Rebellion, FAQ on the Black Seminoles, John Horse, and Rebellion*, Johnhorse.com, 27 Feb. 2017 <http://www.johnhorse.com/Black Seminoles/faq-Black Seminoles.htm>. In the 20th century they became known as Black Seminoles.

[5] *Encyclopedia Britannica, Black Seminoles*, Britannica.com., 10 Sept. 2016 <http://www.britannica.com/topic/Black Seminoles>. "Most Black Seminoles lived

"They do. Some call it Afro-Seminole Creole.[6] But my speech comes from my parents. I speak the way they did. My mother—she was a free person, though most of her cousins were slaves—spoke English before she came here from Georgia, before she met my dad. Even after she died a few years back, my dad, maybe 'cause of her, along with the trading he did with the cattlemen and trappers, spoke mainly English. Anyway, I guess I talk the way my folks did."

Private Jackson nodded. "Makes sense."

I had never thought about it much, and to that extent my analysis was a revelation or perhaps, speculation.

"Getting back to your father…" Private Jackson fidgeted with one of his shirt buttons before continuing. "You know that your dad and the U.S. Army weren't always on the same side of things?"

About to stuff a piece of sausage into my mouth, I halted.

"Don't get me wrong. It doesn't lessen my respect for him. Matter of fact, it makes it greater. He was a man of principle, but the kind you could reason with. Anyway, his differences with the government date back to the Seminole Wars…well before I set foot in Florida."

My father had told me about the wars. There had been three. The last of them, which had ended when I was about seven, resulted in most Seminoles, including us Maroons, being driven out of Florida.[7] My father and I were among the few who remained.

"The way I understand it," said Private Jackson, "the first war occurred shortly before 1820, when the army tried to capture runaway slaves who had gone to live with the Seminoles up in what was then Spanish-held Pensacola.[8] That one was led by General Andrew Jackson. No relation to me…I assume. The second war occurred in the 1830s when Seminole-Negro slaves revolted and refused to work. The army was sent in to put down the insurrection. These days the brass is none

---

separately from the [I]ndians in their own villages, although the two groups intermarried to some extent…"

[6] Ibid.

[7] Ibid. There were three Seminole Wars: 1817-18; 1835-42; and 1855-58. *Seminole Wars*, Wikipedia, 10 Sept. 2016 <http://en.wikipedia/Seminole_Wars>. At the end of the "Third Seminole War, the government believed that only about 100 Seminoles were left in Florida."

[8] *The U.S. acquires Spanish Florida – History*, history.com, 9 Sept. 2019 <https://www.history.com/this-day-in-history/the-u-s-acquires-spanish-florida> indicating that Spain ceded the remainder of its Florida territory to the United States on February 9, 1819 in the Florida Purchase Treaty. "Florida was organized as a U.S. territory in 1822 and was admitted to the Union as a slave state in 1845."

too eager to talk about it, how the tumult ended in a stalemate, an embarrassing one for the army."[9]

My father, who was only a boy at the time of the Second Seminole War, had spoken to me about it. The bravery of his own father under the command of John Horse,[10] fighting the U.S. Army to a military draw, was a source of pride. For the Seminole-Negroes, overmatched in numbers and weaponry, it was a moral victory. For the vaunted United States Army, humiliation.

Private Jackson poured me some more juice before continuing. "The Third Seminole War—your father fought against the army in that one—occurred when growing friction between the Seminoles and the Army came to a head. The way I understand it, near the end of '58, forty Seminoles, led by Billy Bowlegs, attacked an army patrol, killing and scalping several men before looting and burning their wagons.[11] That triggered fighting that went on for well over two years until the government troops captured a number of women and children from Bowlegs' band. At that point, the parties reached a settlement. The government paid Bowlegs and another band, about seventy-five warriors altogether, five hundred dollars each, plus one hundred dollars per woman, in exchange for them moving West[12]...to the Oklahoma territory, I think."

While nothing Private Jackson had said contradicted what my father had told me about the Third Seminole War, it failed to reflect the history that had led up to that war. For years, whites, eager to plant cotton on Seminole lands, had harassed the Seminoles; looted and burned their villages; and driven them from their property. My emotional state

---

[9] *Rebellion, FAQ on the Black Seminoles, John Horse, and Rebellion*, op. cit. The Second Seminole War "was anything but a minor event. It was the largest and most costly Indian War in U.S. history—more expensive and deadly than all the famous Indian wars of the American West *combined.* The war was not forgotten because it was minor, but because it was humiliating for the U.S. Army, and in particular for the American South, whose vaunted white yeomen and gentry could not defeat the black allies of the Seminoles." (italics from original)

[10] *Rebellion*, johnhorse.com, 3 Sept. 2019 <www.johnhorse.com/Black Seminoles/synopsis.htm> stating: "[O]f allegedly African and Indian ancestry, John Horse rose to prominence during the Second Seminole War (1835-1842). [4] Several times during the conflict, his daring exploits sparked new life into the allied Seminoles resistance. By 1837, he led the black portion of the uprising in the climactic Battle of Lake Okeechobee. More than any other leader, his actions helped produce the promise of freedom that the U.S. Army extended to black rebels to close out their portion of the war."

[11] *Seminole Wars, Third Seminole War*, Wikipedia, 20 Oct. 2016 <http://en.wikipedia.org/wiki/Seminole_Wars>.

[12] Ibid.

prevented me from supplementing Private Jackson's rendition of the facts. Regardless, discretion likely would have anyway.

"Once the war ended, the soldiers left and the fort was decommissioned.[13] What happened here during the next four years, you'd know better than I."

"Not really. Anyway, as far as I know, it was nothing out of the ordinary…certainly not for my dad and me, living by ourselves in the far reaches of the Everglades." Mention of those times, coupled with the reminder that my days with my dad were history, stirred a fresh pang of melancholy. There was angst and self-pity as well. Conversation about the Seminole Wars, a brief diversion, had temporarily shifted my focus from my loss. Reality had struck again.

"It was…let's see (Private Jackson glanced upward in a thoughtful pose)…'63, when I arrived here. Once the War of Secession began, because of the fort's location along the Caloosahatchee River, not far from where it empties into the Gulf, it became strategically important again. It was on a critical Confederate supply line. All sorts of materials and goods flowed from the Caribbean islands up through the peninsula of Florida, plus a huge amount of meat came from the cattle ranches around here. The army jumped at the chance to block the Reb supplies and raid their ranches."

I shoveled some scrambled eggs into my mouth. As good as they tasted, they did little to palliate my grim circumstances.

"Anyway, when the army returned a year or so ago, they enlisted your dad's help. Word, which proved right, was that he knew the terrain better than anyone."

About to consume another mouthful, I stopped my fork inches from my lips. "He sure did."

"Yeah, the army's gonna miss him." Private Jackson winced. "Uh…course not nearly so much as you. And like I said, I'm real sorry for your loss."

Unlike Private Jackson's earlier praise that had lifted me, the remark spiraled me downward. Sating food, even the drone of uninspiring history, had distracted me from my pain. Condolences did nothing more than underscore the misfortune that had drastically altered my life. I shoved a piece of sausage into my mouth. The brown, ground-up meat mirrored my state of mind.

"You familiar with Sam Jones?"

"I know of him," I said, "not that I've met him."

---

[13] Ibid.

"When the army returned to these parts in 1862, they contacted Jones and agreed to compensate him and his little Seminole band in exchange for staying neutral."[14]

My father, who was not part of Jones' band, had told me of the promise. He had also said it had not been kept.[15] Jones had gone along with the army, not because he supported their cause, but because he disliked the South and their treatment of his people more. Hopes that they would enjoy financial gain, not that his hopes were realized, had won his commitment of neutrality.

"The vittles taste good, don't they?"

I nodded. A question that had percolated since the previous night returned to the forefront of my thoughts. Curiosity overcame reticence. "Do you know how my father died?"

"Yes and no."

Prone though I was to invoke the meaningless phrase, the response irked me, and apparently my pique showed.

"Uh…sorry, didn't mean to give you double talk. I'll tell you everything I know." Private Jackson took a deep breath, as he seemingly collected his thoughts.

I realized how difficult it was for Private Jackson to talk to me about my just-deceased father. Perhaps that helped explain why so much of his conversation had sounded like a history lesson.

"Uh…Your father was shot. An ambush…and whoever did it…got away."

My gut knotted, almost as if I could feel the bullet that had stolen my father's life. Hearing the gory details would only amplify my pain. Nevertheless, I longed for an explanation, the reason my father was gone. "Do you know why he was shot?"

"Not for sure, but we can make an educated guess. He was helping two of our soldiers reconnoiter an approach for a raid on a cattle ranch about a dozen miles northeast of the fort. The two soldiers made it back alive, though one was wounded. Best guess, cattle ranchers—they're mostly Confederate sympathizers—were responsible. Add the soldiers' blue uniforms to all the raids we had conducted, and the ranchers musta figured what the soldiers and your dad were up to."

"Where's my father now?" I knew I was asking about his body but couldn't bring myself to phrase the question that way.

"We buried him…a short distance from the fort. We have a tiny burial ground there."

---

[14] Ibid.

[15] Ibid.

I bowed my head. Tears welled up in my eyes.

"Would you like to see his grave?"

I nodded, though the upward motion was insufficient to make my head erect.

Private Jackson gestured at my nearly empty platter. "Soon as you finish your breakfast, I'll take you there."

I shoveled the final bites of food into my mouth.

He patted me on the back. "Let's go."

Without a word, we left the mess hall. A bright blue sky, stippled with a few puffy clouds, adorned the landscape. Stepping down the mess-hall stairs, the fort's amazing array of finely crafted, meticulously maintained clapboard buildings, caught my eye. Perhaps their quality had escaped me when entering earlier because the morning sun was in my eyes. More likely, downcast spirits had befogged my mind. My propensity for numbers omnipresent, I estimated the total number of buildings at fifty. Most put my cabin home to shame. Walkways, lined with fine shells, provided a stately path from here to there. Near the center of the walled complex, huge parade grounds, bedecked with an impeccably trimmed emerald lawn, still moist with dew, glistened under the canopy of the morning sun. On the parade grounds, uniformed soldiers bearing white gloves, stood in perfect lines, their polished muskets leaning against their shoulders. At the front, officers in uniforms, adorned with gold buttons and trim, issued directions.[16] The panorama, impeccable order in an Eden-like oasis, was unlike any I had ever seen. In an odd way, it was as disconcerting as it was meticulous. The ease of my familiar bucolic surroundings seemed as distant as the Moon.

We circled around the parade grounds to the fort's main gate, a sturdy array of parallel, spear-like wooden poles. We continued out to a

---

[16] F. A. Hendry, *A History of the Early Days in Fort Myers,* undated, reprinted by the Southwest Florida Historical Society (non-paginated pamphlet). F. A. (Francis Asbury) Hendry, for whom Hendry County, Florida is named and who organized and commanded a Confederate cavalry company in the Civil War, described the fort in said *History* as it appeared in 1853 or 1854. "Fort Myers in that day was a veritable oasis in the desert…[T]he forest trees of shade and beauty were then most carefully selected, dressed and trimmed to suit the most fastidious taste for natural scenery…[T]he walks…were shelled with carefully selected shell, not from the common oyster shell banks and bars, but shells from the seashore—the most beautiful. The parade grounds were the most attractive. Except the shell borders, the most beautiful grass lawn, all kept immaculately clean. The long line of uniformed soldiers, with white gloves and muskets as bright as new coin; officers too, with their golden epaulettes and burnished sidearms, their soldierly deportment drilling and exercising on these grounds, were grand and magnificent to behold."

spot about one hundred yards away, where several wooden crosses stood watch over the scrub earth. Private Jackson led me to a wooden marker. Unlike the others, all crosses, it was a "T." Carved into the horizontal crossbar was the name, "John Reinbow."

I laid my hand on the marker. As I did, I began sobbing. I ran my fingers over the carved letters. Much as I longed for my father's touch, it was as close as I could come. I knelt, perhaps hoping it would bring him closer. I buried my head in my hands, in part to hide my tears from Private Jackson. Mainly I wanted to hide from the world and the horrible turn of events. Ever since I had received the news, I was aware my father was gone, but the site of his grave etched the reality into my psyche. Looking back with hindsight, I realize the full impact of his death had not yet set in. I remained on my knees with hands on the marker for what I would estimate was two or three minutes, though my judgment of time, of anything, was too clouded to merit accreditation.

I felt the hand of Private Jackson on my back. I wiped my eyes and, after giving the marker another look, stood up.

"We weren't sure whether your dad was a Christian. We opted for a 'T.' It served double duty, a cross if he was Christian and non-denominational, if not."

My mother had come from a Christian heritage. We had her family's Bible in our home, though from what I knew, she had never practiced the religion. Perhaps the book was simply a keepsake, a connection to her and her past. In any event, my father was not a Christian, and ours was not a Christian home. His religion was founded in moral principles, not organized faith.

"The marker is fine," I said.

"You ready to go?"

I nodded.

We walked slowly back toward the fort in silence. Just before we reached the gate, I halted and said, "Why do people fight wars?"

Private Jackson looked at me blankly, seemingly ruffled by my inquiry. I stared back and waited. It struck me that the question I really wanted to ask was why my father had to die. Voicing it was too difficult.

"I don't know," he said.

"You're a soldier. You must have thought about it."

"Well, yeah, but…"

I waited. My reaction was hardly accidental. I had learned it from my father. Whenever he asked me a question, especially one that probed my conduct, he would impassively await my answer. If my reply proved unsatisfactory, his head would tilt ever so slightly or his brow might furrow. The tiny gesture communicated qualms, prodding me to examine my response.

"They fight because they disagree…you know, over land and boundaries and…"

"But why don't they talk about it?"

"It's not that simple."

"So, they have to kill each other?"

Private Jackson looked away. He shrugged.

His failure to answer my question, whether it was unwillingness or inability, frustrated me. Perhaps he knew my real question, why my father had to die. If so, his reaction made sense. There were no good answers.

Private Jackson ushered me back though the gate into the fort. He said, "I have duties to attend to. I can take you back to your barracks, where you slept last night, or, if you'd rather, you can walk the grounds of the fort."

The idea of sitting alone with my thoughts within four small walls was depressing. "I'll walk around," I said, not because it appealed to me, but because I had rejected the alternative.

"Fine, but understand, you best not go into any of the buildings, since a number of them are off limits. Once you get to know which are open, you'll be able to come and go more freely." Private Jackson headed off.

I gazed at the array of wood-frame structures. I began walking aimlessly among them. A few were like our home, built directly from logs, but most were framed with boards. The vast majority were well maintained, neatly stained in brown. Two smaller ones, far from the parade grounds, were ashen, the effects of weather showing. I paused and leaned against a hitching post. I yearned for my father. I yearned for our cabin. Back there I knew who I was. I was comfortable in my skin. Challenges that pervaded the world beyond our isolated plot were absent. Life there may have been physically hard, but emotionally it was safe. Unlike a white man's fort, it was familiar and secure. I knew what to expect. In the reaches of the Everglades, my skin, brown with the slightest hint of red, was of little moment. Thrust into the world beyond, the likelihood that my race would play a major role in my life became patent. Admittedly the secluded life with my father bore its headaches. Pretending that it was perfect would be disingenuous. There were the days when my father consumed too much of his homemade fermented corn beer. Though never prone to violence, he became a sloppy drunk, falling all over the place. His disconsolate mornings that followed were equally ugly. But with him gone and an alien world replacing that which

I knew, craving my former life, idealizing it, was inevitable. Being consigned to a foreign setting governed by those who three times had taken up arms against people like me was a demoralizing departure from my known, predictable and safe world.

I felt myself spiraling downward. Wishful thinking, contemplation of my misfortune, was a recipe for anguish. Distraction, while far from a panacea, was my friend. Living in the wilderness of the Everglades, spending countless hours alone, I had become adept at occupying myself. I constantly observed my surroundings and nature, trying to ascertain how and why things happened. I counted this and calculated that. Numbers intrigued me. When I was ten, my father had told me there were 5,280 feet in a mile. Unable to visualize that distance, I took my one-foot stick and used it to make and measure my ten and fifty-foot ropes. Armed with the longer piece, I laid it out end to end over one hundred times. I notched trees at one-quarter, one-half and three-quarters of a mile, as well as an entire mile. Repeatedly walking the distance, the quantity, as well as its fractions, grew progressively less abstract.

Just months before my father died, while at the Gulf of Mexico shore, I wondered how many grains of sand there were on the beach. At the time I viewed it as a matter of curiosity, plus a chance to fill my wealth of solitary time. Over the years I've realized that a third element, compulsivity, was at play. I chose a spot where the beach extended about one hundred feet from shore. Using my 50-foot measuring rope and a stick, I scratched an area 100' x 100' into the beach. My goal was to count all the grains to a depth of one inch. From another stick that I squared off, I put together four pieces in a square, one inch on each side, and one-half inch high. I marked the inside in five equal levels. I laid the tiny, four-square vessel on a board and filled it with sand up to the first marker. I then lifted the vessel leaving the sand behind. I began to count grains, but realizing it was a virtually endless process, I divided the pile into two. I brushed one of the two piles off the board and split the other in half. I repeated the process eight more times. It left me with a pile that was only $\frac{1}{2} \times \frac{1}{2} \times \frac{1}{2} \times \frac{1}{2} \times \frac{1}{2} \times \frac{1}{2} \times \frac{1}{2} \times \frac{1}{2} \times \frac{1}{2} \times \frac{1}{2} = \frac{1}{1024}$ of the original pile. I proceeded to count the number of grains in the remaining pile. It took a long time, but for me it was far from tedious. I multiplied the result by 1024 and that result by ten to find the number of grains in one cubic inch. I multiplied that result by 144 (12 × 12), the number of cubic inches in a section one-foot square and one-inch high. I then multiplied the result by 10,000 (100 × 100), the number of square feet in a section one-hundred-feet square. I don't recall the result, mainly because it was a number much larger than billions, the largest for which

I then knew the name. While admittedly my method was far from precise, it gave me a decent estimate and, more importantly, satisfied my boundless curiosity, as well as my compulsive propensities.

I gazed at the array of buildings that comprised the fort. I walked among them, counting each. By the time I had finished, I had counted fifty-seven. Whether I had missed one or two or counted some twice didn't matter. Distraction, not accuracy, was my goal.

Chapter III

ALONG WITH FIFTEEN OTHERS—I HAD COUNTED THEM—I sat in the last row of the one-room schoolhouse, located near the northeast wall of the fort. Except for two children of the fort's officers and two who were orphans like me, all the students were offspring of families who had sought refuge from Confederate persecution. They ranged in age from five to sixteen. The room included twenty wooden desks, five rows of four facing a larger teacher's desk, along with a blackboard covering about one-half of the front wall. My desk, like all but the teacher's, had a seat attached to the writing area, which included an inkwell at its upper right corner. Each desk also had a slate about one-foot square and a copy of McGuffey's Reader.[17]

The teacher, Mrs. Seward, the wife of a Florida farmer whose family had come to escape Confederate oppression, called on a girl, whom I guessed to be about eight.

"Mary, please continue on page fifteen."

With flawless ease, the girl read: "This horse eats hay. The hay is on the ground. Hay is made of grass."[18]

"Mican, please continue where Mary left off."

At the sound of my name, I froze. Not a word did I utter.

---

[17] McGuffey, William Holmes, *The Eclectic First Reader for Young Children*, (Cincinnati, Truman and Smith, 1836), retrieved from *McGuffey Reader's World*, mcguffeyreaders.ipower.com website, 2 May 2017 <http://mcguffeyreaders.ipower.com/1836_original.htm>. McGuffey published his first reader for young children in 1836. Originally with four readers, two were added in 1840. In 1879, he published an entirely new edition of readers. *McGuffey Readers*, Wikipedia, 2 May 2017 <http://en.wikipedia.org/wiki/McGuffey_Readers>. McGuffey's books sold over 122,000,000 copies. William Holmes McGuffey, Wikipedia, 2 May 2017 <http://en.wikipedia.com.org/wiki/William_Holmes_McGuffey>.

[18] McGuffey, *The Eclectic First Reader for Young Children*, Lesson III at p. 5, op cit.

Mrs. Seward waited several seconds. “Mican, do you know the place?”

I shook my head. I knew the alphabet and could write my name. Read, I couldn’t.

Mrs. Seward eyed me. Whether she was put off or wanted to avoid embarrassing me more my first day in class, I couldn’t say. She called on another boy who read something about a horse, I think. What exactly, I don’t know. I was too busy trying to be invisible.

Mrs. Seward called on numerous others. Each time I held my breath for fear she might give me another opportunity. And each time, with misery begging company, when someone else’s name was called, I hoped the reader would duplicate my silence. No such luck. Even the worst readers negotiated their portions, albeit with help. The content of what they read passed vacuously through the auditory holes in my head. One thought dominated my mind. I’m the only one unable to read. Finally, Mrs. Seward instructed the class to continue reading silently. She started toward the back of the room in my direction. I bowed my head, longing to hide, hoping she would go elsewhere. Once again, no luck.

“Mican,” she said in little more than a whisper, “Can you read?”

I shook my head.

“I didn’t mean to embarrass you earlier, especially on your first day.”

At a loss for words, I shrugged.

“Do you know the alphabet?”

I nodded.

“Don’t worry. It won’t be long before you’ll be reading like the others. In the meantime, I won’t put you on the spot.”

“Thank you.”

She smiled and headed back to the front of the room. I heaved a sigh, one of relief. What moments before had seemed an ordeal eased. Mrs. Seward was not my enemy.

About fifteen minutes elapsed when Mrs. Seward directed several of the older students to read independently. The rest of us were told to take out our small blackboards and chalk. On the blackboard at the front of the room, she wrote the following problem: 16 × 21. She said, “Raise your hand, once you know the answer.”

I raised my hand.

“Yes, Mican. Can I help you?”

Though her question seemed curious, I said, “336.”

Eyes wide, Mrs. Seward stared at me. The rest of the class turned and stared as well.

I kicked myself, incredulous that I had again made a spectacle of myself.

"That…That's right," said Mrs. Seward. "How did you get the answer so quickly?"

Most of the class, independent readers included, were staring at me.

For an instant, I froze, unsure if I was being ridiculed or lauded.

"Mican, please tell us how you arrived at your answer."

"Well…ten times twenty-one is 210. Six more 21s is 126. Add that to 210, and you get 336."

A beaming Mrs. Seward nodded slowly. "Students, I believe your newest classmate is a whiz with numbers."

I felt a rush. Minutes earlier, a doltish hermit crab exposed on a sunlit beach, I was the bright ray that beamed from above.

"I'm going to put several more multiplication problems on the front blackboard," said Mrs. Seward. "Please do them silently at your desks on the left side of your blackboards, saving just your answers on the right side. Once you have finished, you may go outside for recess, during which I'll go around and check your answers. Those of you who have been reading independently may go outside as soon as someone completes the multiplication."

I zipped through the problems in no time. I looked around. No one had gotten up. No way would I, at least until others had. A couple minutes went by before a boy, about fourteen, headed out the door. A minute later, a girl did too. As inconspicuously as possible, I followed. Once outside, I spotted the two who had left ahead of me. Each was balancing a stick on the tip of a finger. I found a stick. I was about to place it on my finger, but second thoughts halted me. Might the duo think that by copying their behavior, I was mocking them? I headed off to my right about twenty yards in the opposite direction from the pair. I knelt and, after breaking off about a one-foot twig from my stick, began drawing with it in the dirt. I made a circle. I drew a line down the middle, dividing it in half. I drew another splitting it into quarters. Why?—because I didn't know what else to do. Using my foot, I scratched out the circle, so that it was all but invisible. I carved a square into the dirt and drew one diagonal. I was about to add another when a voice from behind drew my attention.

"Whatcha doing?"

I turned and observed a girl about my size, a shade over five feet.

"Uh…nothing." I glanced at my scrawl, conscious of my absurd response. "Uh…just drawing in the dirt."

"Can't believe how fast you did that multiplication in your head. You must be mighty good with numbers."

I shrugged.

"By the way, I'm Abbey Parker."

"Nice to meet you, Abbey."

She gave me a funny look and, after waiting a couple of seconds, said, "Aren't you going to tell me your name?"

"Uh…sorry." An embarrassing sense of stupidity negated the esteem I had enjoyed a moment before when she had praised my mathematical prowess. Like the classroom, I had gone from dullard to genius in a flash, but this time, in reverse order. "I'm Mican…Mican Reinbow."

"Mican…that's a…uh…nice name."

"Thank you," I said, though I wondered if the compliment was sincere.

"Did you and your family just arrive at the fort?"

"My dad—he was a scout for the army—was killed the other day. My mom died when I was very young."

"I…I'm sorry." Her abashed expression suggested her response related as much to her inquiry as my circumstances.

"It's not your fault." The words no sooner leapt from my tongue than they echoed in my ears. *Why would I even suggest such a thing?*

"I know, but…"

She was seemingly having as difficult a time with our conversation as I. In my case, it made sense. Living out in the woods, I rarely talked to girls. For that matter, most of the time, I rarely spoke with anyone apart from my father. The thought, a reminder that I would no longer have his company or the security of his aegis, triggered loneliness, along with trepidations.

"You'll be living here in the fort?"

"I guess so…based on what they've told me."

"I think you'll find it's good…well, for a fort. And our teacher, Mrs. Seward, is nice."

I nodded, not so much from agreement as an inability to fashion a verbal response. I took note of Abbey's heart-shaped face, decorated with high cheekbones, turned-up nose, blue eyes and blond hair. Add her dazzling smile, and she was pretty…very pretty. I said, "Thank you for coming over here and joining me."

"It's the least I could do. Being part of a military family—we've moved around more than once—I know what it's like to be an outsider. Kids can be cliquey…and worse yet, mean. Some go out of their way to exclude newcomers, rather than welcome them. After the loss you've suffered, no way should you be put through that." Abbey looked me in the eye. "If there's anything I can do to make you feel more comfortable here, just say so. It would—"

The ring of a bell drew our attention. Mrs. Seward stood in the schoolhouse doorway, brass bell in hand.

"Our recess is over," said Abbey. "Time to go back inside." She headed toward the door, and I followed. I returned to my seat in the last row. My palms were sweaty. I looked over at Abbey who was seated one row to my right, near the front. I was glad she had joined me outside. Given my circumstances, I needed friends. But something more was going on. I gazed at the long locks that draped the back of Abbey's head. Rays of sun shining through a window on her side of the room glistened on the silky strands. A part of me felt confused.

***

For the balance of my first day in school, my attention repeatedly drifted. Normally well focused, my brain was fickle, shifting unpredictably. At times I heard what Mrs. Seward said. Often, I did not. At times my gaze was focused on her. But just as frequently, I was staring off into space, longing for my father. Other times I was staring at the back of Abbey Parker's head. When first she had joined me during recess, I had found her cute. Nicely proportioned, she exhibited hints of the adult female form. Back inside the class, from the rear of the room, her face was invisible, but my mind, its precipitous vagaries holding sway, easily conjured her portrait, a sublimely beautiful canvas.

With the end of the school day near and everyone working silently at their desks, Mrs. Seward asked me to come forward. I nervously negotiated the path, so I stood in front of her desk.

"You're very good at math," said Mrs. Seward.

"Thank you."

"With a little help, we'll teach you to read."

Behind me someone said, "I'd be glad to help."

Even before I glanced over my shoulder, I recognized the voice.

"That would be very nice, Abbey." Mrs. Seward turned to me. "Abbey is an excellent reader, well beyond her age level. Let me introduce you to her."

"I met her at recess."

Mrs. Seward smiled.

Perhaps she was percipient. More likely, my attribution to that effect was spurious.

Mrs. Seward glanced at the large, round clock that hung from the wall to her right. "We still have fifteen minutes until school lets out.

Abbey, you may push a chair next to Mican's desk in the back row where you can help him with the first lesson in McGuffey's reader."

Abbey grabbed her book, and we headed to the back. She opened to page one, the first lesson. She said, "Can you read any of it?"

I shook my head. My brain was boggled. My heart was racing.

Pointing at each word, she read: "'Here is John.'"[19] She turned to me. "Now you do it."

"Here is John," I said, merely echoing what I had heard a moment before.

"Good, but more slowly. Point at the words as you say them. Try to learn them, so when you see them again, you'll recognize them. That's how you'll learn to read."

My finger traversing the words at a pace that matched a deliberate cadence, I said, "Here is John." Memory of the phrase remained the basis of my recitation.

Abbey moved her index finger along the second line as she very slowly read: "'There are Ann and Jane.'" With her finger still on the page, no more than an inch from mine, she turned my way. "Let's see you read it."

With my focus directed to our hands, which were all but touching, absent was the echo that had guided me to a successful reading of the preceding line. I stared at the first word: *There.* I recognized all the letters, but I had no idea how to pronounce it. It was strikingly similar to the first word in the first sentence. I said, "Tŭ-here," using two syllables.

"Good try, but together the letters 'T' and 'h' are pronounced 'Thŭ.'" She said, "The word is *There.*"

I looked at the book, first at *Here*, and then, *There*. "Wow...this is hard."

"I assure you. It'll get easier. Let me read the line to you again." She read it more slowly than before, putting her finger on each word. "Now you try it."

This time I had listened and watched intently. I had made sure to memorize it. I read it back to her, pointing as I did, though relying on memory, more than reading skills. As I finished the last word, *Jane*, I noted its spelling, slowly reciting the letters. I turned to Abbey. "How do you spell your name?"

"A-b-b-e-y."

I repeated the letters and said, "Now I can spell your name."

"Then you're ahead of me."

---

[19] Ibid. The first two lines of Lesson I of *The Eclectic First Reader for Young Children* are as follows: "Here is John. There are Ann and Jane."

I gave her a look. “You’re making fun of me.”

“No, I’m not. Earlier you told me your name, *Mee’-can,* but I’m unsure how you spell it.”

“M-i-c-a-n,” I said, thankful there was one word I could already spell.

“Oh, the second letter is ‘i.’ Did I say your name incorrectly?”

I shook my head.

She pronounced it again: “*Mee’-can,*” after which she spelled it with an “i.” “Do I have it right?”

“Yup.”

“It’s a nice name.” She gestured at the book. “Try reading the first line again.”

“‘Here is John.’” I pointed at the words.

“Now read the second.”

Only one minute removed from a successful rendition, it should have been easy. I messed it up. Abbey helped me with it again.

“Don’t worry,” she said. “I struggled just like you when I started. I promise it’ll quickly get easier.” The warm smile that punctuated her encouraging words mitigated my self-consciousness.

We managed to do one more line before Mrs. Seward excused the class for the day.

“Time to go,” said Abbey. She got up from her seat.

I glanced at the book. The possibility that after an intervening night, with the lines forgotten, I might embarrass myself, kept me in my seat. “I think I’ll read what we’ve done a few more times.”

“Good for you…See you soon.”

“See you too…Oh, and thanks.” Whether she heard my belated expression of appreciation, I couldn’t say. She was already on her way to the door. I watched her every step. The instant she disappeared from view, I looked at the reader, but instead of the words on the page, I whispered, “Abbey.” I spelled her name, repeating the appellation several more times. I heaved a sigh. Tempted though I was to drift deeper into glorious reverie, trepidations that I might forget what I had read prevailed. I focused on McGuffey’s and read the first three lines over and over. Then I jumped around reading the words randomly, until I was sure I recognized each. Once satisfied, I put my book away, got up from my seat and headed out the door. I looked upward. A blue sky dotted with puffy clouds greeted my gaze. I strolled along, adjacent to the fort’s wall. A gentle zephyr caressed my cheeks. I inhaled the invigorating scent of pine. I briefly closed my eyes. “Abbey, Abbey, Abbey,” I uttered. Again and again, I whispered her name, a seemingly magical key loosening the shackles of my otherwise grief-stricken mind. Did it set me free, vanquish my pain? Definitely not. But these new emotions, a delightful distraction, were a welcome haven from the sepulchral world into which fate had thrust me.

Chapter IV

SATURDAY MORNING, THE DAY AFTER MY FIRST IN SCHOOL, McGuffey's reader in hand, I walked along the beach adjoining the Caloosahatchee River, not far from the fort. While others decried the heat that accompanied the advent of Florida's summer, it rarely bothered me, and on that day, aided by a breeze from the waters and a mostly cloudy sky, I felt comfortable. Edging along the narrow sands that separated river and woods, I continued along. The trunk of a fallen live oak, shaded by the canopy of a larger one that still stood tall, caught my eye. I plopped down onto the log and opened my reader. The evening before, a soldier in the barracks where I was being housed had helped me decipher the last four sentences of Lesson I. Its words, all monosyllabic, were randomly listed at the end of the lesson. Out of context, they were more difficult to recognize. Much harder ones, polysyllabic, were yet to come.

Alone in the tranquil riverside sanctuary, I read Lesson I aloud. What was choppy at first, grew smooth with repetition, until I could almost recite it by heart. I practiced the list of words at the lesson's end and soon could jump from one to another recognizing each immediately. I was excited about the ensuing week when I could surprise Abbey with my progress. I was also excited, indeed more so, at the prospect of having her tutor me again. I closed my reader, gripping it firmly. A thought interjected itself. How wonderful it would be to display my new ability to my father. No doubt he would be proud. I missed him so. I needed him. Life had deprived me of my security blanket, stolen my best friend.

I closed my eyes. My brain was schizophrenic. Never had I felt such extreme feelings, rhapsodic and depressing, simultaneously. Wonderful emotions, thoughts of Abbey, the kind I had never experienced, were brewing, but sadness and pain, the worst ever, remained rampant. I squeezed my book even harder and began to weep. Big boys, twelve years old, weren't supposed to cry. I looked around, making sure that no one was near. I sobbed uncontrollably.

***

Abbey slid a chair next to my desk and sat down beside me in the last row. Except for a small group with whom Mrs. Seward was working near the front, most of the class was reading silently at their desks.

"Let's see if you can still read what we covered last Friday," said Abbey.

I opened McGuffey's to the first lesson and took a deep breath. I was strangely jittery. I read the first three lines, half by eyeing the words on the page and half from rote memory.

"That's very good."

Her approbation, her warm expression, mitigated my tension.

"Would you like to try the next sentence? I'll help you with it." Abbey leaned in closer.

I read: "'It is the first book.'" Rather than stop, I continued with the next sentence: "'Ann must keep it nice and clean.'"[20]

"Gosh, that's amazing. You've learned to read already."

I shrugged, though the blasé reaction hardly reflected my excitement.

She gave me a look, a curious one. "Were you faking last week when you said you couldn't read?"

I shook my head, recalling the mortifying moment when Mrs. Seward had called on me. "Why would I do that, humiliate myself on my very first day?"

"I don't know. But how can you read this new part?"

"A soldier in the barracks where I'm staying helped me."

"What? You doubted I'd be able to teach you?"

"No…uh…not that at all." I worried that I had offended Abbey. "I…uh…wanted to be prepared. I was eager to learn."

Abbey eyed me, appearing to weigh my veracity. "You ready for some more?"

"Okay," I said, unsure if Abbey was miffed. I turned the page. As I did my elbow came to rest against Abbey's arm. I froze. Well, I tried to freeze, but nervousness had me shaking. I might have inched away, but I didn't want to. The touch was too wonderful to forgo. Abbey must have felt it too. That she didn't break the contact made the connection all-the-

[20] Ibid., Lesson I, sentences 4 and 5.

more thrilling. I took a deep breath and read: "'John must not tear the book. He may see how fast he can learn.'"[21]

"Good. Can you read more?"

I shook my head. "That's as far as I went, apart from the list of words at the bottom of the page."

"Let's hear you read them."

I did so with ease.

"Are you ready to try Lesson II?"

I was…and I wasn't. I turned the page with my right hand, although I was lefthanded. With Abbey on my left, no way did I want to sever Abbey's touch. I eyed the first word in Lesson II. I hadn't seen it before. I opened my mouth, but nothing came out.

"Try sounding it out."

I stared at her blankly.

"Do you know how to sound out a word?"

Familiar words and rote memory had made me look like a champ. One unfamiliar word had turned me into a chump, a stupid one at that. I shook my head.

"I'll help you." Abbey pointed at the word. "Do you remember that the letters 't' and 'h' together make a 'thŭ' sound? And the last two letters, 'i' and 's,' make up the word *is*, which you already know. Put the two pairs together, and what do you get?"

"Thŭ…is," I said, with incomprehensible separation.

"This," she said.

I repeated "this" and went on to the next word. The balance of the sentence, two words I knew and two that were unfamiliar, was less than smooth, but far better than the opening word. Once completed, I read the sentence aloud again: "'This boy had a bird.'"[22] We continued on with Lesson II. Despite some struggles, with Abbey's patience and help, I got through the remaining five sentences. By the end, I was sounding out words on my own, sometimes correctly, but others not. We had finished re-reading Lesson II for the third time when Mrs. Seward asked Abbey to return to her seat.

As she got up, I said, "Thank you for helping me."

"It's fun for me."

She smiled and walked forward.

I shut my eyes, and reaching with my right hand, felt my left elbow. It wasn't Abbey's touch, but the reminder was nice. Mrs. Seward moved on to history, something about Thomas Jefferson. Exactly what, I don't

---

[21] Ibid., Lesson I, sentences 6 and 7.

[22] Ibid., Lesson II, sentence 1.

know. A different person preoccupied me. Silently, I repeated her name, a rapturous melody filling my head.

***

I had been at the fort for over a month and was making the adjustment to my new life. Helpful as the soldiers were in aiding my transition, more than anything Abbey was the key to what otherwise would have been a slower and more difficult process. My first crush was taking me to new heights, counterbalancing the loss of my father and upheaval from my home. Through most of my childhood, my emotions had maintained an even keel. Not so at the fort. Graphically depicted, the relatively flat line of my past had morphed into a curve with significant modulation. But gradually, both the frequency and depth of the troughs were diminishing.

Garrisoning the fort was Florida's second cavalry, a conglomeration of a company from the 110th Infantry, black soldiers from the 2nd United States Colored Infantry and numerous refugees.[23] Among the last group, there were both Caucasians and Negroes, the former, mostly farmers and their families escaping the abuse of the secessionists, and the latter, escaped slaves seeking asylum.[24] The stronghold was remarkably diverse, though I only made that observation retrospectively when I was older and had been exposed to the prejudice pervading the world beyond.

Hot and humid, it was a typical Florida summer day. I was at the stable assisting Grover Calhoun, who was working the stalls, putting hay into the feedbags. The medium-build, runaway slave become freedman, with expresso skin and lines etched into his timeworn face, appeared older than his forty-plus years.

"Yuz a damn good worker, Mican. Most kids yo' age do stuff half-ass."

I smiled, endeavoring to pick up my pace, one that was little more than half the rate at which Grover worked. Even so, I welcomed the compliment, knowing it was an endorsement of my effort, not a left-handed jab at my inefficiency. I said, "Watching you, as fast as you are, I feel like a slowpoke."

"With any job, yuh always get faster, once yuh get de hang. Hell, when I wuz yo' age, I wuz slower dan a turtle wid no place tuh go. 'Course, up in Tampa—dat's where I wuz befo' I came here—I didn't

---

[23] *Battle of Fort Myers*, Wikipedia, op. cit.

[24] Ibid.

rush none. It wuz my way of rebellin'. Worked just fas' 'nough tuh skip a whuppin'."

"You like it better here than Tampa?"

Grover stopped shoveling and looked at me wide eyed. "Yuh muss be kiddin'? Up in de North, Tampa, I wuz a slave, chattel of a bastard widda mean streak. Son of a bitch kept folks like me alive, jus' so he could use us, kinda like he used his mule. It wuz damn hell. Once de war broke, and I heard I could get protected if I got tuh a Yankee fort, I ran. Ran fast as I could. Befo' dat, it weren't no use. Even dem dat made it tuh de North wuz sent back.[25] And when dey wuz, der massers made an example of 'em. Next tuh dat, Hell wuz like Heaven."

"Here at the fort, your life is better?"

"Yep, it's good. I'm a second-class citizen."

His comment, a seeming contradiction, befuddled me. "I thought you said it was good."

"I did."

"But you said you're 'a second-class citizen.'"

"Sure 'nough. But leas' I'm a citizen. Dat's a whole lot betta dan chattel."

It was the second time he had used the term. I was unsure whether it was a word unfamiliar to me or a product of his inelegant diction. I said, "They treated you like cattle…like a cow?"

Grover laughed as he shook his head. "If only it wuz dat good…but no, dey treated me like chattel."

"What's chattel?"

"Property. As a slave, I belonged tuh my massa, kinda like an ole bucket…or a stick of firewood dat he could turn into smoke and ash."

The explanation erased my confusion. More significantly, it brought home the inequity, as well as the iniquity, of slavery. My naiveté, owing mainly to a sheltered youth in the unpopulated hinterlands of Southwest Florida, was evident.

"I'm glad tuh be fightin' wid de men in blue, fightin' 'gainst dem Rebs. While it don't come wid all de rights I oughta have, it's a step dat way. Like my granny used tuh say, 'A slice of bread may not be a loaf, but it beat a crumb any day.'" He looked me in the eye. "Yuh black, ain't yuh?"

---

[25] *Dred Scott v. Sandford*, 60 U.S. 393 (1857), in which the Supreme Court held that Dred Scott, an African-American slave who had lived for several years in Illinois, then the Wisconsin Territory where slavery was prohibited under the Missouri Compromise of 1820, was not entitled to his freedom. The Court ruled that under the Constitution, as enacted in 1787, slaves were chattel, not citizens, and Scott's owner rights to his property could not be taken away without due process of law.

"Sorta…I guess. I'm a Seminole-Negro. Some folks say were Maroons, though our skin is far more brown than red."

"Maroon?" His brow knitted. "Ain't never heard of nobody called Maroon." He studied my face, perhaps trying to ascertain my color. "Well, no matta. Color of a man's skin shouldn't count fo' nuttin'…leas' yuh aks me. Oughta be judged by how he goes 'bout his business…if he decent or not. Yuh git what I sayin'?"

"Yup." My spontaneous concurrence lacked thought. The complexity of his message went over my head. Having lived in solitary surroundings far from the world beyond, bigotry was more conceptual than concrete. Little did I realize that in years to come, prejudice would cross my path, and Grover's words would acquire greater meaning.

"Yuh happy here in de fort?"

I shrugged. The answer was a resounding *yes*, but an equally resounding *no*. Absurd as that was, it described how I felt. New emotions, the thrill associated with Abbey having come into my life, provided moments that took me higher than I had ever been; yet the affliction owing to the loss of my father generated painful lows. Put on a teeter-totter, the latter, the negative, outweighed the former.

"Folks here treat yuh good?"

"They've been nice." Once again, my response was spontaneous. But it instantly echoed in my head. Indeed, people at the fort, particularly the soldiers, had endeavored to ease my transition into life as an orphan.

Grover gestured at a nearby shelf where I had laid my McGuffey's reader. (I took it almost everywhere.) "Is dat a special book yuh got, like de Bible, maybe?"

"Sorta…It's my reader from school. Didn't know how to read when I came here, but I'm learning."

Grover sighed. "Damn. Wish I could read. Never got de chance. Massa didn't want us slaves tuh learn. Apt tuh beat us if he caught us widda book. Guess he figured de more we knew, de harda we be tuh control."

"Would you like to learn to read?"

Grover's eyes widened. "Could yuh teach me?"

"I'm…uh…willing to try."

"What? Yuh think I'm too dumb tuh learn?"

"No, it's not that at all. But I'm just learning myself. I'm hardly ready to be a teacher."

"But yuh willin' tuh try, ain't yuh?"

I nodded.

"Good." He tossed some hay into a feedbag. "Lez get dis hay done, and den yuh can start teachin' me."

With quickened pace, we finished the chore. I took McGuffey's from the shelf and opened it to the first lesson.

"Lemme hear yuh read," he said.

I read the first page.

"Damn. Yuz good."

"You want to try?"

His look of disbelief underscored the absurdity of my question. But teaching was not among my skills. "Do you know the alphabet?"

"A few letters…'a' and 'b' and 'c'…and 'g'. I know my name begins with 'g.'"

His response convinced me the challenge would be even tougher than I had imagined. When Abbey had begun teaching me, both teacher and pupil were more advanced. Abbey was better equipped than I to instruct, and unlike Grover, at least I knew the alphabet and how to write my name. I glanced at the first line of Lesson I: "Here is John."[26] Not one of the letters that Grover had recited was in the three-word sentence. Common sense told me I needed to teach him the alphabet first, but if I were in Grover's place, I would prefer to read, rather than learn twenty-six symbols. I focused on the four letters he had mentioned. It took a few seconds, but I came up with a word. I scratched "bag" into the dirt floor of the stable and said, "Can you tell me these letters?"

He nodded and identified each.

I pointed at each letter, making its sound: "bŭ …aa…gŭ." I made the sounds again in quicker succession and then, pointing at the entire word, said, "When you put them all together, you get 'bag.'"

Grover recited the three letters. He eyed them, and with a little help from me, made their respective sounds. He then said, "Bag."

"You got it!" I grabbed a feedbag and said, "Feed…bag." I recited the three letters of the second syllable and said "bag" again.

Grover duplicated my recitation.

I said, "Now you can read and spell the word *bag*."

He beamed.

I scratched an "a" into the dirt a couple inches to the left of the word *bag*. I pointed and said, "A bag."

Grover pointed at the dirt and said, "A bag."

"You're reading."

He pointed again. "A bag." He turned to me. "I'm reading!"

"You sure are."

"Show me mo'."

---

[26] McGuffey, p. 1, op. cit.

I thought about the four letters he knew. I scratched "gab" into the dirt. I made the sound of each letter, just as I had done with the word *bag*, and then said, "Gab."

Grover made the sounds of the letters and said, "Gab."

"You've got it!"

He nodded enthusiastically. "Mo'!"

I shuffled the four letters in my head but came up empty. I said, "To make up lots of words, you need plenty of letters. You need to know the alphabet."

"Let's do it!"

I scratched all twenty-six into the dirt. One by one I recited each, after which Grover repeated it. His enthusiasm was infectious. We had just reached "z," on what was our fifth time through the alphabet, when Grover said, "Gosh, yuh only been here fo' a few weeks, and already yuz a teacher. A real good one."

"A teacher?" I laughed. My words, my reaction, were both instinctive. But Grover had a point. I was a teacher—his teacher. And it felt good. On second thought, it felt great. A part of me recognized that my excitement was mainly owing to Grover's zeal, not my skill as an educator. But the detail failed to quell my ardor. The possibility of one day becoming a teacher crossed my mind. Though common sense suggested it was an evanescing fancy, I consciously etched the thought into my psyche to be considered at the appropriate time.

"De teacher dey got at de school here in de fort muss be mighty good."

"She is…but I've got someone else helping me."

Grover looked me in the eye, seemingly reading beyond my words. "Who yuh got helpin' yuh?"

"Just a girl in my class."

"Yuh got a twinkle in yuh eye." The pitch of Grover's voice was inordinately high. "Yuh aks me, yuh got a thing fo' her."

I felt my face flush as I shrugged.

"What's her name…de girl dat be teachin' yuh?"

"It's uh…Abbey."

Grover's eyes were watermelons. "Abbey?…Dat wouldn't be de First Lieutenant's daughter, would it?"

I nodded sheepishly.

"Well, whad'ya know?…She got a thing fo' yuh too?"

"What do you mean?" I said, though I understood his question.

"Well, plain as de nose on yuh face, yuh got a thing fo' her." Grover looked me in the eye. "Yuh can't deny it. So, de only question: Duz she got one fo' yuh?"

"I…I think maybe."

Grover patted me on the back. "Good fo' yuh…and good luck."

"Good luck?"

Grover laughed.

I waited.

Finally, he said, "De female sex. Damn…dey is great. Can't live widout 'em. But livin' wid 'em ain't no walk down easy street."

"I'm not sure what you're saying."

"Dat ain't none too surprisin'…seein' how I ain't sure myself."

The odd response baffled me. But at my age, having lived alone with my father, that was to be expected. With hindsight, however, after I had been exposed to the world beyond, the comment made perfect sense.

Grover smiled, as he appeared to study me. "I suspect wid time yu'll git what I'm sayin', but…ain't no use me tryin' tuh explain. De only way yuh gonna understand is livin' it." He gazed upward and shook his head. "Lordy be, luv is de bes'…and Lordy be, luv is…" He heaved a sigh and shook his head again.

Though his message was cryptic, I understood it better than before, at least I thought I did. It struck me too that Grover was a thoughtful person. In all probability, he was wiser than his flawed grammar and shabby diction suggested.

***

"You've mastered that thing," said Abbey, seated next to me on a log about twenty feet from the Caloosahatchee River.

"Well, when you've read it as much as I have, it's not surprising." I had been through McGuffey's First Eclectic Reader a half-dozen times.

"That may be, but I've never seen anyone learn to read as fast as you." She reached into a cloth bag she was carrying and pulled out a book. "You're ready for this." She displayed an edition of "The Eclectic Second Reader."[27] She opened to the first lesson and handed me the book. "Go ahead. Read it to me."

Even before I looked at the print, I felt the heft of the volume. I suspected it had the best part of two hundred pages, more than double

[27] McGuffey, William Holmes, *The Eclectic Second Reader; consisting of Progressive Lessons in Reading and Spelling for the Younger Classes in Schools,* (Cincinnati, Truman and Smith, 1836); retrieved from googlebooks.com, 8 Oct. 2017 <http://books.google.com>.

the reader I had been using. Nervously, I eyed the page and read: "'1. Frank, what a fine thing it is to read! A little wh…'"

"While," said Abbey.

The challenge presented by an unfamiliar book with new words had immediately become apparent. I took a deep breath and continued. "'A little while ago, you know, you could only read little words, and you had to spell them—c-a-t, cat; d-o-g, dog. 2. And you were a long time getting through with the 'First Reader.' But now you can read quite well.'"[28]

"You certainly can." Abbey smiled broadly.

I felt a warm glow. I had confronted unfamiliar text and, save for one hiccup, had negotiated it competently.

Abbey pointed at the page. "Let's hear more."

I read the four remaining sections of the first lesson with little difficulty. I continued with Lessons II, III, IV, V and VI. Occasional new words interrupted my reading, but only briefly. I was quickly back on track.

"Have you noticed," said Abbey, "that longer words are creeping in as the lessons move ahead?"

I nodded.

"And you handle them quite easily."

I did indeed. I really had learned to read.

"Can you summarize what Lesson VI is about?"

A lump filled my throat. Even though I had finished reading it seconds before, I didn't have a clue. I said, "I…I wasn't listening."

Abbey rolled her eyes.

I felt silly. But my statement was accurate. My only goal had been to recite the words that appeared on the page. What they had communicated when put together had been irrelevant.

"Knowing what you read is a critical part of reading."

My shoulders slumped. "So, what you're telling me is that I'm not actually reading yet."

"That's not what I'm saying. Just that there is more to it than recognizing the words. But don't be disappointed. Soon enough you'll take in the content. And just between you and me, lots of what I read in church passes my lips, along with those of everyone else, without a thought." Abbey looked upward toward the Heavens. "I hope the Lord isn't listening, not that I can keep a secret from him." She heaved a sigh. "Scary, the likelihood he knows my thoughts and when I'm not paying attention in church." Still gazing skyward, she pointed. "Mighty strange that we can see the Moon during the day."

---

[28] Ibid., Lesson I, p. 9.

I looked upward at what was little more than a crescent. "It still reflects the light of the Sun. It just doesn't look as bright because the Sun is out. Kinda like a kerosene lantern. It lights a place at night, but if it were lit during the day, you would hardly know."

"Yeah, that's what they told me in school, the part about the Moon, not the kerosene lantern." Abbey turned and appeared to study me. "But how did you know about the Moon and stuff?"

"What—you think the Moon didn't glow over my cabin?" I poked her in the side.

"You know that's not what I meant. But how'd you learn about the Moon, that its light is reflected from the Sun?"

"There was this man who used to trade with my dad. He'd come around about once a month, and most times he'd go fishing with my dad and me. And when he did, he told me all kinds of things about the sky and nature and everything." I eyed Abbey. "You know how far the Moon is from the Earth?"

A blank expression graced her face.

"About 240,000 miles."

Her face was no less blank.

"You don't find that interesting?"

"Uh…maybe, but I have no idea how far that is. And I'll bet you don't either."

I shrugged. "Well, yes and no."

"That's quite an answer. And I suspect it's almost all *no*."

"Well, I admit I can't really picture 240,000 miles, but I have a good idea what it is."

Abbey threw her hands up. "That's the kind of double talk I'd expect from Wilbur Ormley." Wilber was the dullest kid in the school.

"Well, let me show you, and then you can judge." I took her hand—it was the first time I had held it—and guided her down to the beach. I picked up a stick and drew a circle in the sand about three-feet wide. I said, "This is the Earth. It's about eight thousand miles in diameter. The man who traded stuff with my dad told me so, along with the other numbers I'm gonna show you." I stood alongside the circle representing the Earth and took one giant step. It took me from one side of the Earth to the other. I said, "The Earth's diameter equals one giant step, eight thousand miles. Eight thousand goes into 240,000, thirty times. So, 240,000 miles would be thirty giant steps." I headed down the beach thirty giant steps. I drew another circle in the sand, a little less than a foot wide. I said, "This is the Moon. Its diameter is a little over two-thousand miles, about one-quarter of the Earth's." After pointing at the circle representing the Moon and then the one representing the Earth, I said,

"We have a model showing the relative sizes of the Earth and Moon, as well as the distances separating them."

"Wow!"

I studied Abbey for a moment. "Are you making fun of me?"

"Not at all. I'm impressed. I doubt the older kids in our class know this stuff."

I shrugged, but my seemingly blasé reaction masked self-satisfaction.

Abbey studied my circles in the sand before refocusing on me. "Can you add the Sun to your model?"

"Uh…yes and no."

She started to throw her hands up again but froze. She muttered just loud enough to be audible. "The last time I pooh-poohed that response, my foot ended up in my mouth. Don't need to chew more leather." She looked me in the eye. "Explain this *yes and no* about the Sun."

"It's like this. The Sun's diameter is a little more than one hundred times that of the Earth. We'd need a circle that's about one-hundred giant-steps wide to represent the Sun. The beach isn't broad enough to draw it."

"Gosh, next to the Earth, the Sun is huge." She looked up into the sky. "It doesn't seem so big…especially compared to the Moon."

"That's because it's so far away."

She eyed the beach, her eyes moving from the circle I had drawn for the Earth to the one I had drawn for the Moon. "If you could scratch a circle for the Sun into the sand, where would it be?"

I chuckled.

"What's so funny?"

"The Sun is ninety-three million miles from the Earth. Just one million miles is more than four times the distance from the Earth to the Moon. Ninety-three times what we have in our scale model would be about…2800 giant steps, and four times that would be more than 11,000 giant steps…a number of miles."

Abbey's jaw dropped. "You didn't just figure that out…did you?"

I smiled broadly.

"Really?"

"No. I made this same model and did the calculations last year. Did it more than once."

"Boy, you really are smart."

"Yes and no."

She groaned. "You, with your yeses and noes…What does it mean this time?"

"I know a lot about numbers and nature and stuff like that because that's what my dad and his friend taught me. But I'm just learning to read and to write words. Most of the kids in school were doing that by the time they were six years old, half my age. Whether someone appears smart depends upon what he or she was taught and when."

"Maybe," said Abbey, "but I've never seen anyone learn to read as fast as you. And when it comes to numbers, you're faster than kids two or three years older than you. And the things you know about science and…whatever. You're definitely smart."

I was aglow.

"Aren't you going to say something?"

I longed to kiss Abbey. I didn't dare. I shrugged.

"Is that a *no*?"

"Yes."

Abbey looked me in the eye. "Do you realize you just said *yes* to a *no*?"

"Uh—" I stopped myself, before another *yes* crossed my lips. *Yes* and *no* were making me nuts. On second thought, rather than the tiny words, the culprit was Abbey.

Chapter V

NERVES ABOUNDING, I APPROACHED THE HOUSE of First Lieutenant William Parker. Having dinner at the home of the man who was second in command at the Fort Myers' stronghold was intimidating. Doing so on the invitation of Abbey, the First Lieutenant's daughter, compounded my anxiety. This was my first courting call…ever. Adding to my angst was concern that Abbey's parents might reject me because of my race. I tried to tell myself that like Abbey they would be openminded. The separation of whites and Negroes at the fort contradicted the argument.

In the week that preceded, Abbey had educated me about dinner etiquette, the location of silverware and the placement of a napkin on my lap. Much as the lessons were invaluable, they amplified my apprehension, underscoring my ignorance of social graces. In our family cabin, amidst a solitary existence in the hinterlands of Florida's Everglades, such niceties had been non-existent.

I ascended the stoop of the Parker residence. Though the two-story structure was small, at a fort where most everyone lived in shared barracks, it stood out. Next to the cabin that had been home to my father and me, it was high class. I reached for the door knocker, a brass star, and lifted it. Poised to rap it, I hesitated. I looked down at my shoes. They bore a glossy spit shine. Back in the barracks, Private Jackson had trained me in the art. He had also made certain that my trousers and shirt were neatly pressed. I took a deep breath and allowing gravity to have its way with the knocker, let it fall. It clacked. My hands, as if they had a mind of their own, sought out my pants' pockets. The instant my sweaty fingers touched the cottony fabric, I pulled them out. I stood up straighter, almost as if I had been called to attention.

The door opened. Abbey, her golden locks in curls, stood inside the threshold, a smile on her face. She wore a pink, crinoline-supported, narrow-waisted dress that hung below the knee, beneath which lacy pantaloons were visible. Gray braid trimmed the bottom hem of her frock. Sleeves puffed at the wrists and bedecked with lace adorned her arms.[29] Always pretty, Abbey was lovelier than ever. I considered communicating the thought. I only managed, "Uh…hi."

"Hi."

I stood frozen, almost as if I were a soldier waiting for the sergeant to give the at-ease order."

"Please, come in." Abbey ushered me into the parlor, where her father, a handsome gentleman with a sinewy frame, was seated on a blue velvet armchair.

"Hello, Mican. We're glad you could come for dinner."

"Thank you, Sir." With several months having passed since I had arrived at the fort, the term of respect came naturally. Indeed, I used it whenever I addressed anyone with stripes and, for that matter, any time there was a possibility it might be appropriate.

"Abbey has told us a lot about you, how good you are with numbers and how fast you've learned to read."

"Uh, thank you, Sir. Uh…most of the credit is hers. She's an excellent teacher."

Lieutenant Parker winked at his daughter before refocusing on me.

"I'm very sorry about your father. He was a fine man. He helped us greatly, especially when we first arrived here and were unfamiliar with the area."

"Thank you, Sir." The Lieutenant's sentiments were gratifying. I was happy that he was doing most of the talking.

"As I said, we're happy you can join us for dinner. It's the least we can do after what your father did for us."

"Thank you, Sir." My redundant words reverberated in my head. I longed to say something more astute, but my otherwise facile tongue was tied.

Abbey's mother, a vision of Abbey two decades hence, stepped into the parlor. "Hello, Mican. I'm Mrs. Parker, Abbey's mother. Welcome to our home."

Her arrival, an interruption of my exchange with the Lieutenant, was welcome. "Hello, Ma'am. It's nice to meet you."

"Dinner is ready." Mrs. Parker led the way to the dining room, a small room furnished with a rectangular table, four chairs and a hutch. A blue tablecloth, blue and white dishes, crystal goblets and shiny

---

[29] *Children in Costume History 1860-70 – Victorian Fashion for Girls*, fashion-era.com, 11 Oct. 2017 <http://www.fashion-era.com/Childrens_clothes/1860_1870_girls_costume_pictures.htm>.

silverware adorned the table. Lieutenant Parker and his wife seated themselves at the ends. They directed me to one side, with Abbey locating herself on the other. Never had I dined in such elegance. The luxury magnified my discomfort.

Mrs. Parker served a delicious meal…I think. I told her so, though, in truth, I ate it mindlessly, all but the apple pie with cinnamon-flavored ice cream and a dollop of whip, the most scrumptious dessert I had ever consumed. As for the rest of the meal, it was largely a blank. Lieutenant and Mrs. Parker took turns asking me questions. They were pleasant, but their queries did anything but reduce my tension. However well intended they may have been—and I believe they were—it felt like an inquisition. Now and then, I gave Abbey a glance. An occasional smile and some blank looks, along with a few words, were all she mustered. Though she appeared poised, I suspected she too might be uneasy.

Dessert had barely been finished, when Lieutenant Parker, after checking the clock that occupied a shelf opposite the hutch, said, "Reveille, as it does every morning, comes early tomorrow, and you kids have school. It's best we call it an evening." He focused on Abbey. "You want to show Mican to the door?" He turned to me. "We're pleased you came."

"Thank you, Sir…uh for having me…And thank you, Ma'am, for a wonderful dinner."

"Our pleasure."

I got up from my chair and followed Abbey to the door, a portal located midway between the parlor and dining room, no more than ten feet from the dining-room table.

As I stepped outside, Abbey whispered, "I'm sorry."

"For what?" I said, though I had more than an inkling what she was trying to communicate.

"Uh…you know." Her soft words were barely audible.

I nodded. I turned, and as I started back to my barracks, I breathed a sigh. Ninety minutes earlier when I had arrived at the Parkers' home, I was nervous. But I had told myself that once I got past the entranceway and settled in, the evening would be much easier. I really believed that I would be returning home excited, perhaps on cloud nine. Contrary to my expectations, anxiety had amplified. Joy had never manifested itself. My first exposure to courting had been hard work. Around the fort, soldiers had said that courting, the world of romance, was wonderful, but complicated, more often than not, a puzzlement. They were right on all accounts, but they had neglected to mention a critical aspect. It was terrifying.

***

The morning following dinner with the Parkers, I arrived for school several minutes early. More than two months had elapsed since I had come to the fort. Adjustment to my changed life had progressed at a remarkable rate. The speed with which I had learned to read had won me praise, not just from Abbey, but also Mrs. Seward and my fellow classmates. Their plaudits, coupled with my inherent curiosity, had turned me into a voracious reader. My progress was a vicious cycle, but one that was positive and self-sustaining.

Minutes after I entered the schoolhouse, Abbey came in, followed by Mrs. Seward moments later. As the students raced to their seats, Abbey started toward the back of the room, to the seat next to me.

"Good morning, class."

"Good morning, Mrs. Seward," we rejoined in unison.

"Be seated." She looked around the room. "Abbey, I think it best that you take your former seat, up here in the front."

"But Mrs. Seward, I always help Mican with his reading."

"That was good of you, and I appreciate that. But Mican has learned to read quite well. He no longer requires special help."

Abbey glanced at me and whispered, "I'm sorry…about last night." She sighed before moving forward with book and chalk tablet in hand.

Much as I longed to protest the modified seating arrangement, I dared not. I slumped in my chair.

Mrs. Seward went to the blackboard where she wrote several math problems. "Those of you learning division, please do these on your slates. Those who are still working on your times tables, recite them silently. Check any answers you're unsure of with the sheet on the side wall. The rest of you, please do the decimal problems I put on the blackboard. I'll come around the room and provide help where needed."

Where normally I copied the blackboard problems and determined their answers in a flash, I worked at a snail's pace. My mind remained focused on Abbey. Frustration, owing to her changed seat, simmered. Why, I wondered, had Mrs. Seward moved her? Even when Abbey had helped me with reading or I had helped her with arithmetic, we were never disruptive. If anything, we made Mrs. Seward's job easier, freeing her to assist others. She had told us as much. What had I done to cause the change? Nothing…at least nothing that I was aware of. That left Abbey. But that was even harder to fathom. She was a model student. If Mrs. Seward had a favorite, not that she ever suggested as much, it was Abbey. Over and over, I weighed the facts. Over and over, I asked myself, why was Abbey moved away from me? Could it be that Abbey's parents rejected me because of my race? The possibility galled me. Regardless, I had no choice but to wait until recess for a possible explanation.

At long last, recess arrived. I immediately started forward toward Abbey. I no sooner did than Mrs. Seward called Abbey to her desk. I hesitated, but, with no other option, headed outside. Instead of joining the others, I stayed close to the door, waiting for Abbey. Five…ten…fifteen minutes elapsed. Still no Abbey. Another five minutes passed, and Mrs. Seward rang the bell, the signal for everyone to return to the classroom. Along with the rest, I went inside.

"Take your seats promptly, so we can get back to work," said Mrs. Seward.

The instruction, delivered with characteristic finality, negated any possibility that I could stop and speak with Abbey who was already at her desk. I drifted to the rear of the room and sank into my seat, more frustrated than before.

"All of you, please take out your reading materials," said Mrs. Seward. "McGuffey's First or Second…or other book for those of you who are more advanced, and read silently at your desks."

I took out my Second Reader and opened to the page where I had left off. I read a few words…very few. I stewed. Once again, I tried to figure out why Abbey and I had been separated, but mainly I stewed. The possibility that Abbey no longer wanted to sit near me crossed my mind. But that made no sense. When she had first arrived in the morning, she had tried to take the chair adjoining mine.

About five minutes after we had begun reading—I was still on my first page—the boy in front of me slipped a small, tightly folded note onto my desk. Hiding it behind my McGuffey's Reader, which I tilted upward as a shield, I unfolded the note and read:

> Mican,
>
> I'm sorry. Meet me after school by the big oak behind the storehouse.
>
> Abbey

I read it a second time. I tried to analyze what it meant. On the positive side, Abbey had said she was sorry and that she wanted to meet me. But might the phrase, "I'm sorry," be a polite preamble to her ending our relationship? I thought about dinner at her house the evening before. My nervously voiced staccato answers to her parents echoed in my head. I had made a lousy impression. I wondered how Mrs. Seward fit into the equation. Why had she changed Abbey's seat? Explanations, I had several, but not one that was convincing. Where earlier in the school day, I had been frustrated, confusion superseded. Regardless, I realized that explanations would have to wait until after school.

***

The instant the school day ended, I was out of my seat. Impatience had me yearning to go directly forward to Abbey, but Mrs. Seward was reviewing some materials with her and several others in the room's front corner. As I walked out the door, I paused, considering whether to wait for Abbey. Judgment told me I best follow the instructions in her note. If she had a problem with me, no need to compound it. And too, the possibility existed that she had some other reason for arranging a seemingly clandestine meeting. The storehouse was at the farthest end of the fort and saw fewer people than most anywhere. The big oak behind it was as obscure a site as one could pick on the expansive grounds.

I hurried to the designated spot and seated myself alongside the giant tree that adjoined the wall encompassing the entire fortification. Five…ten minutes slipped by. I drew Abbey's note from my pocket, just to make sure I had not misconstrued the appointed time and place. Given the message's brevity and that I had read and re-read it carefully while in school, checking it was beyond redundant. More than once I peeked around the rear corner of the storehouse. No Abbey. Might she stand me up? I eyed my McGuffey's. I was in no mood to read. Another five or so minutes passed. Concern that Abbey might not show mounted. Regardless, I was not about to leave. Finally, she arrived.

"Sorry it took me so long to get here." Her countenance was somber. "Mrs. Seward enlisted several of us to organize the bulletin board and clean the blackboards."

"But why the secrecy?" Containing my impatience was difficult.

"I had to…It has to do with last night."

"What about last night?" Even as I voiced the question, scenarios, many of which I had been contemplating throughout the day, raced through my brain.

"My…my parents…" She heaved a sigh. "How should I say this?"

"They didn't like me?"

"It's not that at all."

I waited a moment. "Then what?" The edge that slipped into my voice was patent.

"They…they don't want me to spend time with you anymore."

"So, I was right. They disliked me."

"I already told you. It's not that. In fact, after you left, they both said you were very nice."

"That makes no sense." Contrary to my words, a logical explanation reared its odious head. The color of my skin was the problem. In the back of my mind, another possibility stirred. Obfuscation might be Abbey's method of pushing me away.

She took a deep breath and said, "After you left, and after they said nice things about you, my father asked whether I liked you. I said, 'Of course.' And he said, 'I don't mean that way. I'm asking whether you *like* him…really like him. Are you infatuated with Mican?'"

Her recitation of the conversation was as exciting as it was unnerving. My heart raced.

Abbey looked away. Her discomfort was palpable.

Impatience, compounded by curiosity, got the best of me. "What did you say in response to your father?"

"I…I didn't say anything. I simply stared down at my feet."

I read between the lines, at least I thought I did. Joy, tempered by trepidation, bubbled forth.

"My father waited me out. When I didn't respond, he put his hand under my chin and gently raised my head. He said, 'You're infatuated with him, aren't you?' His tone was demanding. My response, a meek nod." Abbey glanced at me, but quickly looked away. Several seconds slipped by. Finally, she said, "Aren't you going to say something?"

With my mind at two distant poles, one of elation, but the other, fear, I needed to hear what had next transpired with her father. I said, "About what?"

Abbey looked at me incredulously. "I just admitted that I'm stuck on you, and you don't say anything."

"Oh…I'm stuck on you too."

She beamed.

Our eyes, filled with yearning, fixated on one another. We inched closer. An instant later our lips met. The kiss lasted little more than a second. But brevity could not diminish its ecstasy.

As we drew apart, Abbey said, "You're the first boy I've ever kissed."

"And you're the first girl."

Abbey's face bore the rapture I felt. My brain forked back to her conversation with her father. "What did your father say once he knew you…uh…how you feel about me?"

"Nothing, at first. My mother jumped in. She said, 'It's nice that you welcomed Mican into the school and helped him after he lost his father.' No sooner did my mother praise me than her tone became stern.

'But boyfriend and girlfriend, that's out of the question!' Though I suspected the reason, I asked. My mother looked at me in shock. Before she could respond, my father said, 'Obviously, you've noticed the color of your young friend's skin. He's a Seminole-Negro. While your mother and I abhor slavery and we believe in equal rights for all people, when it comes to courting and ultimately marriage, each race needs to keep to its own. You're white and any suitors who come your way must be white.' My father gave me a look, one that I had rarely seen, but one that made it clear that his words were not open to discussion. They were the law." Abbey eyed me sheepishly. "I…I'm sorry."

"You agree with your parents?"

"No, but…"

"But what?"

"I don't know."

"That's no answer!" I caught myself, knowing it was unfair to take my choler out on Abbey. I said, "But the difference in our race causes you no misgivings. Right?"

Abbey broke eye contact.

"So, you do have qualms." My pique was evident despite an effort to curb it.

"I…I wouldn't, but…knowing how my parents feel, I…I can't help it."

"Can't help it!"

Abbey heaved a sigh. "I know. It makes no sense, but…" She shrugged.

"Do you intend to obey your parents?"

"I have no choice."

"That's not true." Even as I voiced the uncompromising response, I knew it wasn't that simple. Abbey's father, Lieutenant Parker, was the second-highest-ranking officer in the entire fort. People took orders from him. Insubordination was not tolerated. I said, "You met me here today, and you just kissed me."

"And I'm glad I did. I will cherish the moment. And yes, I had to explain to you how I feel and why I can't allow you to court me. But beyond that, I can't defy my parents." Her gaze shifted toward her feet, and she emitted a beleaguered sigh. "I apologize."

Her expression of remorse was disarming. "For what?" I said, unsure what had prompted her words of regret.

"I promised I would be your friend. And here I am, abandoning you."

I took her hand. "Don't beat yourself up, not after all you've done for me. It was your kindness that got me through those most difficult weeks when I first came to the fort. Without your help, I would have been lost. Popular as you are with all the kids, you could have ignored me. But instead, you made sure I felt welcome. For that I will always be grateful."

Abbey exhibited a slight smile, a hint she had taken my words to heart.

Mixed emotions gripped me. That Abbey felt about me as I did about her was glorious. But feelings alone with no relationship were vacuous. I yearned for a way to circumvent the roadblock. Nothing came to mind. I said, "Is this why Mrs. Seward changed your seat in school?"

"My parents spoke with her early this morning, before school. You might say she has her marching orders. And unfortunately, I have mine as well."

"Does that mean it's over between us?" If my tone was insufficient to communicate that I was begging her to say *no*, my face must have conveyed the plea.

"What can I say?"

"But you…you aren't closing the door?"

Abbey hesitated. "It was probably closed for us."

I was desperate for a flicker of hope. "But maybe…maybe we still have a chance?"

She shrugged.

Though her reaction was anything but a *yes*, I took solace that it was less than a flat-out *no*.

***

The heat and humidity of summer, with nights when one often slept in one's own sweat, had waned. Autumn, a fine time in Southwestern Florida, was well underway. But my nights had turned more difficult. Weeks earlier, even when the days of October had been inordinately hot, I had luxuriated in my bunk, succored with euphoric thoughts of Abbey. Images of her at my side the following morning, helping me learn to read, had eased the most intolerable heat. And too, they had helped me drift off into blissful slumber.

For the first few days after Abbey had informed me of her parents' ultimatum, I held out hope our relationship would resume. Knowing that she liked me as much as I liked her kept me optimistic. But as one week ran into two, and two into three, hope waned. Any contact between us was nothing more than a passing hello. Coping with my circumstances grew harder. Once again, I missed my father more. Hindsight suggests that my emotions may have been a product of self-pity. Disconsolate over the circumstances that had deprived me of my former life, I idealized it, wallowing in my inability to resurrect it.

It was Friday of the third week after Abbey and I had shared that glorious kiss. As the day progressed into afternoon, typical restlessness for the upcoming weekend pervaded the classroom. Mrs. Seward called on Andrew Varner to read aloud from his McGuffey's. Varner, who was thirteen and still mired in the First Reader, read at a level below most who were four or five years younger. With help on several words, mixed with repeated stammering, he crept through three lines before Mrs. Seward called him to a halt. She ran her eyes over the room and said, "Mary, please exchange seats with Andrew."

Mary Smith, an otherwise quiet ten-year-old, who sat next to Abbey, said, "Do I have to?"

Saying nothing, Mrs. Seward displayed an expression of finality. Mary and Andrew exchanged seats.

"Abbey," said Mrs. Seward, "Andrew could use some help with his reading. I'd like you to work with him."

Abbey exhibited no audible reaction. Whether her face showed anything, approval or disapproval, I could not tell from my seat in the back. Regardless, I was miffed. Why did this lunk get to sit next to my Abbey? What bothered me more was that he was tall, strapping and handsome. Though hardly the brightest coal in the schoolhouse stove, the girls warmed up to him.

All during the ensuing weekend, I simmered over the turn of events. It crossed my mind that Lieutenant Parker and his wife may have importuned Mrs. Seward to use their daughter as a tutor with the goal of pushing her further from me. Though admittedly no evidence buttressed the dubious idea, it intensified my pique. The more I ruminated, the angrier I became.

By Monday afternoon, having watched Abbey tutor Varner, her desk pressed tight to his, I could no longer remain passive. I had to do something. Patience and silence had failed. I needed a new approach. I dipped the pointed nib of my steel-tipped pen[30] into my inkwell and, on a small piece of paper, wrote:

---

[30] *Nib Pens – Facts and History of Dip Pens*, historyofpencils.com, 6 Feb. 2018 <http://www.historyofpencils.com/writing-instruments-history/dip-pen-history/> stating: "A metal pen point was patented in 1803 but nothing came out of it. Bryan Donkin tried to sell his patent for the manufacture of metal pens in 1811 but no one bought it. When the patent expired, in 1822, John Mitchell of Birmingham started to mass-produce steel pen nibs and their popularity took off."

Abbey,
Meet me by the big oak behind the storehouse right after school.
Mican

I repeatedly folded the note until it was less than one-inch square. I waited for an opportune moment when Mrs. Seward was preoccupied with several younger students. I handed it to the boy immediately in front of me, instructing him to pass it forward to Abbey. It worked its way to the second row, to a girl who tapped Abbey on the shoulder and gave her the note. Much as I tried, I was unable to discern Abbey's reaction. I hoped she might turn back to me and at least nod, but no such luck. Hope that she might respond with a note of her own was dashed as well.

As the minutes ticked, I reconsidered my plan. Might it be wiser to approach Abbey immediately after dismissal? The possibility that Mrs. Seward would intervene discouraged me from changing my strategy, especially since I had already sent the note. The moment class was dismissed, I hurried to the oak, where I seated myself, my back against the giant timber. I wondered if Abbey would show. I tried to guesstimate the odds. On the positive side, Abbey liked me. She had made that clear. And she herself had chosen the oak as a meeting point, even after her parents had forbidden our relationship. On the other hand, Abbey had shown no subsequent propensity to disobey her parents. Passing minutes amplified concern she might not meet me. I tried to remain positive. Perhaps Mrs. Seward had asked Abbey to stay after class. And too, she had to be careful that no one saw her sneak behind the storehouse. Her father, as the fort's first lieutenant, no doubt, had many eyes and ears. The minutes continued to tick. No Abbey. What had seemed a fifty-fifty proposition grew iffier. I opened my McGuffey's. I had already done all the lessons in the entire second reader, some more than once. I flipped to one of the last lessons. I read two lines and slammed the book closed. I was in no mood to read. I eyed the sky. Puffy white clouds, nature's mutable art, painted the azure canvas. My trusty imagination refused to conjure shapes. I simply waited. Finally, with more than an hour having passed, I stood up. I peered around the storehouse. Abbey was not in sight. I kicked the ground. I kicked it again, harder than before. That racial disparity prevented Abbey and me from having a relationship was infuriating. I stared at my arms, focusing on their pigment. Anger at an unfair world, confusion and self-deprecation fused into an overwhelming hodgepodge. A part of me sensed that the hate society propagated was entrenching itself into my psyche, impelling me into self-loathing. The perception was maddening. But emotions begging to be requited were too difficult for me to address. Burying them was easier. Shoulders slumped, I trudged back to the barracks.

Chapter VI

FOR THE BALANCE OF THE WEEK following Abbey's failure to respond to my note, I was downcast. Days in school dragged. Disquieting questions spawned sleepless nights. Why had Abbey declined to meet me? Had she wanted to, but couldn't? Was fear of her parents controlling the narrative? Might she no longer have feelings for me? Might another boy have captured her fancy?

Encumbered by the weight of another discomposed night, on Saturday morning I went to the stable seeking the sympathetic ear and counsel of Grover Calhoun. I might have sought out Private Jackson, but for two reasons: First, I feared he might report the conversation to Lieutenant Parker. Whether my concern was justified or merely irrational paranoia,[31] I was unwilling to take the risk. Second, I wanted to make a special bookmark, one that took advantage of Grover's skill in shaping gemstones into polished beauties. Armed with the tiny sack of rocks I had collected over several years, I headed to the stables. As expected, Grover was there.

"Good morning," I said, as I stepped through the open barn door.

Grover looked up from a horse he was brushing. "And mornin' tuh yuh."

"Would you have time for some talk and a little help?"

"Jus' as soon as I finish shinin' dis here fella."

I waited while he continued to brush the stallion for another minute or two.

---

[31] Harper, Douglas, *Online Etymology Dictionary*, etymonline.com website, 15 Oct. 2017 <http:www.etymonline.com/search?=paranoia> regarding the etymology of the word "paranoia" as follows: "'mental disorder characterized by systematized delusions,' 1848 (earlier paranoea 1811), from Greek **paranoia** 'mental derangement, madness…**Paranoia**, Verrücktkeit, and Wahnsinn'" (emphasis from original).

He slipped what I assumed was a sugar lump into the horse's mouth. Petting the big steed, he said, "Yuh look fine 'nough tuh be marchin' on Innapenance Day." Grover turned my way. "So, whatcha wanna talk 'bout?"

"Well…uh…"

Grover studied me with narrowing eyes. "Muss be sometin' real sticky, seein' as how yuh came down here jus' tuh say it, and yuh can't spit it out."

I took a deep breath. "It's…uh…'bout Abbey."

Grover nodded, the pronounced motion of his head more demonstrative than a simple *yes*. "Women…dat is sticky…stickier dan honey, fresh from de bees' nes'." He took a deep breath. "I glad tuh hear yuh out, but jus' so yuh know, I ain't no expert. Yuh aks me, when it come tuh women, ain't no experts. Fella could live a million years, and he still wouldn't have no answers." He waited, perhaps anticipating I would be more forthcoming. Finally, he said, "So, yuh gonna clue me 'bout yuh problem?"

"Abbey's father, Lieutenant Parker, as well as her mother, has forbidden Abbey from seeing me."

"Whoa, dat is a sticky one…Whaz Abbey say 'bout it?"

"Not much."

"But she still talkin' tuh yuh?"

"Not really. This past Monday in school I passed her a note asking her to meet me behind the storehouse. She didn't show. And she didn't say a word to me the rest of the week."

"Don't mean tuh hit yuh widda hamma, but any chance she don't like yuh no mo'? Maybe found her anudda fella?"

"I don't think that's it." As I spoke the words, I realized wishful thinking, more than evidence, was behind them. I said, "About the time that her parents nixed our relationship, she told me she was stuck on me."

"Dat's good. Real good…She say how come her parents don't wan' her seein' yuh no mo'?"

"Because I'm not white. On account of I'm a Seminole-Negro."

Grover chuckled. "Jus' as I 'spected."

I waited, hoping he would amplify the comment. When he didn't, I said, "You agree with them?"

"'Course not. But dat ain't no matta. Nobody cares what I think."

"That's not true. I care. That's why I came here."

"Yeah, yuh did, didn't yuh." Grover grew momentarily pensive. He shook his head before continuing. "Ain't use tuh folks aksin' what I think. Doin' der biddin', dat's all I sposed tuh do. Dat's how it is when yuz a slave, a no count." His mien, a canvas whose lines made him appear older than his years, again became thoughtful. Unlike moments earlier, hints of pain, long endured, seemed to emerge.

Comments my father had made about the evil of slavery bubbled forth. Much as I was aware of his view, my understanding was superficial. Amidst the freedom of our solitary home, slavery was a distant abstraction. Even so, the possibility loomed that as I had roamed the beaches of my childhood, I had long buried my head in the sand. Whether that had been occasioned by an unwillingness or lack of necessity, I couldn't say. Regardless, I had never confronted my feelings about my own mixed race. Where did I fit in? How did I feel about being a Maroon? Were issues crying for attention seething beneath my dispassionate surface? The questions begged attention. The moment was wrong. Other issues were on the table, not only mine, but also Grover's. Reluctantly, I put my concerns onto the back burner. I said, "It must have been hard being treated like dirt."

Grover shrugged.

I suspected a life of forced submissiveness, not uncertainty, precipitated his reaction. "You care to talk about it?"

"Sure, if yuh cares tuh listen?"

"Absolutely."

"How 'bout we sits down?" He motioned toward a couple of hay bales along the near wall. Once we were seated, our backs to the bales, he said, "Mo' dan forty years, e'er since I wuz born, I been owned by my massa. Ain't ne'er known nuttin' else…leas' 'til I run away and come tuh de fort las' year." He sighed. "Don't ne'er wanna go back. Dat's why I is helpin' de Yanks. Always hoped tuh be free, but as dem years flew by—saw my ma and pa die befo' der time—began believin' I might ne'er be free. 'Course, in one way, I always been free." Grover looked me in the eye. "Yuh knows what I mean?"

I was as curious as I was clueless. "Can't say that I do."

"I had my dreams. Couldn't no one steal 'em away. Fact is, weren't no one dat knew I wuz dreamin', all de while dat I wuz workin'. Dat pleased me a whole lot, knowin' I wuz puttin' one o'er 'em. Not dat it wuz near as good as real freedom, comin' and goin' when I wanted." Grover paused, appearing to study me. "Yuh got somethin' on yuh mind, don'tcha?…Yuh judgin' me?"

"Yes and no." My habit of resorting to the phrase had come from my father. He had often used it, and I mimicked him. At our cabin, *like father, like son*, the ambiguous technique, worked. Not so at the fort. Folks found my sidestep annoying. Perhaps Abbey was among them.

"Dat ain't no answer."

"Well, it is and it isn't."

Grover's brow furrowed.

I said, "You misunderstand me. What I meant was *yes* to your first question, and *no* to the second."

"Wid all yuh double talk, I ain't sure what I aks yuh…let alone two questions."

"Well, let me clear it up. The answer to your first question, whether I had something on my mind, is *yes*. And the answer to the second, whether I was judging you, is *no*." For a change, my reply of *yes and no* was responsive. Rather than a vacuous hedge, I had answered two questions.

Grover furrowed his brow. Been easier if yuh said dat right off. But befo' yuh put me back in a tizzy, what wuz it yuh had on yuh mind?"

"When you were talking about imagination and freedom, it struck me that you're quietly thoughtful—what my dad called philosophical. As he used to say, you can learn from everyone. And I was learning from you."

"Wish yuh coulda told dat tuh my massa. He always called me stupid, 'specially when he whupped me. I got de scars on my back tuh prove it, if yuh wanna see 'em." He started to pull up his shirt but halted. "Hold on. I'm gettin' carried away. Yuh come down here fo' a reason, and it weren't tuh hear me jabber like a goose. So, lez get back tuh what yuh aks me, befo' I get de runs of de mouth."

His sentence dispatched my brain on two paths: a nauseating image and a question I could not recall. "Your memory is better than mine. I don't remember what I asked."

"Yuh wanted tuh know if I agree wid Abbey's parents, 'bout der barrin' yuh from courtin' her."

"Yeah, I did ask you that." As I spoke the words, I silently lauded his ability to juggle multiple thoughts. I said, "So, do you agree with her parents?"

"Nah, I don't agree wid dem…but dat don't mean I think dey's wrong."

His inconsistency rankled me. Unfortunately, my use of *yes* and *no* answers had undermined my right to protest. Regardless, I wanted a more meaningful explanation. I said, "You can't be on both sides of the fence at the same time."

"I ain't."

I shot him a look.

"Yuh aks me if I agrees wid 'em. I don't. Color of a man's skin shouldn't matta none."

"Then you must think Abbey's parents are wrong."

He shook his head.

The seeming incongruity made me wonder if I had given him too much credit moments before.

"Lemme explain. Way I seez it, skin color ain't nuttin'. What's in a man's heart, how he treats folks, dat's what mattas…But dat's jus' my view. I gets dat lotsa folks, both white and Negro, seez it different. Dey want der chillens marryin' der own…I don't agree wid dat, but I respect it."

Though his position was not what I had hoped to hear, condemning it was impossible. It was supported by logic. What made it even harder to challenge were the echoes of my father's voice. Repeatedly he had emphasized that no one has a corner on the truth. An open mind is the doorway to greater knowledge. Grover had displayed an open mind.

"Yuh don't like my answer, and dis time yuh is judgin' me."

My gut reaction was a *no* and a *yes*, but with too much of that already, I was not about to go there. "Your answer was fine, even if it wasn't what I wanted to hear…And as far as judging you, I was. Very positively…thinking that you're open-minded. And according to my father, who was very wise, that's a wonderful trait."

"'Preciate de fine words. And 'bout what I said. Dat's how I feel 'bout chillens. But once dey growed up, dey should be free tuh marry who dey please. Dat's der freedom."

Grover's words mitigated what he had said earlier. But with Abbey and me still eons away from adulthood, the solace was minimal. I said, "You've thought about freedom a lot, haven't you?"

"Ev'ry day. Hell, when yuz a slave, it's what yuh long fo'."

"When you were in the fields working, is that what you were thinking?"

"Sorta…but my dreams wuz mo' dan dat. I 'magined what I'd do once I wuz free. Out der pickin' cotton, I kept an eye for stones, now and again, a gem. Put 'em in my pocket. Saved 'em. Back in my shack, I practiced filin' and shapin' and polishin' 'em. When Massa learned I could do it, he buys hisself some stones, semi-precious, and has me fix 'em. He give some tuh his wife and he e'en sold some. But I wuz glad tuh work on 'em. It wuz betta den dem fields. Helped me betta my skills. All de time, I wuz thinkin' ahead, tuh de day when I be free and I could have me a little bizness, makin' and sellin' jew'lry. When I hear dat Presiden' Lincoln sez we free, I seen my chance. I wuz near Tampa and I heared de North had a fort down here. Weren't nuttin' safe dat wuz closer. So, dat's where I run. Maybe if de North wins de war, my dream of a little jew'lry bizness 'll come true."

I soaked in every word.

"Whatcha thinkin'?"

"You've got a big stake in the outcome of this war."

"Lotsa folks do. Too bad dey ain't all de same."

That not everyone wanted a jewelry business was self-evident, but I suspected Grover was implying more than that. "What do you mean when you say they're not all the same?"

"Folks like my massa got a big stake. Dey need us slaves. Widout us, dey can't make der money. Dey is fightin' fo' der cotton bizness, jus' like I is fightin' tuh have a jew'lry bizness. Diff'rence is, dey's aksin' me tuh pay fo' ders. Wanna have it on my back."

War, its prudence, was rarely an easy issue. I had heard soldiers at the fort speak of the reasons for fighting the War of Secession, but this was the first time I had heard the views of a former slave. Reduced to property, his dignity stolen, his justification for fighting was undeniable.

"Damn," said Grover, "I keep yakkin'. Fo' sure, yuh had mo' on yuh mind. So, tell me."

I reached into my pocket and pulled out my little pouch. I bent down and dumped the contents onto the dirt floor.

"Ooh-ee. What's we got here?" Grover knelt and studied the twenty or so stones that were spread before him. He looked at me. "Jeezum, yuh ain't fixin' tuh be a jew'ler too, is yuh?"

"Nope. I just want to make a bookmark, a fancy one, with a stone at the top. I was hoping you could help me."

"Be glad tuh, but…yuh stick stones on a bookmark, it may look fine, but it ain't gonna work none too good. Books won't hardly close."

"I plan to use only one stone, up at the top. The bookmark, the part that will go inside the book, will be the tan bark of a river birch.[32] The stone will be attached with fine twine at the top. I was hoping you could help me shape and polish the stone…and put a hole through the middle for the twine. I'll pay you, give you a couple of my stones."

"Far as helpin' yuh, I'd be glad tuh. But 'bout that payin' stuff. Fo'get it. Be my plezur." Grover knelt even lower. He ran his hand among my stones, eyeing them closely. "Yuh knows what yuh got here?"

"A couple," I said. "I know there's coral, limestone, garnet and mica, but mainly I picked them for the colors. I keep the best of each, two or three. If I find a better one, I keep that and throw another away."

Grover eyed the stones again and pointed. "Dis one here be coral, and dis one, moonstone. And dis one…whoa!" He picked up an aquamarine-colored stone. "Dis here be turquoise…semi-precious."

---

[32] *River Birch*, University Kentucky website, 21 Dec. 2019 <https://www.edu.uky/hort/River-Birch> indicating that river birches have a native habitat from Massachusetts to Florida.

"You mean valuable?"

"Well, ain't like diamons, but ain't sandstone neither. Folks pay a pretty penny fo' a nice one." Bearing a puzzled look, Grover rotated it up to the light. "Where'd yuh find dis?"

"Didn't actually find it. My dad gave it to me. Got it from a cattleman, on a trade."

"Dat clears de fog."

"Come again?" I said.

"Didn't make no sense yuh found it, not 'round deez parts. Fa' as I know, ain't no turquoises in deez woods." Grover shuffled through the rest of my stones. "Dat turquoise be yuh best."

"Could you shape it and polish it for me, so it looks really nice?"

Grover examined the jagged stone, over a half-inch wide and nearly as broad from top to bottom. He held it up, rotating it in his fingers. "Yup, I 'spect I could…'Course, I could do it best, if yuh helps me."

"You don't need—" Grover hardly required my help. "You mean you'll let me do the stone with you?"

"Wouldn't want it no udda way."

Grover checked the stone again. "Yuh got yaself a nice stone. Got a good blue-green color and not bad fo' clarity. Like I said, not sometin' yuh generally find 'round deez parts. Turquoises is lots mo' common in Nevada and Arizona."[33] He repeatedly rotated the stone in his hand. "What shape yuh wanna make it?"

"Whatever you think best."

"Ain't never fixed a gem fo' a bookmark. And yuh wanna stick a cord thru?" Grover pawed his scraggly jaw. "Could make it like a tube, 'cept 'stead of round, make it wid six faces, A hexa…hexa somethin'. Sound okay?"

I nodded.

Grover twisted the stone in his hand. "Yuh see how de color is pretty much de same runnin' in dis direction." He slowly moved a finger across the stone. "We'd wanna cut it de long way, like dis, so it don't look like a miz-maz. Whad'ya think?"

"Sounds great to me."

"Good. So, lez do it." He motioned me to the far wall where a collection of tools hung above a workbench. "Be a might easier if we had a lathe. Massa had one. Den we could make us a long tube and flatten de edges afta. But no mind, we can shape it dat way, make it long, wid a

---

[33] *Gem Hunting: Where to Find Gems in the* US, accessgems.com, 26 Jun. 2021 <https://accessgems.com/where-to-find-gemstones-united-states/>.

saw and a hammer and chisel, and den flatten de edges." Grover took down several tools and said, "Yuh do it."

I jerked back.

"Jus' kiddin'. Dis part takes practice. Did hundreds of worthless rocks, befo' I took tuh hackin' sometin' good." He selected a fine-bladed coping saw, and holding the turquoise between his thumb and index finger, cut into one edge. He rotated the stone and again cut on the same plane. After one more similar rotation, he placed a chisel into the incision and tapped with a hammer. The stone split, a small, flat-edged piece breaking off. He held up the remaining stone and eyed it. Following a quick nod, he cut another groove into the stone. He handed me the saw. "Yo' turn."

"Me?"

"Yup. Jus' falla de groove."

I made sure the blade was in the channel and gently moved it back and forth. My only concern was avoiding deviation. How rapidly the cut deepened, if at all, was no matter.

Soon enough, Grover stopped me. "Good job." He made small cuts on the same plane. He said, "Yuz gonna split dis one. And don'tcha gimme dem big eyes." He placed the chisel into the channel I had helped carve. "Tap de chisel jus' like dis." He demonstrated a short stroke and handed me the hammer.

I took a deep breath. Ever so gently, I tapped the stone. Nothing happened.

"Yuh gotsa hit it harda. Don'tcha be 'fraid."

That was exactly what I was. I envisioned the stone shattering into multiple pieces. I gave Grover an irresolute look. A tiny, but stern shake of his head convinced me I had to face the challenge. I tapped the stone, likely not much harder than before. Nothing happened. I rapped again, more decisively. The turquoise split.

Grover held up the stone. A small, flat-edged piece that had separated remained on the table. "Perfect." He rotated the stone in his fingers. "Yuh done great!" He handed me the stone.

Though he had done everything to make my success all but inevitable, I reveled in my contribution. I examined the gem, repeatedly rotating what had generally become a triangular prism. It was a step up from the rock that had come from my sack, but it was hardly a masterpiece. "I thought you said it would have six sides."

"I did, and I jus' remembered de word...hexagon. And de way we gonna do dat is by filin' down de three edges. But firs' we gotsta stick a hole down de middle fo' de cord." Grover looked me in the eye. "I betta do dis."

Much as I enjoyed my success moments before, I had no desire to roll the dice again, especially when the newest challenge presumably carried longer odds. I handed the stone to Grover. He filed the top end until it was flat. He slipped it vertically into a vise at the end of the workbench, placing some cloth between the jaws of the vise and the faces of the stone to avoid marring it. Using a drill and the tiniest of bits, Grover began drilling a small hole down through the length of the stone. He went about halfway before turning the stone over and drilling from the other end. The process was tedious, but finally the two holes connected.[34] He removed the stone from the vise and peered through the hole. "Lookin' good." He handed it to me, along with a file. "Go ahead. File de ends."

I rubbed, keeping the file as close to perpendicular to the adjoining sides as possible. I handed the file back to Grover.

"Yuh gonna file de corna edges." He readjusted the stone in the vise. "Run de file up and down 'em like dis." He demonstrated before returning the file to me.

I began filing the edges.

"Keep checkin' dat yo' new edge be at de same angle wid de edges nex' door."

Every few strokes I checked.

"Betcha yuh thought de facets wuz done wid a hammer and chisel."[35]

Not having thought about it, I shrugged.

"Dat's how dey do it wid diamons not dat I e'er done none of dem." Grover took the stone and checked my work. "Yuh doin' good." He put the stone back into the vise. "'Cause yuh gonna put it on a cord, we ain't be needin' a cullet."

"A what?"

"A cullet. It's de bottom of a stone. What lets it sit good in a settin'. Ain't gonna have no crown neither." Grover sighed. "Be nice if we had a grindin' wheel. Makes it a damn side easier tuh do dem edges. But yuh be doin' fine."

Once I finished filing, Grover took the stone. "Nice…real nice." He checked every edge and face. Yuh mind if I smooth 'em jus' a bit?"

---

[34] *How to Make Holes to String Turquoise Stones*, ourpastimes.com, 26 Jun. 2021 <https://ourpastimes.com/how-to-make-holes-to-string-turquoise-stones-12303714.html>.

[35] *Faceting a Gemstone—the whole cutting and polishing process from start to finish*, Nevada-outback-gems.com, 13 Oct. 2017 <http://Nevada-outback-gems.com/faceting_example/FACETING.HTM>.

I jumped at the offer. Minutes later, he handed the gem back to me. A half-inch long, the small, tube-like stone had six faces. They were less than perfect, but more than adequate. Grover handed me a dampened emery cloth. "Now we gonna polish it. Yuh gotta rub de emery cloth against de stone dis way and dat and ev'rywhere."

I followed his example. What originally had been a varying, craggy mass of colored rock had acquired shape and clarity.

He handed me a soft buffing cloth. "Give it de final shine."

I rubbed the cloth all around the stone and examined it. "It's beautiful. Even better than I had hoped."

"Yuh done a great job!"

I gave him a look. Acknowledging that he had done the real work, that which required skill, was unnecessary. We both knew it. I said, "Thank you…Thank you so much."

"My plezur." Grover took the stone and studied it one more time. "Dem pages in yuh books gonna get marked real fine."

"The bookmark isn't for me."

Eyes narrowed, Grover studied me. "Might it be fo' Abbey?"

I nodded.

"She a lucky girl…Hope yuh be jus' as lucky…Guess dat'll 'pend on her daddy, if he come 'round. He nice, real nice, but…" Grover heaved a sigh. He handed the gem back to me.

***

The day after Grover had helped me cut and polish the turquoise for Abbey's bookmark, I gathered some superb pieces of bark from a river birch. Having several allowed me to try different shapes and to start anew in the event of any mistakes. As it turned out, I stuck to my original idea of a strip about two-inches wide and seven-inches long. I cut several hearts from paper until I had a perfectly proportioned one. Using it as a pattern, I cut an identical heart from the best of my bark. I dyed the heart with red-cedar stain and pasted it near the bottom of the bookmark. At the top of the bookmark, I folded a lap, just wide enough for a cord to pass through, and sewed it. Using a straight edge, I put a uniform black border about 1/8-inch wide around the four outer edges. I ran a five-inch leather cord through the turquoise and, after putting glue on either end of the cord, pushed the ends into either side of the lap, so they met in the middle. I allowed the glue to dry overnight.

The following morning, just two days after Grover had helped me, the bookmark, more impressive than what I had first imagined, was finished. I was anxious to give it to Abbey, but I needed an opportune time. Unfortunately, she was avoiding me. Apart from an occasional, indifferent *hello*, she refused to engage in any conversation. I told myself that Abbey still cared for me, but with the passage of time, my doubts mounted. I went back to Grover, seeking further counsel. Though mainly he provided an advice-free, patient ear, I read between the lines. Discretion, a wait-and-see approach, might be best. I kept hoping that Abbey would sway her parents. Or maybe she would secretly defy them. That she would do so openly seemed farfetched.

All the while that I delayed giving Abbey the bookmark, I read more than ever. Part of my motivation was to impress her. From the collection of books in the school's storage area, I started with several easy ones. Fortified by my progress, I embarked on *Oliver Twist*.[36] More than anything, Abbey's endorsement of the novel led me to tackle it. Challenge though it was at the outset, page by page my skill and confidence grew. By the time I finished the extraordinary novel, reading had become a joyous pastime. I had become an avid reader.

As days of postponement flowed into weeks, patience proved futile. I weighed the possibility of sending Abbey a note, asking her to meet me, but having traveled that fruitless route before, dismissed the idea. I considered going to her home and giving her the bookmark there. Fear that her parents would turn me away nullified the approach. After numerous starts and stops, I slid the bookmark into a copy of *Jane Eyre*[37] that I took from the schoolhouse storage area. I knew little of the book, except that Abbey loved it. I included the following note:

Abbey,
I made this bookmark for you.
Mican.

On a Friday, the instant the school day concluded, I hurried forward. As I passed Abbey, I slipped the book, together with the bookmark and note, onto her desk. I hurried out the door, allowing no opportunity for a reaction. Expectations low, I nevertheless held out hope that over the weekend I might hear a response. That I didn't, though disappointing, was not shocking. Monday morning would be the real test. I was already in my seat when Abbey entered the schoolhouse and took her place. A minute later, Mrs. Seward began the day. Midway through the morning,

---

[36] *Oliver Twist*, by Charles Dickens, was published serially from 1837-1839 and in a three-volume work in 1838. *Oliver Twist, Novel by Dickens*, britannica.com, 28 Sept. 2019 <https://www/britannica.com/topic/Oliver-Twist-novel-by-Dickens>.

[37] *Jane Eyre*, by Charlotte Bronte, was published in 1847. *All About Jane Eyre*, wordpress.com, 28 Sept. 2019 <https://www.janeeyrebookclub.wordpress.com>.

as we took out our reading materials, I tried to see if Abbey was using the bookmark. As best as I could observe, not that it was much since her back was to me, she wasn't.

We were deep into the morning when I saw Abbey—I had been watching her every move—hand a small, folded paper to the girl behind her. Row by row, but only when Mrs. Seward was not looking, the paper was passed back until it was delivered to me. A second later, Mrs. Seward, who had been writing on the blackboard, turned toward the class. I clutched the note tightly, sliding my hand below the level of my desktop. Mrs. Seward gazed in my direction. I feared that she had seen me trying to hide the note. Much as I strove to remain inconspicuous, my guilt-ridden face was palpable.

"Mican," said Mrs. Seward.

The sound of my name, an ominous crack of thunder, terrified me.

"What is the least common denominator to add these three fractions?"

The question, a rainbow in a storm, was welcome. "Uh…uh…" I said, looking to the blackboard and checking for the first time the denominators, 4, 2 and 3. "It's…uh…" My otherwise lightning-fast mathematical brain struggled to solve the easy problem. "Uh…it's twelve."

"That's correct." Mrs. Seward looked at me for another second or two. It was as if she suspected that something was amiss.

I sat motionless, afraid the worst of the storm was yet to pass.

"Mary, for each of the fractions, using the least common denominator of twelve, give me the numerator."

I breathed a sigh of relief. My attention refocused on the folded paper, but concerned that Mrs. Seward recognized that I was up to something, I dared not open it. My hand still clutching it, I rested my arm on my thigh. When finally Mrs. Seward began writing a new problem on the blackboard, I lifted my hand from beneath the desk and, while keeping an eye out in case she turned around, unfolded the paper. The brief note read: "It's beautiful. Thank you. Abbey."

Through the remainder of the school day, I was transfixed on Abbey. During our independent reading period, I read the same page three times, absorbing no more than a quick skim would normally yield. Several times I re-read Abbey's note. Given that I had already committed the five-word message to memory, why or what I was looking for was unclear. Perhaps the chance to see her appreciative words written in her own hand—Abbey had the finest penmanship in the class—was a motivating factor. The piece of paper was tangible evidence, providing hope that our relationship could be renewed. The end of the day would provide the next test.

Nearly an hour before the school day ended, I began plotting strategy. Going directly to Abbey's desk before she had a chance to leave seemed unwise. With Mrs. Seward close by, Abbey could hardly risk an encounter. Even if she did, Mrs. Seward, Lieutenant Parker's watchdog, was likely to intervene. With impatience influencing judgment, I decided to approach her as soon as she departed the schoolhouse. Several minutes before the day ended, I organized my personal belongings so that I could dart forward to the door the instant we were excused. Primed and ready, I waited. When Mrs. Seward finally dismissed us, I charged toward the portal. Only Homer Dooley who sat in the front row beat me there.

I stationed myself outside, a short distance from the door, a location that allowed me to observe everyone who came out but obscured me from anyone inside. One by one the students left, but no Abbey. Because the building had only one door, doubtless she was still inside. Though I had not counted those who had left, no more than two or three students could have remained. Perhaps Abbey was the only one. Was she trying to avoid me? Might Mrs. Seward accompany her? If so, I would need to abandon my plan, allowing for a more propitious moment. I shifted my position, moving adjacent to the front corner of the building farthest from the door. Several minutes later, Abbey, accompanied by Penny Jones, came out. While I preferred to approach Abbey alone, anxious as I was, I refused to shun the opportunity. As the duo headed away from the building, I raced their way.

"Abbey...Abbey," I said, though not too loudly, lest Mrs. Seward hear. "May I talk with you?"

She briefly slowed her stride and said, "It's beautiful."

"What's beautiful?" said Penny.

"Oh...uh...nothing," said Abbey. She turned my way. "Thank you so much. But I...I have to be going." Her pace quickened.

Mixed emotions, elation and dejection, collided. The amorous glow that had painted Abbey's face when she had labeled the bookmark *beautiful* thrilled me. No doubt, Abbey loved my gift. But would it change the status quo? The probable answer, an arrow piercing my heart, caused it to bleed. I started back toward the barracks. The farther I walked, the more I hemorrhaged. Delight owing to Abbey's reaction evanesced. The bottom line, circumstances remained unchanged. Abbey and I would not be together.

Chapter VII

MONTHS DRIFTED PAST, and before long, autumn rolled into southern Florida's balmy winter. Most mornings, a light jacket yielded to an afternoon with short sleeves. Christmas and New Year's came and went. Hardly a day passed that I didn't see Abbey. But hardly a day came that I spoke to her. And when I did, it was never more than a passing hello. Time had mitigated my pain, not that my feelings for her had lessened. Opinions at the fort indicated the war had turned. General Sherman had captured Atlanta in September and had begun his march through Georgia to the sea.[38] Lincoln had won reelection. And word had recently come that the Union Army had captured Fort Fisher, isolating Wilmington, North Carolina, the only remaining port that could supply General Lee's army.[39] Newly arriving Union sympathizers, having been driven from farms, as well as fleeing slaves in need of refuge,[40] spoke of destruction and carnage. Still for the most part, the war seemed distant.

At Fort Myers soldiers recounted their raids, how they had confiscated cattle from nearby ranches, cutting off the supply of beef to the Confederate forces in Georgia,[41] but their forays bore little resemblance to Gettysburg, Chickamauga, Spotsylvania and the like,[42]

---

[38] *American Civil War Timeline, 1864*, historyofwar.org, 27 Oct. 2017 <http://www.historyofwar.org/articles/timeline_acw_1864.html>.

[39] Ibid., American Civil War Timeline, 1865.

[40] Ibid.

[41] *Battle of Fort Myers*, thecivilwarbattles.blogspot.com, posted by Peace Keeper, 10 Oct. 2017 <http://thecivilwarbattles.blogspot.com/2011/08/battle-of-fort-myers.html>. "By 1865, it was estimated that more than 4000 head of cattle had been taken from cattle farms by the Union cavalry units from similar raids."

[42] *10 Bloodiest Civil War Battles*, thoughtco.com, 29 Sept. 2019 <https://www.thoughtco.com/ten-bloodiest-civil-war-battles-104527>. Bloodiest was the Battle of Gettysburg, Pennsylvania, July1-3, 1863, that reported "51,000 casualties, of which 28,000 were Confederates soldiers." Next was the Battle of Chickamauga, Georgia, September 19-20, 1863, that "reported 34,624 total casualties of which 16,170

the bloody battles that had been fought far to the north. Compared to those horrific confrontations, the scene at the fort was peaceful; that is, until the 20th of February 1865. That morning I was near the southwest end of the Parade Grounds when an atypical call to arms rang out. Unlike the usual stolid readiness drills, this was frenetic. Word spread that several Negro Union soldiers out on picket duty had been ambushed.[43] At least one was dead and others wounded.[44] Soldiers readied for a possible attack or to mount an offensive. For the first time, the war, hostilities other than tactical cattle raids, had reached Fort Myers. Though discretion dictated that I return to the security of the barracks, thirst for the action superseded. Where an attack by ships navigating the Caloosahatchee would presumably come on the northwest side of the fort, one by land was more likely from the south or east. Given the ambush in the woods, the latter seemed more probable. I chose a tiny window-like cutout in the fort's wall. The spot, near the bakery, located along the southeast margin of the fort, allowed for observation of events inside and outside the stronghold, as well as the firing of a weapon, not that I had one.

Soldiers scurried about. Activity at the nearby stables was constant. But the scene remained benign until suddenly the thunderous blast of a field piece rang out from well beyond the walls.[45] I peeked through the opening. Nothing unusual was transpiring, at least nothing I could see.

"What's happening?" I said to a passing Union soldier. "A minute ago, I heard a blast."

"Yeah, those damn Rebs fired a warning shot. Demanded we surrender the fort."

"Surrender the fort? Would we do that?"

The soldier shot me a look. "'Course not. Captain Doyle told 'em to stick their call for surrender up their gray asses,[46] though not quite in

---

were Union soldiers." Third highest was the Battle of Spotsylvania Court House, Virginia, May 6-21, 1864, which reported "30,000 casualties…of which 18,000 were Union soldiers."

[43] *Battle of Fort Myers – February 20, 1865*, civilwartalk.com, 26 Oct. 2017 <http://civilwartalk.com/threads/battle-of-fort-myers-florida-february-20-1865.75212/>.

[44] Ibid.

[45] Ibid.

[46] *Battle of Fort Myers*, worldhistoryproject.org., 26 Oct. 2017 <http://worldhistoryproject.org/1865/2/20/battle-of-fort-myers>. Fort Myers Commanding Officer Capt. James Doyle sent back a message to the Confederates' demand for surrender reputedly stating: "'Your demand for an unconditional surrender has been received. I respectfully decline; I have force enough to maintain my position and will fight you to the last.'"

those words. Last I saw, soldiers were rolling two cannons outside the fort…per the Lieutenant's orders."[47]

"You think we're in for a big battle?" For months I had heard men talk how they were itching to fight. Their bravado was contagious. But with a fight on the doorstep, the possibility became more frightening. Gory descriptions of battles elsewhere, in which soldiers, their guts ripped out by bayonets, spouting blood and screaming in pain, filled my brain.

"Ain't sure what's next. But one thing is damn certain. If dem Rebs are lookin' for another Gettysburg, we'll give it to 'em!"

"You bet we will!" My bombast masked fear.

"That's the spirit," said the soldier. He started for the stables. Glancing back over his shoulder, he added, "You need to shelter in a safe place."

Alone again, I took another peek through the opening in the wall. The scene was peaceful. Perhaps another area of the fort manifested more activity. Curiosity cajoled me to search it out; judgment derailed the idea. Bad enough, I'd be in the way. Worse yet, I'd likely get disciplined, having ignored a soldier's behest that I shelter. I needed a middle ground, a site sufficient to protect me from sanction, but one where the ever-changing scuttlebutt flowed. The stables filled the bill. Hurrying there, I found Grover busily working.

"How come yuh ain't in yuh barracks, what wid fightin' likely?"

"I was near the bakery, and this seemed safe."

Grover shot me a doubting look. "Long as yuh here, help me saddle deez hosses. Gotta get 'em ready. My guess, dey gonna send out de cavalry."

I joined Grover in the task. "You think the fighting is happening now?"

"Ain't sure, but it gonna happen. When Sergeant told me tuh ready de hosses, he sez both de white and Negro squads wuz bein' rolled out. Said dat once Captain Doyle 'fused tuh hand over de fo't tuh de Rebs de way dey demanded, shootin' be a sure bet."

"Gosh, a battle here…Talk about exciting."

Grover momentarily interrupted his labor. "Yuh ain't celebratin' bloodshed, is yuh?"

---

[47] Ibid. A historic marker erected in front of the library in Ft. Myers indicates: "Shortly after noon of Feb. 20, 1865, Maj. Footman approached the fort under a flag of truce and gave the Federals 20 minutes to surrender." Williams, Amy Bennett, *The Civil War Battle of Fort Myers, 150 years later*, news-press.com, 27 Oct. 2017 <http://www.news-press.com/story/news/local/amy-williams/2014/06/15/field-notes-amy-williams/10521403/>.

Even if I were, and I wasn't, given Grover's reaction, I would not have admitted it. "Oh no. Just that the soldiers have said they want a piece of the Rebs…more than raids on cattle ranches."

"Well, dey got it. And can't say I blame 'em, but…" Grover returned to saddling.

"But what?"

"Prob'ly bes' I keep ma trap shut, but ain't right tuh leave yuh hangin', not afta I spun de rope." He heaved a sigh. "It like dis. I ain't got nuttin' against fightin' fo' freedom. If dat what it take tuh end slavery, I is all fo' it. Gotta fight de Devil. But wantin' a fight jus' 'cause der ain't 'nough action is loco. War be horrible. Ain't no game." Grover went and got another saddle.

As he walked away, I contemplated what he had said. Although not phrased with the erudition found in the books I was reading, his philosophical analysis equated. I was still weighing his words when, armed with another saddle, he returned. He hoisted it onto the back of a big gray mare.

"Yuh havin' any luck wid Abbey?"

I shook my head.

Grover looked around before responding in a lowered voice. "Lieutenant Parker…he be a good man. He treat me good. But damn, puttin' de color of a body's skin befo' der happiness don't make no sense…no sense at all."

I glanced at my hands, the tiniest tinge of maroon visible. The lily-white Lieutenant Parker was as pigheaded as the stubborn sorrel in the end stall. Grover, on the other hand, may have been as dark as the difficult chestnut, but when it came to personality, the officer had more in common with the equine than did the stablekeeper.

"What sense it make, judgin' folks on de color of der skin?" Grover gazed off into space and shook his head. "Why I even wastin' time aksin' such? Ain't no use. Not in a world where folks think dey is betta dan de nex'."

Seconds before when Grover had posed his questions, I was ready to respond, even knowing the queries were rhetorical. His added comments silenced me. As much as I hated the prejudice that blocked my relationship with Abbey, I realized it paled when compared to what Grover had endured. Unlike him, I had always been free. I could find another girl, not that I wanted to. He, on the other hand, had been treated as chattel, demeaned and robbed of his fundamental rights.

"Sorry," he said.

"Sorry? For what?" I could not imagine what had precipitated his apology.

"Whinin' worse den ol' Stoney down der in de third stall…An' don'cha be denyin' it. I seen how yuh gone quiet afta I quit carryin' on."

"No, no. That's not it at all."

Grover's furrowed brow confirmed he gave no credence to my denial.

Much as I hated to explain my earlier reaction, allowing him to believe he owed me an apology was even more intolerable. "A minute ago, when you were talking about prejudice, I was inclined to react because I felt sorry for myself. But next to you, I've had it great. If anyone needs to apologize, I'm the one."

Grover shook his head. "Yuh ain't got no cause fo' sorries. Ain't no cause fo' me neither. Dey dat stood wid slavery oughta be beggin' pardons."

I welcomed the shame-lifting assessment. It corroborated a separate observation I had made. Grover's locution masked wisdom.

"By de way, dat book yuh gimme las' week is real nice. Lotsa words I can't hardly figure, but I git 'nough dat I knows what's doin'. Read near fifty pages a'ready." He looked me in the eye. "'Preciate what's yuh done…teachin' me tuh read."

The gleam in his eyes warmed me. Moments before, I had been feeling shame. With only a couple of brief comments, Grover had shifted my emotions. My propensity for numbers at play, I visualized it on a number line. His first comment had elevated me from negative to zero. The second had moved me into positive territory. "Thank you," I said.

Grover smiled. He tossed a saddle onto a pinto. He pulled the cinch tight and buckled it. I grabbed a brush and shined the horse's coat. Cavalrymen arrived and took most of the horses. Throughout the afternoon, I worked alongside Grover. Reverberations of shots were few and distant.

As dusk arrived, a soldier dismounted just outside the stable. Eager for information about the battle, we hurried his way as he led his horse toward the stable door. "Looks like the fighting is over. The 'Cow Cavalry' [the term Confederates used to describe themselves as they tried to stop Union raids on their Florida cattle ranches],[48] appears to have headed back north."

"Who de winna?" said Grover.

---

[48] Ibid. *See also*, February 20, 1865, *Battle of Fort Myers*, worldhistoryproject.org, 26 Oct. 2017 <https://worldhistoryproject.org/1865/2/20/battle-of-fort-myers> stating: "The Confederates organized a special battalion of the state militia with the sole purpose of stopping Union raids. The battalion, commanded by Col. Charles Munnerlyn, was made up of cattle drovers who were exempt from the Confederate Army…They became known as the Cattle Guard Battalion or 'Cow Cavalry.'"

"Ain't no doubt. We were."

"Yuh mean dem Rebs surrendered?"

"Well, no…but think about it. The Rebs came here demanding we surrender the fort. We're still holding it, and from all appearances, they're headed back where they came from."

To my mind the battle seemed more like a standoff than a victory. No way was I about to contradict the soldier.

"Any chance dey might try again?" said Grover.

The soldier shrugged.

The noncommittal reaction reinforced my assessment.

"Many die in de fightin'?"

"From what I know, not that I'm sure of the final count, one of our men was killed—that happened in the initial ambush of our guards—and three others were wounded in the skirmishes throughout the day."[49]

"What 'bout de Rebs?"

"Not many. Maybe one or two wounded…I guess."

Compared to the war's other battles, the carnage was miniscule, grounds to be grateful. But for the man who was killed, that was hardly a silver lining. His life, his future…everything was over.

"Can't imagine de war has seen a battle deepa in de South."[50]

"I suspect you're right." The soldier headed toward the stable door. "Gotta get back to my post, 'less I want the sergeant to give me hell."

Once the soldier was out of earshot, Grover said, "Look like God done shine on us pretty good. Dem dat wuz itchin' fo' a fight, wantin' action, got it, but widout sheddin' much blood. We be lucky dat it weren't no Olustee."

More than once I had heard soldiers at the fort speak of Olustee, a bloodbath in northern Florida that had occurred when Union troops,

---

[49] *Battle of Fort Myers – February 20, 1865*, op. cit., indicating: "Union troops suffered 1 killed and 3 wounded. It appears southern troops suffered one wounded." Cf. *The Civil War battle of Fort Myers, 150 years later*, op. cit., to the effect: "What's not in dispute is that the Confederates withdrew that night. Casualty figures vary, but most agree fewer than 10 men died."

[50] Ibid., *Battle of Fort Myers – February 20, 1865.* The Battle of Fort Myers has been referred to as the "'southern-most battle of the Civil War,' but that claim is up for debate obviously." (The Battle of Palmetto Ranch, Texas, also known as the Battle of Palmetto Hill, was fought at a latitude almost a full degree further south than Fort Myers. Intriguingly, it occurred from May 12-14, 1865, well after the Civil War ended when Lee surrendered at Appomattox. *Battle of Palmetto Ranch – Civil War Battles,* thecivilwarbattles.blogspot.com. 31 Oct. 2017 <http://thecivilwarbattles.blogspot.com/2011/09/battle-of-palmetto-ranch.html>. See also, *Battle of Palmetto Ranch*, Wikipedia, 6 Nov. 2017 <http://en.wikipedia.org/wiki/Battle_of_Palmetto_Ranch> to the effect: "Why this final battle at Palmetto Ranch even took place is still debated.")

hoping to cut off the South's rail supply lines, were routed.[51] "You think the Cow Cavalry will attack the fort again?"

Grover pawed his bristly chin. "Don't rightly know."

***

Tension-ridden weeks followed the attack on the fort. But as the calendar page flipped to March 1865, the Cow Cavalry failed to mount another assault. Rumor had it, they had retreated to Fort Thompson, about thirty miles to the east.[52] In the meantime, another rumor, that Fort Myers was about to be abandoned, began to circulate. Like everyone else, I wondered about its accuracy. If true, why? Was there fear a larger Confederate force was preparing to overrun the fort? Perhaps the Union Army had completely cut off the Confederates' southern supply lines, rendering the fort unnecessary. Intriguing as the questions were, a more important issue consumed me. If the fort was shut down, what would be my fate? Might I be left to fend for myself? If not, where might I be sent? An orphanage?

It was shortly after dinner on the 2nd of March when Sergeant Wall visited me in the barracks. In the many months after he had given me the news of my father's death, I had only spoken to him a few times, and those conversations were perfunctory. His personal visit to my quarters was a first.

"Hi Mican. How you doing?"

"Good, Sir."

"Everyone treating you well?"

"Yes, Sir." Soldiers often asked me that question, and I always responded with the same answer.

"Have you heard that the fort is being abandoned?"

Unsure if he was telling me a fact or seeing if I had heard the popular rumor, I said, "Some soldiers, as well as kids at school, have said that, but…uh…nobody was sure."

---

[51] *Battle of Olustee*, battleofolustee.org, 6 Nov. 2017 <http://www.battleofolustee.org/capsule.html>.

[52] *The Civil War Battle of Fort Myers, 150 years later*, op. cit., demonstrating that information about the Battle of Fort Myers remains sketchy. Williams' article notes: "The New York Times had a correspondent embedded with the soldiers there who recorded the events of that Monday in 1865." The article also notes that the reporter "wrote enthusiastically," but "…it's just that enthusiasm (as well as inattention to detail) that makes some area historians skeptical. For example, the report says that to arrive at the fort, 'the enemy had performed a march of about 200 miles'…In fact, they'd come from near LaBelle, just 30 miles away."

"Well, it's true. Matter of fact, in another week, this place will be deserted." He looked me in the eye. "We want to be sure you have a place to go."

I feared what was coming next.

"There's a small orphanage in Tampa."

"An orphanage?" If my words failed to communicate my dismay, no doubt my face did.

Sergeant Wall sighed. "I know, it doesn't sound appealing."

Appealing! He had to be kidding. A prison hardly would have been worse.

"You have any better ideas?"

"Me?" *Was he serious, asking a callow adolescent?*

He waited, much like a judge inviting a convicted felon to make a statement before sentence was pronounced.

"I…I don't know…uh…maybe I could take a day or so to think about it?" One possibility came to mind, but it seemed remote. How to make it happen required some thought.

"Sure, you take some time to think it over…a day or two. But we can't go beyond that. As I said, the fort will be empty a week from now. Those who would take you to Tampa might be leaving sooner." Sergeant Wall put a hand on my shoulder. "Sorry to be the bearer of unpleasant tidings, to turn your life upside down…again."

Whether he was hoping I would ease his conscience by minimizing my disappointment, I remained silent.

"Please, understand, I'm just the messenger…doing my job."

I nodded, though I suspected my expression negated concurrence.

Sergeant Wall headed for the door. Just before leaving, he looked back and said, "If there's anything I can do, just let me know."

You've already done enough. I sank down into my bunk and, digging my head into the pillow, burst into tears. It was the first time I had cried since the weeks after my father had been killed. Idealized images of him and my childhood, devices to drown myself in self-pity, filled my head. If I had to be a victim, I was entitled to vent. I lay there sobbing until gradually I dozed off. Roughly an hour elapsed before I awoke. Having at most two days to avoid the orphanage, I could ill-afford delay. I dragged myself from my bunk and hurried to the stables. I needed Grover's assistance. Unfortunately, there was no sign of him. Calling out his name was as unproductive as a visual check. I went back outside, trying to imagine where I might find him. The nearby blacksmith shop seemed a good bet. I started in that direction. I had gone about forty yards when the sound of my name turned my head. Grover approached from the far side of the stable. I raced toward him. "I was looking for you."

"I wuz in de outhouse. When nature caws, gotta go." He studied me. "Sometin' wrong?"

I nodded.

"Les go in de stable and sit."

I followed Grover into the building and took a seat on a bench alongside him.

"Wat de matta?"

"You're aware that the fort is being abandoned?"

"Yeh, jus' dis mornin' de brass confirmed it."

"They plan to send me to an orphanage…in Tampa."

"Jeezum. Dat ain't right…no how."

"That was my reaction. But I don't know what I can do."

"Mus' be sometin'."

"Where do you plan to go?" I said, unsure how to broach the idea I had in mind.

"Fo' sure, I ain't goin' anywhere near my massa's place. Dat be de las' place I be goin'. 'Spect I'll head tuh Savannah, not dat I know much 'bout it."

"You…you think I might go with you?"

Grover's eyes grew wide. "Wid me?"

"Uh…It was just a thought."

Grover stared at his feet.

Whether he was taking umbrage to my request or considering it, I had no idea. I waited.

"Don't know dat I can do dat."

"I…I understand. I just thought I'd ask."

"No, dat ain't what I be sayin'."

Confused, I waited again.

"Problem is de brass, gettin' dem tuh give de say so."

"But if they did, you would?" I said, grasping at any straw.

"Sure. Fac' tis, I be happy fo' de company. But don't get yuh hopes up. Doubt de brass 'll give de okay. Far as dey concerned, I'm jus' anudda Negro, a no count."

"But going with you would be far better than an orphanage."

"Don't need tuh convince me." Grover scratched his head. "Gotta figure who bes' fo' me tuh aks. Doubt de Cap'in wanna see me, not dat I wanna see him. Don't mean tuh badmout' him. Jus' dat he don't know me from a gator, and I glad tuh keep it dat way."

"The one who spoke to me about the orphanage was Sergeant Wall."

"Ah, Sergeant Wall...Dat be good. I keep Stoney, his fav'rit hoss, in fine shape. Plus, I fixed him a quartz dat he sent home tuh his woman."

"You think he'll give you the okay?"

Grover heaved a sigh. "Suspec' he'll try. But doubt he got de say so. One thing sure, he got a betta chance dan me of gettin' dat okay." Grover looked at me and smiled. "I be right proud tuh have yuh come wid me."

"You would?"

"Yeah...well, on one condition."

"Condition?" A second earlier, I was excited. Apparent qualms dashed expectations. "What's the condition?"

"Yuh have tuh keep helpin' me tuh read...and yuh gotsta learn me 'rithmetic."

The chance to be a mentor to Grover had already proved rewarding. Rather than a burden, the so-called *condition* was a bonus. A glow, likely reflected in the smile I displayed, warmed me. Dejected hours earlier, I had hope—even optimism.

***

A little more than twenty-four hours after I had spoken to Grover, the good news arrived. The powers that be had given their blessing for me to accompany him to Savannah. Activity at the fort, soon to be empty, was vigorous. Unlike most, I had little to do during the three days before my departure. Packing my few things took no more than a half-hour. I took one of two translucent light blue stones from my collection of rocks. Grover had told me each was a lapis. Next to the turquoise I had given to Abbey, he considered them my finest stones. According to him, their hardness lay much closer to red coral, a soft gem, than a diamond, the hardest of all gems.[53] Using tools at the blacksmith's shop, I drilled a hole through the middle of the stone. I filed it, making it as round as I could, after which I polished and buffed it. I took it back to my barracks where I placed it onto a leather tether that I sewed onto a rectangular piece of bark from a river birch.

I took the completed product to the stables where I found Grover, whittling knife and wood in hand, on a bench outside.

"What's up?" he said, as I approached.

---

[53] *Gemstones A-Z with detailed gemstone descriptions*, makermends.com, 13 Jun. 2021 <http://www.makermends.com/gemstones.html> indicating that the color of lapis (lapis lazuli) is "[d]eep azure blue to light blue, bluish green." The hardness of lapis is 5.5 to 6. Coral, which is soft, is 3.5, while the diamond, the hardest gem, is 10.

"I've got something for you." I might have waited until we left for Savannah, but impatience got the best of me. I handed him the bookmark.

"For me?"

I nodded.

"I love it." His eyes showed a tear. "But yuh shouldn't have."

"And why not?"

"It's yo' bes', yo' bes' lapis. Wastin' it on me, a guy dat can't hardly read, don't make no sense."

"First, you read just fine. Second, you're getting better all the time. Regardless, those reasons miss the point. You deserve the lapis. And there's nothing I could do with it that would give me greater pleasure."

"Well, yuh makin' me real happy...Bes' gift anyone ever give tuh me." Grover held the bookmark up and smiled. "It gonna be in ev'ry book I read. And I gonna read a lot. Dat's a promise."

***

Shortly after noon on my last day at Fort Myers, I headed to my favorite fishing spot on the Caloosahatchee. Had it not entailed a time-consuming, five-mile hike, I might have opted for a visit to the cabin that had housed my father and me. The truth be known, a rationalization motivated my decision. Returning to my childhood environs was certain to provoke memories that hindsight had conveniently colored with diffracting rainbows. Images of a past life, one that hindsight had unrealistically idealized, would trigger melancholy, compounding consternation owing to my upcoming move. Thankful though I was to have escaped consignment to an orphanage, Savannah, a far better alternative, was still a voyage into the unknown.

Excited, but apprehensive, I plopped myself down onto a log overlooking the river. As I dangled my line into the water, I contemplated an apparent irony that I had gleaned when reading between the lines that had communicated my good fortune. Because I was a Seminole-Negro, not Caucasian, with whom or where I went mattered less. That lack of concern may have facilitated the approval that allowed me to accompany Grover. Whether my surmise had efficacy or was merely the fatuous observation of a kid remains unclear to this day. That said, however, the intervening years have taught me that children are more discerning than adults realize, which itself is an interesting anomaly, given that each of us was once a child, who shortly after birth began to develop not only insight, but also manipulative skills.

I had been fishing for about fifteen minutes with nary a bite. A focus centering on introspective reflection, rather than fishing, likely contributed to my lack of success. More than once I closed my eyes, giving ear to the rustle of leaves in the adjacent woods. I savored the clement breeze slithering through my long wavy hair. The extended squawk of a great blue heron seated on an outcropping drew my attention. The statuesque blue-gray bird took flight. A choppy liftoff with flapping wings transmuted into a graceful glide, followed by a precipitate dive into the sun-drenched waters. An instant later, the heron emerged, a fish in its beak. As it looped back to the outcropping, the noble bird, its prey on full display, soared past me, as if to confirm the obvious—it was the superior fisherman.[54] To the victor, I nodded, a salute of respect, unencumbered by jealousy. Whether or not I hooked a catch, back at the mess hall a sating dinner awaited.

I shut my eyes and drifted into renewed reverie. I pondered who I was, a question about which I had previously given limited thought. My analysis was far from deep. With my parents gone, first and foremost, like Pip, the character from "Great Expectations," my second Dicken's novel, I was an orphan. That was who I was. The observation was disheartening. I wafted further away from reasoned thought. I began to doze, when I thought I heard a voice, barely audible, call my name. I assumed my mind was playing tricks. But moments later, more awake, I heard the call again. I turned toward the sound's source, the edge of the woods behind me. Peeking around a cedar, Abbey Parker was beckoning me. Still regaining my senses, I did a double take. Abbey beckoned again. I got up and hurried her way. She glanced around before motioning me to a denser spot about twenty feet into the woods.

"I hear you're leaving for Savannah tomorrow," she said. "I had to see you."

"I'm glad you came."

"I can only stay a few minutes." She looked around, confirming that no one was near. "If my parents, especially my father, knew I was here, I would catch the dickens." She drew two brown volumes, decorated with gold, from a paper bag she was holding. "These are for you."

"*Uncle Tom's Cabin*,"[55] I said. "Your favorite."

"Yes. I want you to have it, to remember me by."

I clutched the volumes. "This is my best gift ever, my most prized possession."

She smiled broadly.

---

[54] *Great Blue Heron, Identification, All About Birds – Cornell Lab of Ornithology*, www.allaboutbirds.org, 3 Nov. 2017 <http://www.allaboutbirds.org/guide/Great_Blue_Heron/id>.

[55] Stowe, Harriet Beecher, *Uncle Tom's Cabin*, (Boston, John P. Jewett & Company, 1852, two volumes, 1st Ed.).

"Now that the fort is being abandoned, do you know where you'll be going?"

"Back up north to New York."

"New York City?" It was the only place I knew in New York State.

Abbey shook her head. "About one hundred fifty miles further north, a city with a long Indian name, one I can't even pronounce. It's not far from the state capital, Albany. My father will be stationed there, at least for the time being."

"When do you leave?"

"A day or two after you. My father wants to wait until the fort is all but empty. Make sure that everyone gets off okay." Abbey reached into her pocket. "Like you, I have a most prized possession." She took out the bookmark that I had made. "Every night when I finish reading, I use it to mark my place. It's beautiful. I love it. I will use it always...and when I do, I'll think of you." She pointed at the turquoise tethered to the top. "Where did you get the stone, and how did you shape it, complete with a hole through the center?"

"A man who traded with my father gave it to him. And Grover...Grover Calhoun—I'm going with him to Savannah—helped me fix it. He's very skilled with jewelry. He hopes to have a jewelry business someday. Maybe I'll ask him to teach me. Perhaps I could be a jeweler too." The idea, one spawned on the spur of the moment, echoed in my head. Would I seriously pursue it down the road? I had no clue, and with my last moments with Abbey at hand, that assessment merited no immediate concern. I gazed deeply into her lovely blue eyes. "Will I ever see you again?"

She shrugged.

Though the gesture was neither a *yes* nor a *no*, paradoxically it carried an unequivocal message, one we both knew. With Abbey going to upstate New York and me, to Savannah, Georgia, places that I suspected were separated by close to 1,000 miles, our paths would never cross. That said, she would forever be a part of my life. Whenever I looked back on the horror of losing my father, I would recall that Abbey Parker, kind, selfless and egalitarian, had enabled me to survive those first dreadful weeks of the demoralizing trauma. The books she had given me would be a tangible reminder.

Abbey heaved a sigh. "I...I've got to go." She leaned forward and pressed her lips to mine.

The kiss lasted no more than two or three seconds, but they were the longest and most magnificent seconds of my roughly thirteen years.

"That's my second kiss," she said.

"Mine too, and like the first, it was perfect...No, better than perfect."

She nodded, smiled broadly and hurried out of the woods.

I followed several steps behind, to the edge of the woods. As she headed down the beach in the direction of the fort, I watched until she disappeared around a bend in the river. I returned to the log where earlier I had been fishing. I sat down and stared up at the feather-mottled sky. A glow, as ardent as any I had known, engulfed me. But rapture quickly intermingled with sadness, the knowledge that Abbey was gone forever; that never again would I know the ecstasy of her kiss. I bowed my head and shut my eyes, slipping into a self-contradictory land of ineffable joy and unmitigated heartache. For several minutes, I sat motionless, lost in my thoughts.

When finally, I opened my eyes, I looked at the two volumes I held in my lap. Several times I read the title on the first, all the while thinking of Abbey. I flipped open the cover and found an inscription on the first page:

Dear Mican,
I will remember you always. I love you.
Abbey

"I love you too." I mouthed the words silently. I drew in a deep breath and, staring down the deserted beach, softly uttered, "Abbey, I love you."

Chapter VIII

THREE MONTHS HAD ELAPSED SINCE I HAD ARRIVED in Savannah with Grover. Much had transpired since we had left Fort Myers in early March. General Sherman had stormed north into Virginia, prevailing in the Battle of Five Forks. Richmond, the capital of the Confederacy, as well as Petersburg, had fallen. And ultimately, on April 9, 1865, Lee had surrendered to Grant at the Appomattox Courthouse.[56] A mere five days after the conclusion of the war, John Wilkes Booth, an actor and Confederate sympathizer, had assassinated Abraham Lincoln at Ford's Theater in Washington, D.C.[57] The time and area encompassing these events were far from great, but their reverberations echoed everywhere throughout the divided nation. Savannah was no exception. The war, four years of horrific bloodshed, had ended. What lay ahead was a huge question mark.

Back in January, Sherman had issued a special field order, no. 15, enabling any freedman to acquire forty acres of land along the coast, just for the asking.[58] When we had arrived in Savannah, Grover had weighed

---

[56] *American Civil War Timeline, 1865*, op. cit.

[57] *Abraham Lincoln's Assassination*, history.com, Oct. 27, 2009, updated May 16, 2019, retrieved 9 Sept. 2019 <https://www.history.com/topics/american-civil-war/abraham-lincoln-assassination>. John Wilkes Booth, a Confederate sympathizer who remained in the North during the Civil War, had planned, along with co-conspirators, to kidnap Lincoln, among others. When Lincoln failed to appear at the appointed spot, Booth and his cohorts adopted a new plan to assassinate Lincoln and others. On April 14, 1865, at Ford's Theater in Washington D.C., Booth slipped into Lincoln's box during a production of *Our American Cousin* and shot the President in the back of the head with a ".44-caliber single shot derringer pistol." After shooting Lincoln, "Booth leapt onto the stage and shouted, 'Sic semper tyrannis!' ('Thus ever to tyrants!'-the Virginia state motto)."

[58] Taylor, Col. Samuel, U.S.M.C. (Ret.), *Reconstruction Georgia, Georgia History 101,* ourgeorgiahistory.com, 16 Feb. 2017 <http:/www.ourgeorgiahistory.com/history101/gahistory08.html>.

the possibility of taking advantage of the opportunity. Reluctant to become a farmer, concerned the land would be as much an onus as a boon, he had passed up the chance. In the interim, in exchange for maintenance services, Grover had gotten us room and board in the rear of an unimpressive, wood-frame house about three miles south of the Savannah River. Situated in a Negro area of town, our quarters, a crowded 12' × 14' room, included two beds, a rickety chest of drawers, several shelves, a tiny table and two timeworn wooden chairs, along with a fireplace for cooking and, in winter, a source of heat. Drab though it may have been, it was no worse than my former homes, a dirt-floor cabin in the woods and the barracks at Fort Myers.

Each week, Monday through Friday, Grover and I walked west from our new home to Montgomery Street,[59] where we turned north until we reached the First African Baptist Church, located at the street's terminus on Franklin Square. Grover left me off at the church, where I attended school. He continued north of the Square to a mill on Factor's Row, the center of commerce on the Savannah River. There he loaded cotton onto steamboats. When school was over, I had to wait several hours until he finished work. I used the time to read and study. Once Grover picked me up, we walked back to our living quarters, a trek of three miles. On Saturdays, we stayed near our place where Grover, with my help, earned our keep doing chores. Now and then, I squeezed in a few hours at a farm stand where I earned pocket money. Come Sunday, our day of rest, we walked to the church where we attended services. Sunday afternoons were leisurely spent together. Hindsight indicates the routine was more blessing than burden. New to Savannah, it provided us with order and stability, all the while integrating us into the community. The arrangement enabled me to pursue my education, while Grover, who only required four or five hours of sleep, found time to advance his jewelry-making and reading skills.

It was the second Sunday of June 1865. Shortly after services ended, my teacher, Mr. Charles Wright, a white man who had come from the North to educate southern Negroes, pulled Grover aside.[60] I stepped

---

[59] Montgomery Street runs parallel to what is today Martin Luther King Blvd., about one hundred yards east of the latter.

[60] Even before the Civil War had ended, steps had been taken to provide education for Savannah's freedmen. On the 9th of January 1865, the city's Negroes formed the Savannah Education Association, an association that included reverends and teachers, among others "for the purpose of establishing free schools for themselves and their children." *The Freedman of Savannah, Savannah Education Association*, January 1865 (AMA 19356), drbronsontours.com, 18 Feb. 2017 <http://www.drbronsontours.com/bronsonfreedmenofsavannahsavanaheducationassociation>. (Note: The drbronsontours website, named for Dr. Oliver Bronson, the first

outside into the typically hot and humid June conditions. Still in awe of the urbane city, I gazed south down Montgomery Street. Physically my move from a dirt-floor cabin to a wilderness fort with over fifty structures had been a big step, but coming to Savannah with its impressive homes, numerous squares, busy riverfront and tree-lined streets was a giant leap. I walked about fifty yards from the church before turning and looking back toward it. Just six years earlier, in 1859, the congregation, originally formed in 1773, but formally established in 1788, had made major renovations to the house of worship.[61] The structure's stately, pristine 100-foot steeple, seven tiers, the top of which was a hexagonal pyramid, pointed nobly at God's heavenly cobalt realm.[62]

The better part of a half-hour had elapsed when Grover finally joined me outside the church.

"Yuh ready?" he said, his face bearing a peculiar look.

"Been ready for a while."

"Les go."

We started down Montgomery toward home.

"What did Mr. Wright want? Did it have anything to do with me?"

"Uh…yeah…"

The unease in Grover's manner disconcerted me. Mr. Wright had repeatedly praised both my ability and work, but something seemed amiss. "So, what did he say?"

"He…uh…hit me widda proposa."

"Proposal?...What kind of proposal?"

---

public school superintendent of St. John's County, Florida, was developed and maintained by the late Reverend Gil Wilson. While the website, "[o]ver 1000 web pages" (per Gil Wilson's *Linked in* webpage), is no longer available, portions of its material are still accessible at *bronsondrbronsonstaughistory*, https://bronsondrbronsonstaughistory.wordpress.com/2011/12/15/dr-bronsons-st-augustine-history/).

[61] *First African Baptist Church, Savannah, Georgia (1773-)*, blackpast.org, 5 Nov. 2017 <http://www.blackpast.org/aah/first-african-american-baptist-church-savannah-georgia-1777>.

[62] Ibid. In the First African Baptist Church, which still stands, "the solid oak pews in the main sanctuary, made by enslaved church members" remain. "Beneath the auditorium floor is another sub-floor, evidence that the church was used as an Underground Railroad station." See also, Historic First African Baptist Church, visit-historic-savannah.com, 5 Nov. 2017 <http://www.visit-historic-savannah.com/first-african-baptist-church.html> stating: "The church was a haven for runaway slaves during the turbulent years of the Civil War. The runaways were hidden in a 4-foot high space between the basement and the foundation below. The air holes can still be seen in the basement floor. During the 1960s, the church served as a base for the Civil Rights Movement."

Grover took several more steps. He stopped and looked me in the eye. "He aksed if yuh might wanna live wid him and his family."

"Why would I do that?"

"Sez yuh got great…potenzul. Dat's what he call it. Said it mo' dan once."

"But why should I live with him, rather than you?" Distaste for the idea, not an inability to grasp its logic, occasioned my exasperation.

Grover shrugged. "We bot' knows dat I ain't de bes' when it come tuh schoolin'."

"But you care for me well."

"'Preciate yuh feel dat way."

"You don't want me to live with you anymore?"

"Ain't dat at all. And yuh knows it."

The rare pique in Grover's voice tempered my choler. I had no business insulting the man who had gone to bat for me at Fort Myers and taken me to live with him, saving me from a Tampa orphanage. "Sorry, I didn't mean that the way it sounded."

"I knows dat yuz upset wid wat Misser Wright wanna do. And jus' tuh set de record right, I gonna miss yo' comp'ny if yuh go."

"Then why should we do it?" Once again, dislike of the proposal, not a lack of understanding, begot my inquiry.

"'Cause it be good fo' yuh. Give yuh a betta start…de kind I wish I had."

The regret reflected in Grover's last phrase keep me silent. He was sacrificing his own desires, putting my future ahead of them.

"Les give it a go…leas' fo' a while. If it ain't tuh yuh likin', den yuh can move back wid me…And jus' tuh put some honey on yuh plate, how 'bout yuh come tuh my place ev'ry Sunday afta church. Yuh can stay de night 'til Monday, when yuh walks tuh school and I goes to work."

Having assumed the arrangement was a done deal, its temporary nature, plus Sundays with Grover, ameliorated an otherwise bleak picture. "Well, okay (my groaning inflection all but contradicted my acquiescence), I'll give it a try. But it's only a try. And if I don't like it, I can come back with you. Right?"

"Suppose we cross dat bridge when we comes tuh it?"

I shook my head. "If I don't like it, you've got to take me back. And I spend Sundays with you in the meantime."

Fair 'nough…But yuh gotta give it 'til de firsta August."

"All right. But give me a week before we start." Even with the delay, I was agreeing to a stretch of roughly six weeks.

Conversation grew briefly sparse as we continued down Montgomery. I gazed off to my right, in the direction of the scarred terrain of nearby West Broad Street.[63] Just four months earlier, an explosion at the Confederate Naval Arsenal had spawned a conflagration that had destroyed close to one hundred buildings.[64] People in the wrong place at the wrong time had died. I could only wonder—was I making a mistake? Should I, a Seminole-Negro, forgo the security of life with Grover, my Negro pal, and move in with a white family from the North? With the War of Secession barely over, was it the wrong time and the wrong place for a person of color to make such a move? The questions left me wondering where and how I fit in. With black wavy hair, high cheekbones, almond-shaped eyes, a Roman nose, a Negro mother and Seminole father, I viewed myself as a Black Seminole. But with medium brown skin, bearing at most a dubious hint of red, the world treated me as a Negro. My time at Fort Myers, along with my months in Savannah, had educated me how the white world viewed people of color. Harsh reality supplanted childhood naiveté. That awareness pressed me to look into the mirror, explore my feelings about my color. Conflicting reactions emerged. I was proud of my Black-Seminole heritage. But white society deprecated me because of my race, both as an Indian and a Negro. Throughout the Caucasian-dominated South, bigotry's belittling barrage bashed the self-esteem of people of color. Much as it infuriated me, the risk of internalizing the prejudice loomed. Avoiding it was all but impossible. Even the Bible, what purported to be God's word, avouched my inferiority. How such bias would influence my life was difficult to predict. Time would tell. Whether the world would define me or I would define myself remained an open question. More likely, both would play a role, and the answer would go far deeper than my skin. It would penetrate the depths of my soul.

***

By the light of a kerosene lantern, most every night since I had arrived in Savannah, I had read five to ten pages of *Uncle Tom's Cabin.*

---

[63] That which was West Broad Street in Savannah in 1865 is today Martin Luther King Boulevard.

[64] *The Fire in Savannah, Harper's Weekly*, February 18, 1865, p. 99, retrieved from Savannah Fire, sonoftheosouth.net, 13 Nov. 2017 <http://www.sonofthesouth.net/leefoundation/civil-war/1865/february/savannah-fire.htm>. "On the night of the 27th of January an extensive conflagration broke out in Savannah, in the western part of the city…There was a series of explosions during the next two hours. Several squares were destroyed by the fire." (Harper's Weekly).

Just a few days shy of moving in with the Wrights, I arrived at the final paragraph of the second volume. I paused, conscious of mixed emotions. I was sad to see the amazing saga, roughly six hundred pages, end. I yearned for more. But pride, knowing that I had completed such an enormous undertaking, overshadowed any sadness. I took a deep breath, steeling myself for the final lines. And then, with all the focus I could muster, I slowly read the last paragraph aloud. The moment I finished, I reread it, focusing on its second sentence: "Both North and South have been guilty before God; and the Christian Church has a heavy account to answer."[65] Harriet Beecher Stowe had made her case. A decade before the War of Secession, she had demanded "repentance, justice and mercy," as conditions necessary to saving the Union.[66]

With the book still open in my lap, I closed my eyes and pondered the cogent prose. Stowe, her pen a sword, had denounced injustice and exposed herself to attack.[67] I clutched the volume tightly. It was Abbey's favorite book, her gift to me, an eloquent declaration of her support for human rights. Already in love with Abbey, I esteemed her all the more.

I placed the volume back on the shelf above my bed. I tried to imagine where she might be, that far off place with the Indian name she could not pronounce, not far from Albany, the capital of New York. The information was too vague to conjure a meaningful image. I reached for Volume I and opened to the inscription Abbey had written inside the cover. I silently mouthed her message. "I love you too," I whispered before returning the book to the shelf. I extinguished my lantern and lay down for the night. Life's vicissitudes, hundreds of pages, replete with misfortune, iniquity and slavery, faded amidst glorious memories of Abbey. The two kisses we had shared were palpable. Armed with the unbridled freedom of my imagination, I exulted.

***

The 4th of July fell on a Tuesday in 1865. I had been living with the Wright family for sixteen days. My stay with them had begun one week after the Sunday when the arrangement had been made. I was keeping a

---

65 *Uncle Tom's Cabin*, Vol II, p. 322, op. cit.

66 Ibid.

67 *Harriet Beecher Stowe–New World Encyclopedia*, newworldencyclopedia.org, 11 Nov. 2017 <http://www.newworldencyclopedia.org/entry/Harriet_Beecher_Stowe> indicating: "Stowe wrote the work in reaction to the Fugitive Slave Act of 1850, which made it illegal to assist an escaped slave." Stowe (1811-1896), who was born "in Litchfield, Connecticut…was the seventh of 11 children born to Rev. Lyman Beecher, an abolitionist…."

calendar, each morning marking off one more day until August 1st, the day when I could return to live with Grover. But by the end of the second week, I had let the calendar be. The bridge determining where I would live once July ended could be crossed then. Ceasing to put *X's* over calendar dates changed nothing. That is what I told myself. But deep down I knew it was symbolic. I was happy living with the Wrights. Was it better than living with Grover? Not really. But I spent time with him every week. And for the first time in my life, I had my own room. Amazingly, I was the only one in the Wright household who did. But lest I create false illusions, I need to clarify. The Wrights, Charles and his wife Elma, and their two children, Michael and Nora, respectively nine and eight, enjoyed a lovely flat on the third floor of a fine home on Montgomery Street, about a half-mile south of Franklin Square. The flat included a small kitchen, dining area, parlor, two bedrooms and an area sectioned off in what was an alternative-use, walk-in closet or "room." The 6' × 7' space had a bed, along with shelves on both the bed side and opposite wall. But given that it had a door, it was a room—my room.

Mr. Wright, a shade over six feet, bore an oval face with an aquiline nose and ample brow, all of which exuded his resolute and forthright character. His wife, of average height, with a round face and button nose, was decidedly attractive. Nora was a smaller version of her mother, while her older brother was a wiry young man whose blue eyes and blondish hair hinted that in a few years young ladies would be seeking his affections.

The sultry summer evening of July 4th found us, the Wright family and me, out on Montgomery Street in the area fronting the Wrights' living quarters. For most youngsters it was summer vacation; less so for Mr. Wright's students. Needing to make up for years without education, Mr. Wright deemed vacation, summer or otherwise, a luxury. The breaks he allowed were brief and included homework.

"Nora, Michael, Mican," said Mr. Wright, "today is the eighty-ninth birthday of our country...almost like the four score and seven years about which Mr. Lincoln spoke when he freed the slaves. Our nation is now four score and nine years old."

Precocious as the children were, I suspected they understood what their father was saying.

"This year is a special celebration. For four long years, a large chunk of your lives, our nation has been at war...divided. This year, as we begin the road back to unity, we can celebrate with optimism." Mr. Wright took three sulfur-headed wooden matches, each nearly a foot long. He drew one across a dried phosphorous-soaked paper.[68] The match ignited. He used it to light the other two matches and handed one to each of us. "Hold them at the end, very carefully, and raise them high overhead."

We followed the instruction, relishing the chance to play with fire.

"Unlike the flaming bursts of cannons and guns that have blazed throughout the war, you hold lanterns of peace…beacons beaming a bright future for a reunited country."

Like Michael and Nora, I waived my match. Though the spirit of Mr. Wright's message was not totally lost on me, it faded into the back burner of my mind. The glow of a flaming plaything captivated me. As our matches burned short, within inches of our hands, we extinguished them. I hoped that each of us might get another. Mrs. Wright had a different idea, a better one.

"Suppose we walk to the river and watch the fireworks?"

Before Mr. Wright could react to the proposal, Michael, Nora and I endorsed it enthusiastically. We were on our way. Fifteen minutes later, just as darkness descended, we arrived at the river's edge. Hoards, mostly Negroes, lined the banks. Since white businessmen ran Factor's Row, for an instant the makeup of the gathering surprised me. But on second thought, especially with my experience living in the walled confines of Fort Myers, it made sense. The tradition of July 4th fireworks, a hallmark of the nation ever since its infancy,[69] had been maintained at the fort. But the movers and shakers of Savannah, a staunch component of the Confederacy, were in no mood to celebrate. Less than three months earlier, the army of the Union, a nation from which they had seceded, had vanquished them. That Sherman on his march to the sea had spared Savannah from the ravage he had wreaked on Atlanta,[70] while some

---

68 *The Chemistry of Matches*, compoundchem.com, 7 Nov. 2017 <http://www.compoundchem.com/2014/11/20/matches/> stating: "Matches…have been around for a long time. Sulfur-based are mentioned as far back as the 1200s in texts of the time, and in the 1600s a process involving drawing sulfur matches through dried phosphorous-soaked paper was devised." The first friction matches "were developed by the English chemist, John Walker, in 1826."

69 *The Rockets' Red, White and Blue*, slate.com, 8 Nov. 2017 <http://www.slate.com/articles/life/explainer/2012/07/history-of-fireworks-in-america-why-do-we-celebrate-fourth-of-july-with-fireworks.html> states: "The first commemorative Independence Day fireworks were set off on July 4, 1777. The Pennsylvania Evening Post wrote that in Philadelphia 'The evening was closed with the ring of bells, and at night there was a grand exhibition of fireworks (which began and concluded with thirteen rockets) on the Commons, and the city was beautifully illuminated.'"

70 *Savannah | New Georgia Encyclopedia*, georgiaencyclopedia.org, 16 Feb. 2017 <http://www.georgiaencyclopedia.org/articles/counties-cities-

consolation, was insufficient for merriment among southern whites. Cargoes of cotton and rice bound for ports on both sides of the Atlantic, the lifeblood of Savannah's economy, were down more than ninety percent.[71] White businessmen had descended into a world of financial and emotional ruin. Negroes saw it differently. Slaves had become freedmen. And freemen, Negroes who had never been slaves, were buoyed as well. A better life, though still a distant flickering star, had become possible. Like the rockets that would climb for the Heavens, new hope was destined to burst into a rainbow of glorious hues.

Minutes after we arrived at the river, the pyrotechnics began. Brilliant bursts painted the sky. Variegated fountains leapt from the river.[72] Oohs and aahs accompanied the percussion of exploding missiles. A brass band, its bass drum a rejoinder to the thunderous blasts, accompanied the fireworks, transforming them into a rhapsodic symphony. Roman candles rocketed upward exploding into starry umbrellas. As their cascades drifted earthward, they lit the night, the Heavens bright, a splendid sight, whose sparkles rained, then slowly waned, until their sequels did ensue, indeed outdo the prior view, with starbursts yet, that did beget the last vignette, a coronet upon the day, a perfect way to last survey the grand display, a Claude Monet.

As the last of the glowing embers faded and the reverberations dwindled, off to my left, a man, about eighteen, waved a blue cap overhead. "Lot betta than the flash and boom of cannons I been hearin' fo' too long," he said. "We spilt enough blood deez past four years to last til…" He heaved a sigh, as his voice trailed off.

His comment shifted my thoughts to my days at Fort Myers when news had come that tens of thousands had died on battlefields in both the North and South. Soldiers at the fort had lamented the bloodshed, but itching for a fight, a chance to feed the dirty Rebs a repast of lead, decried their peaceful surroundings. Not until Grover had set me straight did I value the dearth of combat the fort had faced. That casualties there could be counted on one's fingers was a blessing.

---

neighborhoods/savannah>. On December 22, 1864, when Sherman completed his march to the sea, he sent his famous telegram to President Lincoln presenting "'a Christmas gift, the city of Savannah with 150 heavy guns and plenty of ammunition; and also about 25000 bales of cotton.'"

[71] Ibid., *Reconstruction in Georgia | New Georgia Encyclopedia.*

[72] *The Rockets' Red, White and Blue*, op. cit., stating: "By 1783 a large variety of fireworks were available to the public. In 1784 one merchant offered a range of pyrotechnics that included 'rockets, serpents, wheels, table rockets, cherry trees, fountains, and sun flowers.'"

Amidst my musing, thoughts of my father came to the forefront. More than a year had elapsed since he had been killed, since my life had been altered. Nostalgia superseded celebration. Melancholy supplanted merriment. A yearning to be back in our wooded cabin emerged. I glanced at the Wrights, both parents and children. I had a new family. Undeniably, I was in a good place. But at that moment, given my druthers, I would have opted for my former life, deep in the remote reaches of the Everglades.

***

"Whatcha wanna do t'day?" said Grover, as we stood outside the First African Baptist Church following Sunday services.

I shrugged. Spending the day with him, whatever we did, was welcome.

"Wanna gimme a numbers lesson?"

I groaned. The free Sunday afternoon begged something better, not that I objected to teaching him. On the contrary, one evening each week, on his way home after he finished loading cotton, he stopped by at the Wrights' place, where I would help him with his reading and arithmetic. Playing the role of mentor, especially at my age, burnished my self-esteem. Mr. Wright was well aware of this. As part of my chores, he had me help Michael and Nora with their homework. Though it was seemingly a duty, I suspected it was a device to ease my transition, make me feel like a member of the family. Perhaps it was also a lesson, an opportunity for me to discover that work and responsibility need not be burdens. They could be sources of joy. Mentoring his children may have been an obligation, but it was a welcome one, a privilege.

"So, what we gonna do?"

"No schooling. Not on a beautiful Sunday."

"Good by me," said Grover. "How 'bout we go tuh de park. De Baltimo' Hann'buls, a Negro baseball team from up north is in town.[73] Dey gonna play our local boys, mos'ly soldiers dat fought in de war."

"Wow, a professional baseball team…here?"

"Well, I dunno if dey be profess'nal, but dey a real team. Game be in de big park…o'er on de west sida town."

---

[73] *Negro Baseball League, Historical Timeline*, cnlbr.org, 9 Nov. 2017 <cnlbr.org/Portals/0/RL/Historical%20Timeline.pdf>.
Negro League Baseball Chronology, baseballchronology.com, 9 Nov. 2017 <http://www.baseballchronology.com/baseball/Leagues/Negro/>.

"Let's go," I said. Back at Fort Myers the soldiers were known to play baseball on the parade grounds, but by their own admissions, their skills were meager compared to the masters of the game.

Less than a half-hour later, we arrived at the field. We managed a couple of seats on the wooden bleachers that paralleled the first-base line. Grover bought us each a bag of peanuts from a vendor. As I cracked the nuts, allowing the shells to drop to the ground below, I surveyed the growing throng. By the time the game began, I estimated the crowd at a thousand, about three hundred in the bleachers (seven rows, each with forty or so) and another six or seven hundred standing outside the margins of the field. I arrived at that number by counting heads in a small area and multiplying by the total number of such groups, allowing for uneven density as best I could. As I carried out the process, one of Mr. Wright's lessons came to mind. Unlike curiosity, which could be fed with mere convenience, fundamental principles of mathematics and science demanded detail and accuracy. Valid though the point may have been, on an indulgent day at the ballpark, convenience sufficed.

The Savannah locals took the field first with the Baltimore Hannibals up to bat. With one out and runners on first and third, the fourth Hannibal batter, their clean-up hitter, Bull Broman, stepped to the plate. With shoulders as broad as his bat was long, the hulk of a man, about 6'6", took his stance. A moment after the pitcher threw the ball, the Bull unleashed a prodigious swat. The cannon blast echoed as the ball flew high and far, way over the center fielder's head. The roaring crowd stood as one as Bull circled the bases. He doffed his cap as he touched home plate. The Hannibals grabbed a quick 3 – 0 lead. They added two more runs before the initial half of the first inning ended.

The locals came up to bat. An energized crowd chanted the name of Herman Blake, a diminutive, but speedy infielder, exhorting him to get a hit. The lanky Hannibal pitcher unleashed his first offering, a fireball, bearing no similarity to the earlier snail-like deliveries of the Savannah pitcher. Blake's bat still on his shoulder, the umpire bellowed, "Strike one!" Pitch two saw Blake frozen again, the umpire shouting, "Strike two!" Blake rapped his bat against his spikes and dug in. The Hannibal hurler wound up and unleashed a rocket, one that made his first two pitches seem slow. Blake swung, but so late that the ball's thump in the catcher's mitt preceded the vain effort. Savannah's next two batters duplicated Blake's debacle.

"Ain't no contest," said Grover.

"That's an understatement," I said, invoking a phrase that Mr. Wright had used in school a few days earlier. His pervasive influence was undeniable. Bits of knowledge from one subject were integrating into others. Lessons in English, history, mathematics and science, formerly compartmentalized collections of disparate knowledge, interconnected, synthesizing themselves into my reasoning, views and daily life.

As the innings slipped by, that which was obvious in the first stanza, grew into a *fait accompli.* (Mr. Wright's erudite articulation, often dressed with French and Latin phrases, was knitting itself into my thoughts.) There was no doubt the Hannibals would prevail; the sole question, by how much. Even as the locals continued to cheer the minuscule successes of their hometown favorites, they roared approval for the Hannibals' prowess. By the time the contest reached the final inning, with the score 21-0, Grover and I, like many around us, were engaging in increasing conversation unrelated to the game. Surveying the throng, I saw only Negroes. Not one white could I find, though some out beyond left field, too distant for identification, could not be ruled out. "Have you noticed there isn't one white person here at the game?"

Grover gave me a look. "Dat su'prise yuh?" He pointed at the ballfield. "Case yuh ain't been watchin', deez be Negro teams."

"I know, but you'd think some white folks would jump at the chance to see a slugger like Bull Broman."

"Ain't de way I seez it, not here in Geo'gia."

This time I shot Grover a look, one that I assumed expressed even greater skepticism than he had shown a moment before.

"De whites. Dey don't care 'bout Negro baseball. I know dat 'cause I hear 'em talk when I be loadin' cotton. While I be sweatin', de boss man and the ship cap'in, dey gab…pol'tics, baseball, aw kinds of stuff. Dey sez de Negro ballplayers ain't good 'nough tuh wash de white boys' privates."

"You believe that?"

"Course not, but what yuh 'spect me tuh do? Bang a bale a cotton on der heads?" Grover fired a peanut shell between the foot boards of the grandstand. "It be de same when dey be talkin' 'bout smarts. Dey sez we dumb. But it ain't true. If yuh don't let a body learn nuttin'—whup 'im if he try—he gonna seem dumb."

"If that's the way they treat you, why do you work for them, loading their cotton?"

Grover heaved a sigh. "Gotta eat. Gotta live…Gotta do what I gotta do. But likes I told yuh, I got goals. Doin' my jew'lry. And I can read now. Yuh knows dat. Jus' 'cause I don't talk good—years and years sayin' stuff one way, I ain't gonna change. But dat don't mean I dumb."

"Is it better for you here in Savannah than it was at the fort?"

Grover gazed at the ballfield, though presumably introspection, not the game, occupied his thoughts. “Betta?…Hard tuh say. Course life don’t always move de way yuh wants. I tries tuh take two steps fo’wad, befo’ I take one back. When I come tuh Fo’t Myers, dat wuz two giant steps fo’wad. I went from bein’ chattel and gettin’ whupped tuh bein’ free. Yeah, dey treat me secon’ class, but nex’ tuh my massa, it wuz good…not dat I ain’t ’titled tuh betta. But once dey shut de fo’t, I got no choice. I gotta find me a place, and dis here wuz de bes’ I know. Maybe I takes a step back. But I don’t quit. I gonna take mo’ steps fo’wad.”

The resolve in Grover’s voice convinced me of his determination. I also realized that he was looking out for me; that he wanted me to have the opportunities that had been stolen from him; and that having me live with the Wrights was his way of affording me those opportunities. Much as I had delighted in the chance to help him learn to read, to be his mentor, it struck me that he was much more of a mentor to me, fathering me after my dad’s death and guiding me to circumstances that would enable me to take many steps forward with the fewest back. “Thank you,” I said. “Thank you so much.”

Grover pulled back, a puzzled look on his face. “Fo’ bringin’ yuh tuh de baseball game?”

“That too…but much, much more.” From the bottom of my bag, I pulled out a rare shell, one with three humps. I cracked it open and dumped all three peanuts into his hand.

The Hannibals’ second baseman caught a pop fly, the last out of the contest. The Baltimore Hannibals had bested Savannah’s locals 24-0. But of all the brilliant exploits on the field that day, one stood out. Grover Calhoun had hit a grand slam.

***

Nearly six months had elapsed since my arrival in Savannah. I was among the lucky ones who was enrolled in school. My prowess with numbers—I was quicker than most who were two and three years older—had earned me a place with those who were fifteen and sixteen years old. The school differed from Fort Myers where all the children participated. In Savannah, only the brightest were able to attend the Negro school. Our classroom was overcrowded. With books and materials scant, education was reserved for those exhibiting the greatest potential. Down the road, when economic conditions improved and more facilities became available, education could be enjoyed by a broader population. But for the moment, we were the fortunate ones. The idea was drummed into our heads, and we took it to heart. What we lacked in materials, we made up for in dedication.

When the War of Secession had drawn to a close, educational remnants of the antebellum era remained. Apart from a school tax that had previously assisted poor white children with tuition at private schools, Georgia had no system of public education.[74] Negroes received no help from the State. In January 1865, some literate Negroes in Savannah had banned together and formed the Savannah Education Association.[75] They raised funds, recruited teachers and opened schools for Negroes. Three-quarters of the teachers were white, and most, like Mr. Wright, came from the North. In March 1865, Congress had created the Bureau of Refugees, Freedman, and Abandoned Lands, commonly referred to as the Freedmen's Bureau. Although it "did not hire teachers or operate schools itself…[i]t rented buildings for schoolrooms, provided books and transportation for teachers, superintended schools, and offered military protection for students against the opponents of black literacy."[76]

Apart from knowing that many in the community had made my education possible, I was unaware who had funded my learning opportunities. At the time, little did I realize that Grover, despite his meager income, had made a tiny contribution. My teacher, Mr. Wright, though never providing specifics, made certain we appreciated our benefactors, even if we were ignorant of their identities.

Where the school at Fort Myers had been comparatively relaxed, Mr. Wright ran a tight ship. A graduate of Dartmouth College, he employed the Socratic Method. Question after question, he bounded from student to student. Amidst a tension-filled room, he forced us to maintain focus. Exactly how the ancient Greeks had employed the technique, I did not know, but Mr. Wright turned it into a highly effective learning tool. With his broad liberal arts background, including ample studies in theology, he integrated diverse subjects. Where English, history, arithmetic and science had been separate disciplines in the Fort Myers schoolhouse, Mr. Wright constantly intermingled them. Such was the nature of a lesson he delivered on a typical day in early fall.

The broad-shouldered, sinewy teacher stepped down from the First African Baptist Church pulpit, the place where he delivered lectures. His move from the altar, closer to the pews where we were seated, signaled

---

[74] *Freedmen's Education During Reconstruction*, georgiaencyclopedia.org, 18 Feb. 2017 <http://www.georgiaencyclopedia.org/articles/history-archaeology/freedmens-education>.

[75] *See*, footnote 60, supra.

[76] *Freedmen's Education During Reconstruction*, op. cit.

an intention to engage us. "Aaron," he said, "now that you have completed *The Scarlet Letter*, tell us, is it more than just a tale of sin and repentance?"

"Uh…I believe it's about vengeance too."

"How so?"

"Well, vengeance becomes Roger Chillingworth's all-consuming, driving force as he seeks to punish the two adulterers, Dimmesdale and Prynne."

"And should we condemn Chillingworth for seeking vengeance?"

"Absolutely." Aaron sat tall in his seat. "The Bible teaches in Romans 12:19: 'Vengeance [is] mine; I will repay, saith the Lord.'"[77]

"So…" Mr. Wright walked down the center aisle and stared down at Aaron who occupied the end seat. "We should ignore the words in Matthew 5:38-39: 'An eye for an eye, and a tooth for a tooth.'"[78]

"Uh…no…but…"

As the seconds ticked, Mr. Wright simply nodded. Finally, he turned to the other side of the aisle.

Fearing he was about to call my name, I froze.

"Amabel, is the Bible simply a mass of inconsistent gibberish?"

"No, Sir."

Experience had taught that an easy question, the type Amabel had just faced, was hardly reason to celebrate. Even if not a trap, a blunderbuss was likely to follow.

"So, enlighten us mortals. Which is right, the words of Romans or the words of Matthew?"

"I…I guess they both are. Blind vengeance…uh…the kind pursued by Roger Chillingworth is wrong, but sometimes retribution is necessary; for example, to stop an unrepentant murderer from killing again."

Mr. Wright pawed at his chin. "If I understand you, we should execute such murderers, get that eye for an eye…For what other wrongs should we extract vengeance?"

Amabel sat motionless. Worse yet, she was silent.

"Mican…" The sound of my name had me reeling. "Tell me the list of wrongs for which we should demand vengeance."

"I…uh…don't think it's by list."

"If not list, then how?"

"The facts and circumstances of the wrongful conduct. Uh…the risks that the conduct will recur. The danger to others…The…" I drew a

[77] Bible, King James version, *Romans* 12:19.
[78] Ibid., Matthew 5:38-39.

blank. A platitude was better than nothing. “The…uh…dictates of justice.”

Mr. Wright pirouetted. “Aaron, do you agree with Mican?”

The question, one that would have seemed harmless several months earlier, was an all-too-familiar visit by the Seven-Headed Monster of Revelation.[79] No matter what direction Aaron went, whatever position he chose, a snarling head of the monster would confront him. Aaron was doomed.

“Well, not exactly…”

Aaron had refused to take the bait. Unfortunately, Mr. Wright was a patient man, and the silence was deafening.

Mr. Wright spread his arms wide. “Not exactly, what?”

“Well, I guess Mican has a point, that we need to look at the facts and circumstances.”

“So, you agree with Mican?”

Aaron nodded.

“No doubt you’re all familiar with Leviticus 19:18.”

Whether or not I was depended on its content. Unfortunately, the citation alone was insufficient for me to identify how it read. I held my breath for fear Mr. Wright would ask me.

“In case any of you have forgotten the passage, I will save you embarrassment and remind you. It says: ‘Thou shalt not avenge or bear any grudge against the children of thy people, but thou shalt love thy neighbor as thyself.’”[80] Mr. Wright walked to the last row. “Emma, we have three biblical principles. Help us make sense of them.”

“Well…when individuals sin, break the law, punishment may be necessary. But punishment should be a means to justice, not vengeance. To paraphrase Colossians 3:13: As God forgives us, he wants us to forgive.”[81]

---

[79] Ibid., Revelation 13:7. The Seven-Headed Monster of Revelation “represents the worldwide political system.” *What is the Seven-Headed Wild Beast of Revelation 13? | Bible Questions*, jw.org, 12 Oct. 2019 <https://www.jw.org/en/bible-teachings/questions/revelation-13-beast/>. The beast “rules over ‘every tribe and people and tongue and nation,’ so it is greater than a single national government.” (Revelation 13:7) “…the seven heads of the beast of Revelation 13:1 represent seven governments: the primary political powers that have dominated through history and have taken the lead in oppressing God’s people—Egypt, Assyria, Babylon, Medo-Persia, Greece, Rome, and Anglo-America.” *See also*, *The Beast (Revelation)*, Wikipedia, 13 Oct. 2019 <http://en.wikipedia.org/wiki/The_Beast_ (Revelation)> for other interpretations of the Seven-Headed Monster including, among others, its link to the diabolical number *666*.

[80] Bible, Leviticus 19:18.

[81] Ibid., Colossians 3:13.

"Not bad, Emma. Not bad at all." Mr. Wright's assessment was seemingly mediocre. But have no doubt, Emma had chalked up a gold star.

For a moment, Mr. Wright stood pensive. The unpredictability of his next volley kept everyone, including me, still. A squirm would put one in his sights. He said, "Emma mentioned God. That begs the question. How do we know there is a God?"

I was shocked. Why would Mr. Wright, a man who in the privacy of his home unambiguously proclaimed his belief in God, doubt the existence of the Lord? No sooner did the question dart through my brain than an answer emerged. Mr. Wright was a proponent of the scientific method. He taught us to question everything. Even when we were sure of a position, we were urged to entertain contradictory arguments. As he had often put it, "An open mind can learn. And even if that mind does not change, it may see matters under a brighter light."

Mr. Wright walked toward the altar but stopped just short and turned. His gaze seemingly focused on each of us, one-by-one. The scene was familiar. No one moved a muscle. No one wanted to face the theological challenge.

"Peter, is there a God?"

"Absolutely."

Had I been called upon, I would have given a similar answer, though I would have couched it less categorically.

"And how do you know there is a God, Peter?"

"Anselm of Canterbury, a man far wiser than I, demonstrated it with his ontological argument, roughly eight hundred years ago in his Proslogion."[82]

Mr. Wright scratched his head. "Hmm…Refresh my recollection as to Anselm's reasoning."

No doubt the reaction and comment were for effect. Mr. Wright knew Anselm's argument, indeed, far better than Peter.

"Anselm," said Peter, "defined God as a being no greater than that which could be conceived. Anselm said that the concept exists either in our mind, or both in our mind and in reality. But if it only exists in our mind, then a greater being can be conceived, i.e., one that exists in reality too. But that is a contradiction. Ergo, God must exist in reality, as well as in our mind."[83]

---

[82] *Ontological Argument*, Wikipedia, 13 Nov. 2017
<http://taggedwiki.zubiaga.org/new_content/9189c4f222ce4a4331f74e425d79aef5>
citing Leaman, Oliver; Peter S. Groff,
"Islamic Philosophy A-Z," (Edinburgh Univ. Press, 2007).
[83] Ibid.

Mr. Wright nodded repeatedly.

As good as Peter's recitation was, I was surprised it enjoyed an immediate stamp of approval.

"What if God doesn't exist?" Mr. Wright looked Peter in the eye.

A puzzled look appeared on Peter's face. "But God does. I...uh...just proved it."

"So, you did...purportedly. But help me to understand. Does a turtle with three shells and nineteen legs that can travel from Earth to the stars and back in a second...exist?"

"Of course not." Peter struggled to contain laughter.

"Well, I can conceive of it." Mr. Wright folded his arms. "But if it only exists in my mind, and if God is not such, then isn't my turtle something greater than that which can be conceived...greater than God?" Mr. Wright looked around the room. He shook his head. "Surely, we can clear this up...with mathematics, perhaps." He looked my way. "Mican, no one has a quicker mathematical mind than you. Tell us, is there a God?"

Six months earlier, I would have viewed the link between God and mathematics as non-existent. But with Mr. Wright, matters of knowledge and the intellect had boundless links. Unfortunately, I had no clue what link he had in mind. My brain blank, my stomach churning, I remained mute.

Seconds...painful seconds ticked. Finally, Mr. Wright said, "Let me help you. Think of Descartes, the mathematician. Perchance you chose to read that lovely brown book on the end of the first shelf, one of several suggested extra readings." Mr. Wright gestured toward a bookshelf on the far wall.

Conscientious though I was, I hardly had time for most of the extra readings. I suspected the same could be said for my classmates, but that was irrelevant. None of them were on the hot seat. "I'm sorry, Sir," I said. "I'm not familiar with it."

"Then let me fill you in. Descartes invoked geometry to prove the existence of God. Just as the angles of a triangle, their total always 180 degrees, can be precisely deduced, God's existence can be deduced from his nature. The concept of God engenders a supremely perfect being. The very idea of a supremely perfect God that does not exist is a contradiction. Phrased otherwise, God would not be supremely perfect if he did not exist."[84] Mr. Wright paused, seemingly allowing the logic to sink in. "Mican, I assume Descartes, brilliant mathematician that he was, has proved God's existence to your satisfaction."

---

[84] Ibid.

Experience in Mr. Wright's classroom precluded me from treating the comment as rhetorical and responding with an unequivocal *yes*. Countless lessons had taught me that more than anything Mr. Wright wanted us to think. I said, "Much as I would not presume to disparage a great mind like Descartes, I believe his argument is woven from whole cloth."

"Whole cloth?" Mr. Wright's eyes were baseballs. "Please elucidate."

I took a deep breath. "Descartes' argument borders on circular, assuming that which he seeks to prove."

Mr. Wright nodded…sarcastically. "Can it be that the *au fait* Mican Reinbow is wiser than René Descartes?"

"By no means, Sir. I…I believe in God. But much as I try to prove God's existence, I can come up with nothing that comes close. Descartes' argument is far better than anything I could muster."

"But you reject his argument."

"But only because it is impossible to prove or disprove God's existence…To my mind, it's a matter of faith."

Mr. Wright turned and ascended the altar. A tension-wielding silence gripped the room. He stepped behind his lectern. He looked my way and said, "Mican, I agree with you…Class dismissed."

***

By the time we embarked on the first days of 1866, I was well ensconced in my Savannah life. I had chores in the Wright home, the most important of which was tutoring Michael and Nora, both of whom were academically advanced for their ages. When first I moved in, I feared the family might treat me like a servant. Even when the siblings referred to themselves as my charge, I suspected that the reference might be in name only, not reality. But circumstances quickly proved the Wrights had no intention of taking advantage of me. From the outset they emphasized that my primary responsibility was my own education. Add to that their welcoming nature, an unequivocal message that I was part of the family, and my adjustment was easy. Though in many ways I was unworldly, the mixture of good and bad fortune that had been my life did not escape me. Indeed, I had suffered dreadful losses, the deaths of both my mother and father. But thanks to Grover and, more recently, the Wright family, I had avoided the hate, bondage and economic disadvantage that infected the lives of most people of color.

Dinner in the Wright home was always a family affair. The five of us remained at the table until everyone and everything was finished, and that included Mr. and Mrs. Wright's tea, often a second cup. Lively conversation on a wide range of topics, many with an academic bent, prevailed. It was the first Thursday following the commencement of the New Year, and Michael and I had just delivered dessert, a large serving of peach pie, to each seat. With all of us back in place, Mr. and Mrs. Wright at either end of the table, the siblings on one side and me on the other, Mr. Wright said, "Nora, what do you think of our president?"

"Yuck, he's awful." The sentiment, an echo of her parents' view, was predictable.

Mr. Wright pawed at his chin. "If you ask me, he's not that good." Ignoring the chuckle he drew, he turned my way. "Mican, what do you think?"

Months of exposure to his Socratic classroom, as well as his dinner table, shaped my response. "I agree…but given Scripture, the need to mind our tongues, to be charitable, I'll forgo the chance to denigrate him more." I would have buttressed my answer with reference to a specific Biblical passage, including chapter and verse, had I been able to think of one. Regardless, my choice of verb, "denigrate," a word I had learned in school the day before, sparked self-satisfaction.

"Michael, why don't we like this man?" said Mr. Wright. "After all, he is our president."

"He's a bigot!"

"But he's a populist, like Andrew Jackson. Admittedly, he supported slavery, but his purpose was noble, preservation of the Union."[85] Mr. Wright looked down to the end of the table. "What do you think, Dear?"

"That the kids are right. And by the way, he's been a big supporter of states' rights, even while trying to keep the Union together."

"Unless I'm mistaken," said Mr. Wright, "President Johnson came from the North. A Republican, right?"

"He's from Tennessee,"[86] said Michael.

"Tennessee?" A piece of pie on Mr. Wright's fork nearly tumbled off as he stopped the utensil just short of his mouth. "He was Vice-president under Abraham Lincoln. Why would Lincoln choose a southern Democrat who supported slavery as his running mate?" Mr. Wright glanced at his children.

---

[85] *Andrew Johnson – U.S. President*, biography.com, 22 Nov. 2017 <http://www.biography.com/people/andrew-johnson-9355722>.

[86] *Andrew Johnson*, whitehouse.gov, 22 Nov. 2017 <http://www.whitehouse.gov/1600/presidents/andrewjohnson>. Johnson was born in North Carolina. He was "apprenticed to a tailor as a boy, but ran away" to Tennessee, where he ultimately opened a tailor shop.

Their blank looks suggested the question was well above their grade level.

Mr. Wright turned my way. "Care to venture an explanation?"

With no clue as to the answer, I eyed my dessert.

Fortunately, Mr. Wright was more indulgent at the dinner table than in school. While benevolence was a factor, his wife's influence played the greater role. Spoiling a meal with a no-nonsense cross-examination would earn him a reprimand.

"He is from Tennessee," said Mr. Wright. "And let me explain how this unlikely man became Lincoln's running mate. Heading into the 1864 election, Lincoln was worried, and with good reason. Many in the North were unhappy with his Emancipation Proclamation. They were tired of war. Johnson, despite his baggage, had gained popularity fighting for the common man and criticizing wealthy plantation owners. And most significant, when Tennessee had seceded from the Union, Johnson had remained in the United States Senate, the only senator from a seceding state to do so. That act made him a pariah in the South, but a hero in the North."[87] In 1864, the Republicans, eager to demonstrate that their National Union Party welcomed all who were loyal to the Union, nominated Johnson, a southern Democrat, for Vice-president."[88] Mr. Wright shoveled a piece of pie into his mouth. Once he finished chewing, he said, "Based upon the facts, as I just outlined them, should we rethink our views about President Johnson?"

"No way!" said Michael.

"Okay, tell me why."

"He doesn't want Negroes to have rights."

"Can you be more specific?"

Michael shrugged.

Mr. Wright turned to me. "Any idea?"

"He's fine with the Black Codes, laws limiting the rights of Negroes, that are being enacted in most of the southern states. If I remember correctly from school, Georgia is the only one that hasn't enacted one."[89]

Mr. Wright nodded. "These past eight months while Congress has been in recess, what has our kindhearted President Johnson done to solve the post-war issues of the South?"

Michael and Nora dug forks into their pie, a non-verbal message begging a reprieve from their father's grilling. Mr. Wright needed to honor their time-out requests, lest he evoke the ire of his wife. Such was

---

[87] Ibid.

[88] Ibid.

[89] *Reconstruction in Georgia | New Georgia Encyclopedia*, op. cit.

the silent interplay at the Wrights' dinner table. Irony and comedy, education and indoctrination, intertwined amidst exchanges governed by unwritten rules, both subtle and patent, seasoned their meals.

"Mican, care to help…give us some insights into what President Johnson has been up to these past eight months?"

I welcomed the question, an issue we had examined in school during the preceding week. That Mr. Wright was tossing me a softball did not escape me. "President Johnson has issued pardons to those Confederates who have taken an oath of allegiance. He even pardoned high officials, men like Alexander Stephens, who served as Vice-president of the Confederacy.[90] In doing so, he restored their political and property rights, except those incident to slavery.[91] But he has turned a blind eye while most southern states have been enacting their Black Codes, rules that all but maintain slavery by requiring Negroes to sign labor contracts that preserve past plantation order."[92]

"Very good." Mr. Wright eyed his children. "You were listening, I presume." He turned back to my side of the table. "Earlier you mentioned that Georgia was an exception. How have actions here differed?"

"Laws have been enacted that allow Negroes to own property, sue and be sued, inherit and…do things like that."[93] Experience in school had taught me that my last catch-all phrase would not sit well with Mr. Wright, but when nothing specific comes to mind, desperation yields to ill-chosen alternatives.

"Can you name any rights that Georgia has denied Negroes?"

"They can't vote, serve on juries or testify against whites."[94]

"So, even here in Georgia, where treatment of Negroes has been relatively benign, it's hardly equal." Mr. Wright turned to Nora. "What do you think about that?"

"It's not fair."

"Michael, you agree with your sister?"

He nodded.

"Why?"

"Because everyone should be treated the same. The color of one's skin shouldn't matter."

That the Wright children, precocious as they were, could give the desired responses to the questions was no surprise. Egalitarian concepts,

---

[90] *Andrew Johnson – U.S. President*, op. cit.

[91] *Reconstruction (National Park Service)*, nps.gov, 14 Sept. 2016 <www.http://www.nps.gov/articles/reconstruction.htm>.

[92] Ibid.

[93] *Reconstruction in Georgia | New Georgia Encyclopedia*, op. cit.

[94] Ibid.

as well as principles like the Ten Commandments, had been drilled into their heads.

Mr. Wright raised his teacup but stopped before the vessel reached his lips. “Now that Congress is back in session and a New Year is soon to begin, will we see a shift in policy? Will whites dominate the South in a way that will replicate the past? Will Negroes, apart from slavery, be consigned to antebellum oppression? Or will equality for all become both the law and reality of our country?” He sipped his tea before peering blankly into space. “What do you think, Dear?”

Contrary to my expectation that Mrs. Wright would respond by suggesting that the discussion yield to a quiet enjoyment of dessert, she bit into her husband’s bait.

“Hard to say…but given that the Republicans control Congress, there’s reason to hope that Negroes will enjoy a more equitable landscape.”

Prognosticating the future offered a challenge I had no desire to tackle, not when I would have to defend my position. I prepared myself with an echo of Mrs. Wright’s view, just in case I was asked. If nothing else, there would be an adult supporting my argument.

As it turned out, Mr. Wright did not press us for predictions. Instead, with gaze again directed into empty space, he said, “God help us if President Johnson’s version of Reconstruction prevails. If so, the question why we fought the War of Secession will be incredibly painful.” He dug his fork into his pie. He started to raise the utensil but stopped. “Regardless what the future brings, given all the blood that was shed…pain, an abundance of it, is inevitable.”

Chapter IX

IT WAS THE LAST SATURDAY IN MAY 1866. Spring came early in Savannah, as too did summer. Comfortable days in the seventies rapidly morphed into humid ones in the eighties, not that the graph was linear. Were I to describe it mathematically—I had learned algebra and geometry and was embarking on trigonometry—a sine curve would not have sufficed. An equation incorporating at least the seventh or eighth power would have been needed to properly chart the irregular ups and downs of springtime weather. Such was the way I viewed the world around me. Much as it came naturally, my mathematical skills would not have advanced so rapidly were it not for Mr. Wright. Though he leaned toward English, philosophy and theology, logic was an ever-present element of his methodology. Equally important was his bent toward integrating all areas of knowledge. He encouraged me to take advantage of my scientific and mathematical acuity, to view the arts, religion, literature and the world in general through a numerical and scientific lens. When my analysis of a subject diverged into numbers, graphs, equations or geometric shapes, he willingly followed my unconventional path. Still he demanded that I also travel more familiar roads. The upshot was that I saw matters in diverse lights and ways. He analogized it to the scrutiny one might give a painting. Different perceptions emerge as a consequence of observations made from afar and up close, even under a microscope.

The night before, we had celebrated Nora's ninth birthday. Saturday morning, I had spent a few hours picking fruit, earning some pocket money. I had just finished lunch and was preparing for my Saturday afternoon ritual, tutoring Nora and Michael in arithmetic, when Mr. Wright pulled me aside.

"Mrs. Wright promised Nora she could help make an apple pie today. And Michael needs to catch up on some chores he skipped this morning. How about you and I taking a walk down to the river?"

Almost never did I spend time alone with Mr. Wright. Presumably he had a purpose, but what, I had no idea. "Okay." The instant I spoke the word, it reverberated in my head. His proposal, a seemingly casual suggestion, was tantamount to a directive. My response, instinctive, was a product of what I assumed I was supposed to say.

Together we headed down the two flights from the flat and out the front door. We went north on Montgomery in the direction of the river.

Mr. Wright gestured at the blue firmament, sparsely splashed with cottony whites. "Nice day for a stroll, isn't it?"

"Yes, Sir."

We ambled two more blocks without uttering a word. The silence unnerved me. Perhaps he was expecting me to initiate conversation. If so, should I talk about school, his lecture the day before? Maybe small talk, the ruts in the road or rustling in the sycamores, would be appropriate. I said, "That was a nice party last night for Nora's birthday. She really liked the dress Mrs. Wright made for her."

"She did indeed. And speaking of birthdays…when is yours?"

"In the fall."

Mr. Wright stopped. I did the same. He looked me in the eye. "Your birthday…What month? What day?"

I shrugged. Perhaps more accurately, I cringed. Everyone I knew, even Grover, knew his or her birthday.

"You don't know your birthday?" Mr. Wright's eyes were wide.

"Not exactly, except that I was born in the autumn."

He looked away and mumbled just loud enough to be audible. "We need this walk even more than I realized."

Already perplexed about the motive behind the outing, I grew more antsy.

Mr. Wright looked around before mumbling again. "Down by the river will be soon enough."

We continued north on Montgomery, past the First African Baptist Church, past the bluff that housed Factor's Walk, to River Street. We turned east, paralleling the edge of the Savannah River. About three hundred yards beyond the turn, Mr. Wright pointed to a solitary bench that faced the river. "That looks like a good place."

A good place for what? I could not imagine.

We eased over to the bench and seated ourselves kitty-corner at either end.

"Hard to believe, it's been nearly a year since you came to live with us." Mr. Wright gazed across the river in the direction of a steamboat that was moored along the opposite shore. He turned back my way. "When first you came, I avoided pressing you with what might seem like prying queries. But by now, I should know you…know you a whole lot better than I do. Hell, I don't even know your birthday."

The curse word, something I never heard in the Wright household, stunned me. As to my birthday, how could he? I didn't know it.

"Time we have a talk. Time I get to know you. Tell me about yourself, what your life was like before you arrived at Fort Myers."

The request caught me by surprise. Since my early days at the fort, rarely had anyone expressed an interest in my background. In Savannah my classmates often talked about themselves. Some had been slaves. A couple had been orphaned during the war. One, born free, had lived in Savannah his entire life. Two of the oldest had fought in the war. They all had stories. I guess I had mine, not that I had told it.

I thought for a moment, uncertain where or how to begin. "I lived with my father, at least until he was killed. That's when they took me in at the fort."

"Did you and your father live in a village near the fort?"

"There wasn't a village there. Just the fort. My dad and I lived out in the woods, about five miles south of the fort…a hundred or so yards inland from the Caloosahatchee River."

"What was your home like?"

"It was nice…not that it was fancy."

"Tell me about it."

"Well…it was a cabin, a wood cabin…with a dirt floor." The image of the old haunt was vivid. Living there had been nice. But a dirt floor hardly fit the term *nice.* The Wrights' flat had impressive tongue-and-groove, pine-planked floors. Even the barracks at Fort Myers had wooden floors. I stole a peak at Mr. Wright's face, endeavoring to determine if he was judging me. His countenance gave no clues.

"Did you have any neighbors?"

"Uh…yes and no." The incongruous response, one that I had invoked far less than when I had first arrived at Fort Myers, rolled off my tongue in advance of better judgment. "There were some other cabins and the like, but the next closest was more than a mile away."

"How did you like it there?"

"It was good." My response sparked mixed emotions. A vision of my dad and me enjoying dinner alongside a roaring blaze in the fireplace kindled joy. Knowledge that he was gone and we would never again share such moments doused the image with melancholy.

"You miss your childhood home."

Even before I uttered a sound, sadness had me choking on my words. Aware I could not speak without putting my despondency on display, I froze. Lips locked, I endeavored to suppress emerging sobs.

"It's okay. There's nothing wrong with crying."

If you're seven years old. Or maybe if you're a girl. But not when you're fourteen, approaching manhood.

"No, really. Adults cry…and they should."

I gave Mr. Wright a skeptical glance.

"They do. But not for trivialities…for example, when they don't get their way. Adults, mature ones, reserve tears for real loss or pain. Sometimes it's physical and others, emotional…loss of a loved one…or lost love."

His last phrase triggered thoughts of Abbey. When her parents had barred our relationship, that was painful, and I had cried. But that sobbing was reserved for the night when only my pillow could see it.

"I recall that shortly after you arrived here you told me you were a Seminole-Negro. Were both of your parents Seminole-Negroes?"

"My father was Seminole and my mother was Negro. She died when I was very young. I have almost no recollections of her. What I recall of my childhood was with my dad."

"You miss him a lot, don't you?"

I nodded. With the passage of two years since his death, the wound was no longer raw, but scars endured. "I liked our life alone together in the woods. But since his death, people…those at the fort, Grover, and you and your family, have been very good to me." As kind as folks had been, were it possible to bring my father back to life and live with him, I would have jumped at the chance. Afraid of appearing thankless, I kept the thought to myself. A part of me recognized that since my father's death, I had idealized my formative years. On many occasions I had mused about the positive. The negative, my father's propensity to binge, had remained buried. The concession might have led me to reevaluate my time in the Everglades, but I preferred to maintain my romanticized memories.

Mr. Wright laid his arm across the back of the bench, so he faced me more directly. "Do you realize that you're an extremely bright student?"

"Thank you, Sir."

"I'm not sure you understand what I'm saying."

I had heard him, and the point seemed self-explanatory. But knowing Mr. Wright, a seemingly self-evident statement could entail a subtle message.

"Much as I don't want you to get a swelled head, you're my smartest student."

While I knew I was among the best, some, especially those older, were more advanced and far more knowledgeable about history, literature, theology and the arts.

"You don't believe me. I see it on your face."

I shrugged, mainly from discomfort. Ungraciously arguing with my teacher in the face of such high praise was unthinkable.

"Some of your fellow students are two or even three years older than you. That alone gives them a big advantage. But beyond that, some benefited from schooling at an early age. It may have been home schooling, but it was education nonetheless. You, on the other hand, began your lessons much later." Mr. Wright appeared to study me. "Based upon your reaction or lack thereof, it seems I've failed to convince you."

"Well…not exactly." The lull that followed my comment communicated a need for me to explain my conclusion. "In some respects, I had an advantage over the others."

"Advantage? How so?"

"My dad constantly explained how things work. The world around us, nature, was a laboratory. And my dad loved numbers. That rubbed off on me. While I may not have had classroom lessons, every day I was learning science and arithmetic, and not in the abstract. The principles were an integral part of everything I did."

Mr. Wright nodded slowly. "Though I still believe you were at a disadvantage for lack of formal schooling, your point is well taken. And might I add, it is a quintessential example of mine: That you have an exceptionally keen mind." His expression drifted into an opaque, distant realm. "I…probably shouldn't be telling you this but…"

I had no idea what secret he was about to reveal. Nor was I sure I cared to hear it.

"You, Mican, are smarter than I."

Doubtless my face reflected the absurdity of his assessment. *Why would he say something so ridiculous?*

"I'm serious."

"You can't be." My ears disbelieved my mouth's spontaneous utterance. "In class, you play me like a yo-yo,[95] leaving me spinning at

---

[95] "It is believed that the yo-yo likely originated in China. The first historical mention of the yo-yo, however, was from Greece in the year 500 B.C.…The first recorded reference to any type of yo-yo in the United States was in 1866 when two men from Ohio received a patent for an invention called an improved bandalore…" *Museum of Yo-Yo History*, yoyomuseum.com, 13 Oct. 2019

the bottom of a string, only to be jerked upward whenever you please or to be left hanging until you rewind my tether."

"True…But what do you think my professors did to me roughly a dozen years ago when I was a freshman at Dartmouth? And their professors did the same to them. But you, at fourteen, with very limited schooling meet my Socratic challenges with reasoning and prowess, as well as a command of the language, that belies your age and background. Your class is the cream of the crop, and you, Mican, are the crème de la crème."

His accolades left me speechless. The *thank you, Sir,* I knew I should utter, failed to materialize.

"You're probably wondering why I'm telling you this."

Until he had made the point, I had been too overwhelmed to entertain the thought. "Uh…yes."

"When one has a gift, it cannot be wasted. That said, to accuse one of wasting a gift of which one is unaware would be unfair. And so, I feel obliged to put you on notice. You have a gift…Waste it not."

Mr. Wright's message, a laudatory syllogism, adorned with morality, had my brain in a quandary. Praise was nice, but did it have to carry such a heavy onus?

"I'm sorry. I didn't mean to burden you."

If so, you could have lessened the praise, omitted the gift and lightened the load. Allowing the sarcasm to cross my lips was never a consideration. Mr. Wright meant well. Regardless, my responses to him were never peppered with acerbity.

"Enough…at least for today…on that subject. Let's talk about something else."

I was happy to shift the discussion. Whether I would like the new topic remained to be seen.

"I owe you an apology."

Apology? The word dumbfounded me.

"As I mentioned before, I haven't taken the time to learn your background. A while ago, before we got sidetracked, we spoke briefly about your life prior to Savannah. Tell me more…about your way of life and your people."

Still discombobulated, I did not know where to begin.

"Tell me about the Seminole-Negroes. Were they a separate tribe, distinct from the Seminoles?"

<http://www.yoyomuseum.com/museum_view.php?action=profiles&subtraction=yoyo>. Given that the yo-yo only appeared in the United States in 1866, Mican's use of the term in that year involves the exercise of literary license, albeit minor.

A vacuous *yes and no* spilled from my brain. I managed to stem it. That Mr. Wright wanted to hear what I knew was exciting. Rarely, if ever, had anyone shown an interest in my roots. Back when my father was alive, he frequently related tales of our ancestors. His motivation was twofold. He loved telling me the lore, and he wanted to preserve our heritage. I said, "The Seminole-Negroes, or what folks commonly refer to as Maroons, were Seminole Indians who aligned themselves with free blacks and runaway slaves. For the most part, they had their own communities, but often they intermarried.[96] According to my dad, the Seminoles' ancestors came to the Southeastern United States more than ten thousand years ago.[97] What they called themselves, I don't know. The term 'Seminole' has only been used for about one hundred years."[98] Anyway, these original ancestors grew and prospered. By the 16th century, there were about one hundred thousand of them living in Florida. But after the Spanish arrived, battles and disease all but wiped them out. Less than one hundred were left.[99] Gradually their numbers grew, and the Seminoles, along with the Choctaws, Creeks, Cherokees and the uh…oh yeah, the Chickasaws, became known as 'The Five Civilized Tribes.' They got the name because they 'lived in cabins or houses, wore clothes similar to the white man and often became Christians.'"[100]

"Interesting," said Mr. Wright. "And do you know when Negroes began to join the Seminoles?"

"I believe it started over one hundred fifty years ago."[101]

Mr. Wright nodded. "Makes sense."

"Pardon me?" I said, unable to follow his comment.

"Slavery was abolished in Spanish Florida just before the end of the 17th century…1693, if I recall correctly. That made it a logical destination for slaves on the run.[102] But enough of my asides. Please tell

---

[96] *See*, footnotes 4 and 5, supra.

[97] Murray, Dru J., *Florida History, Native Peoples, The Unconquered Seminoles, retrieved from Seminole Indian History,* abfla.com, 17 Nov. 2017 <http://www.abfla.com/1tocf/seminole/semhistory.html>. "The Seminoles occupied the Southeastern United States for 12,000 years."

[98] Ibid., stating: "…in 1771, the first recorded usage of the name 'Seminole' to denote an actual tribe was recorded."

[99] Ibid.

[100] Ibid.

[101] *Encyclopedia Britannica, Black Seminoles,* op. cit.

[102] Ibid. "The word they used to describe themselves—Seminole—is derived from a Creek word meaning 'separatist' or 'runaway.' Because slavery had been abolished in 1693 in Spanish Florida, that territory became a safe haven for runaway slaves."

me more. How did these Seminoles and Negroes—I believe you called them Maroons—get along?"

"Quite well. They aligned themselves against foes, and they farmed and hunted and raised cattle…and from what I know, accumulated considerable wealth, land included."[103]

"Based upon my meager knowledge—I've heard of the Seminole wars—I assume they did not fare well in the first sixty years of the 19th century, the period leading up to the War of Secession."

"To say that the Seminoles didn't fare well is an understatement. By the end of those wars—there were three—their numbers had plunged again. Only about two hundred remained in Florida.[104]

Mr. Wright leaned back, his focus fully on me. "Tell me about those wars."

His manner bore no semblance of that which he displayed in the classroom. He was asking questions, but only to get information. His queries were anything but Socratic. Student-crushing intimidation, cross-examination and counterarguments were absent. He was plainly engaged. His interest in my knowledge was validating. What was also nice, his inquiry zeroed in on an area of history, dates included, that I knew well. My father had detailed the three Seminole wars for me. He considered them fundamental facets of our heritage. I said, "The First Seminole War occurred in 1817 and 1818. Andrew Jackson, then a General, wanting to capture runaway slaves, invaded Seminole villages in Florida, ravaging them.[105] The Second Seminole War, by far the longest and bloodiest, ran seven years, from 1835 to 1842. The Indian Removal Act of 1830, a device to seize prized Seminole lands, precipitated it.[106] For seven long years, the vaunted United States Army failed to win victory as they fought to relocate Florida's 4,000 Seminoles

---

[103] Ibid. *See also*, *McCall, George A., Letters from the Frontier*, (Philadelphia: J.B. Lippincott 1868) p. 160, retrieved from Black Seminoles, Wikipedia, 27 Feb. 2017 <http://en.wikipedia.org/wiki/Black_Seminoles> stating: "Under the comparatively free conditions, the Black Seminoles flourished. U.S. Army Lieutenant George McCall recorded his impressions of a Black Seminole community in 1826: 'We found these negroes in possession of large fields of the finest land, producing large crops of corn, beans, melons, pumpkins and other esculent vegetables…I saw, while riding along the borders of the ponds, fine rice growing; and in the village large corn-cribs were filled, while the houses were larger and more comfortable than those of the Indians themselves.'"

[104] *Florida Memory, Timeline of the Florida Seminoles*, floridamemory.com, 27 Feb. 2017 <http://www.floridamemory.com/onlineclassroom/seminoles/timeline/>.

[105] *Seminole Wars | United States history | Britannica.com*, brtiannica.com, 10 Sept. 2017 <http://www.britannica.com/topic/Seminole-Wars>.

[106] Ibid.

and 800 Maroon allies[107] to the Indian Territory west of the Mississippi."[108]

Mr. Wright glanced skyward.

Were I in the classroom, I would have assumed that his reaction was derisive. But given the events of the afternoon, interpreting it was impossible.

"Funny," he said, "when I was in college studying American history, the Indian Wars in Florida were mentioned, but they were nothing more than footnotes to our nation's Manifest Destiny." Mr. Wright peered pensively off into space. "I guess that's the nature of history. Jaundiced pens, generally those of victors, write it. An immoral invasion becomes a glorious quest. Illegally seized lands are well-earned prizes. And murder, pillaging and rape…collateral trifles, disregarded in the wake of self-congratulatory accounts." He heaved a sigh. "God, I can only imagine how the Confederates would be writing history had they prevailed in the war. Confederate flags might be waving, not only in the South, but also over the hallowed halls of Washington D.C. Statues honoring Robert E. Lee and Jefferson Davis, men who sought to destroy the Union in order to preserve slavery, might be rising throughout the South." He refocused on me. "Fortunately, those scenarios went out the window once Lee surrendered at Appomattox…Of course, that doesn't mean equality won't take time. But at least we've started down that road. Just a little more than a year removed from the war, and already we have the Thirteenth Amendment to the Constitution abolishing slavery,[109] and only a few months ago, in April, Congress, overriding a presidential veto, passed the Civil Rights Act, guaranteeing citizenship and property rights to all persons born in the United States. As I said, it may take time before these laws rewrite the status quo, but I'd lay champagne to moonshine that fifteen or twenty years down the road, the races will enjoy substantially equal rights."[110] An odd expression appeared on Mr. Wright's face.

---

[107] *Black Seminoles, Seminole Wars*, Wikipedia, 27 Feb. 2017 <http://en.wikipedia.org/wiki/Black_Seminoles>.

[108] *Oklahoma Territory*, Wikipedia, 18 Nov. 2017 <http://en.wikipedia.org/wiki/Oklahoma_Territory>. The Indian Territory was essentially lands "granted to certain Indian nations under the Indian Removal Act, in exchange for their historic territories east of the Mississippi River." By 1856 it had been reduced to what is today "the State of Oklahoma, except for the Oklahoma Panhandle and Old Greer County."

[109] U.S. Const., amend. XIII.

[110] Civil Rights Act of 1866, 18 Stat. 27-30 (enacted April 9, 1866). The Civil Rights Act of 1866 was enacted when a two-thirds majority overrode the veto of President

When he failed to continue, I said, "Something the matter?"

"I'm not a very good poker player."

Yet to learn the game, the remark bewildered me more. "Come again?"

"An unsavory thought just crossed my mind and...oh well, having tipped my hand, I might as well lay my cards on the table. That newly enacted Civil Rights Act, the one I just mentioned—I'm not sure you get its benefit."

Was Mr. Wright joking? If not, why was I excluded?

"You know how I said that the law applies to all persons born in the United States. Well...that's not entirely accurate. There's an exception. Indians not taxed aren't covered."[111]

"Are you suggesting that I don't get the rights given to almost every person in Georgia?"

Mr. Wright shrugged.

Rarely had I seen the decisive educator resort to the ambiguous gesture.

"I don't know...It raises a bunch of issues. Are Maroons classified as Indians? Or are they Negroes? Because you're still a minor, does that place you among those not taxed? And once you start working, will that change? My guess is yes, given that you're not living on a reservation. But I'm not a lawyer. All I can do is guess."

"What do you think I should do?"

His face bearing an apologetic look, Mr. Wright shrugged again. "For the time being, given that you're living with us, I doubt it's a problem."

What if it is? Aware that the query bore a ring of sarcasm, I left it unsaid.

"We can look into the matter. Sherwood Parkens, a lawyer—he belongs to First Baptist—might be able to help us out. For the moment, the best we can do is put it on the back burner."

"I suppose you're right." My acquiescence did not reflect my feelings. It irked me that I might not enjoy the rights of other citizens. Still I could not deny the irony of my frustration. Living in the Everglades, at Fort Myers and in Savannah, rights had never concerned me. But suddenly knowing that I might be in a uniquely disadvantageous position made it troublesome.

Andrew Johnson. *See, Civil Rights Act of 1866*, uscivilliberties.com, 18 Nov. 2017 <http://www.uscivilliberties.org/legislation-action3601-civil-rights-act-of-1866.html>.

[111] Ibid.

"Where were we…I mean before my meandering thoughts took us on a tangent?…Oh yeah, you were telling me about the Seminoles, their three wars. And if I recall correctly, you were yet to tell me about the last one."

I pushed the issue of my status aside but made a mental note to address it at a more opportune time. I said, "The third and last Seminole War occurred shortly before the War of Secession, from 1855 to 1858, when the United States Army revived its campaign against Florida's Seminoles.[112] Casualties were few, if only because the number of Seminoles still in Florida was small. By the end of the conflict, just a couple hundred Seminoles remained there,[113] only a fraction of which were Maroons. The few that were left, much like my dad, lived in the Everglades. Some farmed or raised cattle, while others traded skins and hides."[114]

Mr. Wright gazed across the river reflectively. Finally, he said, "I love my country, but the painting is ugly, a repetition of an age-old story. A more powerful nation invades a weaker one, taking their lands and assets, purging their culture. So very sad." He heaved a sigh. "On the bright side, with the War of Secession behind us and the Thirteenth Amendment enacted, we seem to be moving in a positive direction, particularly here in Georgia."

I knew the reasons behind his point. He had explained it in school. Georgia had "repealed the Ordinance of Secession, abolished slavery and repudiated the Confederate debt."[115] Indeed, the Georgia Legislature stood alone among the states of the Confederacy that did not establish a Black Code.[116] They had enacted color-blind laws that theoretically provided civil equality.[117] But economic realities gainsaid legal progress. While Savannah had been spared the destruction that Sherman had wreaked elsewhere, particularly in Atlanta,[118] like the rest of the Confederacy, the city's economy was devastated. According to Grover, white businessmen, themselves victims of hard times, were paying Negroes less than what they had received as slaves before the war.[119] Where Mr. Wright justifiably pointed to the political and legislative

[112] *Encyclopedia Britannica*, Black Seminoles, op. cit.
[113] *See*, footnote 7, supra.
[114] *Seminole Indian History*, abfla.com, op. cit.
[115] *Reconstruction in Georgia | New Georgia Encyclopedia*, op. cit.
[116] Ibid.
[117] Ibid.
[118] *See*, footnote 70, supra.
[119] *A Time of Reckoning (U.S. National Park Service),* nps.gov, 14 Sept. 2016 <www.http://www.nps.gov/articles/a-time-of-reckoning.htm>.

actions that were leveling Georgia's playing field, Grover, though far less erudite, knew the pragmatics. On farms and in enterprises, Negroes continued to suffer the inequity and iniquity of racial discrimination. I said, "On paper the rules have changed, but out in the streets, are Negroes better off than before?"

Eyes wide, Mr. Wright jerked back, a seeming prelude to a harsh rejoinder. A momentary hiatus yielded to a more relaxed posture. "Your question raises a legitimate issue, not that I concur with its implication. Change takes time. And mind you, I understand that is hardly a satisfactory answer to those who are slaving—no pun intended—under cruel and arbitrary conditions. But reforming the rules is a first step toward greater equity. As I said earlier, I expect that fifteen or twenty years down the road, recent political and legislative seeds will bear fruit. It's why I came here from the North. These seeds, coupled with education, represent the keys to equality. What you and your classmates learn today will alter minds tomorrow. Down the road, it will enable you, and I use the word collectively, to alter the world."

Mr. Wright's argument had merit. But so too did Grover's. Rather than being mutually exclusive, their points, when properly juxtaposed, interlocked like pieces of a jigsaw puzzle. Times were tough. But current political, legal and educational steps could bring about change. I felt optimistic about the future. As for the present, contrary to the norm, mine was good. I may have been an orphan, but I was no Oliver Twist. (Our class had recently read the Dickens' novel, a book already familiar to me.) And Mr. Wright was hardly Mr. Bumble or Fagan. I said, "I see your point."

Mr. Wright chuckled. Before I could inquire as to the source of the odd response, he said, "Given your earlier Socratic question, your concurrence caught me off guard."

His comment, confirmation that I had briefly stepped into his shoes, was a remarkable revelation. I laughed, my guffaw more vigorous than his moments earlier.

Mr. Wright extended his left arm, pointing west. "By the looks of the Sun, three hours, maybe more, have passed since we left home. Time we head back." He smiled broadly and rose from his seat. As I did likewise, he slipped an arm over my shoulder. "I'm glad we spent the afternoon together."

I was too, even more so than Mr. Wright.

***

The last Monday in October 1866. Beneath the shade of an elm in the backyard of the property that housed the Wright's flat, I had given Nora and Michael an arithmetic lesson, fractions for her and decimals for him. As we approached the doorway leading to the two flights that accessed the third-floor quarters, the duo giggled. The moment we entered, Michael charged up the stairs, taking them two at a time. In the meantime, Nora, just ahead of me, spread her arms, inching upward at a snail's pace.

"At the rate you're going, we'll miss dinner," I said, not that I objected to joining their silliness.

Arms still wide, she turned my way and halted. "Mican, did anyone ever tell you that you're prone to hyperbole?"

Even coming from the precocious youngster, the quip might have caught me by surprise were it not for the fact that for two weeks the Wright children, mimicking their father, had been repeating the line whenever anyone exaggerated. For that matter, they were invoking it merely to voice disagreement, even when there was no overstatement.

"You plan to pick up your pace?" I said.

Nora shrugged before slowly working her way up to the first landing. Once there, she did a jig, all the while making sure I couldn't pass. She slowly climbed the second flight, after which she rapped on the flat's door and shouted, "Ready or not, here we come!"

The door swung open. Mr. and Mrs. Wright, who stood just inside, along with Michael, all screamed, "Happy Birthday!"

I did a double take, momentarily confirming there was no one behind me.

"We're celebrating your birthday, Mican," said Mrs. Wright.

"My birthday?" Had they discovered something I didn't know? If so, how?

Michael pointed toward the dining area where a cake and a package sat on the table. "They're for you."

"Me?" I remained outside the threshold, too stunned to move.

Nora grabbed my arm and pulled me inside toward the dining area.

"What makes you think it's my birthday?" I moved my gaze from one member of the family to the next.

"You were born in the fall. True?" said Mr. Wright.

"Yes, but that…that's a big chunk of the year."

"Well, from now on your birthday is the 29th of October."

"That's—" I stopped myself. October 29th was as good as any other date. More important, it was better than having no birthday.

Nora pulled my arm again. "Open your present! Open your present!"

With ham hands hindering me, I slowly tore off the wrapping. Inside was a Bible with my name etched in gold at the bottom of the front cover. Though I was not religious, for one who loved books, but owned only two, the volumes of *Uncle Tom's Cabin*, any new book was welcome. But that was not the point. In all my fifteen years, this was my first birthday gift. That was special. "Thank you." I held the Bible up in front of me. "Thank you so much. I'll cherish it."

"Look underneath," said Nora. She pointed at the spot where the Bible had rested.

Atop the lower portion of the torn wrapping paper was another sheet of paper, folded in half. I picked it up and unfolded a painting, admittedly amateurish, of five people standing under the glow of a big yellow sun. From left to right was a man, a woman, a boy, a girl and another taller boy, all holding hands. In the bottom corner, it bore the name, *Nora.*

"It's our family. I drew it, all by myself," said Nora.

"I love it. I absolutely love it." My voice cracked, as I reiterated my reaction. The Bible, a birthday gift, was exciting; the picture, Nora's statement that I was a member of their family, indescribable.

A smile, an arc so broad it approached semi-circle proportions, etched Nora's face.

"C'mon, let's cut the cake," said Michael.

"What? And spoil your dinner?" said Mrs. Wright.

Pouty faces appeared on each of the two youngsters.

"Oh...okay," said Mrs. Wright. "Everyone can have a tiny sliver now."

"And a big piece after dinner!" said Nora.

Mrs. Wright nodded. She winked at her husband.

I stored the diplomatic lesson in my memory bank. By raising the specter that there would be no cake until after dinner, Mrs. Wright won easy acquiescence for the tiny pre-meal taste. Michael and Nora, astute as they were, may have recognized the strategy too. And armed with their wisdom, they also recognized that demanding big pieces immediately might result in nothing now and less later. For me, it made no difference when the cake was served. I had my cake...and I was eating it too.

Chapter X

SUNDAY AFTERNOON, FOLLOWING CHURCH, Grover and I, fishing poles in hand, headed east to a quiet spot along the margin of the Savannah River. Before seating myself on the bank, I stared down the shoreline. Number freak that I was, I wondered about the slope of the bank. Pointing my index finger straight upward, I formed a 90° angle between my thumb and index finger. I swung my index finger in an arc, bisecting the right angle. With my free hand I marked a spot in the air identifying the 45° angle I had created a moment before. I again swung my index finger in an arc, so it bisected the 45° angle, theoretically at an angle of 22.5^o to my thumb.

"What the hell you doin'?"

I ignored Grover as I held my thumb and index finger in front of my eyes, comparing it to the angle formed by the water and the bank. I guessed the latter angle to be about two-thirds of the former. "Best as I can judge, the bank has a slope of about fifteen degrees."

Grover, who had already plopped himself down, said, "As if I give a hoot."

I shot him a look.

"You gonna fish, or you gonna play protracta?"

His use of the word *protractor*, one that never would have come from his mouth when first we had arrived in Savannah, reflected the progress he had made in the more than two years that had elapsed. A night class, one evening each week, plus my tutoring, and mainly hard work on his own had greatly advanced his education. Even his speech reflected the progress. Though still colloquial, it was inching in the direction of the "King's English."

I seated myself next to Grover and, taking a worm from a container we had brought, baited my hook. I gripped my fishing pole, the cedar rod

I had fashioned in the woods south of Fort Myers, so the end of the line penetrated the surface of the water.

"Damn nice day. More like summer, dan late September."

With the temperature in the eighties, his point was well taken. I found it hard to believe that nearly a year had elapsed since I had celebrated my birthday. 1867 was…one week less than three-quarters complete, roughly 73%. I would have made the point to Grover, were I not loath to have him call me a nutcase.

"Gotta get me a new job. Dem wages dey pay loadin' cotton is as bad as what we got as slaves, not dat dey called 'em wages back den. Dat teacher of yours, Mr. Wright, he still convinced dat Negroes gonna get a fair shake?"

"Yes, though he admits it may take more time than he originally thought. Says it's because the economy is bad. Cities and towns are in shambles. Farms, both homes and barns, are a wreck, and with so much equipment destroyed, cotton and rice production, not to mention wheat and corn, are way down."

Grover shook his head. "I thought dat if de North won de war, things would change. Maybe I was whistlin' a tune on de moon, but I expected better." He mumbled inaudibly for a moment before continuing. "Don't mean to be goin' off at de mouth, complainin' like it's worse den it is. 'Cause, if nuttin' else, just de fact I ain't a slave no more is better den what it was." He pulled his line from the water and pointed at the worm on the end. "I used to be as bad off as dat critter. Least I'm free now."

"Have you considered sharecropping?"

Were Grover's look a dagger, I would have been stabbed. "What you been drinkin', Mican? Ain't you heard? Sharecroppin' is whitey's way of givin' us Negroes water in a rainstorm. Dey charge such high rent for de land and tools and stuff dat by de time you done payin' for it, dey all but own your whole crop. You may not be a slave, but whate'er you are, ain't much better."

"Would it help if you started your jewelry business?" Even as I asked the question, I knew the answer would not provide a satisfactory solution.

"Like I told you before, I can't just do dat, least not right off. Maybe once I'm established, I can live off it. But startin' out, it just a way to grab a few bits."

I longed to offer a suggestion that would help Grover realize his dreams. He had done so much to help me. He had befriended me at Fort Myers, brought me to Savannah and pushed me to live with the Wrights, so I could get the education he had missed. I stared at my fishing line.

Ideas were as hard to come by as fish on my hook. Having already made two useless suggestions, I thought better of adding another.

"Dat fella Johnson dat took over for Lincoln in de White House. His plan for fixin' stuff here in de South…What dey call his plan?"

"Presidential Reconstruction."

"You aks me, his plan is a kick in de ass. Course whad'ya expect when you stick a fox in de hen house. A Tennessee two-timer, a fella who likes slavery, decidin' if we get rights. It's a helluva way tuh run de egg farm." Grover tugged his line, seeming to check if there was anything on the other end. "You think dem boys in Congress gonna make it right for us?"

Presidential Reconstruction, a period of about eight months, had ended when Congress had come back into session in 1866. Much more than a year had elapsed since then, and from what I could surmise, though admittedly my views were influenced by Mr. Wright, Congress, in what was termed Congressional Reconstruction, was determined to level the playing field. In March 1867, it had placed the South under military rule.[120] Georgia, along with Florida and Alabama, was placed into the Third Military District.[121] Laws designed to effectuate equality had been enacted. I said, "They abolished slavery and last year they passed the Civil Rights Act, giving Negroes citizenship and property rights, and they did it over President Johnson's veto. And if that wasn't enough, they amended the Constitution to include, among others, the Fourteenth Amendment.[122] Of course, a few more states need to ratify it before it takes effect. But once it does, it'll prevent the states from depriving any citizen of 'life, liberty, or property, without due process of law;' abridging the 'privileges and immunities of citizens;' and denying 'any person within its jurisdiction equal protection of the laws.'"[123] In school Mr. Wright had drummed the provisions of the Fourteenth Amendment into our heads. I proudly displayed my memorized knowledge.

"Yeah, I know 'bout all dem great laws—well, maybe not what dey say exactly—but what I'm aksin', will we enjoy dem rights? One thing to put 'em on paper, another to make 'em happen."

Grover's comment put a knot in my erudite line. My recitation of principles from rote memory ignored the real world. The possibility that

---

[120] *Andrew Johnson*, Whitehouse.gov, op. cit.
[121] *Reconstruction in Georgia | New Georgia Encyclopedia*, op. cit.
[122] U.S. Const., amend. XIV, retrieved from *14th Amendment to the U.S. Constitution: Primary Documents of American History*, loc.gov, 26 Nov. 2017 <https://www.loc.gov/rr/program/bib/ourdocs/14thamendment.html>.
[123] U.S. Const., amend. XIV, §1.

I had fallen hook, line and sinker for brilliantly drafted rhetoric could not be denied.

"Case you ain't noticed, all through de South, dey passin' Black Codes, laws so nasty dat dey look like slavery. Doin' stuff like stickin' Negroes into forced labor for minor, even made-up offenses.[124] Dem fellas in Washington may be passin' laws dat say we equal, but it gonna take more den ink on paper to make it so."

Grover's reiteration of his point rattled me with the jerk of a 200-pound tuna, at least the way I had imagined such a catch. (The largest I had ever hooked—it had occurred back in my days along the Caloosahatchee—was a twenty-inch bass, about five pounds.) A determined student, I had absorbed the lessons of my teacher Mr. Wright. No doubt he had gotten me to think. But what I had failed to recognize was that I was also eager to please, to gain his approval. At times my responses reflected what I assumed he wanted to hear. Mr. Wright was optimistic about the future, and that was fine. I was optimistic as well, but was it for the right reasons? Was my view a product of well-thought out, independent analysis? To what degree had a desire to win my teacher's approbation skewed it? A defensive streak argued, or should I say rationalized, that Mr. Wright was far more knowledgeable than I. Ergo, at my age, with more limited information, it made good sense to adopt the views of one with expertise. Candor forced me to concede my need to be more autonomous. Whether I would was an open question. Broken New Year's resolutions from past years left me less than sanguine about the prospects.

"So, you agree wid me?" said Grover.

His question compelled me to confront my silent dilemma much sooner than I had anticipated. No way would I allow my newest resolution to fall by the wayside in the very minute it had been made. I said, "Your point is well taken. It's great that Congress is enacting laws providing equal rights, but that's a far cry from making them a reality…On the other hand, if Congress simply sits back and lets the South do as it pleases, inequality, a continuation of an ugly past, is a sure thing." For an instant, I chastised myself for having hedged. But my point had merit. I was thinking through the issue, and perhaps that approach, not sycophancy, was what Mr. Wright preferred.

"I hear you. I just hope dey got more den words. 'Cause you aks me—" Grover stopped midstream. "Damn, wid all dis talk 'bout dem codes and Congress, I almost forgot dat der somethin' important I gotta

---

[124] *Reconstruction*, howard.edu, 22 Nov. 2017 <http://www.howard.edu/library/reference/guides/reconstructionera/>.

discuss wid you today." He looked me in the eye. "You listen up good. You hear?"

Unable to imagine what prompted his sudden shift, I lowered my pole and gave him my full attention.

"You know I ain't got no kin. You de closest to it...If somethin' happens to me, I want you to have my stuff."

"Nothing is going to happen to you."

"Not too soon, I hope. But you ne'er know when your number be up. Dats why folks make a will, not dat I gonna. But I got some stuff, a few gems, nuttin' real good, and a few dollars. I got it stashed in a little metal box 'neath de floor of my room, jus' above de ceilin' of de floor below. De box be under de first floorboard, right in de corner of de room, 'neath de head of my bed...You clear on de spot?"

I nodded.

"Good. You keep dat in your head, case somethin' happen to me. It's real—" Grover jerked back, his focus shifted to the river. "Whoa! Looks like I got one. And from de tug it be puttin' on my line, it be de real deal." He leaned back. His line was taut, his pole bent. He eased forward and then drew back. He repeated the action several times, battling whatever hung at the end of his line. Finally, he pulled a fish, over a foot in length, from the water.

"Great catch!"

"Thanks." He took hold of the fish and removed it from his line. "Look like we gonna have a fine dinner tonight." He held the squirmy creature in both hands. "It be a white catfish."[125]

"I suspected it was a catfish, but how do you know it's the white variety?"

"It ain't so big as a channel catfish, and it got a blue-gray back and sides, wid a white bottom." He rotated the fish so I could see the underside.[126] "And it's got dis here adipo' fin—I think dat's what dey call it—'tween the tail fin and dis one here." He extended his finger toward the dorsal fin.[127] "Anyway, what e'er it be, we gonna eat good."

---

[125] *Savannah River Fishing in Georgia*, n-georgia.com, 25 Nov. 2017 <http://www.n-georgia.com/savannah-river.html>. "Fishing for catfish is excellent in the Savannah. White catfish make up the majority, but channel cats tend to be a bit larger."

[126] *White catfish Fish Identification, its habitats, characteristics, fishing methods*, allfishingbuy.com, 25 Nov. 2017 <http://www.allfishingbuy.com/Fish-Species/Catfish-White.htm>.

[127] *Fish Fin*, Wikipedia, 25 Nov. 2017 <https://en.wikipedia.org/wiki/Fish_fin>. "The adipose fin is a soft, fleshy fin found on the back behind the dorsal fin and just forward of the caudal fin."

***

Along with the Wright family and Grover, I strolled south on Montgomery Street and, after turning left on East Gaston, a walk of nearly a mile, we arrived at the north entrance to Forsyth Park. Armed with our picnic baskets, blankets and a couple of balls, we settled on a spot about one hundred yards from the magnificent fountain that had been added a decade earlier. With plumes of spraying water radiating inward toward its tall centerpiece, the fountain, emulating that of the Place de la Concorde in Paris, gave Savannah the cosmopolitan atmosphere that the Parisian paradigm had made famous.[128]

While Mrs. Wright unpacked a spread of fried chicken, mutton and ham, pickled veggies, jam and bread, stuffed eggs and an apple pie, Grover, Mr. Wright, Michael, Nora and I joined in a game of Keep Away. Four of us encircled the fifth, throwing a rubber ball, bouncing it and rolling it to one another, as we tried to keep the person in the middle from getting it. That Grover was adept at snagging the ball was expected. Back at Fort Myers I had seen his agility. But Mr. Wright surprised me. A pedagogue who rarely found time for lighter pursuits, he was not only quick, but could snatch the ball with one hand.

Only minutes after our game had commenced, Mrs. Wright's call drew us all to the two blankets laden with food. Where ordinarily she might have needed a second request to get us to the dinner table, with stomachs hungering for the mouthwatering spread, we raced her way.

"Where did you learn to play ball like that?" I said.

"Back at my days at Dartmouth, we didn't study all the time." Mr. Wright glanced at his children who were charging toward the food. He heaved a sigh. "I need to find more time for Michael and Nora."

"Give yourself a break," said Grover. "You work hard. Teach all day, and den you do night classes, like de one I take."

"I appreciate your kindness. But those two (Mr. Wright pointed) should be my priority. A parent owes that to his children. But enough about me. Let's get those eats."

The six of us sat down to a wonderful repast. Warm summer sunshine with a welcome breeze complemented great food. A cup of white wine, the first the Wrights had given me, put me in an exceptional mood. Having Grover join us was special. In the three years I had been living with the Wrights, it had only occurred a couple of times.

---

[128] *Forsyth Park*, Wikipedia, 26 November 2017 <https://en.wikipedia.org/wiki/Forsyth_Park>.

Once everyone had their fill, including a large portion of apple pie, we headed to the fountain. While Michael and Nora splashed in its spray, Mr. and Mrs. Wright and Grover seated themselves on a nearby bench. I plopped down on the adjacent grass.

"How they treating you down at the loading docks?" said Mrs. Wright.

Grover's mouth turned down.

"That bad?" said Mr. Wright, who was positioned, elbow on knee and chin in hand, like Michelangelo's marble sculpture of Lorenzo de' Medici.[129]

"You got eyes in de side of your head?" said Grover.

"No, but very good ears. I heard you groan."

Grover turned to Mrs. Wright. "Don't be whisperin' no secrets when your husband is around, 'cause he gonna hear 'em."

"Funny you should say that…When I speak to him, even in a loud voice, he often responds with: 'Did you say something, Dear?'"

The familiar scene, vivid, I burst out laughing.

"If I knew you'd take her side," said Mr. Wright, "you wouldn't have had that wine." A smile punctuated his comment. He turned to Grover. "Is it really awful at the docks?"

"De wages dey be payin' is worse dan what dey did before de war. I know de economy be real bad, and business ain't what it used to be, but damn—" Grover caught himself. "Sorry, Ma'am. Didn't mean to go foul, 'specially on de Sabbath."

"Tell them what you and some others are doing about it, Grover." Even before I finished the sentence, I worried I was saying something I shouldn't.

"Well, me and 'bout five others are fed up. We talkin' 'bout goin' on strike. Demandin' better pay."

"Isn't that risky?" said Mr. Wright.

Grover laughed.

"That's a mighty cavalier reaction."

"Cava…What dat mean?"

"That you're very nonchalant, indifferent," said Mr. Wright.

"Hey, wid de boss man treatin' me like dirt when he payin' me next to nuttin', what I got to lose?"

---

[129] *"Lorenzo de Medici" by Michelangelo*, artbronze.com, 27 Nov.2017 <http://www.artbronze.com/lorenzodemedicibymichelangelo.aspx>. Rodin's *The Thinker* is a more familiar rendition of the posture, but could only be referenced with later hindsight, because that sculpture was not conceived until 1880. *The Thinker | Rodin Museum*, Musée Rodin Website, 27 Nov. 2017 <www.musee-rodin.fr/en/collections/sculptures/thinker>.

"He has a point," said Mrs. Wright.

"I suppose," said Mr. Wright, "at least from a financial standpoint. But some of these businessmen, bitter and hurting from the war, are lashing out at what they refer to as uppity freedmen."

"Yeah, so I hear," said Grover. "Matter of fact, one of de fellas at de job says he heard de foreman say, 'If der be a strike, Grover's ass is grass.' 'Scuse my cuss word, but dat's what de foreman said."

A puzzled look showed on Mr. Wright's face. "Why would he single you out?"

"Maybe 'cause he know dat I de one pushin' de fellas to strike."

"Do you think he was threatening to fire you or something else?"

I knew what Mr. Wright was thinking, but I also suspected how Grover would react.

"Not sure, but knowin' de foreman—he one mean swine—he'll do worse den fire me. Exactly what, I can't say."

"Perhaps you should take things slowly to avoid putting yourself in jeopardy." Mr. Wright's tone underscored his concern.

Grover shook his head. "Maybe if you been a slave like me, you'd see it different. Bein' chattel to a massa dat beat you, ain't livin'. Workin' for my new boss ain't neither. What e'er de risks, gotta make 'im treat me like a man."

The rationale, one Grover had previously voiced to me, was difficult to accept. But having never walked in his shoes, questioning it was even harder. Still I anticipated Mr. Wright would.

Instead he remained silent, his only reaction, a furrowed brow. Whether it reflected disagreement, thought or something else, escaped me. The better part of a minute passed before he finally said, "Thank you, Grover."

"I miss somethin'?" Grover glanced at me, presumably seeking clarification.

Equally mystified, I shrugged.

"Let me explain," said Mr. Wright. "Hearing firsthand what you've faced, knowing it moves you to risk your safety, validates my decision to come south. Good folks like you shouldn't have to endure such abuse. Individuals, like me, who were born into privilege, who received a good education, need to right the wrongs you've suffered…wrongs whose repercussions persist." Mr. Wright pawed at his chin. "Would you mind, Grover, if I asked you a few questions about Congressional Reconstruction?"

The query, coming out of the blue, flummoxed me. Grover was hardly the one to educate Mr. Wright on such a subject.

"You free to aks. But don't expect no great answers."

"What do you think of the actions by Georgia's legislature and Congress to level the playing field here in the South. I'm referring to enactments like the Civil Rights Act.[130] I imagine you're familiar with them because the Pastor spoke about them at length in his sermon last week."

"Ain't sure what you're lookin' for, not when you're far more versed dan me 'bout dem laws."

"Dear," said Mrs. Wright, "don't make Grover uncomfortable. He's our guest."

I was certain that Mr. Wright had no desire to embarrass Grover. Even when his Socratic questions left us students tongue-tied, we never considered him a sadist.

"Let me explain the purpose of my question. As a Negro who was once a slave, Grover is better equipped than I to judge how these new laws are working. What I'm asking is whether they are making his life and that of his fellow Negroes better?"

The rephrased question alleviated my concern. Curiosity, however, persisted.

"I'm glad dey doin' what dey is…but far as I can tell, it ain't made much difference." Grover put up a hand as if to signal he had more to say. "De way I sees it, we got a tug-a-war goin' on…wid folks like me caught in de middle."

"When you say tug-of-war, can you be more specific?"

"Well, it be like dis." Grover extended his right arm toward Mr. Wright. "On de one side, you got Congress makin' rules dat supposed to make us equal." He extended his left arm in the opposite direction. "On de other, you got de ole southern white boys fightin' to keep de past. Most southern states been passin' Black Codes. Makin' sure Negroes worse dan second class. Dey givin' us de holes in de doughnuts." Grover dropped his arms. "One thing sure, can't be both ways. Ain't possible. But I tell you dis. 'Less Congress put some teeth into all der fancy laws, ain't gonna do no good. Whitey gonna win."

"Teeth?…What do you mean?" said Mr. Wright.

---

[130] *Reconstruction in Georgia | New Georgia Encyclopedia*, op. cit. Georgia, along with Florida and Alabama, became part of the Third Military District under General John Pope pursuant to the First Reconstruction Act passed by Congress in March 1867. In accordance with the law, Pope "registered Georgia's eligible white and black voters, 95,214 and 93,457 respectively." By March of the following year, a Georgia constitutional convention, whose delegates were over 20% black, had adopted a new state constitution that included "a provision for black voting. The constitution also called for the establishment of a free public school system…"

“De army…men dat’ll enforce deez great laws dey makin’. Stuff on paper be nice, but ’less you got folks enforcin’—and I don’t mean local sheriffs—yuh might as well burn de paper.”

Mr. Wright nodded repeatedly. “You’ll get no argument from me.” He mumbled just loud enough to be heard. “We fought the War of Secession. We emancipated the slaves and restored the Union. Equality is now the law of the land…on paper. But what will it take to make it a reality? Another war?”

The barely audible question shook me. Back at Fort Myers, the bloody battles had been distant. But since I had come to Savannah, countless tales of carnage from those returning from the fight had made the horror patent.

“De other thing we need is for de economy tuh come back. Widout dat, it be bad for Negroes…and whitey too.”

Mr. Wright looked down at me. “What do you think?”

Far more adept at responding to tricky issues than when I had come to Savannah three years earlier, I should have responded easily. I drew an embarrassing blank.

“Sorry,” said Mr. Wright. “Having cooked this pot, I have to eat its contents. And I’ll be damned if I’ve got an answer.” He looked at Grover. “I came here to the South, optimistic that good laws from Washington, coupled with education—that’s my job—would change the landscape. I was convinced we were on the right road. After listening to you, I’m less sanguine.”

“Didn’t mean to stick weevils in your cotton, especially when you nice enough to aks me to your picnic.”

“The last thing you need to do is apologize. On the contrary, I should be thanking you.”

“Thankin’ me?”

“Yes, for forcing me to face facts.”

A silence, with each of us left to our own thoughts, ensued. What I observed was mutual respect between Mr. Wright and Grover. Irrespective whether my assessment was accurate, my regard for both, already high, magnified. Mr. Wright had shown a remarkably open mind. Doubtless he was far more knowledgeable than Grover. His elocution was, of course, superior too. But Mr. Wright was not above listening to Grover’s arguments and giving them credence, even when they differed from his own. And Grover, though his parlance may not have been the King’s English, did not shy away from discussing the issues with Mr. Wright. Unfortunately, unlike these two men, others with prejudice-warped, intransigent minds and hearts would never relent. A war pitting antebellum norms and mores against equality may have been fought and won, but formidable battles remained.

***

A balmy afternoon in the spring of 1869 found me, accompanied by Sarah Jones, on the Savannah horse-drawn streetcar en route back from the Isle of Hope. In my roughly four years in Savannah, my courting had been limited. With school, chores, Sundays with Grover, a few hours here and there picking fruit to earn some pocket money, and tutoring Michael and Nora, time for social life was limited. When I had courted, the calls were one and done, or two and adieu. But this was the fourth time I had called upon Sarah Jones. The first three had been at her parents' home on Jefferson Street, about one-half mile south of the Wrights' flat on Montgomery. Were it not for the new streetcar, a fashionable addition to Savannah's landscape, I doubt Sarah's parents would have okayed the outing. Back then, a potential suitor, after informing a young lady of his interest, had to hope she would invite him to her home. Courting, not going out, was the rule.[131]

Just a few months before, in early 1869, the Savannah, Skidaway & Seaboard Railway had opened its horse-drawn service. The railway, the first of its kind in Savannah, traveled from the West Bay Street Station, south on Whitaker, where one could transfer for the Isle of Hope, about nine miles beyond.[132] With mulberry trees, fragrant pink azaleas and majestic oaks, bedecked with Spanish Moss, lining streets that housed the impressive summer homes of Savannah's wealthiest, the Isle of Hope, along the shores of the Skidaway River, was itself an attraction.[133] But the excursion there on the new streetcar was more exciting than the destination. Drawn by a single horse, with seating for twelve, the

---

[131] *Comparison Between 19th and 20th Century Courtship*, reocities.com, 30 Nov. 2017 <http://reocities.com/rpowerangers/editorspick/courtship.html> indicating: "In the 19th century, courtship consisted of a system of calling in which the courting occurred mostly at the woman's house…This system was very class oriented…At first only the mothers of girls would invite young men to call, but after the girl reached a certain age, she could invite guys to call on her herself. The guys would never initiate the call, although they would have to inform the girl that they were interested in calling on her."
[132] *Streetcars in Savannah*, railga.com, 29 November 2017 <http://www.railga.com/oddend/streetrail/savannahstr.html>.
[133] *Savannah, Georgia Historic Places – Isle of Hope Historic District,* nps.gov, 29 Nov. 2017 <https://www.nps.gov/nr/travel/geo-flor/7.htm>.

impressive tramway, complete with a stove to combat the chill in winter,[134] accorded ordinary folks a taste of the high life.

Seated in the rear, the section mandated for people of color, Sarah and I soaked in the grandeur of our chariot ride. We had left her home at one o'clock in the afternoon, and with our four-thirty curfew, had time to stroll the Isle of Hope's streets, savor a dish of ice cream and skip a few stones along the bank of the Skidaway. Paltry as our 3½-hour allotment may have been, to us it was a largess. Approval of the excursion in lieu of an afternoon at Sarah's home had been anything other than a sure bet.

As the horse clip-clopped its final steps, arriving back at the Whitaker Street station, Sarah said, "It's been a wonderful day."

"Indeed, it has." I took her hand.

She smiled. "We have to do this again."

"Absolutely."

We got up from our seats. I led the way from the streetcar in order that I could help her down. Rays of sun beaming from the west shined on her, a complement to her large brown eyes, high cheekbones and sand-colored skin, so light she could have passed for white. Outfitted in a magenta dress, with puffy sleeves, lacey white collar and flouncy white ruffles encircling the lower third,[135] she was even more radiant than usual. "You look beautiful," I said.

"Seems you told me the same thing before we left my house."

"Well, it was true then, and it's true now. But if you prefer, in the future I'll keep such thoughts to myself." I punctuated the remark with a haughty look, one plainly feigned.

"Uh…no. Forget what I said. Anytime you wish to bestow bouquets, yours truly is thrilled to accept."

Her hand still in mine, we headed west toward Jefferson Street. Soon enough we arrived at her home, a half-hour ahead of our curfew. The sight of her mother enjoying the glider on the bungalow's porch suggested a wiser strategy would have been to dawdle in Forsyth Park where we could have shared a romantic interlude beneath the shade of a secluded elm.

"Glad to see you're back early."

"Just as we promised." If I had to forgo an amorous respite, at least I could score points for good behavior.

---

[134] *History | Chatham Area Transit (CAT)*, catchacat.org, 29 November 2017 <http://www.catchacat.org/about-cat/history>.

[135] *1860s in Western Fashion*, Wikipedia, 30 Nov.2017 <http://en.wikipedia.org/wiki/1860s_in_Western_fashion>.

"Did you enjoy your afternoon?"

"Very much so," said Sarah. "Riding the streetcar into the Isle of Hope, I felt as if we were in London or Paris, not that I know what those places are like…just that they're very cosmopolitan. The homes on the Isle are stunning: Victorians, in all colors of the rainbow, with turrets, belly porches and gingerbread trim; Greek Revival, bright white and pillared; and bungalows that put the term to shame.[136] Add to that the many formal gardens, lovely marshes and the sweet scent of pink azaleas,[137] and it's a paradise. Someday I'd love to have a summer home there."

"Wouldn't that be nice?" Even as I echoed Sarah's words, the idea of owning a second home was beyond credulity. For that matter, just having one seemed a stretch.

Mrs. Jones halted the glider and gazed off toward the southeast, almost as if she were trying to envision the Isle of Hope. "Someday soon, I'll have to get George to take me for a ride there on the streetcar." She turned back to us. "Well, I'm glad you two had a nice day. We look forward to seeing you again, Mican."

I took her words as a not-so-subtle hint that my time to leave had arrived. With Mrs. Jones sitting but ten feet from us, I bid Sarah goodbye, pecking her on the cheek. She pecked me back. I headed off toward Montgomery Street and the Wrights' flat. Though the abrupt end to the afternoon was less than perfect, I floated down the street. Not since my days with Abbey had I been so excited about any female. Maybe love was just around the corner.

---

[136] *Savannah, Georgia Historic Places – Isle of Hope Historic District*, op. cit.

[137] *Periclymenoides Deciduous Azaleas*, rhododendrons.co.uk, 2 Dec. 2017 <http://www.rhododendrons.co.uk/azaleas/deciduous-azaleas/deciduous-azalea-periclymenoides>.

Chapter XI

WE WERE NEARING THE END OF THE SCHOOL DAY in the last week of May 1869, when Mr. Wright asked me to remain after class. By itself, nothing about the request stirred concern, but something about his manner, a seeming disquiet, disconcerted me. As I purported to work on an essay about Emanuel Kant, I tried to imagine what issue had prompted the oddity. Minutes later, with the day ended and the other students having departed, I approached Mr. Wright's desk.

"You wanted to see me, Sir?" At home I called him Mr. Wright, but in school we all addressed him as *Sir*.

"Yes." He stuffed some papers into a folder and muttered to himself, "Be direct."

I waited anxiously.

"Mican, I'm sure you're aware that my coming to Savannah to teach was never intended to be permanent."

I nodded. Within the four walls of the Wrights' flat, suggestions to that effect had been voiced more than once, though always with ambiguity as to if and when his departure would occur.

"It seems the time has arrived for my family and me to go back north."

Having lived with the Wright family for nearly four years, the news shook me.

"Before explaining the reason for this decision, I want you to know that we would love for you to accompany us. We consider you part of our family."

"Thank you, Sir. I appreciate that." My brain, still vague for lack of details about the move, rattled with pros and cons.

"Mrs. Wright and I have been mulling this over for weeks and finally made up our minds last night. In fact, I'm yet to tell Michael and Nora. I'll do that after dinner tonight. But unlike you who will have to make a decision, they go where we go. Rather than putting you on the spot in front of the whole family, I wanted you to know the situation in advance, the rationale of the move, as well as the *where* of it."

"I appreciate that."

"We'll be moving to Meriden, New Hampshire, where Mrs. Wright's parents have their farm. I love teaching here in Savannah, but she has looked forward to returning to New England. Several months ago, I learned of an opening beginning in September on the faculty of the Kimball Union Academy, a very prestigious boarding school in Meriden.[138] It was founded more than fifty years ago. Anyway, I applied for the job and, to make a long story short, landed the position. Given that Mrs. Wright was good enough to accept the move here, one that was intended to be temporary, it would be unfair for me to ask her to stay. And to be honest, I have yearnings to return to New Hampshire and would hate to pass up this wonderful opportunity. And too, it will allow our children to better know their grandparents. It's as if all the stars have aligned for us."

"I understand…and I'm happy for you." That said, I disliked what it meant for me.

"You're very kind. And before we go any further, I'm telling you this, so you won't be blindsided. Take your time deciding what you wish to do. As I said earlier, we would be happy to have you come with us, but it's strictly up to you. We won't be making the move until the end of June."

If Mr. Wright had approached me with the same information several weeks earlier, I would have taken my time before deciding. But timing is everything. I said, "I've heard how cold it gets in New Hampshire." The weather was not foremost in my mind, merely a device to circumvent a direct response. "On the rare occasions that it drops below freezing here in Savannah, I find it unbearable. The thought of surviving twenty below zero or colder yet is ineffable."

"*Ineffable*. You're using one of the new vocabulary words we learned this week. Excellent, but before I diverge, I hope you don't base your decision on the weather."

"I assure you. I'm not."

---

[138] *Kimball Union*, kua.org, 16 Oct. 2019 <https://www.kua.org/about-kua-history> stating: "Established in 1813, Kimball Union Academy is one of the nation's oldest boarding schools…In the nineteenth century, Kimball Union was a co-educational school, its social life integrated with the village of Meriden, where many students traveled from their local farms…Kimball Union has always maintained a close relationship to the community, and specifically with nearby Dartmouth College, to provide the best environment for learning into the twenty-first century."

Mr. Wright studied me. “You…uh…put that in the present tense. Does that mean you’ve already made a decision?”

I thought for a second. Remarkably, I had. “Yes, but let me explain. Cold temperatures, not that I would relish them, are not the reason.”

“Would you care to tell me why?”

Whether or not I wanted to, I felt obliged. It was not because Mr. Wright had asked, but the likelihood that otherwise the Wrights might conclude I didn’t want to live with them. After the kindness they had shown me, such a slur was unthinkable.

“Like you and your family, Grover has done so much for me. I would hate to leave him. If I did, I would feel as though I had abandoned him. And I’ve grown very fond of Sarah Jones. Our relationship would have little chance were I to move north. Add to the equation, warm and familiar Savannah, as opposed to cold and unknown New Hampshire, and the scales lean sharply toward staying here.”

“I understand. If I were in your shoes, I suspect I would make the same decision.” He put an arm over my shoulder. “Time for us to get out of here.”

We started to leave. “Wait a second,” said Mr. Wright. “I almost forgot. There’s another matter I wanted to take up with you.” He backtracked to his desk.

I could not imagine what else awaited me. Based upon what had preceded, I would have willingly skipped the additional agenda.

“This past semester I’ve done little to expand your mathematical knowledge. You’re way ahead of your classmates. At this point, I lack the wherewithal to challenge you.”

“I feel challenged.” Though my response echoed with unctuous insincerity, I meant it. “As you’ve often said, review, especially with tougher problems, helps cement mathematical concepts.”

“Well, be that as it may, you’re too talented not to press forward. Unfortunately, few in Savannah have the expertise to guide you. I suspect you’ll have to do it on your own.” Mr. Wright took a book from the far corner of his desk. “I got this for you.” He handed me the volume.

“Thank you, Sir.” I eyed the cover: “Elements of the Differential and Integral Calculus.”[139]

“It’s by Charles Davies. Have you heard of him?”

---

[139] Davies, Charles, *Elements of the Differential and Integral Calculus* (New York, Wiley & Long; Collins, Keene & Co., 1836), retrieved from Internet Archive (archive.org, Col. Americana; Dig. Spon., Google; from the collections of the U. of Michigan), 2 Dec. 2017 <https://archive.org/details/elementsdiffere03davigoog>.

"Uh, yes, that he wrote some books about mathematics, but that's all I know."

"It was written in 1836, long after Newton and Leibniz developed calculus almost two hundred years ago.[140] I gather the notation is more like that of Leibniz, though it's all Greek to me…On second thought, that's not quite true. I know some Greek. Calculus, on the other hand, is totally foreign."

"That makes two of us."

"Perhaps," said Mr. Wright. "But unlike me, I'm confident that you, with your wonderful mathematical mind, will figure it out."

I shrugged abashedly as I flipped open the book, somewhere near the middle. Equations, replete with unfamiliar symbols, left me agog. "Don't be so sure."

"You underestimate yourself."

Maybe…But maybe not. Regardless, I was eager to test my wits against the daunting text. And too, I was thrilled to have another book, one that swelled my library by one-third. I now had four: A Bible that was very special; a calculus book, a ticket into the world of advanced mathematics; and my favorite, my two-volume set of *Uncle Tom's Cabin.*

***

Sunday afternoons, time normally reserved for Grover, had changed. More and more, I was spending them with Sarah. I had courted her on six occasions. But for the second time in four weeks, we had to miss our Sunday meeting. She and her family had commitments that prevented us from being together. Disappointing as that was, it had a silver lining. It eased my conscience, knowing that I was not stealing every Sunday from Grover. Having sacrificed so I could live with the Wrights, he was entitled to some of my time, indeed more than I allotted him. (Much as I loved spending time with Grover, as I mathematically described it in my mind, where D = Disappointment and S = Silver Lining, I could not deny that $D > S$.)

---

140 *History Topic: A History of the Calculus*, groups.dcs.st-and.ac.uk, 4 Dec. 2017 <http://www-groups.dcs.st-and.ac.uk/~history/PrintHT/The_rise_of_calculus.html> stating: "Leibniz was very conscious that finding a good notation was of fundamental importance and thought about it a lot. Newton, on the other hand, wrote more for himself and, as a consequence, tended to use whatever notation he thought of on the day. Leibniz's notation of *d* and ∫ highlighted the operator aspect which proved important in later developments. By 1675 Leibniz had settled on the notation $\int y dy = y^2/2$ written exactly as it would be today."

With church behind us, and Sarah occupied, I cajoled Grover into joining me on an undisclosed adventure—my treat. Knowing that I had only the scant funds I earned on the rare days that I picked fruits and vegetables at a nearby farm, he rarely allowed me to bear the costs of anything. But once I assured him the adventure would involve minimal expense, he consented. After leaving the First African Baptist Church, rather than heading south on Montgomery Street, I directed him north towards the nearby Savannah River.

"Where you takin' me? Can't be fishin', 'cause we ain't got our poles."

"Impressive deduction. You, my friend, are detective material."

"Ain't you gonna tell me?"

I stopped in my tracks. "We've just come from church, and already you're sinning."

"What are you talkin' 'bout?"

"Patience. You're aware that it's a virtue."

"Maybe tis, but dat don't mean impatience be a sin."

"Virtue and sin are opposites. The opposite of patience is—" I bit my tongue. In school we had learned a long list of virtues. According to the great Roman orator Marcus Tullius Cicero,[141] eloquence was among them. If its opposite constituted a sin, then Grover's inept articulation was a sin. Labeling him a sinner for such would be outrageous. Pride, as well as logic, be damned. I abandoned my nicety-laden argument and said, "I see your point."

"Next time, you better think stuff through before you spout off."

Though the smile that punctuated Grover's reply left no doubt his jab was good-natured, I could not resist poking him back. "Well, now you have sinned."

A wide-eyed look of incredulity greeted my words.

"You gloated."

"You're damn right I did. Ain't often I get de best of you when we be debatin'."

I patted him on the back and pushed him forward. Another fifty yards and we arrived at the West Bay Street Station. "I'm taking you for a ride on the new streetcar."

"Oo-ee…I like dat. Ain't never been on it."

---

[141] *Eloquence as a Virtue*, st-eutychus.com, 17 Oct. 2019 <http://st-eutychus.com/2015/snippet-cicero-on-eloquence-as-a-virtue-and-the-importance-of-integrity/> stating: "Eloquence, after all, has its own place among the supreme virtues. Of course, all the virtues are equal and equivalent, but still, one is more beautiful and splendid in appearance than another."

I bought two tickets, round trip, a mile each way, down Whitaker Street to the SS&S Terminal. Unlike the day I had transferred from there to the Isle of Hope, the short excursion, an opportunity for Grover to experience the tram, was the entire goal.

About ten minutes later, we boarded the streetcar. The entire way, Grover gazed out the windows on either side. Conversation was sparse. Part way down the line, he quipped, "Dis travelin' in style beats walkin' any day."

The comment brought a smile to my face. With all Grover had done for me, the chance to turn the tables warmed my heart.

Once the streetcar pulled into the station and we disembarked, Grover said, "Dat was great!"

"We still have the ride back later. For now, suppose we get some pecans?"

"Long as I de one buyin'."

I was about to balk, but a quick assessment quelled my instincts. Affording Grover a wonderful afternoon was my goal. Allowing him to pay would advance that aim. "You've twisted my arm." I pointed. "Just up ahead, by the southern end of Forsyth Park, there's a fellow who sells pecans from a pushcart—sells them really cheap."

"In de shells?"

I nodded.

"Jeezum, widout a nutcracker, a body could lose a few teeth tryin' to break 'em open."

"Not if he uses a rock to do the job."

Grover bought us a bag of pecans from the vendor. I found a couple of rocks, and we settled in on a bench near the south end of Forsyth. I got down on my knees on the adjoining sidewalk and began cracking. My first blow sent a pecan bouncing three feet sideways.

"You got dat down real good." Grover laughed.

A second try was equally unsuccessful. But the third was a charm. I looked up at Grover, who was seated above me. "Smart mouth that you are, I oughta make you beg." I handed him the nut.

He dug out the contents and put it into his mouth. "Wid no cracker and no pick, it be lots harder to get de meat, but de effort make 'em taste even better…Guess it be like squirrel stew."

"Huh?" I interrupted my work long enough to give him a look.

"Tastes far better to one dat's starvin' den one dat got a ham, corn and a punkin pie on his table."

The analogy, though dubious, somehow made sense. I nodded before dumping many of the pecans, still in their shells, onto the sidewalk. With ever-increasing skill, one-by-one, I broke them open, depositing the meat-laden halves back into the bag. Once I had cracked a good supply, I joined Grover on the bench, where we dug out the meat.

"You making any progress, trying to get your boss to pay you more?"

Grover shook his head. "Nah, still de same ole story. Tried a bunch a times dis past year, but nuttin'. But push 'll get to shove real soon. All ten of us gonna walk off de job next week if de boss man don't sing our tune."

"What do you think he'll do?"

"Don't know, but suspect he gonna look my way. Knows dat I de one stirrin' up de boys. Said I was lookin' to lose my job, maybe worse, less I change my ways…I ain't 'bout to do dat." Grover paused, gazing off into space. "If de boss man fire me, I'll do somethin'. Worse be worse, I'll sharecrop and maybe give my jew'lry business a go. Anyhow, bettin' man I is, I say pecans to pig dung, boss man be bluffin'."

"What makes you so sure?"

"If he fires me, he knows de rest of de boys gonna walk." Grover leaned back. "Boss man may be de dealer, but I'm holdin' de deck." Grover displayed a self-satisfied smile before reaching into the bag. He shuffled through the contents. "Time come to crack some more."

"I'll do it." I reached for the bag.

Grover pulled it back. "Oh no. You ain't hoggin' all de fun." He climbed down, grabbed a rock and began cracking. "De way I sees it. We makin' gains. But like I told Misser Wright. It be like a tug of war. If we stop pullin', we'll be back where we was. Boss man, and dem like him, wanna keep us as der niggers."

Grover's rare use of the term, a word I knew he despised, caught me off guard. It did, however, underscore his point.

"Last fall, I told de boys dat votin' be important. Dey laughed at me til dey seen what happened. De Republicans took one house of de Legislature. And Bullock beat de Democrat for Gov'nor. Folks said it weren't possible here in Geo'gia.[142] But now dat dey seen it, dey eager to vote, come de next election."

---

[142] *Reconstruction in Georgia | New Georgia Encyclopedia*, op. cit. In the 1868 gubernatorial election, "the Republican candidate, Rufus Bullock, defeated the Democratic candidate…In the elections for the General Assembly, 84 Republicans (29 of them black) fell 3 seats short of a majority of the 172 House seats. In the state senate [sic], however, the Republicans (3 of them black) took control, with 27 seats to the Democrats' 17 seats." (*Bookmarks'* author's comment: Today in the 21st century, it is remarkable to see the turnabout that over time has occurred in the nation's political parties. The Democratic Party, which was so closely linked to the Ku Klux Klan in the South after the Civil War, enjoys support in the neighborhood of ninety percent among African-Americans, who have long since abandoned the Republicans, the party of their

"The Republicans would never have made those gains if Congress hadn't enacted the Reconstruction Act and put the South under military rule."

"Dat's what worries me."

"You're...you're concerned about military rule?"

"Not dat. But when dey end it. Fear dat whitey gonna turn back de clock."

Grover's concern was well founded. White Democrats yearned for the day when the troops of the military districts left. Only four years removed from the War of Secession, the South had seen dramatic political changes. The vast majority of southern whites longed to undo those changes. I said, "We're getting rights, not the least of which is the vote. Too bad we still can't earn a decent living."[143] (When speaking with others, I classified myself as Negro because that is how others saw me. In my own mind, the issue was more complex. I was Negro and I was Seminole. I lived in a white home. Race was akin to eye color, merely a matter of appearance. However unrealistic my perception may have been, that was the world I wanted. Regardless, such was not the world in which I lived.)

"We gotta stand up to whitey, men like my boss man. 'Cause if we don't..." Grover's voice trailed off. He ate another pecan before continuing. "Damn, I wish dat Congress had finished impeachin' President Johnson. If he get his way, we'll be back where we was."

---

emancipator, Abraham Lincoln. Hardly coincidental, this dramatic change is rooted in the policies the parties support.)

[143] *A Time of Reckoning (U.S. National Park Service),* op. cit., stating: "Perhaps Reconstruction's greatest shortcoming was its failure to anticipate the economic needs of freedom. Millions of ex-slaves, possessing little more than the ragged clothing on their backs, were at the mercy of their former masters for survival. Amid the general poverty of the South at war's end, wages paid to freedmen in 1867 were lower than those paid earlier for hired slaves. Under the sharecropping system in which the agricultural worker received life's bare necessities and a share of the crop in exchange for his labor, blacks, as well as poor whites, became permanently indebted to the landowner for their maintenance." (*Bookmarks'* author's comment: In latter portion of the 20th century, the world saw firsthand the effect of granting political freedom without economic freedom and visa-versa. In the former Soviet Union, Mikhail Gorbachev tried to extend political freedom, but without concomitant economic freedom. The Soviet Union collapsed, though in large degree from the weight of its own bureaucracy. By way of contrast, China granted its citizens limited economic freedom, while retaining tight political control. The result was enormous economic growth. It is important to emphasize that these examples by no means constitute cause-and-effect blueprints regarding the effects of economic and political freedom. Many other factors, both internal and external, were at play in the Soviet Union and China. Nevertheless, their differing approaches and outcomes provide excellent case studies.)

Aware of what Grover meant, I restrained the urge to point out that the House of Representatives had indeed impeached Johnson. Unfortunately, the Senate had acquitted him by a single vote.[144] "On the bright side," I said, "whenever Johnson has tried to block Congress, they've overridden his vetoes."

Grover shrugged. "Maybe so, but havin' a president dat likes slavery be like havin' a creep dat paws young'uns guardin' de playground here in Forsyth Park."

Grover's point had too much validity for me to disagree. I swallowed hard, tasting humble pie, rather than pecans.

"Wid de military here, we makin' progress," said Grover. "But once dey, along wid de Carpetbaggers[145]—fellas like your friend, Mr. Wright—hightail it back north, dem good ole boys gonna rise again. De Scalawags[146] still be here, but der ain't enough of 'em to do much. Suspect Washin'ton, and dat means Congress, gonna lose int'rest." Grover chewed the last remaining pecan. "What scares me most is dat new white group, de one dat calls itself de Ku Klux Klan.[147] Gangs of white boys ridin' horses, wearin' masks in de night, burnin' crosses and spookin' decent folks. Won't surprise me none if next dey be settin' fire to homes and churches here in Savannah. If nuttin' else, dey is scarin' folks from votin'. And if dey do dat, dey gonna get back in power…and we (Grover held up the crumbled remnants of a shell) gonna go de way of dis here nut."

***

[144] *Andrew Johnson – U.S. President*, op. cit. Johnson outraged Congress in 1865 with the Presidential Reconstruction policies he adopted while Congress was not in session. In 1866 he vetoed the Freedmen's Bureau bill and the Civil Rights Act. Congress overrode both vetoes. "Congress also passed the Tenure of Office Act, which denied the president the power to remove federal officials without the Senate's approval." Johnson viewed the Act as a violation of his constitutional authority. "In August 1867, he fired Secretary of War Edwin Stanton." In February 1868, the House voted eleven articles of impeachment against President Johnson for violating the Tenure in Office Act and other misconduct. The Senate acquitted him by a single vote. *See also*, *Andrew Johnson*, whitehouse.gov, op. cit. (*Bookmarks'* author's comment: The Andrew Johnson impeachment for firing Stanton bears similarity to Watergate and the "Saturday Night Massacre," when President Richard Nixon, a populist who claimed the support of the so-called "Silent Majority," ordered the firing of Special Prosecutor Archibald Cox. That firing helped drive Nixon from office. Similar issues were at play during the two impeachments of President Donald Trump.)

[145] *Reconstruction in Georgia | New Georgia Encyclopedia*, op. cit.

[146] Ibid.

[147] *Ku Klux Klan,* Wikipedia, 6 Dec. 2017 <https://en.wikipedia.org/wiki/Ku/Klux/Klan>.

The school year had ended two days earlier, and it was moving day for the Wrights. Along with Nora and Michael, I sat on the front stoop of the home that housed the third-floor flat they had occupied since shortly after the war. Nearby, the Wrights' bags awaited the arrival of the wagon that would carry them to the train.

"You sure you can't come with us?" said Nora.

"I'd like to, but…"

"You've become part of the family," said Michael. "Why not come?"

"I can't abandon Grover. And I'm courting Sarah now."

"Girls, what a pain!" Michael stuck a finger down his throat.

"A lot better than stupid boys." Nora stuck out her tongue at her brother.

Mrs. Wright, who, along with Mr. Wright, came around from the back of the house, said, "What is going on? We could hear you two as we passed the side yard."

"Michael's being a jerk!"

"Nora, you know better than to call people names." Mrs. Wright gave each of the kids a look.

"Well, he—"

"Enough," said Mr. Wright. "You both heard your mother."

"What did I do?" said Michael.

"I said, 'Enough,' and that's it!" Mr. Wright displayed his legendary stare, an expression notifying the kids to cease or face punishment. He turned to me. "There's still time to change your mind."

I rolled my eyes, a reaction I had never directed at Mr. Wright. "I've already moved my things to Grover's place."

"All of a couple of boxes, and not big ones," said Mrs. Wright.

"Thank you, but I need to stay here with Grover."

"And because he's stuck on Sarah." Michael giggled.

"You'll write to us," said Mrs. Wright.

"Absolutely." I gestured to Michael and Nora. "And both of you will write to me. You'll tell about your new home and all you've learned, especially about math." I pointed at Nora. "How much is thirteen times twelve."

Her face went blank.

"You know twelve times twelve from your times table. All you need to do is add one more twelve. Right?"

"Oh yeah." She thought for a few seconds. "156."

"You got it." I turned to Michael. "How do you divide a fraction into another number?"

"Invert and multiply."

"That's it," I said, displaying a clenched fist.

"I think we better take you with us," said Mrs. Wright.

I smiled. We both knew the final decision had already been made. The wagon to take them to the train pulled up. Mr. Wright and I loaded their things onto the rear.

"We'll miss you," said Mrs. Wright.

"And I'll miss all of you."

Mr. Wright shook my hand, but then drew me in for a hug. "Should you change your mind, you'll always be welcome."

"I appreciate that." The *Sir* with which I still punctuated my responses to him in the classroom had otherwise ceased. "And thank you all for everything you've done for me."

One after another, I hugged Mrs. Wright, Nora and Michael. They climbed aboard the wagon. A tear dripping from Mrs. Wright's eye choked my voice. I waved. They waved back as the wagon drove off. I watched it head down Montgomery Street until it disappeared from view. I stared off into space, telling myself that I had made the right decision. I believed I had. But doubts were inescapable.

***

The day the Wrights had moved to New Hampshire, I had moved back in with Grover. A little over a week had elapsed since the changes had occurred. Having enjoyed my own space in the Wrights' flat, tiny as it was, I had anticipated that returning to a shared 12' × 14' room would require adjustment. Much to my surprise, the former quarters fit like a comfortable old shoe whose leather had been softened with wear.

I had spent the morning studying my calculus book. Deciphering the advanced mathematics without the aid of a teacher was arduous. But next to what Newton and Leibniz had done when developing the abstract concepts, my task was simple. It began with the definition of a limit.[148] While the concept made perfect sense and it took but minutes to memorize the definition, most times when I purported to prove a limit, the possibility of circular flaws was undeniable. Unfortunately, there was no one to confirm if my work was right or wrong.

---

[148] A function $f(x)$ has a limit A as $x \to a$, if given any $\epsilon > 0$, $\exists$ a δ such that $| f(x) - A | < \epsilon$ for $0 < | x - a | < \delta$. (*Bookmarks'* author's comment: As a math major who taught calculus roughly a half-century ago, all too often, after finding a "δ" that satisfied the foregoing definition, I found it hard to dispel a queasiness about possible circular reasoning. Recalling that bygone experience, I incorporated it into Mican's learning process.)

Back when I had studied algebra, geometry and trigonometry, not only had their concepts made sense, but I had a teacher who checked my equations and calculations. Now that I had entered a new world, one whose theoretical principles were far more abstruse than those I had previously learned, doubts and, worse yet, frustration stirred. I feared my foray into self-study might be short-lived. Fortunately, my next step in the world of calculus, the definition of a derivative,[149] made sense not only as an abstract concept, but more so when I applied it to a specific mathematical function. Put in simple terms, I understood how and why the definition represented the slope of a function at any given point. When I finished a problem, I felt confident about my work. Ironically, though it was the cart before the horse, it eased my misgivings with limits. In just ten days I had progressed from intimidated novice to confused birdbrain to promising enthusiast. My brief stint in the middle category was far from a waste. The mathematical phobia that several of my former classmates had displayed grew easier to understand. I had gotten a taste of the turmoil, even fear, that mounts when mathematical principles do not come easily. Unlike a tough essay question where half-baked verbiage might be sufficient to sneak by, mathematics had hard-and-fast, right and wrong answers. Hedging, invoking one of my yes and no answers, was impossible. Bluffing was vain.

Pleased as I was with my progress, as the noon-hour approached, I happily returned my calculus book to the shelf above my bed. A far more exciting pursuit, courting at Sarah's home, was on my afternoon schedule. It would be the first time I visited her on a weekday. After grabbing a bite and cleaning myself up, I put on my linen shirt with turnover collar and sack coat.[150] Before heading out the door, I donned my "John Bull" straw top hat,[151] a recent hand-me-down from a classmate. I stepped out into the sunshine and headed west toward Jefferson Street. Along the way, as I passed the Emporium, my vanity arrant, I checked out my reflection in the storefront window. (Grover's 8" × 8" mirror, while adequate for combing my black wavy hair, was hardly sufficient for a full view of myself.) The vague image visible in the stylish shop confirmed that I was at my best.

Just before turning onto Jefferson Street, I purchased a half-dozen peaches from a pushcart vendor. On my last visit, I had brought flowers

---

[149] The definition of the derivative dy/dx of a function y = f(x) is: $\lim_{\Delta x \to 0} \frac{f(x + \Delta x) - f(x)}{\Delta x}$.

[150] *1860s in Western fashion*, Wikipedia, 8 Dec. 2017 <https://en.wikipedia.org/wiki/1860s_in_Western_fashion>.

[151] *MEN'S CIVILIAN HATS*, historyinthemaking.org, 9 Dec. 2017 <http://www.historyinthemaking.org/catalogue/menhat.html>.

to Sarah. Though the peaches were purportedly for her, their primary purpose was to gain her parents' good graces. Minutes later, arriving at their bungalow, I rapped the front door's molded brass knocker. Sarah answered the door. Attired in a flouncy blue dress with gold-trim embroidery and a white hat bearing a blue ribbon, she was lovely.

"Wow, you look so pretty," I said, even before we could exchange words of greeting. "But of course, you always do."

Sarah blushed, though her sand-colored skin all but disguised the reaction. "We could go inside or, if you prefer, sit out here on the glider."

I gestured toward the sky. "As nice as it is, I vote for the glider."

She started to step outside when I said, "I almost forgot." I handed her the bag of peaches. "These are for you and your parents."

She peaked into the bag. "Thank you. They're my dad's favorite. He'll love them."

I whispered, not that anyone appeared close enough to overhear. "That's the idea. Help win him over."

We seated ourselves on the glider and began to sway back and forth.

"How has your week been?" I said.

"Okay."

I waited a moment, anticipating some details. None were forthcoming. "Did something go wrong?"

"No."

The terse answers were atypical for Sarah, not that she was garrulous. "You sure?"

She looked at me but said nothing.

"Something is amiss…You can tell me."

She heaved a sigh.

The non-reply did itself belie. My prodding eye, a tacit *why*, begged for her to amplify. But sensing that patience was the more prudent course and that she was edging to a more meaningful response, I bided my time.

"There…there is a problem." Her fingers fidgeted with the trim on her dress.

"I want to help. You can tell me."

"It's not that easy."

"Try me." I welcomed the opportunity to lend a patient ear and hopefully alleviate the situation.

She stared straight ahead into empty space. "These past few weeks…uh…sometimes during the week and…uh…the Sundays when I didn't see you, I…I've been seeing another fellow."

Her words, a blast from a blunderbuss, rattled my brain. "What are you saying?" My response reverberated in my head. I knew what she was saying. Accepting it was another matter.

"Jerome Flowers—I'm not sure you know him—has been courting me."

"And?" I stilled the glider and sat motionless, dreading the next volley.

"I…I like him…a lot." She looked away.

Impatience for further clarification goaded me to voice another *and?* Fear of the response, the need to avoid redundancy or whatever kept me silent.

"I think it would be better if we…uh…stop seeing one another."

Sarah had communicated her bottom line. I struck bottom, though paradoxically, I was still falling. "You…you like him better than me?" My inflection suggested a question; it was largely a statement, the closest I had come to grasping the distasteful reality.

"Well…yes and no."

The irony of her words, a phrase I had often invoked, did not escape me. My rational side, the one cultivated in Mr. Wright's class, longed to censure the absurd response. But my emotional side reached for the glimmer of hope it conveyed. "Since you're unsure whom you like more, why not continue to see me too?" Two minutes earlier, the idea of sharing Sarah with another man would have been anathema, but desperate for half a loaf, even a crumb, anathema had become hope.

"Continuing to let you court me wouldn't be fair."

"You let this Flowers fellow start courting you while you were seeing me."

"That…that was different."

A churning volcano within, my face must have reflected exasperation.

"You don't understand. I like you both…but I'm choosing Jerome for other reasons."

"Other reasons…What do you mean?"

"Where you, like me, are seventeen, Jerome is twenty-one. Unlike you, a student, Jerome has a very good job."

"This past week, since the Wrights moved, I've been working part time, picking fruit. It's more than just a few hours now and then."

The furrow in Sarah's brow denigrated my limited, low-paying employment.

"Jerome works in his father's butcher shop, a very successful one at that. He earns an excellent income, and someday he'll take over the business…And then there's the matter of my parents."

"I thought they liked me."

"They do. But they also like Jerome. They consider him an extraordinary catch, one whom I would be foolish to let slip away."

"So, it's because of your parents you're choosing Jerome."

"That's not what I said, and that's not true. Even if my parents had no opinion, I would pick Jerome. I want a good life, a nice home and things. I know he can provide that…As for my parents, I have no desire to make them angry. They simply provide another reason to choose Jerome."

Unable to find words, I heaved a sigh and shook my head.

"Please…please don't take it personally."

Don't take it personally. She had to be kidding. I longed to change her mind, but that seemed impossible. I said, "I…I'd better go."

"Yes, I guess that's best."

I got up from the glider.

"Would you like your peaches back?"

I shook my head. I stepped down from the porch and headed north on Thompson Street in the direction of the Savannah River. I walked aimlessly, east along the river. I wished I had my peaches, not that I was hungry. I wanted to hurl them, one after another, into the depths of the dark waters.

***

For two days after Sarah gave me the heave-ho, I wallowed in my misery. On the third, with despair yielding to melancholy, I took my calculus book down from the shelf and renewed my study. Owing to a divided focus, each page demanded several repetitions before any portion could be digested. Still I welcomed the text's distraction. Anything that turned my mind from disheartened thoughts was helpful. With each day my emotions inched along the number line from minus infinity closer to zero. Positive values remained distant.

Following church on the first Sunday since I had last seen Sarah, Noah Carter, who had been a classmate my entire time in Savannah, badgered me into meeting him for lunch the next day at The Pirates' House.[152] Aware that I was languishing under the burden of heartbreak, he refused to take *no* for an answer. Shortly after noon, I stepped through the doorway of the storied haunt. Opened as an inn more than one hundred years earlier, the Broad Street icon, a block south of the

[152] *The Pirates' House*, thepirateshouse.com, 17 Dec. 2017 <http://thepirateshouse.com>. The Pirates' House website states: "Since 1753 The Pirates' House has been welcoming visitors to Savannah with a bounty of delicious food and drink and rousing good times. Situated a scant block from the Savannah River, The Pirates' House first opened as an inn for seafarers, and fast became a rendezvous for blood-thirsty pirates and sailors from the Seven Seas."

Savannah River, had subsequently become a favorite of sailors and pirates when stopping off in the city. As I began to gaze around the wooden interior, off to my right I spotted Noah waving to me from a booth. I hurried over and slipped into the side opposite him.

"Glad you could make it," he said.

"I appreciate the invite."

He gestured at the board of fare that hung on the near wall. "What's your poison?"

I shrugged. "Whatever you say…with a couple of brews."

"House stew?"

I nodded.

Noah motioned to the barmaid and placed the order. "So, how you doing?"

"Not too bad…I guess." My inflection gainsaid my words.

"Better than yesterday, I hope."

"A little."

"I've got a proposal…and before you react, give it some thought."

"Okay." My gut told me I wouldn't like it, but negativity could at least be withheld until I knew what he had in mind.

"In ten days, I'm heading south to St. Augustine. They're building a big hotel there, and they need workers. The pay is decent, a whole lot more than what you get picking fruit. I'm hoping you'll join me."

The pitch was more interesting than I had expected, not that I was sold. "You mean to say after all this education, you're not gonna use it?"

"Hey, don't get me wrong. It's not the way I expect to spend my life, but being seventeen, I figure it's time to see the world." Noah looked me in the eye. "Whad'ya say?"

I gulped the brew the barmaid had just put before me. Education was wonderful, but becoming an independent, money-making adult, rather than being dependent on others' good graces, was appealing.

"Piqued your interest, haven't I?"

I nodded, though halfheartedly.

"That mean you'll go with me?"

"Can't."

Poised to indulge in his brew, the skinny, yet broad-shouldered Noah drew back his narrow head, atop which curly, coarse hair reigned. "Why not?"

"I can't abandon Grover, not after all he's done for me." Whether I would have bitten at the opportunity were Grover not part of the equation was hard to say. But with him a factor, the matter was an inequality, with the reasons for staying greater than those to go…much greater.

"I hear what you're saying, but before you make a final decision, keep in mind that St. Augustine is a great city. Not only is it the oldest in the nation, having been founded in 1565,[153] but for three hundred years it was a place where our ancestors, especially escaped slaves, found safe haven.[154] And in case you haven't heard, it's a growing place."

I tilted my head, furrowed my brow and forced an odd look.

"What's the matter?"

"That patter you just delivered on St. Augustine...You did your homework and came prepared to do a selling job, didn't you?"

Noah shrugged. "Hey, you can't blame a guy for trying. And by the way, St. Augustine is a terrific place, and you know it."

"Why? Because the Spanish gave refuge to Negroes?"

"You think that's bad?"

"Before you get carried away, let's remember, you're talking about the 16th, 17th and 18th centuries. And the Spanish required that the Negroes become Catholic.[155] That's not my version of freedom." Sensing Noah was about to debate the issue, I held up a halting hand. "Before you get lost in ancient history, keep in mind that since Florida, St. Augustine included, became part of the nation, and later a state, it has embraced slavery. And need I mention that it was part of the Confederacy. Oh…and one more minor detail, I'm a Maroon. Three Seminoles Wars in this century hardly put history on your side of the argument."

"Fair enough. We'll put history aside…My point is that St. Augustine is a great place, a growing city, and it offers an opportunity to make some dough."

I chuckled, but only to myself. Mr. Wright had trained Noah well. Rather than pressing a bad argument, he had switched to a different justification. "You could say the same about Charleston, and you're not headed there."

"I can't go everywhere."

---

[153] *St. Augustine, The Nation's Oldest City*, staugustine.com, 19 Dec. 2017 <http://staugustine.com/history/nations-oldest-city> stating: "The City of St. Augustine is the nation's *oldest permanently occupied European settlement,* having been founded by the Spanish in 1565." (emphasis added)

[154] *Florida Historic Places – St. Augustine Town Plan Historic District*, nps.gov, 14 Feb. 2017 <https://www.nps.gov/nr/travel/geo-flor/24.htm> stating: "During the 16th, 17th and 18th centuries, free blacks and slaves found Florida a haven—the Spanish Crown granted refuge to blacks if they embraced Catholicism."

[155] Ibid.

"True…but as cities go, Savannah is nothing to sneeze at." Among southeastern coastal cities, along with St. Augustine and Charleston, Savannah arguably topped the list.

"Excuse me, but the last I heard they won't be building the St. Augustine Hotel here in Savannah. And in case you hadn't noticed, around these parts, job opportunities, less you care to pick peaches for a song, are none too good."

Noah had a point. A change of scenery to St. Augustine had appeal. But my original calculation proved it didn't add up. I said, "As I indicated earlier, I can't abandon Grover. I can't go."

***

After a morning picking fruit—a few shekels were better than nothing—I spent the afternoon studying my calculus book. I was moving forward rapidly. Formulae that enabled me to take derivatives of the simplest expressions, ax^n, as well as derivatives of products and quotients, had advanced to differentiation by parts. While I was yet to explore the many practical applications of the powerful tool, the mere ability to determine the ever-changing slope of a function at any of its infinite points was mind-boggling. Specifics still beyond my ken, the possibilities of building mathematical models of real-life phenomena, were intoxicating.

With the Sun high in the sky, I had found a shade-yielding willow fronting the house where Grover and I roomed. With my back to the tree's trunk, I ingested the brilliance of Leibniz. About an hour had elapsed, when I observed a patroller, a police officer, entering the house. The unusual occurrence drew my attention from my work. I waited and watched. Minutes later, the officer exited the building. Having no desire to insinuate myself into police business, I lowered my head. Footsteps, coupled with peripheral vision, told me the officer was coming my way.

"Would you know where I could find Mican Reinbow?"

"Uh…I'm Mican."

"They tell me you live with Grover Calhoun. Is that right?"

"Yes, Sir." This was the longest conversation I had shared with a patroller since coming to Savannah, and already it was too long.

The patroller, about my height, roughly six feet, but outweighing my slim physique by about forty pounds, crouched in front of me.

I had considered standing up when first he had spoken to me. Inertia, along with concern that rising might appear threatening, had kept me in place.

"I have some bad news."

"Bad news?" I held my breath.

"Grover...Grover Calhoun drowned in the Savannah River this morning."

"He...he what?" I said, though the officer's words were clear.

"He drowned in the Savannah River."

"Is he...dead?" My question had already been answered, but my brain was unwilling to digest the horror. It darted back to the day when the soldier had delivered the news of my father's death. The mere memory was dreadful; reliving it with another rendition, unspeakable.

The patroller nodded. "Sorry to be the bearer of bad tidings."

A knot seized my stomach. I longed to scream, to pound the earth. The presence of the patroller shackled me. People had warned me to be wary of patrollers. The uniformed man had done nothing to intimidate me, but I was intimidated. I choked back emotions, driving them into the distant reaches of my frazzled brain. I said, "How...how did it happen?"

"It was an accident. He was on the bank, near the edge of the river. He tripped and fell. His head struck a rock as he tumbled down the bank—it's very steep there—into the water. By the time folks were able to pull him out, he was gone."

My mind raced. The story raised questions. To win higher wages, Grover, joined by his coworkers, had gone on strike. The work stoppage had enraged his boss. Subsequently, the job foreman had threatened Grover. I said, "Did anyone see him fall?"

"Yeah, the second in charge."

"The foreman?"

"No, his assistant."

"He...he's white, isn't he?"

"Yeah. So what?" The patroller's face was stone. He stood up.

I followed his lead, knowing I had ventured into dangerous waters. I was rarely one to be confrontational, particularly on matters of race. Like most persons of color in the South, I knew better. Add to the calculation, the presence of a white patroller—around town, there were none of color—and if I was not careful, I could be the next to drown. I said, "Did anyone else see him fall?"

"No." The patroller looked me in the eye. "We talked with the witness. We checked out his story. We're satisfied...Case closed." The deliberate cadence with which he voiced his final two words underscored his message.

Nevertheless, I felt the need to question. "Falling on a rock and drowning in the river...it's hard to imagine—"

"I said the case is closed." The patroller folded his arms across his chest. "Before you say or do something you might regret, let me give you some friendly advice." His steely eyes, intimidating tone and menacing posture made it clear his message was anything but friendly. "Don't stick your nose where it doesn't belong."

Much as I wanted to pursue the issue, the time and circumstances were wrong. Whether I might try under other conditions remained to be seen. I said, "What happened to Grover's body?"

"I'm glad you asked. That's part of the reason I'm here. We hoped you could direct us to his next of kin."

"Grover didn't have any. I was the person closest to him. He brought me here from Fort Myers."

"Then you're the one to claim his body, assuming you want to."

"Absolutely…but I…I guess I need to make burial arrangements first, if that's okay."

"Of course." The patroller peered off into space. "I think that about covers it." He looked back at me. "You take care." He headed on his way.

I dropped to the ground and sobbed. Reluctant to accept the harsh reality, unable to drag myself from beneath the willow, I lay there until finally I nodded off.

***

Several hours had elapsed since I had received the horrible news. I had no idea how I would deal with the situation. After fruitless attempts to confront the issue, I headed over to Noah's place. I needed to talk to someone. Unfortunately, the right candidates were unavailable. The Wrights were up north in New Hampshire. Sarah had discarded me. And Grover was dead. Noah was the next best alternative. I went to his family's home, a block south of Jackson Park, and knocked on the door. An instant after a woman opened it, Noah approached.

"I got it, Mom." Noah directed his focus to me. "A welcome surprise. What brings you?"

Struggling for the right words, I hesitated. My expression likely reflected my discomfort.

"What's wrong?" Noah stepped outside.

I fought back tears. "Grover is dead."

"My God…I'm so sorry." Noah stroked my shoulder. "How…how did it happen?"

"I…I'm not sure…The patroller who notified me said that Grover fell and hit his head on a rock along a steep bank of the river and drowned, but…"

"But what?"

I heaved a sigh. "It happened near Grover's place of work, where he had been leading a strike. The foreman had threatened him. The patroller insisted it was an accident. I have my doubts, not that I have any proof."

"I'm sure they'll investigate it."

I shook my head. "The patroller said the case is closed. And when I expressed qualms, he all but threatened me. From what Grover had said about his employer—he owns Walton's Cotton Lading—he had connections with both the police and the powers that be."

"I assume the patroller was—" Noah cut himself off midstream before mumbling, "Of course, he was white…unless he came from another planet and was green."

"What do you think I should do?"

"What do you mean?"

I thought I had been clear. I said, "Should I press for a further investigation?"

Noah shook his head slowly, but demonstratively. "Bad idea. You could end up like Grover…and your body might never be found."

The assessment mirrored my own. "But how can I simply ignore Grover's death?"

"I understand how you feel, but…" Noah looked me in the eye. "Let me put it this way. Grover wouldn't want you to sacrifice yourself in a futile gesture. And we both know it would be futile."

Noah's point was well taken. Were I doing a mathematical proof, I would have stamped it, Q.E.D. (*Quod Erat Demonstradum;* That which is to be proved.)

"My grandmother—she spent nearly sixty years as a slave—always told me that you have to choose your battles. When I was only seven, I watched my aunt being mercilessly whipped for no reason. When I asked why no one stepped in, my grandmother said, "My daddy tried that years ago. It earned him, as well as other members of the family, beatings…severe ones."

With an argument akin to theoretical mathematics, Noah had already proved his theorem. Supplementing it with an example from his family history, a compelling practical application, added the imprimatur of applied mathematics. I said, "You're right…not that I like it."

"What do you plan to do now?"

I assumed I had answered his question the moment before he had asked it. "Didn't you hear me?"

"Oh…sorry. I wasn't talking about that. I was referring to your plans, now that Grover is gone."

The matter had barely crossed my mind, and when it briefly had, I had ignored it.

"Sorry again. It's none of my business. If you had raised it, that would be different."

"No, it's fine. And to answer your question, I haven't begun to think about it. Given the events of the day, it's much too early."

"Understand…and hopefully, I haven't put another problem on your plate. It's already full."

"You're right about my plate, but as far as adding problems, no way. I needed to talk to someone. I appreciate you being there for me." I took a deep breath. There was nothing left to discuss. I said goodbye and started for home. Over the first block, I tried to mount a strategy. Enervated and with no good ideas, procrastination prevailed. Reality, as well as a plan, would have to wait.

About ten minutes passed before I ascended the steps and reached my room. I eyed the beds and small table and chairs where Grover and I ate. I considered sitting down but dismissed the idea. I went over to the bookshelf and took down the first volume of *Uncle Tom's Cabin*. I flipped it open to Abbey's inscription, "I love you." I clutched the book to my chest. I needed a hug. Pulling the volume close to my heart was the best I could manage. I stood motionless, listening to the eerie silence that enveloped me. A minute later, I returned the book to the shelf.

After locking the door, I walked over to Grover's bed, eyeing its emptiness with melancholy. I moved it about a yard from the wall. Guilt gave me pause, but desperate for any activity that could distract from anguish, I continued. Using a screwdriver and a hammer from a storage box that Grover kept under his bed, I pried the tongue-and-groove floor in the corner where the bed had stood. I no sooner removed the first board than a small metal box revealed itself. I levered one more board before lifting the box from beneath the floor. I carried the box to the table on the other side of the room and seated myself. I turned the box's latch and opened it. Inside was an envelope and a drawstring cloth bag. I loosened the drawstring and peered into the bag. It contained a variety of rocks and stones, about twenty-five, ranging from tiny to an inch in diameter. I had no idea whether any were gems of value. I put them back into the bag, retightened the drawstring, and, after returning the bag to the box, took the envelope. I carefully unsealed it. A stack of currency greeted my eyes. I thumbed through the collection of ones, fives and tens. Never had I held such a huge sum of money. I slowly counted it—all $117. Knowing my new-found wealth came at the expense of Grover's death, compunction had me stuffing the bills back into the envelope. I returned the envelope to the box and closed the cover. I put the box back beneath the floor, replaced the boards, and, using the hammer, pounded them back into place.

I plopped down into a chair and closed my eyes. I needed a plan, if only to begin to deal with the issues facing me. Delay, if anything, would exacerbate my plight. Within seconds, a solution to the first of my problems emerged. Grover deserved a decent burial. The money he had saved was more than sufficient. I opened my eyes and gazed skyward, not that I could see beyond the ceiling. Long with doubts if Heaven existed, I hoped it did. If so, no doubt, Grover was there. I whispered, “Rest in peace, my friend.”

***

Amidst predominating sorrow, for the next three days, from morning until night, I devoted myself to confirming whether Grover’s death was an unfortunate accident or another pernicious device to preserve antebellum white supremacy. I spoke with everyone, both white and Negro, who knew anything about the matter. It became clear that there was only one eyewitness, and that eyewitness, the foreman’s assistant, was adamant that there had been no foul play. Though he was solid and credible when he described the occurrence, I harbored doubts. The coroner was insistent that death had come from an accidental fall. He was as categorical as the eyewitness. My examination of the accident site yielded nothing that would contradict the story of the foreman’s assistant and the findings of the coroner. Grover’s fellow workers had doubts, but they were based only on distrust of the system. Not one scintilla of evidence did they offer to show that a homicide had occurred. They did, however, urge me to abandon my investigation. No good could come of it. Grover’s employer and his foreman were tight with the patrollers, coroner, prosecutor and judge. Even if foul play had occurred, prosecution of a white man for a crime against his Negro employee was an impossibility. Not only was the system rigged, but efforts to buck it would be deemed seditious. Consequences, not justice, would ensue. On that they all agreed.

Despite the foregoing, a need to pursue one last avenue drove me to the office of the local prosecutor. I arrived just after noon where I waited in the hallway for his return from lunch. He showed up around 1:30. A half-dozen people, all white, most with no appointments, came and went. Just after five o’clock he exited his office and started down the hall.

I raced toward him. “Excuse me,” I said. “May I speak with you, Sir?”

“My day is done.”

"I've been waiting here since noon."

The prosecutor scowled. "Okay, but make it quick."

I introduced myself and explained that I had come about Grover's death.

"I know about it," he said. "I've seen the coroner's report and the statement of the eyewitness. Rather than a basis for prosecution, one that would require proof of foul play beyond a reasonable doubt, the evidence demonstrates it was an accident. Matter done." He started down the hall but came back my way. "I'm going to give you some friendly advice, and I don't mean it as a threat." His cordial manner manifested sincerity, not an ultimatum. "There is no case here, but if you push the matter, some of your late friend's co-workers will lose their jobs and/or worse. As I said, it's not a threat, just reality." He headed off.

A moment later, I headed out of the building. If, by chance, an injustice had occurred, it had become clear that it would not be righted. Challenging the white-controlled establishment would not bring Grover back. It would only endanger his co-workers. I could hear him making those very arguments, making them his final testament. I gazed upward at the overcast sky. A narrow ray of sun, a message beaming from Heaven, seemingly confirmed Grover's wish. A part of me still wanted to pursue the matter, but only to alleviate my own guilt. Justifying the self-interested motivation was impossible. The concession, coupled with a want of evidence to launch a challenge, especially one that could be proved beyond a reasonable doubt, compelled me to accept the verdict.

***

Back in my one-room home, I revisited the issue of Grover's death. Though I was convinced that I had made the right decision, guilt was inescapable. Gradually my thoughts shifted to another question. What should I do with myself, my life? The issue quickly transformed. Where did I want to be? Four possibilities emerged: Fort Myers, Savannah, St. Augustine and Meriden, New Hampshire.

The first, Fort Myers, had no chance. With the fort abandoned several years earlier, it was a wooden corral in a desolate wilderness, a lifeless haunt that had likely decayed over time. Returning to the cabin where I had spent my formative years would have been wonderful were my father alive. But with him gone, the cabin offered nothing more than a hermit's life in the woods. That was a non-starter.

Savannah was a nice place. I had received a good education there. But my connections to the city had all evaporated. The Wrights had moved to New Hampshire. Sarah was no longer in my life. If anything, she had become a reason to leave. Crossing paths with her would rekindle depressing memories. And with Grover gone, I had no reason to stay. Savannah had ceased to be the place for me.

That left two choices: Meriden, New Hampshire and St. Augustine, Florida. Over the ensuing hour, I debated the pros and cons of each. I weighed them sitting in a chair and walking in circles within the room's narrow confines. The Wrights were wonderful people. Living with them would be nice. But what would I do in New Hampshire? And for one who abhorred the cold at forty degrees, how would I bear months when the thermometer rarely got that high? The idea of embarking with Noah on a new life where I could earn some money was appealing. But I knew almost nothing about St. Augustine. Apart from Noah, I would know no one there. St. Augustine was a crap shoot, though admittedly an intriguing one. Back and forth I vacillated. One minute I leaned toward New Hampshire, and the next I favored St. Augustine. When logic and security came to the forefront, New Hampshire seemed the choice. When thoughts of possible adventure and independence kindled and images of Northeast winters stirred, my leanings shifted to St. Augustine.

With my brain in a quandary, I headed downstairs. I no sooner stepped outside than a solution struck. I could have the best of both worlds…almost. I would join Noah on his escapade to St. Augustine. I could earn some money and, at the same time, continue studying calculus in the warmth of the South. And where Meriden, New Hampshire was roughly one thousand miles away, St. Augustine was only one hundred fifty. If things went well in St. Augustine, I could stay. If not, Meriden remained a viable option.

I continued down the street, rehashing the plan. The more I contemplated it, the better I liked it. I paused in front of a storefront window and gazed at my faint reflection. Unlike the day when last I had visited Sarah, my physical appearance, attire included, was of no moment. I was looking deeper, searching for my identity, questioning who I was. Echoes of Grover's voice, buoying me, reverberated in my head. The sky was the limit. The world far beyond Savannah awaited me. Grover would want me to take it on. Vibrant and intelligent, armed with an education, I should have been ready…I wasn't.

Chapter XII

TEN DAYS AFTER GROVER'S DEATH, Noah and I departed Savannah. Five days before leaving, I had buried Grover in a fine oak coffin in the Negro cemetery not far from where we had resided. Before his interment, I had lengthened the tether on the lapis bookmark I had made for him. I had turned it into a necklace and draped it from his neck. I told myself that Grover would be happy to wear the token into eternity. Deep down, I knew my real motivation. I wanted him to take a part of me with him.

His coworkers and lots of folks from the First African Baptist Church, along with friends of mine from school, attended the funeral service and burial. After everyone had left, I returned to the gravesite where I read several blessings that I had copied from a prayer book at the First African Baptist Church. I recited a brief eulogy, recounting Grover's good deeds and character, that he was hard working, kind and generous, and merited rewards beyond his earthly life. I thanked him for all he had done for me, not that words were sufficient. I took the shovel from the gravedigger who had patiently waited nearby. I dumped a scoop of dirt onto Grover's coffin before giving the shovel back to the gravedigger who finished his work.

As I left the cemetery, I recounted my history of misfortunes. Still over two years short of twenty, I had lost my mother at a very young age, my father when I was only twelve and, most recently, Grover, my stepfather, if not by law, *de facto*. Self-pity emerged. Guilt superseded. These individuals, my benefactors, were the real victims. An odd notion mitigated my bother. As a consequence of the war, countless families, both Yankee and Confederate, bore pain like mine. Why that fact eased my burden made no sense, at least at first blush. Brief analysis, recollection of the adage, *Misery loves company,* clarified the anomaly. The mental exercise, a constructive distraction, coupled with the knowledge that I had much to be grateful for, provided additional relief.

People say that time heals all wounds. With my loss of Grover less than two weeks in the past, perhaps the process had begun. Though melancholy persisted, it no longer bore the all-consuming nature of its first few days. It was early July when Noah and I traveled to St. Augustine by steamship on the Black Star Line, one of four that connected the two port cities.[156] For us, neither of whom had previously traveled by steamship, the voyage was exciting. Upon arrival at the port, near Fort Marion, the continental United States' "oldest permanent seacoast fortification,"[157] we solicited information about housing. We found a buckboard driver who told us about "Little Africa," a Negro section south of the city that had begun to develop following the War of Secession.[158] For two bits, the driver agreed to shuttle us there. Rather than heading directly to Little Africa, located along the west bank of the Maria Sanchez Creek, at his suggestion we proceeded down the waterway's east side. He spoke of a nice home with rooms for rent at an excellent rate. Green as we were, we abided his counsel.

As we negotiated our way, nearly a mile, the terrain grew progressively more rural. Bumps and potholes lined the woodland road. Occasional paths branching on either side were often narrower than the wagon. Increasing skepticism became apprehension when the driver turned onto a path through what seemed a thicket to nowhere.

"You sure this area has good rooms for rent?" I said.

"Relax. We're almost there."

Noah flashed me an uneasy look.

---

[156] *Reconstruction in St. Augustine*, drbronsontours,com, 13 Feb. 2017 <http://drbronsontours.com/bronsonhistorypageamericastaugustinereconstruction.html> In 1873 there were four steamship lines, "Murray's Line," "Atlantic Coast Mail Steamship Co's," "Empire Line" and "Black Star Line." (*See*, footnote 60, supra.)

[157] *Florida Historic Places — Castillo de San Marcos National Monument*, nps.gov, 14 Feb. 2017 <https://www.nps.gov/nr/travel/geo-flor/23.htm>. The Castillo de San Marcos remains the "oldest existing permanent seacoast fortification in the continental United States. The present star-shaped fort, surrounding moat, and earthworks were constructed between 1672 -1756 to protect Spanish territory in Florida and the shipping routes along the Florida coast." *See*, footnote 237 to the effect that when Congress made Fort Marion a National Monument in 1924, it reverted to its original name, Castillo de San Marcos.

[158] *OUR HISTORY — Lincolnville Memorial & Cultural Center*, lincolnvillemuseum.org, 21 Feb. 2017 <http://www.lincolnvillemuseum.org/cultural center/> states of Lincolnville: "The community was established in 1866 when Peter Sanks, Matilda Papy, Harriet Weedman, Miles Hancock, Israel McKenzie, Aaron Dupont and Tom Solana leased land for $1.00 a year on what was then the west bank of Maria Sanchez Creek. The rest of the peninsula consisted of orange grove plantations. The settlement was originally called Africa, or Little Africa. After streets were laid out in 1878, it came to be known as Lincolnville, named after Abraham Lincoln."

I was thankful I was not alone with the driver. That he was diminutive and three or four times my age might have eased my trepidations, were it not for the looming possibility that he could have cohorts lying in wait. I made a decision. One more minute, and I would demand that we return to town.

The driver negotiated a curve, and there, just ahead, was a house with a handwritten sign out front, "Rooms to Let." The quaint Victorian, an edificial oasis in the sylvan surroundings, was a pleasant surprise.

"I think you gents will be quite pleased with this place. I know the owner. He lost his wife, 'bout three months ago."

It was the first time anyone had ever referred to me as a gent. At seventeen and eager to get on with my adult life, I welcomed the denomination.

"It looks nice," said Noah. "Though I doubt it'll fit our budget."

"Don't wanna promise nothin', but I'd bet a rack of ribs at Sunday's barbeque you'll like the price."

"Can't hurt to check," I said. Even as I voiced interest, concerns persisted.

Noah and I climbed down from the buckboard. We approached the neat, two-story green structure, its porch and gabled roof both bordered with red gingerbread. I knocked on the front door. A minute later, a man, whom I judged to be in his seventies, opened the portal.

"Afternoon. Can I help you?"

"We're looking for a place to stay and our wagon driver…" Noah gestured toward the wagon.

"Oh, Jasper brought you." The man waved. "Hey there, Jasper?"

The driver waved back.

The man refocused on Noah and me. "I live here alone. My wife died recently. The place is more than I need, not that I'm itching to go elsewhere. Problem is, I got a bum knee." He gestured at his left leg. "Can't do the maintenance the way I used to, and I can't make it up and down the stairs no more. Got two rooms upstairs that ain't much use to me now. I'm lookin' for tenants, good ones. You fellas from St. Augustine?"

"Savannah. We just arrived today." I took the measure of the man. He was tall and very thin. He had an angular face and nose, a profile akin to Abraham Lincoln, not that the two could be confused, given their racial disparity.

"What did you do in Savannah?"

"We were students," said Noah. "We came here hoping to find work on the St. Augustine Hotel. We're looking to get on with life…Earn a few dollars."

"Youth…impetuous youth." The man chuckled as he looked us up and down. "I get it. I was the same way when I was your age." Nostalgia dripped from his words. "Would you be willin' to spend some time talkin' to an old man?"

"Don't see why not," I said, assuming he was referring to himself.

The man stroked his double chin. "You seem to be decent sorts. So, here's the deal. In exchange for help maintainin' the house and the pleasure of some company, I'll rent you the rooms. Won't charge you no rent. This stage of life, with no kin, the money don't mean much to me."

I glanced at Noah. With the offer eclipsing our most optimistic expectations, words were unnecessary.

"Before you fellas react, you need to check out the rooms." He led us into the house and gestured for us to go up the center staircase. At the top, on either side of the landing, we found two similar rooms, each about twelve-feet square, with a bed, armoire, small desk and chair.

"Can you believe this?" whispered Noah.

"A lot nicer than what we thought we'd get, and you can't beat the price."

"You prefer one room over the other?"

I shook my head. "Six of one, half-dozen of the other." We headed down the stairs.

"So, what do you think?" said the man.

"You got yourself a deal," said Noah.

The man shook Noah's hand. "My name is Walter…Walter Sanders."

"Noah Carter."

"And I'm Mican Reinbow. Nice to meet you." I shook Mr. Sander's hand.

"The pleasure is mine...I'd offer to help you bring your things up, but…" He pointed at his knee.

"No problem. We've got it," I said. Noah and I headed out to the buckboard.

"You like the digs?" said the driver.

"Absolutely." I slipped the driver an extra two bits. "We appreciate the ride and the great recommendation."

Noah and I unloaded our belongings and carted them upstairs. He took the room on the right, and I, the one on the left, not that it made a difference. We put our things in our rooms, leaving it until later to stow them away. We started back downstairs.

"I'm in here…in the parlor," called out Mr. Sanders. "It's left of the hall…uh…right when you're comin' down the stairs."

We no sooner entered than he got up from a wood-framed chair with green velvet back and cushion. “This is the parlor.” He gestured in all directions. “Let me show you the rest of the house.” With a noticeable limp, Mr. Sanders guided us into the hallway that paralleled the stairs. As we moved toward the rear of the structure, he motioned to his left through an open door. “That’s my room. I’d take you in, ’cept it’s kinda messy.” He turned to the right. “This is the kitchen. You’re welcome to the run of it.”

With a sink, black iron stove, counter space and several cabinets, it was better than anything I had previously experienced, even nicer than what the Wrights enjoyed in their Savannah flat. Off in the corner was a hard-rock maple table with three matching chairs, two on the longer side and one on the shorter.

“Very, very nice,” I said.

“Glad you like it.” Mr. Sanders pointed to his right. “Over there’s the pantry.” He led the way out of the kitchen into the dining room. The bright space with two large windows sported a fine table, hutch, and a corner cabinet in each front-wall corner. “Ain’t been usin’ this room much since my Wilma passed.” Melancholy filled his voice as he slowly moved his gaze around the room.

Though clairvoyance was hardly among my purported talents, I assumed he was recalling good times spent there with his late wife.

“You have a lovely home,” said Noah.

“It’s yours now too.” He gestured across the hall. “Now that you’ve had the tour, suppose we go back into the parlor and get to know one another.

As we returned to the formal room, Mr. Sanders took the same chair in which he was seated earlier. Noah and I went to the settee on the opposite wall.

“Have you checked out jobs at the St. Augustine Hotel?”

“Not as yet,” said Noah.

“Not that I’m the best source, but from what I’ve heard,” said Mr. Sanders, “your chances oughta be good. Rumor has it, they’re short on help.” He surveyed us for a couple of seconds. “You fellas strike me as havin’ more on the ball than just construction, not to demean hard labor…What I mean is you got education. Our people need more like you in jobs demandin’ brains, rather than brawn. Hope you ain’t plannin’ on wastin’ whatcha learned in school.”

“No, Sir, Mr. Sanders,” I said.

“Please, call me Walter.”

My face must have reflected my reluctance.

"I'm much more comfortable with Walter. Calling me Mr. Sanders makes me feel my age…old."

His argument overcame my need to afford the elderly man what I considered proper respect. I said, "Even though we'll be working, we plan to keep up with our studies. Noah is focusing on philosophy and architecture, and I'm teaching myself calculus."

"Calculus. Damn, that's heady stuff. Way beyond what I know. Fractions and decimals are as far as I got. Taught myself. Tried algebra after I retired, but it was too hard. That, plus I couldn't see no use for it…Not that I think it ain't useful. Just that it wouldn't be for me, bein' retired and all."

"What did you do before you retired?" said Noah.

"Had a buildin' and roofin' business with 'bout eight employees. Thanks to St. Augustine's growth, it was profitable. Made enough to buy ten acres here, 'bout an eighth of a mile square. The land was dirt cheap. By the time I was fifty, I sold my business to my top employee, and me and Wilma retired. We built this here house. When we moved in, we was pretty much alone. Weren't no one else near. After the war, in '66, some freedmen started comin' to the area, mainly on the far side of the creek. Built themselves mostly one-room cabins. Fortunately, we still had all our land; so, no one could move in on top of us.[159] The wife and me enjoyed near twenty-five good years of retirement before she passed. Miss her a lot…but I ain't complainin'. Can't. Ain't got no right. Altogether, me and Wilma was married fifty-six years." He breathed a wistful sigh. "Didn't know it at the time, but she did me a real good turn before we got married. She pushed me to read. Didn't do much of it over the years, but since we retired, I done loads. And now that I'm alone, I read every day. Can't compare to havin' Wilma by my side, but it beats countin' the chirps of the crickets."

The information explained an anomaly I had observed in his speech. While his discourse was laced with slang and double negatives, his expansive vocabulary suggested he was literate.

"Gotta tell you. I'm real happy to have you fellas here. Mighty lonely, sittin' all day by myself, 'specially after havin' Wilma by my side all those years. She was a great listener, and for me, one who loves to

---

[159] *Florida Historic Places — Lincolnville Historic District*, nps.gov, 14 Dec. 2017 <https://www.nps.gov/nr/travel/geo-flor/23.htm> stating: "The Lincolnville Historic District is St. Augustine's most prominent historically black neighborhood and is associated with many significant events in the city's African American history. Founded in 1866 by former slaves, the district remained relatively static until the late 19th century."

talk, she was perfect. And speakin' of talkin', I been goin' on like a mina bird."

"On the contrary," said Noah. "Listening to you is very interesting. And we're thrilled to have found such a lovely home. Far better, not to mention cheaper than anything we could have expected."

Walter gazed off into space. "Reminds me of my workin' days."

"How so?" The instant the question rolled off my tongue, I doubted its wisdom. In the face of a rhetorical remark, displaying curiosity with someone I had just met was presumptuous. "Please, ignore my inquiry. It's none of my business."

"Relax. Be my pleasure to explain...Case you forgot, I'm a talker...Anyway, I was referrin' to the method I used when I was in business. It was never my goal to beat the other fella. Don't get me wrong. I was always lookin' for a deal, a real good one. But that didn't mean the other fella had to lose. I searched for somethin' that was more valuable to him than me, and vice versa. Goal was for us both to get more than we gave. Most times, there was a way. And it had a bonus. Me and the other fella was happy to do business in the future. Rather than walkin' away resentful, we built trust."

"I can see why you were a successful businessman."

Walter smiled.

I found it difficult to interpret his expression. Appreciative acceptance of a compliment was possible. Judging me a brown-nose was equally viable.

He said, "Don't really know what's happenin' elsewhere in the South, but from what I hear economic conditions in St. Augustine are better than other places. St. Augustine was lucky to be spared the worst of the war, as well as its aftermath durin' Reconstruction."[160]

"Savannah was like that too, at least as to the war itself," I said. "The city is pretty much intact. Unfortunately, economic conditions there are dreadful."

"Probably would have been like that in St. Augustine, 'cept that Washington picked it as the army's district headquarters for Reconstruction.[161] Havin' the soldiers here prevented the violence

---

[160] *Early American Florida History*, visitstaugustine.com, 13 Feb. 2017 <https://www.visitstaugustine.com/history/american-florida.php> stating: "Fortunately, St. Augustine was spared much of the violence and hatred that Reconstruction brought to much of the South. The presence of Northerners, even Northern landowners, was nothing new to St. Augustine. The economic benefits of having Northerners visit or even purchase property in the community were well-known by most residents long before the war."

[161] Ibid.

plaguin' southern cities. Also brought money here. Businesses did better. Folks was less resentful of the carpetbaggers from up north.[162] Money has a way of doin' that. Stick a buck in a guy's hand and he'll...Damn, there I go again, waggin' off at the mouth. You boys will have to stop me when I get carried away."

I doubted I would, certainly not until I knew Walter better. Regardless, I found his confab interesting. I might have voiced the sentiment were I not conscious of my seemingly obsequious behavior only a minute before. I said, "How are people of color fairing here in St. Augustine?"

"Where do I start?" Walter grew briefly pensive. "With the obvious, I guess. Negroes are definitely second-class. But that said, I suspect we got it better than most places in the South. Don't know it personally, just from what I hear. But it makes sense for the reason I mentioned, that the army's Reconstruction headquarters are here. A decent economy eases the effects of prejudice, lessens the need for scapegoats. 'Course the whole thing is delicate. Could go either way."

"What do you mean?" said Noah.

"Well, the way I see it, Reconstruction could change things. Already has. The state's Reconstruction Constitution puts public schools in every county. It also gives all men the vote.[163] Just this past year, the Sisters of St. Joseph came here from France to teach the freed slaves.[164] These are all good things. But the progress could halt in a heartbeat."

"Why so?" I said, eager to compare circumstances to Savannah. The latter had seen progress, albeit far slower.

"Well, I ain't no seer or nothin', but I can't help worryin'. Once the army leaves—they was supposed to last May, but fortunately, our Governor, Reed, got 'em to stay.[165] But anyway, once the army goes, the Democrats, all them good old conservative white boys, plan to flip things back the way they was. That they could bring back slavery is a long shot, but you aks me, equality is longer yet."

The assessment struck me as well reasoned. In the fraction of an hour I had spent talking with my new landlord, I had made assessments of my own. He was, as he had indicated, talkative, but he was anything but boring. From a shelf on the front wall, the melodious chime of an elegant clock, its wave-like frame curving downward from its round face, drew my attention.

---

[162] Ibid.

[163] Florida in the Civil War and Reconstruction, Florida History Internet Center, 28 Feb. 2017 <http://floridahistory.org/civilwar.htm>.

[164] *Reconstruction in St. Augustine*, op. cit.

[165] Ibid.

"Five o'clock," said Walter. 'Bout time I start makin' us dinner. In the meantime, you boys might wanna head upstairs and organize your things. Soon as you're done, come back down and we'll eat."

***

The following morning, Noah and I were up early. After a flapjack and sausage breakfast, compliments of Walter, we hiked the wooded road to the site of the St. Augustine Hotel, roughly a half-mile north of Walter's home. Located at the Plaza de la Constitución at Bayfront, a few hundred yards south of the fort, the structure, whose bottom story had already been framed, was about two hundred feet long.[166] Noah and I approached a man hammering a timber.

"Excuse me, Sir," said Noah. "My friend and I are looking for a job working on the hotel. You know where we might apply?"

The man pointed. "'Round the corner, little over fifty yards. Before you get to the cathedral, cut right, toward the bay. Out back, you'll find a shed where they run the show, includin' the hirin'."

We thanked him and followed his directions to a small structure, about 10' × 14'.

"This must be the place," said Noah. He knocked on the door.

"C'mon in. It's open."

We stepped inside where a burly white man in work clothes greeted us. "What can I do for you?"

"We're looking for work," said Noah.

The hulking man with robust arms and a stone face looked us up and down. "You boys got experience?"

I assumed the limited time I had spent picking peaches didn't count. "We've been going to school the past few years."

"School?" The man gave me a look. "What you been studying?"

"Philosophy, English, history, math…most everything. These days I'm teaching myself calculus."

"Calculus?" The man laughed. "Don't know what it is, but we sure don't need it here."

---

166 *The St. Augustine Hotel Corner of Plaza and Bayfront St. Augustine Florida, Reconstruction in St. Augustine*, drbronsontours.com, 13 Feb. 2017 <http://drbronsontours.com/bronsonstaugustinerehotel.html> indicating: "**Hotel St. Augustine** was built in 1869 by a partnership of Captain E. E. Vail, F. H. Palmer, and Dr. Andrew Anderson. T. P. House was the architect and builder. The hotel had gaslights, was 200 feet long, three stories high, and contained 80 rooms (140 rooms were added in 1875). This was the first major hotel built in St. Augustine after the close of the War of Rebellion." (emphasis from original; *See*, footnote 60, supra.)

I swallowed hard, shifting my gaze to my feet. What folly had led me to think that my studies would impress a boss looking for real-world work experience?

The man turned to Noah. "You studyin' calculus too?"

"Uh…no."

"You ever done carpentry?"

Noah shook his head.

"We could use more workers, but the kind with skills, not those lookin' to get some."

"We're quick learners," said Noah.

"I don't think so."

"Just a second," said a gentleman who, attired in a fine suit, was seated at a desk in the farthest corner. "You say you're studying calculus?"

"Uh…yes. But I…I understand that's not what's needed here."

The gentleman shrugged. "If I dropped a rock off a cliff, and I expressed the altitude of the rock as a function of time, what would the first derivative of my function represent?"

"Velocity," I said.

"And the second?"

"Acceleration."

The man in the suit nodded slowly. "One doesn't get to calculus unless he's done a lot of studying. Indicative of a hard worker. Doesn't mean he's good with his hands, but odds are he'll try. Truth is, we want carpenters…skilled carpenters, but we need more hands. Tell you what. I'll give you fellows a chance. Here's the deal: laborers' pay, $8.27 per week. That's ten hours, six days, a sixty-hour week."[167]

"Gee thanks," I said.

"Before you get too excited, understand, it's a trial run. And Sherm here (he gestured at the other man) will keep close tabs on you. If he doesn't see quick progress, you get the heave-ho. It's nothing personal. Just a matter of simple arithmetic, something you fellows can understand. It's like this. The two of you together will be costing me the equivalent of one skilled carpenter. And let me tell you, right now, that carpenter can produce a helluva lot more than the two of you combined. Though normally I'm not a gambling man, I'm willing to take a chance that you're quick learners. And if you are, who knows, six months or a

---

[167] *Typical wages in 1860 through 1890 | Outrun Change*, outrunchange.com, 28 Feb. 2017 <https://outrunchange.com/2012/06/14/typical-wages-in-1860-through-1890/> indicating that for a sixty-hour week a carpenter earned on average $10.92 in 1860, $24.60 in 1870 and $16.56 in 1880, while a laborer earned $5.88 in 1860, $9.36 in 1870 and $8.10 in 1880.

year from now, you might be making a whole lot more, maybe double, carpenters' pay." He pointed at me and then Noah. "But keep in mind, if a week or two down the road, Sherm doesn't like your progress—and that progress better continue—you're history."

"We'll work very hard, Sir," said Noah.

"I suspect you will…How good you'll be remains to be seen." He pawed at his beard. "And now I leave you to Sherm's capable hands." He turned back to his desk.

A scowl on his face, the burly man who had first greeted us motioned us to a table at the opposite end of the shed. "I'm Sherman Hooker, foreman of this project."

"Noah Carter."

"And I'm Mican Reinbow."

"You boys is mighty lucky. Ain't sure why Mr. House—he's the builder and architect on this here project[168]—decided to give you a shot. But what he says goes."

"We appreciate the opportunity," said Noah.

"Don't let your hopes outrun your prospects." The burly man with no neck eyed us imperiously. "'Cause I'm gonna keep my eye on you. And 'less you pull your weight, you'll be gone faster than a hare with a pack of bloodhounds on its ass."

"We'll do our best," I said.

"That may be." Hooker's drawl, more measured than before, hinted at sarcasm. "Of course, that ain't the point. Question is whether you got the right stuff, the physical kind." The fists of his blacksmith-like arms clenched. "Around here, calculus, whatever the hell that is, don't cut the mustard. You get my drift?"

While it was possible Hooker was merely laying the ground rules, I feared he was looking forward to firing us. Whether it was because he didn't like Mr. House superseding his hiring authority or because Noah and I were of color or a sadistic need to disparage those who were more educated or a combination of such factors, his determination to give us a hard time seemed apparent.

"Let's go outside, onto the site, where I'll introduce you to Bill Styles. He'll get you started."

As Hooker led the way from the shed, Mr. House, who had been working at his desk, looked up. "Just a second. Before you fellows start work, you might like to see what the hotel will look like once it's done."

---

[168] *The St. Augustine Hotel Corner of Plaza and Bayfront St. Augustine Florida*, op. cit. (*See*, footnote 60, supra.)

"Boss, these are laborers and, for that matter, rookies. Ain't nothin' they need to know about the big picture to do their jobs."

"Understand that, Sherm. But it never hurts when you're cutting a tree to know the forest, especially if you're the type with curiosity." Mr. House turned to Noah and me. "You fellows like to see the plans?"

"Absolutely." Even if I hadn't been interested, no way would I have responded otherwise, not when the preference of the head honcho apparently differed.

Mr. House motioned us over and unrolled a large paper on his desk. "This is how the building is projected to look when finished."

Seeing the drawing of the impeccable three-story structure, the still-fresh image of the bare-bones, wide-reaching frame I had seen outside metamorphosed into a majestic edifice. "Wow…that's impressive."

"I think so," said Mr. House. "And those who are financing it, Mr. Vail, along with his partners, Messrs. Palmer and Anderson, concur. It'll be St. Augustine's premier hotel, the biggest for miles around." Mr. House pointed at the plans. "With its location on the Plaza overlooking the bay, coupled with its overhanging balconies, it'll be a mecca. Add Florida's weather, the ocean and a growing tourist business, and the hotel is St. Augustine's future waiting to happen."

Even more than his words, Mr. House's enthusiasm struck me. Clearly, he relished the project and believed in its potential.

"What's the population of St. Augustine?" said Noah.

"About 2000, give or take," said Mr. House.[169] "But don't let that fool you. Keep in mind that it's a resort destination. At any given time, we have many non-residents here."

The caveat about non-residents notwithstanding, the number was less than I had expected, far less than Savannah's 28,000 inhabitants. Since arriving in St. Augustine the day before, I had realized that it was smaller than I had imagined, but a population of 2,000 shocked me. The realization underscored that I had come to St. Augustine on a whim. Advance investigation of my new hometown had been skipped. Still the move made sense. With nothing left in Savannah to hold me there, I wanted out. St. Augustine was the best of imperfect alternatives.

"Excuse me, Boss," said Hooker. "If we're gonna pay these greenhorns, ain't it time they get to work?"

---

[169] *Florida's Lineup Of Largest Cities Has Shifted Over The Years*, orlandosentinel.com, 3 Jan. 2018 <http://aticles.orlandosentinel.com/1991-09-22/news/9109201145_1_florida-cities-population> stating: "Up until 1900, Key West was Florida's largest city. In 1890, it had 18,000 hearty residents…Florida's second largest city for most of the 1800s was St. Augustine with a couple of thousand people."

"Yeah, I suppose so." Mr. House turned back to Noah and me. "Hope this is the start of a good relationship with the St. Augustine Hotel project. And with that, I leave you to the trusty hands of Sherm...that's Mr. Hooker, who will get you started."

"Thank you again, Mr. House," said Noah.

"We appreciate this opportunity," I said.

"This way," said Hooker, as he led us from the shed. Once we had gone about twenty yards, out of earshot of the building, he said, "Work here starts at seven-thirty, every Monday through Saturday, ten hours a day. Like the boss said, pay is $8.27 per week for sixty hours." He delivered the message while still marching forward, never looking at either of us.

We followed Hooker, turning east, so we faced the bay. He stopped. "Just so there ain't no misunderstandings, had it been up to me, you boys would be gone already. The kinda work you'll be doin' demands these." He displayed a pair of huge forearms. "The stuff you find in books ain't gonna drive a nail straight into a two-by-four, let alone lift a four-by-eight. 'Less you prove to me you're better than you look, your stay 'll be short. Mr. House may have let you in the door, but I can show you the way out. He don't never second guess me on who's good and who ain't." Hooker glared, a look that was to become familiar. "We clear?"

"Yes, Sir," I said, echoing Noah's response.

"Good. Then let's see what Bill Styles—you'll report to him—has for you." Hooker entered the construction site. A minute later, he returned, accompanied by a tall, sinewy white man. "These here are the rookies...Whad'ya say your names are?"

"I'm Noah, and he's Mican."

"Nice to meet you. I'm Bill Styles." He shook our hands.

"Bill here tells me it ain't a good day to be trainin' greenhorns. Just what I feared. We're payin' dead weight to distract our best from their work." Next to the puss that Hooker displayed, sour milk would have been sweet.

"It's okay. I'll find them something to do."

Styles' tone, far more accommodating, helped mitigate my discomfort.

"C'mon with me," said Styles.

He took us around to the bay side of the building to a stack of lumber. "These boards need sanding, just on the top side. You fellas know how to sand a board?" The look he gave us suggested he had serious doubts. "Here, let me show you, in case you ain't sure." He laid a board across a pair of sawhorses. He took a piece of sandpaper and ran it back and forth over the board. "Always move with the grain, not across it." He laid a second board across the sawhorses and then handed us each a piece of sandpaper. "Let's see you do it."

Noah and I rubbed the boards.

"Looks like you got the idea, not that it demands a cabinetmaker." He grabbed a hand brush. "When you finish a board, dust it clean like this…You got plenty of sandpaper in the box. So, if no questions, get started. Later, I'll check and see how you're doing." He headed back into the interior of the worksite.

Noah and I began sanding.

"This isn't too bad," said Noah.

"Seems okay." Continuing to sand, I looked around. There were no other workers in close proximity. I whispered, "Hooker didn't seem to like us."

"That's an understatement."

"You think he'll give us a hard time?"

Noah shot me a look. "I assume that was a rhetorical question."

"Styles seemed a whole lot better. Glad he's the one supervising us."

Noah shrugged.

"You disagree?"

"No. Just that Hooker is likely to decide our fate. Don't forget, he's Styles' boss."

I silently conceded the point. "But on the bright side, Mr. House seemed to like us. Heck, he took the time to show us the hotel plans."

"Yeah, I really liked that, and not just because it was good to have the big boss show an interest. Seeing what the finished product will be explains why we're sanding this pile of boards."

"Speaking of the finished product, what did you think of it?"

"Impressive, especially for a place the size of St. Augustine," said Noah.

"About that. Didn't you expect St. Augustine to be bigger?"

"Not really."

The response underscored the impulsivity of my decision. For one who purported to be rigorously analytical, the admission was disconcerting. "Returning to the drawing of the hotel—you know more about architecture than I—how would you describe it…its style?"

Noah momentarily interrupted his sanding. "Not Gothic or Romanesque. Guess you'd have to call it Victorian…Stick Style.[170] You've got the gingerbread trim. And the balconies that line the exterior

---

170 *Study of Stick Style Architecture and History*, oldhouseonline.com, 2 Jan. 2018 <https://www.oldhouseonline.com/articles/a-study-of-stic-style>.

are very much Stick, what with their white-post railings. On the other hand, the concave lines on some of the balcony roofs, coupled with the flat roof of the overall structure, add a touch of Italianate. But looking at the building as a whole, its vertical lines and exterior woodwork, I'd stay with my original label, Victorian Stick."[171]

"You ever think of being an architect?" I posed the question, not sure whether it was in jest or serious.

"Actually, I have," said Noah, "though I rarely talk about it, because it seems like pie in the sky that isn't meant to be."

"Why so?"

Noah furrowed his brow. "You need a mirror?"

"Come again?"

"We're black…well, in your case, maroon."

"And?"

"Buildings, most all of them, are financed and built by white people. Since when does whitey hire people of color as architects? It just doesn't happen."

"So, you've abandoned your dream without giving it a shot?"

"Wrong! I'm pursuing it now. It's a key reason why I came to St. Augustine. What I've learned about architecture from books is important, but I want to understand the hammer and nails of it. And St. Augustine, a growing tourist area, seemed right. Negroes have fared better here than most any place in the South. As we discussed before we came here, it's been that way for three centuries, ever since the ruling Spanish turned it into a haven for people of color, both freemen and slaves.[172] With the army's Reconstruction headquarters here, there's no place in the South where a Negro entrepreneur is more likely to undertake a construction project. And face it, only a Negro entrepreneur would hire someone like me as his architect." Noah resumed sanding.

For a while, neither of us spoke. Back and forth, board after board, I rubbed, occasionally switching from my left hand, my stronger, to my right. Both my arms grew increasingly sore. The task grew more and more tedious. "You getting tired?"

"Damn well, yes."

"Me too. This is tougher than I thought."

"Yeah. You think they'll have something more interesting for us to do?"

"Given our lack of carpentry skills, I doubt it." I glanced at the humongous pile of lumber that sat just feet away. There were enough

---

[171] Ibid.

[172] *See*, footnote 102, supra.

boards to keep us rubbing for…God knows how long. Enervated as I was, I eschewed mathematical proclivities to determine my rate per board and calculate the time needed to sand all the lumber. Curious about how much we had earned, I made a quick estimate. I said, “On the bright side, assuming we’ve been working for about an hour, we’ve each earned roughly fourteen cents. Not bad.”

Noah rolled his eyes. “You and your numbers.”

“Hey, don’t you want to know how you’re doing?”

“Not every fifteen minutes.”

I would have pointed out that I had waited four times that long before doing a calculation, except I got Noah’s point. Repeated estimates of what we had earned would only make the days seem longer. I eyed the board on which I was working. To ease the ache in my arms, I needed to vary my sanding technique. I tried shorter strokes. Dreadfully inefficient, it provided no relief. Longer, slower strokes worked no better. I moved to the opposite side of the board, a meaningless gesture. With just a couple minutes of testing alternative methods, less than a penny’s worth of earnings, I concluded that sanding a board with the grain was a one-dimensional enterprise with no appealing options.

Hour by hour, I struggled through the day. Two types of relief emerged: Conversation with Noah and the distraction of my own thoughts, many of which were nebulous daydreams. Around the middle of the day, a worker approached and told us we could take a brief break for lunch. Unfortunately, we had not brought one. The worker eyed our sanded boards, felt a couple and walked away without uttering another word.

Five more agonizing hours dragged by. My arms ached. I was starved. Out of the corner of my eye, I spotted Styles approaching. I rubbed harder and faster, the way I did on my initial board.

“How you boys doin’?”

“Okay,” said Noah.

Styles took a board from the pile constituting our completed work. He ran his hand over the surface. He eyed the many boards that remained undone. His eyes narrowed, their lines parallel to his straight-line lips.

I anticipated words that would clarify his opaque expression. They were not forthcoming.

“So, we’ll see you boys tomorrow morning…7:30 sharp.” Styles walked away.

Once he was a safe distance, Noah said, “What was that about?”

“Got me.”

“Are we done for the day? Can we go?”

"I think so." I went to the corner of the structure and took a gander. I returned to Noah. "We must be good to go. Everyone is leaving."

We circled to the south side of the Plaza and headed south on St. George Street. Just fifty yards from the Plaza, a man stood behind a large pushcart laden with vegetables, fruits and other comestibles.

"We should pick up some food before going home, don'tcha think?" said Noah.

"Sure...But I'm famished. Rather than wait, let's have something now." I reached into my pocket and pulled out coinage from my brief Savannah work. I had kept it separate from the money Grover had left me. Spending what he had worked so hard to save didn't feel right.

"Good idea. I've got two dollars with me." Noah checked out the merchandise. He selected a few apples.

I got a loaf of bread[173] and a couple pounds of sweet potatoes.[174] Noah added a dozen eggs.[175] The items' cost totaled 57 cents (apples, 15¢; bread, 11¢; sweet potatoes, 7¢; and eggs, 24¢). I tried to pay the entire amount, but Noah insisted on contributing two bits. From the loaf's heel, I tore off a large chunk, and Noah followed with an equally big piece from the same end. We devoured the portions immediately. We each took an apple and, after one bite, continued down St. George Street in the general direction of Little Africa.

"So, how would you rate our first day on the job?" said Noah.

"Boring and my arms ache." A chunk of apple in my mouth garbled my words. "What's your assessment?"

"Not the best. We were total outsiders. Hardly a word from anyone all day."

I thought of Grover and his experience on the Savannah docks. "Having a browbeating boss watch us like a hawk would have been worse."

---

173 *Another Androsphere Blog: How much did things cost in 1850's USA?*, Another Androsphere Blog, 8 Jan. 2018 <http://anotherandrosphereblog.blogspot.com/2013/03/how-much-did-things-cost-in-1850s> indicating hard bread cost 22¢ per kilogram in 1853. *But see*, *Cost of loaf of bread in 1870?*, answers.com, 8 Jan. 2018 <http://www.answers.com/Q/Cost_of_loaf_of_bread_in_1870?> stating: "In 1870 bread wasn't sold in a loaf like today. Most people made their own rolls/bread."

174 Ibid., *Another Androsphere Blog.*

175 *Prices for 1860, 1872, 1878 and 1882 — Groceries, Dry Goods & More*, choosingvoluntarysimplicity.com, 8 Jan. 2018 <http://www.choosingvoluntarysimplicity.com/prices-for-1860-1872-1878-and-1882> indicating a dozen eggs cost 20¢ in 1860 and 30¢ in 1870.

"True…but the fact it could have been grimmer, doesn't make it good. A boss who complimented our work, along with some contact with our coworkers, would have been nice."

"What do you think Styles and Hooker thought of us?"

"As for Styles," said Noah, "I have no clue. Hooker, on the other hand, was transparent. He despises us."

"Not necessarily. Maybe he's just gruff on the exterior."

About to take another bite of his apple, Noah frowned.

I silently conceded my appraisal had been grounded on wishful thinking. "Well, perhaps he'll give us a fair shake."

"Maybe." A cynical inflection in Noah's voice was less than reassuring.

We continued on our way, arriving at Walter's about five minutes later. He greeted us at the door.

"You was gone the whole day. That mean you was hired?"

"We were," said Noah, his tone matter of fact.

"Not the kind of enthusiasm I'd expect from two fellas who started the mornin' unemployed and returned with a job."

"Guess it's because we're tired." The need to avoid sounding like a complainer shaped my response.

"So, you like the work?"

Like it? Not really. I hoped Noah would field the question. He didn't.

"Well, the first day is always tough," said Walter.

His effort to turn a jerky turkey into a slick chick was obvious.

"You must be hungry," said Walter. "Let's go into the kitchen."

"Oh," said Noah, holding forth a bag with our purchases. "We bought a few things on the way home." He tilted the parcel, so Walter could see inside.

"We ate some of the bread and a couple of apples on the way," I said.

"You fellas didn't need to bring food here, 'specially your first day workin'. I was plannin' to feed you."

"That's mighty kind, but board wasn't part of the deal," I said.

"Not specifically. But I kinda thought I could help you out, least till you got paid. Like I told you yesterday, I'm happy to have company. Me and Wilma didn't have no children. It gets mighty lonely here. Wasn't that way when she was alive. We had—damn, here I am runnin' off at the mouth when you fellas wanna eat." He led the way into the kitchen. "I made a lamb stew this afternoon. Made it with Wilma's favorite recipe. You know what that was?"

His question drew a double shrug, one from Noah and one from me.

"Take most everythin' and anythin' from the pantry. Pour in water, add loads of spices and slow cook it." Walter chuckled. "It's a great recipe…one that produces somethin' different every time."

"Sounds like it's a recipe that's made with love."

My comment drew a puzzled look from Walter.

I pointed at the big pot housing the stew. "The whole time you were fashioning that epicurean delight, I suspect you were entertaining fond thoughts of Wilma."

Walter appeared to study me. "Damn, just one day workin' on the hotel, and already you're a carpenter."

"Come again," I said, replacing him as the one with confusion.

"You hit the nail on the head." Walter smiled. He took three large bowls from a shelf and laded them with a healthy portion of stew. We each carried one into the dining room where a table, a French provincial, was already set with utensils. Walter circled to the far end. He gestured us to either side.

"Wilma always sat at the end nearer the kitchen."

I started to reach for a utensil, but hesitated, glancing to see if Walter chose a fork or a spoon.

"Wilma and I always said grace before dinner. These days I kinda talk to her or say a little prayer before I eat. You mind if we have a moment of silence…or maybe one of you would like to say a few words."

I gave Noah a look, a not-so-subtle message, encouraging him to take the lead.

"Dear Lord," said Noah. "Thank you for the food we're about to eat. Thank you for the peace our nation has enjoyed these several years since the great war. Thank you for the freedom folks now enjoy. And thank you…uh…for…uh…all our other blessings."

"Amen," said Walter.

"Amen," I echoed. A second later, I added, "And thank you, Lord, for bringing us here, where this fine gentleman has welcomed us into his lovely home."

"Amen," said Noah emphatically.

Walter smiled again, this time broadly. He picked up his spoon. Noah and I followed his lead. I dug my utensil into the mound that filled my bowl. "It's delicious!" Regardless how it tasted, manners learned from the Wrights had ensured that my comment, if any, would be positive. However, the tasty dish, its appeal compounded by hunger yet unsated, obviated the need for a white lie.

"You're right about your wife's recipe," said Noah. "It's excellent."

I thought of pointing out that each stew was unique, and, therefore, Walter deserved all the credit. Better judgment suppressed the compliment. Crediting his late wife, helping him maintain his connection to her, was worth more than a boost to his ego.

"So, wha'd they have you fellas doin' at the hotel today?"

"Sanding boards," said Noah.

"All day?"

"Yeah. Don't mean to whine, but…" The banality made me cringe. Complaining, what I had avoided minutes earlier, was exactly what I intended to do. Mr. Wright would have taken me to task, but with him far distant, I was free to vent. "It was boring as Hell."

"Ain't never been to Hell," said Walter. "But from what I hear, it's anythin' but borin'. Hot and horrible, maybe."

Walter's retort exposed the absurdity of my comment. I was guilty of invoking a cliché; I was whining; and I was claiming to do one thing, all the while doing the opposite. Were I up to bat at the ball field, my three strikes would have shipped me back to the bench.

"Who hired you…a supervisor or…?"

"Mr. House, the builder and architect, gave us the job," said Noah. "Another man, Sherman Hooker, the foreman, spoke to us first. He was surly. If Mr. House hadn't stepped in, we would have had no chance."

A curious expression, the type that hints at brewing thoughts, appeared on Walter's face.

I waited several seconds, hoping he might clarify his reaction. No such luck. "Whatcha thinking?"

"Wilma always said my face was an open book." Walter started to dig his spoon into the stew.

"You didn't answer my question." My bold quip underscored how quickly Walter had made us comfortable in his home. The way things were going, in less than a week, good-natured sarcasm might be acceptable.

"Fair enough. You got me…Here's what I was thinkin'. 'Bout a year ago, I met Mr. House. He surprised the hell outta me. Came 'round here, to my house. Wanted to pick my brain 'cause someone told him I knew the ins and outs of St. Augustine construction better than anyone. Aksed 'bout coquina, water table and drainage, and stuff like that. Don't know that I helped him much, but he was mighty appreciative. Struck me as a decent sort."

"That was our reaction too," said Noah. "What about Hooker?"

"Can't say I ever met him, though he's the reason I reacted funny a moment ago. From what I hear, he's fine, if he likes you. But if he don't, he's a tyrant, as well as a bully. Don't mean to be gossipin'. Ain't somethin' I normally do. But only fair I warn you, 'specially after tippin' my hand when you mentioned his name."

"Based upon how he treated us today, Noah and I figured he was a tough nut. Going over his head to Mr. House, not that we meant to, seemed to rub him the wrong way."

"He also appeared to resent the fact that we're educated, presumably better than he." Noah glanced my way. "Maybe he was just sending a message to put us in our place, let us know who's boss." Noah eyed me more demonstratively, perhaps hoping I would voice a more optimistic assessment or at least concur with his evaluation.

Far from sanguine, I remained mute.

Chapter XIII

NOAH AND I HAD ARRIVED IN ST. AUGUSTINE on a Tuesday. Wednesday, Thursday, Friday and Saturday we had sanded what seemed like enough boards to build the entire hotel. (A mere glance at the huge skeletal structure that adjoined our labor would have proved my assessment gross hyperbole. Regardless, four days of the mind-numbing toil had been awful.) Each day was a repetition of its predecessor. One or two brief visits each from Hooker and Styles was typical. They ran a hand over a board or two, said nothing or grunted before moving on.

Our production the first day nipped that of the second. The culprit, sore arms, portended bad news. But by Saturday, the tide had turned. Muscles in forearms and biceps had expanded. Stamina had escalated. Our output increased. Hopes that it might draw a favorable reaction when Styles stopped by late in the day were not realized. Pursed lips accompanied a taciturn visit.

Sunday, our one day off, was a welcome break from the tedium. In the several evenings that had preceded, we had grown comfortable in Walter's house. Already, he was a friend. Though he owned the abode and we were mere roomers, it felt like home. We had just finished a tasty breakfast of oatmeal, orange juice, toast and coffee.

"Would you fellas like to join me for church services this mornin'?"

"Sure," I said, after catching a quick nod from Noah.

"If we leave early, we can take the scenic route along the creek bank.[176]

---

[176] The site selected for the home of Walter Sanders lay on a peninsula located between the Matanzas River to the east and a creek to the west that ran south from King Street to the Matanzas River. In the 1880s a project dredged the creek and created Lake Maria Sanchez, which exists today. *Flagler NAS – Lake Maria Sanchez Project*, wikispaces.com, 11 Jan. 2018 <httpp://flaglernas.wikispaces.com/Lake+Maria+Sanchez+Project>. Lincolnville,

"Whatever you say," said Noah. "But you okay walking, especially along the bank, what with your bum knee?"

"Ain't a problem. I do it every week. And for that matter, walkin' is good for my knee. Stairs, kneelin'…stuff like that kills it. As for ladders, they're suicide."

We donned our Sunday best, and Walter led the way out the back door. It was the first time Noah and I had used the rear portal. We headed across the backyard onto a winding path through the woods. We had gone roughly sixty yards from the house when we reached a creek. Its quiescent waters, a mingling of salt and fresh, gently wound between margins lined with cedars, their knee-like root systems rising from the shallows. Salty air permeating the estuary filled my lungs.

Walter pointed toward the top of a tall pine, a beanpole with a few small limbs near the acme. "Up there, on the highest branch, there's an osprey, guardin' its nest."

Facing west, with the morning sun to our backs, the scene was perfectly lit. Details that might have washed out on a gray day or at a different hour were vivid. "That's a big nest," I said.

"Yup, at least three-feet across," said Walter. "And it's got a couple of babies."

"How can you tell? I don't see them."

"You don't?" Walter gave me a look.

I stared intently. Still, I saw only the nest and one large osprey. Afraid of embarrassing myself, I said nothing.

"Relax," said Walter. "I can't see them neither. A few days ago, they poked their little heads and beaks over the edge. That's when I spotted 'em." Walter chuckled as he slapped me on the back.

I laughed, savoring our rapidly blooming camaraderie.

"Over there." Noah pointed. "There's a big alligator, half-in and half-out of the water."

"Must be close to ten feet," I said.

"Here at the creek, you see 'em all the time." Walter drew out his pocket watch, giving it a glance. "Lots more to see along the way. If we don't want to be late for church, we best move ahead." He led the way north along the path adjoining the creek. We went about one hundred yards when Walter stopped and pointed. "See the loggerhead turtle over there?"[177]

---

which was referred to as "Africa" or "Little Africa" in 1868, developed on the west side of the creek.

[177] *Florida Ecosystems: Swamps*, floridanature.com, 11 Jan. 2018 <http://www.floridannature.com/SwampsEcosystem.htm>.

I gazed in the direction he was pointing but saw no life. I stepped behind him, so I could sight down his arm. On the nearside of the creek's muddy bank, I spotted the turtle, at least one hundred pounds. Its hard shell nearly matched the land on which it was parked. "How did you see it while walking?"

"Hey, when you travel these banks day after day, year after year, you develop a keen eye. More important, the wildlife got their favorite spots. With time you get to know 'em…both the animals and their spots." Walter gestured again, this time toward the creek itself. "You see that growth in the water. That's turtle grass, a source of what turtles need to survive…why you find 'em here."[178]

"Is this part of your land?" said Noah.

"Yup. Like I said a few days ago, me and my wife bought 'bout ten acres. Runs 'bout two hundred yards along the creek from a spot just south of the house to that bend up ahead." He looked back in the direction from which we had come. He smiled.

"You love this place, don't you?" said Noah.

Walter nodded. "But I loved it a whole lot more when Wilma was alive…Walkin' this path is real nice, but can't compare to doin' it with Wilma's hand in mine." He continued forward along the path.

After several minutes, we swung right for about one hundred feet and then left, north on St. George Street. Another third of a mile and we came alongside the site of the St. Augustine Hotel.

I gestured to my right. "You bringing us to sand more boards today?"

Walter pointed just ahead to our left. "Nope, we're going there, to the cathedral."

"You're kidding?" said Noah.

Walter shook his head.

"You pray at the cathedral, the basilica next to the St. Augustine Hotel?" Noah's eyes were wide.

"Somethin' wrong with that?"

"It's…it's a Catholic church."

"And?"

My reaction was identical to Noah's. "Uh…we kinda assumed you were Baptist."

"Fair assumption…for newcomers to St. Augustine. But keep in mind, the city was founded by Spain, a Catholic country, way back in the 16th century. Right off and all through the seventeenth and eighteenth, the Spanish Crown gave refuge to Negroes, so long as they

---

[178] Ibid.

became Catholics.[179] The upshot, when Florida, St. Augustine included, came under United States' rule, the city's Negro population, unlike other places in the South, was largely Catholic." Walter hesitated, eying Noah and then me. "You fellas got objections to prayin' in a Catholic church?"

"Not I," said Noah.

"Me neither." During my time in Savannah attending school at the First African Baptist Church, I had been exposed to Baptist theology. While I valued the religion's moral compass, influences of my early childhood, largely secular, remained. A chance to visit a different house of worship intrigued me. Dogma, a likely entrée on the menu, would pass my ears with negligible impact.

"You fellas know anythin' 'bout St. Augustine? I'm referrin' to our patron Saint, not the place."

I duplicated Noah's shrug.

"Well, let me tell you. His mother was an 'African woman of great faith.' In his thirties, he 'turned back to God and was baptized Catholic.' He wrote loads of books and sermons and was later ordained as a priest."[180] Walter led the way closer to the church's entrance.

"Very interesting structure," said Noah, drawing to a stop. "Front façade is Spanish mission. Reminds me of the Alamo. But the doorway, with its pillars and triangular pediment, is neoclassical, while the tower over there (Noah gestured to the left) is baroque...Quite the conglomeration."[181]

"Jeezum, I've been prayin' here for decades, and you know my church's architecture better than me."

"That assumes he knows what he's talking about." I winked and said, "Much as I hate to admit it, he does. In fact, he—" I clipped my tongue. Noah was the one to decide whether to share his desire to be an architect.

"Our congregation has met here, not in this building, since 1586. The original burned. One of straw and palmetto that replaced it went up in flames as well...1599, I think. Over the next two centuries there was

[179] *See*, footnote 102, supra.

[180] *African American Catholic History*, catholiccincinnati.org, 10 Jan. 2018 <www.catholiccincinnati.org/wp-content/uploads/2011/10/African-Catholic-Heritage-Facts-2011.pdf> stating: "St Augustine was born in Tagaste, Africa, and was the son of Moinca. At the age of 33 he turned back to God and was baptized Catholic. Augustine was ordained a priest and later Co-Bishop of Hippo. He led a holy and simple life, writing over 200 books, letters, and sermons."

[181] *Cathedral Basilica of St. Augustine (St. Augustine, Florida)*, Wikipedia, 10 Jan. 2018 <https://en.wikipedia.org/wiki/Cathedral_Basilica_of_St._Augustine>.

two more. A fifth version, what you see today, was completed in 1797[182]...You fellas know what it's made of?"

Stone hardly seemed an intelligent answer. Rather than show my ignorance, I looked at Noah.

"Cement?"

"Well, in part. It's coquina and stone."[183]

"I've heard of coquina," said Noah. "What exactly is it?"

"It's a limestone made up of 'shelly fossils.'[184] But unlike most limestones that 'consist of fossils or other carbonate grains held tight,' often by cement from the grains, coquina's only got a little cement, along with lotsa empty space."[185]

"Where'd you learn such technical stuff?" I said.

"In case you forgot, I made my livin' as a builder and roofer in St. Augustine. I may not know architectural styles, but I know materials, 'specially coquina. 'Round here, it's the material of choice." He gestured to the north. "That huge fort, 'bout a quarter-mile ahead, is mostly coquina."

I swallowed hard, realizing my question, the surprise it had engendered, was presumptuous. When it came to construction, with years of hands-on experience, Walter was an expert. The embarrassing scenario bore a striking familiarity. As with Grover, I had equated flawed syntax and grammar with a lack of intellect. Arguably the current affront was more egregious than its predecessor. Not only was Walter's elocution, however imperfect, far superior to Grover's, but, more important, given my past blunder, I should have known better. "I...I apologize," I said.

---

[182] *The Cathedral Basilica of St. Augustine Florida,* 10 Jan. 2018 <http://www.drbronsontours.com/bronsoncathedral.html>. The Cathedral Basilica of St. Augustine is the oldest church in Florida. The 1797 rendition is in large degree the structure of the Cathedral one observes today. "A fire on April 12, 1887 gutted the Cathedral. It was rebuilt with the help of architect James Renwick who added the Spanish Renaissance Bell Tower out of poured concrete with coquina in the Flagler Era (and Flagler's money). Renwick was the architect of St. Patrick's Cathedral in New York City. Renwick kept the original façade of la Rocque only changing the choir window and the clock into a niche." (*See*, footnote 60, supra.) *See also*, footnote 181, supra, *Cathedral Basilica of St. Augustine (St. Augustine, Florida)*, Wikipedia, indicating: "On April 12, 1887, just as fire had destroyed previous church buildings in St. Augustine, the structure burned once again. The damage was not total, and the exterior shell of the building was still salvageable because the coquina blocks and cement used to build the masonry walls were fireproof."

[183] Ibid.

[184] *Buildings and building stone: Castillo de San Marcos, St. Augustine, FL,* gly.uga.edu, 12 Jan. 2018 <http://www.gly.uga.edu/railsback/BS-SA.html>.

[185] Ibid.

"For what?"

"An impertinent question."

"You did nuttin' wrong." Walter motioned us along. "We better go in. Father ain't no fan of latecomers."

I suspected that Walter, kind gentleman he was, had played dumb and changed the subject in order to mitigate my discomfiture.

We stepped through the doorway and seated ourselves on the left end of the lower gallery.

"This section is where the slaves sat before the war," said Walter. "It's where I've always sat, even though I weren't never a slave."[186]

"It's a lovely church," I said, surveying the interior. Though not overly ornate, its adornments exceeded that of Savannah's First African Baptist Church. Two impressive crystal-pendant chandeliers hung from the ceiling. Behind an ornate wooden altar table, a line of candles stood tall. Symmetrically spread across the front wall were three arched cutouts, each of which contained a statue of a religiously dressed man.[187] I suspected the figures might be popes or saints, though both distance and ignorance made it impossible for me to verify the assumption.

"It's very special to me. I was baptized here, and my parents, as well as Wilma and me, was married here. When I come here to pray, I feel their presence. During Mass I talk to 'em, silently of course."

Walter's spirituality, that his religion provided greater meaning to his life, was undeniable. Envy, an inapropos companion given the setting, invaded my psyche. I had spent many days at Savannah's First African Baptist Church. I had studied theology. But I lacked Walter's spirituality. Perhaps if my childhood had included services in a house of worship frequented by parents and ancestors, I would have shared Walter's religiosity. Intriguing as the hypothetical may have been, it failed to alter the facts. I was who I was; and at that moment, a pang of jealousy was undeniable.

As the last parishioners straggled in and I prepared to witness my first Catholic Mass, I surveyed the assembled throng. I counted the rows, as best as I could. I estimated that eight to ten people could sit on either side of the center aisle. A quick calculation led me to speculate that the cathedral could hold over five hundred. I guesstimated the sanctuary to be two-third's full, attendance well over three hundred. The priest commenced the Mass. Occasionally, portions of the prayers were

---

[186] *Cathedral Basilica of St. Augustine (St. Augustine, Florida)*, op. cit., stating: "In the beginning the slaves were assigned to the slave gallery. It is not know [sic] where free people of color sat during the services."

[187] Based upon a photo of the "Original Cathedral Interior, New York Public Library," contained in *The Cathedral Basilica of St. Augustine, Florida,* op. cit.

familiar. I mouthed the words, not that I was actually praying. I compared it to my prior Baptist experience, observing the differences. Those distinctions interested me more than the service itself. Structure and ritual played a greater role. Symbols and mystery, difficult for me to interpret, were manifold. The Eucharist or Holy Communion was the highlight. A sermon, a minister's preaching from the Bible, was conspicuously absent.[188]

I watched the congregants. They were attentive. Their recitations, plainly familiar, were voiced with conviction. If any were skeptics like me, they gave no hint. Their supplications appeared genuine. Doctrine that had little meaning to me made the time grind slowly. My mind drifted. I found myself analyzing the proceedings. I wondered if perhaps others might be daydreaming. I looked down the row where I sat. All were fully engaged. My rational approach, a demand for evidence, made perfect sense. Yet faith, wonderful faith, had undeniable appeal. A simple truism shed light on the matter. Faith...required faith. Either you had it or you didn't. I fell into the latter category. Ironically, my logic, or should I say illogic, demonstrated my point. Reasoned analysis, exactly what I was engaged in, was the antithesis of faith.

At long last, the final amen was spoken. People close by offered good wishes and we returned the kindness. We headed out the door.

"So, whad'ya think?" said Walter.

Lying, telling him the experience was uplifting, was unseemly, particularly in a holy setting. I hoped that Noah would field the inquiry. It didn't happen.

Walter turned my way. "You disliked the Mass?"

"Oh, no," I said. "It was very enlightening." The sugar-coated misrepresentation beat an all-out lie. Liked it, I hadn't; but enlightening, it was. An irony struck me. Were I Catholic, I would have already generated fresh grist for my next confession. I glanced at the exiting throng. Odds were, I was unique, the only one to mar the fresh slate I had brought from the Mass.

"Have you fellas had a chance to see our town, the historic part?"

"Not really," said Noah.

"After we grab a bite, I'd love to show it to you." Walter gestured north on St. George Street. "Up ahead, by the city gates, there's a street vendor. Hawks the best fish and chips this side of the Atlantic."

"Lead the way," said Noah.

---

[188] *The Differences between Protestantism and Catholicism*, exploregod.com, 13 Jan. 2018 <https://www.exploregod.com/difference-between-protestantism-and-catholicism>.

I echoed Noah's vote.

Five minutes later, we approached the city gates. The closer we got, the taller the finial-topped, rectangular stone towers appeared. I estimated their height at twenty feet, about twice the distance that separated them. Walls about eight feet high extended east and west from either tower. About ten yards beyond the gates was a moat with a causeway over it.[189]

"Just over there is our vendor." Walter led the way to a man with a cart and a fiery caldron, a few feet inside the left gate.[190] "Three fish and chips?" Walter reached for his pocket purse.

"Oh no," I said. "Noah and I have this one."

Walter started to balk.

"It's two against one," said Noah. "And we know you believe in democracy."

Minutes later, armed with three man-sized orders, each wrapped in heavy paper, we seated ourselves on the ground, our backs to the wall just outside the gates.

"As good as advertised?" said Walter.

"Even better," I garbled, my mouth laden with crisply coated fish. "What is it?"

"Redfish or snook, maybe…or perhaps it's bass." Walter shrugged. "Ain't no expert on fish. Only know it's mighty good."

His point was indisputable. I shoved a chunk of fried potato into my mouth. Conversation ebbed. The scrumptious repast took precedence.

Finally, as we neared our last bites, Walter said, "Ready for another?"

Noah, otherwise renowned for a huge appetite, was wide-eyed.

"It was great, but…" I grabbed my stomach.

Walter laughed. He stood up. "Time I show you fellas the sights."

---

[189] *City Gate, St. Augustine Florida*, drbronsontours.com 14 Jan. 2018 <http://www.drbronsontours.com/bronsoncitygate.html>. The original gate was built in 1718. The current gate was built by the British in 1809. In 1827 a bridge over a moat that lay beyond the gates was replaced with a causeway. Early in the 20th century the moat was filled in. (*See*, footnote 60, supra.)

[190] *Street Food History – Facts about Street Food Vending*, historyoffastfood.com, 14 Jan. 2018 <http://www.historyoffastfood.com/fast-food-history/street-food-history-and-facts/> stating: "People sold ready-to-eat food since the earliest civilizations. Ancient Greeks had street vendors that sold small fried fish…In China (also ancient) street food was also intended for poor but the wealthy citizens would sometimes send their servants to buy them street food. Street vendors of 14th century Egypt sold lamb kebabs, rice and fritters, Even the Aztecs had vendors…In North America, during the American Colonial period, street food that was sold was tripe, oysters, roasted corn ears, fruits and sweets."

We disposed of our garbage and began strolling south, down St. George Street. Earlier, coming the opposite way, I had taken little note of the surroundings. Well sated, my attention drew to the tightly packed Spanish-style homes that lined either side of the street.[191] Shutters of green, red and black adorned the façades. Balconies that overhung the street offered occasional shade.

"Some of these coquina houses been 'round for over two centuries," said Walter. "They seen lotsa history. Behind them, as well as alongside some, like this beige one here (he gestured at a high wall adjoining a house), are beautiful gardens. They're filled with fruit trees: orange, guava, mango, apple, pomegranate and even banana. Add to that, lovely fountains and colorful flowers, and they're wonderful."

Just ahead, a wall with stunning pink and red azaleas draped over its top hinted at the splendor about which Walter spoke. As we passed, I drifted closer, gazed upward and inhaled the perfumed air.

We continued south, passing narrow side streets. As we reached Cuna Street, Walter said, "This little section is known as Minorca. 'Bout a hundred years ago, a Scottish physician, Andres Turnbull, brought a thousand Greek colonists from Minorca and Corsica. They were servants, indentured to his British land grant 'bout sixty miles to the south. Seems they had no idea what was in store for 'em. Turnbull treated 'em like slaves. Next thing you know, they rebelled. That didn't change things much. So, 'bout ninety marched here to St. Augustine. Another six hundred followed, a couple months later. Their descendants still live here."[192]

A little further on, we came to the quaintest of streets. I stopped and peered down the tiny thoroughfare. "This is the narrowest street I've ever seen."

"It's Treasury Street," said Walter. "Folks claim it's the narrowest in America."[193]

---

[191] Woolson, Constance Fenimore, *The Ancient City*, *Harper's New Monthly Magazine* (No. CCXCV.-December 1874-Vol. I; Pt. I of II), retrieved from The Project Gutenberg eBook of *The Ancient City*, gutenberg,org, 7 Jan. 2018 <http://www.gutenberg.org/files/52770/52770-h/52270-h.htm>.

[192] *Tour the Museum | St. Photios Greek Orthodox National Shrine,* stphotios.org, 15 Jan. 2018 <http://www.stphotios.org/about-us/tour>. In detailing the dreadful conditions endured by these Greek colonists, the St. Photios website indicates: Only 1255 of the 1403 original group survived the ocean voyage. Scurvy, crowded conditions and bad weather took their toll." Thereafter finding conditions on land "deplorable," they rebelled. "The revolt did not bring about improvement. By the end of the first year 450 men, women and children were reported dead."

[193] *Treasury Street – St..Augustine, Florida – Atlas Obscurua*, atlasobscura, 14 Jan. 2018 <https://www.atlasobscura.com/places/treasury-street> stating: "Measuring under

I pressed my back and the heel of my shoe against the wall of a building on one side of the street. Using my shoes, each roughly a foot in length, I took baby steps across to the opposite wall. "Gotta be less than seven feet."

Noah pointed at a wagon that was passing on St. George. "I doubt that wagon could fit between these walls."

"That's the idea," said Walter.

"Come again?" I said, reacting to the seeming lunacy.

"The Royal Spanish Treasury was located just up the street. Piracy was a big problem. Legend says they built it 'just wide enough for two men to lug a chest of gold to and from ships,' but too narrow 'for a horse-drawn carriage to squeeze through and ride off with the money.'"[194]

"Let's give it a look," said Noah.

We walked east a couple hundred yards. As we approached the sea wall, the breeze grew stronger. Waves breaking against the wall testified to nature's inimitable might. Salt-laden air filled my lungs. I gazed across the watery mass, beyond the north end of an island, what I later learned was Anastasia Island. I focused on the point where the cumulus-flecked azure met the dark blue of the ocean. I closed my eyes, picturing the curvature of the Earth and the several thousand miles of growling liquid that stretched to Europe. The image boggled my mind. What anomalous thoughts…fear, hope, lament and insignificance…must have consumed those who had made the first voyage across the seemingly infinite unknown. I said, "St. Augustine is a fascinating place."

"Thought you'd like it," said Walter.

I looked north where the massive Fort Marion stood guard; east to the ocean; and south along the sea wall. I turned back and gazed down the myopic telescope of Treasury Street. I murmured, too softly for Walter and Noah to hear, "I like this place."

We headed back on Treasury to St. George Street. Walter led the way south around the corner. The cathedral was only a hundred feet ahead, and another hundred feet beyond was the skeletal frame of the first floor of the St. Augustine Hotel. As we approached the Plaza de la Constitución, Walter gestured to his right, to the area of the Plaza inland from the burgeoning hotel. "You know what that is?"

"The city marketplace," said Noah.

I would have voiced a similar answer had I been quicker.

"Yeah, I suppose." Walter chuckled.

---

seven feet wide, St. Augustine's Treasury Street may be the narrowest street in the United States."

[194] Ibid.

“That’s an odd way to say *yes*, assuming that’s what you meant,” I said.

“You know what was sold there?”

“Food, various goods…uh…I think.” Walter’s question, coupled with his earlier reaction, had me second guessing myself.

“Can’t say you’re wrong.”

“So, why you playing a cryptic game of look and tell?” said Noah.

Walter sighed. “Not all the meat marketed there was edible.”

“What do you mean?” Despite my question, I had a suspicion.

“Slaves…colored folks was sold there.”[195]

I gazed at the open pavilion. Three broad stairs led to a flat base, from which seven rectangular stone piers about ten feet apart supported a gabled roof with an unadorned triangular pediment at either end.[196] I could all but see an auctioneer facing Matanzas Bay, standing alongside a beleaguered Negro, while a crowd of white vultures bid on the meat. “Wait a minute,” I said. “I thought you told us that St. Augustine was a safe haven for slaves.”

“I did.”

I shot Walter a look. “People of color being sold as slaves…I’d hardly call that a safe haven.”

---

[195] *Public Market Plaza St. Augustine Florida HABSNo. FLA-131*, drbronsontours.com, 15 Jan. 2018 <http://www.drbronsontours.com/bronsonpublicmarket.html>. Whether the pavilion was actually used as a slave market has been debated for many years. The issue was examined by Gil Wilson in his very comprehensive website, “Dr. Bronson and Friends: A History of St. Augustine.” He concludes that some slaves were sold at the market, but it was not a “slave market,” the type that existed elsewhere in the antebellum South. He asks: “Was it a slave market? Absolutely not. New Orleans, Charleston, Alexandria, Virginia had their slave pens as identifiable buildings where *only* slaves were sold (emphasis added). St. Augustine did not. Most important St. Augustine did not sell enough slaves. What slaves were sold were sold throughout the city. In stores, on boats, at the courthouse and yes in the public market…However I do not believe it should be called the slave market.” To understand how the pavilion may have earned its reputation as a slave market, *see*, *St. Augustine’s “Slave Market”: A Visual History | Southern Spaces*, southernspaces.org, 21 Feb. 2018 <http://southernspaces.org/2012/st-augustines-slave-market-visual-history> relating how W.J. Harris, who did not arrive in St. Augustine until 1898, produced a popular picture postcard of the pavilion, labeling it the “OLD SLAVE MARKET, ST. AUGUSTINE, FLA.” So too did William Henry Jackson with photographs identifying the pavilion as the “Old Slave Market.” And in an 1883 novel “Down South,” British author Lady Duffus Hardy wrote about St. Augustine: “In the center stands a curious old market place, roofed in at the top, but open on all sides; this was the ancient slave mart where, ‘God’s image, carved in ebony’ was bought and sold in most ungodly fashion…” (*St. Augustine’s “Slave Market”*); (*See*, footnote 60, supra.)

[196] Ibid., describing the pavilion, including its dimensions: 33’ 3” × 60’ 9¼”.

"Well, it was," said Walter, "at least under Spanish rule. But that ended once the United States bought Florida from Spain…in 1819, if I recall. Years later, Florida joined the Union as a slave state."[197]

"So, from what you're saying, after the United States took over, St. Augustine was as bad as the rest of Florida."

"I suppose…when one views slavery purely as a matter of principle. But here in St. Augustine, the pavilion included, the number of slaves bought and sold was small, 'specially compared to the rest of the South."

Noah eyed the structure. "Jeezum, a damn slave market."

Walter held up both hands. "Hold it. Don't turn a drizzle into a monsoon. Slaves was sold in the market, but mainly it was a place where folks bought and sold food, 'specially meat and vegetables."

The clarification mitigated my feelings, but only a little. It rankled me knowing that a building on the very Plaza where I worked, people, perhaps even Maroons like me, were chattel, exchanged for money. I found solace knowing the Emancipation Proclamation, the end of the War of Secession and subsequent constitutional amendments had changed the landscape. "Doesn't it bother you, Walter?" I said.

"In some respects." Walter heaved a troubled sigh. "On the one hand, I hated slavery. Always have. But never a slave myself, I didn't suffer its horror. But that don't excuse how I felt, that I didn't do more to fight it. Told myself that St. Augustine was better than most places, 'cause it had fewer slaves." Walter bowed his head and muttered, "Truth be known, I was easin' my guilt, knowin' I was free. 'Course, that ain't what I told myself. Claimed I was just acceptin' the world the way it was. It's kinda like this here bad eye I got." He gestured at his right eye. "Ain't got no sight in this here eye. Most would say I'm half blind. Not me. The way I views it, I'm blessed with sight. I can see. And that's how I see life. Father, over at the cathedral, calls me an optimist." Walter momentarily pursed his lips before muttering, "And you're also longwinded, Walter." He shook his head. "Anyway, my point, before I rudely interrupted myself, is that I got hope for the future. Slavery's gone, and with the army here, I believe folks like us got a shot at a square deal. But whatever goes down, no complaints from me. Had well over seventy years, most of 'em with Wilma. More than any man could aks. Any more that come my way is whipped cream on pie à la mode." Walter smiled.

---

[197] Florida became the Nation's 27th state in 1845. *The American Period (1821 - Present) - Fort Matanzas National Monument*, nps,gov, 21 Feb. 2017 <https://www.nps.gov/foma/learn/historyculture/am-period.htm>.

His stream of consciousness begged a reaction. Conjuring one was another matter.

"Don't mind me," he said. "I always talk to myself, 'specially since Wilma crossed over. But damn, I sure got carried away. Like one of them speeches in a play, when the actor jabbers on and on. What they call a sol…a solo somethin'."

"Soliloquy?" said Noah.

"Yeah, that's the word. Though it hardly fits. No actor worth his salt would babble the way I do."

"You'd be surprised," I said.

"Oh, actors babble too?"

"Uh…no, I…uh…meant that what you said was interesting."

"I knew what you was sayin'."

Walter's reaction brought a smile, if not to my face, to my psyche. Sardonic repartee with this elderly man, more than four times my age, was already permissible. "Walter, you're like fine wine at a Sunday picnic."

"You mean well aged?"

I shook my head. "You can't fool me. You know exactly what I mean." This time I smiled broadly. The beaming face that my words evoked proved my point. It also confirmed the observation I had made a moment earlier.

***

The following day, Monday morning, Noah and I were on the job a few minutes early. An excellent Sunday had amplified positive vibes regarding our move to St. Augustine. A reinvigorating day off had primed us for the challenge of our sixty-hour workweek. The Sun still low in the eastern sky, the temperature yet to climb, afforded auspicious conditions for sanding the many boards that sat close by. We had been working for nearly an hour when out of the corner of my eye I spotted Sherman Hooker approaching. Upping my sanding speed a notch, I pretended not to see him.

"Good morning, Mr. Hooker," said Noah, continuing to rub as the boss drew near.

"I wish it was." Hooker's icy tone turned the tropical paradise into a frozen tundra.

"Is something the matter, Sir?" I stopped sanding, not wanting to appear as if I were ignoring him.

"You tell me," growled Hooker, folding his arms across his massive chest.

As surly as he had been during the preceding week, that comportment was affable next to this newest iteration. I wanted to say something to ease the tension, but ignorance of what riled him dictated silence.

Hooker stared at Noah and then at me. "Here in St. Augustine, we hate thieves!"

Was Hooker accusing us of stealing? If so, what and when? My face likely reflected my disbelief.

"You niggers arguin' with me?"

"Uh…no, Sir," said Noah.

Hooker glared at me. "I didn't hear nuttin' from you."

I suppressed the rage his odious epithet had ignited. "No, Sir."

"Then tell me why you niggers stole our nails and bolts."

"We didn't take anything," I said, echoing a similar reaction from Noah.

"You callin' Styles and Wood liars?"

"No," I said, though I had no idea who Wood was.

"So, you admit you stole the stuff."

"We don't know what Styles or the other fellow said, Sir. But we didn't take anything." Noah's attempt to restrain exasperation was patent.

"Fine. You boys wanna do this the hard way…then that's how we'll do it." Hooker stormed off, disappearing around the corner.

"Do you believe that bastard?" Noah's frustration added volume to a purported whisper. "Accusing us of theft and calling us niggers!"

"He's even meaner than we thought, hard as that is to imagine."

Moments later, Hooker reappeared, accompanied by Styles. "Bill, tell these dirt bags whatcha you told me Friday after work."

"Johnny Wood, one of my best men, said he saw these two (Styles pointed at Noah and me) stealin'. The next day, shortly before quittin' time, armed with binoculars, I staked out an inconspicuous perch on the top of the frame. Sure enough, I seen 'em stuffin' bolts and nails into their lunch bags, just before they left."

"So," said Hooker, "whad'ya have to say for yourselves now?"

"I can't explain what Mr. Styles claims he saw, but we didn't take anything. I assure you."

Ignoring Noah's denial, Hooker turned to Styles. "Thanks Bill. You can get back to work." As Styles headed off, Hooker said, though to no one in particular, "There goes a good man, the kind you can count on." Hooker turned to us. "You want to hear it from Wood too? Your choice."

I glanced at Noah. His face confirmed the futility of challenging the kangaroo court.

"Just as I expected. Your silence confirms your guilt." Hooker spit, the execrable mass striking the ground with the finality of a judge's gavel. "So, let me give you niggers the score."

The reiterated epithet had me fuming again.

"Your days here are over. The only question is how you leave."

I disbelieved my ears. In a matter of minutes, Noah and I had been accused, convicted and fired. "What do you mean, *how*?"

"Just what I said. You can go quietly. And 'cause I'm a nice guy, with four-days' pay. Or you can leave kickin' and screamin', claimin' you're innocent. But get this, you pick the latter, and we're pressin' charges. Rather than a paycheck, you'll get time in the lockup, a spot on the chain gang. Round here, strangers, especially niggers, don't beat the system." Hooker smiled, but the diabolical look was anything but cordial. "Oh, by the way, I forgot to mention, if you don't leave quietly, you'll never get another job in St. Augustine. It's a small place. Word that a guy can't be trusted spreads quick. And special for you two, I'll give the word an extra shove. Guarantee, you'll be blackballed."

I glanced at Noah. His expression, one of hopeless resignation, mirrored my thoughts.

"Fair man that I am," said Hooker, "I'm gonna give you time to consider my offer. I'm goin' 'round the corner. Be back in five minutes. So, take your time decidin'…even the whole five minutes."

"Gee, thanks," I muttered under my breath.

The glare Hooker sent my way before heading off suggested that he had heard my sarcasm.

"What do you think?" said Noah.

"We're between Scylla and Charybdis." I had no doubt that Noah understood my mythological literary reference to Homer and the treacherous Strait of Messina. More than once, Mr. Wright had referenced the perilous passage, with Scylla, the shoals (stylized as a six-headed monster) on the Italian side, and Charybdis, the menacing whirlpool, on Sicily's side.[198]

"So, what do you recommend?"

"As if we have a choice. We gotta take the four-days' pay and leave."

"Damn. That's how I see it too. But no way will I admit I took something that I didn't."

[198] *Between Scylla and Charybdis*, Wikipedia, 16 Feb. 2020 <https://en.wikipedia.org/wiki/Between_Scylla_and_Charybdis>.

"Point well taken," I said. "We'll go on record denying the accusation." Off to my left, I spotted Hooker coming our way. I whispered, "The bastard gave us less than two minutes."

"Time's up. Whatcha gonna do? Go quietly or get booted in the ass?"

"We're gonna leave, but not because we took anything," said Noah. "We didn't!"

Hooker laughed, punctuating the inexplicable reaction with a sly expression. He looked around. "Since we're alone, and you've agreed to go, what the hell…I might as well be up front. I know you didn't take anything."

"Then why you firing us?" Amidst my rage, hope of saving our jobs sparked.

A sneer, arguably more demonic than his earlier one, painted Hooker's face. "You boys did the unthinkable. You made a fatal blunder."

"What do you mean?" said Noah.

Hooker pointed at Noah and then at me. "You went over my head. Nobody does that to Sherman Hooker and lives to work on this hotel." Hooker eyed me. "You look confused. Shouldn't be, not for a hotshot who knows…calculus. But that's okay. Don't feel bad if you're kinda slow. I'll spell it out for you." Hooker rapped a demonstrative finger against his massive chest. "I decide who works here. I hire. I fire. You walked in the door lookin' for a job. I said *no*. And what kinda crap did you pull? You went over my head, to Mr. House." Hooker shook a clenched fist. "Nobody, least of all, niggers, gonna walk in my door and show me up. Ain't gonna happen!"

"But how can you fire us when you admit we didn't take anything?" My question made perfect sense; yet it was foolishly rhetorical. Forget calculus. The answer was easier than simple addition.

Hooker snickered.

His disdain enraged me. "Suppose we go to Mr. House and tell him that you're firing us for a theft that you acknowledge never occurred?"

"Do it. I don't give a shit!"

His cavalier response flummoxed me. My spontaneous threat made seconds before reverberated in my head. Was he bluffing? Was I bluffing when I threatened to go to Mr. House? We needed to weigh the consequences. Might Hooker be able to have us blackballed throughout St. Augustine? I needed to discuss it with Noah.

Hooker gestured in the direction of the shed where Mr. House worked. "You gonna pay the big boss a visit?...Oh, before you do. Keep in mind, you'll be prosecuted for theft."

"What do you mean?" said Noah. "You just admitted that we're innocent."

"That's between you and me…and the nails you never took. You see, when I talk to Mr. House, I'll deny this conversation ever occurred. And Styles and Wood 'll both confirm you stole the stuff. They're good old white boys. They know where their bread is buttered. They're loyal, and I take care of 'em. Of course, it don't hurt that the three of us share the same view. Niggers, like you boys, ain't welcome on our beach."

A minute before, I thought Noah and I had a shot. Not so. Hooker had a noose around our necks. Without compunction, he was prepared to lynch us.

"By the way, Mr. House hates crooks. He also hates troublemakers. Knowin' him, he'll go out of his way to ensure you don't work in St. Augustine. Even if he don't, like I said, I will." Hooker folded his arms.

I looked at Noah. A tiny nod of his head confirmed what I knew. Our fate was sealed.

"Appears we see eye to eye." Hooker waited several seconds, an unmistakable opportunity for Noah and me to balk. "Follow me to the shed and collect your four-days' pay."

Ten minutes later, Noah and I headed south across the Plaza. We each had $5.52 more than when we left for work in the morning. But we were poorer than when we had started our day. We no longer had jobs. Worse yet, a browbeating boss had stolen our dignity, pulverizing it like the dust that kicked up as we dragged our feet over the pothole-ridden road. A sluggish pace testified to our despondency. Conversation was non-existent. I looked off to my right at the marketplace. My knotted stomach was a gurgling pit. I could all but see a bumptious white man bidding on a vulnerable, young Negro girl. Admittedly, slavery had been less widespread in St. Augustine than most places in the South. Amendments to the Constitution had abolished the abomination and guaranteed due process and equal protection. And Congress had enacted laws prohibiting discrimination. Documents in black and white confirmed that equality was the law. Those were the facts. But reality belied the facts. Equality was an abstraction, a distant one whose time lay far in the future…years…centuries…or maybe never. As Grover had contended, egalitarian laws inscribed on paper, even scads of them, were a far cry from equality.

We continued south until we turned onto the path that led to Walter's home. It struck me that I had negotiated the route oblivious to the environs I had passed. My ears had been deaf to the birds; my eyes, blind to the colorful vegetation; and my nose, indifferent to the fragrant woods and marshes. The observation, confirmation of my mood, was no surprise. My fixated brain was unreceptive to the engaging stimuli.

As we approached the neat Victorian, Walter called out from his porch rocker, one of two. He always occupied the same one. The other had been Wilma's. "You fellas are home early."

I nodded, preferring to let Noah deliver the bad news. We ascended the three stairs that led to the green-railed, balustered porch.

"We were fired," said Noah.

Walter stilled his rocker.

"It's not like it sounds." Noah detailed our exchange with Hooker and how he had pushed us into a corner.

"A fella told me Hooker was a scurvy rat...Seems that fella owes the rats of the world an apology." Walter muttered inaudibly before continuing. "I understand you're disappointed, losing your jobs, but don't take it personally. You can't when dealin' with an ass who's got a hate-filled heart and a dung-filled brain."

Though the blunt analysis failed to win my job back, it permuted my thinking. I had suffered an injustice. But I bore no responsibility for that injustice. I was blame free. Frustration persisted, but self-flagellation ceased. "Thank you," I said.

Walter showed no reaction. Nevertheless, I suspected he understood my message.

"We'll have to look for another job tomorrow," said Noah.

"No. Give it a rest for a day," said Walter. "Wednesday will be soon enough."

The approach, a day to rejuvenate ourselves, had definite appeal.

The remainder of the day, I was relatively relaxed, considering the outrage I had borne in the morning. As I climbed into bed, rather than turning onto my side, the way I normally slept, I lay on my back. I gazed at the darkened ceiling before closing my eyes. The morning's misfortune still stuck in my craw. But with Walter's message fresh, I refused to allow the inequity to define me. Others, many of them slaves, who had been raped, pillaged and/or killed, some in the war, had suffered far worse than I. Compared to the horrors that most people of color had endured, I had been fortunate. Part of it had to do with where I had lived. Most of my years had been spent with my father alone in the woods of Southwest Florida. After his death, my exposure to bigotry had increased. Still location had insulated me from the tribulations faced by most people of color. While the Union stronghold in Fort Myers had evinced biases, it was a rare oasis in the world of the Confederacy. More recently, living with Grover and the Wrights and attending school at the First African Baptist Church, racial prejudice had invaded my life with growing frequency. That said, as a part of a welcoming white family, I had remained sheltered from bigotry's most heinous consequences. My recent experience in St. Augustine had altered my perspective. My resentment of racial bias amplified. Regardless, I refused to succumb to Sherman Hooker's abuse. He was a scum bag. That he could sadistically wield his authority was beyond my control. But Walter was right. No way should I allow Hooker's turpitude to eat me up. Like Walter, I focused on that which made me grateful. The resolve in no way lessened the wrong I had sustained; it did, however, mitigate my resentment. I had lost my job, indeed a battle, but thanks to Walter, I had won a moral victory. I turned over onto my side, buoyed by the solace that peaceful slumber might be near.

Chapter XIV

WHAT ON MONDAY HAD ME WONDERING if my stay in St. Augustine might be short lived had turned positive by Thursday. Walter, who was fast becoming our guardian angel, had bailed Noah and me out. He had found us jobs with a friend, Norwood Hanks, who had worked for Walter more than two decades earlier. Hanks was building homes south of the heart of St. Augustine in Little Africa. While our new employment was less than full time, it fit our needs, particularly because of the generous housing arrangement Walter had given us. Hanks agreed to pay us seventeen cents per hour, about three cents more than our rate at the St. Augustine Hotel. Hanks anticipated that he would need us an average of thirty hours per week, doing a wide range of housing construction work. As our skills improved, and he anticipated they would, he would gradually adjust our pay upward toward a carpenter's rate, roughly double that of a laborer.

The arrangement was an immediate success. Over the first month, Noah and I averaged nearly thirty-five hours. We helped frame, side and roof a small cabin not far from the west bank of the Maria Sanchez Creek. We did similar work on a four-room farmhouse nearby. The work schedule, coupled with the five to ten hours per week we spent performing chores at Walter's place, left ample time for my studies, as well as relaxation. It was a perfect balance, one that allowed me to contribute a couple dollars each week toward the household food stocks, enjoy a similar sum for spending and still save a dollar or so each week. The job had two major bonuses. The diverse tasks were far more appealing than sanding plank after plank, hour after hour. And unlike Hooker, a Simon Legree (the cruel slave driver from *Uncle Tom's Cabin* was etched into to my psyche), our new boss, Mr. Hanks, was a nurturing and appreciative mentor.

Week by week, month by month, the time flew. Our weekly hours grew to an average of about fifty. Our skills progressed and so too, our hourly rate of pay. Like a train chugging forward on steel rails, my life was on solid footing. It had direction. What it lacked, however—and this was anything but a complaint—was a destination. Construction was not where I wanted to be in twenty years. A profession, the kind that demanded mental, rather than physical skills, was my ambition. But inertia, very comfortable circumstances, pushed the issue into the background; that is, until one day, Mr. Hanks brought it to a crossroads. Noah and I had been working for him for well over a year, during which we had progressed from neophytes to highly skilled carpenters. It was the last Monday before the winter solstice of 1870, a wonderful time for construction work in St. Augustine. Daytime highs in the seventies, coupled with far less precipitation than the rainy summer season, were conducive to high production. We had spent the day painting a new Victorian a fashionably delectable purple. More than once, it had struck me that Mr. Hanks was not his usual convivial self. As we stowed the last of the paint cans in preparation for the next day's work, he said, "I…uh…need to talk with you fellows." He gestured toward the stairs of the yet unpainted porch. "Let's go sit over there." Once we were settled, he continued. "Over the weekend, Ruth (Mr. Hanks's wife) and I did lots of talking. This past month I turned sixty-eight."

His age surprised me. He had never mentioned it. Had I guessed, I would have said late fifties.

"Anyway, we…uh…think it might be time to…uh…call it a career." He gestured over his shoulder. "This house…it's gonna be my last."

The sledgehammer left me speechless. From time to time, I thought about my future, but it was always *the future*. There was no immediacy. That was no longer the case.

"I'm leaving you both in the lurch, aren't I?" The remorse in his voice was palpable.

As good as he had been to us, not just with raises, but respect and praise as well, I felt obliged to come to his defense. I said, "No, we're just surprised...Isn't that right, Noah?"

"Uh…yeah."

Mr. Hanks gave us each a look. "You're both very kind."

"That's what you've been to us," I said. "You hired us when we didn't have jobs. You trained us. And you've paid and treated us well."

"Do you have any plans for retirement?" said Noah.

"Yup, I'm going out to pasture…both literally and figuratively. The literal part will involve working our little farm. It's only a few acres. As for the figurative part, for a change, I expect to kick back and take it easy. I also hope to spend more time with my Bible. For years I've talked about reading it from cover to cover. Unfortunately, I've never gotten to it. But maybe now will be the time...What about you fellows? Any thoughts, though I understand you've had no chance to mull it over."

"I'll have to see," said Noah.

Though at times I had contemplated the matter, perhaps going to college or otherwise pursuing a professional career, vague as any such reflections had been, I shrugged.

"In recent weeks, as I was weighing retirement, I explored possible avenues for the two of you, as well as my other two regulars. One in particular has real possibility. Perhaps you've heard that there are plans to replace the lighthouse on Anastasia Island."[199]

"Someone told me that the government had provided funding for a new lighthouse," said Noah. "Whether that's accurate, I have no idea."

"It is," said Mr. Hanks. "Owing to soil erosion, the existing tower is expected to wash into the ocean. Congress recently appropriated $100,000 to replace it.[200] Construction on the new tower is expected to begin in about six months. I took the liberty of speaking with William Russell. I know him well. He's the keeper of the current lighthouse and is anticipated to get that position in its replacement.[201] He has considerable influence. They need skilled workers for the construction. I told him about you fellows. If you're interested, I believe you'd have a great shot, not that I can promise anything."

The possibility intrigued me. Whether I would bite in the event of an actual offer was impossible to say. Compensation would be an issue. A bigger one was what I wanted to do with my life. Already nineteen, I needed to weigh the alternatives carefully.

"Sounds interesting," said Noah. "I'll think about it."

"Me too," I said. "Regardless, I appreciate your trying to get us the opportunity."

"You've earned it, both of you. I couldn't have asked for better employees."

"And we couldn't have asked for a better boss," said Noah.

---

[199] *St. Augustine Light*, Wikipedia, 19 Jan. 2018 <https://en.wikipedia.org/wiki/St._Augustine_Light>. The present lighthouse, which stands on the north end of Anastasia Island off the St. Augustine coast, was begun in 1871 and completed in 1874.

[200] *Lighthouse History*, staugustinelighthouse.org, 19 Jan. 2018 <http://wwwstaugustinelighthouse.org/ourstories/LighthouseStory>.

[201] *St. Augustine Light*, op cit., stating: [William] "Russell was the first lighthouse keeper in the new tower, and the only keeper to have worked both towers."

"That goes for me too." My words echoed in my brain. I had been fortunate to have worked for such a kind man. It had made an otherwise good job, excellent.

***

Walter, Noah and I seated ourselves at our usual places in Walter's dining room. Walter occupied the head of the table, the end closest to the front of the house. Noah sat on one side and I, the other. As always, Wilma's seat, the end nearest the kitchen, remained vacant. Each of us had a platter with mutton, along with beans and squash from Walter's garden. Three weeks had elapsed since Mr. Hanks had announced his retirement. New Year's Day, 1871, had come and gone less than a week earlier.

"Those hiring for the new lighthouse offered Mican and me jobs as carpenters," said Noah. "It pays over seventeen dollars a week."

A chunk of mutton on his fork, Walter halted just before the tidbit reached his mouth. "Great!"

"The question now for each of us," I said, "is whether to take the offer."

"Be hard to turn it down," said Walter.

"True," said Noah. "But I think I will. When I came to St. Augustine to work on the hotel, it was a way to earn some money. A life doing construction was never the goal. A cousin of mine is opening an emporium in Atlanta. For three hundred dollars I can buy in, a one-third interest. With the money I've saved, I can put $150 down and the pay the balance over time. While it's not the architecture career I dreamed of, it's a chance to move up from laborer to boss, to have my own business."

A plaintive expression prominent, Walter turned my way. "You gonna leave me too?"

Until that moment, I had seen my decision purely through my own eyes. Concern in my landlord's voice put a new twist on the issue. Guilt might have kicked in, but fortunately I was leaning toward taking the job at the lighthouse. Staying with Walter, affording him the benefit of continued company, provided an additional reason. I said, "I still want to pursue a higher education, study mathematics and science. But the lighthouse opportunity is too good to pass up, especially when I have no idea where I'd go to college."

"I'm glad you plan to stay," said Walter. "Havin' you here means a lot."

"The feeling is mutual." Still I wanted to be sure Walter understood that the day for my departure might not be far off. "Of course, six months, a year or so from now, I anticipate I'll move on to pursue other goals."

"Hey, I wouldn't want you to do any different. But in the meantime, I'm glad one of you is stayin'. It'll give me time to find a tenant for the room that's bein' vacated, not that I'll find someone as nice as you two."

"You've treated us royally, Walter," I said. "No doubt, we've gotten the long end of the stick."

"I could debate the point," said Walter. "But instead, I'll put it this way. Each of us has gotten more out of this deal than we put in. That's how the best relationships work."

Had Walter not made the point, it would have escaped me. Once he did, my mathematical lens kicked in. Simple arithmetic said: The whole is equal to the sum of its parts. But Walter had demonstrated the contrary. He had seemingly cut a single pie into three halves. For a moment, the anomaly boggled my mind. Recollection of one of Mr. Wright's philosophy classes resolved the paradox. Millenia earlier, Aristotle had said that the whole is greater than the sum of the parts.[202] The philosophical principle had survived centuries of scrutiny. Its reverse was equally viable, if not mathematically, at least philosophically.

***

Two weeks earlier we had finished the interior details on the purple Victorian, and Mr. Hanks had retired. Shortly thereafter, Noah had packed his bags and moved to Atlanta to join his cousin at their new emporium. Still with several months until I commenced employment on the St. Augustine Lighthouse, I was awash with free time. It was my first vacation since I had left Savannah, and I welcomed the respite. With Noah gone, I did extra chores around Walter's house, not that they were burdensome. I studied for hours and volunteered at a Negro school that had recently opened in St. Augustine. The two-story institution, 33' × 15', referred to as the Bronson School (Public school, No. 2, colored), was located on Cordova Street about two hundred yards north of the Plaza.[203] It faced east toward Spanish Street.

---

202 *Metaphysica, 10f-1045a*, Retrieved from *Quotations by Aristotle*, history.mcs.st-and.ac.uk, 21 Jan. 2018 <mathshistory.st-andrews.ac.uk/Quotations/Aristotle.html>.

203 *Dr. Oliver Bronson St. Johns County 1st Superintendent of Public Schools*, drbronsontours.com, 22 Feb. 2018 <http://www.drbronsontours.com/bronsonoliverbronson.html> (*See*, footnote 60, supra.)

Following a day helping students learn to read, I returned home to Walter's place. He was seated in his porch rocker, enjoying a mug of ale.

"How'd it go today?"

"Good, all things considered. The kids are willing, but they're way behind. Eight, nine, ten years old, and some barely know the alphabet. They're using McGuffey's, the same book I learned from about seven years ago."

"They have the ability to learn?"

"Yes, but they need to make up lots of ground. They've lost their early years, the time when their brains were sponges. Add a shortage of books, too few teachers, especially with experience, tough conditions in their homes, inadequate food and whatever, and it's a monumental challenge."

"Yesterday, when I was gettin' some lamb at the marketplace, I was talkin' to Billie Bordell. He knows Oliver Bronson. Says the good doctor is tryin' real hard to make the schools good. That what you hear at the schoolhouse?"

"Yeah, the teachers say it's much better than a couple years back when classes were held in the churches and wherever. The state constitution enacted in '68 requiring education of all children, coupled with the funding law, has improved the landscape.[204] Negro children finally have real school buildings. Unfortunately, they're segregated and far from equal.[205] But it's a helluva lot better than a decade ago."

"You ever consider teachin' as a career?"

The idea had crossed my mind, but that was as far as it had gone. "Teaching, seeing a youngster learn, is rewarding, but not what I want to do with my life. Volunteering now and then, what I'm doing now, is a possibility." I went inside and got a brew. I came back out and seated myself on the porch railing across from Walter. "You were born when Washington was still President. You've seen it all, the nation in its infancy, Jackson and the Trail of Tears, Manifest Destiny, more than three scores of slavery, the War of Secession…What do you think?"

"'Bout what?"

---

[204] 1868 Constitution of the State of Florida, Art. VIII, Sect. 1 provided: "It is the paramount duty of the state to make ample provisions for the education of all children residing within its borders, without distinction or preference."

[205] Legislation passed in 1869, though not mandating segregated schools, authorized counties "to create separate schools for blacks and whites." *State Politics and the Fate of African American Public Schooling in Florida,* Howie, Sheryl Marie, p. 35, Institutional Repository @ UF, *1863-1900,* 30 Apr. 2011 <https://ufdc.ufl.edu/UFE0006780/00001>.

I suspected he understood my question, albeit vague. "Where we're headed. Will Reconstruction change things, or will we end up back where we were?"

"Slavery?"

"Not that, God forbid. But will the new constitutional amendments, 13, 14 and 15, bring about equality, or something close to it, the way they're supposed to?"

Walter started to get up from his rocker.

"Where you going?"

"To get a crystal ball." He laughed as he sank back into his seat.

"C'mon, humor me."

Walter took a swig of his ale. He rocked back and forth.

I waited.

His pensive look hinted he might be summoning transcendent wisdom. "Don't matter how long you've lived, not when you're talkin' 'bout the future. Only thing predictable 'bout that…it ain't predictable."

The point, hard to argue, was not what I wanted to hear. "I understand, but you must have some opinions."

"Everyone does. But opinions are like watermelon pits. Ain't got value. Folks love to spit 'em…But if you want, I'll give you mine."

"Your watermelon pits?"

Walter ignored my jibe. "The way I see it, we're in a tug of war. On the one side, you got the Republicans and Congress fightin' discrimination…pressin' for equality. On the other, you got the damn Democrats and groups like the Ku Klux Klan pushin' their Black Codes, laws limitin' our rights to own property and jailin' us for bein' unemployed. Slavery may not be their goal, but the old order, keepin' us second class, sure is."

Irony did not escape me. Several years before, Grover had invoked the same game when making a comparison. I said, "Tug of war…Good analogy. But it begs the question: Who's winning? I submit, we are. We've got guarantees of equal protection and due process. And Congress showed its backbone when it enacted the Civil Rights Law in '66. They kyboshed southern codes that restricted our right to own property and access the courts."[206]

Walter eyed his mug after indulging. "Yup. No arguments with your points…And all that's great. For the moment the hatemongers of the South been yanked nearer the mud pit than the folks seekin' equality. But the tug of war ain't over. Just imagine if the Democrats win back

---

[206] *See, Civil Rights Act of 1866*, uscivilliberties.com, 18 Nov. 2017 <http://www.uscivilliberties.org/legislation-action3601-civil-rights-act-of-1866.html>.

Congress and the White House. That Civil Rights Act you talked 'bout 'll be a dinosaur—extinct. And for that matter, I'm even nervous with Grant as president. He may be a Republican, but he's no Lincoln. Wouldn't shock me if he forged some compromise with the Democrats. They may not turn the clock back to the antebellum days of slavery, but what we get may not be much better. This president might even do it without Congress."

Walter had made valid points; his last, however, a glaring exception. "How do you figure that? In case you've forgotten, Congress makes the laws." A viscous sarcasm coated my message.

"I'm quite aware...But we got a divided Supreme Court. Some of the judges are along in years. And in case you've forgotten, the president picks any new justices. Sure, they gotta get Senate approval, but the wrong president could produce a court with a swine-filled majority. And maybe you're too young to recall the Dred Scott decision.[207] It was decided in the late fifties, back when you was a child. The Supreme Court ruled that Negroes, even freemen, wasn't citizens. And before you balk..."

I was not about to balk. Eat crow and apologize for a mocking tongue was more like it.

"I follow stuff. I know 'bout the Thirteenth Amendment. It abolished slavery. I also know 'bout the Fourteenth, that it overcame Dred Scott by makin' all folks born in the United States citizens. But stick the wrong folks on the Supreme Court, and everythin' could change. Hell, given the chance, good old southern boys will declare the 1866 Civil Rights Act unconstitutional. They'll bless segregation...a fancy name for discrimination."[208]

Walter's civics lesson had me reeling, as well as embarrassed. Discussions of other subjects had demonstrated he was smart. But contrary to my haughty assumption, he knew more about political science than I. "You know a lot about the government and the Constitution. Where did you learn that?"

"Hey, I didn't go to school, but I wasn't a slave neither. Like my parents, I was a freeman. They knew how to read, and they taught me too. They was concerned with their rights. They took me to the library

---

[207] *Dred Scott v. Sanford*, supra, footnote 25.

[208] In *Plessy v. Fergusson*, 163 U.S. 537 (1896), the United States Supreme Court did, indeed, uphold state laws that mandated segregated facilities based upon the doctrine of "separate but equal." That principle continued for more than a half-century when the Supreme Court in *Brown v. Bd. Of Education*, 347 U.S.483 (1954), unanimously overruled *Plessy v. Fergusson,* ruling that "segregated facilities are inherently unequal" and violative of the Equal Protection clause of the Fourteenth Amendment.

and taught me 'bout the Constitution. And like I told you before, Wilma pushed me to read too. I may not speak perfectly—colored folks around these parts don't—but I can read and write…and I can think."

"You can indeed." It struck me that Walter's parlance confirmed his assessment. Though his prose lacked the polish of Mr. Wright, his vocabulary was impressive, and more important, his comments about complex issues were astute.

"I've got a question for you," said Walter. "Of the three recent constitutional amendments, which do you think is most important?"

Mr. Wright had taught us about each, required us to learn the rights and protections that each provided. But over time, working on construction, my recollection of their details had grown foggy. As the one who was formally educated, I was embarrassed to exhibit my ignorance. "That's an excellent question. What would you say?" I sought refuge in slow sips of my brew.

"Unless I'm mistaken, I asked the question first."

With my dodge, a colossal failure, I swallowed hard.

"But if you like, I'll answer it." Walter rocked back and forth. "Not to put the Thirteenth and Fourteenth down—God, they're so important—but in the long run, the Fifteenth, the right to vote,[209] comes first. Without it, them that hate us would control the government. And God help us, if and when they do…Even with the vote, we got no guarantees, but least we got a fightin' chance."

***

A week earlier I had begun employment on construction of St. Augustine's new lighthouse on Anastasia Island. Located east of the mainland across the Matanzas River, the island was a half-mile ride on a wood-floated ferry.[210] The lighthouse would rise at the north end of the island, near the Atlantic Ocean side. Because the site was more than a half-mile from where the ferry docked, for the first few weeks on the job, most days I stayed at the workers' encampment. Once or twice a week I took the ferry back and forth to Walter's home, where I managed to do several hours of chores around his property and, more important, provide him some company, what he wanted most.

---

[209] U.S. Const., amend. XV prevents federal or state governments from denying any person the right to vote based upon "race, color, or previous condition of servitude."

[210] *Santa Anastasia – the Island of Adventure – HISTORIC CITY NEWS*, historiccity.com., 23 Jan. 2018 <https://historiccity.com/2016/staugustine/news/florida/santa-anastasia-the island-of-adventure>.

Not far from the worksite stood the old lighthouse, constructed by the United States government in 1824, shortly after purchasing the territory of Florida. The structure, a two-story, masonry house with an adjoining rectangular tower, was in imminent danger of being washed into the sea owing to progressive soil erosion. Word was that it occupied the same site as the Spanish watchtower Sir Francis Drake had described when he had attacked St. Augustine in 1579.[211]

With the new lighthouse's completion three years away, interim preservation of the 1824 lighthouse was imperative. Even before the new construction began, we added a jetty to protect the old tower. Anastasia Island's abundant supply of coquina obviated the need to ferry stone for the jetty from elsewhere.[212] Once the old lighthouse was secured, we built a trolley track to carry supplies from the dock on the west side of the island to the new construction site.[213]

After several weeks, I modified my routine, not that it was cast in stone. Workdays I stayed at the encampment. Once work was completed on Saturday, along with many coworkers, I ferried across the Matanzas to the mainland. Whites went off in one direction, while we Negroes chose another. Into the wee hours we caroused at a favorite saloon, often staying overnight with seven or eight of us in a single room. All but one slept on the floor. But the one who got the bed paid double what each of the others kicked in. Every other Sunday, even if I only squeezed in a few hours of sleep, I made sure to attend church with Walter and spend the afternoon with him. Late Sunday afternoon or early the next morning, I ferried back to Anastasia.

We had been on the job for about six weeks when I got lucky. Saturday evening, along with several others, I went to St. Augustine to the Jackstar Saloon, a joint laden with poker tables and cigar smoke. Everything about the watering hole screamed low class, with one exception, the artfully crafted cypress-wood bar, about twenty-five feet long, that paralleled the rear wall of the establishment. Behind the bar was a long, handsomely framed mirror and numerous shelves stocked with liquor. What began for me with a shot of whiskey turned into conversation with a barmaid, a cute lass, slim-waisted and well-endowed, more than a decade my senior. Words flowed between us as smoothly as her flawless bronze skin. Several whiskies later, considerably more than I normally consumed, and after lots of

---

[211] *St. Augustine Light*, Wikipedia, 19 Jan. 2018 <https://en.wikipedia.org/wiki/St._Augustine_Light>.

[212] Ibid. The 1824 lighthouse "crashed into the sea in 1880, but not before a new lighthouse was lit. Today, the tower ruins are a submerged archeological sight."

[213] Ibid.

conversation, much of which was flirtatious, she said, "I hope you didn't plan to return to Anastasia tonight, 'cause I doubt you'll get a ferry at this hour."

I gestured to a table in the far corner where a half-dozen of my buddies had been engaged in a poker game for several hours. "No problem. We'll get a room upstairs for the night."

"You're welcome to stay at my place. I got a flat, nothing fancy…just three small rooms on the second floor. It's down on Washington Street." She eyed the clock on the wall that was approaching midnight. "I get off in a little more than an hour…at one."

"Sounds good. I'll take you up on the offer." Exactly what the proposal entailed, I was unsure. For the next hour I speculated, wondering if she was inviting me to sleep with her or merely providing a place to bed down or, perhaps, she was a prostitute. At various times my best guess was each of the three. A fourth possibility, that maybe she intended to rob me, crossed my mind. I put little credence in the alternative. Regardless, if robbery was her goal, she'd be disappointed. I had just six bits remaining in my pocket.

Finally, the one-o'clock hour arrived. She came around from behind the bar and said, "You ready?"

As we headed for the door, I told my pals I would not be joining them for the night. Fearing taunts, especially with a crew that had imbibed heavily, I departed as quickly and unobtrusively as possible. Once the barmaid and I were outside, I said, "You lead, and I'll follow." I no sooner spoke the words than I realized I didn't know her name. "I'm Mican."

"Yes, I know. You told me earlier."

Failing to evoke the response I wanted, her name, I was forced to be more direct. "I don't know yours."

"I told you. It was about the time you had your fifth drink."

I waited a moment. "You gonna tell me again, or do I have to guess?"

"Hadn't thought of that, but it's not a bad idea." She jabbed an elbow into my side. "It's Opal."

We strolled south on Cordova Street. Conversation was sparse. The silence stood in stark contrast to the easy exchanges we had shared during her free moments at the Jackstar. We turned west on Bridge Street to Washington, where we soon reached a modest two-story frame structure.

"This is it…my home." She led the way into the gray, weathered building to the second-floor walk-up. We stepped inside, into a combination dining room and parlor, where Opal lit a kerosene lamp.

"Very nice," I said, looking around the neat, but simply appointed room. To the left of the side-hall entrance was a small table and three chairs. On the right, along the front wall was a settee and an easy chair, both of which showed wear.

"Would you like a drink?" The smile that punctuated her offer hinted she might be teasing.

"No thanks. In case you hadn't noticed, I consumed my share at the Jackstar."

"Really? I never would have known." She smiled before eyeing the clock that hung on the far wall. "Been a long day. Don't know about you, but I'm ready for bed." She gestured at the settee. "You're welcome to sleep there, but let me warn you, it's short and hard...If you prefer, my bed's available. It's a double. Let me show you, and you can decide."

Sight unseen, the bedroom was my choice. The time-worn cushions of the main room's tan settee could not compare to the two lovely pillows I envisioned...the ones that lay beneath Opal's yellow blouse. Cleavage behind the vee of her top's red-laced trim testified to the accuracy of my conclusion. My imagination, stimulated to staggering heights, furnished irrefutable proof.

Opal started to lead the way. "I might as well give you the full tour."

A *full tour*...was exactly what I wanted.

Past the dining-room table, she guided me through a galley kitchen. As we came out the other end, she said, "That was the kitchen, and here's the bedroom." We stepped through the doorway into a small room where Opal lit another kerosene lamp. Green walls and an armoire complemented a double bed bearing a quilt, patchworked with embroidered trees: palm, oak, cedar, maple, elm and a couple I could not identify.

"Very nice." I gestured around the room and then more directly at the quilt. "The bed looks far more comfortable than the settee. If it's okay, I'll choose that."

She shrugged. "You want me to sleep on the settee?"

"Oh...uh...no, I..." Telling her that I assumed we would sleep together when, apparently, she had other ideas would have been mortifying.

"I'm only kidding. I'm glad you prefer the bed. I do too. And I'm sure we'll be very comfortable here...together." She inched closer, pressing one of her voluptuous pillows against my arm.

I looked her in the eye. The yearning I felt radiated from her large browns. A moment later we melted into each other's arms. Lust converged with lust. Lips met in a passionate kiss. So began a night flaming with ardor, the details of which I leave to imaginations. Suffice it to say that hours before, we were strangers. By morning we knew one another well. Indeed, in the biblical sense, not that either of us was especially religious.

Over the ensuing weeks, Saturday nights bore striking similarities. Alcohol and conversation at the Jackstar presaged a voyage whose crescendo climaxed in carnal intimacy. Week by week the relationship progressed. What had originated as an enchanting temptress's seduction of a willingly naïve young man evolved into recurring excursions bearing mutually requited lust. Gaps in worldly wisdom, though admittedly not age, evanesced.

Sunday morning, following my sixth Saturday night with Opal, we sat at her dining table, each with a platter of scrambled eggs. She poured me a cup of coffee and then one for her before seating herself across the way.

"What do you think?" she said.

"About what?" Contrary to my response, uncanny intuition told me what she intended.

"Where are we going?"

"Excellent question…Are we there already?"

She nodded. "I think so."

Ambiguous as our dialogue had been, I knew exactly what she was saying. And she was right. The matter had been simmering in the back of my mind for two weeks. But reveling in sexual satisfaction, I had refused to face it. Nevertheless, I was glad Opal had brought it to the forefront. It allowed us to savor what we had shared and yet end our relationship without rancor and, more important, with neither of us hurt. Looking back, we both knew from the get-go that the affair was transitory. An existential experience of transcendent proportions was the antithesis of what we had shared. Carnal pleasure, plain and simple, was the totality of what we had enjoyed. A lasting relationship was never on the table. Great as the nights had been, in the six weeks we had spent together, never…not once, had either of us uttered the phrase, *I love you.* Sex was an enticing aphrodisiac; but an aphrodisiac, no matter how seductive, did not a bond create. "We had a great run, didn't we?"

"We sure did." She looked me in the eye, "You still gonna stop in at the Jackstar now and then?"

"Absolutely." I sipped my black coffee, debating whether to pose a stirring question. Curiosity how she might respond superseded judgment. "You think we might dance a little in the future?" I glanced over my shoulder toward the bedroom.

Opal shrugged. "Your guess is as good as mine."

A part of me was certain it would happen. Another part was equally certain of the contrary. The inconsistency of my analysis brought a conscious smile to my lips.

"What does that mean?" she said.

"That I have no clue what lies ahead for us."

"Well..." she said, with thoughtful hesitation, "whatever the future holds, I'm grateful for what we've had. It's been terrific."

"Ditto here." I looked into her lovely browns. The yearning I had seen our first night, weeks earlier, was absent, not just from her eyes, but my emotions too. Love of another kind, an enduring affection was evident. There was, however, no need to question the end of our relationship. We were at different stages of our lives. We had different goals. Paths that had intersected needed to fork. Intimacy, no matter how fine, did not equate to a lifelong commitment. Euclid might have explained it as a matter of simple geometry. A round peg does not fit a square hole.

Chapter XV

FOLLOWING THE FIRST WORKDAY AFTER OPAL, I took the late-day ferry to the mainland and went directly to Walter's house. I found him dozing in the parlor.

"Long time no see," he said, as he got his wits.

"Yeah, two weeks." Although I had spent repeated Saturday nights with Opal, only half the time had I made it to Walter's on Sunday afternoon.

"Had I known you was comin', I would have delayed my dinner."

"Glad you didn't. I grabbed a bite at the encampment before I left."

"Good news. I found a new tenant, a maintenance man for the Hotel Magnolia. He plans to move in here next week. He's not Noah or you, but it'll be nice to have daily company again."

I was happy for Walter, but also for myself. Leaving him alone, sometimes for two weeks at a time, had spurred guilt.

"Oh, speaking of Noah, I almost forgot. I got a letter from him the other day. Things are going well at the Savannah emporium. He also sent a letter for you." Walter went to the credenza along the front wall and got an envelope that he handed to me.

I pried it open and read:

June 6, 1871

Dear Mican,

All is well in Savannah. My letter to Walter will fill in the details. A matter that might interest you prompted this additional correspondence. Last week I bumped into your former girlfriend, Sarah. Her husband's family business went broke, and he took off. She thinks he went west to Nevada to prospect for silver. Sarah described him as a mean drunk. She indicated that choosing him over you was a big mistake. She wondered if you might consider putting bygones into the past...By the way, she gained at least thirty pounds.

Warm regards,
Noah

I laughed before rereading the letter. Even without the final tidbit, I had no interest in resurrecting a relationship with Sarah. When she had dumped me a few years earlier, heartache had followed. But I had gotten over her quickly. Blinders, occasioned by attraction, yielded to open eyes. Evaporation of olfactory-deceiving perfume unmasked a hidden stench. A self-centered gold digger was not for me. My recent relationship with Opal helped me see the matter more clearly. I had grown toward manhood, not merely in a physical sense, but emotionally as well. The chance to sow my proverbial wild oats had ushered me across a bridge. Unlike so many of my young coworkers who week after week would ferry from Anastasia for a wild weekend on the mainland, I had moved beyond. Though I would still cross the Matanzas River on Saturday evenings, my destination and purpose would be different. I would travel directly to Walter's house. I was back to studying. I was saving my earnings, not simply because it was wise, but for college. My time with Opal, a chance to experience what theretofore had been a desired and imagined unknown, had enabled me to refocus. I no longer wondered what I was missing. I no longer needed to chase the magic that others recounted in stupefying terms. I knew firsthand. I was worldlier than just a few weeks earlier. More important, I was much older. That's not to say that I was no longer looking for love. But the Jackstar was hardly the place to find it. I would need to look elsewhere...church, the library or maybe a park, not that the place was consequential. What mattered was the person, a woman of substance with whom I could share more than physical pleasures.

***

Up with the Sun, after a hearty breakfast of eggs and sausage, I took the short walk from our encampment to the lighthouse construction site. Coming from the direction where the ferries docked, I spied Sherman Hooker, my former boss at the St. Augustine Hotel. Though I immediately looked away, eye contact had occurred. Each of us had seen the other. I continued toward the construction site. Out of the corner of my eye, I discretely followed Hooker's progress. He turned north, so his back was to me. I slowed my pace to a near standstill, pausing in an area where I could track him with strategic glances. Hooker headed into the small structure that adjoined the existing lighthouse, a building that was being used as headquarters during the initial phase of our project. Whenever a stranger went there, it was a good bet he was seeking a job. Odds were that was Hooker's purpose.

I continued to the worksite. My thoughts remained on Hooker. An uneasy feeling disquieted me. Working alongside the ogre would be bad enough. But his hiring would probably auger a worse consequence. Hooker was more than a mere worker. If hired, he would likely be a foreman. He could be my boss again. My job could be in jeopardy.

All through the day I ruminated. Had Hooker applied for a job? Was he hired? Would he victimize me again? With dusk's advent, along with my coworkers, I returned to the encampment. I was about to get in line for food when I spotted George Wall, a supervisor who would know about any new hires. Judgment counseled restraint; curiosity superseded. I hurried Wall's way, seizing the chance to address my concern. "Are they still adding men to the crew?"

"A few. You looking to recommend someone?"

Just the opposite, but I had no intention of badmouthing an applicant. It would be my luck that Wall knew Hooker and liked him. "No, but I was just wondering."

"We had a couple of applicants this morning. Even hired one."

That Hooker had joined the St. Augustine Lighthouse team became more likely, but I needed to be circumspect. "This new guy have good skills?"

"Very. He's been laying bricks for several years...mainly in Jacksonville."

The location turned Hooker into a longshot. "You mentioned a couple of applicants. The other wasn't as good?"

Wall laughed.

"Did I say something funny?"

"Not that. The other guy had an impressive background. He was the foreman at the St. Augustine Hotel, as well as the Drayer Building."

The possibility that Hooker might be under consideration for a higher position, the kind that could involve multiple interviews and a wage negotiation, rekindled my worries. Still discretion guided my fishing. "This other fellow have a shot at a job?"

"Nope. He was given a quick goodbye."

"Really?" Spontaneity hinted I was pleased.

"Yup. The weasel's reputation from the Drayer project preceded him. They canned him, caught him extorting his workers, demanding kickbacks from their pay." Wall shook his head. "Bad enough the area has seen an influx of carpetbaggers and scalawags. Last thing we need is a snake like that."

I thought out loud. "His black mark will make it tough for him to land another position."

"Certainly around a place the size of St. Augustine. Word spreads. A bad rep is worse than incompetence." Wall gestured toward the food line. "Enough shop. It's been a long day. I don't know 'bout you, but I'm starved."

"Me too." A full day's work, plus news that Hooker had gotten his comeuppance, that he would not be making my life miserable, sparked a ravenous appetite.

***

Month by month the new lighthouse began to rise from the Anastasia earth. Across Florida, a largely agrarian state, difficult times persisted. The economic consequences of the war remained manifest. Whites had been unable to reclimb the pecuniary mountain down which defeat had driven them. Freedmen's compensation often left them poorer than when they were slaves. Carpetbaggers from the North lined their pockets at the expense of antebellum residents.

St. Augustine, which had been spared destruction during the war, continued to fare better than most of Florida and the vast majority of the South. A pre-war fledging tourist industry breathed new life thanks to warm winters and an oceanside location. Hotel construction, as well as projects like the new lighthouse, provided jobs. Though insurgent white organizations such as the Ku Klux Klan, employing violence, assassination and voter intimidation, sought to restore white supremacy throughout the former Confederacy,[214] the continued presence of the United States military curbed such lawlessness in St. Augustine. Bolstered by the Fifteenth Amendment's guarantee of the right to vote, in 1870 Northern Florida had elected Josiah Thomas Walls as the state's

[214] *Ku Klux Klan*, op cit. The Ku Klux Klan played the role of "military arm of the Democratic Party." *See also*, *Reconstruction Timeline*, thomaslegion.net, 25 Mar. 2020 <www.thomaslegion.net/reconstruction_timeline_reconstruction_era_timeline.html> indicating that in April 1871 Congress enacted the Ku Klux Klan Act responding "to President Grant's request for more federal authority to combat anti-black violence in the South…"

first Negro to serve in the United States Congress.[215] Such anecdotal progress buoyed Negro hopes for the future, even as the weight of the evidence belied that optimism.

I had spent Saturday night at Walter's and accompanied him to the cathedral for Sunday services. Elmer, the tenant who had replaced Noah, had declined an invitation to join us. His refusal was no surprise. Elmer had turned out to be a laconic loner, hardly the ideal tenant for Walter.

Services at the cathedral had little impact on me. If anything, I identified myself as Baptist, but only because of my time at Savannah's First African Baptist Church. Deeply held religious beliefs, I still had none. Amidst the recitations of time-honored prayers, my mind drifted. Principles and equations of Newtonian physics I had been studying in recent weeks commanded my attention. Hours of scrutinizing my calculus book had boosted my ability to rely on reasoned analysis, rather than memorized formulae. In some respects, the concepts occupying my thoughts were similar to those of the supplicants. Both had come from a distant day. Both involved fundamental principles. Both commanded the utmost respect. But their dissimilarities were greater. Those of the supplicants were based on faith; mine, reason. Theirs were regurgitated, often reflexively; mine emerged from step-by-step analysis. At times, church and science had clashed. Science had contradicted scripture's dogma, rejecting its categorical principles. The church had responded decisively. Heresy, unmitigated evil, had to be silenced, if only to preserve God's good name and message. Protection of the Lord justifed, indeed required, death for the apostates.

The congregation kneeled, closing their eyes in prayer. I knelt and shut mine too. Unfamiliar with the foreign devotion, no way could I recite it. Regardless, my mind was otherwise preoccupied. I was contemplating a differential equation describing the velocity of a falling projectile under the influence of both gravity and the opposing force of air resistance, a vector that escalated as the speed of the projectile increased. Minimizing complexity, I assumed that the atmosphere was of uniform density; the rate of change in air resistance was linear; and the projectile, perfectly round. I imagined the moment of equilibrium, when the force of gravity and air resistance matched, and the projectile attained its constant, terminal velocity. "Amen," I said, concluding with the identical word the congregation was voicing. I opened my eyes.

"Good Sabbath," said Walter.

I shook the hand he extended. "Good Sabbath, and peace to you."

---

215 *WALLS, Josiah Thomas | US House of Representatives: Art & Archives*, history.house.gov, 20 Jan. 2018 <http://history.house.gov/People/Detail/23324>.

Along with the rest of the congregation, we wended our way out into the May sunshine.

"I'm glad you joined me today. I know services, 'specially with a liturgy, ain't your thing."

"A little religion never hurt anyone." My comment masked how little I had absorbed.

"What did you think of today's homily?"

"Well…it was a—"

"Walter."

Our heads turned with the call of Walter's name, a welcome distraction. Coming up behind us was Walter's long-time friend Herman Slack. Once we exchanged pleasantries, I said, "You still helping out at Cordova Street?" Herman had tutored at the school during my days volunteering there.

"Yup. Any chance we can lure you back? We need help, especially with math and science."

"I'd like to, but can't, not with my long hours on Anastasia, working at the lighthouse."

"Understand…You still thinking about college?"

"That's the plan, once the lighthouse is completed. Of course, finding a school that accepts people of color may be tough."

"Don't know if it would interest you, but the other day at the school, a fellow mentioned a place where Negroes might have a shot at higher education."

"Something here in Florida, maybe?" My question was grounded upon hope, not the expectation of a positive reply.

"Nope. The University of South Carolina. Before closing during the war, it was called South Carolina College. It reopened in 1866."[216]

"And they're accepting Negroes?" The possibility excited me.

"Not as yet."

Walter shot Herman a look. "Jeeze, you know how to take a guy up a mountain…only to shove 'im off a cliff."

"Walter…Walter, it's Sunday. Display some grace." The broad smile that punctuated Herman's words reflected the good-natured teasing between the cronies. Herman redirected himself to me. "From what I was told, the University of South Carolina has appointed Negroes

---

[216] *Our History*, University of South Carolina website, SC.edu. 1 Sept. 2016 <sc.edu/about/our_history>. South Carolina University was founded in 1801 as South Carolina College. Owing to a lack of students, it closed in 1861 during the Civil War.

to its Board of Trustees. They want a diverse campus, including people of color."[217]

"Really?" I said.

"You gonna hard time me too?"

The absence of a smile left me unsure if Herman might be serious. "Sorry. I wasn't questioning you. Merely surprised."

"I knew that." Herman slapped me on the back.

"Herman…I'm waiting." The shrill voice of Herman's wife turned our heads.

"Seems someone wants you, Herman." Walter supplemented his histrionic, high-pitched message with a smirk.

Herman pointed a finger at his buddy. "Not another word from you." He hurried to his wife.

"See what you're missin'." The instant Walter completed the quip, he sighed. "Damn. Don't I wish someone was still callin' me?"

The melancholy in Walter's voice froze my tongue. Clever banter, appropriate seconds before, became unthinkable. I started in the direction of our favorite fishmonger, staying a step ahead of Walter, affording him the privacy of his thoughts. A strange irony crossed my mind. Hard as it was to endure the loss of such a wonderful life partner, one was fortunate to be in that position. I could only hope to find a special someone with whom I too could build decades of sublime memories.

***

Armed with the information that the University of South Carolina had Negro members on its Board of Trustees, my hopes of a college education mounted. Though I preferred to pursue my studies in Florida, anywhere in the South was fine. During my shifts at the lighthouse, I contemplated the best way to gain admission to the new institution. My construction job hardly seemed the ideal platform. Some limited studying on my own was nice, but next to full-time presence in school, it was feeble. To have a chance, I needed help. Mr. Wright was the one person of stature who knew my background and abilities. Come the end of the workweek, when I had time, I would seek his recommendation. Common sense told me I was getting ahead of myself. The University of

---

[217] Ibid. "State leaders revived the institution in 1866 as the University of South Carolina with ambitious plans for a diverse University that included the first African-Americans to serve on the board of trustees and the first African-American students (1873)…The University of South Carolina became the only Southern state university to admit and grant degrees to African-American students during the Reconstruction era."

South Carolina had not begun to accept applicants of color. The point had merit. Regardless, common sense could not douse enthusiasm.

Out of the corner of my eye, I noticed a supervisor. He appeared to be watching me. For how long, I could only wonder. Odds were he had taken note of the inefficiency occasioned by my ruminations. I needed to get down to business, lest I get walking papers. I grabbed a brick and, using my spade trowel, buttered the brick with mortar, including the ends that would join adjacent bricks. I laid the brick in place,[218] making certain the mortar on its sides was a tad thicker on the outer edge in order that it could ease around the lighthouse's curved exterior.[219] With my trowel's handle I tapped the brick to locate it perfectly and eliminate bubbles of air.[220] I scraped away any mortar that extended past the joint. I took another brick, eyeing it briefly. Like all the others, it had come from a brick-making factory in Birmingham, Alabama. St. Augustine's lighthouse may have been a local project, but its construction was the product of diverse contributions. The iron for the circular staircase and the upper structure supporting the light had been ordered from Philadelphia. And the crowning element, the nine-foot Fresnel lens, capable of projecting a beacon well over twenty miles, had been ordered from Paris.[221] It struck me that the project could serve as a lesson to the University of South Carolina, an institution that had previously shut its doors for want of sufficient students. Success, indeed quality, could be achieved with diversity. Accepting a Maroon from Florida would be the paradigm of such diversity. That my reasoning was predicated on personal interest and, worse yet, short on logic, did not escape me. Nor did it trouble me. My sole concern was the result. I wanted an acceptance letter.

I troweled more mortar onto the course and installed another brick. I repeated the process over and over. I glanced at the people working on the project. There were Caucasians, Negroes and even another Maroon like me. Why was our encampment segregated? What relevance did the color of one's skin have to do with where one ate and slept? It made no sense. Yet those were the rules. But what if the rules weren't there? It was all but certain the Caucasians would have congregated together. So too, the Negroes. For the most part, people of the same religion, ethnic

---

218 *How to Lay Brick | how-tos | DIY*, diynetwork.com, 30 Jan. 2018 <http://www.diynetwork.com/how-to/skills-and-know-how/masonry-and-tiling/>.

219 *How to Build a Short Curve Brick Wall,* | Hunker, hunker.com, 30 Jan. 2018 <https://www.hunker.com/13424830/how-to-build-a-short-curved-brick-wall>.

220 *How to Lay Brick*, op. cit.

221 *St. Augustine Lighthouse and Museum*, stfrancisinn.com, 29 Jan. 2018 <http://www.stfrancisinn.com/st-augustine-lighthouse-and-museum/>.

background or color associated with one another. The concession beckoned me down an unpleasant path. The Constitution guaranteed individuals the right to associate. If individuals preferred segregation, wasn't that their right? I jammed a brick into place. Mortar oozed excessively, requiring me to remove the brick and restart the process. I thought back to my days at Fort Myers. Caucasian and Negro soldiers occupied distinct companies. They slept in separate barracks. At the time it seemed unfair. But my analysis moments before suggested otherwise. I restrained the urge to slam the same brick down again. Having to apply the mortar in the same location a third time was a punishment I preferred to eschew. Worse yet was the possibility the supervisor might see me. I laid the brick carefully, along with several more.

My thoughts drifted back to Fort Myers and the segregation there. Though seemingly expected and accepted, on one occasion I had heard a Negro soldier grouse about the inequality associated with it. White privates received "$12.00 per month plus a clothing allowance of $3.50," while Negro soldiers were paid "$10.00 a month, with an optional deduction for clothing at $3.00."[222] The inequity was patent. The point would have proved the unfairness of segregation, except Congress had cured the injustice, granting equal pay to all soldiers in 1864. Arguably, Congress had rendered the military's segregation fair. Nevertheless, something about the conclusion stuck in my craw. As I wiped away some excess mortar along the edge of a brick, it dawned on me what. Equal pay was a step in the right direction. It did not, however, constitute equality. In the wake of slavery's abolition, segregation became the alternative device to ensure that Negroes remained second-class citizens. That Negroes congregated separately did not prove otherwise. No way did they choose a segregated society in which they were relegated to inferior employment, education, accommodations and life in general. Hate, violence and threats to their lives influenced their willingness to accept the state of affairs. The point underscored the importance of anti-discrimination laws enacted by the federal government. It also underscored the risk posed if Democrats regained control of the government. Elections, the vote or denial of the vote, could turn back the hands of time. The observation reminded me of something Walter had said. The Fifteenth Amendment, the right to vote, was the most important

---

[222] *Military history of African Americans in the American Civil War*, Wikipedia, 29 Jan. 2018 <https://en.wikipedia.org/wiki/Military_history_of_African_Americans_in_the_American_Civil_War>.

of the Reconstruction laws. Whether he was right, I didn't know. Regardless, no way could I argue that he was wrong.

***

Sunday morning, I was up early, even before Walter. I grabbed a quick breakfast. Rather than readying myself to accompany him to the cathedral, I went to work. With the utmost care I drafted a letter to Mr. Wright. It was hard to believe that more than four years had elapsed since I had last seen him and his family, and more than a year had passed since I had corresponded with them. After inquiring how they all were, particularly Michael and Nora and their schoolwork, I detailed my employment for Mr. Hanks and at the lighthouse, along with my volunteering at the school. I told him of my progress with the calculus book he had given me, both to show my appreciation and to ensure he knew that I still valued academics. All this was a prelude to my purpose, asking him for a college recommendation. Informing him that my application was probably a year or more away gave me pause, but I deemed it wiser to be up front rather than face embarrassment if, a few months later, he inquired how I made out. With fastidious scrutiny, I repeatedly revised the letter, checking punctuation, spelling and grammar, as well as content. Once satisfied, I copied it in my neatest hand, making an extra copy for myself using a sheet of carbonated paper.[223] The clever device, one of so many invented since the start of the Industrial Revolution, forked my brain. I could only imagine the amazement of the country's early colonists were they able to observe late 19th-century technology. Arguably progress during the last one hundred years had exceeded the total of the preceding millennium. The observation begged the question: Might the ensuing hundred years do the same, dwarfing the accomplishments of the Industrial Revolution? I laughed out loud at the offbeat thought. Perhaps another millennium would slip by before a period of such rapid technological growth would arrive. The musing, replete with irony only visible with hindsight, hinted how fascinating a glimpse into the future would be.

I read my letter one more time…with trepidation. A single error would force me to recopy the entirety. Fortunately, my considerable care had yielded a satisfactory product. I placed the letter into an envelope,

---

[223] *The Exciting History of Carbon Paper!*, kevinlaurence.net, 2 Feb. 2018 <kevinlaurence.net/essays/cc.php> indicating: "The first documented use of the term 'carbonated paper' was in 1806, when an Englishman, named Ralph Wedgewood, issued a patent for his 'Stylographic Paper.'"

which I sealed, addressed and stamped for mailing the next day. An urge to begin college sooner, not later, gripped me. Reality forced me to quell the desire. It was not in the cards. But in the meantime, I would study harder. I went upstairs to my room to the shelf that housed my books: *Uncle Tom's Cabin*, the Bible and my calculus book. I had made tremendous strides learning integral calculus. I had even played around with differential equations, though admittedly my knowledge of the subject was rudimentary. Spending my day-off digging deeper into the complex discipline's more challenging aspects had little appeal, especially after having worked so hard on the letter. I glanced at my Bible. When first I had gotten it, I had tried several times to read it. No more than ten or fifteen minutes elapsed before ennui reigned and my mind wandered. Twice I dozed off. The Bible was staying on the shelf. That left only one choice, *Uncle Tom's Cabin*. Seven years had elapsed since Abbey had given it to me. Most of its details had long since evaporated from my memory bank. I took the first volume down to the porch and seated myself in Wilma's rocker.

I opened the cover. I read Abbey's inscription:

> Dear Mican:
> I will remember you always. I love you.
> Abbey

I read it twice more, slowly mouthing the words. I closed my eyes and conjured an image of the scene where she had given me the volumes. The spot, hidden in the woods, where we had spent our final moments, was vivid. The glorious touch of her lips, the kiss we had shared, was palpable. I pictured the turquoise-decorated bookmark I had given her. Did she still have it? Did she use it to mark the numerous books, no doubt, she read? I drew in a deep breath. A calm, an awesome serenity, captivated me. I closed my eyes again and for several minutes basked in memories of our time together.

Opal popped into my head. I opened my eyes. My time with her had been great. But it was a fling, built exclusively on sex. By way of contrast, my relationship with Abbey constituted love. Would I have liked more of a physical relationship with her? Doubtless. But that in no way diminished what we had shared. To the many who would contend that Abbey and I were too young to understand the meaning of love, I would demur. Admittedly, we were too immature for a permanent relationship. Our youthful inability to handle the complexities of life together was hard to deny. But that concession failed to negate the depth of our connection. We were in love.

I turned the pages of *Uncle Tom's Cabin* past its preliminary folios, to the first page of the story, and began to read: "Late in the afternoon of a chilly day in February, two gentlemen were sitting alone over their wine, in a well-furnished dining parlor, in the town of…"[224] I reached the bottom of the page and turned to the next. I had no recollection of what I had read. My mind was still transfixed on Abbey. I thought back to the days when I had first arrived at Fort Myers, how she had befriended me and taught me how to read. My comprehension, or should I say lack thereof, harked back to the days when I started my initial McGuffey's Reader. The analogy, however, did not extend far. Back then I could not pronounce, let alone digest, the words. In contrast, my inability to absorb what I had read a minute earlier was strictly a product of focus. I closed the book, allowing it to rest in my lap. I rocked back and forth. Scenes of time spent with Abbey drifted through my mind: the enthralling touch of her arm against mine when tutoring me in the rear of the schoolhouse; the sun-drenched glow of her golden locks as we strolled hand in hand along the banks of the Caloosahatchee; and her reassuring smile in the face of her parents' disapproval at their dinner table. I savored the moments, endeavoring to ensure that they would never fade into oblivion, victims of time.

The best part of a half-hour passed before my reverie subsided. I reopened *Uncle Tom's Cabin* and read. I absorbed the content. Indeed, I took in the content with greater understanding than when I had previously read it. Details and subtleties that had gone over my head seven years earlier intrigued me. Maturity and experience enabled me to better understand how the novel had cast a bright light on slavery's brutality; how it had ignited the nation's conscience; how it had helped precipitate the War of Secession; and how it had altered America's social and economic landscape.[225]

***

---

[224] *Uncle Tom's Cabin*, op. cit., p.1.
[225] *Uncle Tom's Cabin (1852) | The Black Past: Remembered and Reclaimed*, blackpast.org, 3 Feb. 2018 <http://www.blackpast.org/aah/uncle-toms-cabin-1852> indicating that next to the Bible, *Uncle Tom's Cabin* was the second-widest-sold book of the 19th century, and so significant as to prompt President Abraham Lincoln, upon meeting the book's author Harriet Beecher Stowe, to say, "'so this is the little lady who made this big war.'" Stowe, a determined abolitionist, did much to rouse the Nation's conscience about the immorality of slavery. By focusing on Negroes' Christian values, she challenged the nation to acknowledge Negroes' humanity. But her novel did not escape social criticism for creating characters who were caricatures that fostered stereotypes inimical to Negroes' fight for equality.

1872 rolled by with amazing alacrity. Summer wafted into autumn, something we workers at the lighthouse appreciated. Even with the benefit of the Atlantic's breezes, months of enervating days in the nineties were grueling. Slightly cooler temperatures, coupled with the knowledge that December, January and February would deliver more comfortable highs, averaging near seventy, not only enhanced efficiency but also improved dispositions. Progress had enabled dreams of a tower, once as nebulous as the clouds that floated above, to metamorphose into reality. Among the workforce, a manifest sense of accomplishment stirred contagious pride. What had been nothing more than an income-generating job had become meaningful. We grew increasingly connected to what we were building. As one worker phrased it, "The lighthouse will be our legacy." Admittedly, our pay remained the foremost motivation for our labors, but intangible gratifications had become a significant bonus.

In my free time, I had delved into all manner of knowledge: mathematics, science, literature, history and philosophy, mostly from borrowed books. But more than anything else, I had remained focused on calculus. It was a Saturday night when, into the wee hours, with the benefit of a kerosene lantern, I had been studying partial differentials in Elements of the Differential and Integral Calculus.[226] Minutes after I put the text away and extinguished my lantern, sleep overtook me. It was well past noon the following day when I arose. Walter had already arrived home from church, and we enjoyed an excellent dinner—for me brunch—that he had prepared. Following the repast, we strolled to the Maria Sanchez Creek, to our favorite spot, a rock comfortably shaded, but perfect for viewing the wildlife that frequented the sunlit waters and their adjoining banks.

"You hear anythin' from Mr. Wright?" said Walter.

"Not as yet." Three months had elapsed since I had sent my letter requesting a recommendation, and I had grown antsy. On second thought, I was downright worried. Without his recommendation, all I had was my claim that I had studied hard over a number of years. That was hardly the prescription for gaining admission to the University of South Carolina or, for that matter, any college. "What do you think?"

"'Bout what?"

"C'mon. You know...Do you think Mr. Wright is avoiding me because he's unwilling to give me a recommendation?"

Walter shrugged. "You're aksin' the wrong guy. I never met him."

---

[226] *Elements of the Differential and Integral Calculus,* Chapter IV, op. cit.

His point was valid, but it was likely a dodge. Walter saw the situation the same as I. The lapse of time was a bad sign. But confirming what we both knew would only make me feel worse.

"Maybe your letter got lost in the mail…never reached 'im."

The possibility, which had crossed my mind, provided hope, though not a lot. It was a longshot.

"Have you considered writin' to 'im again?"

"I have…but not for now. Since I plan to stay here for the foreseeable future—maybe even till the lighthouse is completed—I won't be looking for admission to college until the fall of seventy-four. That gives me roughly two years, enough that I can put it on the back burner."

"You mean procrastinate?"

The question forced me to reassess my analysis. "I'm known to do that, but in this case, I think it makes sense. Don't want to appear pushy, especially when Mr. Wright might be reluctant to recommend me." I gazed across the waters of Maria Sanchez where an anhinga stood in the sunshine drying its unfurled wings. Like so many of its brethren, it was apt to remain parked and motionless for an hour or more. Diving into the creek for a fish, finding its next meal, could be delayed until later. For the time being, basking in the glorious sunshine, be it procrastination or not, was fine. What was good for the bird was good for…whatever.

"How things at the lighthouse?" said Walter.

"It's getting taller every month."

"Ain't what I meant. I was referrin' to how things are for you…the job and the folks you work with?"

"It's gotten better with time." The spontaneous response reflected my feelings. But exactly why was more subtle, and the inquiry pressed me to explore the reasons. "When we started, there was nothing there. As the lighthouse has grown taller, it's become a source of pride." The comment was not a revelation. I had been conscious of the fact for some time. But something else had shifted my mindset about the job. "There's been a change at the site, partly, I guess, because the men have gotten to know one another, but it's…it's more than that…We're less divided than when we started…the whites and the Negroes. Don't get me wrong. The whites still hang out together, as do the Negroes, and we're mostly separate in the encampment, but…" I visualized the manner in which the job was done. "We work together, as a team. We have a common goal. Matter of fact, we have more in common…" I paused, as I endeavored to put my finger on it. "Maybe I can best describe it this way. It's like a subtraction problem, where that which unites us, the minuend—"

"I thought a minuet was a dance."

"Not minuet…minuend. It's the number from which one is subtracting another number, termed the subtrahend. Anyway, the way I see it, the minuend, that which unites us, is growing, while the subtrahend, that which divides us, bigotry, is decreasing." The glaze coating Walter's eyes communicated that my analogy had provided anything but clarification. For that matter, subtraction involving both a variable minuend and subtrahend was an inapt, indeed dreadful, analogy. An equation expressing unity as a function of prejudice would have been better. Its first derivative would be negative, and the second…I burst into laughter.

"You laughin' at me?"

"Gosh, no. I was laughing at myself." I eyed the anhinga that continued to bask. Unlike the graceful bird, I was no longer in the sunshine. My brain had gotten worthlessly mired in the giant swamp grass that grew not far from where the graceful bird stood. "Ignore my ridiculous example. Instead, let me leave it this way. Relations at the lighthouse have improved. Unity has increased, and bigotry is down. That's not to suggest it's all good, that everything is copasetic. It's far from that, but bottom line, it's much better than it was."

"I got another question," said Walter, "though I think you've answered it already."

"What's that?"

"Since you're gettin' to like your construction work more, any chance you might stick with it?"

"What do you think?"

"You'd rather be doin' mathematics and stuff."

"You got that right!"

"Much as I hate to, I gotta concede that you're makin' the right decision. Workin' with your brain beats workin' with your hands. Havin' spent my life doin' the latter, I oughta know. I ain't complainin', but given my druthers, I would have gotten an education, been a doctor or engineer. And for that matter, if I had my druthers, you'd just stay here and keep me company. And before you get shook up, relax. I want you to pursue your dreams. Wouldn't want my own son, if Wilma and me had one, to stay here, rather than makin' somethin' of hisself."

Walter's words were gratifying. The time for me to leave would inevitably come, and knowing it would be with his blessing was itself a blessing. But his words also underscored how much he valued my company, which had become more important with the sudden departure of his newest tenant. The maintenance man, the loner whom I had barely gotten to know, had taken up full-time residence at the Magnolia Hotel where he worked.

I glanced at Walter but avoided eye contact. He had been very good to me. The observation prompted me to take stock. I had faced my share of misfortune, losing both my mother and father before adolescence. But in that aftermath, at each stage, I had been lucky. Someone—Grover, Mr. Wright, Walter—had stepped in to help me through the ensuing years of my youth. They had also sheltered me from much of the bigotry and disadvantage that most people of color faced. As an adult I needed to do for others as my benefactors had done for me. When the time came to consider moving on, the mathematical inequality evaluating the pros and cons had to include the effect on Walter. Would it be the end-all? Absolutely not. But it would count.

Chapter XVI

REPUBLICAN PRESIDENT ULYSSES S. GRANT had just won a second term defeating Horace Greely, editor of the "New York Tribune." Greeley had run under the standard of the Democratic/Liberal Republican party,[227] the latter largely consisting of Republicans who had grown disenchanted with the policies of their former affiliation. With so many southerners excluded from politics owing to their involvement in the Confederacy, carpetbaggers from the North suffused the South, seizing the chance to make a quick buck, not necessarily an honest one. St. Augustine was not immune to the influx. Growing tourism, a plus to the economy, also escalated St. Augustine's numbers.

Thanksgiving, 1872, was but a week away. I had begun to worry that Mr. Wright might never respond to my request for a recommendation. The concern inveigled me to rethink my plans to attend college, not that I was abandoning them. Construction of the lighthouse, a three-year project, was into the second half. As my satisfaction with the job increased, so too did the appeal of staying until its anticipated completion in 1874. The ability to save additional funds added another reason for delay. Just when I had seemingly decided to wait, a letter from Mr. Wright arrived. It read:

> October 30, 1872
>
> Dear Mican,
>
> Please accept my apologies for the delay in responding to your request for a recommendation. At the end of June, only days before your letter arrived, our

[227] *Reconstruction Timeline*, op. cit. See also, *Election of 1872*, u-s-history.com, 5 Feb. 2018 <http://www.u-s-history.com/pages/h215.html> indicating that "Grant won an overwhelming victory." Greeley died before the electoral college votes were counted. When they were, "only three remained loyal to the deceased candidate."

family went on a two-month camping and hiking trip throughout New England. It was something we have wanted to do for some time, and this was likely our last opportunity. Michael graduated Kimball a year early and began his studies at Amherst College in September.

When we returned home from our trip—it eclipsed expectations—I was behind in my work, which now includes administrative duties, in addition to teaching. This past weekend, I finally managed to write your recommendation, which, together with a carbonated copy, is enclosed.

We were happy to learn that you are doing well and plan to attend college. Everyone here is fine. Nora is in high school and earning high marks. Mrs. Wright, Michael and Nora all send their best.

With highest and warmest regards.

Sincerely,
Charles Wright

I flipped to the recommendation and read:

October 30, 1872

To whom it may concern:

It is with great pleasure that I recommend Mican Reinbow for admission to college. Mican was my student at the First African Baptist Church school in Savannah, Georgia from 1865 to 1869. During that time he lived with our family and tutored our two children. Accordingly, I know him not only as a pupil, but also as a person of utmost character. We were proud to consider him part of our family.

Mican is extremely bright, curious and dedicated. Though his formal education did not commence until he was orphaned at age twelve, by the time his studies under my tutelage ceased at age seventeen, he was well ahead of most of his classmates, particularly in mathematics and science. In mathematics he surpassed the area I could teach (algebra, geometry, and trigonometry) and was studying on his own. Before I left Savannah, I gave him a calculus book. I understand he has been teaching himself that discipline. Neither as a student at Dartmouth College, where I earned my degree, or in my years of teaching have I observed a finer mathematical mind.

Mican is an extraordinary student who is capable of great things. He is modest, kind and generous and would be an asset to any college class. I wholeheartedly recommend him without any reservations whatsoever.

Should you desire further information, please feel free to contact me.

Sincerely,
Charles T. Wright
Instructor and Administrator
Kimball Union Academy
Meriden, New Hampshire

Gratification of the nth degree engulfed me. The stunning approbation was hard to fathom. Over my twenty-one years, I had received compliments, but never, ever had I been described in such glowing terms. I placed the letter and recommendation back into the envelope from which they had come and walked outside. Correction: I floated out the door, down to the banks of the Maria Sanchez, where I seated myself, my back against the trunk of a sprawling weeping willow. I drew the recommendation out of the envelope and read it again. I basked in euphoria. It was incomparable…almost. Objectivity forced me to concede that my two kisses with Abbey, their immediate aftermath, ranked higher. The concession, however, did nothing to diminish my rapture.

I drew in a deep breath, absorbing the delightful fragrance of the sublime riverside. I gazed skyward where the profile of a broad-winged bird, perhaps an eagle, hawk or osprey, gracefully circled above. Far beyond in the vast infinity of the Heavens, a white billowy mass floated aimlessly. I followed its drift as it gradually transformed into a nebulous soul of eternity. The flow of the creek as it silently meandered through the tranquil estuary draped me in its peaceful veil. The idyllic setting exceeded its normal magnificence. It was paradise personified…perfect. That my state of mind prejudiced my perspective did not escape me. But it also failed to diminish my euphoria. For the ensuing hour, I luxuriated. I read Mr. Wright's recommendation twice more, but mostly I recounted the good times and kindnesses the wonderful family had shown me. The date on Mr. Wright's letter and recommendation, so close to my "October 29th birthday," triggered fond images of the surprise party they had staged.

Finally, my brain shifted into a more typical gear. A question came to mind. Should I reconsider my plans to delay college until after the lighthouse was completed? Armed with Mr. Wright's recommendation, might it be the time to pursue my higher education? The idea was enticing. But I wanted to see the lighthouse to consummation. It had become a part of me, a tribute to those of us who were raising it from the depths of Anastasia's sands to ever loftier heights. For the moment, my decision was made. I would stay. But like Anastasia's coquina that served as the tower's base, it was porous, full of holes. I liked it that way. I had my course of action. Down the road, if I changed my mind…so be it.

I closed my eyes, blissfully contemplating the thank you note I would pen to Mr. Wright. My mental draftsmanship had barely begun before I nodded off.

***

As 1872 passed into 1873, and the months of the latter slipped by, construction of the lighthouse rolled on. Originally a mélange of workers with disparate backgrounds, little of which involved the likes of a lighthouse, our team had grown increasingly efficient. A common goal, once a distant image, visible only on the paper plans of an architect, had risen high above the island's sands. The time that had elapsed since the project had begun dwarfed that which remained until the august beacon reigned over the ocean below.

Across the South, portents of the future were mixed. The Ku Klux Klan Act, enacted by Congress in 1871, was contributing to what was fast becoming the Klan's demise.[228] But the Freedman's Bureau, established in 1865 to help freedmen get food, clothing, health care and jobs, among other things, had been "effectively shut down" in 1872, when Congress had refused to renew its authorization.[229] At the ballot box, results varied as well. The 43rd Congress, which began its session in March 1873, included seven Negroes, two more than the 42nd

---

[228] *Ku Klux Klan,* Wikipedia, op. cit. *See also*, *Ku Klux Klan Act*, legal-dictionary.thefreedictionary, 6 Feb. 2018 <https://legal-dictionary.thefreedictionary.com/Ku+Klux+Klan+Act> indicating that the criminal penalties of the Ku Klux Klan Act [42 U.S.C.A. §1985(3)] were subsequently declared unconstitutional by the United States Supreme Court in *United States v. Harris*, 106 U.S. 629 (1883) "on the ground that protecting individuals from private conspiracies was a state and not federal function."

[229] *Freedmen's Bureau*, Wikipedia, 6 Feb. 2018 <https://en.wikipedia.org/wiki/Freedmen%27s_Bureau>.

Congress and four more than the 41st.[230] But 1873 also saw Texas elect a redeemer government, candidates who supported a return to white supremacy.[231] St. Augustine was not exempt from the divided outcomes that pervaded the South. The local Ladies Memorial Association, motivated by a "sacred objective," sought to construct a monument to the "Confederate Dead" on the Plaza de la Constitución. The military governor, Colonel Sprague, banned the monument from public property.[232] Not to be denied, in 1872, the southern traditionalists erected their monument on St. George Street between Bridge and Francis.[233]

Christmas, 1873, one of our rare paid holidays, fell on a Thursday. Almost never did I take a day off from work, not that my coworkers did either. But unlike them, I had been saving most of what I had earned. Apart from food, I had few expenses. Many of my coworkers had families and struggled to make ends meet. Those who were single generally blew their pay on wild Saturday nights filled with women, booze and gambling. I, on the other hand, deposited my money at the bank where I enjoyed a small but steady return. Christmas time, I took my first vacation since I had begun work on the lighthouse. A work-free Friday and Saturday, at my own expense, yielded a welcome four-day weekend, what by my standards was hedonistic. I fished with Walter in the Maria Sanchez Creek, where we bagged two catfish and a bass. Twice I slept in past eleven. Not once did I pick up a book. For hours Walter and I rocked on his porch. And on Sunday I accompanied him to the cathedral for services. Once they concluded, we stepped outside into what was a chilly St. Augustine day. A stiff breeze made it feel colder than the temperature, little more than fifty. We were about to start down St. George Street when Herman Slack came rushing over.

"I'm glad I caught you fellows."

"Good Sabbath," said Walter. "Hope you had a good Christmas."

---

[230] *Black-American Representatives and Senators by Congress, 1870-Present*, historyhouse.gov, 25 Mar. 2020 <https://historyhouse.gov/Exhibitions-and-Publications/BAIC/Historical-Data/Black-American-Representatives-and-Senators-by-Congress/>.

[231] *Reconstruction Timeline*, op. cit.

[232] *The St. Augustine Confederate Memorial*, drbronsontours.com, 11 Feb. 2018 <drbronsontours.com/bronsonconfederatememorial.html>. In 1879, after Reconstruction had ended, a larger monument, a 25-foot-tall obelisk, was erected on the Plaza, replacing the original. Two marble plaques from the original were placed on the 1879 monument. Despite demands for its removal, the obelisk continues into the 21st century. (*See*, footnote 60, supra.)

[233] *Confederate Monument - St. Augustine | American Civil War Forums*, civilwartalk.com, 20 Jan. 2018 <https://www.civilwartalk.com/threads/confederate-monument-st-augustine.112296/>.

"I did, thanks." Herman turned to me. "I saw you during services. Glad you're here."

My immediate thought was that Herman wanted to reengage me as a volunteer at the Cordova Street School. They were always short on teachers.

"We've been tracking colleges in the South," said Herman, "looking for those that might open their doors to our best. This week we got word that the University of South Carolina, what used to be South Carolina College before the war, accepted its first Negro student."[234]

"Holy—" I clipped my tongue before voicing the expletive, one of many that had become prevalent in my lighthouse vocabulary. Not only was it the Sabbath, but the possibility the Priest, among others, might be within earshot, forbid the utterance.

"As best I know, they're the first public college in the South to do so."[235] Herman eyed me. "Don't mean to be nosey, and feel free to tell me to mind my own business, but...whad'ya think...I mean about the University of South Carolina...You interested?"

"Definitely." My brain was already in high gear. With a little luck, the lighthouse might be completed by the end of the upcoming summer. There was still time for me to apply for the 1874 fall term.

"Does that mean you're thinking about applying?"

"It's a possibility." The measured response minimized my expectations. I was all but certain I would apply. "I greatly appreciate the information."

"My pleasure. And by the way, I hear the University has a beautiful campus. Sam Garner—doubt you know him—spoke with a fellow who saw it. Said it was the nicest he'd ever seen." Herman turned to Walter. "Sorry to rain on your parade."

"Pardon me?" said Walter.

"Well, I'm sure you'd prefer that Mican stay right where he is. And for that matter, I can't say I blame you. We'd be real happy to have him back at the school volunteering."

---

[234] *1873 – 1877: The End of Reconstruction | OMSA*, sa.sc.edu, 14 Sept. 2018 <https://www.sa.sc.edu/omsa/1873-1877-the-end-of-reconstruction> stating: "On October 7th, 1873, Henry E, Hayne, the black Republican Secretary of State of South Carolina, registered as a student in the Medical Department of the University. His enrollment marks the first official matriculation of an African American student in the University of South Carolina."

[235] *University of South Carolina Reconstruction Records*, sc.edu, 14 Sept. 2018 <http://library.sc.edu/digital/collections/reconstruct.html> stating: "In 1873, the University of South Carolina became the only state-supported Southern University to fully integrate during the Reconstruction Era that followed the Civil War."

As much as I appreciated the compliment, guilt overshadowed positive feelings. Numerous times it had crossed my mind that I should make time to again help at Cordova. I doubted it would happen. Work around Walter's place, along with studying, took precedence. And too, I wanted to preserve a few hours for self-indulgence.

Herman glanced over his shoulder. "I better get to the wife. One more minute, and I expect she'll be calling. If only she'd come over and tap me on the shoulder. Unfortunately, she prefers to yell." He shook his head and muttered, "God, it's embarrassing, especially when folks mimic her…*Herman, someone's calling you*…or some such thing."

"Let Flora know how you feel," said Walter. "I'm sure she'll handle it differently."

"Oh, really?" Herman's snarl could have sliced a beefsteak tomato with a single stroke. "Just so happens, I tried that years ago. You know what it got me?"

The pause that punctuated Herman's question offered Walter the chance to hazard a guess. The tone, however, dared him to do so.

"Flora became indignant. Said a man so touchy that his wife couldn't call his name could make his own dinner and sleep—"

"Herman!" Flora's familiarly shrill voice turned countless heads, not the least of which was Herman's.

"Damn! See what you guys have done, delaying me." He raced to his wife.

Along with Walter, I laughed. Herman may not have been clairvoyant, but he had accurately predicted the taunts his wife's call would evoke.

Walter pointed north in the direction of the City Gate. "You wanna get a fish and chips? Ain't had one in months."

"You're on," I said, "provided I buy."

Walter, ever generous, stiffened.

"C'mon, for a change, humor me."

He sighed. "You've twisted my arm."

"Well, at least I didn't kick your bum knee."

We headed up St. George Street to our favorite stand, just inside the City Gates, where we got our meals, each in a paper bag. With the inordinately chilly weather, we passed up the opportunity to dine on the nearby ground. Instead, we turned south toward Walter's Victorian. But roused appetites, further stimulated by the enticing aroma of fried fish and crispy potatoes, refused to postpone our gastronomical pleasure. We dug into our bags as we walked. By the time we arrived home, our meals were nearly gone. My bag contained only a few remaining chips. I nibbled them slowly, trying to make them last. As I did, my mind shifted to another task. No sooner had I finished my final swallow than I hurried up the stairs to my room. I began writing an application letter, detailing my life history, especially my educational background. Critical though my letter was, it was also self-serving. More important was the enclosure, Mr. Wright's recommendation.

***

The 1st of February 1874. High above the surface of Anastasia Island, at the top of the St. Augustine lighthouse, another day's work had just ended. Exterior work, including painting, along with interior tasks remained, but the bulk of the lighthouse was constructed. One hundred sixty-five feet tall, it towered over the expanse. Before climbing down from my lofty perch, I surveyed the panorama in every direction, traversing the circular, iron-railed platform that protruded just below the acme, the place that would ultimately house the Fresnel lens. To the north, looking right to left, I eyed the coast of Florida; the margin of the great Atlantic; Vilano Beach, the reputed home to pirates and marauders;[236] and the Tolomato River. Moving counterclockwise around the platform, I gazed west at the City of St. Augustine, where at its north end, stood the massive Fort Marion, dating back to the 15th century, when the Spanish had constructed the original rendition, Castillo de San Marcos.[237] From my vantage point, about a mile from the fort, its strategic advantage as sentry to the entrance of Matanzas Bay and the sea's access to St. Augustine, was evident. My distance from the fort allowed the walls to belie their unique character. Seeming bastions of dense stone, the barriers of porous coquina hid the many cannonballs they had swallowed.[238] Unlike typical stone walls that shattered under

[236] *St. Augustine Vilano Beach Basis*, vacationrentalpros.com, 10 Feb. 2018 <https://www.vacationrentalpros.com/St-Augustine-Vilano-Beach-Basics/> stating: "Vilano, 'villain' in Spanish, may have once have been an area known for pirates, marauders and ship-wreckers. So goes the rumor of its name. Its reputation changed toward the end of the 19th century…"

[237] *Castillo de San Marcos | Visit St. Augustine*, visitstaugustine.com, 11 Feb. 2018 <https://www.visitstaugustine.com/thing-to-do/castillo-de-san-marcos> stating of Fort Marion: "The fort was officially taken off the list of fortifications in 1900 and it was preserved and recognized as a National Monument in 1924. Congress renamed the fort in 1942, reverting to the Spanish name, the Castillo de San Marcos."

[238] *Buildings and building stone: Castillo de San Marcos, St. Augustine, FL*, op. cit., stating: "Given its light and porous nature, coquina would seem to be a lousy building material for a fort. The Spanish probably used it solely because it was the only material resembling stone on Florida's sandy coast. However, coquina's porosity turned out to make it an ideal material for the walls of the fort. Cannon balls failed to shatter the

the assault of cannons, coquina absorbed the onslaught. The heavy iron projectiles embedded themselves in the walls, leaving the latter intact. I continued counterclockwise around the platform, moving my gaze south along the sea wall that protected the city. I peered down Anastasia's backbone, where vegetation, mostly diminutive, decorated the largely primeval landscape. Another ninety degrees around the platform brought me to my final stop. Beyond the shore of Anastasia, lay the endless expanse of the Atlantic. I drew in a deep breath of the pristine salt air. I closed my eyes, envisioning scores of blissful sunbathers who, with St. Augustine's burgeoning tourism industry, would one day dot Anastasia's eastern sands. The benevolent breeze slithered through my long jet-black locks. Earth, so far below, seemed remote, as if I had ventured into the uncharted world of endless space. For more than a minute, I remained motionless, sojourning through the farthest reaches of the universe. Out of the solar system, past stars and endless galaxies, amidst the uniqueness of my mind, I traveled where no man had gone.

I opened my eyes and beheld the indomitable Atlantic. A hundred times farther than I could see and much more, the waters continued. I focused on the most distant visible point, where sky and sea kissed. I envisioned the curvature of the Earth, my line of sight tangent to the surface at that point. How far away was it? With the several years I had spent working on the lighthouse, I wanted to know. I wanted to be able to tell others.

I descended from my perch to the ground. I went directly to the encampment. Dinner would have to wait. I got a pen and paper and seated myself. I drew a large circle, the Earth. I drew a radius to the top of the circle, marking it with a length of 4000 miles, half the approximate diameter of the planet. I extended the radius with a tiny line segment, representing the 165-foot-tall lighthouse. I drew a line segment from the top of the lighthouse, so it was tangent to the circle. I added another radius, one which ran to the point of tangency. Using the principle that a radius and a tangent to a circle form a right angle at the point of tangency, I had a right triangle. The hypotenuse was 4000 + 165/5280 (the height of the lighthouse in miles). The longer of the two legs was 4000 miles. The shorter, the one I wanted to know, how far I could see from the top of the lighthouse, remained to be determined. Lacking trigonometric tables, I had to depend on the Pythagorean Theorem: $a^2 + b^2 = c^2$. The method engendered arithmetic inconvenience, but the mathematics was much easier than what I had tackled in recent years. I converted the

---

coquina and instead were absorbed into the rock, much as jabbing a tool into styrofoam results in holes but not in breakage of the styrofoam..."

fraction, 165/5280 to a decimal: .03125 miles. I plugged my numbers into the Pythagorean Theorem.

$$(4000)^2 + b^2 = (4000.01325)^2$$

$$b^2 \cong 16000250 - 16000000$$

$$b^2 \cong 250$$

$$b \cong 15.81 \text{ miles}$$

With my measure of the Earth's radius only an approximation and my eye level not exactly 165 feet (my eye level was a few feet below the peak of the lighthouse, but the structure's base was several feet above sea level), I realized my computation was imprecise. But that was fine. I had an answer. It was roughly sixteen miles to the furthest water I could see from the top of the lighthouse. It crossed my mind that I could see a ship from its top down to the water level at that distance; but the distance before the top of its mast would disappear would be far greater and depend on the height of the ship. Of course, such a sighting would require the clearest of days, especially with a tall ship.

***

For the second time in three months, I was taking time off from my job at the lighthouse. It would be a full week. I would be traveling further north than ever before, all the way to Columbia, South Carolina, over four hundred miles. Though the distance from St. Augustine to Columbia was roughly three hundred miles for the proverbial crow, unfortunately that straight shot was problematic. Despite proposals for a rail route north from St. Augustine, nothing had materialized. Compounding the difficulty, there were no convenient connections from Savannah, roughly the midway point, to Columbia. Rail lines or river waterways connecting the two cities were non-existent. The most convenient way to get from Savannah to Columbia was a steamboat to Charleston, followed by a train to Columbia.

The obvious question: Why was I making the trip? The University of South Carolina had invited me for an interview. Mr. Wright's recommendation had impressed them, but because I had been away from school for roughly five years and was not from South Carolina, they would not consider me without an interview. Whether to go was an easy decision. Forgoing the chance for a college education at the magnificent campus—I had seen a sketch—was unthinkable. To do so would have spawned interminable regrets. Though concerns about the treatment of persons of color at the formerly all-white institution were undeniable, I was ecstatic about the potential opportunity.

Cost of the trip was never an issue. Over the past five years, with minimal expenses, I had saved an average of six dollars per week. My time at the lighthouse, with a weekly pay of seventeen dollars, had skewed the average upward. Coupled with the money Grover had left me, I had accumulated over fifteen hundred dollars. The price of the round trip, roughly thirty dollars, was no burden. The University's invitation for an interview included free room and board for a two-night stay.

Saturday afternoon, following work, I boarded the St. John's Railway, the only train service from St. Augustine. Travel on the fifteen-mile track running west to Toico Landing on the St. John's River[239] took the better part of an hour. Damaged by Union gunboats in the War of Secession, the short track had reopened in the late 1860s,[240] but poor maintenance rendered it considerably slower than most rail services. From Toico Point, I boarded the St. Matthews, a finely appointed packet steamer, which transported me to Savannah, and then, following transfer on the daily line, to Charleston.[241] From there I boarded the South Carolina Railroad on its route west to Hendersonville and then north to Columbia.[242] While the actual travel time on board trains and steamers was about twenty-four hours, getting from stations to port and visa-versa, along with layovers, turned the trip into two full days.

I reached the University of South Carolina well after dark, too late to see the campus or the surrounding area. I was taken to Legare College, an addition to the Pinckney College building. The original structure had been named for Charles Pinckney, a Revolutionary War General and member of the school's first Board of Trustees.[243] Weary from the journey, I went to sleep soon after arriving. With an important endeavor awaiting me the next day, a good night's rest was imperative.

The letter inviting me for an interview indicated my application and recommendation appeared impressive, but admittance would require confirmation of my academic potential. The University's admissions' staff wanted me to meet with professors in multiple disciplines.

---

[239] *Saint Johns Railroad Collection | Florida Historical Society,* myfloridahistory.org., 20 Mar. 2018 <https://myfloridahistory.org/collections/manuscripts/saintjohns_railroad>.
[240] Ibid.
[241] *St. John's River*, drbronsontours.com, 20 Mar. 2018 <http://www.drbronsontours.com/bronsonstjohnriver.html> (*See*, footnote 60, supra.)
[242] *South Carolina Railroad*, Wikipedia, 20 Mar. 2018 <https://en.wikipedia.org/wiki/South_Carolina_Railroad>.
[243] *History of the Horseshoe,* sc.edu, 14 Sept. 2018 <sc.edu/about/our_history/horseshoe_history/index.php>.

Monday morning, I was up early. I donned my Sunday, go-to-church suit. Following an excellent breakfast of eggs, sausage, grits and orange juice, Johnnie Grant, a Caucasian sophomore, escorted me from Legare for my first meeting. The instant we stepped outside into the beautiful March sunshine, my jaw dropped. The sketch I had seen had failed to do justice to the stunning horseshoe-shaped campus.[244] Structures, some of brick, some draped with ivy, and others with tall columns, resembling the Parthenon, wrapped around a bucolic center. In a matter of seconds, I had fallen in love with the University of South Carolina. It was where I wanted to be.

"Majestic, isn't it?" said Johnnie.

"That's an understatement."

Johnnie guided me along the inner edge of one leg of the Horseshoe. "The campus has lots of history, not all of which makes me proud." He gestured in all directions. "These buildings were built by slaves. Prior to the war, both faculty and students brought their slaves to the campus. The slaves cleaned the rooms. Antebellum presidents and faculty were among the nation's strongest supporters of slavery. Fortunately, we're in a new chapter. We're in the forefront of change, an integrated campus."[245]

Uneasy as I had been as to how persons of color were treated on the campus, Johnnie's remarks were a welcome beginning. Time would reveal if others would be as hospitable.

We had gone about one hundred yards when Johnnie pointed up ahead on our right. "That building, Rutledge, is where I'm taking you. It's the oldest and, perhaps, most storied building on campus. It was completed in 1805. We refer to it as *South Building*, *Old South* or just *South*.[246] It's named for two brothers, John and Edward Rutledge, both

---

[244] Ibid. The Horseshoe, the heart of the University of South Carolina campus, still exists. Some of its buildings date back to the first decade of the 19th century.

[245] *Slavery at South Carolina College, 1801-1865,* 2 Mar. 2018 <https://delphi.tcl.sc.edu/library/digital/slaveryscc/index.html> stating: "The primary buildings of South Carolina College survive as the historic heart of the modern campus—known today as the Horseshoe—and were constructed by slave labor and built of slave-made brick…Slaves were essential to the daily operations of the antebellum institution…Whether they were owned outright by the faculty or college itself, or hired from private parties, slaves maintained campus buildings, cleaned student tenements and faculty duplexes, and prepared meals at the student dining commons, faculty residences, and the president's house…Slavery also shaped the contours of the intellectual and political world at South Carolina College. Presidents and faculty members became some of the nation's most ardent defenders of slavery, even as a handful emerged to oppose the institution."

[246] *Slavery at South Carolina College, 1801 – 1865*, 25 Mar. 2020 <https://delphi.tcl.sc.edu/library/digital/slaveryscc/rutledge-college-1805.html>.

of whom served as governor of South Carolina, among other public offices. Edward was the youngest signer of the Declaration of Independence.[247] During the War of Secession, when the college was closed, the building was used as a hospital. These days it's being used, among other things, to train Negro teachers."[248]

I eyed the impressive, three-story, symmetric structure, which I estimated over one hundred feet in width. With sections set back on either side of a taller center section, it bore a small triangular pediment over the main entrance and a much larger pediment spanning the roof of the entire center section. Atop the building was a tall cupola.

Johnnie pointed across the way at the opposite leg of the Horseshoe. "That three-story building with the flat façade and shutters is where I live. It's a decent place. You'll see more of it later, but for now, let's get you to your first destination." He guided me to a first-floor Rutledge classroom, where he delivered me to Professor Jackson, an English professor.

The lanky, bespectacled gentleman, attired in a three-piece suit, went directly to substance, wasting little time on niceties. After shaking my hand, Professor Jackson said, "I read your application letter and the recommendation of Mr. Wright. Please tell me about yourself."

"What exactly would you like to know?"

"Your life history. And I'm aware that you summarized it in your letter, but I want to hear you speak of it."

I felt as if I had walked into a courtroom and been called to the witness stand. Only an oath was missing. The formality unnerved me. I took a deep breath before beginning my narration. Step by step, I related my background: my childhood in the woods and swamps of Florida's Everglades; my father's death; my time at Fort Myers and the start of my education; the several years I had spent in Savannah under Mr. Wright's tutelage; and my time in St. Augustine. I repeatedly mentioned my independent study. My chronicle took the best part of fifteen minutes, during which Professor Jackson rarely interrupted and, even then, with only the briefest of comments or questions.

When I finished, Professor Jackson said, "You've had an interesting life thus far."

His choice of the word, "interesting," echoed in my head. Like unripe fruit, was the bland comment a euphemism veiling an opinion that I was ill-prepared for the university?

---

[247] *History of the Horseshoe*, op. cit.

[248] Ibid.

He handed me a pen and paper. "I'd like you to write a brief essay, about two hundred words, why you believe your admission to the University of South Carolina will benefit both you and the school. You will have twenty-five minutes."

Mentally I had prepared myself for the possibility I might be tested, not that I could anticipate the questions or problems that might be selected from a myriad of disciplines. Explaining how admission would benefit me, turn me into a mathematician, scientist or, perhaps, a teacher, was manageable. The words flowed with reasonable efficiency. The second aspect, how my admission would benefit the university, produced a blank. I did a quick count of the words I had already written, roughly 140. I was thankful I was limited to a few more sentences. Unfortunately, nothing came to mind. Suggesting that I hoped to accomplish great things that would bring prestige to the university would be the height of arrogance, and, worse yet, Professor Jackson would not buy it. For that matter, nor would I. A glance at the large round wall clock indicated I had less than six minutes remaining. My hopes of attending the University of South Carolina were rapidly ticking away.

I rubbed the palm and fingers of my sweaty left hand on my pant leg. I grabbed my pen and dipped it into my desk's inkwell. I tried to write. My hand balked. My brain delivered nary a thought. My heart raced. I stole a peak at Professor Jackson. Our eyes met for only a fraction of a second before I looked away. Presumably he had been watching me, observing and judging my idle ineptitude. I peaked at the clock. The second hand raced with seemingly deviant alacrity. I had three minutes left. *Write!...Write something!* I silently screamed at myself. I eyed my frozen left hand, the one holding the pen. The hue of my skin sparked an idea. Good, bad or otherwise, I had to go with it. I wrote: "The University of South Carolina has ventured down a courageous road, becoming the South's first public institution of higher learning to admit Negroes. I would welcome the opportunity to participate in this noble experiment, one with the potential to knock down racial barriers and foster greater unity for the benefit of all society. I am eager to learn. I am prepared to work hard."

I started to proofread what I had written. I made it to the second sentence when Professor Jackson, his voice resolute, declared: "Pen down." He immediately came to my desk and took my paper. He eyed it for a second, perhaps to see if it was blank or legible or...whatever.

"I think that about does it for me," he said. Professor Jackson led me from the room into the hall where Johnnie, who was waiting, guided me up to the second floor.

"You'll be meeting with Professor Hopkins. Not to frighten you, but he's eccentric. He teaches math. I had him last year. No sense of humor…and tougher than buffalo hide when it comes to grades."

Johnnie's avowed intent may not have been to scare me, but he had made me even more nervous than I already was. Fresh from what, at best, had been an ambiguous reaction from Professor Jackson, I was terrified that my next stage would be in front of a crueler audience. We arrived at a classroom, the door of which was closed. Johnnie knocked.

"Come in," a croaky voice responded.

I followed Johnnie inside.

"What can I do for you? Make it quick."

I was thankful Johnnie was ahead of me and the one being addressed. Unfortunately, my turn before the stubby man with round face and wire-rimmed glasses, seated at the large desk, would come quickly.

Johnnie gestured my way. "I've brought Mican Reinbow here for his interview."

Professor Hopkins lurched forward. "Interview?"

"Uh…yes, Sir," said Johnnie.

Professor Hopkins reached to the corner of his desk for a black log. He eyed it, grumbling inaudibly before turning back toward Johnnie and me. After directing Johnnie to leave, he said, "I've got a meeting (he glanced at his watch)…in seventeen minutes and thirty seconds…Well, we can make this quick." He pointed at the front row, a desk directly in front of his. "Sit."

I was halfway into my chair when Professor Hopkins said, "Where have you been doing your studies?"

"On my own. I've been working on the construction—"

"Oh, you're the one who's been building houses." The bald, bespectacled, round-shouldered man, bearing a protruding midsection, turned his mouth down.

"I was building homes, but the past three years I've been employed at the lighthouse in—"

"Houses, lighthouses…they're all the same, work with your hands, not your brain."

I swallowed hard. Compared to this, my experience with Professor Jackson had been a leisurely Caloosahatchee cruise in my childhood dugout. Professor Hopkins was turning my dream of attending the University of South Carolina into an ill-fated voyage across the roiling waters of a tempest-plagued ocean.

"How long have you been doing this…*construction*?"

"About five years. Since 1869. But before that I was in school in Savannah at the First African Baptist Church. I took algebra, geometry, trigonometry and after—"

"We don't have much time. Unfortunately, you did, during which you probably forgot much of what you learned at the church." He cleared his raspy throat. "If I recall from your application, you claim you've been studying on your own, learning calculus." His sardonic tone suggested that he gave little credit, let alone credence, to my efforts.

"Yes, Sir, though I still have a lot to learn." The last thing I wanted was to create excessive expectations.

"Well, let's see what you know. And given our time constraints, maybe we can hit algebra, a little geometry and calculus all at once." Professor Hopkins got up from his seat and gazed blankly into space. After a seeming eternity, probably no more than fifteen seconds, he wrote on the blackboard: "A projectile is shot into the air at an angle. Its path is described by a function $y = 4x - x^2$, where x is the distance from where it was launched over flat ground and y is its altitude." Professor Hopkins turned to me. "What is the path of the projectile?"

"A parabola, Sir. Like a camel's hump."

"Perhaps you arrived at your answer because that's how projectiles generally fly?"

"That too, but mainly because of the equation. It was in the form $y = ax^2 + bx + c$, where $a = -1$, $b = 4$, and $c = 0$."

"So, it is...From its starting point, at $x = 0$, how far would the projectile travel along the x-axis before striking the ground?"

The question, an easy one, merely required me to find the other point where $y = 0$; that is, when $4x - x^2 = 0$..."When $x = 4$, Sir."

"Okay. Now let's put some sophistication into this problem. "How would you find the maximum height of the projectile? And explain your reasoning."

"I would take the first derivative of the function, set it equal to zero and solve. As for the *why*, it's because the derivative, dy/dx, is the slope, and at the maximum height—what one might call the top of the camel's hump—the slope is zero. At that point, there is no change in y."

A sound, a cross between a snort and the word "hmm" emerged from between Professor Hopkins' lips. Interpreting its meaning was impossible. I stood mute.

"Okay. Take the derivative and find the maximum point. Of course, any dimwit can do that, given such a simple equation. What I want to know is whether you understand the theory behind a derivative. Kindly go to the blackboard, and take the derivative...**from definition**." Professor Hopkins began stuffing papers into his briefcase.

The action disrupted my slowly mitigating discomfort. I suspected he was anxious to rid himself of me and get to his meeting. I hurried to the board. I grabbed a piece of chalk and took two deep breaths. I began my work by writing the definition of a derivative on the blackboard and continued from there, applying the definition to the given equation.

$$\frac{dy}{dx} = \lim_{\Delta x \to 0} \frac{f(x + \Delta x) - f(x)}{\Delta x}$$

$$\frac{dy}{dx} = \lim_{\Delta x \to 0} \frac{4(x + \Delta x) - (x + \Delta x)^2 - (4x - x^2)}{\Delta x}$$

$$\frac{dy}{dx} = \lim_{\Delta x \to 0} \frac{4x + 4\Delta x - x^2 - 2x\Delta x - (\Delta x)^2 - 4x + x^2}{\Delta x}$$

$$\frac{dy}{dx} = \lim_{\Delta x \to 0} \frac{4\Delta x - 2x\Delta x - (\Delta x)^2}{\Delta x}$$

$$\frac{dy}{dx} = \lim_{\Delta x \to 0} 4 - 2x - \Delta x$$

$$\frac{dy}{dx} = 4 - 2x = 0 \; (at\ the\ maximum\ point)$$

$$2x = 4$$

$$x = 2$$

Since y = 4x - x^2, for x = 2, the value of y = 4.

The maximum point for the projectile is (x,y) = (2,4)

I turned away from the blackboard. Professor Hopkins, his briefcase in hand, was almost to the door.

"How would you find the area under the curve above the x-axis between $x = 0$ and $x = 4$?"

"I'd take the integral from 0 to 4 of the binomial $4x - x^2$ with respect to x."

"I'm due at my meeting." Professor Hopkins charged out the door, leaving me standing alone in his classroom.

I looked around the deserted room. I gazed at the open door. Was Professor Hopkins done with me? Should I wait for his return? Would Johnnie come for me? Would he tell me what to do or where to go? Or should I simply leave? I walked to the door and looked up and down the quiet hallway. I stepped outside the room and waited. Several minutes passed. I poked my head back into the doorway and checked the clock. I decided to wait ten more minutes. I gazed at the desk where Professor Hopkins had sat. The word *curmudgeon* popped into my head. In lieu of a definition, Webster should put Professor Hopkins' photograph next to the word. Time continued to tick. No one came…Ten minutes elapsed. I gave it two more and left. I went down the staircase to the building's main entrance. Outside there were individuals milling around, walking here and there. Where should I go? What should I do? Was I supposed to meet with another professor? I looked back over my shoulder, considering whether to return to Professor Hopkins' classroom. I rejected the idea. I contemplated a return to Legare where I would again be staying at night. Perhaps someone there could tell me what to do. Amidst my discombobulated self-debate, I spotted Johnnie approaching Rutledge. I waved, getting his attention.

"Done already?"

I nodded.

"I was on my way to get you. Matter of fact, I assumed I'd have to wait. Professor Hopkins is usually longwinded. Goes off on tangents—no pun intended—all the time. Talks about the weirdest things…how fishing and mathematics are interrelated; the link between fried eggs and mathematics; the…He ties everything to mathematics…So, how'd your interviews go?"

"No clue. Professor Jackson gave no hint. He was like a stone statue, though that was better than Professor Hopkins' response. He was less than enthusiastic about the fact that I've been working construction and studying on my own the past few years. He gave me a problem to do at the blackboard, and the next thing I knew he was out the door. Apparently, he was late for a meeting…Whad'ya think?"

"Uh…well, not being a professor, let alone a mind reader, it's hard to say."

I read between the lines. Johnnie had opted for a diplomatic dodge. "Am I supposed to see any more professors today?"

"No, you've had your inquisition."

The term, not reflective of how I had envisioned my visit to the university, was apt.

"I have a quiz today. I need to do some cramming. In the meantime, you might wanna grab a bite at Pinckney (he pointed) and perhaps view the campus."

For lack of a better idea, I took Johnnie's suggestion. Following a leisurely lunch, I returned to the eastern end of the Horseshoe, the top of the arc, where the President's House stood.[249] With a center stoa, the

[249] *University of South Carolina Libraries*, library.sc.edu, 14 Feb. 2018 <http://library.sc.edu/socar/exh/evol/demo1.html> stating: "The original President's House was built in 1807 and was used as a residence by University presidents until the 1920s, when it was converted into offices…It was torn down in 1939 while a new library, now McKissick Museum, was constructed just behind it."

gabled home had four large windows across each of its two floors. I turned and faced the interior of the Horseshoe. Draped on either side by a line of impressive buildings, the center, extending about two hundred yards, was bedecked by tree-lined walkways, both rectangular and diagonal, traversing the otherwise green landscape. The pristine premises in the heart of Columbia, South Carolina's capital city integrated nature and manmade structures into an academic Eden. A venue more conducive to pedagogic endeavors was hard to imagine.

Apart from a shift in my gaze, I stood motionless. I shut my eyes and savored the tweets and chirps of birds singing in the trees. I drew in a deep breath of pure air. I wanted to be a student at the University of South Carolina. I wanted to learn there. It was a glorious dream, but a dream that I doubted was destined to be realized. Based upon the reactions of Professors Jackson and Hopkins, the lack of interest they had shown in me, my chances of admission appeared miniscule.

I opened my eyes and walked down the center of the Horseshoe, sometimes strolling across the fescues, while other times opting for the crisscrossing paved paths. The temperature, much warmer than when I had arrived the day before, enhanced the appealing surroundings. I passed a white girl lying on a blanket reading a book. A little further on, a Negro fellow sat cross-legged, writing in a notebook. The mixture of races and sexes sharing the learning environment complemented the appealing physical aspects of the campus. The apparent absence of racial conflict was remarkable. Equally surprising was the dearth of people on the campus. At a later date, I would discover the reasons behind these anomalies.

When I reached the westerly wall at the mouth of the Horseshoe, I looked back and surveyed the territory I had walked. Rays of sun, emerging over my shoulder from the southwest, lit up the scene, enhancing that which had already seemed perfect. Mixed emotions seized me: blissful joy owing to a heavenly site; but melancholy that my time there was destined to be brief. I glanced to my right, in the direction of Legare. Returning to the place where I was being housed made little sense with the afternoon far from complete. I headed out of the Horseshoe, through what was the only break in an otherwise continuous wall.

What I observed was anomalous. In every direction, except behind me in the Horseshoe, was devastation. Here and there were traces of post-war construction, but mainly there were ruins, the result of cannonballs and, more so, fire. I glanced back at the Eden that lay within the wall. The brick barrier separated Heaven from Hell.

In the years after the war, I had heard people talk of the destruction left by Sherman's march to the sea,[250] the hardscrabble life that had been left in its wake, but this was the first time I saw it. It was the first time I stood amidst the aftermath. It was the first time I walked the burned-out streets. Others who had traveled Sherman's war-torn path had told me how fortunate Savannah and St. Augustine were to escape ruin. My eyes gave new meaning to that which my ears had previously heard.

I headed south along Sumter Street, which paralleled the wall. At roughly seven feet, it topped out about a foot above me.[251] I followed it for over one hundred yards to the corner of Greene Street. Looking east, the wall bordered the entire leg of the Horseshoe before it bent north on another street whose sign was too distant to identify. I turned around and walked back north on Sumter, proceeding past the mouth of the Horseshoe to Pendleton Street, where the wall again turned east, encasing the campus in an idyllic cocoon. I might have followed the turn of the wall were I not drawn by the sight of a huge building set on a hill about five hundred yards to the northwest. Like the Horseshoe, it was an oasis in a desert of destruction. I continued north on Sumpter, wending my way until I was about one hundred yards from the massive structure. With roughly forty broad cement stairs leading to the ten pillars that adorned its Parthenon-like center front, the symmetric edifice bore duplicate sections on either side, each of whose width approximated the center section. I estimated the breadth of the entire front at two hundred feet. I continued closer, taking in the triangular pediment with impressive dental molding that decorated the center section. Rising high, perhaps fifty or more feet from the middle of the roof, was a magnificent cupola,

---

250 *South Carolina State House | The State House History*, scstatehouse.gov, 19 Sept. 2017 <http://www.scstatehouse.gov/studentpage/Explore/history.shtml>. General William T. Sherman captured the capital of South Carolina on February 17, 1865. *See also*, *Columbia, South Carolina*, Wikipedia, 19 Sept. 2018 <https://en.wikipedia.org/wiki/Columbia_South_Carolina> stating: "Controversy surrounding the burning of the city started soon after the war ended. General Sherman blamed the high winds and retreating Confederate soldiers for firing bales of cotton, which had been stacked in the streets...Firsthand accounts by local residents, Union soldiers, and a newspaper reporter offer a tale of revenge by Union troops for Columbia's and South Carolina's pivotal role in leading Southern states to secede from the Union."

251 *History of the Horseshoe*, op. cit., stating: "The Horseshoe Wall, constructed out of solid brick, originally stood 6 feet 9 inches high. It wrapped around the campus on Sumter, Greene, Bull and Pendleton Streets, and the only entrance was on Sumter Street. The wall failed in its original purpose to prevent students from sneaking into Columbia's taverns at night, but helped save the campus during the burning of Columbia during the Civil War on the night of February 17-18, 1865, by keeping flames off the college grounds."

a series of three concentric sections, the first with oval windows, the next with round, and at the apex, a finial whose apertures were again oval. At each level, adornments, what I guessed to be copper and bronze, highlighted the structure.[252]

As I moved through the manicured grounds, closer to the staircase that led up and into the structure, I reached a circular walkway. I followed it clockwise around the building's exterior. To my surprise, the opposite side duplicated what had seemed the front. Once again, a classical Greek pillared section protruded in the middle. I realized the building was cross-like, even more symmetric than I had imagined. The possibility that I might be viewing the most impressive manmade structure I would ever see was inescapable. The edifice spoke with the eloquence of fine prose; flowed with the harmony of mellifluous music; and reigned over the locale like a regal palace. I stared long and hard, storing as many details in my memory bank as I could.

"Spectacular," said a voice from behind. "Isn't it?"

I turned and observed a Negro gentleman, about sixty. "That it is."

"Let me guess. You're a student at the university. Right?"

"Don't I wish. I'm a…would-be student. I had interviews today." I heaved a sigh. "And based upon reactions, I suspect *would-be* will be as far as I'll get."

"You're from South Carolina, I presume?"

"Wrong again. Florida…St. Augustine to be exact."

"Darn. I'm doing worse than when I played baseball. Even in my twenties, I was never too good, only a two-hundred hitter. But with you I'm batting zero."

"Well, don't feel bad. Based upon my interviews, that's probably my average as well."

The gentleman gestured at the building again. "The State House is part of my constitutional every day. Don't always take the identical route, but one way or another, I come past here. The building still isn't quite finished. They started construction about a decade before the war. Nothing got done once the fighting started. And since the war ended, they haven't done much, least what would add the final touches any time soon."[253]

---

[252] *Cupolas of Capitalism, Picture Gallery, South Carolina State Capitol Building,* cupola.com, 7 Apr. 2020 <http://www.cupola.com/html/bldgstru/statecap/slide/sccap1e.htm> showing an aerial view of the South Carolina State Capitol ("postcard from the Gervais St. side, courtesy of Chris Miller").

[253] *SC State House – Columbia South Carolina,* sciway.net, 14 Feb. 2018

"Looks good to me," I said. "Are they using it?"

"Absolutely. They need to, especially 'cause the old State House was shelled and burned in the war."

"How come this one is still standing?"

"Good question. Folks here in Columbia have been trying to figure that one out for nigh on a decade. For some mysterious reason, maybe dumb luck, Sherman let it be when he torched the city." The man eyed the building, seemingly trying to ponder the conundrum. Once he looked back my way, he said, "You aware that Negroes hold the majority here in the South Carolina legislature?"

"Really?" My mouth was agape.

"Been that way since 1869. We're mighty proud to have the only state legislature in the entire country that's ever been controlled by Negroes."[254]

The anomaly was hard to fathom. "Who would expect, of all places, a southern state, the first to secede from the Union, would be the first to be controlled by Negroes? How'd it happen?"

"The power of the vote. Once folks, ones that never had it, got the right, they used it. Course it didn't hurt that the military government has been watching over things throughout Reconstruction." The man looked up at the sky, off to the southwest. "Old Sol says it's time I get a move on. Still got more than a mile left on my constitutional."

As he headed off, I added his tidbits to what I had already learned about the University of South Carolina. Besides being a rare oasis where people of color could become students, the body dictating its fate, the state legislature, was controlled by such people. The ruminations might have brought joy to my psyche, were I not so pessimistic about my chances of winning admission.

<https://www.sciway.net/sc-photos/richland-county/sc-state-house.html> indicating the structure was begun in 1851. The Civil War and post-war poverty delayed completion, which took fifty-six years.

[254] Ibid. The South Carolina legislature remains the only statehouse in America to have majority African American control.

Chapter XVII

SEATED WITH WALTER ON HIS PORCH, we leisurely swayed on the rockers, both of which bore a bright white coat of paint, one I had applied only a week before. A typically comfortable March day, high in the seventies, provided an excuse to lazily lounge. Clement conditions would continue for another two months before sweltering days with showers, heat and humidity would dominate.

"The end's in sight," I said, sipping our version of a mint julep: bourbon, spearmint and sugar, but no crushed ice. A cold one would have been preferable, but the trade off, living up near the Canadian border where ice was plentiful, was intolerable. "Looks like the lighthouse will be done by the end of summer."

"You reach a decision what you'll do, once it's finished?"

"Not yet, though I'm still hoping to attend college. Last week a fellow told me about a Negro school in North Carolina—coed like the University of South Carolina. When it opened at the end of the war, it was known as Raleigh Institute. These days it's called the Shaw Collegiate Institute. I understand it's Baptist, with a narrow curriculum, one that emphasizes theology.[255] Don't know if they teach advanced mathematics or physics, things I'd be interested in. I sent a letter requesting information, for a pamphlet or brochure, assuming they have one."

"What if it don't pan out? What then?"

---

[255] *Shaw University | The First Historically Black University in the South*, docsouth.unc.edu, 18 Feb. 2018 <http://docsouth.unc.edu/highlights/shaw.html> indicating Shaw University is "the South's oldest historically black University…Located in Raleigh, North Carolina, the Baptist-affiliated, co-educational liberal arts institution was known as the Raleigh Institute from 1866 to 1870. The school changed its name to the Shaw Collegiate Institute in 1870, after Elijah Shaw funded the construction of the campus's first building, and five years later, the campus became known as Shaw University."

"Maybe I'll run for president…Damn. That'll be tough. I have to get the Constitution amended to permit candidates under the age of thirty-five."

"Seriously, you got any fallbacks?"

"Well, I might try teaching at one of the new Negro schools. Their need is undeniable. Unfortunately, they pay next to nothing." Accustomed to the good wage of my job at the lighthouse, the idea of a big cut irked me.

"You ever consider goin' into the home-buildin' business?"

The thought had crossed my mind, but never long enough to be deemed serious.

"Hell, you got all the skills, what with your experience with Hanks and the lighthouse. And I know you're good, 'cause I seen your work 'round here."

"I suppose it's a possibility." My words were more receptive to the suggestion than my brain.

"Little Africa is growin'." Walter gestured behind himself, nearly spilling his mint julep in the process. "Across the creek, they're buildin' businesses as well as houses. Folks there are a lot more comfortable hirin' someone of color. And you could still live here…keep the overhead down."

Low overhead, plus the benefit of Walter's company, rendered the inertia of staying in place appealing.

"Better yet, you could teach math part time here in St. Augustine, at the Bronson School or the one on Cordova Street, all the while startin' a construction business. If it grows like I think it will, you can dump teachin' and build full time. Either way, you can live here cheap…and I'll be real glad to have you."

Walter had outlined an excellent plan. If I adopted it, at worst I would have a tolerable job with no concerns about my next meal, and at best, I might develop a lucrative business. Though the strategy fell short of my dreams of getting a college education and using my brain to solve complex problems in mathematics and science, it was a viable option. I sipped my mint julep before resuming my rocking. "You've painted an interesting picture. I'll think about it."

***

April 1874. As I occasionally did, rather than wait for Saturday, at the conclusion of the midweek workday, I took the ferry from Anastasia across the Matanzas and made the walk south to Walter's house for the night. It was close to seven when I arrived, still with plenty of daylight in the ever longer days of the nearing summer solstice. The front door was open wide. With the invention of the screen door[256]—I had installed one the previous weekend—Walter could leave the front door open, even after dusk. Before the advent of the device, forgoing outside ventilation had been more tolerable than succumbing to the evening swarms of mosquitos.

"Pleasant surprise," said Walter, who was seated in the dining room. "I just finished my lamb stew. There's lots in the pot…on the stove. I'll get you a bowlful, and while I'm at it, I'll grab a second helpin'." He got up from his seat.

"How was your day?" I said, as we entered the kitchen.

"Seems I'm the one who should be aksin' that question, given that my days are all the same."

I laughed.

"What's so funny?"

"Mine at the lighthouse are pretty much alike as well."

We laid our bowls onto the dining-room table and were about to seat ourselves when Walter said, "Oh, I almost forgot, a letter came for you yesterday. I'll get it." En route to the parlor, he said, "You remember when letters didn't come in an envelope?"

"Sure…and fish came pre-fried from the ocean."

"No, I'm serious," Walter called out from the parlor. "They was written on one page of a folded, double-wide sheet. The addressee, like the sender, was added after the thing had been folded for mailin'. Envelopes started 'round the start of the War of Secession."[257] Walter returned to the dining room and slid an envelope down to my end of the table.

"Sit down, before your stew gets cold." I shoveled a forkful of stew into my mouth with my left hand. With my right, I reached for the envelope. I flipped to the back where a red wax seal protruded. Above it was the name and address of the sender, the University of South Carolina. Excitement converged with trepidation. I held out the envelope in Walter's direction. "It's from the University of South Carolina."

---

[256] *Screen Doors a new invention!*, kristinholt.com, 3 May 2020 <www.kristenholt.com/archives/5031> stating: "'Wove wire for window screens' were referenced in the American Farmer in 1823." During the Civil War, Gilbert, Bennett and Co., a sieve manufacturer, coated "wire cloth with paint to prevent rust and sold it for window screens."…By 1874, E.T. Barnum of Detroit, Michigan advertised screens that were sold by the square foot."

[257] *How to Post a Letter, 19th Century Style | Parks Library Preservation*, parkslibrarypreservation.wordpress.com, 19 Feb. 2018 <https://parkslibrarypreservation.wordpress.com/2011/02/14/how-to-post-a-letter-19th-century-style/>.

"So, I noticed."

"Wanna bet what it says?"

"No. And you shouldn't neither."

"Hey, as long as I have to suffer bad news, I might as well make a few bits."

"Since when did you become a doom merchant?"

I breathed a sigh. "High expectations with low odds are a formula for disappointment. I can put it in the form of a mathematical equation if you prefer."

"Spare me…please."

I jabbed my fork into a chunk of lamb and stuffed it into my mouth. The extra bit of tasty sustenance in advance of the preordained letdown was welcome. I laid my fork down and broke the wax seal. I opened the envelope, removed its contents and read:

> March 30, 1874
> University of South Carolina
> Columbia, South Carolina
>
> Dear Mr. Reinbow:
>
> I am pleased to inform you that we have accepted you for admission to the University of South Carolina for the upcoming school year beginning in September 1874.

"They…they've accepted me!" I shouted.

Walter stared at me wide eyed.

I went back to the letter, rereading the opening sentence, before continuing with the remainder.

> I am also pleased to inform you that your matriculation will be tuition-free and you have been awarded a scholarship of $200 to defray your room and board.[258] If you wish to accept our offer of admission, please let us know no later than June 1st, 1874. If you accept, I will send you more information.
>
> While not a condition of your acceptance, I invite you to serve as a student tutor for pupils who come with weaker backgrounds in mathematics. Your decision

---

[258] *History of the University of South Carolina*, Wikipedia, 7 Mar. 2018 <http://en.wikipedia.org/wiki/History_of_the_University_of_South_Carolina> indicating that the South Carolina legislature in February 1874, provided for 124 scholarships of $200.

whether to serve as a tutor may be left until you arrive on campus in the fall.

I look forward to hearing from you. Congratulations.

Sincerely,
William N. Dowdett
Admissions Officer

"They're giving me a $200 scholarship, in addition to tuition-free acceptance. Can you believe it? And they've invited me to be a tutor for students needing help with mathematics."

"Sounds like they really want you."

The comment mirrored my reaction. I took another forkful of stew. The otherwise flavorful morsel tasted incredible. I scanned the letter once again before handing it to Walter.

Once he finished reading it, he said, "You gonna accept the offer?"

"I assume that was a rhetorical question."

"Re…what?"

"I assume you know the answer, but just in case you have doubts, I'll dispel them. University of South Carolina, here I come!" The image of the Horseshoe, indelibly stamped in my brain, emerged. I counted on my fingers. "Roughly five months, and I'm off to college!"

"The timin', completion of the lighthouse, oughta work out perfectly. Right?"

"It could be close, but…I think so."

Walter appeared pensive as he went back to eating his stew.

An inkling of his ruminations crossed my mind. A minute later, he confirmed my suspicions.

"I'll miss you," he said.

"I'll miss you too."

His face scrunched.

Examination of the facts kept me from debating the issue. Indeed, we would miss one another, but suggesting our emotions were alike was folly. Where I was thrilled to be embarking on a new adventure, he would again be left alone in his old age. "I'll try to find you a new tenant…And look on the bright side, whomever you get has to be better than the clod you have now."

"When you put it that way, it does have a silver linin'." Walter grinned.

"You needn't be so agreeable."

He continued to smile.

I savored the moment. Our relationship was special. Each of us had benefited, getting far more from the relationship than we had put in. I said, "This fellow who works at the lighthouse...he might be an excellent replacement for me. He's honest, hardworking and a great listener. I think you'd enjoy his company. As for him, he'd be damn lucky, not merely because of the deal you offer, but because of the terrific guy he'd be living with. Assuming he's interested—and I'll be surprised if he isn't—I can bring him by some weekend, so you can meet him." I finished my stew. Once I cleaned my bowl, I went up to my room where I penned the following letter.

April 5, 1874
15 Matanzas East
St. Augustine, Florida

Dear Mr. Wright,

Today I received a letter from the University of South Carolina accepting me for the school year beginning in the fall. Without your wonderful recommendation, I would not have gained admission. I am so grateful for your help, not only for the recommendation, but also all you did in Savannah to educate me and help me grow as a person.

I hope that all is well with you and your family. Please give my fondest regards to Mrs. Wright, Michael and Nora.

Thank you again.

Sincerely,
Mican

***

May, June, July...the months sailed by. The day after I had received the University of South Carolina's offer, I had sent my letter of acceptance. From that day on, my focus on studies had intensified. Evenings after dinner, I read whatever I could get my hands on. Sundays were divided three ways, time for Walter, chores and mathematics. Rather than trying to press ahead learning more about calculus, I devoted myself to review. Come September, when I arrived at the university, I wanted to be as prepared as possible to tutor.

It was the second Sunday in August. With the commencement of my college education less than a month away, it had become apparent that the final touches on the lighthouse would occur after my departure. With only a few Sundays left before I would be off to South Carolina, I decided to spend them in a variety of ways. An economist from

Jacksonville was giving a talk at the Government House about the state of the economy. After attending morning services with Walter, plus our traditional fish and chips, I took the very short walk across the Plaza de la Constitución to the King Street coquina structure, once the governor's residence, but since the War of Secession, a federal courthouse and customs house.[259]

I arrived about ten minutes prior to the talk's scheduled time and went directly to the room where it was to be held. I approached the only person there.

"Is this where Mr. Hillson is giving his lecture today?"

The bearded man gestured at himself. "I'm Mr. Hillson. Whether I'll be giving a lecture remains to be seen."

Uncertain how to respond, I took a seat in the first row. Another ten minutes elapsed, during which one other man, at least twice my age, arrived. Mr. Hillson stood alongside the lectern.

"Given the enormous crowd (Mr. Hillson surveyed the empty room), rather than a lecture, come on up and we'll talk informally."

Along with the other man, I got up and joined Mr. Hillson near the lectern. He said, "Looks like we're in for a rocky ride."

"When you say we," said the other man, "are you referring to St. Augustine or something more?"

"Much more. The entire industrialized world."

"Really?"

The man's reaction echoed my thought. The idea that economic impacts would spread across oceans was difficult to imagine. I wondered if Mr. Hillson was referring to something other than economics. I would have posed the question were I not afraid of displaying my ignorance.

"I assume you're both aware of the financial collapse that occurred this past September."

Like the other man, I nodded, though I knew almost nothing about the subject.

"Ever since Germany switched from silver and backed the deutschmark with gold about three years ago, the rumblings have been escalating."[260]

The information underscored my need to keep my mouth shut. I had no idea how the deutschmark was backed, let alone that there had been a change.

---

[259] *Government House (St. Augustine),* Wikipedia, 21 Feb. 2017 <https://en.wikipedia.org/wiki/Government_House_(St._Augustine)>.

[260] *Panic of 1873 |Teachinghistory.org*, 24 Feb. 2018 <http://teachinghistory.org/history-content/beyond-the-textbook/24579>.

"Once Germany abandoned silver, the world supply shot up and, as a result, the price tanked. The United States, whose dollar was backed by both silver and gold, felt the need, like numerous other countries, to prop up its currency. Last year Congress followed Germany's lead, passing a law directing the purchase of silver to strengthen the dollar.[261] That caused capital to dry up. Land speculators stopped buying, and overextended industrialists, whose stocks were flying high, failed to meet payments. Defaults on bonds were rampant and the stock market crashed.[262] With capital unavailable, economies of the industrialized world, many of which had been booming for years, slumped. And here we are."

"Do you think things will get better soon?" I asked the question in an effort to be part of the discussion.

"As I said earlier, we're in for a rough ride. The lack of capital, the unwillingness to commit money for the long term has slowed growth. That's bad news for jobs and bad news for the economy…The way I see it, this dip is here to stay. We're sinking into a depression."[263] Hillson eyed the other man and me, as if studying us. "Have you fellows felt the impact of the downturn?"

"That's why I came today," said the other man. "I work for the railroad, but I was thinking about opening a little business. When I went to my bank—I've been with them for over twenty years—they turned me down."

"That's what I'm talking about." Hillson turned my way. "You experienced the effects?"

"Not really, though I've heard grumblings that what was a fast-growing tourist business here in St. Augustine is taking a hit. As for me personally, there's been no impact. I work construction, at the new lighthouse that's being built on Anastasia Island. We haven't had any layoffs. I guess that's because the federal government is behind the project. Congress funded it before we began."

---

[261] Ibid.

[262] Krause, Jeff, *Stock Market Crash of 1873,* prezi.com, 7 Feb. 2018 <https://prezi.com/1zesl06yri_n/stock-market-crash-of-1873/>.

[263] *1873: America's Mortgage and Banking Meltdown, The Motley Fool,* fool.com, 7 Feb. 2018 <https://fool.com/investing/general/2008/10/20/1873-americas-mortgage-and-banking-meltdown.aspx> indicating that the collapse of 2008 was more like the downturn of 1873 than the crash of 1929. The Great Depression of the 1930's "had much more to do with overlarge inventories of industrial goods." The panic of 1873, which began on Wall Street on September 19th, saw a run on banks, with people seeking "liquidity by redeeming every paper asset for gold and currency." The fault lay with "bad mortgages" associated with a "housing bubble."

"It's almost finished. Isn't it?" said Hillson.

"Yup. About two more months, and we'll be operational."

"What do you plan to do then?"

"I've been accepted to the University of South Carolina."

If Hillson played cards, I doubted he fared well. Though he said nothing, his face, rife with skepticism, gave him away.

"They began accepting people of color this past December," I said.

"Really…a public university in the South?"

"They're the first."

"Congratulations. You're fortunate to have the opportunity to attend such a fine institution. That's a lot better than looking for work when employers aren't hiring. With a little luck, by the time you graduate, the economy will pick up…not that I'd bet a gram of silver on it."

With several years of education in my future, the possibility of an extended downturn caused me minimal worry. Little did I imagine the impact it would have on my life.

***

The 29th of August 1874. The sunny Saturday was my last day working on the lighthouse before I headed north to the University of South Carolina. Near as the final touches on the lighthouse were, it had become apparent that it would not be completed before I departed. As I rode the horse-drawn rail carriage across the wooden bridge spanning the Matanzas River,[264] melancholy mixed with excitement. Eager as I was to begin my college education, I was sad to leave St. Augustine, the lighthouse and, most of all, Walter. As the carriage approached Anastasia Island, I gazed at the structure that towered skyward near the top of the island's spine. With its fresh coat of black and white paint, it was an immense spiral candy cane of licorice and peppermint. Anomalous as the merger of the two flavors might have been in a confectionary delight, equally so was the selection of black and white for the lighthouse. Red or blue, rather than black, would have seemed more apropos, but the unique striping of St. Augustine's lighthouse had rapidly grown on us workers. More typical colors would have been banal.

My last day at the lighthouse was much like the many that had preceded. But in my mind the day was unique. I repeatedly wondered

[264] Woolson, Constance Fenimore, *The Ancient City*, *Harper's New Monthly Magazine* (No. CCXCV, December 1874, Vol. L, Pt. I of II), retrieved from The Project Gutenberg eBook of *The Ancient City*, gutenberg.org. *See*, p. 24 of the Guttenberg eBook for a drawing of the horse railroad.

how I would feel when it ended, knowing I would not be coming back to the job, that a chapter of my life had closed.

Soon enough, the sound of the horn ending the day reverberated in my ears. Ordinarily, I would have stopped immediately. Instead, I picked up another walkway brick and pressed it into the ground. A desire for closure pressed me to finish the course on which I had been working. As I knelt to put another brick in place, I felt a hand on my back.

"Whad'ya doin'?"

"Uh…nothing," I said, as I looked up and saw all 250 pounds of 6'5" Jeff James standing over me. Even as camaraderie had grown at the site, almost never had I shared a word with the muscular Caucasian.

"Yuh deaf?"

"Uh…no, but I—"

"Didn't yuh hear the horn?"

"Yeah…but I was—"

"C'mon with me."

His sharp tone overcame my preference to do otherwise. I stood up and followed him. I found it hard to believe that having avoided trouble during my several years at the lighthouse, I was finding it at the conclusion of my last day. James led the way to the building where we workers ate our mess. I was tempted to ask him what he wanted with me, but he hurried along, staying a step ahead. When we reached the building, he opened the door and, without a word, gestured for me to enter. The instant I stepped inside, the entire throng of workers leaped up singing, "For he's a jolly good fellow…"

On a table about fifteen feet inside the door was a big round cake, from which rose more cake, a model of the lighthouse, bedecked with spiraling chocolate and vanilla icing from bottom to top, except for a small area of solid yellow, emblematic of the light, at the apex.

As I stood frozen, unable to catch my breath, tears welled up in my eyes.

James put his arm over my shoulder. "All us guys wanna wish you the best. Real great that you're goin' to college. We're all proud of you."

The rest of the throng raced my way offering similar wishes. A part of me felt the urge to run before I burst into unmanly tears. Most of me savored ineffable joy. Regardless, with the entire crew surrounding me, I was hemmed in.

"C'mon, we want some cake!" yelled someone.

"Mican has to make the first cut…And he gets the first piece," screamed another.

I made the initial cut, and a huge piece was served to me in a mess kit. Slices were rapidly delivered to all. I looked around the room. We mirrored the lighthouse with its beautiful spiral of dark and light. White and colored had joined as a team and built a magnificent structure. What had mattered was our willingness to work together, accomplish a common goal, not the color of anyone's skin. Much as licorice and peppermint appeared to be flavors that could only clash, when properly interwoven, they created an exemplary combination. Perhaps the lighthouse, our work there, presaged the future of the nation. Maybe unity would replace the divide that culminated in the War of Secession. Perhaps "Life, Liberty and the pursuit of Happiness," the promise of the Declaration of Independence, would be realized by all Americans.

One after another, coworkers approached me with good wishes. I was halfway through my cake when one said, "Any chance you'll make it back for the lighting ceremony, once the lens has been installed?"

I shook my head. "Much as I'd like to, I can't see it. I'm sure they'll keep me mighty busy at college, too much so to make a quick trip here. It is, after all, over four hundred miles."

From the rear of the room, someone shouted, "Speech…speech!"

The entire throng took up the chant. It continued until some called for everyone to quiet themselves. The din yielded to silence.

I had no desire to orate, but I had no choice. I said, "Thank you…thank you all for this wonderful surprise. I…I'm at a loss for words…overwhelmed. This is all so unexpected…but I assure you, it means so much to me. Your kindness has given me a memory I will cherish." I wanted to say more, but only nerves, not ideas, were forthcoming. I said, "Thank you all."

Applause and shouts filled the room.

Joy filled my heart.

"You gonna stay here for mess this evening?" said a coworker.

"I'd like to, but…uh…I can't. I promised Walter, my landlord, that I would join him for dinner." I finished my cake and took my leave. I began the walk from the lighthouse back to the horse railroad. I went just a short distance when I passed a sabal palm. I gazed up its spindly trunk, to the top where its fan-like leaves spread as if dusters ready to sweep the clouds from the sky. Walking backwards from the palm, I continued until my perspective eliminated the illusion that made the palm appear taller than the lighthouse. After crouching so my head was nearly on the ground, I inched closer to the palm, so its peak and the top of the lighthouse were aligned along the line of my view. I pictured similar triangles, one created by my view, the ground and the palm, and the other, by my view, the ground and the lighthouse. I put a mark in the sand before standing up. Taking strides as uniform as possible, I started walking toward the palm and, ultimately, the lighthouse. At ten paces, I was alongside the palm. I continued walking and counting until I reached the lighthouse, a total of 51 paces. I again pictured my similar triangles. The ground forming the base of the palm's triangle, ten paces, was a little less than one-fifth of the ground forming the base of the lighthouse's triangle, 51 paces. That told me the palm was almost one-fifth the height of the lighthouse or just over thirty feet. No doubt, many would have deemed the exercise useless and bizarre. I could not debate the point. But the activity was who I was. And too, it was symbolic. The lighthouse, at least on the exterior, was complete. My work there, physical labor, was done. The time to transition to more cerebral matters, the kind embodied in the geometry of similar triangles, had arrived. Still buoyed by the unexpected outpouring of my fellow workers, I knew who I was, a thoughtful, cerebral adult, well-prepared to become a mathematician and scientist.

Chapter XVIII

THE PRECEDING AFTERNOON, I had arrived at the University of South Carolina and settled into my new home in Legare College, the same building where I had been housed for my interviews. I was yet to meet my roommate, a Negro student from Charleston, South Carolina, who was expected to arrive a day later than I. Our room, on the third floor, had beds, desks and armoires, one for each of us. The furnishings, all pedestrian, were time worn. Located on the south side of the Horseshoe, the building, an 1848 add-on to Pinckney College, housed dormitory rooms in its westerly half. The most easterly portion of the structure, Legare, housed dormitory rooms for Negroes and apparently a Maroon like me. Near the building's center, each floor had a large hall, a museum on the first, a library on the second and society hall on the top floor.[265] The fellow who had guided me to my room when I had arrived had indicated that rooms like mine had been shared by three before the college had closed prior to the War of Secession. The disclosure stirred an image of an overcrowded spartan space. I was thankful our quarters would house only two.

Following breakfast, I headed to Rutledge College. Owing to familiarity acquired during my prior visit, I negotiated the Horseshoe with relative ease. That ability, albeit trifling, aided my acclimation. As I walked the tree-lined grounds, to my surprise, a majority of those I observed were Negroes. I went to Room 105 where student tutors were told to meet at nine o'clock. I arrived early, took a seat and, along with about fifteen others, waited. Ten minutes later, nine on the dot, a man about fifty entered and stepped to the front of the room.

"Good morning, and welcome to the University of South Carolina. My name is Professor Peters. It is my hope your next four years here will

---

[265] *History of the Horseshoe,* sc.edu, 25 Mar. 2020 <https://sc.edu/about/our_history/horseshoe_history/index.php>.

be rich and rewarding, an experience that will see you work hard and expand your intellectual abilities, knowledge and horizons. Each of you has been invited to serve as a tutor based upon acumen you have demonstrated in a particular discipline. You will be asked to help two or three of your fellow freshmen, each of whom you will assist for an hour or two each week.

"Since admitting our first Negro students, the Board of Trustees has taken major steps to bring more Negroes to our campus. Owing to the nation's history, slavery included, for years Negroes had little or no educational opportunities. Following the end of the war, conditions have improved, but only slowly. A lack of teachers and books, as well as funds, has continued to disadvantage Negroes. As a result, many with potential are behind where they would otherwise be. You are tasked with helping these students make up their deficits.

"On the blackboard I've identified the room here in Rutledge where each of you should go to meet the professor who will supervise the academic discipline that you will tutor. These professors await you. So, without further ado, except to wish you a wonderful college experience, please proceed to your designated rooms."

After checking the blackboard, I headed to the second floor and room 219, the meeting place for those tutoring mathematics. As I entered, I realized it was the same room where I had undergone the mathematics segment of my interview. It was not that I recognized the room. Instead, I recognized the man seated at the front desk, Professor Hopkins, the curmudgeon who had interviewed me.[266] Along with the others, two males and one female, all Negroes, I took a seat and waited. Pen in hand, Professor Hopkins worked at his desk. Several minutes elapsed during which he did not look up.

As I waited, I recalled my discomfort when he had tested me. The memory unnerved me. I told myself that despite his eccentric manner, he had apparently approved of my work. Nevertheless, I felt uneasy.

Finally, Professor Hopkins stood up. "With the four of you, my charges, present, let us begin." He came around from behind his desk

[266] Professor Hopkins is a fictional character. At the commencement of the 1873-74 school year, the actual Professor of Mathematics was the Rev. B. B. Cummings, who had replaced Dr. James Woodrow. Cummings was "an informer against alleged Kuklux in Spartanburg…He was a man of ordinary intelligence and small scholarship, and was otherwise unfit for a professorship in any reputable college." Reynolds, John S., *Reconstruction in South Carolina, 1865-1877*, Columbia. South Carolina (The State Co. Publishers 1905) p. 233, retrieved from Internet Archives, archive.org, 14 Mar. 2018 <http://www.archive.org/details/cu31924028792O8>.

and stared for several seconds. "Might as well be up front…call a spade a spade."

Was the comment intended as a racial slur? For the moment, I gave Professor Hopkins the benefit of the doubt. I assumed he had made a poor choice of words. However, rescission of my beneficence came quickly.

"Antebellum, I was a professor here, back when this institution was known as South Carolina College. A more distinguished site of higher learning could not be found in the South. Slaves were common on the campus. They cleaned the residences, prepared meals and the like. They served both faculty and students. This campus was an illustrious place…hallowed grounds. Then came the war, and the college closed. When it reopened several years after the war, I was invited back. Little did I imagine the extent to which this erstwhile noble institution would be turned upside down. Reconstruction divided the South into military districts. Carpetbaggers and scalawags leveraged the circumstances for personal profit. Laws banning discrimination were enacted. So it is that the foundations of lunacy, a mixed-race campus, were laid. And suffice it to note that many Negroes, preferring their own facilities, concur that the current state of affairs is, indeed, lunacy.

"Much as I yearned for a segregated campus, I was willing to endure the indignity of integration. But I assumed the university's standards for admission would remain high and only a handful of rare, qualified Negro students would be accepted. But alas, my assumption proved folly. A shift in power enabled the aforementioned lunacy to bear ill-begotten fruit. Our legislature (Hopkins gestured to the northwest, presumably at the Capitol) currently has a Negro majority, which, in turn, has encumbered this university with a Board of Trustees bearing a Negro majority. Three of my colleagues, Professors LaBorde, Talley and Gibbes, resigned after Henry Hayne, a person of color, the first of his kind, was admitted to the university last fall.[267] This year the Board turned the campus on its head when it adopted a policy of attracting many more Negroes. That had a perverse effect on the campus population. Small when the university reopened, it shrank dramatically. Countless qualified white students eschewed the opportunity to enroll. Many white upperclassmen refused to return. The foregoing is problematic, but the fruit we are harvesting is far more squalid. For want of competent Negro students, the admissions committee accepted many unqualified Negroes. They now constitute the vast majority of our campus population. In numerous respects, we have been reduced to a high school. The students

[267] Ibid., *Reconstruction in South Carolina, 1865-1877*, p. 234.

you will be tutoring need help with elementary algebra; some, I suspect, are barely proficient with fractions. Our institution, once a proud bastion of education, has been emasculated.[268] Personally, I despise it. For now, I must live with it. But don't assume it is permanent. The war may be over...but the fight continues." He circled behind his desk. "I hope we understand one another."

I tried to imagine what twist of serendipity had saddled my tutoring responsibilities with this bigoted supervisor. I glanced at my fellow tutors. Their stoic faces showed nothing. Regardless, their ruminations were patent. Like me, they were surely bemoaning misfortune.

Professor Hopkins seated himself. "On perchance that I have confused you about the relationship upon which we are embarking, permit me to clarify with a mathematical inequality. On the right side of the inequality sign, we find you student tutors, none of whom, from my standpoint, should be here. Unfortunately, forces of war and subsequent politics, as aforesaid, have dictated otherwise, at least for the present. On the left side of the inequality, tis I, not that I would be here had I known in advance the extent of irrationality that would pervade this campus. As I noted earlier, three professors have already resigned. A number of white upperclassmen have quit the University.[269] I have stayed because I believe the insanity will be undone. I intend to work toward that goal. In the interim, however, we occupy this asylum—and I use the term advisedly—together. But understand, I am the professor, and you, mere students. Between us lies an inequality sign." He got up and drew a huge *greater-than* (>) symbol on the front blackboard. "So, irrespective of the politics of both the state legislature and this campus, inside the four walls of this room, *my* classroom, *I rule*." Professor Hopkins smiled, though the silence accompanying the expression suggested it was a sneer. "With our ground rules laid, our work today is complete. If there are no questions, you are excused."

The probability that anyone would pose a question was the definition of the quantity *infinitesimal*. Still the four of us tutors sat motionless, each apparently waiting for someone else to get up. Finally, the lone female in our group inched out of her seat. The rest of us sheep followed.

---

[268] Ibid. Within a short time after the first Negro was admitted, "The number of students greatly increased, so that it soon exceeded 200—more than nine-tenths being [N]egroes. The requirements for admission were so lax—the regulations in this matter were so flagrantly disregarded—that the so-called University soon became little more than a high school, whose chief aim was to inculcate and illustrate the social equality of the black race with the white." p. 236, 237.

[269] *History of the University of South Carolina*, op. cit.

As I, the last in the procession, headed for the door, Professor Hopkins called to me: "Mican, I want to speak with you."

I jerked around in his direction. "Uh…yes, Sir." I stepped alongside his desk, terrified that he had singled me out.

"You impressed me the day of your interview, and I don't impress easily."

"Thank you, Sir." The unexpected praise deescalated my fear, not that it vanished.

"When I saw your application indicating you were a self-taught Negro, I was enraged that the administration would waste my time with such frivolity. When you successfully answered my first question, I gave you a problem requiring you to find a function's maximum point using the definition of a derivative. I was certain you could not solve it. It was my intent to rid myself of you without further waste of time. To my shock, you solved it easily, something you could only do with an understanding of the theory underlying calculus. As I said, that was impressive."

"Thank you, Sir." My redundant response echoed in my ears, but I was still too intimidated to say anything else.

"Lest you get a swelled head, let me set the record straight. Happy about your presence here, I am not. But as long as I must tolerate the tribulation that has befallen this institution, I prefer to concentrate on the best of the distasteful crop." Professor Hopkins shook his head and muttered. "Crops, like cotton…an interesting way to characterize the colored swarm that has invaded my classroom. If they were white, the term would be apt." He heaved a sigh. "Weevils more closely describe this swarm." He refocused on me. "Fair-minded and magnanimous as I am, I'm giving you a chance. Don't cause me to rue that decision."

"I'll try my best, Sir."

"You're excused." His attention shifted to an open book on his desk.

I headed out the door feeling better than when he had asked to see me a minute earlier. But better was a relative term. I felt much worse than when my day had started. Roses, with their sweet fragrance and magnificently hued petals, adorned the University of South Carolina, but roses had thorns, sharp and treacherous. Professor Hopkins had labeled himself fair-minded and magnanimous. Arguably his claim had merit…in a subjective, narcissistic world in which bigotry was the gospel. I negotiated the stairs to the first floor. As I departed the main entrance, a woman approached. I would not have recognized her, except that she was the only female tutor in our group of four.

"Hi, I'm Lucinda Brown, one of Professor Hopkins' tutors."

"Yes, I know. Not your name, though I know it now, but that you're a math tutor."

She shrugged. "As the group's only female, I guess I stand out."

"Kinda." I noted the slim woman's large emerald eyes and high cheekbones. Well proportioned, about six inches over five feet, with flawless tan skin, she was very attractive. "I'm Mican Reinbow."

"Nice to meet you, Mican. You make out okay with Professor Hopkins? The reception he gave us was less than welcoming."

"That's an understatement." At that moment, I had no idea that down the road I would discover that Lucinda was a master of the understatement. "To answer your question, Professor Hopkins, even as he complimented me for solving a problem at my interview, made it clear that I was persona non grata."

"He tested you at an interview?"

"You weren't?"

She shook her head.

A possible reason for the difference crossed my mind. "The last five years I've been working construction. And I'm not from South Carolina. That may explain why he examined me."

"You must have shown well. If not, you wouldn't have been chosen as a tutor."

"As the only female selected, you must have impressed the committee too."

"Perhaps…though based upon what transpired a while ago on the second floor (she gestured at the building), they may just be sadists, singling us out for abuse under a tormentor…what they euphemistically refer to as a mentor."

Her outspoken criticism of Professor Hopkins was bold. Admittedly, he had done nothing to hide his prejudice, but her willingness to be so open with me, a stranger, was audacious. It emboldened me, though admittedly, with her cards already on the table, my need for courage was minimal. "Hope we haven't been dealt a bad hand."

"By a Jack who dishes the cards from the bottom of the deck?"

I was unsure whether she might be alluding to Professor Hopkins' first name or, more generally, the picture card of the knave. Rather than showing my ignorance, I made a mental note to check the list that bore the full names of the faculty. I said, "Would you like to get a cup of coffee?"

She hesitated. "Yes, that'll work. It'll leave me time to see the campus before my first class this afternoon."

"I know you weren't tested, but did you at least come for an interview?"

She shook her head. "They admitted me based upon my grades, along with the recommendations of my teachers."

"Let me guess…unlike me, you didn't do construction for five years before applying?"

With a puzzled look, she scratched her head. "Not that I recall."

"You have a sense of humor." The assessment added to what I had already learned about Lucinda. She was sharp, far from shy and very attractive. I pointed about one hundred yards to the west. "We can get coffee at the Pinckney-Legare building, up on the third floor."

"You sure you're a freshman?"

"Really, I am."

She gave me a look. "I know. If you weren't, you wouldn't have been in Professor Hopkins' group of newbies…I was teasing."

I shrugged…sheepishly. Keeping up with Lucinda was a challenge.

We headed to Legare and climbed the stairs to Society Hall. Once we had gotten our coffees, we seated ourselves at a long table. I kept my beverage black. Lucinda loaded her cup with cream and sugar.

"You opting for coffee-flavored sweet cream?"

"I…uh…I'm not much of a coffee person. The few times I've had it, I…I didn't like it all that much."

I welcomed her sudden lack of ease, not that I wished her discomfort. But the hint of vulnerability in her otherwise confident mien rendered her less intimidating. I said, "You'll be surprised. Coffee grows on you." Lucinda was growing on me, much faster than had the caffeinated beverage I was imbibing.

"I feel very fortunate to be here. It's amazing how the vote has turned things around in South Carolina. It's fast becoming a progressive state, at least in the large cities. We've seen it in Charleston, and here in Columbia, what with the legislature controlled by folks of color. It's a whole new world."

"The federal government has a lot to do with it," I said. "The military districts established by Reconstruction have altered the landscape. We saw it in St. Augustine. That's where I've been living the past few years. The Democrats have tried to regain a stronghold, turn it back into the old South, but they haven't had a chance, not when the headquarters of the Third Military District are located there."

"Here in South Carolina, lots of whites, the vast majority of them, would love to restore the old order. They prefer slavery, but failing that, they want a two-tier society, with folks of color on the bottom. They can dream about it all they want. It's not gonna happen. Now that their balloon has burst, no way can they put the air back inside."

I heaved a doubting sigh. "I hope you're right."

"You disagree? You looking to resurrect the past?" Her tone had an edge.

"No way do I want to go backwards…but I can't say I'm as confident as you that the hump is behind us."

Her cup, about to meet her lips, stopped. "Don't get me wrong. I know it won't be easy, not with the likes of Hopkins around. But lots of blood was shed to lift the shackles of slavery. Matter of fact, I was born a slave, and I was one until my ninth birthday when the Emancipation set me free. My daddy died fighting for the Union Army. And I'll do the same, if that's what it takes to preserve my freedom."

Her irrepressible determination moved me. It also silenced me. We bore striking similarities. We were both of color; we had lost our fathers at a young age; and we were freshman mathematics tutors. But I sensed that we were also very different. Placed on a linear spectrum, with shrinking wallflowers at the far left, Lucinda was at the far right. As for me…

"I apologize."

The rueful words coming out of the blue stunned me. "For what?"

"Your silence hints that one of my worst habits has reared its nasty nose. I got on my soapbox and attacked you for no reason. Fine that I have strong convictions, but that hardly justifies a harangue, not with the first person, apart from my roommate, I meet on campus…one who was kind enough to invite me for a cup of coffee."

"You have no reason to apologize. You didn't attack me. You simply voiced your views."

She looked me in the eye. "Be honest. Deny you didn't deem my carrying on a harangue. And keep in mind, I saw your face and your silence."

"First off, you did not carry on. As for my silence, I was impressed by your steadfastness."

"Sure." A furrowed brow underscored the word.

"Really. As a matter of fact, I viewed your comments on a mathematical scale."

She sipped her coffee. "Mathematical scale? Please tell me. I'm all ears."

"It's nothing dramatic. Just a simple linear range, reflective of resoluteness. Far to the left are the mice of the world. You, on the other hand, are way to the right."

"And where, may I ask, are you?"

"Somewhere in the middle…I guess."

She smiled.

"What does that mean?"

"That you're far more tactful than I."

"You're not so bad yourself." The words, meant as a compliment, reverberated in my ears. "I didn't mean that the way it sounded."

"What—your insult was even more vicious than your words?"

"You know I was implying the opposite."

She smiled again.

I realized she was poised beyond her years; that she could fence with one who was older and more experienced, who should have been more worldly. "You ever consider a career in the law?"

"Not my thing. Math and science are my passions." She peered into her coffee cup and muttered, "Two-thirds gone. That's as much as I can take."

Having finished mine, I said, "How 'bout I show you around the campus." With the familiarity garnered during my prior visit, coupled with a sketch I had studied back in St. Augustine, I was confident. I led the way outside and guided her around the Horseshoe. Once we had circled the entire interior, I pointed toward the wall. "The area outside the campus is also worth seeing. Just a half-mile over there (I pointed again) is the State Capitol. Would you like to see it?"

"I would, but not today. Having gotten in late, I didn't have time to get settled. And I told my roommate—I've barely met her—I'd join her for lunch."

"Can I walk you back to your dorm?"

"No need. It's right over there in Rutledge, at the opposite end from Professor Hopkins' room."

"Do you have him for math?"

"Yes, calculus, at ten A.M., every weekday, except Thursday. What about you?"

"Me too," I said.

"You nervous about it?"

"Not really. Is there some reason I should be?"

"From what I've heard, calculus is tough stuff."

I shrugged. "Maybe."

Her brow furrowed, dipping closer to her radiant eyes. "And I suppose you're speaking from personal knowledge."

I hesitated to brag, but my comment demanded clarification. "I've studied some calculus already, and it's quite logical."

"You attend college before this?"

I shook my head.

"So, how'd you learn calculus?"

"My teacher at the Baptist Church, when I was in Savannah, gave me a calculus book before he moved back north."

"And?"

"I studied it on my own."

"Impressive." She looked me in the eye. "If and when I run into problems—pun inadvertent, but apt—would you mind if I pick your brain?"

"Not in the least." My response neglected to disclose that I would love for her to seek my help. Spending more time with her would be a pleasure. "Besides math, what other courses are you taking?"

"English Literature, American History, Physics and…what's the last one? Oh yeah, Philosophy. How about you?"

"In addition to Calculus…English Composition, Economics, Chemistry and…Philosophy." I had been debating between Religion and Philosophy. Up to that moment, the decision was an evenly balanced scale. That Lucinda was taking Philosophy was enough to tip it.

"Looks like we may have a couple of classes together…For now, I better be on my way." She headed in the direction of Rutledge. I watched her, noting her shapely figure, the swivel of her hips, as she gradually disappeared beyond a huge maple.

***

Following breakfast, with two nights of campus life behind me, I embarked on my initial day of classes. The strikingly cool, gray September morning hinted that autumn was drawing near. Crossing the Horseshoe, I headed to Harper, which owing to its common wall with Elliot was sometimes referred to as Harper-Elliot College.[270] I negotiated my way to the third floor, Room 302, to my first class, Introductory Philosophy. Excitement, but also jitters, accompanied me as I entered the room. More than half a decade had passed since I had been a student. Three rows back, near the windows, I spotted Lucinda, one of only four people already in the room. I went directly her way and pointed at the desk to her left.

"Mind if I join you?"

---

[270] *Slavery at South Carolina College, 1801-1865,* op. cit., indicating that Harper, which was built in 1848 when enrollment at the then South Carolina College had risen to 221, was used as a Confederate hospital during the Civil War and that four interior rooms were used by the federal military as a prison in 1865. The use of campus buildings such as Harper as a hospital spared them from destruction when Sherman marched through Columbia in February 1865.

"Please do." She gestured around the room. "Not many students. I thought Philosophy would be a popular course."

I checked the large circular clock that hung on the opposite wall. "We still have eight minutes before the class starts. Presumably more will arrive."

"I suppose, though you'd think everyone would be here early the first day."

I would have made more conversation, but unable to find something to say, I opened my notebook. I put a small bottle of ink into my desk's well and laid my pen down. Another student entered the room, and a minute later, a man, clad in a tweed suit, about fifty with a full beard, stepped through the doorway. My assumption that he was our professor was confirmed when he placed his satchel on the large walnut desk at the front. Following a look at the clock and a perusal of the room, he said, "Since it appears we're all here, we might as well begin, even if we are a few minutes early."

I quickly counted the students, not that it was necessary. I already knew that we numbered six. Why, I wondered were so few taking philosophy? Possibilities crossed my mind. Perhaps the class was difficult and/or boring or the professor was a hard marker. The explanations made little sense, given that incoming freshman were unlikely to have advance knowledge about a particular course or professor.

"Good morning. I'm Professor Nelson, and this is Introductory Philosophy. If by chance anyone belongs elsewhere, please take your leave."

No one moved. One by one, Professor Nelson called our names, and we responded, "Here."

"An auspicious start. Those, and only those, who belong here are present…By any chance, does anyone know, as a matter of logical parlance, the contrapositive of the statement I just made?"

I had no clue what a contrapositive was. Apparently, none of my classmates did either, or at least no one volunteered an answer.

"Worry not," said Professor Nelson. "I did not expect you to know. But before this course is done, you will. And as long as I asked the question, the answer is: "All those who are not present do not belong here. And for your information, my original statement and its contrapositive, like all statements and their contrapositives, are logical equivalents."[271]

I dipped my pen and took notes as fast as I could, hoping the cryptic concept would make sense once I had time to examine it more closely.

"Having finished attendance, complete with a digression into a principle of logic, a fundamental element of philosophy, let us embark upon our first lesson, an esoteric subject, the existence of God. Professor Nelson casually plopped himself atop his desk, dangling his legs above the floor. "Who among you believe in God?"

All my fellow classmates, except for Lucinda, raised a hand. Uncertain how to react to what should have been an easy question, I raised my hand…halfway.

Professor Nelson surveyed us. "It appears we have four believers, one non-believer and one, call him, a half-believer." He focused on me. "Let me guess. You believe on weekends, but not weekdays. Or perhaps you're a non-believer, but reluctant to admit it."

My first class had barely begun, and, consistent with a nasty knack, I had managed to get myself singled out.

"You care to share the reason for your half-armed response?"

Not really. I might have voiced the reaction had I thought it would win me a reprieve. I said, "Uh…for me, it's…uh…a matter of semantics."

"Semantics? This sounds interesting. Tell me more." Professor Nelson's intonation bore a devilish cast, but more impish than diabolical.

First class jitters might have led me into panicked silence had Mr. Wright's Socratic examination of the issue years before not armed me with a reasoned response, along with the confidence to deliver it. "Uh…whether I believe in God is a function of how one defines *God.* If God represents forces in the universe beyond our ken, then…uh…yes, I believe in God. If, on the other hand, God is defined as a being who listens to the prayers of individual supplicants, I have serious reservations."

Professor Nelson abandoned his perch and moved to the head of my row. "Earlier I indicated that we have an auspicious beginning. We have more than that. Your response has transported us directly into the substantive facets of philosophical discourse. And having done so—not that I mean to single you out unfairly—by chance, can you tell me what is meant by the term *ontological argument*?"

---

271 The contrapositive of a statement, "A implies B," is "not B implies not A." A statement and its contrapositive are logically equivalent. The two can be expressed as follows: $(A \rightarrow B) \leftrightarrow (\tilde{}B \rightarrow \tilde{}A)$.

"Yes, Sir. It's a logical argument proving the existence of God."[272]

Professor Nelson's eyes were wide. "That's correct, at least for our limited purposes today…And thank you, not just for the astute contribution, but also for helping dispel a disheartening view many of my colleagues have been voicing. According to them, our crop of freshmen, now that the university actively seeks students of all races, is a sad collection of uneducated riffraff who are totally unprepared for the rigors of higher education. Before we move forward, may I inquire how and where you acquired the information you've shared with us?"

"At the First African Baptist Church in Savannah. My teacher—it was right after the war—was Mr. Charles Wright. The past five years he has been teaching at the Kimball Union Academy in New Hampshire."

"Aah Kimball…an excellent preparatory institution with an outstanding reputation." Professor Nelson eased back to his desk and continued his lesson.

Much as I endeavored to maintain focus on his words, from time to time, I found myself preoccupied. I was celebrating the praise Professor Nelson had heaped upon me. Before I knew it, the class concluded.

"Impressive," said Lucinda, as she got up. "Looks like you're way ahead of the rest of us."

"Not really. I just got lucky. Professor Nelson selected a subject with which I was familiar. I was like the animal from African folklore that is confronted by a seemingly harrowing trial. The trial, however, turns out to be just what the animal loves."[273]

"You're too modest."

I soaked in the compliment. Something about Lucinda, her disarming magnetism, cajoled an awkward admission. "You know why I raised my hand halfway?"

"Because your answer was more than a simple yes or no. It depended on the definition of God."

"Don't I wish."

"Then what?"

---

[272] An ontological argument is an argument proving the existence of God using ontology, "the philosophical study of the nature of being, becoming, existence or reality…" Ontology, Wikipedia, 16 Mar. 2018 <https://en.wikipedia.org/wiki/Ontology>.

[273] Songofthesouth.net, 5 May 2020 <https://songofthesouth.net/movie/background.html> stating of the Uncles Remus tales: "While it is for certain that most, if not all, of the tales were brought over to America from Africa during the slavetrading [sic] era, it has been speculated that some of the tales originate from India or even Egypt." Joel Chandler Harris immortalized the tales in his 1880 book "Uncle Remus: His Songs And Sayings."

"I was afraid to admit that I didn't believe in God, especially with the other hands going up. But when I saw that yours stayed down, I felt reassured, enough that I only raised mine halfway. Professor Nelson picked on me because he suspected I was an indecisive sheep. He was right. But kismet be praised, his ensuing question was clover, just what a sheep loves to eat."

***

With three weeks behind me at the university, I had settled into my new life in South Carolina. Finding many poorly qualified students occupying the seats of my classes, some of which were remarkably small, was a double-edged sword. It raised concerns that the curriculum might get watered down, but it attenuated my fear of failure. As a nervous newbie, the trade-off was, on balance, positive.

Besides sharing philosophy and calculus classes with Lucinda, the two of us ate together now and then. But the last Saturday of September was different. For the first time I was formally courting her, an invitation that would take us off campus. We headed out of the Horseshoe past the Capitol, turning north on Main Street, which was the perpendicular bisector of the magnificent governmental seat. We continued for a half-mile to 1623 Main, the location of John C. Seegers' Saloon, a German establishment.[274] The new, two-story Victorian, built in a section of Columbia that had been devastated during Sherman's march to the sea, bore a narrow portico with slim, embedded columns decorating the front, along with four windows, each about seven feet high, spanning the second floor.

As Lucinda and I entered the building, a gray cloud of cigar and cigarette smoke engulfed us. Its foul flavor permeated my lungs. We found ourselves a table in the front corner, far from the long wooden bar that faced the entrance. We each ordered bratwurst and sauerkraut, plus a stein of German beer.

---

[274] *Luke Drake Opens Nov. 29 | Restaurants | free-times.com*, free-times.com, 16 Mar. 2018 <https://www.free-times.com/food/food-feature/lula-drake-opens-nov/article_20729f52-1433-57f3-9387-96c11906584e.html>. 1635 Main Street, Columbia, South Carolina is a historic structure "built in 1873 as a saloon by a German immigrant and prominent Columbia businessman John C. Seegers." In November 2016, the Lula Drake Wine Parlor opened at said address. *See*, *Lula Drake wine bar and bistro to open at 1635 Main Street in July 2016 | The State*, thestate.com, 16 Mar. 2018 <http://www.thestate.com/news/business/biz-column-blogs/shop-around/article88154342> for a photograph, *circa* 1880, of the building.

"So, now that we've been at the university for a few weeks, what do you think?" I said.

"It's not as hard as I had expected."

The observation echoed my sentiments. "The competition is less than I anticipated. The two students I'm tutoring don't even know algebra. Nice fellows, but academically short of what you'd expect to see on a college campus."

"Back home in Charleston, I heard that the Legislature was providing lots of scholarships because quality students were hard to come by. The opportunity for a free education should have had them flocking from the woodwork. But apparently not. Even with a free ride, an integrated campus has proved too revulsive for most whites to bear. As for us Negroes, who could have imagined we'd be in the majority just a year after the first of our kind was admitted?"

"Actually…I'm a Maroon." Reticence accompanied my disclosure. Attracted as I was to Lucinda, I worried it might sabotage my chances with her. But judgment counseled I face the issue sooner, rather than later.

"What's a Maroon?"

"A Black Seminole. My mother was Negro. She died when I was very young. My father, a Seminole Indian, was killed while serving as a scout for the Union Army."

"I'm sorry."

Our food and beverages arrived. I tasted my brew. "Does it matter to you that I'm half-Seminole?"

Her eyes, the big emeralds, expanded. "Why would it?"

"Because I'm mixed race."

Those same emeralds turned icy. "You realize you just impugned me."

Her unexpected indignation left me flustered, unable to fashion a response.

"I don't judge people by the color of their skin. For that matter, I suspect I'm partly white, not that I know. But common sense suggests it. Given my family's slavery background, odds are their masters had their way with my ancestors." She held out a hand and wrist. "My skin is quite light."

"It's lovely." I reached out and caressed her arm. "A moment ago, when I asked if it mattered that I was part Seminole, I was trying to be up front, not disparage you."

"I appreciate that, and causing you discomfort is not my goal. Just the opposite. I enjoy your company. You're the most interesting person I've met since arriving in Columbia." She smiled.

Her kind words and warm expression melted me. “Ditto,” I said, for want of a more suitable response.

“Thank you…I think.”

I gulped. Having already stuffed a left and right foot into my mouth, I needed to do better. “You’re very pretty…intelligent and you have a wonderful personality.”

She blushed. “Uh…ditto.”

We both laughed, joyful guffaws wrought with sexual tension, at least from my standpoint. For the next few minutes, we ate, mainly in silence. Sausage and cabbage, flavored with perfect company, tasted exceptional.

“What do you think of Professor Hopkins?” I said.

“He’s an excellent teacher…despicable bigot that he is.”

Her succinct and comprehensive assessment exceeded my expectations. “Wow, that touched all the bases.”

“You disagree?”

“Not in the least. For that matter, I couldn’t have said it better…Correct that. I couldn’t have said it as well.”

“How do you think he feels toward us?”

Apart from his bigotry, I hadn’t thought about it. “I guess he respects our mathematical abilities, but that’s as far as it goes. To him…we’re barely human.”

“You sure he gives us the benefit of that doubt.” She sipped her brew. “Yuck,” she said. “Might even be worse than coffee, what with its bitter taste. Don’t know why I order this stuff.”

“Kinda like Hopkins. You tolerate it.”

She shook her head. “Your analogy doesn’t float. With Hopkins, I don’t have a choice.” She held out her stein. “What’s in here is strictly the product of my own stupidity. I could have opted for a sarsaparilla.”

The truth be known, I would have preferred...well, not a sarsaparilla, but a vanilla-flavored root beer. Apparently, I lacked her courage, a willingness to openly duplicate her admission.

“Where do you think the university is headed?”

Less than one month into my freshman year, trying to find my way, the question was not one I had entertained. “What do you mean?”

“What do you think the campus population will look like a decade from now?”

She had to be kidding. “I don’t even know what it will look like when, with luck, we graduate four years from now.”

“I plan to do it in three years. When first I thought about it over the summer, it was pie in the sky. But now that I’m here and I’ve seen the competition, I believe it’s doable.”

"That's a great idea, one that never had crossed my mind." Approaching my twenty-third birthday and anxious to get on with my life, it struck an intriguing chord.

"You never answered my question."

"I might try…if I could remember it."

"What will the campus population look like a decade from now?"

I shrugged. "Half-and-half, colored and white…maybe?"

She gave me a look.

"Hey, when you're guessing, something in the middle, a hedge, makes sense."

"That may be, when dealing with a normal curve. If, on the other hand, the curve is inverted, the middle is not a hedge."

"Spoken like a true mathematician, not that I get your point."

"Well, the way I see it, we have two strong opposing forces, one of which will prevail. On the one hand, you have the Republicans and the powerful thumb of the military's presence guaranteeing that folks like us can be here. On the other, you have the pushback from the Democrats and the traditional southern whites who are looking to make this campus white again. Unless I miss my guess, one of these forces will prevail. Either the campus will be open to all races, in which case, it will be predominantly Negro because few whites will attend, or bigotry will prevail, and it will be lily white."

"So, you see it like the Law of the Excluded Middle that Professor Nelson spoke about in philosophy class this week." Having missed the subtlety of Lucinda's question when first she had asked it, I was pleased with my ability to link it to newly learned principles.

Lucinda shook her head. "It's not that type of *either-or*. The graph is U-shaped, not a discontinuous function. While it's far more likely that the campus will be either black or it will be white, the possibility of 50-50, though a longshot, can't be ruled out."

The self-satisfaction I had felt a moment earlier evaporated. I had duplicated my failure to get Lucinda's first point by missing her second. I realized that she was very astute. The observation flew in the face of the common conviction that females were less adept when it came to analytics. Using principles of mathematics and logic, Lucinda had synthesized a political and social issue in a way that I never would have considered. I said, "You are one very intelligent lady."

She eyed me skeptically. "You patronizing me?"

"Not in the least. I'm simply giving credit where it's due…And just for the record, I believe your analysis of the issue was far more incisive than mine."

Lucinda sipped her beer. "This stuff tastes a little better, not that it measures up to sarsaparilla."

I followed her lead and imbibed, but with much more than a sip. "So, once you get your sheepskin, what do you plan to do with your degree?"

"I'm not altogether sure, but for me that's secondary."

Her response was not surprising. Even if she had no specific plans, she desired to be educated.

"Don't get me wrong. Much as I'm not career driven—though I might like to teach—I have definite goals."

I read between the lines. She was likely looking to marry, someone of substance. But she would be more than a silent wife. She would be a well-spoken partner. Discretion guided me to voice a circumspect inquiry, rather than a presumptive conclusion. "So, what are these goals?"

"I want to be an activist. I want to fight for civil rights…not just for Negroes, but people of all races. And I want to press the causes of women. The idea that half the population should be rendered second-class citizens based on their sex is no less outrageous than doing so based on the color of their skin." She looked me in the eye, perhaps weighing whether I concurred.

My presumption that marriage topped her list of goals was all wet. I was thankful I had opted for a question, rather than a declarative presupposition. I said, "Your point is well taken. But convincing the men of the world will be one tough battle."

"No tougher than the fight to abolish slavery."

The irony in her words caught me off guard.

"In case you've forgotten, we won that one."

Yeah, after centuries of suffering and persecution that culminated in unimaginable bloodshed. I might have voiced the sentiment had her face and tone been less resolute. "To what extent do you want to change things?"

"Simple…All people, regardless of race or sex…or for that matter, other arbitrary classifications, should be treated equally. People should be judged as individuals, by their conduct, not physical classifications."

"I take it you would support enactments similar to the Fourteenth amendment to the Constitution and the Civil Rights Act of 1866."

"I'm familiar with the Fourteenth Amendment, but not the Civil Rights Act. Unless the latter covers the right to vote, I'm talking about more than those two enactments. The right to vote, given to folks like you in the Fifteenth Amendment, must be expanded to include women."

Her position reminded me of Walter's comments about the importance of the Fifteenth Amendment. It also reminded me of Mr. Wright's assessment that as a Maroon, I might not enjoy the benefit of that amendment. Rather than focus on my own circumstances, I said, "Is getting women the right to vote number one on your list?"

"Not to diminish it, but no. Other rights, such as property rights, are equally important."

Discrimination based upon race had long stuck in my craw, if only because I was among the victims. My relationship with Abbey had been quashed because of my race. Though I could not prove it, I believed that Grover, my surrogate father, had been taken from me owing to his race. Hooker had fired me because of my race. The inequity was familiar. But the idea that discrimination based upon sex was equally unfair was not something I had seriously contemplated. I had grown up with certain assumptions. Men and women were different. Men took care of women. They had different roles in society. Men were breadwinners, while women bore children and were nurturers. The set of postulates made perfect sense…at least to men in a patriarchal society. But whites, male and female, had made similar arguments, not the least of which was the inferiority of people of color, in order to maintain an inequitable, racist society. The analogy to sex-based discrimination rattled my brain. A few seconds was insufficient to examine the complex issue. What was clear, an intelligent young woman, whom I found incredibly attractive, had seduced me to weigh questions I had not previously entertained. "Are you hoping to get women the rights of men, all in one fell swoop?"

She shrugged. "Naturally I want them all and quickly. But if it must be one at a time, so be it." She appeared to study me. "What kind of look is that?"

"Sorry, I didn't mean to appear cynical. I was trying to imagine how you plan to go about it. Progress on racial discrimination, far from a fait accompli, required a war."

"Admittedly, and I suspect the fight for women's rights will involve tough battles."

"Violence?"

She heaved a sigh. "Personally, I don't believe in it, but others have a different view. And much as I disagree with them, crazy, they're not. To date, polite requests for rights have been met with lip service. Women, in this Victorian world, are told to tighten their corsets and sew their samplers. Leave politics and business to men. I, for one, find that insulting."

"Wow, you are a feisty one." The remark no sooner spoken than I regretted it. Intended as a compliment, it reeked of sarcasm.

"That's exactly what I was referring to: men refusing to take us women seriously."

I swallowed hard. Having to excuse my discourtesy was becoming a habit. "I didn't mean that the way it sounded."

"That's okay. I'm used to it."

Whether she had taken offense was hard to ascertain. Having put my foot into my mouth too many times, I was not about to seek clarification.

"Are you familiar with the Grimké sisters?"

"Who?"

"Sarah and Angelina Grimké."

I shook my head.

"They're from Charleston. They were at the forefront of the fight that won my freedom. Their father, a colonel in the Revolutionary War and a judge on the South Carolina Supreme Court, had a plantation there.[275] My grandfather was his slave. His daughter, my mother, was sold to another Charleston plantation owner. Anyway, the Grimké sisters rebelled, abandoning the wealth and advantage of the white aristocracy into which they had been born. They went north, became Quakers and outspoken abolitionists. During the first half of this century, they wrote and spoke out against slavery.[276] They attacked religious demagogues who distorted scripture with claims that God intended that Negroes be slaves. In their later years, the Grimkés wrote books and articles promoting women's rights. Sarah, the older sister, died this past December.[277] She can no longer wage the war for equality. Sarah died for me…and now, I'm obliged to carry her torch, the fight to end all discrimination. Before coming to the university, I became an activist. My education here will hopefully equip me to become an effective one."

The motivations behind Lucinda's passion had become apparent. "The world needs more people like you."

She eyed me. "I'll take that as a compliment, though it may have been sardonic, and if so, understandably. I often climb atop my soapbox."

"In support of a cause for which you're passionate…And just to set the record straight, it was a compliment." I gazed deeply into her lovely eyes.

---

275 *The Grimké Sisters, Abolitionists From South Carolina*, history1800s.about.com, 19 Sept. 2018 <http://history1800s.about.com/od/abolitionmovement/a/Grimke-Sisters.htm>.

276 Ibid.

277 Ibid. Sarah Grimké died on December 23, 1873. Noted abolitionist William Lloyd Garrison spoke at her funeral. Sarah's sister, Angelina, died on October 26, 1879.

Lucinda smiled…warmly.

"You're beautiful." I reached across the table and took her hand. I drew it towards me and kissed the back of it. Her fingers drew tighter around my hand. I responded in kind. Desire raged. Rapture ruled. Transfixed gazes articulated adoration. Lips, motionless, spoke more than words. Silent seconds communicated emotions.

When finally I released her hand, smiles were again exchanged. We finished our bratwurst and brews with little conversation. I paid our bill, and we left the quaint establishment. Hand in hand, we strolled back toward the campus. High above, the seven-starred canopy of the Big Dipper ladled us with benevolent sparkle. Past the Capitol, we negotiated our way into the Horseshoe and to Rutledge, her dorm. Standing outside the entrance, our eyes engaged, much as they had earlier at Seegers' Saloon. Longing lips, silent before, drew closer and met in a tender kiss. Seconds, perhaps no more than two or three…glorious seconds ticked before lips parted.

"Sweet dreams," said Lucinda.

Of that I had no doubt. "Sweet dreams to you, my dear."

Lucinda stepped inside Rutledge. I turned and floated down the Horseshoe's southerly leg to my dorm, Legare. Above, on high, a starlit sky, my gait so spry, did testify, her sweet goodbye, a lorelei upon Sinai, sublimely perfect lullaby.

Chapter XIX

A WEEK EARLIER I HAD RECEIVED A LETTER from Walter that the completed St. Augustine Lighthouse was scheduled to be lit in a ceremony on Saturday, the 18th of October 1874. Daft as it seemed, immediately after classes on Wednesday the 15th, I boarded the South Carolina Railroad and began the two-day trip to St. Augustine. That I would travel back to Florida only six weeks into my college education would not have been predictable before I had left St. Augustine. But so too, the level of academic challenge, far below my expectations, had not been predictable. Past experience, proving I could make the trip missing only three days of classes (Thursday, Friday and the following Monday), provided the impetus to venture forth. Two days would get me to St. Augustine late Friday, where I would spend two nights, including that of the Saturday ceremony, followed by a departure Sunday morning for an arrival back on campus early Tuesday.

Right on schedule, I reached St. Augustine on Friday afternoon. I went directly to Walter's home. I had a key, not that one was needed. Walter rarely locked his door. No longer his tenant, I knocked, if only because it seemed the thing to do. Moments later, he opened the portal.

His eyes widened. "Mican…Is everythin' okay?"

"Absolutely. I couldn't miss the lighting ceremony. Once I got your letter, I had to come."

"Glad you did, not that I expected you." He motioned me in.

"How things here?"

"Good. Bill (the lighthouse worker I had recommended as a tenant) is workin' out well…not that he could replace you."

Concerned for potential embarrassment, I gestured up the stairway.

"Don't worry. He's stayin' at the lighthouse the whole weekend. Didn't want to miss none of the excitement, now that the job is endin'…How's college?"

"Excellent. It's easier than I expected...mainly because so many of the students have weak backgrounds. The truth be known, they don't seem ready for college. They may be smart enough, but another year or two in high school wouldn't hurt...Strange though, the campus is predominantly Negro. Not the faculty—there's only one Negro professor—but the students."

A puzzled cast showed on Walter's face. "A public college in South Carolina, a great bastion of the Confederacy, got mainly Negro students?"

"I know it sounds strange, but there's a logical explanation. South Carolina's State Legislature, as well as the university's Board of Trustees, has a Negro majority."

Walter chuckled.

"What's so funny?"

"Negro majorities in the Legislature and on the Board may explain why the campus is mainly Negro, but those majorities are weirder yet. But enough of that for now. After your long journey, I'll bet you could do with a good meal and a lemonade." Walter pointed up the stairs. "Your room is just as you left it. Stick your bag up there, and I'll meet you in the dinin' room. I got a nice lamb stew simmerin' on the stove."

Walter limped into the kitchen, as I started up the stairs. "How's that knee of yours?"

Walter called back. "Creakin' worse than a mismounted door."

Minutes later, I joined him in the dining room, where he already occupied his traditional seat. A bowl of stew, along with a glass of lemonade, fronted our respective places. As always, what had been Wilma's seat, the one nearest the kitchen, remained vacant.

"So, whad'ya like best 'bout school?"

Though I suspected he was referring to my courses, I said, "I met an incredible girl. Her name is Lucinda."

Walter eyed me.

As well as I knew him, I read his face. "Yes, I've fallen for her, big time." I anticipated a verbal response, but when his silent gaze persisted, I said, "And yes, I believe it's mutual."

A broad smile painted his face. He stared at the far end of the table, Wilma's seat. "Ain't nothin' better than love. I'm happy for you. Hope it's the start of many decades like I enjoyed." His tone became wistful. "If it is, just one warnin'. Don't make the mistake I made."

To what he was referring, I could not imagine. Anytime he had referenced Wilma, wonderful, affection-suffused memories had been evident.

"Make sure you don't outlive your sweetie. 'Cause once you do, your world gets hollow." He took a bite of his stew. "Strange...always thought I could get along without much. Didn't realize I was spoiled...spoiled real bad."

Clarifying the apparent anomaly that Walter had posed would have been easy. Material wants and needs...Walter had few. Wilma's love was entirely different. When she died, Walter lost a part of himself. Fascinating as the intellectual nicety may have been, Walter had no need to hear it from me. Chances were his philosophical musing had been rhetorical. He was well aware of the distinction. I kept my mouth shut, at least no words crossed my lips. A tasty chunk of stew, however, did.

"The lighthouse ceremony gonna be held early tomorrow evening, close to dark. Understand they want folks to enjoy the full effect of the new light."

"Would you like to go with me?" I said.

"Ever since you showed up, I was hopin' you'd aks. Just 'cause I didn't work on the lighthouse don't matter. Lived 'round here my whole life. Bein' at the ceremony 'll be real nice...How long you plan to stay?"

"Till Sunday morning. That way I can make it back for classes Tuesday."

"Wish you could stay longer...but a scoop of ice cream, even if it don't compare to a big bowl, sure beats none."

***

Bum knee and all, Walter walked with me up St. George Street to the ferry that took us across the Matanzas River to Anastasia Island. From there we hiked the half-mile to the new lighthouse. With dusk on the brink, we emerged from the tree-lined path where the structure came into full view. "Wow," said Walter. "It's magnificent. First time I seen it up close. A lot different than lookin' across the river."

I stopped and marveled as well. I focused on the huge glass section at the top. A welling sense of pride confirmed my decision to return for the ceremony. A crowd, as best I could judge, three or four hundred, encircled the base. Walter and I drew closer, about forty yards from the lighthouse, where the crowd began.

"Hey, Charlie. Look who came back for the ceremony. It's Mican." Lloyd *something* (I only knew many of my fellow workers by first names) hurried my way. "You graduate already?" Lloyd slapped me on the back.

"Uh...almost, but not quite," I said.

"Great to see you, Mican," said Charlie. "Things goin' well in South Carolina?"

"Very." I introduced Walter to them.

His hand to the side of his mouth, as if shielding me from his conversation, Lloyd focused on Walter. "Between you, me and that big black and white barber pole (he gestured), besides being one of the best workers, Mican was mighty popular here." He turned my way. "Glad you could make it back."

"Now that the lens is in place, you gotta go up to the top," said Charlie. "From here it's impressive, but that ain't nothin' compared to up close. Damn thing is amazin'."

With a few more pleasantries exchanged, Walter and I worked our way among the throng to the lighthouse. Four or five times we were corralled. Enthusiastic welcomes and plaudits repeatedly came my way. As we reached the lighthouse, Walter said, "Seems you made as big a mark with the guys as with me."

"Apparently, my coworkers are as bad as you when it comes to judging people."

"Yup, that's how I see it." Walter winked before gesturing at the structure. "Shall we go up?"

I shot him a look. "Minor detail, the climb to the top is 219 stairs." All the workers knew the number, not merely because we had been told; we had counted them.

"I know. I'm gonna take the elevator."

"There's no—" I clipped my tongue. Obviously, he was teasing. "You mind waiting down here while I go up?"

"No problem. Jake and Peggy Turner—they worship at the cathedral—are right over there." He pointed. "I'll go say hello."

I entered the lighthouse and, following behind others, began climbing the spiral staircase to the top. Unlike some who stopped at the eight landings,[278] mostly to catch their breath, I pressed forward uninterrupted. At irregular intervals I passed individuals going down.

"Tough climb," said one. "But you won't be disappointed. Well worth the view at the top."

I nodded. Headed in the opposite direction, time was insufficient to inform him I had made the ascent and seen the view many times. But what I had not seen was the landmark's crowning jewel, the Fresnel lens.

Further up, another man said, "Just a little more, and you'll be there." He called back over his shoulder. "It's a lot easier going down."

---

[278] *St. Augustine Lighthouse and Museum*, op. cit.

No fooling. A minute later, I reached the apex. I climbed out onto the wide platform that served as a base for the lens, which was sandwiched between a pedestal and cap, both bright red. Others who arrived at the top just ahead and behind me oohed at the magnificent view in every direction. After the many hours I had spent at the lofty perch, the distant sights were no surprise. Admittedly they were awesome; nevertheless, my focus directed inward. I looked through the steel-framed, circular, glass-walled chamber that housed the incredible Fresnel lens. I slowly followed the outer rail of the bright red platform that encircled the lens. I had read about its inventor, Agustin Fresnel. When he was eight, he could barely read. No one could have predicted that his dogged study of the behavior of light would enable him to develop lenses and advance lighthouse effectiveness in ways that had not occurred in two thousand years.[279] I had seen his diagram with concentric rings of glass and countless beehive prisms, with bullseyes, that bend light into a narrow beam.[280] I knew that an open flame lost 97% of its light; that rear reflectors had reduced that loss to 83%; but that Fresnel's lenses had lowered it to an amazing 17%.[281] And too, I knew the dimensions of Fresnel's St. Augustine lens: nine feet tall and six feet wide, consisting of 370 hand-cut, beehive prisms.[282] Diagrams, dimensions and statistics…I knew them all. But plans, measurements and data were one thing. Seeing the Fresnel lens up close, another. The ensuing ten minutes, I studied the masterpiece from every angle, circling it repeatedly, committing the details to memory as best I could.

I turned to the west where the Sun had already sunk halfway beneath the horizon. A minute later, the flaming disc vanished, a golden glow in its wake. It struck me that sunset had arrived at the lighthouse base a minute or two earlier. Very deliberately, I circled the platform, taking time to observe the Lilliputians below. After dawdling a bit longer, I slowly descended the staircase, joining Walter outside the lighthouse.

---

[279] *Fresnel Lens History*, dunkirklighthouse.com, 29 Jan. 2018 <http://www.dunkirklighthouse.com/fresnel_lens_history.htm>.

[280] Ibid.

[281] Ibid.

[282] *Lighthouse History*, staugustinelighthouse.org, 9 Jan. 2018 <http://www.staugustinelighthouse.org/ourstories/LighthouseStory>. While the St. Augustine Lighthouse is today lit by a 1000-watt bulb, the Fresnel lens installed in 1874, with its prodigious capacity for light refraction, continues to function. *But see, History - Fresnel Lenses, Coast Guard Compass*, coastguard.dodlive.mil, 29 Jan. 2018 <http://coastguard.dodlive.mil/2009/09/history-fresnel-lenses/> indicating: "The lighthouse lens of yesteryear has today been superseded by handheld GPS devices, although some locations around the country still use Fresnel lenses as working aids to navigation…"

Minutes ticked by. The dark veil of night had all but gripped Anastasia's terrain. Eyes aloft, a buzz raced through the throng encircling the lighthouse. The magic moment finally arrived.

High above, the chief keeper, William Russel, who had long maintained the old St. Augustine lighthouse, lit the new one.[283] Oohs and aahs pervaded as the breathtaking beam rotated from water to land and around again. I basked, not just in the glow that stretched to the vista where the Heavens caressed the sea, but also from inner pride. The stunning tower represented three years of my life, as well as that of my coworkers. With the task complete and jobs few, many of them were apt to wander aimlessly like the waves on the great Atlantic expanse, searching for their next beach. Not so for me. I had already found my place at a new port, a beautiful college campus. My future mapped, I savored the moment. Any doubts about my decision to return for the ceremony vanished amidst the shadows far beneath the brilliant beacon.

***

Summer hot, its juggernaut had since begot a kinder slot, the gordian knot of heat forgot, a blessing sought, a Camelot.

Thanksgiving, proclaimed a national holiday by President Lincoln back when the country was in the throes of the War of Secession, had come and gone the week before. The oaks and elms and other deciduous trees had shed all but a few recalcitrant leaves. Beneath a gray sky, the Horseshoe, lush with greenery only weeks earlier, bore a stark mantle. I headed into Harper for Professor Nelson's Philosophy class. I climbed the stairs to Room 302, where I took my seat next to Lucinda. My other four classmates had already arrived.

"Hi Sweetie. How was your trip home to Charleston?" Lucinda had taken a long weekend, the first time she had missed any class and her first trip home since school had commenced.

"Very nice. On Saturday evening, I visited my cousin Henrietta. She served a wonderful ham dinner with all the fixings. How was your—"

"Good morning," said Professor Nelson, who had just arrived. "Before returning to the reading of Kant that we began in our last meeting, in recognition of Thanksgiving, which came in the interim, let us take a few moments to acknowledge our blessings and examine, philosophically speaking, how our little world fits into the greater world." Professor Nelson came around from behind his desk, and, as he was wont to do, seated himself atop the walnut furnishing. "We here on

[283] *St. Augustine Light*, Wikipedia, op. cit.

this beautiful campus, a site conducive to learning, are indeed fortunate. Look beyond the walls of this haven, and to the north, east, south and west, devastation prevails. War's horrible vestiges scream. Widespread ruins pervade. Somehow, be it the will of God or serendipity, this iconic institution was spared. Our campus, a seat of exemplary pursuits, can be the font of better days. As the only southern state institution of higher learning open to all races, it can prove to the former Confederacy that Caucasians and Negroes can build a better social and economic future together.

"Friends have asked me why I, a white man, am willing to teach on a campus that has become predominantly Negro. Their questions offend me. Admittedly, a more balanced population would be preferable. The refusal of many whites to study on an integrated campus deprives us of that benefit. It cannot, however, stop us. We have sown the seeds of the future."

I looked around the sparsely populated room. All six of us students were colored. Professor Nelson was the only white. Still I was glad he was there. Whether he was jousting with windmills, pursuing a quixotic dream, remained to be seen.

"The mountain we must climb is indeed tall. Economics, always an underlying force, pushes back against us. Since the crash of the stock market a bit more than a year ago, the nation has been driven into deep recession. This dim outlook superimposes itself on what was already a bleak South Carolina landscape. Of the roughly $400,000,000 worth of property that our state enjoyed when the war began, only $50,000,000 remains.[284] Nearly ninety percent was destroyed. Moreover, the abolition of slavery, righteous as it was, has hit South Carolina harder than any other state. It was one of two states, the other Mississippi, that had more slaves than whites, and South Carolina's excess, over 111,000, was the largest.[285] The foregoing confirms that South Carolina's road back to prosperity will be arduous.

"Compounding the difficulty are perilous political winds seeking to propel us backwards. Congressional elections held earlier this month have placed both houses of the United States Congress under Democratic control.[286] These Democrats will likely dam the flow of funds that finance Reconstruction. With recession shrinking federal tax receipts and

---

[284] *Reconstruction in South Carolina – NY Times.com*, nytimes.com, 14 Sept. 2018 <http://www.nytimes.com/1865/09/13/news/reconstruction-in-south-carolina.html>.

[285] Ibid., to the effect that South Carolina had 402,406 slaves and 291,388 whites, an excess of 111,018 slaves prior to the Emancipation Proclamation. The estimated value of South Carolina's slave population in 1860 was $200,000,000.

[286] *Reconstruction Timeline*, op. cit.

Congressional focus directed to restoring the Union, both money and political will to rebuild the South will be scant.[287]

"Other electoral events presage the risks that past gains will evaporate. Alabama and Arkansas have joined the ranks of states electing redeemer governments.[288] Earlier this month, Andrew Johnson, the president who was voted out of office after surviving conviction in the Senate following impeachment, was elected as a United States Senator from Tennessee.[289] That Johnson, the ultimate symbol of a determined white aristocracy, will be returning to Washington is ominous.

"All of the foregoing notwithstanding, I suggest that we here on the campus of the University of South Carolina are extremely fortunate. In the face of vast hurdles, we have made great strides toward a more just society. But if progress toward equality is to continue, if the demons of an iniquitous past are to be repelled, we must remain vigilant. We cannot take our good fortune for granted. Beyond our respective duties to study and teach, we must set an example and press the cause of righteousness. And with that said, unless you have questions or comments, let us return to our discussion of Immanuel Kant."

As I flipped open my notebook, I stemmed the urge to clap. Professor Nelson exemplified what the nation needed, more men willing to stand up for the cause of righteousness. Off to my right, out of the corner of my eye, I saw Lucinda's hand go up.

"Yes, Miss Brown."

"Regarding the progress that has been made with respect to civil rights, do you believe that equality for women has been wrongfully ignored?"

Professor Nelson climbed down from his desk. "No. In the first place, overcoming discrimination based upon race is a huge challenge. Muddying it with other matters, even valid ones, would be a mistake. But muddying it with a specious one would be madness."

"You don't believe that women should enjoy the same rights as men?" Lucinda's question was delivered in a clement, rancor-free voice.

"Absolutely not." A steely-eyed Professor Nelson moved toward the windows and took a step forward in Lucinda's direction. "Discrimination based upon race is inherently wrong. Distinctions based upon sex simply recognize the undeniable differences between males and females. Don't get me wrong. I'm not saying men are better than women

---

[287] *South Carolina after the Civil War*, SC Digital Academy Website, 29 Mar. 2018 <library.sc.edu/blogs/academy/files/2011/08/South-Carolina-after-the-Civil-War-3-4-6.pdf>.

[288] Ibid.

[289] *Andrew Johnson – U.S. President*, op. cit.

or visa-versa. I'm simply acknowledging that they're different. You don't dispute that, Miss Brown, do you?"

The amiable professor had willingly entertained Lucinda's question. But he had also made his position eminently clear. Irrespective of the merits of the issue, judgment dictated abandoning it.

"Shouldn't women be able to vote? Why should husbands have a right to their wives' property? What—"

"Miss Brown!" Pique replaced Professor Nelson's normally placid demeanor. "To answer your questions, *no*, *no*…and to the one you were yet to complete, *no*!"

"Why?"

Lucinda's persistence stunned me.

"Why?...I'll tell you." Professor Nelson took a deep breath, seemingly to ease elevating ire. His voice soft, his cadence measured, he delivered an emphatic response. "In case you haven't noticed, men and women are different. Men are physically strong. Men are breadwinners. And men are leaders." His icy stare communicated that these were facts, not opinions open for debate. "Women, on the other hand, bear children. They are nurturers. They care for the home. I reiterate, I'm not saying men are better than women; merely that they are different." Professor Nelson took a couple of steps in Lucinda's direction, enabling him to look down at her. "Allow me to refer you to the greatest of all wisdom, the Bible. It is written in Colossians 3:18, 'Wives submit yourselves unto your husbands, as it is fit in the Lord.' And in Corinthians 14:33-36, 'Women should remain silent in the churches. They are not allowed to speak, but must be in submission, as the law says. If they want to inquire about something, they should ask their own husbands at home, for it is disgraceful for a woman to speak in the church.'" Professor Nelson folded his arms. "I trust the word of the Lord suffices to curtail your presumption."

Lucinda remained defiantly stone faced.

"Your reaction appears to be less than a resounding *yes.*"

I quavered for Lucinda. Professor Nelson's thermometer had elevated. Explosion was all but imminent.

"So, even God's message doesn't satisfy you." Professor Nelson repeatedly shook his head. His thundering voice resounded. "Rarely does a student draw my ire. You, however, have accomplished that uncommon feat…Here I am, a white man, fighting to win equality for people like you, of color, and what do you do? You attack me. You, Miss Brown, are an ingrate!"

A pervasive silence draped the room. Footsteps of a fly crawling on the windowsill were all but audible. Lucinda remained motionless, a stoic statue. Professor Nelson moved slowly back toward his desk, resuming his lesson on Kant. My eyes directed to him, but my mind stayed focused on what had preceded. Much as he had claimed to be a champion of people of color, and he was, Professor Nelson was a bigot. And his bigotry was racial, as well as sexual. That Lucinda, enjoying the privilege of attending the formerly all-white university, had less of a right than a Caucasian to voice objection was the definition of bias. For a moment, the observation seemed paradoxical. But a familiar mathematical concept dispatched the illogic. Prejudice lay on a continuum. Professor Nelson differed from the hatemongers of the Ku Klux Klan. He also differed from Professor Hopkins. Much about his views was laudable. But free from prejudice, Professor Nelson wasn't. Then again, even the most fair-minded person, while decidedly fairer than Professor Nelson, was less than perfect.

Amidst my wandering thoughts, the class continued until Professor Nelson finished his lecture. The instant he dismissed us, Lucinda raced for the door. As I followed in hot pursuit, she passed in front of Professor Nelson, never looking his way. I caught up to her in the hallway.

"Can you believe that bull-headed blowhard? Chastising me because I refused to thank him for his prejudice."

"It was offensive…and not to excuse it, but from his perspective, he's going out on a limb for people of color."

"Jesus, you're taking his side."

"I'm not. I'm merely trying to explain how he sees the situation."

"As I said, you're taking his side." Lucinda charged down the hall and the stairs, leaving me well behind.

I caught up to her outside. "I wasn't saying he was right."

"You damn well weren't saying he was wrong!" The look that punctuated her remark was more telling than her words.

We were having our first fight. What made it absurd was she was right, and I knew it. Regardless how Professor Nelson felt about race, when it came to women, he was biased. Lucinda had reason to be outraged. Not only had he demeaned her position, but he had demeaned her as well, and he had done so in front of the entire class. "I'm sorry," I said. "I had no business defending him. He was wrong both on substance and for attacking you."

"I appreciate your saying that. I needed to hear it…even though I understood the point you were trying to make…And by the way, I'm sorry too."

"For what?"

"I lashed out at you, owing to my frustration with Nelson. I needed to vent."

I put my arm around Lucinda, leaned over, and pecked her on the cheek. An amorous smile covered her face. I kissed her on the lips. Our first fight was short lived. “I love you,” I whispered.

“I love you too.”

The exchange of words was special. Even more special had been our kisses-festooned moonlight stroll a week earlier. Just before Lucinda had entered her dormitory, each of us had uttered the iconic three-word phrase, a mere eight letters, for the first time. Armed with that articulation’s magical power, I had headed for my room in Legare, along the way defying the law of gravity...soaring high above the Horseshoe.

***

Christmas and New Year’s Day had come and gone. The second semester had begun. Excellent grades, among the highest in the freshman class, had proved that I had what it took for a successful college career. A cold January day with winds howling through the Horseshoe assaulted me as I headed to physics class. As I stepped into Rutledge, I welcomed the building’s sanctuary. I ascended the stairs to the classroom of Reverend B. B. Babbitt,[290] where I took my seat in the middle of the room. Minutes later, Reverend Babbitt began the class.

“Today we begin our discussion of optics, more specifically, lenses and the refraction and reflection of light. Light is bent as it passes through a material, even air. The amount it is bent is determined by the material’s refractive index. Every material has its own refractive index.[291] Before diving into the scientific details surrounding refraction, let’s briefly discuss the subject as laymen, the way we all observe it in daily life.” Reverend Babbitt looked around the room. “Unlike me, most of you are too young to need eyeglasses. A person who is nearsighted cannot see distant objects clearly because the shape of the eye causes entering light rays to meet at a point in front of the retina, rather than directly on the surface of the retina. In contrast, a person who is farsighted has the

---

[290] *Reconstruction in South Carolina, 1865-1877*, op. cit., p. 232, indicating that the Reverend B. B. Babbitt was chair of physics at the time.

[291] *Snell’s law | physics | Britannica.com*, Britannica.com, 29 Mar. 2018 <https://www.britannica.com/science/Snells-law>. Snell’s Law, promulgated in 1621 by Willebrod Snell, a Dutch mathematician and astronomer, says that when a light ray passes from one material to another, the ratio of the sine of the angle the ray makes with a perpendicular to the first material and the sine of the angle the ray makes with the perpendicular to the second material equals the ratio of their respective refractive indexes ($I_1/I_2 = \Theta_1/\Theta_2$, where I_1 and I_2 are the respective refractive indices of the materials and Θ_1 and Θ_2 are the respective sines of the angles the rays make with the perpendicular to the respective materials).

opposite problem. The curvature of the eye causes light rays to meet, come into focus, behind the retina. Eyeglasses bend light so its rays meet at a point directly on the retina." Reverend Babbitt studied the class, seemingly assessing whether his message was being absorbed. "Who can tell me what bifocals are and who invented them?" Reacting to a raised hand in the back, he said, "Yes, Mr. Grayson."

"Bifocals were invented by Benjamin Franklin. They are worn by people, like my grandfather, who have trouble seeing objects both near and far...people who are both nearsighted and farsighted."

"Correct on the substance...and yes, as to Benjamin Franklin, as best as history suggests.[292] And we will speak more of Dr. Franklin before the class is over. For the moment, let's focus—no pun intended—on nearsightedness and farsightedness. As we shall see when we get deeper into refraction, in the case of the former, a concave lens, one curved inward, is used to bend light outward, so its focal point is farther back, at the retina. In contrast, farsightedness is corrected with a convex lens, one curved outward, which bends light inward, making the focal point closer, again at the retina.[293] Now, can anyone give me another example of refraction?"

"Yes, Miss Wood," said Reverend Babbitt.

"A rainbow."

"Correct...And can you explain how that occurs?"

"Not really. I only recall that someone told me it was refraction."

"Well, let me explain. A raindrop acts like a prism, which is a triangular piece of glass. A light beam is made up of all the colors of the spectrum from red to violet. When light from the Sun moves from air through a raindrop, because air and water have different refractive indexes, the light is bent. But the different colors of the spectrum, owing to the fact they have different wavelengths, are bent in different amounts. And that is why we see a rainbow."

My hand shot up and Reverend Babbitt called on me.

"Why then don't people who wear eyeglasses see things with a rainbow effect?"

"Excellent question...It's because the eyeglasses are so close to the retina that the amount of dispersion of the different colors is too minute to be detected. Where the angle between light entering and leaving glass drops 42° for red light, at the far end of the spectrum it drops 40° for

---

[292] *Benjamin Franklin – Father of the Bifocal*, antiquespectacles.com, 29 Mar. 2018 <http://www.antiquespectacles.com/topics/franklin/franklin.htm>.

[293] *How Glasses Correct Your Vision*, glassescrafter.com, 29 Mar. 2018 <http://glassescrafter.com/information/how-glasses-correct-vision-.html>.

violet.[294] Not much of a difference, especially when projected over the fraction of an inch between the eyeglasses and retina. But technically you are correct. What we term a 'chromatic aberration' occurs.[295] All colors do not meet at a point."

Reverend Babbitt eased back a couple of steps. "I'm sure you've noticed the beautiful reds and yellows and other hues that often paint the sky at sunrise and sunset. Can you tell me what causes these glorious effects?" He waited a moment, and when no response was forthcoming, said, "Without getting too technical, as we merely embark on the subject, suffice it to say that particle matter in the atmosphere refracts the Sun's light, dispersing different colors at different angles."[296]

Reverend Babbitt eyed the wall clock. "We have less than ten minutes, and I want to be sure to return to Benjamin Franklin, one of our Founding Fathers. The good doctor is the epitome of why we are providing you with a broad classical education here at the university. Our nation's Founding Fathers were men of letters, Renaissance men. They had command of the language. They knew history. They were statesmen. They were architects and builders, designing and constructing their homes and other edifices of note. They appreciated both science and the arts. And they understood how to integrate their knowledge, use its many facets together. They were independent, but they were leaders. The education we are giving you here is calculated to arm you with such knowledge and skill, enable you to see the full picture, no matter what issues insinuate themselves, be they of science, history, mathematics, politics, philosophy or whatever. Not only do I want you to learn physics, but I want you to integrate it, so you can use it in conjunction with your other knowledge. This is my goal." Reverend Babbitt checked the clock. "We still have five minutes. Can anyone give me another example where we employ a lens, and perhaps even explain how the lens works?"

A hand shot up in the far corner.

"Yes, Mr. Wilson."

"Some lighthouses have lenses. I live in McClellanville, a little over one hundred miles southeast of here. Nearby is the Cape Roman

---

[294] *What causes a rainbow | How Stuff Works*, science.howstuffworks.com, 29 Mar. 2018 <https://science.howstuffworks.com/nature/climate-weather/atmospheric/question41.htm>.

[295] *Why do I see a red or blue* glow *on certain objects when wearing my glasses? – Quora*, quora.com, 30 Mar. 2018 <https://www.quora.com/Why-do-I-see-a-red-or-blue-glow-on-certain-objects-when-wearing-my-glasses>.

[296] *Optics*, Wikipedia, 29 Mar. 2018 <https://en.wikipedia.org/wiki/Optics>.

Lighthouse.[297] The original had lots of lamps and reflectors, but because it couldn't be seen from a sufficient distance, several years before the War of Secession, they built a new lighthouse, one with a special kind of lens. I believe it's called a…'Freshel' lens, but I don't know what it is or how it works."

"I've heard that modern lighthouses have lenses." Reverend Babbitt shrugged. "But I'm not familiar with their details."

"Mican helped build a lighthouse. He might know."

"Mr. Grove, I appreciate the information, but in this class, we raise a hand and wait to be recognized." Reverend Babbitt turned my way. "Mr. Reinbow, is it true that you helped build a lighthouse?"

"Yes, Sir. The St. Augustine Lighthouse."

"By any chance, do you know if it employs a lens and how it works?"

"Yes, Sir. It has a Fresnel lens." I spelled the name. "It's pronounced *fray-nel´*." I hesitated to go further.

"Can you tell us anything more about it?"

Back when I was working on the lighthouse, I was interested in its design, including the science behind it. Articulating it was easy. "It's glass and has an oval shape, something like a watermelon, except the bottom is flat. The one in St. Augustine is roughly nine feet tall, what's called 'first order,' the tallest. It's an array of concentric annular sections, a series of stepped prisms, each of which bend light a little more than the one beneath it, so all the light rays are parallel, focused into an intensely powerful beam.[298]"

Reverend Babbitt's eyes appeared to glaze over. "Uh…on that extraordinary note, we'll call it a class."

Like my classmates, I got up and headed for the door. As I passed Reverend Babbitt, he said, "A very interesting exposition. Once we get deeper into optics, perhaps you'll share more about the St. Augustine lens. I'd love to hear about it."

---

[297] *Cape Romain Lighthouses*, Wikipedia, 31 Mar. 2018 <https://en.wikipedia.org/wiki/Cape_Romain_Lighthouses>.

[298] *How do Fresnel lenses work? – Explain that Stuff*, explainthatstuff.com, 25 Mar. 2018 <http://www.explainthatstufff.com/fresnel-lens.html> states: "A lighthouse uses similar science to a telescope, but works in exactly the opposite way—with the help of a Fresnel lens. The glass lenses in a telescope refract (bend) light rays… into a powerful and parallel beam so people can see it, with just a naked eye, as far as 30 km (about 20 miles) away or more." *See also*, *Fresnel Lens*, Wikipedia, 26 Mar. 2018 <https://en.wikipedia.org/wiki/Fresnel_lens>.

"I…I'd be happy to." I bounded out the door, celebrating the unpredictable oddity. My extremely knowledgeable physics professor wanted me to educate him and the class…albeit it about a single matter.

***

Armed with a picnic basket, blanket and a bottle of wine, Lucinda and I headed out of the Horseshoe, where we proceeded north on Sumpter, turning west on Gervais, past the Capitol, toward our destination, across the Gervais Street Bridge. The walk, about a mile, beneath bountiful Sunday sunshine, confirmed that spring was in full swing. Pink azaleas and white camellias, their blossoms full, graced our path. In her long ivory dress with off-the-shoulder sleeves and three tiers of pink lace encircling the lower portion, Lucinda exceeded her usual, incredible self. A bustle and corset beneath, accented her superb womanly figure. A pink bonnet covered her pulled-back hair, crowned in a knot.

"You look beautiful," I said, my brain reaching beyond her sartorial splendor to the familiar charms they decorated.

"Flattery will get you everywhere." With a seductive smile, she teased.

With my free hand, I took hold of hers. While occasional new buildings hinted at progress, for the most part, the War's devastation, a mismatch for the colorful vegetation, predominated. But with Lucinda at my side, whatever the scenery, my world was nirvana. About twenty blissful minutes elapsed before we reached the Gervais Street Bridge. The lengthy steel-truss span, supported by rectangular brick pediments, stretched across the breadth of the Congaree River, just south of the confluence of the Broad and Saluda. The august structure, built just four years earlier, replaced the wooden bridge that the Confederacy had burned in a desperate effort to slow Sherman's march from the west into Columbia.

Lucinda and I strolled across, pausing near the middle to take in the gush of the merging rivers. Ripples and foam testified to the waters' inexorable bow to gravity's whim. Upon reaching the west side, we parked ourselves beneath an isolated palmetto palm, just beyond the crest of the bank. We spread our blanket and dined on a simple repast of southern fried chicken, sweet potatoes and mince pie from the commissary. Intermingled with our bites were sips directly from our shared bottle of white wine, chicer than the ever-popular beer and whiskey. Our dining done, we eased down onto our backs with Lucinda perpendicular to me, her head resting on my stomach and my arm wrapped around her.

Lucinda pointed skyward. "You see that big, white furry pussy cat floating overhead?"

"Looks more like a dragon to me."

"Have it your way…but if so, kindly slay it."

"Your wish, my dear, is my command."

Several seconds passed.

"You simply intend to lie there?"

"A little patience. Dragons are formidable…Tell you what. Close your eyes, and I'll see what I can do." I shut my eyes as well. A zephyr caressed my face. I caressed Lucinda's breast, savoring the contour over which my hand traveled. The rippling voice of the Congaree, harmonizing with the chirp of some feathered friends, played soothing music in my ears. Several minutes elapsed as I nearly dozed off. I checked the sky. The dragon had morphed into a nebulous blob. "Awaken, my dear…The evil dragon has met its fate."

"My hero." She drew upward and kissed me.

"I made something for you." I reached into my back pocket and took out a birchbark bookmark with a tethered garnet, much like the ones I had made before. I would have fashioned something different, but neither the arts, nor creativity were my forte. When it came to such, bookmarks included, I was a one-trick turkey.

"I love it."

"And I love you."

She kissed me. "I love you too."

***

Seated in the library, the first freestanding library building in the nation,[299] I waited for Lucinda. I had arranged to meet her there at three, following her two-o'clock class. I had arrived early and was studying when she approached my table in a back corner. Her face bore a worried look. "Is something wrong?"

"Well…uh…" She burst into tears.

I got up and gave her a hug. "What's the matter?"

---

[299] *South Caroliniana Library*, SC Encyclopedia, 18 Nov. 2019 <http://www.scencyclopedia.org/sce/south-carolina-library/> stating: "The South Caroliniana Library building was completed in 1840 as the central library building for the South Carolina College (later the University of South Carolina). It was the first freestanding college library building in the United States, predating those of Harvard (1841), Yale (1846) and Princeton (1873)."

She struggled to get her breath.

I held her and waited a moment. "Sit down and tell me what it is."

We seated ourselves side by side. Lucinda took several deep breaths. "You know that calculus test we had last week?"

"Yes," I said, finding it hard to imagine how that could be a problem. Lucinda had gotten 98%, her grade second only to mine.

Lucinda wiped her eyes. "Someone spread a rumor that I cheated. They claim I took out a cheat sheet during the test. And to make matters worse, someone passed the rumor on to Professor Hopkins." She looked me in the eye. "You know I didn't cheat, don't you?"

"Of course." I rubbed her back. "Any idea how Professor Hopkins reacted?"

"Not specifically, other than I heard he looked upset."

Given the professor's attitude about an integrated campus, I worried that he would unfairly prejudge the matter. Discretion kept me from voicing the concern. In all likelihood, it had already crossed Lucinda's mind. If by chance, it hadn't, mentioning it would only compound her anxiety. I said, "Any idea who started the rumor?"

"Don't actually know…but the two seniors in our class, Jefferson Lee and Sam Rutledge, are great candidates. Their resentment that folks like us have invaded their lily-white institution has never been hidden. Rutledge has been quoted to the effect that he never would have enrolled had he known in advance, 'they'd be admitting niggers.'"

"No doubt it galls him that freshmen like us whip his ass on the tests."

Lucinda managed a half-smile, the first hint of a positive emotion since she had arrived.

"So, what do you plan to do?"

"I don't know…Any suggestions?" Her plaintive tone begged sage counsel.

I had no clue.

"Aren't you going to say something?"

"Perhaps you should just play it by ear…wait and see what, if anything, Hopkins says."

"That's the same idea I had, not that it's a good one. Unfortunately, I can't come up with anything better. I guess I'm stuck with it."

***

Seated in our usual seats near the window, Lucinda and I waited in silence for Professor Hopkins to arrive for class. A common question occupied our minds: How would Professor Hopkins handle the cheating accusation? Two minutes late for class, the stocky pedagogue finally entered the room. He paused at his desk, and then, without saying a word, distributed a blank sheet of paper to each of us.

"Much as I hate to waste time, both yours and mine, we have a matter demanding attention." He went to the blackboard and picked up a piece of chalk. "This is a test, just two problems. You will have exactly ten minutes to complete it. It will separate the wheat from the chaff. And it will probe the truth."

He proceeded to write on the board: "For $1 \leq x \leq 3$, write an integral expression to find the volume (V) of the frustum of the cone formed when the line $y = x$ is rotated about the x-axis."

I pictured the graph of the equation $y = x$, a line at 45^0 to the x-axis. In my mind, I rotated it around the x-axis, visualizing the frustum of the cone formed for x-values between 1 and 3. Summing the volumes of infinitesimal cylinders of width dx and circular base, whose area πr^2 was equivalent to πx^2, over the designated range was easy using integration. I wrote the answer: $V = \pi \int_1^3 x^2 dx$.

I refocused on the blackboard and the second question Professor Hopkins had written there. "Find: $\int lnx\ dx$."

Using the integration by parts formula, $\int udv = uv - \int vdu$, I let $u = lnx$ and $dv = dx$. I applied the formula and with several brief steps arrived at the answer: $xlnx - x + C$.

I was less concerned about my answers than I was about Lucinda's. Much as I was curious how she was doing, I dared not steal a peek. Professor Hopkins was maintaining an eagle eye. From what little I could discern with my peripheral vision, Lucinda was still working on the problems.

"Ten minutes are up. All pens down…Now!" Professor Hopkins scurried around the room collecting the papers. He quickly wrote another problem on the blackboard. "Do this for practice while I take a few minutes to grade your papers."

Five minutes later, he said, "I've checked your answers. Seven of you got one answer right and one wrong. Three got both wrong. And two, Mr. Reinbow and Ms. Brown, got both correct. Professor Hopkins eyed Lucinda and me as he said our names. His gaze shifted to the remainder of the class. "In the future I trust there will be no further fictitious accusations of cheating…And one more thing, rest assured that the results of this test today will be incorporated into your grades." He headed to the blackboard where he resumed the class.

I glanced at Lucinda. I returned the broad smile that painted her face.

Chapter XX

RECENT MONTHS HAD BROUGHT POSITIVE NEWS as the nation continued to digest the aftermath of the War of Secession. In early March, the 43rd Congress, just before the conclusion of its second and final session,[300] had enacted the Civil Rights Act of 1875, outlawing segregation in public accommodations and facilities such as hotels, theaters, railroads and steamships.[301] But with America, like the rest of the world, still mired in recession, and Democrats fighting to regain political power, the only certainty regarding the nation's future was its categorical uncertainty. Whether the cantilevers of constitutional amendments and statutes were strong enough to bridge the divide of hate and enable the nation to realize the principles of its founding documents remained in doubt. Only time would tell.

The final day of our freshman year at the University of South Carolina was behind us. Exams, with all their pressure, were history. Lucinda and I were both near the top of our class. In recent months we had spent hours together every day, studying, eating and socializing, along with the two classes we shared. Our relationship was the most serious and longest that either of us had experienced. Hours earlier we

---

[300] "The Twentieth Amendment (Amendment XX) to the United States Constitution moved the beginning and ending of the terms of the president and vice-president from March 4 to Jan. 20 and of members of Congress from March 4 to January 3." *Twentieth Amendment to the United States Constitution*, Wikipedia, 31 Mar. 2018 <https://en.wikipedia.org/wiki/Twentieth_Amendment_to_the_United_States_Constitution>.

[301] *About the Civil Rights Cases of 1883*, thoughtco.com, 31 Mar. 2018 <https://www.thoughtco.com/1883-civil-rights-cases-4134310>. Several years after its enactment, in the Civil Rights Cases of 1883, the United States Supreme Court, voting 8-1, struck down that portion of the Civil Rights Act of 1875 which prevented discrimination in public accommodations and facilities such as hotels, theaters, railroads and steamships. The Court held "the Thirteen and Fourteenth Amendments did not give Congress the power to regulate the affairs of private individuals or businesses."

had boarded the South Carolina Railroad and traveled southeast to Charleston. With my steamer from Charleston set to sail south at eight in the evening, I had but a few hours to spend in her hometown. I accompanied Lucinda to her house where I met her mother. The lovely lady—Lucinda was a tintype of her mom—welcomed me warmly. Anxiety that stirred before I arrived at their tiny bungalow evaporated in the brief hours I spent there. I boarded my steamer with a smile, convinced that Lucinda's mother liked me and approved of our relationship.

Nearly a day after leaving Charleston, I disembarked my ship as it made a brief stop at Tocoi Point. I had already written my first letter to Lucinda. Summer break was nice, but just two days into it, I was looking forward to being back at the university, back with Lucinda. I caught the final daily run of the St. John's Railroad for the fifteen-mile trip from the St. John's River east to St. Augustine.[302] The train's run ended near the San Sebastian River at West King Street, about a mile from Walter's home. I was hoping to hire a wagon for transport, but arriving after dark, only one was available. A couple, not going my way, beat me to it. With a suitcase in one hand and a small duffle under my arm, I trekked the half-mile east to the Plaza, followed by another half-mile south to Walter's home. The walk, normally about fifteen minutes, took considerably more, owing not only to a slow pace, but two stops to rest. It was nearly ten when I finally arrived at Walter's. I knocked, not wanting to alarm Walter at such a late hour.

Moments later, I heard Walter call out, "Who's there?"

"Mican."

I no sooner said my name than the door swung open. "Great to see you. How come you knocked? You know I don't lock it."

"I was afraid I'd scare you." I carried my things inside. "How you feeling?"

"Good, 'cept my damn knee. Doesn't take to humid June weather. 'Course it don't take to nuttin'. Your room is waitin' for you. I'd help you carry your stuff up, but I can't barely make it to the top, even with both hands on the rail."

I lugged my bags upstairs and deposited them in my room. Before going back down, I poked my head into the room across the hall. Bill wasn't there. I headed down.

---

302 *Saint Johns Railroad Collection,* | *Florida Historical Society,* op. cit., indicating: "The St. John's`Railroad ran from Tocoi Landing on the St. John's River to New Augustine, a village near San Sebastian River [sic]…The only tangible reminder of the Saint John's Railroad existence is a St. Augustine Historical Society marker standing on Florida State Road 214" (West King Street).

"Bill out tonight?"

Walter handed me a tall lemonade, one of two he held. "Nah, he moved out two months ago. Got an offer to work at a warehouse in Jacksonville."

"How come you didn't tell me?"

"I just did."

"C'mon, you know that's not what I meant. You could have put it in your letters."

Walter shook his head.

"What's that supposed to mean?"

"That if I had told you, two things, neither of which was good, mighta happened. One, you woulda worried about me. Worse yet, you mighta come here. Last thing I wanted was for you to miss school."

"Well, I'm here now…for two months. And while I'm here, I'll help you find another tenant."

"You hungry?"

"Nope. Riding the steamship and the train, I ate four or five apple-butter sandwiches. I'm stuffed."

Walter gestured toward the door. "Let's go sit on the porch. It's probably cooler there."

Amid the darkness, he lit a kerosene lantern that hung from the porch roof. He seated himself in his usual rocker, while I took Wilma's.

"You do as well the second semester as the first?"

"Yup."

"Knew you would." Walter sipped his lemonade. "Wish I coulda gone to college…For that matter, wish I coulda gone to school. But I can't complain. I was lucky that my folks had some books, and my mom taught us kids to read."

His comment reminded me how fortunate I was. The kindness of others, my parents, Grover, Mr. Wright and Walter, had afforded me an easy path, free of many of life's vicissitudes. It also underscored that the world had changed dramatically. Opportunities unthinkable for persons of color when I was born had become possible. And with the amendments to the Constitution and statutes enacted during the preceding decade, my children and/or grandchildren might only know racial discrimination as a facet of history. The tantalizingly optimistic rumination, including the idea of having a family, shifted my thoughts to Lucinda, and apparently, Walter's focus moved to her as well.

"You still courtin' that special girl from Charleston?"

"Lucinda...Absolutely. And she's the best thing that ever happened to me."

"Sounds serious."

"It is. En route here, I met her mother, during my stop, albeit brief, in Charleston."

Walter stilled his rocker and looked me in the eye. "Is Lucinda the one?"

"I hope so." My words echoed in my head. The idea of spending my life with Lucinda was spectacular. I took several drinks of my lemonade, savoring the state of my affairs. "Enough about me," I said. "How are things with you?"

Walter shrugged. "Same old...No, not quite. Make that, same older...But I ain't complainin'. Can't." He patted the arm of my rocker...Wilma's. "Yep. I'm grateful for all those wonderful years."

His message was clear. I wanted to react with something profound, something that reflected my recognition of his words. Nothing came to mind. Fortunately, this was not an exam at the university. Leaving the question blank had no adverse consequences. I opted for silence, hoping that an attentive ear abetted Walter's nostalgia.

***

July and most of August had flown by with breakneck speed. I had written to Lucinda roughly twice each week, and she had done so with equal frequency. I had volunteered about fifteen hours per week at the Cordova Street School. Every Sunday I had accompanied Walter to the cathedral, after which we had dined on fish and chips from our favorite vendor. Even spread over several hours, the round trip, more than a mile, was difficult for Walter, but he insisted on walking its entirety. As the weeks passed, it grew harder yet.

Sunday, the 29th of August 1875. Walter and I had just returned home after attending services at the cathedral and eating our fish and chips near the City Gate.

"You want to go fishing this afternoon?" I assumed he would bite at the suggestion.

"Sounds great...provided we can do it in a couple of hours. The walk to and from town wore me down. Need a little nap before I go another round."

An admission related to his bum knee would have been no surprise; hearing him say he lacked the energy was.

"Later, around four," I said, "when the Sun will be lower in the sky, works for me."

Walter headed to his room. I got my calculus book and went out to the porch. In a little more than a week, I would be returning to South Carolina, and the time to brush up before the start of the new school year was at hand. I spent a while reviewing various problems using integration by parts. I looked over a section on the integration of rational fractions before moving to irrational ones. Having just read through the steps of a sample problem, I rocked back, closed my eyes and began repeating the steps in my mind…Apparently, I only made it part way before a siesta supplanted mathematics.

"You plan to sleep right into the evenin' and on into night?"

Walter's voice startled me. I struggled to get my bearings. "Uh, I guess I dozed off."

"Seems I wasn't the only one beggin' a nap."

How long I had been asleep, I wasn't sure, except that it was considerably more than a few minutes. "What time is it?"

"After three. We gonna fish?"

"Absolutely." I climbed out of the rocker and, along with Walter, gathered up the necessary gear. "You have a good nap?"

A blithe smile lighting his face, Walter took several seconds before he responded. "Did I ever? Had this dream…real as could be. Wilma and I was in our boat—we had this little dinghy years ago—driftin' aimlessly at the sleepy-creek's whim. Sittin' side by side, holdin' hands. We was in our early twenties and very much in love. God, she was beautiful…Talk about wonderful." Walter heaved a sigh. "It may have been a dream, but damn, it felt real…almost like it was, way back then. Memories may not be the original, but they ain't bad neither." A smile as blissful as that which preceded his comments, concluded them.

Gear in hand, together we headed out the back door and down the path that led to the Maria Sanchez Creek. During the summer we had fished at various sites, but that Sunday, Walter opted for his favorite, a picturesque spot adjoining a cedar with foliage sufficient to provide shade from the summer heat. Across the way, sabal palms, pines and cedars, draped with lacy gray Spanish Moss, provided a pleasing backdrop to the gently meandering waters.

"Ain't no way better than this to spend a day."

Walter had a point…almost. "Be nice to catch something."

"Yeah, I suppose that might be, but like the priest told us this mornin' when we sipped from the silver chalice. 'Don't wish for a full cup. Savor your sip.'" Walter gestured in all directions. "What we got here is lots more than a sip. Damn close to a full cup. Rather than wishin' for the last ounce, enjoy what we got."

Nearby, I spotted a wood stork. I tossed a worm from our bait can in the direction of the big bird. It stepped closer and snatched the worm with its long beak. After swallowing the tiny meal, the bird emitted a satisfied shriek. It took off in flight, reigning over the idyllic river below.

From all appearances, the wood stork understood Walter's message. A single worm was better than none. Savor even the smallest sip from the chalice. I put an arm over Walter's shoulder. "Don't think I've ever met anyone who knows how to live life better than you."

Walter shrugged, about as much of a response as a compliment could evoke from the modest man.

I pulled my hand from Walter's shoulder, returning it to my pole. I closed my eyes. The cheery chirp of birds, the rustle of the breeze sojourning through the trees played music in my ears. I drew in a deep breath. The subtle, aqueous fragrance of water hyacinth filled my lungs.[303] I opened my eyes and looked down the bank where the lovely purple flowers abounded. Those who navigated waterways where the plant grew despised it. To them the water hyacinth was a noxious weed whose dense mats clogged their routes.[304] I inhaled again. Taking a lesson from Walter, I savored the beautifully hued florets' perfume. Life was good. It was better than good…It was great.

With my hook baited, I cast my bamboo rod, equipped with an old, large-spooled Nottingham Reel (actually Walter's).[305] The fly soared out over the creek's waters where it could freely drift. The pure Florida air caressed my left cheek. My gaze turned south about one hundred yards where the creek bent and the greenery along the edge appeared to meet the sky. Like Maria Sanchez's warm waters, my thoughts drifted aimlessly. Tension on my line jerked me from my reverie.

"Looks like I've got one." I cranked my rod's spool. Tension on my pole increased.

"Reel 'er in," said Walter.

I raised my rod a few degrees, causing the tip to bow. I anticipated my catch would dart about, varying the pull I felt. The resistance remained constant. I turned to Walter and shrugged.

"Caught yourself some hyacinth roots?"

Protesting was futile. I tugged my pole repeatedly until finally the hook broke free. I wound my line all the way in and laid my rod on the ground. I leaned back, yielding to my better talents. A master fisherman, I wasn't. Appreciative of nature's bounty was another matter. I embraced the joy of Maria Sanchez's environs, watching my more skillful compatriot continue to fish. Five or six times, Walter cast his lot into the

---

303 *Water Hyacinth perfume ingredient*, fragrantica.com, 6 Apr. 2018 <http://www.fragrantica.com/notes/Water-Hyacinth-216.html>.

304 *Water Hyacinth Control and Possible Uses,* uniteddiversity.coop, 6 Apr. 2018 <library.uniteddiversirty.coop/Walter_hyacinth_contol.pdf>.

305 *Fishing | recreation | Britannica.com*, britannica.com, 10 Apr. 2018 <https://www.britannica.com/topic/fishing-recreation>.

waters. His luck was no better than mine until, at last, he drew back in response to a yank on his line.

Pulling on his rod, cranking his reel, he said, "This is the real deal."

I stood up in order to see better. "Work him. Let him know who's boss."

"Suddenly you're an expert angler, tellin' me how to reel in a big one?" Walter winked.

I shut my mouth.

Walter raised his pole, almost to vertical. At the other end of his line, a fish emerged from the creek, its tail swishing nearly tangent to the surface.

"Wow, it's gotta be more than a foot," I said.

Just as quickly as he raised his pole, Walter lowered it. He gave the fish more slack and reeled it in again. The fish jumped above the surface, whipping from side to side. Up with the pole and down with the pole…more slack, less slack, reeling in and out…Walter battled the fish until the latter had lost its fight. Relative calm, supplanting rapid swimming and determined thrusts, seemingly communicated, "You win." Walter reeled in the fish the rest of the way.

"It's a largemouth bass," he said, as he took hold of the squirmy catch. "You can tell by the greenish color on the top of its body. Also the lower jaw…it goes beyond the upper."[306]

I held my extended hand up near the fish, using my familiar nine-inch extension from the tip of my thumb to the tip of my middle finger as a ruler. "I'd say it's close to fifteen inches. Must weigh…what, maybe eight or nine pounds?"

"Gotta be my biggest largemouth ever."

"Maybe you should save it as a trophy."[307]

Walter studied his big catch. "At my age, what do I need with trophies?" He continued to eye the fish. "No need to eat it tonight. We had our fish and chips earlier. That was enough fish for today." He freed the fish from the hook.

I grabbed the basket we had brought and opened it.

Walter shook his head. He tossed the bass back into Maria Sanchez. "Ain't his time yet."

We watched the big one swim away. Along with Walter, I remained focused on the rippled waters. Day after day, year after year…century

---

[306] *Largemouth Bass Features and Size | Bass Fishing Gurus*, bassfishing-gurus.com, 6 Apr. 2018 <https://bassfishing-gurus.com/largemouth-bass-features-and-size/>.

[307] Ibid., indicating the average trophy length for largemouth bass is about thirteen inches and that in the South a ten-pound trophy largemouth is not uncommon.

after century, they looked the same. Yet one second to the next, new replaced that which was there but a moment before. That which was unchanging was fleeting. The logic-defying anomaly begged scrutiny. Were I back at the Horseshoe, I might have sought out Professor Nelson on the chance that he could unravel the philosophical conundrum. For want of a better alternative, I grabbed my rod and cocked my wrists, preparing to cast my line into the depths.

Walter shot me a look. “Given what we threw back, we gotta be done.”

I nodded before cranking my spool. Walter had caught the big one. Our fishing was complete. We headed back to the house where, after a light dinner, we took to the porch and our respective rockers. An earlier gentle breeze, as it so often did, yielded to a still evening. Crickets, invisible to the eye, voicing their temperature-dictated rhythms, seemingly coordinated their music to the pendulum swing of our rockers. Peace, a ubiquitous solitude, pervaded the sylvan setting.

“Been a perfect day,” said Walter. “Lovely service at the cathedral. Father gave the best of his sermons. Fish and chips at the City Gates ain’t never been crisper…Caught the big one down at the creek…And best of all, Wilma was back in my arms again…Well, sorta.” He leaned back and closed his eyes. Soon enough, he dozed off.

Not long after, I did too…At least an hour passed before I awoke. Dusk had come and gone, yielding to night. I took a moment to get my bearings. I looked over at Walter, debating whether to rouse him. He was absolutely still…peacefully still. The observation counseled that I not disturb him; allow him to wake in his own convenient time. I would have, except he was too still. He made not a sound. His chest moved not one iota. I put my hand on his shoulder and gently wiggled it. “Walter…Walter, it’s getting late.” I waited, but no reaction. Minor concern shifted to alarm. I jerked his shoulder several times, calling his name. No response. I put my ear close to his nose and mouth. No evidence of breathing. I felt his chest. There was no trace of a heartbeat. My spirits sank. Calling out his name again, I felt his wrist. The absence of a pulse cemented the inescapable conclusion. Walter was gone.

Shaken and confused, I stood motionless for about a minute. I sank down into my rocker. I burst into tears, grief supplanting panic. I began to rock, at first rapidly, but soon at a slow cadence. I wailed repeatedly, longing to alter reality. “Damn…Damn it!” I screamed, unable to address gut-wrenching emotions. The visceral reaction proved no better than wails. I stilled the rocker. I shut my eyes, debating what I needed to do. Waiting for morning crossed my mind. The idea never had a chance.

I got up from the rocker, poked my head inside the door and checked the parlor clock. It was nearly nine o'clock. I went back outside and tried again to rouse Walter. I checked once more for signs of life. None. I went back inside and took the blanket from his bed. I draped it over him from chest on down. Though the summer night was anything but cold, I wanted to keep him warm…or, perhaps, if I'm honest with myself, I wanted to do something for him…something that would ease my pain...my guilt.

I headed down from the porch and hurried to the cathedral. I was thankful to see Father standing alone on the altar. The possibility that I might need to go to his private quarters and, worse yet, awaken him had been avoided.

"Father, may I speak with you?" I said, as I approached him in the center aisle.

"Certainly, my son." He eyed me. "You're Mican, the young man who lives with Walter?"

I nodded.

"He's very proud of you, that you're pursuing a college education and how well you're doing."

"It's Walter that brings me here. He...he passed this evening." A choking sob seized me.

Father put his arm over my shoulder. "I'm sorry, so sorry." Father's voice was weak and cracking. "I…I can hardly believe it. He was here this morning. What happened? An accident?"

I shook my head. "He dozed off this evening on the porch and…and he never woke up."

Father nodded slowly, repeatedly. "He went peacefully. That's good. He's in a better place now."

Skeptic though I was, my longing to mitigate my affliction cajoled me to heed his words of faith.

"Walter was a good man. Our congregation will miss him. I will miss him."

"I miss him already. He was so good to me."

Father stepped around in front of me and looked me in the eye. "You were the son he never had. Walter lives on through you."

Hearing that Walter held me in such special regard was uplifting, but I felt a sense of duty. Maintaining his memory, his legacy, was my responsibility. I said, "Walter caught a huge bass today, trophy size." I held my hands wide apart, perhaps wider than the length of the big fish. "Earlier today he had taken a nap. He had a dream, a wonderful dream about his Wilma. It was as if she were there with him. That's how he described it. What do you think?" My question begged the obvious, a soothing exegesis from the sage man of the cloth.

Father turned toward the rear of the altar, seemingly gazing at the three gold figurines that decorated the sacred scene. He glanced upward. "I'm not prescient…but the fish could be a sign." Father looked upward again, this time longer than before. "Perhaps Walter knew his time had arrived…that Wilma had come for him." Father smiled. He wiped a tear from his eye. "If you ask me, Walter is home…home with Wilma."

The analysis, reasoning predicated upon faith, itself arguably incongruous, warmed my heart. Dismissing Walter's dream as a coincidence was as illogical as buying into it. Father had not proved that Walter and Wilma were together, but he had provided evidence to support the idea. No one could prove the contrary. Why not accept Father's assessment? A curious irony was inescapable. Had Father insisted that Walter and Wilma were together, my skeptical side, my propensity to follow the scientific method, would have balked. By acknowledging that the truth was unknowable, by presenting an interpretation as his belief, debate became futile. The credibility of his surmise, far from proved, elevated. So too, did my willingness to entertain his view. Whatever his goal, Father had displayed the height of religious prowess, a virtuosity that played mellifluous music in my ears. He had mitigated my pain. I said, "I believe you're right. I believe that Walter and Wilma are together…together in a better place."

***

Gray skies, accompanied by light drizzle, hung over St. Augustine as the horse-drawn wagon bearing Walter's casket wended its way west from the cathedral. At Cordova Street, the wagon turned north to the Tolomato Cemetery,[308] where so many of the cathedral's parishioners were interred. Alongside Father, I followed directly behind the wagon. Behind us, a long procession, well over one hundred, silently walked the half-mile to the burial plot. In his eulogy at the cathedral, Father had noted the inordinately large assemblage, citizens of diverse races and religions. Father described it as a testament to the deserved respect and affection that Walter had enjoyed.

---

[308] *Tolomato Cemetery Preservation – Home*, tolomatocemetery.com, 13 Apr. 2018 <http://www.tolomatocemetery.com/>. Burial place from the 18th century through 1884, Tolomato, the parish cemetery for what is today the Cathedral Basilica of St. Augustine, houses the graves of approximately 1000 St. Augustinians, many of whom bear significance to the history of St. Augustine and the United States.

Upon reaching Tolomato, six pall bearers, four Negro and two white, lifted Walter's casket from the wagon and carried it to the burial pit that had been dug adjacent to Wilma's grave.[309] Once the procession had gathered around the gravesite, the pallbearers lowered Walter's body into its final resting place. Father delivered last prayers and words. They passed my ears unheard. My brain was preoccupied, digesting that Walter was gone, but also celebrating the possibility that he was home…not necessarily home as many Catholics might view it, but home with Wilma.

I closed my eyes. Reaching deeply into my psyche, I envisioned Walter in a heavenly place taking hold of Wilma's outstretched hand. Traces of moisture, both rain and tears, intermingled on my cheeks. Emotions, no less disparate than the waters coating my face, gripped me. Grief was undeniable, but hope that Walter could again feel Wilma's touch was palpable. Skeptic though I was, for a few brief moments, I grasped onto wishful thinking, suppressing my beliefs. Much as my yearning was on Walter's behalf, even more so, it was for me, a pretense to mitigate my grief.

Soon enough the burial concluded. People quietly filed out of the cemetery. I remained, preferring peaceful introspection to the distraction of the crowd. A couple of minutes elapsed when I turned and started to walk away.

A man I recognized, though I could not recall his name, approached.

"I'm George Holcum. I was Walter's attorney."

"Yes, I know," I said, his mention of his name jogging my memory who he was.

"My sincere condolences. Walter was an extraordinary man."

"The finest."

"Don't mean to interrupt your thoughts, but I wanted to speak to you…before you head back to college. I understand you'll be leaving in a day or so."

I nodded, wondering what he could want with me.

"I'll cut right to the chase. Walter left his home to the cathedral."

"Don't worry. I only have a few personal items there. I took most everything with me to South Carolina. I can have the balance of my stuff out when I leave the day after tomorrow. Would it be okay if I stay there till then?"

---

309 Ibid., *Monuments and Markers - Tolomato Cemetery Preservation*, indicating the cemetery bears "the graves of veterans that represented both sides of the Civil War, including Freedmen who fought with the Union."

"Absolutely. Matter of fact, you're welcome to stay until the cathedral has a buyer and is ready to close. But that's not why I wanted to talk to you. Walter named you in his will. He left you his intangibles, over two thousand dollars in the bank, plus railroad stock worth roughly twenty-five hundred."

The disclosure knocked me for a loop. The possibility of any such inheritance hadn't crossed my mind.

"Apart from Wilma, Walter didn't have any family. You were very special to him, the son he never had."

Mixed emotions, different from the conglomeration minutes earlier, surged. Excitement owing to the largess was undeniable. Guilt, however, cast a superseding shadow. Once again, I was profiting from the death of one who in life had been my benefactor. "I should have spent more time with Walter."

Holcum shook his head. "Walter was right."

"About what?"

"How you would react. That you might have qualms when I told you. He made sure I was prepared. He instructed me to tell you to be happy and enjoy the funds; to do otherwise, blame yourself in any way, was the last thing he wanted." Holcum heaved a sigh. "Walter phrased it better than I, but I assume you get his message. Remember the good times with Walter. Know that you were special. Enjoy what he left you. And you will honor his memory."

"I'll try…and thank you."

"Don't thank me. Thank Walter."

I wished I could. The rumination spawned a pang. As best I could, in accordance with Walter's wishes, I endeavored to dismiss it.

Holcum pulled a slip of paper from his pocket and showed it to me. "I want to make sure I have your South Carolina address, so I can transfer the property to you."

I confirmed the address, and Holcum was on his way.

I turned and stared at Walter's grave. Were the gravediggers not shoveling backfill into the hole, I might have gone closer. I remained motionless for a minute before uttering, "Thank you, Walter…Rest well. Goodbye, dear friend."

Chapter XXI

THE FIRST WEEK OF SEPTEMBER, I headed back to the University of South Carolina. Walter's passing weighed heavily on my mind, but the return to college was a helpful distraction. Unlike a year earlier when I was a callow freshman embarking on the unknown, I was a sophomore. A year of academic success behind me, coupled with my relationship with Lucinda, buoyed me with confidence. Rather than making the trip from St. Augustine with only the layovers needed to catch the next transport, once I reached Charleston, I went to Lucinda's house where I stayed overnight…on the parlor couch. Lucinda's mother would never have allowed Lucinda and me to share the same room. For that matter, Lucinda, a product of the Victorian era, though a strong advocate for women's rights, would not have shared her bedroom had the decision come down to her. Lucinda believed that ultimate sexual intimacy was reserved for marriage.[310]

As close as our relationship had been throughout the school year, the summer apart had proved the familiar adage. Absence had made our hearts grow fonder. Though neither of us had used the word *marriage*, allusions to spending our lives together suggested that we were moving in that direction. It was where I wanted to go.

The day before classes commenced, after traveling west on the South Carolina Railroad to the Horseshoe, Lucinda and I returned to the same dorms in which we had been housed the preceding school year. The

---

[310] *Women in the Nineteenth Century*, ivcc.edu, 3 Apr. 2018 <http://www.ivcc.edu/gen2002/Women_in_the_Nineteenth_Century.htm> stating: "Women were not supposed to have any real sexual contact before their marriage, especially if they were from the upper and middle-classes. Consequently, most women of these classes learned about sex from their husbands on their wedding nights." The article lists a number of stereotypes for the sexes. Where it describes men of the era, with among other traits, as *powerful, worldly, logical and sexual/sensual*, women are characterized as *weak, domestic, illogical and not sexual/sensual*.

next morning, following breakfast together in her dorm, Rutledge, we headed to room 219 for our first class, Calculus II with Professor Hopkins. Several minutes after nine, the scheduled time for the class, Professor Hopkins entered the room.

He opened his black logbook and took attendance. "All nine of you are here and accounted for." Professor Hopkins came around from behind his desk, appearing to study us. "Before diving into this semester's material, I have a question for you: "What, in your opinion, is the most powerful word in English or any other language?"

After a brief hiatus, with no hands raised, Professor Hopkins went to the blackboard and wrote a huge equal sign. "Mind you, this is only a matter of opinion, but I deem no word stronger than *equals*. Let me tell you why. It is elegant. It is explicative. It is elemental to numerous disciplines. It reduces the most complex of mathematical expressions on its one side into simple incarnations on its other. It is the link that reveals how one variable changes in relation to another; how and why the planets, as well as all manner of projectiles and objects, move; and how to take advantage of the magic of electricity and magnetism. It is the centerpiece, both literally and figuratively, of arithmetic, algebraic, geometric, trigonometric and other mathematical expressions. But lest you think the equal sign's realm is confined to mathematics and physics, let me suggest otherwise."

Hopkins eyed us, as if making sure he had our full attention. "Economies, the entire exchange of goods and services, be it an exchange of currency or barter, are built upon the equal sign. Taking into account supply, demand and circumstances, it communicates: I'll give you this for that. So too, the world of chemistry is built upon equivalence. Though chemists use a yield symbol when writing equations, it is analogous. Allow me to give you an example. Corrosive hydrochloric acid added to caustic sodium hydroxide equals life-sustaining water and ordinary table salt. I could go on and on, but I believe you get my point. *Equals* is a Herculean word. Accord it the respect it deserves."

The exposition was interesting and cogent. Whether it convinced me was another matter. A definitive conclusion would need to await a more appropriate time. Professor Hopkins was moving forward.

"Let me return to the more mundane circumstances that bring us together. You represent the cream of an otherwise dismal crop. South Carolina College, the predecessor of this university, was an esteemed institution where academics were taught at the highest level. These days, rather than teaching calculus, statistics, and solid and projective geometry, most of my time is spent edifying neophytes in algebra and basic geometry. Were that not bad enough, all too many of my charges are ill-equipped for those preliminary courses. The truth be known, what we have is a normal school or less."

Less than five minutes into my first class, Professor Hopkins, despicable, though admittedly proficient, bastard that he was, had quashed faint hopes that a new year might see him mellow.

"Last week I reviewed the records of the incoming class, mainly Negro. Hardly any are ready for Calculus I. Simply put, a grim situation worsens."

I longed to remind Professor Hopkins that slavery had deprived these students of an education, the opportunity to prepare for college. No way did I dare open my mouth. To do so would have been fruitless suicide.

"I've checked your records. All of you are ready for calculus, though several of you demonstrate dubious preparedness for Calculus II. But you are here. Three of you stand out above and beyond your fellow classmates. You can move beyond Calculus II this semester. Rather than hold you back, especially when the majority will require attention to material that is part and parcel of Calculus I, I have decided to put you three into a separate group who will occupy the rear corner of the room and proceed at a much faster pace."

I welcomed the disclosure, certain that both Lucinda and I would be among the three.

"The following students are in the special seminar group: Mican Reinbow, Harold Ward and Thomas Blane. The three of you should take your calculus books to the back of the room and do the problems on page 215."

As I got up from my seat, I glanced at Lucinda, who was seated immediately to my right. Our eyes met. I shrugged before heading to the back row. I quickly worked through the assigned problems. Once finished, I helped Harold Ward, who was struggling. Where Blane was a solid student, Ward was mediocre. His mathematical knowledge did not compare to Lucinda's. Ward and Blane were both white. Of the six students not chosen for advanced work, all five were Negroes. It was inescapable that bias had played into Professor Hopkins' choices. Memories of Grover, how he had confronted his Simon Legree boss in Savannah, pressed me to speak up. Lucinda had been wronged. Foolhardy though it was, I needed to champion her cause. Once the class was done, I would raise the issue. I began rehearsing my pitch.

The class concluded. Professor Hopkins dismissed us. I asked Lucinda to wait for me in the hall. Only the imperious educator and I remained. Anxiously, I approached his desk.

"Sir, may I speak with you?"

From the seat behind his desk, Professor Hopkins peered over the top of his wire-rimmed glasses. "What is it?"

"I think Lucinda should be included in the advanced group."

"You think *what*?"

I swallowed hard. "Uh…that Lucinda deserves—"

"I heard you the first time!" He ripped off his glasses and glared at me. "Since when do you tell me who will or will not do advanced work in my classroom?" His fiery eyes demanded an answer.

"I…I wasn't trying to tell you what to do."

"Really. Then what exactly were you doing?"

"I…uh…just thought you might want to include Lucinda. She's—"

"You want me to include your girlfriend, so you can turn my class into your personal courting hour."

"Uh…no, Sir. Because she's an excellent mathematics student."

Professor Hopkins exhaled disgustedly. "For a woman, she's good. But entitled to special attention, no way."

"But Sir, Lucinda is a much stronger student than Ward."

"Mr. Reinbow…" Professor Hopkins jerked his chair back and stood up. "You have the gall to instruct me about my students…how to run my class?"

In the face of the irate rhetorical question, I opted for silence.

"Even assuming *arguendo*, Miss Brown were as qualified as you suggest—and understand, I make that assumption merely to demonstrate the fallacy of your position—your point reeks of naiveté. As you have no doubt observed, Miss Brown is a woman. Her pursuit of higher mathematics is a voyage to nowhere. Once she completes her education, rather than using it for theoretical or more practical, applied purposes, she will assume her domestic place, making cookies and babies. And before you make a fool of yourself by contradicting my thesis, let me give you the evidence…solid statistical evidence. Look at women, particularly Negro women. What percentage pursue careers involving higher mathematics? I'll tell you. It is roughly zero…or if we put it into mathematical terms, given any ϵ, we could find a δ, such that the limit of a function reflecting the likelihood Lucinda would make meaningful use of her mathematical knowledge is zero! And before you mouth off by telling me my analogy is not a true mathematical limit, disregard any such thoughts. My point is merely, as I said, an analogy, not a mathematical equation!"

Dubious as I deemed his mathematical model, that was secondary. "But Sir, the reason so few women, particularly Negro women, have not engaged in higher mathematical pursuits is the lack of opportunity. Society has not allowed them—"

"You brazen bastard!" shouted Professor Hopkins. "I give you, a colored Indian, an opportunity for the best of mathematical educations, and how do you respond? Rather than gracious appreciation, you challenge me. Worse yet, you do so with specious scapegoating. You blame society for Negroes' inferiority." Professor Hopkins pointed at the door and bellowed, "Get out of here! Get the hell out of here before I axe you from the advanced group!"

Rage, unchanneled rage, begged I lash back. Judgment...perhaps more accurately, fear...stilled my tongue. I retreated into the hallway where Lucinda was waiting.

"What was that about? I heard Professor Hopkins explode a moment ago."

I put a finger to my lips and motioned down the hall. We headed down the stairs. Once outside, I said, "I asked Professor Hopkins to include you in the advanced group."

"You what?"

"I asked Professor—"

"I know what you said. But why would you do that?"

"You belong in the advanced group. You're a helluva lot more qualified than Ward."

"I know, but that doesn't explain why you stuck your nose into my business."

"I wanted to help."

"You wanted to help?" Her mouth taut, Lucinda turned away and gazed skyward.

I longed to defend myself. Unfortunately, good intentions did not justify my insinuating myself into her affairs. "I shouldn't have done it without your permission."

"Let me rephrase that. You shouldn't have done it—period!" She looked me in the eye. "If I wanted the issue raised, I could have done it. I don't need others picking and fighting my battles."

If I were dealing with someone else, I might have argued that a man defends a woman. That was what men, chivalrous men, did. But Lucinda believed in women's rights. She rejected the widely held notion that women were weak; that they needed men to step in on their behalf.[311] "You're absolutely right. I had no business going to Professor Hopkins.

---

[311] Ibid., indicating that men of the 19th century were thought to be *active* and *brave*, while women were *passive* and *timid.* Suffragettes seeking the vote for women, faced these and other biases. So too, did feminists of the 20th century fighting for the right to control their bodies, equal pay, and the ability to work in all fields, especially those that had been traditionally male dominated. Although these biases have been greatly mitigated, their remnants persist.

I should have raised the issue with you." The furrowed brow that greeted me, prompted me to clarify. "I should have raised the issue, not to get your permission to go further, but merely as a sounding board, leaving it for you to decide whether to raise it with Professor Hopkins."

"Now you're talking."

"Forgive me?"

Lucinda briefly displayed a pouty mouth, but then she leaned in and pecked me on the lips. Once she drew back, she said, "Forgiven… I know you were trying to help, but in the future, leave my affairs to me."

"Fair enough." I took Lucinda's hand. Together we strolled the tree-lined walkways of the Horseshoe. The argument, if I could classify it as such, had ended. It was not a wedge. If anything, it underscored the brevity of our rare disagreements. I squeezed Lucinda's hand. "You're beautiful," I said.

She drew to a halt, displaying a puzzled look. "Whatever you say."

Whether the enigmatic comment was an affectionate puff on the pipe of peace or a bit of concluding sarcasm was beyond my ken. I did, however, know enough to keep my mouth shut.

***

The early months of our sophomore year rolled along. Both Lucinda and I were taking extra credits. Were it not for her lead, I might not have done so. Her push to graduate in three years had wheedled me to do the same. That many of our fellow students had come to the university ill-prepared for the rigors of college played a key role. By necessity many courses were less demanding than they would otherwise have been. On balance that worked to my advantage. Higher grades were an obvious benefit. Though watering down diminished what I learned in some courses, my increased load made up for any such deficiency. And the load gave me the chance to expand my curriculum into areas I might have ignored. One in particular, a product of Noah's earlier influence, was architecture. With countless links to mathematics and physics, coupled with my work experience, the discipline's examination of centuries of construction styles fascinated me.

On campus, Lucinda and I were walled, both literally and figuratively, from the politics that persisted outside. In both the South Carolina State Legislature and the university's Board of Trustees the balance of power was tenuous. A small change in political fortunes had the potential to turn back the clock. Insulated as we were in the Horseshoe, we were largely blind to the daily events that could move the needle. Continued hints that the benefits of Reconstruction could evaporate escaped us. We took little note that another southern state, Mississippi, had elected a redeemer government. In part our ignorance was a product of our cloistered college life. Our own naiveté was equally responsible.

With a full year of Newtonian mechanics already under my belt, I doubled up on physics, taking not only Electricity and Magnetism, but also Thermodynamics. My strong mathematical background facilitated my grasp of the theory underlying these disciplines. Apart from philosophy, when it came to the humanities, I took just enough courses to satisfy the requirements for graduation.

It was the first Friday in December. Fall, a glorious season in South Carolina, was yielding to the fickle days of the approaching winter. Campus oaks and maples had seen their variegated foliage tumble to Earth. Days had shortened, with the Sun making its east-to-west daily voyage entirely in the southern sky. With classes done for the week and the dark of evening pervasive, Lucinda and I opted for a visit to John C. Seegers' Saloon. More than a year had passed since we had visited the Main Street establishment, site of our first courting beyond the Horseshoe. As we entered, I pointed to the right. "Let's take that booth along the wall."

"If I'm not mistaken, that's the one we occupied our first time here."

"That's why I chose it."

We seated ourselves, and soon after, a waitress came our way. "What can I get you folks?"

I flashed Lucinda a smile, one I armed with a devious cast. "You mind if I do the ordering? But let me warn you. It'll be different."

Despite a curious look, she said, "Be my guest."

"Two whiskey cobblers[312] and a pair of steak dinners."

Lucinda's eyes widened.

"You still on board?"

"Far be it from me, after giving the okay, to renege."

I nodded to the waitress, and she headed off.

"I've heard of a whiskey cobbler," said Lucinda. "But I have no clue what it is."

Knowledge of cocktails, I had none. But earlier in the day, I had cornered a more sophisticated classmate who had given me the

---

[312] *History - Were there cocktails or mixed drinks in the 19th century? | American Civil War*, civilwartalk.com, 22 Apr. 2018 <https://civilwartalk.com/threads/were-there-cocktails-or-mixed-drinks-in-the-19th-century>.

recommendation, complete with details. "It's whiskey, mixed with fruit, sugar and crushed ice."[313]

"Since when did you become a connoisseur of alcoholic libations?"

"Hey, watch me long enough, and you'll discover I'm full of hidden talents."

Lucinda's brow furrowed.

"Well…the truth be told, I picked Bill Teasdale's brain this afternoon. According to him, the drink became popular throughout the South during the War."

"Cocktails and steak. This is a step up from our usual, sardines and lemonade. Any special reason?"

"C'mon, even bottom-of-the-barrel peons like us can celebrate once in a while."

"Gee, thanks."

After feigning a puzzled mien, I said, "For what?"

"Labeling me a peon."

Our drinks arrived. Lucinda and I clinked our glasses. "To us…our happiness."

She reiterated my words. Each of us sampled the contents of our glasses.

"Ooh, I like it," said Lucinda. "Matter of fact, I could grow to like this a lot."

I nodded before taking another sip of the sweet drink.

"How'd you make out today at your women's rights meeting? You went, didn't you?"

"It was good. The women welcomed me, though I wish the group were larger. Counting me, there were only seven. For that matter, I wish we had a group here on campus."

"Maybe you could start one?"

"Not gonna happen. Not when we have a limited number of women, most of whom believe females should stay at home behind their husbands."

Her assessment had too much merit to debate. "You really are determined to change the world, aren't you?"

"No, just the minds and hearts of all the males who deny women equality." She shook her head. "Let me correct that. Add to that list, the majority of females who concur with those males. And while you're at it, add those who believe that people of color should be second-class citizens."

"Whew, with that agenda, you've got a helluva challenge."

---

[313] Ibid.

A smile on her face, she pointed a finger my way. "You're gonna help me. Right?"

"Sure." I looked her in the eye. "You know I believe that women should get the vote…not that I'm in favor of counting those votes."

"Mican Reinbow!"

"C'mon, you know I'm teasing."

Our dinners arrived just in the nick of time. Conversation grew sparse, and what there was focused on our indulgent repast.

We had finished our meals and were awaiting our bill when I reached into my pocket and drew out a bookmark. The scraggly, gray patch of doubled-over rag bore a frayed piece of string tied in a bow. Next to it, dross was delightful. "I made you a bookmark."

With an askance look, Lucinda held the abomination in front of her. "Thank you…I think."

"Don't you like it?" I said, struggling not to laugh.

"It…it's nice. Though I hope you don't mind if use the other one you gave me with the beautiful garnet."

I reached out and took the bookmark from her. I held it up and summoning a theatrical voice, said, "You're right. It is less than perfect." I reached into my pants pocket and working with my hands beneath the level of the table, untying and retying the string, added an accessory. Cupping the string and trinket in a closed fist, I handed the bookmark back to Lucinda. "Will you marry me?"

Lucinda eyed the diamond ring, one-half carat, that was tied to the rag. She burst into tears.

"Is…is that a *yes*?"

"Of course, I'll marry you. She stood part way and leaned forward, as far as the booth permitted.

I did the same. Our lips met with ineffable joy.

We eased back into our seats. She untied the string and removed the ring. She slipped it onto her finger. "It's beautiful. I love it." She raised it, closer to her eyes. "You shouldn't have. It's too extravagant."

I shook my head.

"Much as I love it, couldn't you make better use of the money?"

I shook my head. "Anyway, we'll be fine."

She eyed me skeptically.

I leaned forward and whispered, "I have a little secret, a good one. I saved a large portion of what I earned while building houses and at the lighthouse. And Grover and Walter also left me money when they died. Between bank accounts and stock, I have over six thousand dollars."

Lucinda's jaw dropped. "Really?"

"Really."

Lucinda sat motionless. A bewildered look, one that had predominated since the moment she saw the ring, subsided. She said, “You don’t mind me marrying you for your money?”

Though I knew she was jesting, I said, “Not true. You accepted my proposal before you knew I had money.”

She shrugged, before holding her engagement ring up to the kerosene lantern that hung from the adjacent wall. She rotated her hand back and forth. Beneath the light’s glow, the diamond sparkled. The smile that lit her face was brighter yet. She said, “Do we need to wait for graduation to get married?”

I shook my head.

“You plan for us to live in dorms on opposite sides of the Horseshoe?”

“Nope.”

“Then what?”

“We can wed at the end of the school year, and in the meantime, look for a house. In case you forgot, we can afford one.”

Lucinda displayed no reaction, at least none I could discern. “Aren’t you going to say something?”

“Wow…wow.” She breathed deeply. “Don’t mind me. I’m overwhelmed. I’ve never experienced anything close to the past few minutes. A proposal, a ring, marriage and plans for a new home, all at once. I can’t believe it.” Her gaze directed toward the ceiling.

“Whatcha looking at?”

“Nothing. Just taking time to appreciate what hindsight will likely show was the most wonderful moment of my life.”

I reached across the table and took Lucinda’s hand, the one bearing the ring. Words were superfluous.

***

Second semester of our sophomore year was everything college is supposed to be and more. Lucinda and I were proven students with excellent academic records. We were taking extra courses, well on our way to a goal of graduating in three years. Studying, because we did it together, was no chore. And there was still plenty of free time, especially on weekends. We had firmed up our plans to wed at the end of the school year. Lucinda had no desire for a big wedding, and with her family tiny and mine non-existent, a private ceremony with her mother and a Justice of the Peace fit our needs.

House hunting had become our favorite pastime. With the nation deep in the recession that followed the stock market crash of 1873, housing prices, having surged during the War of Secession and for several years thereafter, had nosedived. Not only was it a buyer's market, but with credit hard to come by, cash was king. My savings, coupled with the largess given to me by Grover and Walter, put us in an enviable bargaining position. Fortune allowed us to consider more than a simple starter house. Temptation enticed us, but our conservative natures, coupled with the possibility we might leave Columbia after graduation, prevailed. In April we found a two-bedroom bungalow about a half-mile southeast of the Horseshoe. The $800 price tag was below what we had budgeted.[314] The structure, about twenty years old, had been fortunate to survive the flames of Sherman's march. While it needed some work, my construction skills gained in St. Augustine were more than equal to the challenge. The summer months, during which we would be free, except for some independent study, offered the perfect opportunity to make the improvements. A June closing date put a bow on the plan.

It was a Sunday afternoon, the last in April 1876. On a scale of twenty, life for Lucinda and me was nineteen-plus. I'd say twenty, but that would contradict my belief that nothing subjective is perfect. Regardless, our life was as good as it gets. That morning we had attended services at the Bethel African American Episcopal Church. Founded shortly after the War of Secession in what had been an old sword factory,[315] it was located on Wayne Street, west of the Horseshoe, about two-thirds of the way to the Congaree River.

Before college, Lucinda had attended church sporadically, more than I. Since arriving at the university, like me, she rarely went to services. But recently she had joined a small group of Bethel women who were advocating for equal rights. Because the group sometimes met after Sunday services, she had begun attending them. On the Sunday in question, she had convinced me to join her at the church. Once the service ended, I remained in a pew, my physics book in hand, while she joined her group for a meeting. I was studying Coulomb's Law. Propounded late in the 18th century, it stated that the electrical force between charged particles, attraction or repulsion, is inversely

---

[314] *How much did a house cost in the 19th century*, answers.yahoo.com, 23 Apr. 2018 <https://answers.yahoo.com/question/index?qid=20080719193937AA61SHf> stating: "...toward the end of the 19th century, a modest house in a city like Chicago cost about $500." Cf. *$100 in 1875 → 2016 | Inflation Calculator*, in2013dollars.com, 23 Apr. 2018 <http://www.in2013dollars.com/1875-dollars-in-2016?amount=100> indicating that the purchasing power of $100 in 1875 would be more than twenty-one times its purchasing power in 2016. If so, a small house such as a bungalow in Chicago would have cost considerably more than $500 in 1875.

[315] *Our History | Bethel AME Church*, bethelcolumbia.org, 24 Apr. 2018 <http://bethelcolumbia.org/about-us/our-history/>.

proportional to the square of the distance between the particles.[316] I had just finished a problem employing Coulomb's Constant, when Lucinda emerged from her meeting.

"How'd it go?" I led the way south on Wayne Street as we started back to the Horseshoe.

"Good, but it could be a whole lot better if we could get more members. We talked to several from the congregation, but they're reluctant to join."

"They say why?"

"A couple disagreed with our goals. One said it was contrary to the Bible. She argued that a woman's place is in the home; that women should defer to their husbands. Others who sympathize with our cause refused for a variety of reasons. They're too busy. One said we should leave it to the legislators. Even within our group, which is down to six, there's a split. Two members consider women's issues less important than those of race. For now, our primary focus will likely be on the latter."

"You think you can effect change with such a small nucleus?"

"Don't know, but we're determined." Lucinda briefly pursed her lips. "It bugs me when people cite the Bible to deprive others of equal rights."

"No need to convince me. In case you forgot, you, not me, are the one who reads the Good Book."

Lucinda tugged my arm, drawing to a stop. "Yes, I read the Bible…occasionally. But relying on it as a guide to a moral life is different from taking it literally…and, worse yet, latching onto phrases supporting one's biases, while ignoring those to the contrary."

---

[316] *Coulomb's Law*, physicsclassroom.com, 24 Apr. 2018 <http://www.physicsclassroom.com/class/estatics/Lesson-3/Coulomb-s-Law>. Coulomb's Law states: $F = \frac{kq_1q_2}{d^2}$, where F is the electrical force between the two point charged particles; q_1 and q_2 are the quantity of each point's charge; d is the distance between the two particles; and k is Coulomb's Constant. Coulomb's Constant is dependent upon the medium in which the charged particles are located. For example, the value of k in air is much higher than in water, implying the electrical force for the same two charged particles is much higher in air than water. Where the particles are both positive or both negative, the force determined pursuant to Coulomb's Law is repulsive. Where one of the particles has a positive charge and the other negative, the force would be attractive. The formula is very similar to that for gravitational force F: $F = \frac{GMm}{d^2}$ where G is the gravitational constant; M and m, the masses of the respective objects; and d, the distance between the objects.

Her point had merit. Still I yielded to the temptation to play the gadfly. "Hey, he…in this case, she…who lives by the sword, dies by the sword."

Lucinda shot me a look.

"Relax. I get your point. But that said, when it comes to faith, none of us know."

"What does that mean?"

I sensed that Lucinda's question was a product of annoyance, more than substance. I said, "Since joining the church, you've indicated that your skepticism about God has waned; that you now believe."

"So, what's that got to do with anything?"

"You take God's existence on faith, not reason. And don't argue, because you've conceded that arguments, ontological and otherwise, proving God's existence, prove nothing."

"Fine. What's your point?"

"Others, based on faith, contend the Bible is the word of God."

"C'mon, believing in God and taking the Bible literally are…" Lucinda heaved a sigh. "Okay, I see what you're saying, not that I like it."

I pecked her on the cheek, valuing one of Lucinda's untold wonderful traits. Despite a strong will, unlike many, perhaps me included, when confronted with a legitimate argument, she could accede, rather than resort to defensive intransigence.

"Was that little kiss a victor's celebration?"

"On the contrary, appreciation of the one I love."

"Sure."

We resumed our walk home. Shortly before we reached the Horseshoe, we came upon a hot-dog vendor along the margin of a small park. After making our purchase, two dogs doused with mustard, we seated ourselves on a bench.

"The pastor delivered an interesting sermon today," said Lucinda. "I like him. He doesn't pretend to have all the answers. Rather than putting himself on a pedestal, he presents as just another person. Yes, he's a clergyman, and most are educated, but when it comes to esoteric questions—death, God, eternity, whatever—he avoids pretense. He admits he's postulating, just like the rest of us."

"Wait a second. A while ago, you acknowledged your belief in God, one predicated on faith. Now you admit you're guessing. Inconsistent, wouldn't you say?"

About to sink her teeth into her tubular snack, Lucinda halted. "Not really."

"Please, enlighten me." I culminated my words with a mocking laugh.

"I'd be happy to." The sarcasm in her voice exceeded that of my guffaw. "Many with faith-based beliefs treat their views as verified truths. Some of us, despite our beliefs, acknowledge that we don't have proof. Our faith is tantamount to a guess, arguably an educated one…admittedly, influenced by hopes and needs."

Her response made more sense than I had anticipated. "I'll bet you'd be pretty good climbing out of quicksand."

"Why—you planning to stick me there?"

For want of a quick comeback, I bit into my hot dog.

"Returning to the pastor," she said, "I appreciate that he uses religion to promote thought, especially introspection. Too many invoke it as a weapon."

"Weapon?" I garbled with my mouth full. "What do you mean?"

"So much of religion throughout history, and mind you, I'm speaking of all religions, has been a means to control people, exert power. Doctrine, catechism, has often been a device to create guilt, force contributions and otherwise manipulate the masses. The threat of hell has been more powerful than guns and swords."

"If you feel that way, why not reject religion altogether?"

"First, as you know, my belief in God has grown. I have faith. But equally important, religion, despite its shortcomings, has many positive aspects…moral guidance, a sense of community, values, just to name a few. Like every institution of mankind, religion has its pluses and minuses. As best I can, I buy into the pluses, and circumvent the minuses."

"Makes sense, I suppose." Even as I voiced agreement, reservations percolated. "Maybe that's why I prefer mathematics and physics. Prove a theorem or use a formula, and that's it." The thought of an object in free fall compelled me to qualify my statement. "Don't get me wrong. I'm not suggesting that physics is an exact science. A prime example would be the absurd results a first-year calculus student gets when determining the velocity of a falling object when it strikes the ground. The answer may make sense in a vacuum, but not the real world, not when it's supposedly the same for an iron ball and a feather. Ignoring air resistance yields ridiculous results. Even using differential equations, the variable effect of air, with its irregular motion and density, can only be approximated."

"Well, at least your point holds true for mathematics."

"Yes and no." The familiar phrase, an old friend from my childhood, echoed in my head. The years had taught me that under certain circumstances its use was meritorious. But time had also shown that it could be problematic, particularly when responding to an educator's questioning. I said, "Take the principle that parallel lines never intersect." I found it hard to believe I was playing devil's advocate to myself. "In non-Euclidean geometries such as spherical geometry, they can."

Lucinda's eyes were wide. "Now you've lost me."

I thought for a moment, looking for an example that would bridge the gap in our mathematical knowledge. "Picture the globe and the vertical lines of longitude at 10° and 20°. At the equator, they're parallel. Right?"

"Yes."

"But at the North and South poles they intersect."

Lucinda jerked back. "What the…"

"Relax. Mathematics and logic did not turn upside down. Within a given system of axioms, postulates and theorems, that which follows can be absolutely accurate. In two dimensions, the principles of Euclidean geometry, including the non-intersection of parallel lines, all hold true."

"You mean my universe didn't just come crashing down, the victim of a devious proof by contradiction?"

"Nope. All's well that ends well."

Lucinda winked. "For the universe, maybe…but Mr. Shakespeare just rolled over in his grave."

***

The incredibly busy second week of June 1876 foreshadowed that Lucinda and I were in for a wonderful life. Following a simple wedding before a Justice of the Peace and Lucinda's mother—the latter had come by train from Charleston for the day—we moved into our new bungalow, having closed the purchase the afternoon before. The home, on a third of an acre, was far from fully furnished. But with a bed, armoire, table, two chairs and settee, bought from the prior homeowner for a small sum, it was ideal for us to begin our married life.

At the wedding ceremony, Lucinda was even more beautiful than usual. Her styled, textured hair was tied into buns on either side of her head. Her flawless bronze skin contrasted with her white dress, whose hem was encircled with three rows of lace trim and whose flouncy sleeves bore lacey cuffs. Her waist wrapped tightly with a corset, an accessory she had all but abandoned since joining the AME Baptist Women's Organization, turned her naturally incredible figure into a statuesque hourglass. The moment she entered the home of the Justice of the Peace—she arrived separately with her mother in order that I not see her before the ceremony—my hormones raged. Yes, I knew her body and she knew mine. We had touched each other in glorious ways. And contrary to the catechism of the day, we had proved that women, like men, enjoy sex. But consistent with her values, consummate pleasure had been postponed. Seeing her perfectly wrapped and coiffed, knowing that in mere hours we would share long awaited ecstasy, desire elevated beyond that which an ordinary graph could display.

Following the ceremony, Lucinda, her mother and I dined at John C. Seegers' Saloon. Though I had suggested we opt for a classier spot, if only for the sake of Lucinda's mother, Lucinda preferred the mundane establishment, the site of our first outing, the place where we had subsequently become engaged. Shrimp cocktails, steaks, a decadent chocolate cake and a bottle of champagne proved Lucinda right. The normally busy site was quiet at the three o'clock hour. The otherwise commonplace ambiance stirred nostalgic memories of great times shared there. Not unlike so many days spent with Lucinda, the simple celebration delivered a memorable lesson. Fancy and expensive were not necessarily superior to plain and economical. Of course, so much of that principle was a function of Lucinda's humble needs and tastes.

After taking Lucinda's mother to the train and seeing her off, Lucinda and I headed to our new home and our first night as husband and wife. Though the eight o'clock hour had barely arrived, we were ready, indeed eager for bedtime. As well as I knew Lucinda's glorious contours and charms, it was as if I were exploring complete unknowns. Long, we had awaited the moment when our bodies would connect as one. For the first time, we were free to do that which for so long had been forbidden. Intimacy is as much an operation of the mind as the body, the mental no less consequential than the physical. Converting ecstasy into words is problematic at best. Though I was never a slave, Lucinda was. An analogy she drew dwarfs any description I could fashion regarding our experience when, first with license, both literal and figurative, we made love. Accordingly, rather than relate my own recollections of our intimacy, I yield to her rendering, paraphrasing it as best I can.

News of Lincoln's emancipation, freedom delivered, ignited elation so overwhelming as to send shockwaves throughout the body. Freedom bore anomalous similarity to the lifting of the yoke of society's strictures, enabling full engagement in carnal pleasure. But much as love making and emancipation were similar, they differed. The former, its pinnacle, though ephemeral, engendered greater physical joy, while the latter, less fleeting, persisted. Regardless, both were marvelous. Both were rights to be enjoyed throughout one's life…And both were inalienable.

Chapter XXII

AS GOOD AS LIFE HAD BEEN THE PRECEDING SEMESTER, the summer of 1876 turned out even better. Lucinda and I had a ball decorating our new home. Financial cares, we had none. As part of our quest to graduate in three years, we both engaged in independent study. Lucinda was active in her women's-rights group, attending meetings, rallies and protests. I put my construction skills to good use, adding a porch with a rocker and painting several rooms. We planted a sizeable garden, complete with lettuce, carrots, beans, turnups, onions and tomatoes, along with a peach and apple tree. Still we had lots of time to romp about and play…and make love. The state of our lives arguably turned my belief that nothing is perfect into a paradox. Invoking mental gymnastics, coupled with my mathematical propensities, I purported to resolve the inconsistency. On a scale of twenty, our lives merited a score reflected by a discontinuous function f(t) which, for the summer, approached twenty in its limit; i.e., our score was not twenty, *per se*, but fell short by an infinitesimally small sum, one less than any amount, however tiny, that one might select. (The absurdity of the foregoing, my use of mathematical sophistry, afforded my logic a seeming modicum of consistency. Far more dubious was the sanity of my logic.)

On the first day after classes had ended in June, the upcoming summer vacation, two-plus months, had appeared to be a lengthy stretch. But by late August, looking backwards, it had transmuted into a brief break. Such was the nature of things as Lucinda arrived home the last Thursday of August, following a suffrage rally at the State Capitol.

"You win the vote?" I said, seated on the rocker that decorated our new porch.

Her brow furrowed. "Go ahead. Make fun. One day when we women gain our franchise, you men will be sorry. We're gonna vote you boys out of office…On second thought, that should ultimately make you men happy. Things will finally get straightened out…for everyone's benefit."

I might have argued with her, but for two points. I didn't feel like debating, and, more important, she was probably right. "So, how did the rally go?"

"Okay…I guess." A dour expression suggested success was even less than her unenthusiastic words. "Not a single legislator gave us the time of day. Most passersby ignored us. A group of counter-protestors from some gun clubs shouted us down. A few clods—I'm pretty sure they were drunk—called us whores and niggers. They apparently disregarded that two in our assemblage, Mary Smith and Ella Braintree, were white. They even threw stones at us. One hit me in the back."

"You…you okay?" I halted my rocker.

"Yeah…maybe a little bruise, but it couldn't have been all that big…the stone."

"This is getting out of hand. Maybe you—" I bit my tongue, at least for the moment, knowing a suggestion that Lucinda should rethink her involvement would not be well received. "Were any patrollers on the scene?"

"One, I think."

"Did he help protect you?"

Lucinda laughed.

"What's so funny?"

"The lone officer—he wasn't in uniform, but I think it was that Sykes fellow—was among those throwing stones at us."

"Damn, you need to reconsider this whole thing."

"I what?"

"C'mon, I'm serious." The bristling face that met my eyes pressed me to soften my stance. "I'm not saying you should stop pursuing women's rights, just that you should confine—"

"Sure, we should voice our objections in the back room of the church where no one will hear them and nothing will change."

"C'mon, you know that's not what I'm saying."

"Then what are you saying?"

Threading the needle would not be easy. "You need to choose your battles. Safety has to be part of what you stitch."

Lucinda shook her head.

"What, you disagree?" My words rang hollow. I had come nowhere near the needle's minute eye.

"You know as well as I that confrontation is the only way to call attention to our cause. Meetings, fliers, etcetera are nice, but the Legislature rarely moves until issues, especially those that challenge the status quo, threaten to burn out of control. Our legislators won't come to us. They'll treat us as if we don't exist. We need to go to the Capitol and confront them on their own turf. And if that means we'll have to face the gun clubs and other hatemongers, so be it. For that matter, all the better. It'll bring our issues to the forefront."

Much as I wanted to argue that the provocations Lucinda was advocating were the very risks she needed to avoid, I couldn't. She was right. Without such provocations her group's chances of success, otherwise dubious, would be miniscule. I said, "At least promise me you'll be careful."

With lips briefly sealed, she looked me in the eye and said, "You don't want me to lie, do you?"

***

Following our political philosophy class, Jack Philips and I headed to the commissary for a doughnut and coffee. Jack was one of my few Caucasian friends on campus. It was not that I had anything against white people. On second thought, that's not entirely true. Over the years, experience had made me increasingly suspicious of them. Bigots like Professor Hopkins, Sherman Hooker and the patroller who had informed me about Grover's death had given me reason. But my lack of white friends was also a matter of numbers. With the passage of time, the university had become nearly ninety percent Negro.[317] Each year fewer whites applied, choosing other colleges, while other whites transferred elsewhere.

Snacks in hand, Jack and I seated ourselves across from one another at a long table. "If Prof is right," said Jack, "November's elections for both president and governor oughta be humdingers."

"Yeah, seems like the future of the university will be determined by the votes. If the Democrats get control of the State House, there's sure to be a new Board of Trustees, and if that happens, the population here on campus is bound to change."

"I have to admit, I'd love to see it a little more balanced." Jack gave me a look, seemingly checking if he had pricked a tender nerve. "Personally, I feel like an outsider here."

---

[317] *Reconstruction in South Carolina, 1865-1877*, op. cit., p. 236, 237, stating: "The number of students greatly increased, so that it soon exceeded 200—more than nine-tenths negroes. The requirements for admission were so lax—the regulations in this matter were so flagrantly disregarded—that the so-called University soon became little more than a high school, whose chief aim was to inculcate and illustrate the social equality of the black race with the white."

"I understand." He and I had addressed the issue before, though never at length. "Here in South Carolina, we have loads of Negroes and likewise, whites. I'm not sure of the exact percentages, but I suspect Negroes outnumber, roughly 55:45. Be nice if the campus reflected those numbers or something around 50:50."

"Dream on, my friend. And feel free to imagine that folks will be color blind. It's not gonna happen."

Though my vacuous comment had been akin to the hole in my doughnut, I said, "I wasn't making predictions, just saying it would be nice." I bit into my fried delight. It tasted better than the political realities. "Who do you think'll win this fall?"

Jack shrugged. "You're asking the wrong person. I don't follow politics. I only know that whoever wins will pick the faculty and students, and the numbers here on campus won't be close to half and half."

"Perhaps." My tone, still influenced by wishful thinking, voiced more skepticism than I felt.

"Think about it. If the Republicans win, the current board will stay in power. That guarantees the status quo. On the other hand, if the Dems prevail—we're talking ultra conservative men who are still fighting the War of Secession, many of whom would reinstate slavery, if they could—it's a good bet the new board will ban Negroes from the campus."

"Damn," I said. "There's so much room in the middle for sensible compromise, but the idiots, on both sides, turn it into the Law of the Excluded Middle, either-or, with no middle ground."

Jack groaned.

"You disagree?"

"Not at all." With a measured cadence and haughty tone, Jack added, "Just that your purported philosophical erudition…fails to impress me."

My sheepish expression was palpable. "I did get carried away."

"True, but your underlying point has merit."

The compliment, albeit mixed, emboldened me to pursue the delicate subject. "Given what you said about the implications of Republican or Democratic victories this fall, which would you prefer?"

Jack shook his head. "To tell the truth…neither."

"What does that mean?"

"What the Democrats stand for, reactionary oppression, is anathema. But I'm not a fan of the Republicans either. Reconstruction has been a mixed bag. Having South Carolina under military rule is not my idea of utopia."

"C'mon, there are no utopias. Even Professor Nelson conceded that when he covered Thomas Moore's imaginary island of perfect government, politics and social conditions."[318]

Jack finished chewing a bite of his doughnut. "Give me a break. When I used the word *utopia*, I didn't mean it literally, and I suspect you know it." He directed a waiting look my way.

"Fair enough, but what are you saying?"

"That military rule is no way to live. And don't take this wrong, but I wish the campus were a little whiter. And before you react, understand, I'm not looking for a white campus. But as I said earlier, more balanced would be nice."

"Sounds like you want the 'excluded middle,' maybe even the very utopia you scoffed at a minute ago."

Jack heaved a sigh. "Perhaps I'm parsing things, but having something more balanced than we've got is a far cry from utopia...Make sense?"

I nodded. "For that matter, I think we're pretty much on the same page." I thought for a second. "Why can't we get to the middle?"

Jack shrugged. "I'm not sure, but a deeply polarized nation plays a huge role."

"Yeah, unfortunately, it does." An analogy popped into my mind. "I assume you're familiar with a normal curve." I drew one in the air.

"I am, though not like you, math guru that you are."

"We can debate my so-called expertise another time. But here's why you're right. What we have today is the normal curve turned upside down, what one might call an *abnormal curve*." I was well aware that I was co-opting the very argument that Lucinda had made shortly after we had first met. "The Democrats, the conservatives or reactionaries, are way over here (I gestured to my right) and the Republicans, liberals, are at the opposite end of the spectrum (I gestured left). We have too few in the middle to force a consensus. Whichever side gets control will dictate a one-sided policy."[319]

---

[318] *Utopian Socialism - The Utopian Socialism Movement*, utopiaanddystopia.com, 29 Apr. 2018 <http//:www.utopiaanddystopia.com/utopia/utopian-socialism/> stating: "The first utopian socialist was without the doubt the English philosopher and author Thomas Moore (1478-1535). His 1516 novel 'Utopia' (which popularized word [sic] 'utopia' in modern times) described the need for the creation of a state that practiced religious toleration, freedom of marriage, simpler communal life, free education and health care. He wrote this highly influential book guided by his frustration with the current political state in late 15th and early 16th century England..."

[319]*Bookmarks'* author's comment: Highly polarized 21st century politics is reminiscent of the post Civil War era. The sequence of Barack Obama's presidency, followed by Donald Trump with a Republican Congress, succeeded by Joseph Biden and a

"That sums it up pretty well." Jack sipped his coffee. "Care to venture a guess who will win in November's election?"

"For president…or governor of South Carolina?"

"Now that you put it that way, both."

"Well…" I finished the last bite of my doughnut, using the time to weigh my answer. "The best I can do is speculate. Given the way Reconstruction has been collapsing,[320] coupled with a lack of funding to prop it up, my money, not my heart, says Tilden will win. And using the same reasoning, I'd have to pick Hampton when it comes to the State House. What do you think?"

"As for South Carolina, I agree with you. The massacre that occurred during the Independence Day celebration in Hamburg,[321] the Negro hamlet about seventy miles southwest of here, is a strong indicator of the political winds. Hampton and his Democratic friends mean business. Voter intimidation and suppression have become effective elements of their arsenal."

No way could I debate Jack's point. The white paramilitary group's attack in Hamburg had proved it. They had killed a half-dozen and taken four prisoners.[322] I said, "Threats to lives, actual executions, keep lots of voters home."

Jack nodded. "It reflects the level of polarization, in this case, hate, we've been talking about. Even with federal troops still here, we're seeing violence. Imagine how it will be if Washington withdraws the troops."

The thought was chilling, especially knowing that politics, coupled with the recession, had already ended military rule in every other district. Chances were, it was just a matter of time before the last district,

---

Democratic Congress is a repetition of the very "abnormal curve" to which Mican referred. With Democratic and Republican party roles reversed, each election delivered a seismic swing of the political pendulum on issues of social policies, climate, immigration, race, governmental regulation, etc. It is analogous to the period of Reconstruction and that which ensued when it ended in 1877 and the federal military occupation ceased. Once the Democrats regained power, the road into Jim Crow laws was paved. Not until after World War II did the road fork into what became the Civil Rights movement. That the Nation, still struggling from the aftermath of slavery and the Civil War, after coming so far, could backtrack under the influence of populist, autocratic leadership would be sad irony. But only time will tell.

320 *Compromise of 1877 – End of Reconstruction: US History for Kids*, American-historama,org, 31 Mar. 2018 <http://www.american-historama.org/1866-1881-reconstruction-era/compromise-of-1877.htm>.

321 Ibid.

322 Ibid.

comprised of South Carolina, Florida and Louisiana, would see the same result. Perilous consequences stood on the doorstep.

***

The elections of 1876 had been held. Thanksgiving had come and gone. But even as the days of December clicked off, nothing was settled. Democrat Samuel J. Tilden had won a narrow victory over Republican Rutherford B. Hayes in the presidential popular vote, but the electoral college votes of several states remained in dispute, and, as a result, so too the outcome of the election.[323]

In South Carolina, the gubernatorial vote was no less a matter of debate. In the months leading up to the election, Republican Governor Daniel H. Chamberlain had been unable to maintain the peace, as white paramilitary groups known as "Red Shirts," had conducted raids, like the Hamburg Massacre, attacking and intimidating Negro voters, suppressing their franchise. Once the votes were counted, Democrat Wade Hampton III declared victory by the narrow margin of roughly 1100 votes.[324] But in Edgefield County, ballots cast exceeded the voting-age population by 2000. Laurens County ballots surpassed the number of registered voters.[325] And in Aiken County, site of the Hamburg Massacre, when compared to the previous election, Democratic votes increased by a factor of four, while Republican votes fell to fewer than one hundred.[326]

With disarray still bedeviling the political landscape, Christmas Day, 1876 arrived, and so too, Lucinda's mother. She had come by train from Charleston the afternoon before and was staying with us for the holiday. It was her first overnight visit to our new home. During the summer I had upgraded it, so it looked like new. A wreath on the front door, candles all about, and a small evergreen adorned with tinsel and ornaments had added a festive touch.

"Appreciate you newlyweds inviting me for Christmas," said Mrs. Brown. (With limited contact, I still referred to my mother-in-law as Mrs. Brown, despite her invitation to call her Mom.) "By rights, I shoulda done the cooking and had you two in Charleston."

---

[323] *Reconstruction Timeline*, op. cit.

[324] *South Carolina gubernatorial election, 1876,* Wikipedia, 17 Dec. 2019 <http://en.wikipedia.org/wiki/1876_South_Carolina_gubernatorial_election>.

[325] Ibid.

[326] Ibid.

"Nonsense," I said, seated in a chair opposite the settee which Lucinda and her mother occupied. "It's our pleasure…and privilege to have you. We're happy you can finally stay with us."

"Knowing that you've got such a fine place so early in your marriage does my heart good. Hard to believe how rapidly my dream for Lucinda, that she would have a prince and a castle, has become a reality."

Her praise of our home felt good; that she slipped in the word *prince*, better yet.

"Who knows…my days as a grandma might be near."

Lucinda choked on her eggnog. "Mother!"

"Well, I can hope, can't I?" Mrs. Brown looked my way. "Am I wrong, Mican?"

I suspected that an effort to escape the mother-daughter exchange by remaining silent would fail. Opting for the lesser evil, I said, "Uh…yes, you're free to wish for whatever you want."

"There, you see, Lucinda."

"I sure do. My dear husband prefers to please his mother-in-law, rather than voice his feelings."

Caught like Odysseus, between Homer's proverbial Scylla (the six-headed monster) and Charybdis (the whirlpool)—the analogy providing evidence that Mr. Wright's influence persisted—I needed to adopt a different approach. I folded my arms. "Mother and daughter, having started this discussion, can complete it without my assistance." I smiled broadly, wanting to ensure that my dodge was taken in its intended good-natured vein.

Lucinda gave me a look before turning to her mother. "You see what I have to deal with?"

Mrs. Brown rolled her eyes. "Not to change the subject, but you think the politics will mess up your education here?"

"It's a definite maybe," said Lucinda.

Her mother turned my way, and, putting her hand to the side of her mouth as if shielding Lucinda from her comment, said, "You sure your wife has two years of college behind her?" She shifted her gaze to her daughter. "Mind explaining?"

"If the Democrats get control of the Capitol and then, by implication, the university's board, big changes are all but certain on the campus. Fortunately, Mican and I are on track to graduate at the end of the school year. With a little luck, we'll complete our education before any disaster strikes."

Lucinda's mother looked my way again. "Maybe your wife has learned a thing or two."

"You really think so?" I said, adjusting to Mrs. Brown's singular sense of humor. Amidst her repartee, her love for her daughter, her pride in her daughter's accomplishments, was apparent. I glanced at our Christmas tree. A subtler point regarding their relationship exhibited itself. Pinecones that hung by threads were still seeds of the tree.

***

"What a stupid way to run a railroad," said Jack Philips, seated with me on a bench along the wall of a second-floor hallway of Rutledge.

"You got that right," I said. "Having politicians decide the state of affairs is like inviting convicted rapists to safeguard young virgins."

Jack slapped me on the shoulder. "Well put."

Following a moment in which I basked in my cleverness, I said, "If someone had told me back on Election Day that three months later we'd have two governors and two presidents, I would have summoned the men in white coats."

"We don't have two presidents; only that we don't know the rightful holder of the office."

"But we do have two governors," I said. On December 7th, Chamberlain, the Republican, was inaugurated for a second term. Seven days later, the Democratic legislators declared Hampton the winner and inaugurated him as governor. On December 29th, a United States Senator from Georgia introduced a resolution declaring Hampton, South Carolina's governor. South Carolina Senator John Patterson responded with papers asserting Chamberlain had won the governorship.[327]

"We don't actually have two governors, just two who claim the office." Jack shrugged. "What a ridiculous state of affairs."

"The situation regarding the presidency isn't much better. Admittedly, two presidents have not been inaugurated, but it's anybody's guess who won the office. We're three months past the election, and all we have is a new law creating a commission of fifteen, five from each house of Congress and five members of the Supreme Court, assigned to determine who won the electoral votes of the disputed states.[328] If that isn't chaos, I don't know what is."

---

[327] Ibid.

[328] *United States presidential election, 1876*, Wikipedia, 30 Apr. 2018 <http://en.wikipedia.org/wiki/United_States_presidential_election,_1876>. The Congressional portion of the Electoral Commission consisted of five Democrats and five Republicans because each party controlled one house of Congress. Of the five members of the Supreme Court, two Republicans and two Democrats were appointed, with the four of them assigned to select the final independent member, Justice David

Jack heaved a sigh. "It's hard to believe we're less than a month away from Inauguration Day,[329] and we have no clue who won." He looked me in the eye. "Answer me a question. Will the mess get resolved by March 4th, and if so, who will be inaugurated?"

Lacking an answer, I opted for a sidestep. "No fair. You asked two questions."

"Fine. Pick either, and provide an answer."

My sidestep, a failure, I gulped. "It…uh…will maybe…possibly get resolved."

"Thanks a heap."

"You have a better answer?"

"Nope, I left my crystal ball at home." Ignoring my groan, Jack continued, "Any guess what the future holds for our university?"

I thought for a moment. "That's as tough as the ones you asked before. But one thing is sure, politics will play a big role. Depending who becomes governor and which party controls the State House will determine who sits on the university's board, and that board will determine who occupies the seats in our classrooms."

***

Second semester of the 1876-77 school year continued in a fashion reflecting the insular nature of our campus. While political issues on both the state and federal level roiled, inside the Horseshoe, it was life as usual. From time to time in our commissary bull sessions, we discussed the chaos, but our debates were little more than convenient diversions from our studies. Subsequent hindsight did, however, confirm what many predicted: what transpired off the campus dictated the outcome on the campus.

In 1877, Easter fell on the 1st of April. Lucinda had wheedled me to travel to Charleston for the holiday. Her purpose was twofold: visit her mother and see Laura Towne speak at her mother's Charleston Church. During the War of Secession, Miss Towne, an abolitionist, educated in the North as a homeopathic physician and teacher, had opened the Penn School, the first school for freedmen. It was located on St. Helena Island,

---

Davis. "[N]o one, perhaps even Davis himself, knew which presidential candidate he preferred." (Wikipedia, citing Morris, Roy, Jr., *Fraud of the Century: Rutherford B. Hayes, Samuel Tilden And The Stolen Election of 1876*, New York, (Simon and Shuster, pp. 168, 239, 2003).

329 Until 1933, when Franklin D. Roosevelt was inaugurated, Inauguration Day was the 4th of March. *Why the Presidential Inauguration is in January*, daily.jstor.org, 1 May 2018 <https://daily.jstor.org/inauguration>.

off the coast of South Carolina's mainland.[330] Miss Towne was also a feminist and that, more than anything else, enticed Lucinda to attend her talk.

In the interim, before we traveled to Charleston for the weekend, the disarray associated with the presidential election of 1876 had finally resolved itself. Tilden, who had bested Hayes in the popular vote by three percentage points, conceded to the Republican.[331] With Florida, Louisiana, Oregon and South Carolina having all submitted two sets of returns, the special commission of fifteen resolved all twenty electoral college votes of those states in favor of Hayes, giving him a 185-184 victory. In each case, the commission voted 8-7 along party lines, with David Davis casting the deciding vote awarding the states' electoral votes to Hayes.[332] On March 3rd (the 4th was a Sunday), Hayes was inaugurated. The election of 1876, an enduring saga, had involved more rants than substance. The Democrats had railed about the graft and scandals of Grant's tenure, while the Republicans had raged about the Democrats' responsibility for secession and the many injustices wreaked throughout the South during Reconstruction.[333] But at least the election was finally resolved. What we, the citizenry, were yet to discover was that behind the scenes, the politicians had negotiated an unsavory deal.

Lucinda and I arrived in Charleston on Saturday and stayed the night at her mother's home. On Sunday morning, the three of us had attended Easter services and after lunch had returned to the church to hear Laura Towne speak. At first blush a small turnout disappointed Lucinda. However, it turned out to be a silver lining, a better opportunity to meet the activist after her talk. Once Miss Towne was done, Lucinda, with me in tow, approached the dedicated teacher.

"I enjoyed your presentation," said Lucinda. "My husband and I traveled here from Columbia to hear you. You more than justified the trip."

"Thank you," said Miss Towne.

---

[330] *PBS Online: Only A Teacher: Schoolhouse Pioneers*, pbs.org, 1 May 2018 <http://www.pbs.org/onlyteacher/lauratowne.html>. Towne opened her school in the back room of a plantation house in 1862, where "she began her work attending to the medical needs of the freedmen…Unlike most of the schools for freedmen, the Penn School offered a rigorous curriculum, modeled on that of schools in New England." The school operated for forty years.

[331] *United States presidential election, 1876*, op. cit.

[332] Ibid.

[333] *Compromise of 1877: Definition, Summary & Results*, 30 Apr. 2018 <https://study.com/academy/lesson/compromise-of-1877-definition-summary-results.html>.

"No, thank you for all you've done for my race," said Lucinda. "Were there no white folks like you who challenged injustice, slavery would still persist. Few would abandon a comfortable life in Pennsylvania to establish a school to educate poor Negroes in the South."

"All of us, both individually and as a society, have an obligation to right the inequities occasioned by slavery. The power of the vote is critical in that regard. 'Nobody seems to remember that the South is only half-civilized, and that the negroes [sic] are nearly as well informed and a great deal more loyal than the whites.'[334] And this, in spite of centuries of discrimination and disadvantage."

"I belong to a women's group in Columbia that is seeking equal rights for females," said Lucinda. "It's frustrating how the patriarchs treat us. To justify their discrimination, they label us the weaker sex. They insist their odious rules, instruments of oppression, protect us."

Watching Lucinda revel in the opportunity to share thoughts with Miss Towne, I simply listened, affording my wife an exclusive audience with the esteemed progressive.

"Good for you. We women need to press our case for equality." Miss Towne paused, her countenance thoughtful. "Unfortunately, I suspect the political climate is less than ideal for both the rights of women and Negroes. The presidential election confirms it. While it would have been worse had Tilden prevailed, the recent compromise that put Hayes into office—I assume you're aware of it—may be as bad."

"We've heard rumors that the Republicans, Hayes in particular, have agreed to withdraw the remaining federal troops from the South."[335]

"Hayes..." Miss Towne muttered inaudibly before continuing. "'I have been in raging indignation at Hayes. I hope we have not another Buchanan in the President's chair, but I fear we have. He is too easy and ready to think well of everybody. He won't believe in rebellion till he sees it again.'"[336]

Lucinda was wide-eyed. "You're not suggesting the South might try to secede again?"

"God forbid, and no. Though many here in the South are still fighting the war—I say that figuratively, rather than literally—between the devastation owing to that conflict and the state of the economy, the

---

[334] *Letters and diary of Laura M. Towne, Written From the Sea Islands of South Carolina,* Edited by Rupert Sargent Holland (Cambridge, 1912) p. 261, retrieved from archive.org, 1 May 2018 <https://archive.org/stream/cu31924074445267/cu31924074445267_djvu.txt>.

[335] *Compromise of 1877 – U. S. Presidents*, history.com, 31 Apr. 2018 <https://www.history.com/topics/us-presidents/compromise-of-1877>.

[336] *Letters and diary of Laura M. Towne*, op. cit., p. 261.

where-with-all to wage a war is lacking. What concerns me is that if the federal troops leave, and I've heard the rumors too, we're destined to go backwards. I'm not saying that we'll revert to slavery, but no way will we see anything resembling equality."

Miss Towne's assessment reinforced concerns I had entertained for months.

"Bad enough that matters on the national scene are a mess," said Miss Towne. "Do we need to compound that by having two men claiming the governor's house?"

"Much as I despise Hampton," said Lucinda, "you'd think that Chamberlain would finally concede, now that the South Carolina Supreme Court has ruled that Hampton was legally elected."[337]

"You might." Miss Towne's tone suggested less acquiescence than her words. "But from what I've seen, politicians, whatever their party, equate *reasonable* to what's in their personal interest. Anyway, this Hampton fellow, the declared winner, is the devil. In his 'speech at Columbia, he gave an ass's kick at the dead lion, when he said he should not occupy the State House till he had had the fire engines in, and the convicts scrub the place out. I try to smother my rage, but I wish I could speak out or write out what blazes inside.'"[338]

"Being located out on St. Helena Island," said Lucinda, "—if I'm not mistaken, there's no bridge to the mainland, and so, access is only by boat—does that help insulate you from the politicians' folly?"

"To some extent. It also helps preserve the Gullah culture of the people…Are you folks familiar with Gullah history and culture?"[339]

"My husband is a Black Seminole, originally from Southwest Florida."

"Really?" Miss Towne looked my way. "Then you must have grown up with the Gullah culture."

"Not really. The last of the Seminole Wars ended before I was able to understand what was occurring. After that, there were only a handful of us Black Seminoles left in that part of Florida. As far back as I can

---

337 On March 7, 1877, the South Carolina Supreme Court ruled that Wade Hampton III was the legally elected governor of the state. *South Carolina gubernatorial election, 1876*, op. cit.

338 *Letters and diary of Laura M. Towne*, op. cit., p. 261.

339 *St. Helena Island in Beaufort County South Carolina*, discover-hilton-head-island.com, 3 May 2018 <http://www.discover-hilton-head-island.com/st-helena-island-sc.html> stating: "St. Helena Island SC is closely identified with the Gullah heritage. It provides a unique opportunity for tourists to learn more about the distinctive Gullah culture, Gullah history and Gullah people. One of the reasons that the Gullah culture was able to thrive on this small island was because of the relative isolation from the mainland."

remember, my father and I lived in an isolated cabin—my mom had already died—and most people with whom we came in contact were white…trappers, soldiers, cattlemen and the like. I've heard of some Gullah practices, such as 'jumping the broom' to celebrate a marriage,[340] but my knowledge of such customs is not from personal experience."

"It's an interesting culture. It began in Africa where Negroes were kept in holding cells before being shipped across the Atlantic as part of the slave trade.[341] Even as we educate these former slaves, along with providing them 'carpentry classes, blacksmith training, wheelwright instruction, harness making, basic mechanics, basket weaving and cobbling,'[342] we endeavor to preserve their culture." Miss Towne heaved a sigh. "Living on an island with no connection to the mainland is a double-edged sword. Anyone or anything that arrives from the outside must come by water. Someday, way in the future, they'll probably connect us with a bridge. It'll be a great convenience, but I suspect it will do harm to many wonderful traditions. Progress has its price."

***

Brew in hand, along with Jack Philips, Lucinda and I sat in the parlor of our house on the last Friday of April 1877. The political madness occasioned by the elections of 1876 had been resolved. The fallout, however, was yet to work itself out.

"You two were mighty smart to pack your education into three years," said Jack. "Damn, I wish I had gone that route. Unfortunately, I lacked the clairvoyance of some others."

"If you're referring to the rumors that the university may close at the end of the school year, I assure you," said Lucinda, "that was never part of our decision. We did it to get on with our lives sooner."

"Whatever the reason, you look like geniuses. Ever since Hayes met with Chamberlain and Hampton, it's been one piece of bad news after another: Hayes removes the federal troops from South Carolina; Hampton is certified as governor; and now we have one of those damn

[340] *Black Seminoles*, Wikipedia, 3 May 2018 <https://en.wikipedia.org/wiki/Black_Seminoles>.

[341] *Ultimate Gullah – Gullah History*, ultimategullah.com, 3 May 2018 <http://ultimategullah.com/culture.html> stating: "Nearly a half a million Gullah live between Jacksonville, North Carolina and Jacksonville, Florida today. This 500 mile stretch along the Atlantic Ocean and over and between the Rivers [sic] that surround it is home to the descendants of the Africans brought to the Carolina Colony beginning in the late 1500s…The Gullah represent one of the oldest culture groups surviving and living among us today."

[342] *St. Helena Island in Beaufort County South Carolina*, op. cit.

redeemer governments here in Columbia."[343] One can only imagine what's next for our campus. Even if the university remains open, the financial support, requisite to most students, is certain to evaporate. And presumably the Board of Trustees will change, and once it does, all bets are off."

"You paint a bleak picture." I assessed it briefly. "Unfortunately, I suspect it's accurate. And if so, the rumors about the university closing are likely to prove right as well."

"If it does," said Lucinda, "what will you do, Jack?"

"Open my own college." Jack threw his hands overhead, nearly spilling his bottle of brew. "God only knows. Maybe transfer to another school. I try not to think about it. But when I do, I pray they keep the campus open until I get my degree next year." Jack gulped his beer. "What about you two. What are your plans, once you graduate in June?"

"We've been waiting to see which way the wind is blowing," I said. "We'd like to stay here in Columbia, now that we own a home. I'd love to get a job on campus teaching, as well as doing post-graduate study and research. But given the current politics, that dream is a longshot."

"I assume you're checking out other alternatives, if only to know where you'll get your next meal."

Personal privacy kept me from disclosing we would not be under the financial gun. "Hey, like you, we're going along blithely, relying on wishful thinking. Maybe we'll all be lucky. Come June, maybe everything will work itself out."

Jack rolled his eyes.

Qualms notwithstanding, I suppressed loose lips by drawing my bottle to them.

"You still as active in your women's group, Lucinda?"

"Even more so."

---

[343] *South Carolina gubernatorial election*, op. cit., providing the following timeline: "April 3 — President Hayes orders the removal of Federal troops from South Carolina. April 10 — Federal troops leave the State House and return to their barracks. April 11 — At noon, Wade Hampton becomes the sole and official Governor of South Carolina." *See also*, *Reconstruction Timeline*, op cit. On April 10, 1877, the date President Hayes directed General Sherman to withdraw the federal troops, Chamberlain issued a paper which began as follows: "To the Republicans of South Carolina: By your choice I was made Governor of this State in 1874. At the election on the 7th of November last, I was again by your votes elected to the same office. My title to this office, upon every legal and moral ground, is today clear and perfect. By the recent decision and action of the President of the United States I find myself unable longer to maintain my official rights, and I hereby announce to you that I am unwilling to prolong a struggle which can only bring further suffering upon those who engage in it." (Reynolds John S., *Reconstruction in South Carolina, 1865 – 1867*, op. cit.)

"The rise of the Red Shirts and others like them doesn't concern you?"

"Of course, it does, but it's all the more reason for activism. Without it, the reactionaries would not only eviscerate the gains of Reconstruction, but also ensure that women remain second-class citizens."

"I hear what you're saying," said Jack. "But have you considered the increased risks, now that the federal troops are gone? No way will you get a fair shake, what with the Democrats, many of them thugs from the gun clubs, controlling the government." Jack looked Lucinda in the eye. "As a white man, I'm not proud of the situation, but reality is…reality. The sons of the Confederacy have regained control of South Carolina's courts. Crimes against Negroes, women included, are being ignored. Worse yet, all too often, those who wear the badges and robes by day, the sheriffs and judges, perpetrate the crimes by night. Justice is all but non-existent."

A palpable silence pervaded. I imbibed my beer, an escape from the disquiet. Jack's warning, one I had previously voiced, was welcome. In recent weeks I had avoided pressing the issue, knowing Lucinda disliked my meddling. Coming from someone else, especially a member of the white community, perhaps the message would find her more receptive.

Chapter XXIII

GRADUATION DAY, JUNE 1877. On the campus of the University of South Carolina, commencement, an age-old anomaly, was more paradoxical than ever. Graduation, the conclusion of our studies, was the beginning of our lives…after college. But at the university, the word *commencement* made absolutely no sense. It was the end. The university doors were closing.[344] For the vast majority of students, their education had been abruptly cut short. For Lucinda and me, graduation brought mixed emotions. We were elated to receive our sheepskins, but we were sad to see the doors of our alma mater locked.

"I'm so proud of you both," said Mrs. Brown, seated in a rocker on our porch. We now had two, the second of which Lucinda occupied. I sat on the porch rail. "Hard to believe, my daughter and her husband are college graduates. Me, a slave, who had no formal education, has a daughter who went through college." Mrs. Brown rocked back. "Wish your daddy was here to see it." She gazed upward beyond the gingerbread that bedecked the underside of the porch roof. "Sausage to chitlins says he's looking down and smiling."

Though hardly sanguine, I was far less skeptical than I had been before Grover and Walter had died. Arguments disproving God's existence, as well as the afterlife, were as fatuous as those to the contrary. Whatever the truth, at that moment, rational analysis yielded to hope that Mrs. Brown's faith-based belief was accurate. I said, "Lucinda and I are very lucky. Not only were we able to attend the only public university in a southern state open to Negroes,[345] but we managed to graduate just before its doors shut."

---

[344] *A Time Line – History | University School of Law*, law.sc.edu, 31 Mar. 2018 <http://www.law.sc.edu/history/time_line.dhtml>. "The University is closed on June 7, 1877, by a joint resolution of the South Carolina General Assembly."

[345] *Our History*, University of South Carolina, op. cit.

"You think they might reopen soon?" said Mrs. Brown.

"Hard to know." Lucinda brought her rocker to a halt. "But if they do, I suspect the school will be very different. Physically the campus may be familiar, but the makeup of the student body, as well as the attitudes, will probably be poles apart from what we experienced."[346]

"It's good that you two have time to figure out your next venture. Not many enjoy that luxury."

That my mother-in-law approved of us taking a measured approach to our future was pleasing, at least it seemed so for an instant.

"Heck, it oughta give you more time to make me a grandma."

"Mother, we've been this route before. It's none of your business."

"C'mon, can't a body hope?"

"Hope…yes," said Lucinda. "But don't insinuate yourself into private matters."

The smirk Mrs. Brown displayed evidenced that the edict had fallen on deaf ears. She mopped her brow. "Calendar says summer won't arrive for two weeks. Guess the calendar lacks a thermometer." She slowly inhaled the thick air. "Almost makes you think the folks who put up with those northern winters aren't crazy."

"C'mon," said Lucinda. "As bad as several months of endless heat may be, it's better than weeks when the temperature never reaches freezing."

Mrs. Brown shrugged. "You won't get an argument from me."

Lucinda gave her mother a look.

"Hey, I only said it *almost* makes you think the northerners aren't crazy." She mopped her brow again. "Heat may be tough… but fried beats frozen, any day."

I silently laughed at the droll exchange. I tried to remain invisible. The middle of their debate was an unpalatable place; but observing it, fascinating. Lucinda was very much a reflection of her mother. Both were strong personalities. Though only one had a formal education, both had sharp minds. Neither was quick to concede a point. Regardless, mutual, unconditional love was evident.

***

Along with ten others, mostly members of the AME Baptist Women's Organization, I marched clockwise around the South Carolina

---

[346] Ibid., stating the university "reopened in 1880 as an all-white agricultural college and during the next 25 years the institution became enmeshed in the upheaval of late 19th century South Carolina politics."

State Capitol. I carried a sign that read, "Suffrage for Women." A white man, the husband of another AME marcher, walked alongside me at the rear of the group. All of us chanted: "Equality for Women…Equality for all." In what was a spontaneous counterprotest, eight or nine Red Shirts or those of similar ilk followed us closely. The voices of our group were loud, but the vituperative shouts of our pursuing antagonists were equally so. Following the paved walkway, we completed several circumnavigations around the impressive edifice. Here and there onlookers watched us pass, most giving us little more than a curious gaze. One or two offered words of support, while a few derided us with bigoted epithets and obscene gestures.

As we passed the south side of the Capitol for the fifth time, we drew to a halt and discontinued our chants. The newest cry of our antagonists, "Niggers and nigger lovers, go home," resounded. At the direction of our group's leader, a Negro woman in her twenties, we stepped off the walkway onto the grass, making room for our antagonists to go by. Rather than continue, they stationed themselves on the grass on either side of the walkway, no more than fifteen feet from us. Their shouts gradually subsided. Our tension mounted.

A bearded man bearing a shirt with a Confederate flag emblazoned across his chest, yelled, "Nigga whores, go back to your African jungle and eat your bananas!"

Consistent with the instructions we had been given prior to the march, we remained mute, pretending to ignore the invective.

"Apes can't talk!" shouted another of the antagonists.

A burly man, well over six feet and weighing upward of 250 pounds, armed with a baseball bat, stepped forward onto the intervening walkway. He turned to his comrades. "You fellows wanna see a home run? A brew says I can belt an ape's head over the State Capitol." He took a stance as if ready to hit.

The man whose shirt bore the Confederate flag shouted, "Yuh best not do dat, lest you hafta toss yuh bat away. Wouldn't be worth dog dung, coated with Nigga cooties. We might betta lynch de lot of 'em, de way dey done in Gainesville, Texas, back durin' de war. Won't be near as good. Dey hung over forty, from what I heard." He stared at our group. "Course a dozen, give or take, ain't chickenfeed."

I eyed the group of antagonists and counted them. They numbered nine, two less than our eleven, nine women and two men. But we had nothing but signs mounted on thin pine sticks. In addition to the baseball bat, at least two of our antagonists were armed with guns, one a rifle and the other, a shotgun. We were no match. For that matter, even discounting their weapons, we were no match.

Our leader motioned us away from the threat, directing us back onto the walkway, a short distance ahead of our antagonists. We renewed our march. Once again, the hecklers followed, drowning us with vitriol. Gradually they moved closer, shouting at us from the grass on either side. The man with the shotgun hurried ahead. He stepped onto the walkway and pointed his weapon our way.

"Stop right there…or I'll blow you to kingdom come!"

We froze.

The antagonists inched closer on all sides. The man with the bat stood about three steps away on our left, while the one with the rifle took a position on our right. From behind me another called out, "My revolver is locked and loaded, just in case you apes was thinkin' of backin' up."

"Shall we shoot 'em or hang 'em?" said another.

"Seems a shame to waste good ammo on a bunch of jungle bunnies."

"Anybody got a rope?" said the goon with the bat.

"I can fetch one," said another. "We could take 'em to the park (he gestured west). They got some fine hangin' trees there."

"What's going on here?"

The voice off to my right turned my head. A patroller wearing a badge approached.

"These here niggers…and nigger lovers is makin' trouble," said the man with the baseball bat.

"So, I see," said the patroller. He walked up and down alongside us, giving us the twice over. "Lyman," he said, addressing one of the antagonists, "what's goin' on?"

"These rabble-rousers been marchin' 'round the Capitol, disturbin' the peace…causin' trouble."

"I can see that." He gestured at our signs.

"We weren't causing any trouble," said our leader. "We were just exercising our—"

"I got eyes. I can see whatcha doin'." The patroller stepped closer to our leader. "You give me any more lip, and you'll get what's comin' to you." He turned back to the antagonists. "Lyman, what you plannin' to do?"

"We was gonna give 'em what for, maybe string a few up."

The patroller frowned. "You think that's a good idea, out here in broad daylight. Oughta pick you a better time and spot. You know, after dark, when no one's around." He gestured up the street. "Folks, both white and niggers, are out this time of day. They're watchin'." He refocused on our leader. "By rights, I oughta let these boys do their business. City could do with a good lynchin'. But…this must be your lucky day. I'm gonna let you go. Next time 'll be different." He ran his eyes over us. "Now, get your damn asses outta here...before I change my mind."

We started north, past the Capitol.

"And don't you dare raise dem damn signs. 'Cause if you do, your lucky day will have come and gone. You hear me?"

Signs low by our sides, we quietly proceeded to Gervais Street, which ran parallel to the rear of the Capitol. Walking briskly on Gervais, we turned north onto Main away from the Capitol. Once we were well beyond the view of our antagonists, we stopped.

"That was close," said one of the women.

The man who earlier had been marching with me at the rear of the pack said, "Those thugs meant business. If the bastard with the badge hadn't stepped in, likely some of us would be swinging from the wrong end of a rope."

I eyed Lucinda. She showed no reaction. I said, "His point is well taken."

Lucinda shrugged.

"C'mon, this is serious." I looked her in the eye.

"I understand, but the only way we'll get our rights is if we stand up to these animals. So many died so we could be free. If we don't fight, the bigots will restore their antebellum world. Look at the last election. They intimidated folks, scared them from the polls. The Negro vote was a fraction of what it's been in recent years."

"That may be, but..." My brain boggled amidst conflicting logic. Sacrificing ourselves as meaningless statistics was idiotic. But allowing the hatemongers to negate the progress from the War of Secession and Reconstruction was inconceivable. Caught between impossibilities, I turned silent.

Lucinda waited, giving me ample opportunity to tell her why she was wrong. Finally, she said, "Whatever you think...I have to do, what I have to do."

With the protest ended, albeit prematurely, we marchers went our separate ways. As Lucinda and I headed for home, she said, "You know, we're a wonderful match, so similar and yet, so different."

"I agree about the match part, but the second facet confuses me."

"Think about it. Our brains are alike, both enamored with math and physics. But our souls are different. Yours leans toward academics, where mine tilts toward social justice."

"Is that a bad thing?" I said, conceding her point, at least to myself.

"Not at all. We are who we are. And as I said, we're a wonderful match."

"So, neither of us needs to change?"

"Absolutely not. We owe that to each other, as well as ourselves." She smiled.

We stopped and I kissed her. I said, "If ever I try to change you, don't let me. Live your life, follow your soul...even after I'm dead and gone."

"That's a morbid specter."

"Not really, since I have no intention of dying for many years. Why would I, when I have the best wife imaginable? But anyway, promise me, you'll always be true to your soul."

"Fine, provided you promise to be true to yours as well." Lucinda looked me in the eye. "Give me your word."

"I promise," I said, embracing the excellent bargain, one that treasured our love and marriage, while preserving our individuality. I welcomed the obligations it imposed upon me, including the duty to never alter Lucinda's essence.

***

As the days of August 1877 waned, Lucinda and I were living a paradox. Bigotry's tentacles were ubiquitous. Nevertheless, within the confines of our home and property, our lives approached life's apex. As newlyweds, free of financial burdens, the weeks since graduation had been a continuous celebration. It was not that we had been partying *per se*, but our days were ongoing revelry, a luxury few young southern couples of color enjoyed. Lucinda had lined up a job teaching a variety of subjects, math and science, and perhaps even reading, at AME Baptist. Her minimal pay was no concern. It was what she wanted to do, and she was excited for the start of the school year. I had interviewed for a position teaching mathematics and/or physics at the Benedict Institute, a college founded in 1870 under the sponsorship of the American Baptist Home Mission Society in what had been a slave owner's plantation mansion.[347] Indications suggested I would be hired part time with the possibility that my position might become full time the second semester.

---

[347] *Benedict Institute*, gmnupes.com, 8 May 2018 <http://gmnupes.com/gpage2.html> stating: "Mrs. Bathsheba A. Benedict of Pawtucket, Rhode Island, provided the amount of $13,000.00 to purchase the land to open Benedict Institute on December 12, 1870. This new school was established for the recently emancipated people of African descent." In 1894 it was chartered as a liberal arts college and the name was changed to "Benedict College." Today it has 2100 students and 33 baccalaureate liberal degree programs (*See*, Benedict College website).

An inordinately cool, late August day—the high temperature failed to reach eighty—hinted that autumn was nearing. I had spent the day tending to our backyard garden, removing weeds, harvesting a wonderful crop of vegetables and installing a fence. Lucinda had been off with her AME Baptist Church women's group, engaged in a march in support of non-segregated childhood education, along with women's suffrage. The change of the political landscape throughout the South, particularly in South Carolina, suggested that gains made under the Thirteenth, Fourteenth and Fifteenth amendments to the Constitution and the Civil Rights Act of 1866 and 1875 might erode. Inroads upgrading long inferior, underfunded Negro educational facilities were beginning to erode. As they did, Lucinda's organization had broadened its agenda to include the promotion of improved schooling for Negroes.

Dusk drew nigh as I neared the end of my work. I was filling a bushel basket with a final load of vegetables when a woman I recognized—I knew her face, though not her name—circled around to the back of our house.

"Uh…excuse me," she said, her fingers fidgeting. "I…I knocked on the door several times, but…uh…when no one answered, I…uh…took the liberty of coming back here." She avoided eye contact.

"What can I do for you?"

"I…I'm Hannah Woolsey…with the AME Baptist Women's Organization."

"Yes, I recognize you…Where's Lucinda?"

Her uneasiness palpable, her gaze lowered. She shook her head and began to cry.

"What is it? Did something happen?"

"She…" Her sobbing became uncontrollable.

My concern became panic. "Tell me. What happened?"

Hannah shook her head again. She looked up briefly. "They…"

"They what?"

"They…they lynched Lucinda."

"Is she okay?" The spontaneous utterance was a product of my brain's refusal to absorb that which had invaded my ears.

Amidst hysterical weeping, Hannah shook her head.

"Is…is Lucinda…dead?"

Hannah nodded.

I sank to the ground, pounding the earth with my fists. Wails, screaming wails streamed from my mouth. Tears gushed. Harder yet, I beat the loamy dirt until finally I gave way, throwing myself prostrate onto the ground…How long I lay there, I'm unsure, but it was likely several minutes.

When finally I regained a minuscule semblance of—I don't know what—but certainly not reality, I looked up where Hannah was standing nearby.

"I...I'm sorry. So sorry...Is there anything I can do?" The pain etched on her face reflected the inanity of her question.

"Where is Lucinda now?"

"We took her...her body to the church."

My brain raced. Darting thoughts, all incapable of bringing Lucinda back to life, were meaningless. I raised myself to my knees and slowly climbed to my feet. I gazed at Hannah, almost pleading with her to begin anew, negate all that she had told me.

Shoulders slumped, Hannah looked away.

"Do you know who did it?"

She shook her head. Just that there were two of them...men."

My raging brain screamed for vengeance. Stronger yet was unfathomable torment. "I have to go see her," I said.

"You sure you want to?"

"I...I have to be with her." I was sure of nothing, but amidst my seething and grief, logic played no role.

Accompanied by Hannah, I hurried to the AME Baptist Church. With evening drawing close, all was quiet. We circled behind the house of worship where a large, blanket-covered wooden crate sat on the all-but-bare ground. Hannah pulled back the coverlet. I dropped to my knees and wailed at the sight of Lucinda's lifeless body. Rope burns across her grotesquely twisted neck kindled a gruesome image of her dangling from a rope. Though not a witness to the atrocity, I carry the scars of that image with me. My sobbing uncontrolled, I took hold of Lucinda's hand and kissed her lips. Helpless, I closed my eyes, trying to escape the reality I beheld. If anything, it made that reality more manifest. I put my hand to Lucinda's heart, perhaps searching for a beat...begging for life I knew did not exist. "I love you, my dear," I uttered softly. "I love you." I kissed her one last time.

Hannah helped me up. She slid the blanket back over the makeshift casket. She said, "You're welcome to stay with me and my family tonight."

"I shook my head."

"We'd love to have you."

"Kind of you, but no," I said, not that I actually considered her offer. Regardless, had I thought it through, my answer would have been the same. Spending the night in an unfamiliar house with unfamiliar people was not what I wanted. It was not what I needed. On the other hand, nowhere, no one, save Lucinda, could satisfy my needs.

“We’d be happy to walk you back to your home,” said another woman who stood nearby.

“No need. I’ll be okay.” My response echoed in my head. I would be anything but okay.

“We at the church will help you with the funeral arrangements,” said the woman. “The pastor—he’s in Florence, but due back early tomorrow—I suspect he’ll be round to see you then. For tonight, please take care of yourself.”

“I…I’ll try.”

“You sure you won’t change your mind and stay with—”

“I need to be home.”

“I understand.”

Hannah patted me on the back, just before I departed.

As I circled around the church, off to the west, the Sun had dropped below the horizon, but the faint light of evening still painted the sky. I turned east, beginning the long walk home. The veil of darkness rapidly grew. Darker yet were my thoughts. Crying…pleading that I wake up from the nightmare, I trudged homeward. My life had nosedived to zero. I kicked the ground…several times. I grabbed a rock and hurled it wildly past a huge oak, barely visible amidst the descending night. I glared at the tree, little more than a shadow in the dark. Its outline reignited a torturous image of Lucinda dangling from a noose amidst her last agonizing breaths. Rage…unchanneled rage blazed.

***

Home alone, the night I learned of Lucinda’s death was wretched. Detailing it would serve no purpose. Suffice it to say that apart from a few isolated minutes of dozing, I failed to sleep. With the advent of morning, I embarked on an arduous chore. I cleaned myself up in preparation for a train trip to Charleston. Someone had to deliver the appalling news to Lucinda’s mother, and that someone had to be me. I considered sending a telegram, but instantly nixed the idea. Bad enough that Mrs. Brown would have to endure the tragedy. The least I could do was try to comfort her. Ironically, the burden of playing messenger probably helped me. Preoccupation with how I would tell her elevated my mental state from horrific to horrid, though mathematically there was no difference. Emotionally, I remained at zero.

Shortly before I departed, the pastor from the AME Baptist Church paid me a visit. His words and manner were undeniably kind and caring, but their impact on my pain, if any, was negligible. They failed to bring Lucinda back. They did, however, enable me to arrange her funeral to be held two days later. They also added details of Lucinda's murder, details that put the kibosh on my crazed ruminations of vengeance. Two white men had abducted and lynched Lucinda. An outraged white woman had shot the two, after which vigilantes had, in turn, killed the woman. Justice, at least within an absurd definition of the term, had been delivered in an absurd way. Much as I wanted to exact revenge, my opportunity had already been quashed. I will never know what I would have done had the opportunity existed. Fury would have urged me to take the law into my own hands. Lucinda's voice would have demurred. Whether wise counsel would have checked unbridled rage is unknowable.

I headed off to Charleston where I delivered the dreadful news to Mrs. Brown. I took her back to my home. I think it benefited us both. Though we spoke little, we understood the other's suffering. I tried preparing a eulogy but was unable to summon the strength. Even if I had, I doubt I could have delivered it.

Knowing that Lucinda would want the work of her AME women's group to continue, I donated $200 to the organization. I promised myself that I would give an additional $60 each year. The funds that I had inherited from Walter, which I had never felt comfortable spending, could finally be put to good use. The $45 of income they generated annually, plus $15 from the principal, would cover the regular contributions. Offering my services to the organization would have been nice, but its constant connection to my loss was too hard to bear. Perhaps down the road when time had mitigated my pain, I would become an active participant in their cause. My reluctance to become more involved might have triggered guilt but for the promises Lucinda and I had made to preserve our distinct cores; she, in the pursuit of social justice, and I, in the world of math and science. The irony of our promises was not lost upon me. I was the one who had sought the commitment, a guarantee that she would never allow my influence to alter her essence. But with her death, the similar vow that I had made to her had become not only my obligation, but also my umbrella.

The funeral was held on a typically stifling late August day. Heat and humidity without a breath of breeze had folks perspiring profusely. Sadness ensured that moisture flowed from their eyes as well. The pastor, along with two women from Lucinda's activist group, delivered wonderful tributes, not that I digested the entirety of their words. Lucinda was laid to rest in the Randolph Cemetery. Established six years earlier by local Negro legislators and businessmen, it was located a couple hundred yards east of where the Broad and Saluda rivers merged, becoming the Congaree.[348] Knowing that prior to Randolph, Negroes were all buried, along with poor whites, in the local Potter's Field,[349] I was grateful for the well-maintained, park-like burial ground, a rare iota of positivity from the first days after Lucinda's death.

Once the funeral service ended and folks had conveyed their condolences, I took Lucinda's mother to the train. I had encouraged her to stay longer, but she preferred to return to Charleston. Like me, she chose seclusion.

One could rightly question my failure to describe the funeral in greater detail, including the remarks of those who eulogized Lucinda. Three reasons illuminate my decision: to do so would stir pain, not catharsis; grief fettered my recollection; and, at the risk of redundancy, it would not bring Lucinda back.

Immediately after taking Mrs. Brown to the train depot, I returned home. I went to the parlor credenza and took out a bottle of whiskey. Numerous glasses, more than I had ever consumed in a single sitting, left me in a stupor. The binge commenced a new chapter in my life, one dominated by alcohol.

***

A week had passed since Lucinda had been interred. In the interim I had spent countless hours raging. Unbridled fury thwarted rational thought. As it had been with Grover, there was nothing I could do to requite the wrong. The duo who had perpetrated the evil were already dead. More important, nothing could bring Lucinda back. Purpose grew non-existent. I hated the world outside. An occasional notion that I should try to make it better—that was what Lucinda would have done—amplified my fury. No way would I feel guilty, not after Lucinda had been stolen from me. I stormed about the house cursing, banging the wall and occasionally throwing things. Incapable of addressing my feelings, I buried them. I spent more time in bed than not. Even so, I was sleep deprived.

I had not been out of the house, except to the backyard where I picked vegetables from the garden, along with peaches and apples from our trees. I got eggs from our chickens, a couple of which I beheaded, giving me a source of meat. I might not have ventured off our property

[348] *Historic Randolph Cemetery*, historicrandolphcemetery.org, 8 May 2018 <http://www.historicrandolphcemetery.org/histroy/>. Named for Senator Benjamin Franklin Randolph, Columbia's Randolph Cemetery, founded in 1871, was the city's first cemetery established for Negroes.

[349] Ibid.

had my stock of liquor not been exhausted. It was the 1st of September when I finally dragged myself from the cloister of my home. Somewhat disheveled, a deviation from my typically trim appearance, I went to the public marketplace, where I purchased a slab of beef and one of pork. I also picked up two packages of *Granula*.[350] I had previously tried the "rock-hard breakfast bricks" and found them unappealing. But the convenience of the cereal, introduced about fifteen years earlier, was enough to attract me. While some referred to it as the first ready-to-eat cereal, and indeed it was more ready than any of its predecessors, the tough, tasteless nuggets needed to be soaked overnight in water or milk before they were edible.[351] The inventor, a religious fundamentalist, hoped his food for the soul would shift Americans to a more vegetarian diet and reduce the consumption of whiskey.[352] Expediency alone had led me to choose the convenient fare. The meat alternative was well suited to a miserable soul who, consumed by grief and lethargy, was heavily into the hard stuff. But contrary to the inventor's goal, it failed to inhibit my propensity to imbibe.

Armed with my new meal in a package, I embarked on what, with hindsight, was the most unproductive stage of my life. I still ate eggs and chicken and occasionally pork or beef, along with vegetables and fruit, but my two staples, *Granula* and whiskey, accounted for nearly half my diet. Where the days went, I can't say. Many a morning I stayed in bed close to noon, often hungover from the preceding day. Afternoons and evenings found me in a state of limited sobriety. Almost never did I have a visitor, and on those rarest of occasions, I was an indecorous host. Never did I visit someone else. Simply put, I was a drunken hermit. Now and again, I took my calculus book or a physics text I had acquired during college years down from the shelf. After flipping a few pages, I would grab my bottle—I had ceased to use a glass—and drink. Any moments of intellectual analysis were brief, quickly yielding to more vacuous ruminations. Piteous wallowing was easier than complex equations.

---

350 *How cereal transformed American culture*, theweek.com, 29 May 2018 <http://theweek.com/articles/470258/how-cereal-transformed-american-culture> stating: "During the early 19th century, most Americans subsisted on a diet of pork, whiskey, and coffee. It was hell on the bowels, and to many Christian fundamentalists, hell on the soul too…To rid America of these vices, religious zealots spearheaded the country's first vegetarian movement. In 1863, one member of this group, Dr. James Jackson invented Granula, America's first ready-to-eat, grain-based breakfast product."

351 *Period-Granula, the first ready-to-eat cereal | American Civil War Forums*, civilwartalk.com, 16 Mar. 2019 <https://civilwartalk.com/threads/granula-the-first-ready-to-eat-cereal.75757/>.

352 Ibid.

As autumn drifted into winter and winter into spring, I developed a pattern. On roughly a biweekly basis, I ventured out and acquired additional *Granula* and whiskey and, especially during the cold months, additional victuals. About once per month, I would also purchase a newspaper, which, over time, I managed to read in its entirety. The periodical gave me a sense of life in the world beyond my property. Foremost among those events were the continuation of the long recession and the shift of power following the end of Reconstruction. With the Democrats back in control of South Carolina, as well as most of the South, people of color, like me, were driven deeper into second-class citizenship. Auspicious amendments to the Constitution, as well as civil rights acts, remained the law of the land, but in the streets, courts, businesses and other public places of the South, their glorious guarantees of equality were illusory. But for the abolition of slavery, one could label it a return to antebellum days. Post-Reconstruction injustice became my excuse for a barren existence. I refused to participate in the unfair world outside. In sober moments of soul-searching, I acknowledged the hollowness of my justification. I knew that Lucinda would have wanted me to move on. But unable to accept her loss, aided by my bottles, I rationalized. My self-destructive pattern persisted.

Under the bright sun of a late April 1878 day, I ventured forth to restock my supply of food and whiskey. Before doing so, I stopped at a metal engraving establishment where I ordered an 18-inch bronze plaque for the front of my house. It read as follows:

Home of Lucinda Brown Reinbow
Champion of Negro, Women's and Civil Rights

I headed west past the deserted Horseshoe to Assembly Street, which ran alongside the westerly edge of the State Capitol grounds. Shortly thereafter, I arrived at the busy marketplace near the center of Columbia, where farmers and shoppers congregated in what had become a common scene throughout America. The list of available goods at these popular meccas constantly expanded amidst ever-increasing industrialization.

From a vat of whiskey, a merchant filled my gallon jug. Along with *Granula*, a loaf of rye bread and pork, I purchased pickled beets packed in a Mason Jar, a newly available item that came both empty and prepacked with foodstuffs.[353] I picked up the day's edition of *The Daily*

---

[353] *Almanac: The Mason Jar - CBS* News, cbsnews.com, 3 Jun. 2018

Phoenix, Columbia's local newspaper. I was about to start for home when I heard someone call my name. I turned and saw Martin Fredericks, who had attended the University of South Carolina with me.

"How you doing?" I said.

"Pretty good. I…uh…heard what happened to Lucinda. My deepest sympathies."

"Thanks. I appreciate the sentiment." Decorum dictated my words. His condolences, well meant, scratched a delicate veneer, beneath which bottled-up emotions, simmering rage, hungered to erupt. A part of me recognized the need to address the issue. But I was unready. I was unwilling. The bottle, its numbing impact, was easier. "Whatcha been doing this past year?"

"Mostly odd jobs," said Fredericks. "I refuse to sharecrop. You ask me, it's slavery with a middleman, the little plot to which you're tied. It's the white man's way of circumventing the Constitution. No matter how hard you work, you can't grow enough to get ahead, not when the owner of the land takes most of your crop."

I nodded. Even if I had disagreed, which I didn't, I would not have contested the point. Torpor, a woebegone one at that, had soured a taste that once had savored spirited discussion.

"I wish the university had stayed open one more year, so I could have gotten my degree. You were fortunate with the timing."

Fortunate? He had to be kidding. Though I knew he was referring to the fact that I had graduated, fixated as I was on my loss, my brain conflated the issues.

"Not many of our classmates are still in the area, not that its surprising. Once the university closed, no reason to stay. Someone told me your friend Jack Philips went home to Shiloh. You been in touch with him?"

I shook my head.

"You been working this past year?"

"No, I…" An admission that I had been wallowing was embarrassing. "I've kinda taken some time off, tending to my house and garden."

A slight change in Martin's expression hinted that he read between the lines; that he knew I had been doing nothing. He said, "Decent jobs

---

<https://www.cbsnews.com/news/almanac-the-mason-jar/> indicating that John Landis Mason patented the glass jar that bears his name on November 30, 1858. His airtight jar greatly improved food preservation in the pre-refrigeration era. Though his invention was very successful, Mason died a pauper. Once his patent expired, competitors stepped in and took over the industry.

are impossible to come by. I hate to say it, but the politics is taking us backwards."

"You referring to the fact that the Democrats have gotten control of Congress, as well as our state legislature?"

"That's half of it."

"What's the other half?"

"The Supreme Court. I assume you've heard about their decision in *Hall v. Decuir*,[354] the Louisiana case regarding the power of states to prevent discrimination in public transportation."

I shook my head. With my solitary existence and lack of sobriety, my ignorance was no shock, not that it wasn't embarrassing. "When did it come down?"

"'Bout a year ago."

"Really?" I said, aware that my ignorance had been underscored. "What did it say?"

"That the Constitution's Commerce Clause vests Congress with the sole authority to regulate interstate commerce and, therefore, Louisiana couldn't enact a statute banning racial discrimination."

"Admittedly, that's regrettable, but unless I'm missing something, that hardly seems a disaster."

"That was my initial reaction too. But the way it was explained to me—I heard it from a fellow who spoke with a lawyer who teaches this stuff—the case opens the door for private transport companies to make rules segregating passengers. Given that whites own all the transport companies, such rules are virtually certain to become pervasive."

"But wouldn't they violate the Civil Rights Act of 1875?"

Fredericks shrugged. "Hey, I'm only telling you what I heard. Anyway, the fellow claimed the Supreme Court's decision allows the states to discriminate with regard to commerce within their boundaries...*intra-state*."

"But states could also pass laws that prohibit intra-state discrimination." I no sooner made the point than practical realities demurred. One by one, the Democrats had elected redeemer governments throughout the South. Rather than ban discrimination, they would promote it.

---

[354] *Hall v. Decuir*, 95 U.S. 485 (1877). The Supreme Court emphasized that its decision in no way affected states' "regulation of internal commerce, or as affecting anything else than commerce among the States." *Hall* was a steppingstone for states enacting so-called Jim Crow laws that mandated segregation. The door opened wide in 1883 when the Supreme Court struck down the Civil Rights Act of 1875 [The *Civil Rights* cases, 109 U.S. 3 (1883)].

Fredericks bore a blank look. "I don't know. And I guess that's why you've got a degree and I don't."

I shook my head. "The reason you don't have a degree is because the university closed. It has nothing to do with your ability. As for me, serendipity, learning opportunities when I was younger, allowed me to finish my degree early."

"Maybe that's the explanation." Fredericks' tone and look showed skepticism.

"If by chance they reopen the university, you gonna go back and finish?"

"Doubt it, not that I wouldn't want to."

On the chance that Fredericks might clarify, I waited a moment before saying, "Why not?"

"Couldn't afford to, not without a scholarship. These days, the chances of that are zero."

"C'mon, they're not—" I clipped my tongue. His point had merit, at least in substance, if not technically. Expressed as a mathematical limit, his odds approached zero. If the university reopened, itself a longshot, with the Democrats in control, Negroes wouldn't be admitted, let alone awarded scholarships.[355]

***

Several days had passed since I had been to the marketplace. In the interim I had been on a binge worse than usual. Apart from thrown-together meals, mainly Granula with water and a poorly fashioned stew, my days had been devoid of anything other than sleep and alcohol. On the fifth day following my shopping spree, hungover from a particularly dissolute evening the night before, I stayed in bed past noon. When I finally arose, I devoured two jam sandwiches and loads of coffee. Next to what I had eaten the day before, the repast was epicurean. I took the edition of the *Daily Phoenix* I had purchased several days earlier out to the porch. I seated myself on a rocker and perused most everything the newspaper had to offer. My brain displayed little interest in most of what met my eyes. Nevertheless, the mundane activity was significant, surpassing anything I had done since my last marketplace excursion. I had just finished scanning the social notices, when I came upon an

[355] *Our History*, University of South Carolina, op cit., stating: "Following the end of Reconstruction in 1877, South Carolina's conservative leaders closed the University. They reopened it in 1880 as an all-white agricultural college and during the next 25 years the institution became enmeshed in the upheaval of late 19th century South Carolina politics."

advertisement for McKenzie's Saloon, a popular spot known for its delectable ice cream, candies and baked goods. The item spawned a wistful image of the last time Lucinda and I had frequented the colorful establishment. Though more than a year removed, I could see us seated at a tiny round table, each with a blueberry tart, decorated with a dollop of whipped cream and scoop of vanilla ice cream alongside. The aroma of cakes and pies baking in the ovens pervaded the air. I closed my eyes, endeavoring to summon a sharper picture of the scene. Like our scrumptious treats, I savored the memory. But melancholy was inescapable. Yearn as I did to transform reverie into reality, to take Lucinda into my arms, it was impossible. Bliss and sadness intertwined, their respective impact modulating from moment to moment. My emotions ebbed and flowed. The ice cream melted. I opened my eyes. Sadness, the reality that Lucinda existed only in my mind, prevailed.

Temptation, the need to dull emerging pain, goaded me to my whiskey bottle. Inertia kept me in my seat. I rocked back and forth several times before forcing myself to turn the page of the newspaper. An article about Alexander Graham Bell caught my eye. Bell and his newly formed American Telephone Company had constructed a telegraph line between Boston and Somerville, Massachusetts.[356] Two years earlier, in 1876, I had read about Bell's invention of the telephone; how he had adapted Samuel Morse's telegraph into a "harmonic telegraph," capable of sending multiple signals of differing pitch over an electrical wire.[357] The concept's move from the laboratory to everyday use intrigued me.

I read the article a second time before folding the newspaper to a quarter of its full size. I laid it aside and began to rock. My brain went into high gear, arguably more analytic than it had been in over a year. The potential of Bell's invention was beguiling. Morse had sent impulses, short and long, over a wire. Bell had advanced the technology to send sound, a voice. Why couldn't a picture be sent over a wire? The question was easily asked. The answer, however, was incredibly complex. For several minutes my mind meandered aimlessly. The futuristic idea, perhaps impossible, boggled my brain. Amidst my confusion, I invoked a mathematical concept I had used countless times before. I reduced the problem to one already solved. Cameras had been around for years. Rather than imprinting an image on film, what if it were converted to electrical impulses capable of being sent over a wire. The

---

[356] *History of the Telephone,* bebusinessed.com, 6 Jun. 2018 <htpps://bebusinessed.com/history-of-the-telephone>.
[357] Ibid.

idea was excellent. Unfortunately, it bore a missing link. I had reduced the problem to one that was yet to be solved: How could a photograph be converted to electrical impulses? The question appeared overwhelming. Lethargy, rearing its ugly head, poised to supersede. A spark ignited. A photograph was a conglomeration of blacks and whites and innumerable shades of gray in between. Like the telephone, where sounds of differing pitch were sent over a wire, impulses representing the shades of gray from black to white could be sent as well, and thereafter reconverted into their respective shades. The idea was appealing, but just as quickly, problematic. Shades of gray in a photograph change in a gradual continuum. Transmission would require that a photograph be broken down into many minute sections. A grid of ten by ten, one hundred impulses, would be difficult to transmit simultaneously and yet only a small fraction of the number required to convey more than a blotchy image. The complication rekindled confusion. It also provided a great excuse to dismiss the idea. In my disconsolate state, no way was I willing or capable of undertaking the arduous intellectual challenge.

***

I stepped out back to examine my garden. Seeds sowed in early spring, flowers and vegetables planted by me, as well as intrusive flora begotten by nature, had taken root and grown. An overnight rain had given them all a welcome drink. It had also provided me with an excuse to ignore needed weeding. The chore would be easier after the Sun imposed its evaporative powers on the soggy earth. Once industrious, I had adapted to my indolence. Admittedly, I was depressed. But lack of productivity did not produce guilt. One might ask whether I would have been less depressed had I been more productive. Fair though the question may have been, I declined to entertain it. Well, that's not entirely true. It crossed my mind, but I dismissed it because it couldn't bring Lucinda back.

I circled around to the front of the house, where I ran my fingers over the bronze plaque honoring Lucinda. I said, "I'm sorry, Darling. I know I should do better. But without you, I can't."

My mind drifted back to my childhood in the Everglades. It was indeed good, but was it as good as my memory claimed? Had I idealized it? Was I inherently weak? If not, why did I resort to the bottle? The loss of Lucinda was a simple answer. But that was the precipitating event. Horrific as the lynching had been, it had not ordained that I resort to a life of intoxication. Something within me, be it voluntary, inborn or wholly uncontrolled, had guided me down that route. Had I internalized society's scorn for people of color, particularly maroons, who fit in nowhere, causing me to endure irreconcilable conflict? The possibility had merit, but at most it was a single garment in my wardrobe, an amalgam of intricate patterns. Images of my father emerged. With alcohol an omni-present facet of my psyche, I harked back to my father's propensity to consume an excess of corn beer. Years earlier, the day after I had first arrived at Fort Myers, Private Jackson had labeled me a "chip off the old block." Perhaps that explained why I was resorting to alcohol. Maybe it provided a justification. Embracing the exegesis enticed me. Candor gainsaid the idea. Blaming my father was a rationalization. Just as he was responsible for his drinking, I was for mine. That said, without Lucinda at my side, I was anything but ready to address the problem.

I went inside to my whiskey-stocked parlor cabinet, where, using a funnel, I filled a bottle from a gallon jug. I took the bottle out to the porch, along with a newspaper I had picked up at the market the day before. It was the first publication of the newest rendition of the *Daily Phoenix*, the *Straight-Out Democrat*. The *Phoenix*, which had originally appeared just before Lee had surrendered at Appomattox, had brazenly declared in that inaugural edition: "Our city shall spring, from her ashes, and our *Phoenix*, we hope and trust, shall announce the glorious rising! God save the state!"[358] Over the ensuing years, the *Phoenix* had reinvented itself under several different names, the newest of which, the *Daily Phoenix*, the *Straight-Out Democrat*, had just debuted on June 28, 1878.[359]

I sipped my whiskey before diving into the diatribe of Henry S. Farley, the newspaper's editor. Front page, first column, he voiced his view as to the status of South Carolina's legislative body. Farley pulled no punches when evaluating the work of the legislators.

> "Issues which were not anticipated at the election and which should have had the full benefit of the assembled wisdom of the State, were decided contrary to the wishes of the people. Through precipitate and unwise legislation, bills were passed that must be repealed, and much injury was done that may never be remedied."

[358] *Chronicling America, Great American Newspapers, About Straight-out democrat, (Columbia, S.C.) 1878-1879,* Library of Congress, retrieved 11 Feb. 2019 <http://chroniclingamerica.loc.gov/lccn/sn92065612/> quoting the March 21, 1865 inaugural edition of the triweekly newspaper, the *Phoenix*.
[359] Ibid.

My reaction to Farley's contention was paradoxical. Much as I concurred with it, I disagreed. Grave harms had been done. As to the nature of those harms and the appropriate remedies, doubtless Farley and I were light years apart. Such was the divide that split the country. The War of Secession had cleaved the nation. Reconstruction had introduced change. Reactionary forces were endeavoring to restore the old order. The country lay in limbo, arguably unstable. Whether it would gravitate back to its past or move forward to a more egalitarian state was yet to be determined. My heart, of course, lay with the latter. But were I a betting man, my money would have rested on the former. I reached for my bottle. I had problems of my own. Drowning them with a soporific beverage was easier than addressing them.

Chapter XXIV

AS 1878 ROLLED INTO 1879 AND THE LATTER WAS SLIPPING PAST, I acclimated to my stagnant state. During the first year or even two after Lucinda's death, I assumed my dependence on alcohol would be a passing episode; that a few months down the road, I would find my way back to sobriety. But as the seasons came and went, I realized the bottle might be my permanent destiny. Distasteful though the observation may have been, I didn't hate it enough to alter it. I reasoned, or perhaps rationalized, that nothing would bring Lucinda back.

As the months slipped by, my minimal contacts with the outside world diminished. Past friendships grew more distant. Had my garden, plus my chickens—I always kept about a half-dozen—been sufficient to meet my nutritive needs, in all likelihood I would never have left my property. But desire for a broader diet, and, more important, a need for whiskey, motivated trips to the local market. And as long as I was there, I purchased a newspaper.

How I managed to fill so many days remains a mystery, indicative that alcohol dominated even more than I realized. Gradually, however, I made some meager progress, as I began spending one or two semi-sober hours several days per week in pursuit of intellectual matters, particularly those related to physics and mathematics. Occasionally a story in the newspaper about an invention inspired me. The underlying science and mathematics would catch my fancy. At times I even contemplated an idea that would take the invention to another level. But like my thoughts about sending photographs over wires, invariably my deliberations lacked the determination needed to generate anything substantive. Challenging questions, an inevitable element of material progress, were met with whiskey, not cerebral discipline. Ideas grew foggy, yielding to inebriated sleep.

One invention, the light bulb, highlighted on the front page of the newspaper, sparked more than a passing interest. It was November 1879, when I read that three weeks earlier, on October 22nd, Thomas Edison, using a carbon filament, had successfully tested an incandescent light that had burned for over thirteen hours. Using high resistance and a low voltage (approximately 110), he had avoided the flaws that had rendered earlier lights commercially unviable.[360] Little did I imagine that only several months later, he would develop a vastly improved filament of carbonized bamboo that would last 1200 hours.[361] But even before I learned of the improvement, the commercially useful electric light excited me. Electricity, not fire, was destined to illuminate the world. Chances were, it would rule the entire industrial universe as well. Steam engines, still more efficient than their electric counterparts, would face new competition.

With my intellectual side attaining its highest gear in many a fortnight, I decided to take a walk. My sack jacket over a vest—I had not updated my wardrobe to the tighter fitting suit coats that were coming into vogue—was perfect for the comfortable autumn weather that typified Columbia.[362] I headed west to the Horseshoe. Apart from passing its exterior wall, more than two years had elapsed since I had last visited the grounds of my higher education. From time to time, newspaper articles had hinted that the campus might reopen. The rumors, pie in the sky, had failed to materialize.

I continued to Sumter Street before I turned north along the westerly wall of the Horseshoe. Overgrown vegetation marred the once pristine perimeter. Stepping through the open gateway, I was struck by the speed with which the impressive academic bastion had deteriorated into a hollow space of aging buildings. Weeds and cracked walkways had replaced park-like landscape. Leaves from oaks and maples, not to mention litter, covered the ground. How could this have happened? For an instant, the question confounded me...but only an instant. The briefest introspection, a glimpse into the mirror, negated any incongruity. Like me, the campus had suffered a death knell, delivered from without. A lynching, the theft of my Lucinda, had driven me into my downward spiral. Legislative fiat, the withdrawal of funding, had closed the university's doors. The Emancipation Proclamation may have doused the flames of prejudice, but extinguish them, it had not. With redeemer

---

[360] *Thomas Edison,* Wikipedia, 10 Jun. 2018 <https://en.wikipedia.org/wiki/Thomas_Edison>.

[361] Ibid.

[362] *Men's Clothing – 1870s,* University of Vermont website, 23 Jun. 2018 <http://www.uvm.edu/landscape/dating/clothing_and_hair/1870s_clothing_men.php>.

governments having replaced federal troops throughout the South, smoldering bigotry had flared. The ensuing conflagration, albeit flameless, had consumed both the campus and me. The War of Secession had ended more than a decade earlier, but its most abominable remnant, hate, an odious phoenix, had risen from the ashes.

I proceeded into the Horseshoe. A bench in front of Rutledge Hall caught my eye. Back when we were students, Lucinda and I had sat on the cement-based, wooden-back seat countless times. As I approached it, suppressed rage bubbled forth. By the time I seated myself, I was seething. The world of my higher education had been turned into a sty. While the unsightly, abandoned premises contributed to my ire, the absence of Lucinda was the real precipitant. Were I at home, no doubt I would have grabbed my trusty bottle and drowned my emotions in an alcoholic stupor. The want of such mind-numbing liquid compelled an alternative. I ran my gaze over Harper and Elliot College across the way and on toward the library. Recollections of better campus days moderated destructive emotions. I turned and looked behind me at Rutledge, the place where I had learned the principles of physics, including those of electricity. The thought reminded me of the intellectual spark that had spurred my walk to the Horseshoe. A yearning to relive my past life stirred. Mustering drive sufficient to transport me there was another matter.

A short distance from the bench, a squirrel snatched acorns from the ground. The bushy-tailed rodent raced about gathering the oaken fruit in preparation for the long, cold winter. I had watched him for about two minutes when he stopped less than ten feet from me. His gaze met mine. Several seconds elapsed before he briefly broke eye contact, just long enough to pick up an acorn. He stared at me again. Though his look was likely defensive, intended to ensure that I did not make an aggressive move, it made me uneasy. It was as if he saw through me, disdained my slothfulness. A few more seconds of exchanged stares, and the squirrel hurried away.

A sense of guilt seized me. Behind me stood the edifice where I had supposedly become educated in physics. How then could a lowly creature confront me, exhibit greater understanding of nature's scientific principles. Unlike me, who could read books and write equations, the squirrel was illiterate. But he was hardly ignorant. He used his energy to gather food, create a stored source of future energy that would sustain him in the extended, bitter nights of winter. The squirrel may not have been my equal, but he was arguably my superior. The disquieting observation challenged me. Like the squirrel, I needed to harness energy. A glance upward at the sunny heavens delivered a momentary lift. A drifting cumulus suggested that the obliging rays would soon be interrupted. Harnessing energy, especially that which comes from within, was complicated, more than I was willing to contemplate. Self-assessing analysis exceeded what I was prepared to entertain.

The light bulb, Edison's invention that had prompted my walk to the Horseshoe, flashed in my head. Like many devices of the Industrial Revolution, it depended upon harnessing energy, man's increasing sway over his environment. Long before humans, lightning bolts had ignited fires across the planet, but it had taken thousands of millennia before prehistoric man had harnessed the potential energy housed in wood; that fire had become a tool. More than two thousand years had elapsed since people had first used water to drive a wheel to grind grain. So too, wind had become a source of harnessed energy. But progress remained slow, incredibly slow, until the advent of the Industrial Revolution and the invention of the steam engine. Large creatures of iron, capable of working a 24-hour day, had begun performing a myriad of tasks with previously unimagined efficiency. And the rate at which such progress continued, accelerated. Expressed through the mathematical lens with which I viewed the world, with progress "p" as a function of time "t," not only was $\frac{dp}{dt}$ positive, but so too $\frac{d^2p}{dt^2}$, the rate at which it was growing.

With my brain adrift in principles of differential calculus, my eyes again caught the squirrel. Racing about, he drew to a halt, even closer than before. He peered up at me with wide eyes.

"Mind your own damn business! I'm contemplating matters way beyond your scant capacity."

The squirrel failed to budge.

"What! You think you're—" I shut my mouth…tight. Blaming the squirrel for my inability to address my anger was absurd. I heaved a sigh. "I…I was thinking about physics. I know, it falls way short of dealing with my issues…but give me a break. It's a step…okay, a baby step…in the right direction."

The squirrel stood up on its hind legs.

"Don't be judgmental!" My words echoed in my head. They had been directed at the squirrel, but they were intended for me. I was judging myself, and the picture was grotesque. I leaned off to my right, away from the squirrel. I grabbed a couple of large acorns from in front of the bench. I gently rolled them toward the squirrel.

He eyed me for several seconds before inching forward toward the acorns. He snatched them up and scurried off. I watched and waited, hoping he would return. If so, I was determined to give a better account of myself. The opportunity never materialized.

I looked around the otherwise deserted Horseshoe. My mind went into high gear. I imagined the campus alive again, the buildings aglow with incandescent lights. Could it be done? If so…how? The obvious way, a battery, a huge Daniell cell, not so different from the kind I had made in chemistry lab, using a zinc anode and copper cathode, along with sulfuric acid.[363] The idea was simple, but also impractical. No way could it provide large amounts of power over an extended period. My thoughts shifted from direct current to alternating current. Might the problem be solved with a giant, coal-powered steam engine capable of turning a large permanent magnet inside an equally big coil of copper wire. I recalled from my study of electricity that the voltage (electromotive force) of the induced current was proportional to the number of turns in the coil. Logic, based upon rudimentary knowledge, rather than expertise, indicated that by using many turns of wire, a high voltage could be generated. Logic dictated that the simple system could power many light bulbs and, consequently, illuminate numerous buildings. And with coal in ample supply, the system was sustainable.

Straightforward though the idea seemed, its perils were undeniable. It required wires connecting buildings to the coil, plus many more wires, presumably in parallel, so lights could be operated independently. Those wires would need to carry currents of high voltage. Adequate insulation to protect against deadly shocks or fires would be a must. Common sense urged that the idea was fraught with far more difficulties than I could imagine. The concession did little to negate my satisfaction. The concept had possibilities.

I gazed once again at the array of buildings, picturing them all brightly lit. The image no sooner entered my mind than another thought popped into my head. Rather than coal, might water be used to turn the generator's big magnet? I looked off to my left, not that I could see beyond the Horseshoe's wall. I pictured the Congaree River about a mile to the west. Just as it meandered past Columbia, there were rapids and shoals. They were a far cry from the dramatic flow needed to drive a waterwheel and, ultimately, a giant magnet. But a place like Niagara Falls—I had seen photographs of its astounding cascade—could turn many huge magnets, each inside a giant coil, continuously inducing

---

[363] *Daniell cell,* Wikipedia, 8 Feb. 2020 <https://en.wikipedia.org/wiki/Daniell_cell> stating: "The **Daniell Cell** (emphasis from original) is a type of electrochemical cell invented in 1836 by John Frederick Daniell, a British chemist and meteorologist, and consists of a copper pot filled with copper (II) sulfate solution, in which is immersed an unglazed earthenware container filled with sulfuric acid and a zinc electrode."

humongous quantities of current. Many cities, particularly in the industrial North, had grown up along the region's numerous rivers. The same water that had powered the steam engines of the Industrial Revolution could bring light, as well as power, for a myriad of other electrical devices yet to be invented. The possibilities were boundless.

A part of me suspected my imagination had gotten the best of me. But enthusiasm refused to succumb to pessimism...perhaps realism. Electricity could change the world. Admittedly, it would require tremendous investment in a framework. Beyond the large generators, with magnets spinning within coiled wire, manifold wires connecting to homes and businesses would be necessary. The simple formula E = iR, electromotive force (voltage) equals current multiplied by resistance, bolted in my brain. The system would involve powerful currents. Those currents would generate huge voltages, and such voltages would be perilous. A seemingly doable concept grew increasingly daunting. But the hurdles did not deter me. Unlike an actual system, ideas demanded neither sweat, nor financial costs. But ideas, good ones, could not eschew pragmatism. How, I pondered, might one test my concept? A small-scale project could limit costs. Better yet, start with a mathematical model. See what the numbers say. To do so would demand a full understanding of Faraday's Law of Induction, as well Lenz's Law.[364] Manipulation of formulae was fine for purposes of an elementary physics class in electricity, but mathematical models showing the viability of building large-scale electrical circuits demanded proficiency with surface integrals and the partial derivatives associated with the multi-variable functions they involved. To contemplate such problems, I would need to expand my mathematical expertise.

I leaned back and stared upward, where a large cloud had all but obliterated the Sun. Pie in the sky was nice, but tasting it demanded effort. Were Lucinda alive and there to help me work though the complexities, I would have undertaken the challenge. But in my state, surface integrals and concomitant intricacies had no appeal. An easier,

[364] *Bookmarks'* author's comment: A bit more than a half-century removed from when I got my degree in mathematics and studied physics, I began reviewing Faraday's Law and the surface integrals it involved, before starting to write this section of *Bookmarks*. I had spent several hours when, like my protagonist Mican, a light bulb went on in my head. My ignorance was bliss, at least temporarily. Admittedly it was an encumbrance, but ironically, an encumbrance that made it easier to imagine electricity's possibilities from the perspective of one living in the period immediately after the invention of the light bulb. Deferring my review of relevant principles of mathematics and physics helped me step into Mican's shoes. (One could argue that the foregoing reasoning reeked of the very rationalization that dominated the vacuous stage of Mican's life. The argument has too much merit for me to dispute it.)

more familiar approach beckoned me. I got up from the bench and headed out of the Horseshoe. The unseemly campus, its time, if ever, for rehabilitation had not arrived. Neither had mine. I headed back to my house and the security that it, together with my whiskey bottle, embodied.

***

With 1879 fading into the past, a familiar rumor began recirculating: The doors of the University of South Carolina were about to open again. Sure enough, in 1880, it happened. The event might have buoyed me, but with the State Legislature controlled by the Democrats and with Reconstruction a relic, people of color, like myself, were expressly barred. The campus reopened as an all-white agricultural college.[365]

The dawn of what was touted as a bright ray provided me with another excuse to slip back into the depths of my despondency. The truth be known, I had never left it. And so, the first three years of the 1880s encored the wasteland that had closed out the 1870s. With whiskey dominating, one purposeless day bled into the next. Even if I wanted to detail them with distinguishing events, I could not. Each was as pointless as its predecessor. A part of me hoped that at some point I would discard my inebriating crutch and escape my alcohol-fused ennui. The truth be known, I yearned for that day. But yearning is very different from will.

Further inhibiting my rehabilitation was a reluctance to participate in a world replete with antebellum inequities. Legitimate though the reason may have been, admittedly it was also a convenient excuse, one that was certain to persist. Shifts in power had guaranteed that the pendulum of change, having swung to the reactionary side, would not swing back for the foreseeable future. Any doubt about the matter was dispelled by my newspaper's chronicle of the Supreme Court's decision in what was referred to as the Civil Rights Cases of 1883. Confronted with alleged discrimination by a hotel, a railroad and a theater, the Court struck down the Civil Rights Act of 1875.[366] The Court sustained a claim by the defendants that Congress had exceeded its authority under the Thirteenth and Fourteenth amendments. Although those amendments authorized Congress to enact legislation enforcing their provisions, neither prohibited discrimination by private persons or entities. The Thirteenth Amendment only abolished slavery and the Fourteenth

---

[365] *See*, footnote 347, supra.

[366] 109 U.S. 3 (1883).

Amendment proscribed discrimination by the states. To the extent that Congress had purported to regulate discrimination by private persons or entities, the Court held that Congress had exceeded its constitutional authority.[367] The decision left little doubt that the future lay in the past; that asphyxiation awaited folks like me who still held their breath in expectation of a more egalitarian world.

***

Another year slipped by as the calendar moved into June 1884. Following a relatively productive morning weeding my garden, I was seated in my parlor sipping a whiskey-laced tea, an ill-conceived beverage experiment, when I heard what sounded like a knock at my front door. I would have responded had I not assumed it was the product of an animal or some act of nature. About a half-minute later, I heard another rap, louder than its predecessor, followed by a yell.

Filled with curiosity—over a year had passed since my last visitor—I headed to the front door and opened it. A squat Negro man with a full beard, whom I judged to be in his fifties, stood at the portal. “What can I do for you?”

“Understand your house is for sale.”

“Somebody must have given you bad information. Not for sale. Must be another.”

“You Mican…Mican Reinbow?”

I nodded.

“And this, your house?”

I nodded again. “But it’s not for sale.”

“Damn. This fellow at Jake’s Saloon told me your place was on the market.”

“Well, the fellow was mistaken…What was the fellow’s name?”

“George.”

“George what?”

The bearded man shrugged. “Don’t really know. I happened into the saloon and was asking around when this fellow, George, told me your house was for sale.”

Skeptical as I already was, the dubious explanation increased my suspicions.

[367] The United States Supreme Court indicated that it did not decide whether Congress could regulate discrimination by private persons under the Commerce Clause of the U.S. Constitution. (120 U.S. at 119).

"Anyhow, George was right about one thing. Said your house was a beauty, in tip-top shape." The man gestured all around the porch. "Looks brand new. I checked the front and sides before I knocked on the door."

I eyed the porch. It did look great. It struck me that the rest of the house looked great as well. Despite my years of lethargy, armed with broad construction experience, I had meticulously maintained my home.

"If the inside is anything like the outside, I'd be prepared to offer you a mighty pretty price."

I shook my head. "Minor detail. As I told you repeatedly, it's not for sale."

The fellow heaved a sigh.

"Why you so interested in buying my house?"

"I'm a lawyer. I'm taking over Harry Robeson's practice. He died last month. Maybe you knew him?"

"Can't say that I did."

"Anyway, I just moved here from Charleston. I need a place for myself and my daughter and my eight-year-old grandson. My daughter lost her husband to diphtheria a few months back."

"Sorry for your loss."

"Thanks, but the truth be known, he was no prize. Pretty much a ne'er-do-well. Liked the bottle better than work."

I would have commented were my brain not struggling to face the ugly description of myself.

"Robeson had a tiny office on the second floor of a building on Laurel Street, a couple doors from Main. Certainly not big enough for me to live there, let alone with my daughter and grandson. So, I gotta find a place. Knowing that the law practice will keep me mighty busy, I need one that's in excellent shape. Won't have the time to fix it up, not that I've got the skills. My wife, may she rest in peace, used to say that you'd find my name if you looked up 'ham-fisted' in Webster's."

I chuckled, a reaction that echoed in my ears. How long had it been since I had laughed? Weeks, months…maybe years had passed since my home had heard a guffaw. I said, "A body can get mighty thirsty, what with the heat. Can I get you something to drink?" Good sense suggested I send the stranger on his way. Chances were he had fabricated the story that he had heard my home was for sale. The possibility that he was a con man or worse was inescapable.

"Don't want to put you out, but I could use a drink."

I motioned him into the parlor, where I pointed to my glass. "I'm having tea with a shot of whiskey. Can I get you one?"

His eyes widened. "Can't say I've ever tried the combination, but I'm game, especially parched as I am."

"Have a seat, and I'll be right back with your drink." As I headed to the kitchen where I prepared his libation, the folly of inviting him in became more compelling. Desire for company, coupled with the continued reverberations of my earlier laugh, vanquished both qualms and judgment. A minute later, I returned to the parlor and handed him his beverage.

"Thanks." The stranger took a sip. For an instant his lips appeared to purse, but then he nodded. "Not bad...Not bad at all." He imbibed again. "Didn't know what to expect, but it...it grows on you. Matter of fact, if I'm not mistaken, folks in the British Isles pour whiskey into their tea."[368]

"No fooling." I seated myself in the easy chair across from him and reached for my half-empty glass. I sipped it, almost as if I were testing it for the first time. It was better than I had previously realized, or, perhaps, it was better with company. I said, "You know my name, but I don't believe I caught yours."

"Homer Grayson. And please excuse my lack of manners. My Gracie—that's my late wife—would give me what for, accepting your hospitality without introducing myself."

"Don't worry. I won't tell her." The non-plussed expression that greeted my words had me ruing my woeful attempt at humor. "Sorry, I didn't mean to be impertinent...make light of your loss."

"No problem. I was slow on the uptake." Grayson gestured at his glass. "Blame it on the whiskey." He took a gulp. "Your home is just as nice on the inside as it is on the out. Sure wish it were on the market. Be perfect for my family and me."

"You're welcome to a tour, not that I'm gonna change my mind about selling."

"I'd like that, at least the part about a tour."

We got up from our seats. I took him to the dining room which was open to the parlor. I showed him each of the two bedrooms, which were across the hallway. As we headed into the kitchen, he said, "Not often that you see crown moldings in a bungalow, and you've got them throughout."

"I added them myself."

---

368 *Pairing Whiskey and Tea | The Whiskey Reviewer*, 4 Mar. 2019 <http://whiskeyreviewer.com/2012/02/pairing-tea-and-whiskey/>.

He ran his gaze over the kitchen molding, a four-inch Roman ogee. "Now I understand why your home is in such great condition. You've got the very skills I lack."

I shrugged abashedly.

"You're too modest."

We returned to the parlor where we finished our drinks. He got up from his seat. "I appreciate the hospitality. It's time I move along." He pulled a small leather case from his shirt pocket out of which he took a business card that he handed to me. "Just in case you need a lawyer or, better yet, if you change your mind about selling…I'd give you a fine price and do all the paperwork at no charge."

I slipped the card into the vest pocket of my shirt, not that I had any expectation that I would contact him. I accompanied him out the door. From the edge of the porch, I watched him head to the road before turning in the direction of the heart of Columbia. As he disappeared from view, an odd feeling overcame me. Exactly what it meant, I wasn't sure. I eased over to my favorite porch rocker and began to slowly sway. Back and forth I swung, my mind an oscillating instrument. I reached into my pocket and drew out the business card. I stared at it for the better part of a minute. It struck me that my connections to Columbia had long since ceased. The college that had drawn me there no longer accepted, let alone welcomed, people of color. With political power back in the hands of the Democrats, people like myself were at best second-class citizens. And most of all, there was no Lucinda to keep me there. Perhaps the time to leave Columbia had arrived.

For an hour I rocked, wondering if my thoughts were serious or idle fancy. Mostly I suspected they were the latter, but occasionally they seemed serious. A question popped into my head. If I were to sell my house and leave Columbia, where would I go? No way would I remain in South Carolina. Savannah or St. Augustine was no more appealing. Neither offered anything that attracted me. With the Democrats in control throughout the South, life for one like myself would be much like Columbia. Staying in my home—I had kept it in great shape—was preferable. New England crossed my mind. It never got serious consideration. As much as I hated winter and the cold that accompanied it, absent some exceptional attraction, no way would I move to the Northeast.

Fort Myers popped into my head. From the little I had heard, following the War of Secession when the North had abandoned the fort, nothing more than a tiny community, perhaps a few hundred people, had settled there. But that could be a positive. The inequality that dominated the cities of the South might not hold sway. Perhaps there were still a few Black Seminoles in the surrounding area. Returning to the place of my childhood, the cabin where I had spent my formative years was intriguing. Sketchy memories, likely idealized, of days spent fishing, hunting and playing in the woods and along the beaches of the Caloosahatchee, were fond. Add to the equation, winters considerably warmer than Columbia, and the idea had possibilities, enough that I did not dismiss it out of hand. Over the ensuing several days, off and on, I contemplated a move back to Fort Myers. Still it never seemed more than an improbable thought.

***

It was an early autumn day when en route to the marketplace, I detoured twice: first, to make my annual $60 contribution to the AME Women's Organization, something I had done every year since Lucinda's death; and second, to a building on Laurel, a couple of doors from Main. Unlike so many structures throughout the heart of Columbia, it was one of the lucky ones. It had escaped the torch of Sherman's fiery march. With the long downturn that had followed the financial panic of 1873, so much of Columbia remained a devastated canvas.

As I neared the door of the second-floor walk-up bearing a sign *Law Offices of Homer Grayson*, I stood motionless, debating whether to halt my detour and redirect myself to my original destination, the marketplace. I gazed upward at the unimpressive, flat-front, stone building that faced me. The second-floor window bore large gold lettering, the same words as the door. I reached into my pocket and pulled out Homer Grayson's business card. "What the hell," I muttered under my breath. "It can't hurt to see what he's offering. For that matter, it'll be interesting, even if I have no intention of selling." I climbed the stairway that led to the second-floor office. The door to the quarters, about a dozen feet on each side, was open.

Homer Grayson, who was seated behind a large walnut desk, looked up. "Mican…come right in," he said, a twinkle in his eye. "What can I do for you?"

"I was in the neighborhood and decided to stop…One never knows when one might need a lawyer." I suspected he surmised the real reason for my visit. If he didn't, I would be well advised to find a shrewder attorney, if and when I needed one.

Grayson smiled as he reached across his desk and shook my hand. "Have a seat."

I took one of two captain's chairs that faced his desk.

"Perhaps you've reconsidered the possibility of selling your house?"

"Not really…but I'd be willing to listen, assuming you want to make an offer."

Grayson took a deep breath. "Hadn't expected to see you again…hmm…Normally, I start low and give myself room to negotiate. But negotiations take time. Time is a luxury I can't afford. And so, right up front, I'm gonna give you my best figure. That way you can take it home and mull it over. If you like it, you can come back and we'll have a deal, provided I haven't already made another. But understand, I can't afford to pussyfoot around. I need something fast. I found a place near the Congaree. I like yours better, but if it's not available, then yessiree, the Congaree, it'll be."

Admittedly, I was not a businessman, but I wasn't born yesterday. Odds were his pitch was exactly what he said it wasn't, a clever negotiating tool, designed to give him the upper hand.

Grayson rocked back, his hands slipped behind his head. His gaze moved upward, toward the ceiling.

I suspected it might be part of an act, one he had performed in many prior negotiations. I waited impassively, at least on the exterior. Behind my façade, misgivings mounted.

Finally, Grayson refocused on me. "Okay…No beating around the bush. Here's my bottom line…I'll give you $1200, cash money, no mortgage, for your house."

I felt my eyes go wide. I was expecting an offer of $900 or $950. One thousand or $1050, and I would have given it some thought. Twelve hundred, hardly the negotiating ploy I had anticipated, was a shocker.

"So, what do you think?"

With the number rattling my brain, I found it hard to think.

"Good or bad, you must have some kind of reaction?"

I did. How to proceed was another matter. "I…I'll give it some thought." I got up from my seat.

Grayson shrugged. "Not exactly what I hoped to hear, but better than a refusal. But keep in mind, I plan to move quickly, and much as I love your place, once I've signed on the dotted line for something else, that'll be that."

"Fair enough." I turned and headed for the door. I no sooner stepped through the portal than I did a one-eighty. "Twelve hundred cash…you've got yourself a deal, on one condition."

"What's the condition?"

"There's a bronze plaque on the front of my house honoring my late wife Lucinda."

"I noticed it when I visited your house. What about it?"

"Promise me that you won't remove it."

"You've got my word…So, you sure you want to sell?"

"Uh…not really, but yeah."

He eyed me with a puzzled gaze. "Much as I want your house, I don't want to push you into anything you'll regret. If you want to take twenty-four hours to think it over, don't hesitate." He glanced toward the ceiling again and muttered, "With a little effort, I'll talk myself out of a deal I really want."

Rarely rash, I endeavored to take in that which was transpiring. What lunacy would prompt me to sell the house I loved, especially on a whim? The question was far less knotty than it appeared on the surface. My life had become an abyss. A slow climb from the depths was too hard. Time, years of intoxicated stagnation, had proved that I needed to kick myself in the ass. Selling my home and starting anew in Fort Myers would force me to do that. I walked back toward Grayson's desk. "You've got a deal." I reached across and shook his hand.

The instant I left Grayson's office, I questioned myself. The reaction was hardly unexpected. What was surprising, however, I felt relatively sanguine about my decision, more so than I would have predicted ten minutes earlier. I proceeded toward my original destination, the marketplace. As I walked along, I took stock of my life. Over the years I had seen the highs and lows of life. I had smelled the sweet scent of roses, Lucinda's favorite, but I had also spent years consigned and confined to the outhouse with its relentless acrid stench. Where my life might go next remained unknown. Another question, a familiar one, popped into my head. *Who am I?* In the past, when I had embarked on a new chapter of my life, that question had commanded scrupulous analysis. The answer had always been complex, often nuanced. But not this time. As I prepared to leave South Carolina and return to the place of my childhood, one overshadowing word obscured all others. I was a drunkard.

Chapter XXV

CONSUMMATING THE DEAL WITH GRAYSON WAS EASY. He prepared the deed, which I signed, and he paid me twelve hundred dollars in cash. He went above and beyond my condition regarding Lucinda's bronze plaque. He included a provision in the deed that not only barred removal of the plaque, but also required that it be affixed to the front of any structure that replaced the house. He added another clause indicating that the foregoing provision run with the land, thereby obligating future purchasers to preserve the plaque. He bought all my furniture for the reasonable price of two hundred dollars. He was as fair with me as I was with him.

Following a four-day trek by rail, steamboat and wagon, which concluded exactly nineteen days after Grayson and I had shaken hands, I arrived with a single suitcase in Fort Myers. I separately shipped to the Fort Myers' shipping office a trunkful of personal items, which I picked up at a later date.

The fort that had dominated the area when I had departed roughly two decades earlier was long gone. Climbing down from the wagon which had carried me from Punta Rassa, the last 15-mile leg of my journey, I stepped out onto First Street, a sandy, weed-begotten roadway. Irregularly spaced, weather-beaten wooden structures dominated either side of the street.[369] The rural town, miles from any city, with about three hundred inhabitants, bore no similarity to the military outpost that had

[369] Grismer, Karl H., *The Story of Fort Myers,* original Ed. 1949, facsimile reproduction by Southwest Florida Historical Society, 1982, p. 117, describes Fort Myers at the time of its 1885 incorporation as follows: "Not one street was paved, or even graded. First Street, or Front Street as it was more commonly known, was a thoroughfare in name only. It was nothing but a sandy, weed-grown open space stretching between two irregular rows of unpainted, cheaply constructed frame buildings housing general stores, saloons, livery stables, blacksmith shops, and miscellaneous establishments of little consequence."

housed me during the War of Secession. The surrounding fence, impeccably maintained buildings and parade grounds were nowhere to be seen. I suspected that I was standing somewhere within the erstwhile fort's walls. The nearby Caloosahatchee River, about 150 yards away, lent support to my conjecture, but no way would I have bet money on it. I walked northeast, past two properties both of which had split-rail fences around faded wooden homes. Further up the street, a couple of freshly painted structures moderated a negative first impression.

Another fifty yards and I spotted a house bearing a sign, "Rooms to Let." A second sign, "Vacancies," hung from the bottom. I climbed the two steps of the stoop and knocked on the door. A heavy-set Caucasian woman with gray hair answered.

"What do you want?" she said, opening the door no more than a foot.

"I'd like to rent a room."

"None are available."

"But the sign says, 'Vacancies.'"

"Forget what the sign says. None are available." She slammed the door.

I remained on the stoop for several seconds, all but certain she had denied me a room because of the color of my skin. I thought of Lucinda. She had died fighting discrimination. My gut begged to bang on the door again. But what would it get me? Arrested? Perhaps. And if so, as a stranger, a person of color in a rural southern town, in all likelihood, I would face a corrupt legal system. The Civil Rights Cases of 1883 popped into my head. The law was not on my side. The Civil Rights Act of 1875, which prohibited discrimination in privately owned accommodations, had been struck down by the United States Supreme Court. The nation's ultimate arbiter had given its imprimatur to the abhorrent conduct I had just faced. I did not have a leg to stand on. I climbed down from the stoop, encumbered by the burden of a heavy load. In my hand, I lugged my suitcase. In my heart, I bore the weight of guilt. Lucinda's memory demanded I do more than turn tale in the face of prejudice. Common sense told me there was nothing I could do. But common sense failed to quell self-reproach.

I stepped out into the dusty street. I looked left and right, debating what to do, where to go. I drew upon my knowledge of the area, familiarity acquired in my youth. I walked down to the Caloosahatchee and began following it southwest. I passed the wharf, where several schooners were docked,[370] and continued out of town. Following the

---

[370] Ibid., p.132.

shoreline, I found myself on the primeval path I had traversed years earlier when housed at the fort. It was much the same as it had been when last I had left my footprints there, the day before my departure roughly two decades earlier. Here and there, patches of tall feathery grasses, rising from the sandy beach, swayed rhythmically in the breeze. Cedars and mangroves, their feet in the river, repeatedly forced me to shift inland to bypass them. All along, rising in the woods and from scrub land, humungous slash pines, most with branches and needles only on their top quarter,[371] stretched toward Heaven. Bushes with purple, red and yellow flowers and berries colored the landscape. Countless palms, their varieties manifold, opined to the area's tropical character. A stately royal palm caught my attention. Its fifty-foot trunk of nearly uniform diameter led to symmetrical green foliage draping from its apex.[372] I approached the graceful spire, placing my hand on its smooth surface. I stared upward at and beyond its green limbs. The sky's azure blue, coupled with the white of puffy cumulus, provided an ideal background for the verdant image. The view was familiar, but my memory failed to do it justice. Having been born in the area, perhaps I had taken it for granted. I inhaled deeply, imbibing the scene. I continued on my way.

A short distance beyond, I located what had been my favorite fishing spot during my days at the fort. A sycamore, with typically blotchy, peeling bark, still marked the spot where I had so often angled the river. I parked myself beneath the big tree. I opened my suitcase and took out a half-loaf of rye bread and a jar of apple butter. Before making the final legs of my journey, I had purchased the items in Arcadia, a small, southern-Florida mining town that had sprung up a couple of years earlier when phosphate, a substance valuable for making fertilizer, had been discovered in the Peace River.[373] I made myself a sandwich and, leaning back against the sycamore's trunk, ate the meal. Youthful memories of afternoons spent eating and fishing in the identical location bubbled forth. One glorious recollection superseded the rest, my last visit, when I had shared a parting kiss with Abbey Parker. I reached into my suitcase and took out the first of the two-volume set of *Uncle Tom's Cabin* given to me by Abbey. Along with my calculus book, I had brought the novel from Columbia in my suitcase. I gazed at the gold-embossed picture of Uncle Tom and his family standing outside their

---

[371] *Slash Pine Stock Photos & Slash Pine Stock Images – Alamy,* Alamy.com, 10 Apr. 2019 <https://www.alamy.com/stock-photo/slash-pine.html>.

[372] *Are Palm Trees Native to Florida, Native Palm Trees,* Westcoast Landscape & Lawns, 12 Apr. 2019 <westcoastlawns.com/florida-friendly/palm-trees-native-florida/>.

[373] *Arcadia-Viva Florida 500*, 14 Mar. 2019 <http://vivafl500.org/cities/arcadia/>.

tiny cabin. I opened the book to the title page and read the subtitle, *Or Life Among the Lowly.*[374] The War of Secession had been fought and won. The Constitution had been amended. So much had changed. Yet so much remained the same.

Like me, Abbey was now in her thirties. I tried to imagine how her life had turned out. Chances were, she was married, and not to a Black Seminole, certainly not if her father and mother had any say about it. Whatever course her life had taken, books were presumably playing a meaningful role. I closed the volume and stared at the cover again. Perhaps the time had come to reread the story.

***

The morning after I arrived in Fort Myers, I arose with the Sun. My night sleeping under the sycamore had been far from uninterrupted. At least four or five times I had awakened, but each time I had managed to drift off relatively quickly. I might have looked to my whiskey bottle, except I had neither brought nor purchased any on my trip. Once I had agreed to sell my house and leave Columbia, I had supplemented the decision with an attempt at abstinence. The hardest consequence of that effort had occurred during its first few dreadful days. Anxiety, insomnia, nausea and tremors had dominated. Horrible as the period had been, given its relative brevity, I suspect I had gotten off easier than many other drunkards. Details are difficult to relate if only because my memories of that dark stretch are foggy. In its wake, less acute, but perilous cravings for the bottle persisted. That left open how long my temperance would continue.

Armed with a thirst, I walked down the gradual, sandy slope, about fifteen paces, to the river's edge. I squatted down and splashed some water onto my face. Cupping my hands, I imbibed several mouthfuls. I removed my apple butter and rye loaf from my suitcase. I carved a couple slices and slathered them with a thick blanket of fruited spread. I slapped them together into a sandwich that I devoured standing up.

Admittedly, escape from my barren life had been the primary force impelling my departure from Columbia. A desire to retrace my roots, a lesser motivation, had guided me to Fort Myers. I picked up my suitcase and embarked upon that which had brought me there. Retracing my steps from the day before, I headed back toward town. I counted my steps as I walked. I turned away from the Caloosahatchee toward First Street,

---

[374] Stowe, Harriet Beecher, *Uncle Tom's Cabin*, (Boston, John P. Jewett & Company, 1852, two volumes, 1st Ed.).

continuing northeast on the thoroughfare. As I took my 673rd step, I stopped at what was arguably Fort Myers' busiest intersection. Years earlier, I had judged the distance from my favorite fishing spot to the fort's gate at 700 yards. Presumably I was close to where that gate had stood. A sign across the way read, "Hendry Street." On the intersection's northeast and northwest corners were a pair of wood-frame general stores.[375] About a half-dozen folks were milling about the structure occupying the northwest corner. Roughly 150 yards down Hendry Street, a wharf led into the Caloosahatchee. Over to my right, on the other side of First, a building bore a small sign, Brayman Hotel. As I would soon learn, the nondescript building was more of a boarding house than a hotel.[376] I looked up and down the street, debating what to do. I needed some goods, but first I wanted to explore the town, preferably without my suitcase in hand.

I turned back to my left, giving the general store on the northwest corner a closer look. The two-story wood frame had a large gable with a single second-story window facing me. Below the window, a wooden porch, raised roughly a foot off the ground, was shaded by a sloping wood-board overhang. Across the first story's front façade were several windows.[377] The structure was the archetype of the simple Victorians lining the streets of new towns that had sprung up in western America following the discovery of gold. An unimpressive sign on the wall read, "Parker-Blount General Store." A line below read, "Post Office."[378] I approached a bearded man about sixty who was unpacking an orange crate, arranging the fruit atop a frame-bordered table outside the establishment.

"Excuse me," I said. "I just arrived in Fort Myers. I plan to shop some, but first I'd like to give the town a quick look. Might I leave my suitcase here, just for fifteen or twenty minutes?" Except for a few dollars of spending money in my pocket, I had my valuables in a money belt under my shirt. In the unlikely event my suitcase was stolen, my loss, apart from my books, would be small.

---

[375] Grismer, Karl H., *The Story of Fort Myers*, op. cit., p. 101, 199.
[376] Ibid., p. 113.
[377] Ibid., p. 119, displaying a photograph of Jehu Blount's General Store on the northwest corner of First and Hendry Street as it existed in 1886.
[378] Ibid., p. 101, indicating that W. M. Hendry was Ft. Myers' first postmaster, housing the post office at his general store on the northeast corner of First and Hendry Street. Jehou Blount, who opened a general store on the opposite side of Hendry, resented the fact that W. H. Hendry drew in customers because the post office was in his building. Blount "began pulling political strings" and had Howell A. Parker appointed postmaster. Blount formed a business partnership with Parker, and the Parker-Blount General Store became the site of the post office.

"Stick it right over there." The man gestured to the front wall adjoining the door.

"Thanks. I'll be back shortly." After depositing my suitcase, I headed northeast on First Street. Whether it was the bright sunshine reigning in a blue sky, my mood or something else, as I strolled along, Fort Myers impressed me more than the day before. I had walked but a hundred yards, and on my right, a drug store caught my eye.[379] A bit further, on the corner of Jackson Street, I spotted a newspaper office. I would soon learn that the periodical, which had only begun publication days before, was a journalistic paragon.[380] As I neared the intersection of Royal Palm Avenue, on the southeast side of First, my eyes were drawn to a small, freshly painted white church, draped in sunshine. The bucolic house of worship, an impeccable painting lifted from its canvas, captivated me. Crackerjack of construction that I was, its carpenter wood, gothic style tickled my architectural tastes. I drew closer, noting the chamfered edges on the rectangular tower that climbed from its steep, single-gable roof.[381] I stepped inside the quaint structure. The rich tones of its beautiful cabinet organ were all but audible. Rapt in enveloping spirituality, I gazed upward between the rafters of the high gothic ceiling.[382] Skeptic that I remained, I could not deny I was in God's country. Even as my rational side begged to press the patent contradiction, aesthetics quelled reason. I shut my eyes and basked in the seductive harmony of soothing introspection.

Following a couple minutes of reflective quietude, I stepped outside. Fort Myers had more sophistication than I had previously imagined. It also had more personalities than the place I knew in my youth. It was still the primeval wilderness of my childhood, where once a fort with manicured grounds stood guard. But it was rough and tumble cattle country, a tropical paradise and a quaint pioneer settlement, where religious tenets and genteel civility resided. I gazed further up First Street, checking out both sides. Several well-maintained frame homes,

---

379 Ibid., p. 113.

380 Ibid., p.111, 112, stating: "On Saturday, November 22, 1884, the first issue of Editor Cleveland's paper appeared—the Fort Myers Press. And a mighty fine newspaper it proved to be. Few newspapers published anywhere in Florida at that time excelled it in quality. During the years which followed the Press helped tremendously in the development of Fort Myers and the Caloosahatchee region."

381 Ibid., p. 100, 149, the latter showing the church in the upper left-hand corner of a sketch of Fort Myers as it existed in 1885.

382 Ibid., p. 100, quoting Dr. James A. Henshall's description of Fort Myers and its church in his 1882 book *Camping and Cruising in Florida* as follows: "I could not realize I was in the wilds of Florida while gazing upward at the lofty Gothic ceiling, with its chamfered and oiled rafters, or at the new cabinet organ..."

complete with lawns, reinforced my observation. I was about to continue my walk when an intrusive thought, reality, turned me around. Chances were Fort Myers had yet another personality, one less tasteful. With federal troops long gone and Reconstruction ancient history, likely it was a citadel of bigotry. My exclusion from the boarding house the preceding day had evidenced the restoration of antebellum intolerance. Seminoles, most of whom had been driven west on the Trail of Tears to the Arkansas and Oklahoma territories, were *persona non grata*. Negroes, though no longer slaves, were second-class citizens. As for Black Seminoles, like myself, we fit in nowhere—well, maybe, in an all-but-invisible cabin hidden in the dense woods of the Everglades. I headed back to the Parker-Blount General Store and my suitcase.

"Back already? That was quick," said the bearded man, who was putting the finishing touches on what had become a neat pyramid of oranges.

"Just wanted to get a quick overview."

"And?"

"Quite nice." Even if I thought otherwise, I would not have said so.

"Lemme guess. You're here lookin' to punch cattle?"

I shook my head.

"Damn. Generally, with strangers, that's a good bet. You know, dey don't call dis place 'Cowtown' for nuttin'.[383] His eyes narrowed. "Loggin'?"

"Wrong again."

"You ain't a homesteader, is you?"

"You're right…I'm not." I confirmed the assumption he had voiced in the negative in like manner.

"Jeezum, there ain't much left, less you're here to fish. If so, yuh come to the right place. Out in the Gulf, we got the big ones. Matter a fact, we got 'em world class. If dey got fins and swims, yuh can lay beans to boogers, yuh can catch 'em here, 'specially the big ones…tarpon, shark and the Goliath grouper."[384]"

"Well…I'm sure I'll fish, mainly the Caloosahatchee, but that's not why I'm here."

He scratched his head. "By any chance, you get here by takin' a boat south, when you was lookin' to go north…to Canada or some such place?"

---

[383] *Fort Myers History Facts and* Timeline*: Fort Myers, Florida – FL, USA*, 13 Mar. 2019 <http://www.world-guides.com/north-america/use/florida/fort-myers/fort_myers_history.html>.

[384] *Fish in Fort Myers*, H_2O Offshore Adventures website, 16 Mar. 2019 <http://www.fortmyersfishingcharter.net/fishing.html>.

Whether he had exhausted his guesses or was labeling me stupid, I wasn't sure. "You mean to tell me, this isn't Canada?"

For an instant, he appeared nonplussed. "Oh, I get it. You're makin' a joke."

I shrugged.

"Okay. But that don't answer why you come here. You can't be passin' through. Fort Myers don't lead nowhere." He studied me again. "Just to end dis guessin' game. And don't mean to be nosy, but… where yuh from? What brings yuh here…if I may ask?"

Knowing that I might settle in the area, appearing unsociable was ill-advised. Acquiring a bad reputation was easier than a good one. Losing the former was tougher than the latter, especially in a small town where gossip was sure to travel fast. I said, "I grew up in the area. Lived in the fort for a year or so before it closed, near the end of the war. I came back to find my roots."

"Lemme guess. Your father was in the Negro unit based at the fort?"

I shook my head.

"Damn. Ain't never had a worse day with my guesses. Most times they're sharp as a Bowie knife." He scratched his head. "Well, lemme guess one more time. Your folks got a farm and your back to see 'em?"

"My folks are both dead. My dad was killed while scouting for the Union Army."

"Sorry for your losses, not that I care for Yanks."

His last quip negated my willingness to express thanks for his condolences. "Care to hazard anymore guesses?"

"And spoil my perfect record?"

Discretion kept me from telling him that there was little risk of that. I went inside the store and began shopping. I picked up a couple cans of salted meat, one pork and the other beef. I grabbed a box of *Granula*, several pounds each of potatoes and carrots from barrels, a couple loaves of bread and a jar of orange jam, all of which I put onto the counter. I added a bolo knife with a six-inch blade, a timeworn hatchet and, for three cents more, a burlap sack to carry everything. I addressed a man behind the counter, presumably the proprietor. "A pound of coffee, please, and you can total it all up."

The man got my coffee and then figured my bill. "That'll be $4.27."

I paid him and, with the burlap bag over my shoulder, headed outside, picked up my suitcase and went on my way. I worked my way a couple hundred yards to the margin of the Caloosahatchee, where I turned southwest, following the riverbank about one-third of the distance to the river's mouth. Nearly two hours later—owing to my load, my pace was slow—I began looking for a particular towering live oak, a childhood favorite adjoining a broad area of sandy beach. Though two decades had elapsed, reason told me the tree would still be there, not materially different from the way it had looked when I had left the area. Back in Savannah, Mr. Wright had taught us that live oaks, so prevalent throughout the South, had an average life of two hundred fifty years. A score was but a trifle in such a lifespan. And sure enough, the oak stood tall, exactly as I remembered it. The great sentinel, Atlas, with brawny arms and gnarly elbows, had watched over my ancestors at the close of the 17th century, when slavery had been abolished in Spanish Florida.[385] It had reigned during the Seminole Wars when the natives had battled the United States military and Colonel Abraham Myers, the fort's quartermaster, for whom the town of Fort Myers had been named.[386] It had shaded me from the easterly rising sun on mornings when I had fished the Caloosahatchee. And it was there after my father had been taken from me, when I had moved from our cabin in the woods to the fort.

I laid my suitcase and bag onto the ground. Near the top of the beach, a patch of wispy grasses, the tallest as high as my waist, danced with flawless uniformity, their swing and sway dictated by their invisible conductor. I reached down and picked up a handful of sand. As soft and white as well-ground flour, traces squeezed between my fingers, drifting off in what was tantamount to a mist. The sight, the silky feel, so different from the coarser tan and gray material that coated the beaches of Savannah and St. Augustine, triggered nostalgia. Recollections of childhood days, fishing, canoeing, swimming and cavorting at the same site, surfaced. I ambled down to the waters' edge, where I turned back and gazed up at Atlas, its robust limbs dripping with parasitic moss. Following a deep breath of the humid air, I walked back up the gradual slope to the base of the huge trunk. I pressed my hand to its rough bark, caressing the uneven surface. I closed my eyes. Images of my father and Lucinda emerged. I longed to hear their voices, feel their touch. Atlas stood motionless. The chirps of the birds, murmur of the river and whisper of the breeze, all soft and euphonious, a symphony for my senses, drowned out whatever message Atlas had for me.

I picked up my suitcase and burlap bag and started into the woods, heading east. The trail that my father and I had carved with machete and eroded with our feet had dematerialized amidst the vagaries of nature. Step by step, as best I could, I counted my paces. Getting myself the right distance into the woods would facilitate finding our cabin, assuming it

---

[385] *Encyclopedia Britannica, Black Seminoles*, Britannica.com., op. cit.

[386] *Fort Myers History Facts and Timeline: Fort Myers, Florida – FL, USA*, op. cit.

remained. Past several cypress trees, beyond a thicket, the arid, sandy soil, unfriendly to growth, rendered my trek easier than I had anticipated. Continuing through an area with mainly small scrub evergreens, my pace count reached the century mark. I estimated I had another fifty before I would need to look north and south, perhaps as much as fifty yards either way. I struggled through another thirty paces of thick bushes. As I emerged into the shade of a nearby oak, off to my right, beyond more scrub evergreens, I spotted a cabin. Could it be the place where I was reared? My pace total demurred. Nearly twenty more seemed necessary. I hurried toward the structure, veering to my left for a better view. It appeared to be the cabin. Perhaps my paces had grown longer than those of my childhood. Maybe efforts to account for my non-linear path thru and around the numerous bushes had introduced inaccuracy. Past one last small pine, and any doubts evaporated. It was indeed the cabin of my youth. It showed age, but considering the years, it was in decent condition, much better than I had imagined. Skillful as my father was, I should have expected it. I stared at the log structure, eighteen-feet wide and fifteen-feet deep. I knew its dimensions as well as I knew algebra. I burst into tears. Why—was beyond me, at least at that instant. I sank to my knees. My forehead descended into hands whose knuckles melted into the granular earth. For several minutes I bawled. Gradually my sobbing slackened to a whimper. I remained crouched, genuflecting before the wooden monument. Was I in prayer? Definitely not. Was I paying homage? Not really. What was I doing? The answer escaped me. Hindsight, coupled with repeated cogitation of the indelible memory, has provided ample clues. Seeing the cabin, iconic symbol of my past, overwhelmed me. Emotions long repressed, anger never addressed and issues unassessed, burst forth from the depths. Unresolved matters, links to my father, Abbey, Grover, Walter and, most of all, Lucinda, erupted. Subsuming feelings, so long bottled up with soporific alcoholic liquids, streamed to the surface, drowning me in a river of tears.

Even after my crying ceased, I remained still. The five-mile trek, lugging suitcase and bag in the sultry conditions, had exacted a toll. The mournful outburst had been exhausting. Enervation, physical and mental, reigned. I dragged myself to an erect position and plodded to the cabin door. I pulled the portal. It failed to budge. Placing both hands on the wrought-iron handle, I tugged upward and outward. The door, no longer aligned in its jamb, opened part way, enough that I could squeeze inside. I stepped through. The interior was very much the way I remembered it, with one major exception. It looked smaller. The irony did not escape me. Unlike the dimensions, specific numbers that I knew well, my visual recollections were anything but concrete. Intuitively, one could presume the eccentricities of time would make them less reliable. The observation confirmed that which my studies of math and science had long since taught. Unlike the irrefutable logic of mathematics, perceptions and their concomitant analyses were anything but foolproof. The offbeat observation, a brief mental distraction, helped me regain a modicum of composure.

I studied the cabin, moving my gaze over each of its four walls. All had fared well. A dirth of personal property suggested that someone had looted the contents, items such as beds, stove and pans that had been left behind after my father was killed. I glanced down. The dirt floor was still a nondescript dirt floor. I looked upward, scrutinizing the interior of the side-gabled roof.[387] It seemed intact. I stepped back out the door, fetched my suitcase and sack and brought them inside. I wondered about title to the underlying land. Might the plot lie within the distant reaches of one of the huge cattle ranches that dotted the region? Could it have been included in the many thousands of acres that had been distributed under post-war field orders and homestead acts?

A deep breath filled my lungs with musty air. An unsavory odor was evident. I went over to the cabin's sole window and opened it. I returned to the front door and, using my shoulder, pushed it open wider to allow as much cross ventilation as possible. Step by very slow step, I examined the interior, particularly the walls. Tiny twigs, pine needles and other dried-up vegetation hinted that insects and vermin, likely mice, had found refuge in the cabin over the years. Making it habitable, even to a level far beneath that which I had enjoyed in Columbia, would require lots of work. Echoes from days when I was highly motivated wheedled me to embark on the process immediately. The notion had no chance. Years of alcohol dependence inhibited my ability to generate the motivation. Regardless, fatigue rendered the task impossible. Following another cursory look about the cabin, I seated myself cross-legged on the floor. My focus shifted inward. Comforting recollections of a secure childhood tranquilized vexed emotions.

Roughly ten minutes elapsed before I stood up, my mood a bit enhanced. I removed the bolo knife and foodstuffs from my burlap bag and placed them on a wooden shelf on the rear wall. Rather than unpack the remainder of my things, I hung the bag and my suitcase from two large iron hooks adjacent to the shelf. I took the can of salted pork from the shelf and punctured the top with the bolo knife, cutting away about

---

[387] A gable is the triangular portion of a roof. With a side-gabled roof, the gable faces the side. With a front-gabled roof, the gable faces the front. *Gable,* Wikipedia, 19 Mar. 2019 <http://en.wikipedia,org/wiki/Gable>.

seventy percent of the can's top. Knife and can in hand, I went outside and seated myself on a fallen log that I had noticed just before reaching the cabin. Fatigue, a consequence of both the hike and emotions, persisted. I dug the knife into the meat and, using it like a fork, dined. Hungry as I was, the simple cuisine was delicious. The salty repast generated a huge thirst. A tall beverage, flavored with a shot or two of whiskey, would have been perfect. Unfortunately—or fortunately, depending on which side of me was speaking—I had no alcohol, whiskey included. I stabbed my knife into the meat, so the blade stood vertically in the can, got up from the log and worked my way back through the woods to the margin of the Caloosahatchee. I kneeled, and using my knife, stripped away more of the can's top. Still more than half-full of meat, I dipped it into the water and repeatedly imbibed. I ate more meat and imbibed again. When finally hunger was sated and thirst quenched, I contemplated what I should do. Much was required to make the cabin livable. But the work would have to wait. I headed up from the beach to a sandy spot that enjoyed the umbra of Atlas' densest limbs. I lay down and took a welcome siesta. For the ensuing three hours, sleep predominated, interrupted only by brief hiatuses. It was well after five when the Sun, in the course of its daily voyage west, dipped low enough that its rays, sneaking beneath the oak's canopy, shone directly on my face. I briefly shaded my eyes before rising to my butt, keeping my knees bent. I reached for my can of salted meat and consumed its final contents. I went back to the water's edge, using the empty can to get another drink.

Standing on the beach, I debated what to do. Inertia wheedled me to spend the night where I was. Auspicious weather buttressed the idea. Common sense, coupled with concern that animals might pilfer my food and damage my property, sent me back to the cabin. Somewhat refreshed, I surveyed the premises, more conscious of the priorities demanding attention. A bed or some facsimile of such was essential. A chair and table were needed, but I could manage without them for the time being. The same could be said for a stove. A fire amidst a circle of rocks outside would temporarily suffice. I glanced at the dirt floor. A wooden one, the kind I had known for two decades, would be nice, but that was far down the road. Sleeping on dirt that at times could feel damp was a definite problem. But in the short term, simplicity superseded quality and permanency. After emptying the burlap bag, I took it outside, where I began filing it with the countless dead leaves and pine needles that lay beneath the trees. Once it was half-full, I rolled it up. The makeshift pillow, along with dirt floor, would suffice.

My thoughts shifted to the next day. How should I tackle the challenges that life in the cabin presented? Years earlier when my father was alive, he and I were self-sufficient. Well…my father was. Between nature and skills, he satisfied most all our needs. His ability as a hunter and trapper provided furs that he bartered for what little we needed to purchase. Whether with time, I could duplicate his skills, was questionable. Fortunately, I had no need to prove myself. I enjoyed an easier alternative, a plethora of funds. Armed with that luxury, I mapped a plan for meeting my requirements. In the morning I would return to the general store and purchase additional items, foodstuffs included. My initial work, virtually nothing, was complete.

***

The morning after reaching the cabin, I was up before the Sun. With an upcoming ten-mile hike, five each way, I fortified myself with a breakfast of *Granula*, soaked overnight in a half-can of Caloosahatchee water. Milk would have been preferable, but having none, water sufficed to make the rock-hard, so-called ready-to-eat, cereal bricks edible.[388] I got the money belt that I wore beneath my shirt and laded it with my cash, except for ten dollars that I put in my pocket. Carrying a large sum of money was not something I relished, but the alternative, leaving it at the cabin, at least until I had an effective hiding place, was worse. On the bright side, I hardly looked the type who would be flush with cash, and even on the off chance that someone robbed me, the ten dollars in my pocket was likely all the thief would get.

It was shortly after nine when I reached the intersection of First and Hendry Street. I eyed the pair of general stores that occupied the northerly side of First. I opted for the Parker-Blount store, the one I had frequented the day before.

The man behind the counter, whom I later learned was co-owner Jehou Blount, greeted me with a curious look. “Back again already?”

“Yup. Need a few more things.”

“Seems maybe you plan to stay around…not that it’s any of my business.”

Much as I preferred to be circumspect, discretion dictated otherwise. As a Black Seminole, odds were I started with two strikes. Perhaps that was all I got. If by chance, like baseball, I would be afforded the traditional third, I could ill-afford to squander it with a sarcastic quip. I said, “I may stick around. I’ll have to see.”

“You stayin’ here in town?”

---

[388] *Period-Granula, the first ready-to-eat cereal | American Civil War Forums,* civilwartalk, op. cit.

"A few miles south. I grew up in this area, back when the fort was here. Seems like it's grown a bit."

The proprietor shrugged. "Couldn't say for sure. Arrived in '73,[389] well after the war. But we're growin' now. Population is over three hundred."

"That's about the number that occupied the fort during the war." I gestured in the direction of the street. "Town feels bigger, but maybe that's because we were all cloistered in the fort."

"Speakin' of the fort, did it really have a bowling alley?[390] That's what some crackpot claimed."

"It did."

Blount became wide-eyed. "Damn, I woulda bet a ham the claim was hogwash."

I headed toward the back wall where a variety of tools hung. I selected a chisel, saw and hammer. I checked the price of each, keeping a running total in my head. No way would I reach into my money belt. I laid the three items onto the counter and continued throughout the store. I eyed some wooden fishing poles but passed them up. I had the time and skills to make one. I did, however, select several fishhooks. After laying them on the counter, I circled to the farthest front corner. A Confederate flag draped from a wall staff caught my eye. Photographs of Confederate soldiers hung from the wall below. Beneath them, on a table was a variety of Confederate memorabilia, including a pile of neatly folded Confederate flags, along with a small stack of books, all the same. I picked one up and eyed the title, *Lincoln was a Liar*. I thumbed through the paperback, only sixty pages, much of which was photographs. If the store display reflected the town's politics, Fort Myers was very different from the place I had known years before. The blue bastion of federal soldiers was long gone. Cattle ranches still dotted the surrounding area. Along with entrepreneurs capitalizing on a burgeoning citrus industry and an influx of tourist fishermen, the ranches provided the economic engine of the town. But political leanings among the inhabitants had likely shifted toward those represented by the gray uniforms that had fought for secession and the preservation of slavery. Though battlefields had grown quiet, the fight was still being waged in the minds and hearts of the people. The thought gave me pause about my decision to seek my

---

389 Grismer, Karl H., *The Story of Fort Myers*, op. cit., p. 279, indicating that Blount moved to Fort Myers in the fall of 1873 and shortly thereafter "opened a general store…" Blount had "served in two wars: the Seminole uprising of the 1850's [sic] and the Civil War."

390 Williams, Cynthia A., Blog: *Quo Vadis, TIME TRAVELER (Tag Archives: City of Palms)*, 2 Jun. 2013, retrieved 27 Mar. 2019 <https://cyn1020.com/tag/city-of-palms/>.

roots. But the pause was brief. The change was necessary. And too, the roots I was seeking lay outside of town, beyond the dichotomy of blue and gray, off in the verdant woods of a more distant past. I was a Black Seminole. And based upon my childhood recollections, not only did that mean that I was not white, but also it meant that in some respects I was neither Black, nor Seminole. Both groups viewed Black Seminoles as outsiders. That's not to suggest that Black Seminoles were ostracized; but welcomed, they were not. The thoughts stirred recollections of views voiced by my father. Much as he detested the bias, he could not deny its reality. An egalitarian society, where differences in race and culture were embraced, was his dream. But it was merely a dream, one that he acknowledged was, at best, distant, and, at worst, naive. Such was his reason for building a cabin hidden deep in the woods, why we lived separate and apart from whites, Negroes and Seminoles. But at other times, my father was less pessimistic, willing to give starry-eyed hopes a chance. Such was what motivated him to scout for the Union Army. The possibility of ebbing discrimination motivated him to lend support. Even as he did, he was far from sanguine. Equality was at best a long shot. Of that, he left no doubt.

I stared at the flags and books and other Dixie memorabilia. I was even less optimistic than my father. To what extent my recollections were accurate, I was uncertain. It was also possible that projections of my own beliefs and wishes colored my memories. Amidst my ruminations, anger bubbled to the surface. The war, the hate had robbed me of my father. Its aftermath, the bigotry it embodied, had stolen Lucinda as well. The losses were huge. They were permanent. And they remained unaddressed. I took a deep breath. The admissions were a baby step in the grieving process that for years I had judiciously suppressed. Was I ready to face the issues? Perhaps, though certainly not at that moment. I went to the area near the counter and gathered up a wide range of food stuffs: several cans of pork, beef and lamb; a variety of vegetables; a loaf of bread; jars of jam; a paper bagful of peanuts from a barrel; three boxes of *Granula*; a tin of hard candy; and a small block of rock salt. I added the last item after some self-debate. Down the road I could evaporate salt from the brine of the Gulf's waters,[391] but for the time being, a ready supply of the flavor-enhancing preservative was required.

Once I had laid the last of my purchases onto the counter, Blount figured my bill. "All total, it came to $9.08."

---

[391] *Open-pan Salt Making*, Wikipedia, 27 Mar. 2019 <https://en.wikipedia.org/wiki/Open-pan_salt_making>.

I handed Blount a five-dollar gold piece, four silver dollars and a dime.

"Damn, I could do with more folks like you. Big order and you ain't beggin' for credit." He handed me two cents change.

As I stuffed the items into my burlap bag, the same one I had used as a pillow the preceding night, I said, "I paid for the sack the last time I was here."

"You're fine. Matter of fact, with all you bought, I'd be good with givin' you one for free."

"Appreciate that, but I'm all set."

Blount studied me. "Based on looks, I'd say you're Negro, but I see Indian too. Last time here, you said you grew up 'round these parts. By any chance, you a Black Seminole? Ain't many left in Southwest Florida."

With the impertinence of his comments exceeded only by the brazenness of his snooping, I bristled, but only briefly. Discretion kept me in check. "Yes, I'm a Black Seminole…Is that bad?"

Blount eyed me as if I were the rude one. "Ain't good or bad…well, less a body makes it so."

The response did nothing to mitigate what, up to that point, had been controlled pique. With judgment still containing indignation, I said, "Is that how most in town feel, or just your view?"

"Hey, I don't speak for others, least wise, not usually. On the other hand, I got my views, and with lotsa reasons. I fought in two wars, the Seminole War of the 1850s and the War of Secession.[392] Didn't like the outcome of the latter. Don't care for uppity folks in Washington tellin' us how to live our lives. A few of your people, Black Seminoles, still live in the surrounding area. Some camp out on the outskirts of town.[393] Don't bother me none, long as they keep to themselves. They're even welcome, just like you, to buy and trade here, provided they ain't no bother. But Sundays, when my family goes to church, or when my kids go to school, ain't gonna mix with 'em. That goes double when you talk courtin'. It's enough that they banned slavery. No way we gonna mingle and mix. Not about to see our heritage, our way of life, lowered by…" His words trailed off.

I filled in the blanks. Like most of his southern white contemporaries, Blount considered individuals like me inferior.

---

[392] Grismer, Karl H., *The Story of Fort Myers*, op. cit., p. 279.

[393] Ibid., p.118, stating: "The Indians often camped on the outskirts of town or even in the yards of the town residents."

"Anyway, most folks like to keep with their own kind. I'm sure you agree."

I didn't.

"But we here in Fort Myers have been decent 'bout stuff. Long as folks mind their own business, we get along fine. Just 'cause I ain't gonna invite you to sit at my table when I play poker Saturday nights over at the Silver Horseshoe (he gestured down the street in the direction of the saloon), doesn't mean you can't shop here. Matter of fact, folks like you with cash money are welcome here anytime. Most of your kind come with skins and pelts, egret plumes and the like, lookin' to trade."[394] He heaved a sigh. "Too often their stuff is second rate. They expect me to take it in exchange for quality merchandise." He gestured all around the store. "Ain't gonna happen. Life don't work that way." He pawed his beard. "Still, I gotta admit that their comin' here ain't all bad. I got the upper hand. Don't deal less I get the better end." He looked at me funny. "Hope that's not the face you wear when you play poker."

"I don't play poker…and just so there's no confusion…this is my only face."

"Hey, that's you're problem, not mine." His stare was cold. "But just to set the record straight, I wasn't slurrin' you. I was referrin' to your reaction when I told you 'bout getting the better end of a deal. A smart trader keeps his cards close to his vest…and he's tough. Havin' that reputation don't hurt. Folks walkin' thru my door know they gotta give more than they're gonna get." Blount puffed out his chest.

I took my sack, headed out of the store and started walking in a southwesterly direction. Several doors down, I came astride the saloon. Like the worms that had baited my childhood pole enticing the fish of the Caloosahatchee, temptation inveigled me. My tongue tasted the familiar almondy, cedar-infused, smooth flavor of my favorite whiskey. I looked back in the direction of the front façade of the general store. Gone were faint hopes that Fort Myers might still bear the northern influences that had prevailed when it was a Union fortification. The town had become a microcosm of Savannah and Columbia. It was different from the Fort Myers I remembered. Situated in the deep South, it embraced the values symbolized by the Stars and Bars.

I gazed once again at the saloon. Conscious of my sack and, more important, my money belt, discretion…sober discretion subdued

---

[394] Ibid., p 116, indicating that Fort Myers was incorporated on August 12, 1885. *See*, p. 118 to the effect: "Seminoles wandered into town as they had in days gone by, bringing their alligator teeth and hides, their crane and egret plumes, their skins of deer, and their pelts of otter, bear, beaver and panther. In payment they took kettles and knives, thread and needles, tobacco and candy, grits and bacon…"

temptation. A Black Seminole, laden with valuables, would be a fool to enter a den whose alcohol-influenced patrons yearned for restoration of the antebellum southern culture.

Chapter XXVI

FOLLOWING A SECOND NIGHT IN THE CABIN OF MY YOUTH, common sense urged that I begin to tackle the tasks needed to make the structure more habitable. Despite its dirt floor, the cabin had seemed fine back in my childhood. It was all I knew. But in Savannah and St. Augustine, I had become accustomed to better quarters. In recent years, armed with both funds and construction skills, I had enjoyed a comfortable home in Columbia. Arguably, I was spoiled…On second thought, forget the arguably. What once sufficed, failed to measure up. I looked around the cabin. A wooden floor, good stove, better roof, bed, table and chairs, nice stone fireplace and a hiding place for my valuables were but a few of the requisites. A rocking chair had become a necessity as well. But all those items would have to wait. In advance of the structure's rehabilitation, years of pent-up emotions and unresolved issues demanded that a few days be devoted to thoughtful contemplation, initial steps on my road to self-rehabilitation. Perhaps indolence was affecting my thinking, but even assuming it was, its influence paled when weighed against the need to tend to my emotional well-being.

I went over to the shelf that harbored my two-volume set of *Uncle Tom's Cabin*. Armed with the first book of the influential novel, I headed outside, where I seated myself on the same fallen log on which I had eaten my first meal, as well as most since my return. I ran my fingers over the book's brown leather cover. I felt the touch of Abbey's hand in mine. I shut my eyes, resurrecting the fondest memory of my youth. Familiar, short, high-pitched chirps sounded in my ears.[395] Atop a thicket, draped in sunshine, a painted bunting, head blue, breast orange

---

[395] *Painted Bunting Sounds, All About Birds, Cornell Lab of Ornithology*, allaboutbirds.org, 3 Apr. 2019 <https://www.allaboutbirds.org/guide/Painted_Bunting/sounds>.

and adorned with green and yellow,[396] proudly stood, a testament that nature's canvas could outdo the palette of the finest artistic master. For several minutes, I watched the feathered warbler reign over the bush that presumably housed its nest. I gestured at my cabin, communicating that I was its neighbor. Still rapt in song, the bird ignored me. It was as if it deemed me an invading trespasser, unworthy of recognition. Perhaps if it had known my pedigree, the years I had previously spent in the area, it would have been less aloof. As best I could, I mimicked its warble, and after several efforts, its head turned, so one eye was directed my way. Maybe it took note of my music. Perhaps it understood my message. It chirped some sweet notes.

"Thank you," I said, interpreting its song as a message that I was now welcome. Its coat of many colors reinforced my interpretation. It lived harmoniously with all its neighbors, be they black, white, red or multi-colored. The absurdity of my ruminations did not escape me. It was of no matter. I reveled in sublimity, a serenity I had not known since days before Lucinda's death.

I parted the volume's covers. The text opened near the center, to the pages between which lay the birchbark bookmark I had made for Lucinda. I eyed the marker, running my fingers over its soft surface. Between my thumb and index finger, I took hold of the garnet stone that was tethered to the top. I gazed deeply into the red gem. The glowing spirit of Lucinda's soul, the goodness of her heart, engulfed me. Distant though Lucinda may have been, her presence was palpable. Her loving, supportive essence was manifest.

For several minutes, I sat in wistful reflection before finally slipping the bookmark between the front cover and the cover page. I opened the volume to Chapter I, where Mr. Haley negotiated with Mr. Shelby to buy Tom.[397] The words were identical to those I had read a score earlier; yet, they were entirely different. Back when Abbey had given me the book, still learning to read, it was all I could do to follow what was happening. Analysis, let alone subtleties, was far beyond my ken. Years of education and experience cast a new light on the old story. Even as Harriet Beecher Stowe, determined abolitionist that she was, voiced her abhorrence for slavery, she wove a textured fabric bearing multi-dimensional characters. She understood that screaming slavery's evil, declaring slave owners the devil, was an ill-conceived device to abolish the practice. That Mr. Shelby esteemed Tom, that he ensured Tom's well-being after

---

[396] *Song Birds of Florida*, floridiannature.com, 3 Apr. 2019 <https://www.floridiannature.com/songbirds.htm>.

[397] *Uncle Tom's Cabin*, Vol I, pp. 1-13, op. cit.

he was sold, evidenced Mr. Shelby's humanity. It did not, however, negate the ignominy of the reality, that he treated Tom as chattel. Stowe laid bare the fallacy of masters' oft-invoked smokescreen. Claims that they treated their slaves well camouflaged the truth: they turned human beings into property, no different than a cow or a plow.

As I finished the first chapter, I paused. The world of the South was seemingly black and white, both literally and figuratively. But the truth be known, it was far more nuanced. Its canvas encompassed a thousand shades of gray, some far darker than they appeared. Such was the gray of the uniforms the Reb soldiers had worn in the great war. Light on their surface, they masked the soldiers' dark objectives. But much as these soldiers wore uniforms cut from the same cloth, they were not the same. They too came in varying shades of gray. The observation, a global one, induced me to become more introspective. My own view of politics, society, mores and values, had missed the nuances. Unrequited rage had led me down a path of ever-narrowing perspective. The iniquity over which I had seethed was no less evil, any more than slavery was in the eyes of Harriet Beecher Stowe, but my response to that iniquity, my ability to judge facts, had been impaired by a dark veil of anger. Only the day before, it had influenced my reactions when dealing with storekeeper Jehou Blount. Acknowledging the point, the need to address my own issues, was far from a panacea. I was not yet ready to examine the many colors of the painted bunting's world, but at least I could see shades of gray amidst the blacks and whites. I had taken a small step toward rehabilitation. And that step was liberating.

***

Two days had elapsed since I had begun reading *Uncle Tom's Cabin.* Apart from eating and sleeping, I had done nothing other than focus on the tome. I would have reached the end sooner had I not repeatedly taken time to contemplate what I had read and to analyze it in the context of history, both that which had transpired in the nation and in my own life. As I read the final pages, Harriet Beecher Stowe's "Concluding Remarks,"[398] the breadth of her indictment, often far from subtle, sledgehammered me one last time. "Both North and South have been guilty before God; and the Christian Church has a heavy account to answer."[399]

---

[398] Ibid., Vol II, pp. 520-529.

[399] Ibid., p. 529.

Though the text predated the War of Secession and the Emancipation Proclamation by roughly a decade, its charges remained valid. Despite the abolition of slavery, a conflict that had left roughly two-thirds of a million dead,[400] and a period of Reconstruction, remnants of the prior era remained entrenched. Blame, however, lay beyond the South. Confronted with consequences to their personal economic interests, many in the North, like their southern neighbors, voted their pocketbooks. All too often houses of worship provided platforms for the advocacy of white supremacy. Whether the churches were *per se* responsible was a semantic shroud that begged the underlying truth. The people who led and attended those churches, who promoted unchristian values, were indeed responsible, albeit in varying degrees. Some resorted to and/or condoned violence against Negroes. Others, less militant, pushed for Jim Crow laws. And many silently acquiesced in the perpetration of injustice.

I thought of Abbey and Lucinda. When it came to confronting inequality, they were years ahead of me. When first I had read *Uncle Tom's Cabin*, it was just a story. To Abbey, my contemporary, it was a statement of principles, ones she had adopted despite her parents' bias. So too, Lucinda had walked the walk, not just for racial equality, but women's rights as well. She had died fighting for those beliefs. For an instant, guilt invaded my psyche. But flagellation was fleeting. For too long I had beaten myself up. Unlikely that Abbey would have wished that on me. Surely, Lucinda would not.

I closed the cover, allowing *Uncle Tom* to rest in my lap. I thought of my calculus and physics books. Equations, iron-clad expressions built on axiomatic truths, had always been my preference. Religion, philosophy, politics and the social sciences had often left me unsatisfied. A reason, one that had been largely unconscious, revealed itself. Ambiguity, opinion and, worst of all, so-called principles whose validity was a function of their proponent, annoyed me.

The irony of my reflections was too patent to deny. I had always viewed myself as openminded, willing to entertain gradations. Apparently, I preferred the black and white, right and wrong, of mathematics. Yet I wanted the bright, multi-colored world of the painted

---

[400] *But see, Who, What, Why: How many soldiers died in the US Civil War - BBC News*, 4 Apr. 2019 <https://www.bbc.com/news/magazine-17604991> stating: "For more than a century, it has been accepted with a grain of salt that about 620,000 Americans died in the conflict…" However, in the 21st century, "J. David Hacker published a paper that used demographic methods and statistical software…" Based upon his analysis, the BBC news article indicates: "US Civil War deaths therefore could range from 617,877 to 851,066, and [Professor Hacker] settles on an estimate of 750,000 dead."

bunting. Even a thousand shades of gray could not satisfy me. Logic's Law of the Excluded Middle, the principle that I had learned from Professor Nelson, reared its irksome head. The rule fit foursquare with my need for definitive, unambiguous answers. But even as I yearned for such black and white results, I begged for the variegated hues that lay in the middle. The absurdity brought a smile to my face. I shrugged and laughed heartily, something I had rarely done in recent years.

A gust, though far from strong, rustled the nearby leaves. I drew in a deep breath and, armed with my book, got up from the log. I negotiated the path to the beach. After rolling up my pants' legs and removing my shoes and socks, I drew the bookmark out of the volume. With the book in my right hand and the bookmark in my left, I waded into the edge where the water was just deep enough to hug my ankles. No longer sheltered from the Sun, I felt a thirst. Where ordinarily I might have opted for tea laced with copious whiskey, the need for the alcoholic addition was absent. Unlike my experience a few days earlier when I had skipped a visit to the saloon owing to monetary risk, I had no desire for intoxicants. I ran my toes through the fine sand. Alternating left and right, I stood in place, slowly lifting one foot, allowing the mixture of sand and water to trickle between my digits. I strolled along the edge of the river, its gentle waves climbing over my ankles. With Lucinda in my left hand and Abbey, my right, Eden wheedled me to luxuriate. Senses heightened, I willingly obliged. The caress of the breeze, the sand and water, and, most of all, Lucinda and Abbey soothed me. The rustle of the leaves, the babble of the Caloosahatchee and the chirp of its feathered inhabitants sated me with sweet music. The scent of evergreens, infused with the flirty fragrance of the pristine coral-bed river, doused me in an aromatic paradise. Returning to the cabin, searching out my roots, an impetuous decision, was validated. I gave *Uncle Tom* a quick glance. Days devoted to reading, eschewing tasks that demanded attention, had been justified. The catharsis required before I could move forward had begun. As for the path my life would follow, that remained a mystery. But the door to the jail in which I had so long been imprisoned had swung open. I was free to explore that which lay beyond the slavery of my mind. I could disembark the dismal cell whose sinful spell did reason quell and peace repel, to bid farewell, perhaps dispel relentless hell, a liberty bell, its toll the knell to make me well.

***

As the next day dawned, energy, enthusiasm, the likes of which had long been foreign, abounded. I was eager to rehab the cabin, upgrade it beyond what it originally was. As I chomped on a mugful of *Granula*, softened overnight in Caloosahatchee water, I mapped out a plan. The roof needed patching. Installation of a floor was a priority, though far from the top. Lumber from a wide variety of trees was readily available. But hand hewing logs into boards made little sense with a sawmill in town. A rented buckboard could transport them. But several miles from anywhere, I could do with a means of transporting myself. A horse would be perfect. The thought tantalized me, in part for its obvious pragmatic advantages, but also for the companionship it engendered.

Anxious as I was to begin my labors, practical propensities, my mathematical/scientific side, dictated that to the extent possible, groundwork had to come first. I headed toward town. My first stop was at the saloon, not for whiskey, but to check the board outside, where folks posted notices for available services and goods. Nothing caught my eye. I was about to move on when a fellow in a cowboy hat and boots approached.

"Any good bargains on the board today?" he said.

"Depends what you're looking for."

"Not necessarily." He perused the board. "I buy stuff I don't need all the time."

Bad enough the fellow was a spendthrift. Was he so foolish that he advertised his imprudence, even to strangers? "Any particular reason you do that?" I asked the question despite being all but certain of the answer. Like so many compulsives, his behavior was dictated by other than judgment. The same could be said for drunkards. The painful point tempered my disdain for his folly.

"You take me for a buzzard brain, don'tcha?"

"No," I said, but with insufficient conviction to be credible.

"Well, it's like this. I see what folks got for sale. Most times, they need the dough. It's a buyers' market, with me the buyer. But the price gotta be cheap, and the stuff sure to sell or good for tradin' up."

The seeming dupe was shrewder than I had imagined.

"Seein' as how you're checkin' the board, by any chance you lookin' to buy somethin'?"

"A horse." The disclosure unnerved me. Had I made myself a mark in a seller's market?

"Hmm, a horse…Ain't got none for sale." He muttered under his breath, "Well, you can't win them all." He gestured down the street. "Down at the livery stable, Edgar Jones sells them. He's got them all, from ten-dollar nags to better breeds. Not the kind with papers, racers, that might go a thousand or more, but fine mounts."[401]

"Sounds good. Think I'll check him out...Thanks." I started to walk away.

"You're new around here. Right?"

I nodded.

"Well, before yuh go, lemme warn yuh. Edgar deals Jewish."

"That's fine. I've got nothing against Jews, not that I've met many."

"That ain't what I meant. He ain't a Jew. Just deals like one. Won't sell yuh nuttin' on credit. Even white folks that go to church with him is hard pressed to get credit. And when they get it, it's Jew style."

"Pardon me?" I said, restraining the urge to voice umbrage to the bigoted aspersion.

"Yuh know, like when yuh need to borrow money. Them Jewish lenders know you're desperate for dough...that they got yuh by the short hairs. They gouge yuh with interest up the wazoo. Not that I blame them."

"Who?"

The man eyed me incredulously. "The Jews...Ain't that who I was talkin' about?"

"If you say so." I would have gone on my way had temptation not superseded prudence. "You know for whom this town is named?"

"Some guy named Myers, not that I know nuttin' about him."

"His name was Abraham Myers, and he was Jewish."[402]

The man laughed. "You expect me to believe that, comin' from some jamoke who ain't a local?"

---

[401] *How much did a horse cost in the 19th century? | Yahoo Answers*, 6 Apr. 2019 <https://answers.yahoo.com/question/index?qid=20071227101611AAAHlc3>. *See also, Quora, How much did it cost to own and travel with a horse back in the 1850's and 1860's* [sic], Suzanne Marie Realia Sullivan, Answer February 21, 2019, 6 Apr. 2019 <https://quora.com/How-much-did-it-cost-to-own-and-travel-with-a-horse-back-in-the-1850s-1860s> stating: "In the west US it was possible to buy a horse for as little as $10, but a decent riding equine cost around $150, with a range of $120 (1861) to $185 (1865). A pack horse for the Oregon Trail cost $25 in the US in 1850, but a riding horse would run you $75." (Like real estate, though to a lesser extent, the cost of a horse likely varied with location.)

[402] *Jew or Not Jew*, 30 Mar. 2019 <jewornotjew.com/profile.jsp?ID=1596> stating: "As far as we can tell, the largest American city named for a Jew is Fort Myers...ironically one of the less-Jewey cities in the rather Jewey state of Florida." But interestingly, Myers "was buried in St. Paul's Episcopal Church Cemetery, Alexandria, Virginia." *Abraham Myers*, Wikipedia, 30 Mar. 2019 <https://en.wikipedia.org/wiki/Abraham_Myers>.

"Believe what you want. But just so happens, as a youngster I lived in the fort until it was shut down near the end of the war. They taught us the history of the town."

"So, wha'd this Myers guy do that they named the town for him? Part the waters of the Caloosahatchee?" With a self-satisfied look, the man laughed.

"He married the daughter of the commander of Fort Brooke in Tampa."[403]

"Jeeze. Did he at least have a link to Fort Myers?"

I shrugged.

"Damn! Just proves me right."

I did a double take. The buffoon had to be kidding. "About what?"

"About them Jews. Yuh can't trust them. Gotta count your fingers, once they shake your hand." He shook his head. "Damn. Can't believe our town was saddled with the name of some Johnny Come Never. Ain't right, no how." He grumbled inaudibly before continuing. "So, lemme guess. Myers was a money lender."

"I don't know a lot about him, but he graduated West Point and served as a captain in the U.S. Army."[404]

"Damn, our town is named for a lousy Yankee."

"Not quite. During the war, he was a colonel in the Confederate Army."[405]

"A little better. At least he fought in gray duds. Still don't change that the bum's a Jew. Hardly need our town named for one of them." He adjusted his hat. "Powers that be oughta rename this place."

"You're right," I said sarcastically. "Perhaps folks here should rename the town for one of its founders."

"Jeezum—you ain't suggestin' Captain Gonzales?"

"Don't seem so, given that I have no idea who he is."

"He founded this place, shortly after the Yanks abandoned the fort. Set up a tradin' post. Traded furs, tobacco, beads and the like.[406] Did business with the Negro Seminoles." The man briefly studied me. "Less I'm mistaken, that's where you fit in." He muttered under his breath. "Damn, namin' this place for Gonzales would be near as bad as a Jew." He shook his head. "If you wasn't referrin' to Gonzales, then who?"

"One of this area's great leaders, from before the War of Secession."

---

[403] *Ft. Myers, Florida, History*, Stewart Title website, 31 Oct. 2017 <http://www.stewart.com/en/stc/fort-myers/about-us-history.html>.

[404] *Abraham Myers*, Wikipedia, op. cit.

[405] *Jew or Not Jew*, op. cit.

[406] *Fort Myers, Florida,* Wikipedia, 3 Mar. 2019 <https://en.wikipedia.org/wiki/Fort_Myers,_Florida>.

A puzzled look draped the man's face. "Who might that be?"

"John Horse, Billy Bowlegs or one of the other Seminole—"

"You think you're funny. Well, you ain't." He looked me in the eye. "Lemme give yuh some friendly advice. If yuh plan to stay around these parts, yuh best watch your tongue. The war may be over, but some folks, lots of them, are still fightin' it."

"That so?"

"Yeah, that so."

I started to walk away.

"Before you go. I got some more information for you."

"Really?" I said, despite antipathy to entertaining more of his bigoted rant.

"If yuh head down to the livery stable, like yuh said yuh might, assumin' yuh got cash money, yuh oughta be able to make a great deal. Between you, me and this here wall, I happen to know that about now, Edgar has more horses than he can handle. Gotta feed them, and that costs dough."

The tidbit was far better than the dose of bias I had anticipated. "Appreciate the information."

"My pleasure, not that I give two cents if yuh get a good deal. Just that I love when Edgar swallows his own medicine. The bastard screwed me when first I came to Fort Myers. Needed a horse, so I could ride herd. Crummy piker jewed me a lousy deal."

Kinda like what you do to others. Given that he had provided me with useful information, I kept the insult to myself.

The man pointed at the door. "Too much talk. Came here with a purpose. Gotta get me a bourbon." He went into the saloon.

I headed down the street in the direction of the livery stable. Halfway there I slipped into a narrow alley between two buildings. After making sure no one was in sight, I opened my shirt and took out one hundred dollars, the absolute limit I would pay for a horse. I slipped the money into the side pocket of my pants and closed my shirt. After taking a moment to plan my approach, I proceeded to the stable. The barn door was open. Inside, a muscular man, about fifty with a full beard, greeted me.

"Howdy. What can I do for you?"

"Hi. I'm Mican Reinbow. When I was a kid, back during the war, I was housed at the fort for a couple of years. I used to hang out at the stable, around the horses. They've always fascinated me. Passing by, I thought I'd give a looksee, if that's okay?" I gave no clue I was in the market to buy.

"Be my guest." He extended his arm. "I'm Edgar Jones, the stable-keeper."

I shook his hand and then looked up and down the half-dozen stalls. "You've got some nice horses."

He nodded. "Yup, horses are great. You get a good one…it's faithful. Does what you want, when you want it, and without no lip. You get my drift?"

"I hear you," I said, happy to be agreeable.

"Horses ain't like people. Take my ex-wife, if you want proof. If I said it was day, she said it was night. But then if I agreed with her that it was night, she'd tell me I was lily-livered. Couldn't win for nuttin'. But don't get me wrong, I ain't knockin' women. Men is just as ornery. Don't make no difference. But take a horse. He…or she…may have a mean streak, start out buckin' and kickin'. But once you train them, train them good…they're with you one hundred percent." He looked me in the eye. "You gettin' my drift, boy?"

The likelihood that he knew he had demeaned me was undeniable. Rather than choosing the door, I swallowed my pride and played dumb. "You're absolutely right. Horses are like dogs. A faithful one will stand by you, no matter."

He gestured at me. "You got a horse?"

"Never have…but might be nice…someday."

The bearded man's eyes narrowed. "Someday could be today…Get my drift?"

The redundant phrase was tedious, but his failure to punctuate it with "boy" rendered it palatable. "You've got some nice animals." I gestured at the stalls.

"These here in the stable ain't for sale, well…'less you got four or five hundred dollars."

I jerked back, partly from surprise, but more so to give the impression that such means were way beyond me.

"Out back in the corral, I got nine more. They ain't trained. A couple is past their prime. Some others wouldn't be much for ridin', but they can haul, least as good as a mule. And two or three others got pretty good potential. The right owner might turn them into somethin' near as good as what's in the stable." He slapped me on the back. "No harm in lookin'. Right?"

I nodded and followed him out back to the corral.

"You see one that interests you?"

"The roan looks nice…and the dapple, way over there." I pointed.

"Yeah, they're both pretty good. But lemme warn you 'bout the dapple, Spotty—that's what I call him. Looks calm, the way he's standin' there, nice. But he's a mean bastard. Go near him, and he'll kick you where the Sun don't shine. Get my drift?" Jones eyed me, seemingly making sure I was keeping up. "Now, the sorrel, she's pretty good. Ain't trained, least not much. You can feed her some oats. Even put a rope around her neck and lead her a bit. Might let you put a saddle on her back, but try to ride her, and she'll buck up a storm. Ain't the fastest thing on four legs, but you never know, might turn out to be a rider. Get you from here to there. Hard to tell. Kinda like shootin' craps. She might be snake eyes but could be a seven." Jones looked me in the eye. "You could have her for an even hundred…That assumes you got the dough."

I shrugged, if only because I was unsure how to react. My interest was piqued, but showing it was a bad idea, especially when a skilled angler might be luring a naïve fish. "What would you charge for the gray by the gate?" I picked the scruffy, flaccid animal, not because it appealed to me, but to test Jones' candor.

"That bedraggled beast?" Jones snorted. "You want him. You got him for twenty-five bucks. But understand, he ain't good for much, less you lookin' for a companion that can pack a tiny load."

His forthrightness mitigated my defensiveness. "Sounds like I'd be better off checking out the sorrel."

"C'mon, give her a look."

He entered the corral and led the sorrel out. "Like I said, she's a nice horse. Ain't been broken in for ridin', and I ain't sayin' she'd ever be good for that. But she's pretty strong and decent with folks, long as they don't spook her." Jones rubbed his hand over the equine's side. "Run your hand on her, the way I did. Let her know you're friendly."

I followed his instructions, taking note how her soft coat glistened in the sunshine. As I stroked her satiny surface, my mind drifted, unearthing deeply buried recollections. For an instant, I closed my eyes. I imagined that Lucinda was standing alongside. I could all but feel the ecstasy of her velvety bronze skin. Years had passed since I had felt that magnificent sensation. Whether the sorrel would be a rider became less important. How good a workhorse she would be mattered less. I circled in front of the horse, running my hand over the side of her face. Her brown eyes met mine. I was hooked. This was the horse I wanted. I turned to Jones. "I came here to find out what it would cost to rent a buckboard and a horse for a couple of days. I had no plans to buy a horse, but I like this sorrel…I'll give you seventy dollars, cash money for her."

Jones pawed at his beard. "Tell you what. I'll give you a rock-bottom offer. You can have her for eighty…and, what the hell…I'll throw in the use of a buckboard for two days."

I thought for several seconds, not that there was any real debate. "You got a deal." I reached into my pocket and counted out eighty dollars." I heaved a sigh. "At least I still have twenty to buy food and other stuff." Letting him know that I had lots more money would be ill-conceived on two counts: he might renege, thinking I could afford more; and publicizing my wealth was a perilous practice.

"You're welcome to take her today, if that's what you wanna do?"

The question revealed the rashness of my decision. "I guess so."

"I got a buckboard available, if you want it now."

With trees uncut and arrangements for their milling yet to be made, I said, "I'd rather wait."

"Suit yourself. I may need a couple days' notice when you want it...you never know."

"That's fine." I was about to leave, but realized I needed feed for "Cinda." I had already selected her name. For a dollar, I bought a half-bale, enough to get me started.[407] With a little luck, Cinda would be able to graze on the land near the cabin. Before heading home, I made two stops. En route, I visited the general store and purchased some clover and alfalfa seeds to improve that likelihood. I also bought an ample supply of four-inch nails, along with a bowl, plate, knife, fork and spoon, necessaries I had neglected my last time shopping.

Hay on Cinda's back, a rein around her neck to guide her, I wended my way back to the cabin. A sense of calm pervaded me. In recent days, I had taken major steps forward. Halfway home, I stopped and turned to Cinda. With my free hand, I caressed her soft cheeks. I eyed her rein that I held in my other hand. Perhaps the bridle I had worn around my neck the past few years was finally off. A life limited by liquor was ready for days dominated by determination.

Arriving back at the cabin, I looked around, contemplating the projects demanding attention. My industrious side prodded me to attack them immediately. Judgment counseled otherwise. Rest, both physical and mental, would steel me for the tasks. Yielding to judgment, suppressing compulsion, I spent the remainder of the day getting to know

---

[407] "A typical three-string bale of hay weighs 100 to 140 pounds and has dimensions of 22 inches by 15 inches by 44 inches." *What is the Typical Size and Weight of a Bale of Hay*? | References.com, 9 Apr. 2019 <https://www.references.com/business-finance/typical-size-weight-bale-hay-8d319098d43a41bd>. *Quora, How much did it cost to own and travel with a horse back in the 1850's and 1860's* [sic], op. cit., Dale Rose, indicating that at the peak of the Civil War, hay sold "for between $45 and $50 a ton." And *See also, Another Androsphere Blog: How much did things cost in 1850's* [sic] *USA?,* supra at footnote 174, to the effect that hay cost $44.05 per ton (or approximately $2 for 100 pounds).

Cinda and enjoying a leisurely repast. As darkness descended, I took my leaf-stuffed burlap-bag pillow outside to a barren spot. I lay down on my back and stared upward. Amidst the still air, utter silence reigned. Consummate peace and tranquility prevailed. I began to nod off when a thunderbolt rattled my brain. Lying there motionless, or seemingly so, I was racing through space, spinning at over 1,000 miles per hour, owing to the 24-hour rotation of the Earth over its 25,000-mile circumference. If that weren't enough, I was simultaneously hurtling around the sun at a rate 1,000 times faster than the speediest trains, roughly 70,000 miles per hour, based upon a calculation made back during my days at the Horseshoe ($2\pi \times 93{,}000{,}000$ miles to the sun $\div 365 \div 24$). That I could be streaking at such incredible speeds on two distinct paths, but simultaneously be totally at rest with everything still, defied reason. It was chaos personified...but only if I deemed it such. I refocused on the Heavens. Stars twinkled above. Some were stalwart. Other seemingly vanished, only to reappear in an instant. The universe was replete with anomalies. Control them, I couldn't. But I had free will. I could affect my surroundings. I could fashion a better life for myself.

***

Over the ensuing six weeks, working twelve-hour days, I attacked projects full bore. Experience at the St. Augustine Lighthouse, as well as building houses, had equipped me with a broad range of skills. I chopped down three medium-sized pines and one cedar, all of which I trimmed free of branches, leaving lengthy logs. I split the logs into pieces, each just over six feet long. I arranged to use Jones' buckboard and to have my log sections milled. With Cinda—our relationship had grown rapidly—hooked to the buckboard, I made trips to the sawmill where my logs were trimmed into neat six-foot boards, three-quarters of an inch thick. I brought the boards back to the cabin and then returned with another load of logs. I repeated the process until enough logs had been transformed into boards.

Inside the cabin, I dug a series of narrow trenches across the breadth of the structure. Near the beaches of the Caloosahatchee, I dug beneath the sandy surface and extracted an ample supply of karst limestone,[408] which I crushed into smaller stones. I put the crushed stone into the

[408] *Geology of Florida*, Wikipedia, 9 Apr. 2019 <https://en.wikipedia.org/wiki/Geology_of_Florida> indicating: "The Floridian peninsula is a porous plateau of karst limestone sitting atop bedrock known as the Florida Platform...The limestone is topped with sandy soils deposited as ancient beaches over millions of years as global sea levels rose and fell."

trenches, partially filling them. Atop the stone, I laid thin pine logs, a base that allowed a floor to rest several inches above the ground. After leveling the tops of the logs, I laid pine floorboards, nailing them one by one to the pine logs. The technique was inferior to that which we had used when I had worked for Norwood Hanks in the Little Africa section of St. Augustine, but the result was a huge step up from a dirt floor.

From the branches of some previously felled pines, I fashioned a small ladder, sufficient to climb onto the cabin's roof. Still in relatively good shape, the roof took me less than a day to patch. Once completed, the cabin was very habitable. The time had come for upgrades. The cedar boards that had been milled weeks before took center stage. I installed shelves near the lone window and made a bed frame that I placed in the cabin's back left corner. A huge burlap bag stuffed with dried hay provided a mattress, not the likes of which one would find in a fine hotel, but far better than bags of leaves. I saved the finest cedar boards for a six-foot cabinet, nearly two-feet wide, with four shelves. Just beneath its acme, above the top shelf, I installed a false back, behind which a two-inch space provided a hiding place for my valuables. Two short screws held the false back in place. A coat of oak stain over the surface of the cabinet, finely sanded so it was silky smooth, yielded a decent piece of furniture.

The renovation and improvement of the cabin were a significant physical accomplishment, but it was more than that. Once again, my life had purpose. Reading *Uncle Tom's Cabin* had mentally prepared me to move forward. Work on the cabin, accomplished with various woods, provided tangible evidence that I was up to the task. I was indeed getting on with my life.

Chapter XXVII

CHRISTMAS, 1884, HAD COME AND GONE. The best part of two months, remarkably productive ones, had passed since I had arrived in Fort Myers. Years spent in South Carolina, where raw winter days were hardly uncommon, made me appreciate Southwest Florida. Even in January and February, typical daytime highs approached the middle seventies. Most every day, I spent an hour or so rereading my calculus and physics books, mastering their every subtlety. Fishing the Caloosahatchee, my primary source of food, was an almost daily activity. Bass, gar, panfish and catfish were but a few that found my line and, ultimately, my palate. A fine garden, sowed with seeds of carrots, lettuce, potatoes, beans, onions and radishes, had begun to grow. Adjacent to the cabin door, I planted a rose bush, Lucinda's favorite, a fond reminder of our blissful days together. All the while, I continued to enhance the cabin. Lime plaster, filling and coating lath nailed to the original timbers, produced smooth walls. A table and two chairs, plus a rocker, all of which I fashioned from pine, added ambiance. Were my father able to see the home borne from his cabin, no doubt he would have been proud. I was.

Following an ample day of work, I was relaxing at my table with the *Fort Myers Press.* A reference in an item on the back page caught my eye. It was old news, but amidst my years of alcoholic dependence, my tracking of scientific advances, particularly those that were more theoretical than practical, had been patchy. The item referenced an experiment that had been conducted in 1879 by Albert Michelson, an instructor of physics and chemistry at Annapolis. He had calculated the speed of light at 186,380 miles per second, plus or minus 30 miles per second.[409] That anyone could track such incredible speed, more than

---

[409] *Albert A. Michelson,* Wikipedia, 18 Apr. 2019 <https://en.wikipedia.org/wiki/Albert_A._Michelson>. (*Bookmarks'* author's comment:

seven times around the world in a second, boggled my mind. My scientific proclivities, so long dormant, sparked. I sent a letter to the library at Annapolis requesting information about the experiment. After receiving a brief response, I sent numerous additional letters to other sources seeking more information about the nature of light. Was it a wave? Or perhaps a particle capable of moving through a vacuum?[410] In the months that followed, the subject consumed me. On the banks of the Caloosahatchee or seated in my rocking chair, as well as in bed at night, I analyzed the scientific question.

Two hundred years earlier, Sir Isaac Newton had argued that light was a particle. Admittedly, the argument made wonderful sense, if only because the alternative, that light was a wave, challenged logic. Reason suggested that a wave, like sound, required a medium, such as air, for transmission. Scientists had long suggested the existence of that medium. They referred to it as the "ether" (also known as the "aether"). The concept was possible, but no one had proved the existence of the ether. On the other hand, if light were a particle, it could travel through empty space, for example, from Sun to Earth, without a medium. I might have leaned toward the particle theory, rather than the wave, but for information gained in a modern-physics class I had taken my last year at the University of South Carolina. Only a few years earlier, the Scottish physicist James Clerk Maxwell had developed equations showing that a symmetrically changing electric field would produce a changing magnetic field. His equations predicted a sinusoidal electromagnetic wave with electrical and magnetic properties, traveling perpendicular to the direction of the wave propagation.[411] The equations also predicted that the wave would move at a speed approximating that which Michelson had found for light.[412] Maxwell's equations made a strong

---

Over a half century ago, as a college student, together with my physics laboratory partner, I "performed" the Michelson-Morley experiment and "calculated" the speed of light. I can recall almost none of my college labs, but this one remains memorable. In the foregoing sentence, I put the words "performed" and "calculated" in quotes because the data my laboratory partner and I generated led us to a calculation of the speed of light that was off by a factor of roughly of 10^3. With no clue where or how we had gone wrong, even the infamous *fudge factor* could not bail us out. The unmitigated disaster our lab results produced exemplified the familiar adage, "Garbage in, garbage out.")

[410] Fowler, Michael, *The Michelson-Morley Experiment*, 18 Apr. 2019 <http://galileoandeinstein.physics.virginia.edu/lectures/michelson.html>.

[411] *A Brief History of Light | Tge BLOG of the cosmos*, blogofthecosmos.com, 23 Apr. 2019 <https://blogofthecosmos.com/2016/10/31/the-nature-of-light/>.

[412] Ibid., stating: "Maxwell's wave equation indeed showed that the speed of the hypothetical wave in a vacuum would be 2.9986 x 10^8, [sic; 10^8 meters per second] which was very close to the speed of light. Maxwell also predicted the existence of a

argument that light was a wave, irrespective of a medium for propagation. But equations, mathematical models, were little more than a basis for a theory. Proving that theory demanded concrete evidence developed from experiments consistent with the scientific method. Rehashing the matter more than a decade after I was exposed to it, I favored the wave theory. Its mathematical basis was more compelling than the simplicity of the particle theory. Perhaps more than anything, my professor's view back at the university that Maxwell was right influenced my conclusion. My professor knew more than I. Planets to particles, it was a safe bet I would have favored the particle theory, had my professor favored that.

For the most part, my life in 1885 was solitary. At irregular intervals, averaging about two weeks apart, I ventured five miles north to the town of Fort Myers. All things considered, my life was satisfactory, the best since Lucinda's death. Cinda played a key role in my progress. Initially she helped me drag and carry heavy loads. Gradually her role expanded. She became a rider, certainly not a steed with speed, but good enough to carry me, as well as pull and shoulder my loads. She was also there to hear my dissertations on every imaginable subject, even the nature of light as a wave or particle. Did she understand what I said? Of course not. That was of no matter. She was a great listener, an incredible friend. Admittedly she was only Cinda, not Lucinda, but having her as a partner was far better than none.

It was the 15th of August when I road Cinda into town. Though never a conformist, I had grown to like the Stetson hats that so many of the cowboys wore. I hitched Cinda to the rail outside of Hendry's General Store. The Parker-Blount establishment across the street sold Stetsons as well. I had previously compared the wares of the two stores. A particular Stetson I had seen at Hendry's had caught my fancy. Preference of one store over the other played no part in determining where I shopped. The proprietors of both stores never refused my business. That said, each left no doubt that, like other Negroes and Seminoles, I was a second-class citizen.

I headed into Hendry's. The beige suede Stetson I had previously seen still hung on a wall hook. I took it to the counter behind which F. A. Hendry stood.

---

family of electromagnetic waves, of which light is one." Said Richard Feynman, noted American physicist of Maxwell's work (Ibid.): "From a long point of view of the history of mankind, seen from, say, ten thousand years from now, there can be little doubt that the most significant event of the 19th century will be judged as Maxwell's discovery of the laws of electrodynamics."

"Excellent choice. That's a fine hat." He held it up. "You planning to punch cattle?"

I shook my head.

"Good for you. Be a shame to mess such a fine hat on dusty cattle drives, especially for what cowboys make these days. Not like it was back in the sixties when Jake Summerlin and his boy controlled the market down in Punta Rassa. Since Cuba adopted its import tariff, cattle have sunk to ten bucks a head."[413]

I took in what he said without reacting. I paid him for the hat and started to leave.

"Just wondering…You…your people got any views about what we did the night before last?"

"Don't know what you're referring to."

"Unanimous vote, forty-five to none, we incorporated Fort Myers. High time we did it. Only way the town will get decent roads, water and the like. That plus we gotta stop the cowboys from causing trouble on Saturday nights."[414] Gotta do something about the rabble that loiters as well."[415]

I wondered if his last reference included me. Admittedly, bias crept into my perception. Owing to a storied past as one of Fort Myers' leading citizens, Hendry enjoyed high esteem with most everyone in town. I was among the exceptions. During the War of Secession, when Hendry had risen to the rank of major, he had supplied the Confederacy with beef, and in 1863, he had organized a cavalry company.[416] The possibility, albeit remote, that he had been involved when my father was killed while scouting for the army had predisposed me to dislike him.

"The town is growing. The recent census shows it at 349."[417]

"I saw that in the *Press*."

---

413 Grismer, Karl H., *The Story of Fort Myers*, op. cit., p. 83-85, 102. *See also, Jacob Summerlin*, Wikipedia, 19 Apr. 2019 <http://en.wikipedia.org/wiki/Jacob_Summerlin> indicating that Summerlin, known as "King of the Crackers" and "King of the Cracker Cow Hunters," accumulated "a fortune of 15,000 to 20,000 head of cattle…and was considered one of the wealthiest of Floridians."

414 Ibid., p. 116.

415 Ibid., p. 118 stating: "The Indians often camped on the outskirts of town or even in the yards of the town residents. James E. Hendry, Jr., [grandson of F. A. Hendry, Ibid. p. 280] recalls that when he was a youngster he often awakened on rainy mornings to find a family of Seminoles bedded down on the front porch of his home. Occasionally they asked for handouts; they never asked for work. Hard labor was what foolish white people did to make money they worried over; the Indians would have no part of it—it didn't agree with them."

416 Stone, Spessard, *Capt. Francis Asbury Hendry*, 19 Apr. 2019 <freepages.rootsweb.com/~crackerbarrel/genealogy/William3.html>.

417 Grismer, Karl H., *The Story of Fort Myers*, op. cit., p. 118.

His eyes widened. "You can read? Good for you."

The lefthanded compliment, an indication that he expected otherwise from someone of my race, piqued me. As I had so often done, I held my tongue. Knowing that Lucinda would have spoken out stirred guilt.

"Fort Myers has a bright future. Next step, we need to get our own county, separate from Monroe. It's too damn big. The hotshots at the seat down south in the Keys don't even know we exist. And once we get our own county, I'm gonna push that it be named for the great leader of our army."

Despite knowing whom he meant, I said, "Who's that?"

"Lee…General Robert E. Lee!"[418]

My history studies at the University of South Carolina had educated me about the famed military leader. "Not everyone considers him a great man."

Hendry jerked back. "Just what does that mean?"

"For starters, he was a slave owner." My comment was intended to irk. In Fort Myers, it was widely known that two decades earlier, Hendry, like Lee, had owned eight slaves.[419]

"Lee's ownership of slaves was consistent with the country's law at the time. Presidents like Washington and Jefferson owned slaves as well. And fair-minded man that Lee was, he acknowledged that slavery was a 'moral and political evil.' He always treated his slaves well."[420]

"So, he claimed." I let my sarcasm drip. "Of course, Lee considered the evil greater to the white race, than the black. He said the 'painful discipline' slaves faced was 'necessary for their instruction.'"[421]

---

[418] Hendry, F. A., *A History of the Early Days in Fort* Myers, undated and unpaginated exposition. Captain Hendry held General Robert E. Lee in high esteem. Captain Hendry wrote in his exposition regarding the naming of Lee County, where Fort Myers is located: "Proud indeed am I that when a name was discussed that I—even I—made a motion to name it in honor of the beloved Robert E. Lee." Hendry went on to share the following anecdote. "Some one [sic] stepped in and said: 'Judge, some people are protesting against the name of our proposed new county.' The judge's eyes flashed fire and he said: 'Let them protest and be——[sic].' I will leave the dash to be filled in by my dear friend, Judge Cranford. Yes, we are proud of the name of our county and its seat of government."

[419] Stone, Spessard, *Capt. Francis Asbury Hendry*, op cit.

[420] Fortin, Jacey, *What Robert E. Lee Wrote to The Times About Slavery in 1858*, The New York Times, August 18, 2007, retrieved from nytimes.com, 19 Apr. 2019 <https://www.nytimes.com/2017/08/18/us/robert-e-lee-slaves.html>.

[421] Ibid., stating: "[S]lavery was 'a greater evil to the white race than the black race' in the United States, and that the 'painful discipline they are undergoing is necessary for their instruction.'" (inner quotation is from a December 27, 1856 letter from Robert E. Lee to his wife.)

"Many others held the identical view."

The remark was accurate, not that it validated the view. It also begged the question: Did Hendry share Lee's attitude? Emotions that had driven me to instigate the verbal sparring, the image of Lucinda's lifeless body after she had been lynched, implored me to lash out. A countervailing thought challenged the urge. Though Hendry bore responsibility for his sins as a slave owner, his conduct after the War of Secession evidenced that he differed from the bigots who had lynched Lucinda. His reputation for being friendly with area Seminoles was hard to deny. They held him in high esteem.[422] Did he deserve to be attacked? What would it accomplish? Would I walk away with regrets? But what about Lucinda? It was all too complicated to evaluate in seconds. I would be back to his store in the future. If need be, I could pursue the issue then. I donned my new Stetson and went on my way.

***

Months earlier, Thomas Edison had visited Fort Myers. I would have gone into town to catch a glimpse of the amazing inventor had I known he was coming. Frustrated by a miserable winter three hundred miles north in St. Augustine, Edison had come to Punta Rassa on March 6, 1885, arriving in Fort Myers on the 8th. The next day he was gone.[423] Two days later, on one of my shopping trips, I learned of his visit, and that knowledge only came after I returned to my cabin. A tiny three-line personal item in the newspaper indicated that Edison had come to town and was considering the purchase of a tract along the Caloosahatchee from Samuel Summerlin,[424] son of the aforementioned cattle king, Jacob Summerlin.

Six months later, during another trip into town, I learned that Edison had purchased a thirteen-acre parcel from Samuel Summerlin for $2,750, a seemingly outrageous price, given that Summerlin had bought the land for only $500 several years before.[425] Word had it that Edison planned to build a beautiful winter home on the property. The tidbit induced me to

---

[422] Grismer, Karl H., *The Story of Fort Myers*, op. cit., p. 278, stating: "Captain Hendry was friendly with all the Seminole Indians of South Florida and they held him in such high esteem that when they heard he was dying, Chief Billy Conapachee (q.v.) and his brother Billy Fuel walked sixty miles from deep in the Glades to see him before he passed away." *But see*, Hendry, F. A., *A History of the Early Days in Fort Myers,* op. cit., in which Captain Hendry referred to Billy Bowlegs, the great chief of the Seminoles as a "savage."

[423] Grismer, Karl H., *The Story of Fort Myers*, op. cit., p.114.

[424] Ibid.

[425] Ibid.

do something I would not have otherwise anticipated. Comfortable as I was with my life alone in the woods, I had no interest in outside employment. But a chance to meet Edison while working on his home, cajoled me to explore the matter. I approached Edison's representatives and offered my services on a part-time basis. My experience at the renowned St. Augustine Lighthouse, as well as building houses, earned me a job.

***

Prime Maine lumber, selected by Edison himself, arrived in Fort Myers, and construction began in early winter, 1885. Cool mornings, typically in the fifties, with daytime highs in the seventies, provided an excellent environment for the work. The gentle flow of the Caloosahatchee, as it drifted past the front portion of the property, testified that the home would be an idyllic haven. The two-story, single-chimney structure, along with an adjoining guest house, was quickly framed. The main home, largely symmetric, bore a pair of tall windows on the front façade of the second story. Below, a rustic-railed porch extending beyond the side walls of the first story, akin to a top hat, provided character, as well as an aura of stability.[426]

During the first few months of construction, I worked only a day or two each week. Still I managed to get to know the foreman well. A practical man with an interest in science, he had learned of my background when hiring me. After hours, when the day's work was done, he often picked my brain on subjects such as electricity, mechanical advantage and the like. In March of 1886, with the house unfinished, Edison arrived with his bride. Awaiting completion, they stayed at the Keystone Hotel near the foot of Park Street. The 20-room, two-story building, with a large dining room, parlor and wharf, was reputed to be the "finest hotel south of Tampa."[427] Fine as it was, Edison preferred to occupy his home. Expeditious completion became imperative. The foreman convinced me to work six days a week for a month.

About ten days had passed since I had become full time. Several times I had seen Edison on the property, checking the progress. My view had only been at a distance. It was roughly the first of April, while I was

---

426 *Ft. Myers Historic Homes, Edison & Ford Home | Edison Ford Winter Estate*, edisonfordwinterestates.org, 21 Apr. 2019 <https://www.edisonfordwinterestates.org/what-to-see/historic-homes/> displaying a photograph of the home as originally constructed.

427 Grismer, Karl H., *The Story of Fort Myers*, op. cit., p. 108.

putting finishing touches on the fireplace mantle, that he approached me from behind.

"Mican Reinbow…"

The sound of my name turned my head. Stunned by the sight of the great inventor, I said, "Uh…yes."

"I'm Thomas Edison. It's nice to meet you."

Electricity surged through my limbs as I shook the hand he extended. I was thrilled. But I was intimidated. My normally facile tongue knotted.

"Jack tells me you have a college degree, with emphasis on mathematics and physics. Says you know a lot about electricity and thermodynamics."

I shrugged. When it came to accomplishments in the world of science, the contrast between us was sharper than that which distinguished our skin pigments. "I…uh…have studied those areas, not that I'm an expert."

"You're too modest."

"Thank you." I longed to ask him about his incandescent light, phonograph and dynamos. Most of all, I wanted to talk to him about "etheric force," a term he had coined.[428] Not only did I lack the nerve, but face to face with the renowned man, I needed time to frame my questions and thoughts.

"Nothing wrong with doing construction, but with your knowledge, you might want to try something more cerebral."

"Uh…I guess." I feared he was about to ask me what I had been doing since I had graduated. Admitting that I had spent several years in alcoholic oblivion would be mortifying.

"I'd like to talk more, but for the moment, a few matters demand my attention. Perhaps another day we can talk science."

"I would love that." Just before he walked away, I took the measure of the illustrious man. Of medium height, stocky, but not fat, his large heart-shaped face displayed a broad, flat mouth and bushy brows. I estimated him to be about my age, perhaps a few years older. A balding top added an element of distinction, though my foregoing observation may have been influenced by the fame that preceded him. As I watched him walk away, I vowed that if someday fortune provided an opportunity for lengthier conversation, I would be armed with worthwhile thoughts and questions.

---

[428] *Etheric force,* Wikipedia, 18 Apr.2019 <https://en.wikipedia.org/wiki/Etheric_force> stating: "Etheric force is a term Thomas Edison coined to describe a phenomenon later understood as high frequency electromagnetic waves—effectively radio. Edison believed it was the mysterious force that some believed pervaded the ether."

***

Nearly two weeks had elapsed since I had met Thomas Edison. Each day I had hoped that he would visit the worksite and find time to speak with me. No such luck. Twice I had seen him on the premises. Another day, fellow workers had observed him there.

It was a typical April day, temperatures in the low eighties. I was installing molding in the main room of the house. With both sets of double front doors open and windows wide in the rear, a welcome breeze flowed through the structure. As I faced the wall on which I was working, I felt a hand on my back.

"Your work looks good."

I turned and saw Edison. "Uh…thank you."

He gestured all around. "The place is shaping up nicely…Wish it had been completed before Minnie and I arrived in Fort Myers, but results are what matter. On that score, I'm pleased."

"Good results are a product of a good crew." Viewing myself as an add-on, my comment was intended to compliment the regular team, not brag. Unfortunately, my choice of words subverted my intent.

"Indeed, you've all done an excellent job."

"I…I didn't mean myself. I—"

"That's fine. I know what you meant."

Though unconvinced he believed my explanation, I appreciated his effort to mitigate my discomfort.

He drew his pocket watch from his vest. "Your workday will be over shortly. You mind spending the balance with me down by the river. We could have that talk I mentioned a while back."

Did I mind? He had to be kidding. I was thrilled, not to mention that he was the boss. He, not I, decided how my workday was spent. "It would be a great privilege to speak with you, Mr. Edison."

He led the way toward the riverbank, ushering me to the shade of an elm. "I plan to have benches here, but for now the ground will have to suffice."

He seated himself, and I did likewise.

Edison smiled before inhaling deeply. His mien pensive, he gazed out over the Caloosahatchee and began speaking in what seemed a stream of consciousness. "Nature…'Nature is what we know. We do not know the gods of religions. And nature is not kind. or merciful, or loving. If God made me—the fabled god of…mercy, kindness, and love—He also made the fish I catch and eat. And where do His mercy, kindness, and love for that fish come in? No; nature made us—nature did it all—not the gods of the religions.'"[429] He turned to me. "What do you think?"

What did I think? His extemporaneous prose was exquisite. Telling him so would come across as sycophantic, especially when the object of his question was otherwise. "Uh...Nature is amazing." I cringed, knowing my shallow reply was no better than silence.

"Religion...God...nature are subjects I enjoy discussing. And maybe we'll get the opportunity, but today I'd rather talk about science. Okay?"

"Fine with me. I'm just happy for this opportunity."

"Fort Myers is a beautiful place." He gestured at his nearly finished home. "I would not have built here if I thought otherwise. But when it comes to science, there's almost no one in the area to talk to. If I'm going to spend winters here, I need to ferret out the best local minds. Given your background, I'm sure you're at or close to the top of the list."

I welcomed the compliment, even if it did appear a bit lefthanded.

"Not to put you on the spot, but is there some invention or scientific principle you'd like to discuss?"

The question whether light was a wave or a particle immediately came to mind. For the first time I felt on solid ground. Recent readings had the matter fresh in my mind. And I knew Edison was interested in the subject. He had created the term "etheric force" to explain the phenomenon of light.[430] I said, "How about etheric force?"

"Gosh, I hadn't expected something that esoteric, but...great choice!" He looked me in the eye. "What are your views about etheric force?"

"Well...all I can do is speculate, but I'm skeptical that there's an ether."

He gave me a look. Though it wasn't testy, I felt intimidated.

"Do you think light is a particle?" he said.

"It's possible, though the idea is certainly problematic." My answer, one that could be invoked on any issue of scientific ambiguity, was less than substantive, and I knew it.

"Is it because you doubt that a particle could move through the atmosphere at 186,000 miles per second? Air resistance would be huge."

"True, unless the particle was far smaller than that which we have yet identified."

---

[429] Edison, Thomas A., Interview in the *NY Times Magazine*, retrieved from *Thomas A. Edison Quotes*, goodreads.com, 2 Mar. 2019 <https://www.goodreads.com/author/quotes/3091287.Thomas_A._Edison>.

[430] *See*, footnote 429, supra.

"Interesting…"

That Edison would give my comment even seeming credence was pleasing.

"Based upon what you've said, you've left the door open to either a particle or a wave. Which do you think is correct and why?"

My desire to hedge had been challenged. "Well, I lean toward a wave, mainly because Maxwell's equations predict waves traveling at very close to Michelson's calculation for the speed of light." I declined to mention my other reason, that my professor at the University of South Carolina had favored a wave.

"I'm aware of Maxwell's work, not that I'm a theoretical physicist," said Edison.

Neither was I, and I hoped that he had not construed my comments as purporting such expertise.

"Like you, I lean toward a wave. But similar to sound, which depends on air or other matter for propagation, common sense tells me that if light is a wave, it needs a medium. I believe that medium is the ether; that the etheric force enables the transmission."

"Then you doubt that experiments will bear out what Maxwell's equations predict?" I could not believe that I was challenging the great man's view.

"I didn't say that. Maxwell's equations don't preclude the existence of an etheric force."

His point, taken in a vacuum, was accurate. "But if Maxwell was right, there is no need for etheric force. Put another way, the etheric force would be redundant."[431]

"I suppose…But merely because the etheric force is not necessary, does not imply it does not exist." Edison looked me in the eye. "You concur?"

"I see your point." Daunted by his stature, not that Edison had said or done anything to cow me, I declined to press my doubts about the existence of the ether and/or etheric force.

---

[431] Less than a decade after James Maxwell's death in 1879, "…German physicist Heinrich Hertz was able to experimentally detect electromagnetic waves. His discovery of radio waves showed that they have a similar nature of reflection and refraction and similar properties as light and that they indeed move at the speed of light, confirming Maxwell's predictions. Mysteries still persisted, in particular, with regards this ether medium that had long been hypothesized. Since electromagnetic waves were found to be able to travel even in a vacuum, Maxwell's theories had largely made such a hypothetical medium to be redundant. Experimental attempts, however unsuccessful to detect it, followed along and dominated 19th century physics…" *A Brief History of Light | The BLOG of the cosmos*, blogofthecosmos.com, op. cit.

Edison stared at the Caloosahatchee in what I assumed was judicious contemplation. With the aid of a quick peek, I judged that he was detached. Perhaps he was silently contemplating the ether; maybe his mind was focused on an invention; or, more likely, his thoughts were directed to some matter I would never guess. Perhaps he was judging me. The possibility negated any chance that I would interrupt his musing, not that I would have anyway.

One...two…three minutes ticked by. The hiatus unnerved me.

Finally, Edison turned to me and said, "You know what I was thinking?"

I shook my head, barely.

"Oh, sorry, I didn't mean to leave you…figuratively, that is."

"Uh…that's okay. Sitting here along the river with you…uh…with or without conversation, is…uh…fine by me." The juddering with which the words kangarooed from my tongue belied my response.

"Yes, that's exactly my original point."

I had no idea what point he was referencing.

"Sitting here…silently communing in nature's sanctuary." He gestured at the river, trees and sky. "That's why I decided to build here. It's ideal to both rest and stimulate the mind." Following another moment of apparent introspection, this one no more than five seconds, he continued. "'To do much clear thinking a person must arrange for regular periods of solitude when they can concentrate and indulge the imagination without distraction.'"[432] He nodded slowly, his gaze drifting back toward the river.

Once again, we sat in silence, each lost in his own thoughts. Unlike the earlier hiatus when the passage of time made me progressively more antsy, the seconds flowed as easily as the tranquil Caloosahatchee. Like before, I had no clue as to Edison's ruminations. Maybe he was merely resting his mind. Regardless, mine was active. I was savoring the opportunity to sit aside the venerable man and follow his recommendation, commune with nature.

***

Day by day, as we put the final touches on Edison's winter home, I kept hoping he might pull me aside again. More than once, I spotted him on the grounds, but apart from a single passing wave from a distance, I

[432] Edison, Thomas A., retrieved from AZ Quotes website, 24 Apr. 2019 <https://www.azquotes.com/quote/354384>.

had no contact with him. The day before the last details were completed, he finally approached me, seconds after I finished hanging a picture.

"Looking good." Edison eyed the picture before moving his gaze around the main room. "It's really shaped up well, Mican."

"You and your bride should enjoy your winters here.[433] All the folks in Fort Myers are mighty happy that you'll be spending time in this neck of the woods."

"Would you like to talk again?"

"I'd love to!"

Edison ushered me out to the same spot we had sat the previous time. Once we were seated, he said, "I have a little proposition for you. Down the road, would you like to work for me…become a mucker?"

The offer was intoxicating. But it was also offensive. Inviting me to be a mucker, a word rhyming with the most derogatory of terms, suggested that he considered me second-class. I deemed it a racial slur, and apparently my face reflected my umbrage.

"Please, don't misunderstand. Mucker is not a negative term. If anything, it's affectionate."

Sure. Were he anyone else, I would have voiced the sarcasm.

"Mucker is what I call all my assistants. And for that matter, I refer to myself as 'Chief Mucker.'"[434]

That he directed the dubious appellation to himself reversed my thinking. What moments before had seemed blatant bigotry was not. "I'd be honored to work for you. Would it be here in Fort Myers?"

"Yes. And that's why I said, 'down the road,' a moment ago. I plan to have a laboratory here so I can continue my research during the winter months. Much as I want to escape the Northeast when the snow flies, giving up my work as a trade-off is unthinkable."

"Do you plan to install your laboratory next winter?"

"It's possible, though nothing is cast in stone. Regardless, when I do, I'll be in touch."

"I appreciate that."

"And I'm glad you're willing. People with a knowledge of physics are all but nonexistent around here. As for muckers from up north, few are eager to leave their families for a few months each year." He inhaled deeply. "The end of the month, I head back north. It's sure to be a busy

---

[433] Grismer, Karl H., *The Story of Fort Myers*, op. cit., p. 115. On February 24, 1886, Edison married Miss Mina Miller.

[434] *Thomas Edison's Research Laboratory*, Agile Writer website, 24 Apr. 2019 <http://www.agilewrier.com/Biography/EdisonLab.htn>.

year. I'm moving my Edison Machine Works from New Jersey up to Schenectady, New York.[435] On top of that, I'm in for a helluva battle."

My curiosity piqued, but I dared not show my nosy side.

Edison pawed his chin in a moment of quietude. "You interested in hearing about it?"

"Yes, but it's none of my business…unless you wish to tell me."

He chuckled briefly. "It's no secret. It's all playing out in the public square. The newspapers, always eager to make a buck off a lurid story, have been splashing the details across their pages. It's the war between AC and DC current, which one will light and power the country. I suspect you're aware of the matter."

I had indeed contemplated the issue, but I was hardly up to date on the battles. I said, "I'm familiar with AC and DC current. As to all the pros and cons of each, as well as any sensational political or other issues they involve, I know much less. But I've heard that you're a strong proponent of DC current."

"Absolutely." He looked me in the eye. "As one who presumably has no stake in the outcome, any opinion which will prevail?"

Since first I had spoken to Edison, I had grown a bit more comfortable. His question rekindled prior intimidation. Temptation cajoled me to choose the toady response, DC current. The expectation that he would ask me to defend my position prompted a more anodyne stance. "I don't know enough to voice an intelligent opinion."

"Fair enough. I won't press you."

Thanks to the ease with which he let me off the hook, intimidation ebbed.

"DC current has the disadvantage that it can't transmit over long distances. Unfortunately, much of it dissipates along the way. On the other hand, AC involves higher voltages, and renders it much more perilous."

I was already aware of the information he imparted, but it merely outlined the problem, not a solution. Using DC in urban areas and AC in rural ones seemed logical. Suspecting the conundrum was more complex, and not wanting to embarrass myself, I kept the thought to myself.

"Let me give you a bit of history. Once I invented a practical incandescent light bulb, cities raced to construct DC hydroelectric power

---

[435] *Thomas Alva Edison*, Edison Tech Center website, 25 Apr. 2019 <https://edisontechcenter.org/ThomasAlvaEdison.html>.

plants. With my patents, it was a gold mine.[436] But ultimate success begged that I find a way to transmit DC power over long distances. Because I'm an inventor and a businessman, not a mathematician and scientist, I hired this Serbian mathematician and engineer, Nikolai Tesla. Rather than solve my dilemma, Tesla told me to switch to AC, an 'utterly impractical' solution.[437] Next thing I knew, Tesla quit on me and hooked up with George Westinghouse, who bought some of Tesla's patents. As part of Westinghouse Manufacturing and Electric Company, they began installing AC generators. Not only have they gone into rural areas, but they've made inroads into cities like New Orleans."[438] Lips pursed, Edison gazed toward the river.

"So, where do you think this current struggle is headed?"

Edison jerked back, as he gave me an incredulous look. "AC is a blind amputee with vestibular imbalance trying to walk a tightrope of frayed string. Mark my words: 'Westinghouse will kill a customer within 6 months after he puts in a system of any size.'[439] And from there, it will be all downhill. On second thought, it'll be a freefall, from that tightrope I referenced."

"So," I again said, but this time with confidence, rather than to preface a question, "the war you mentioned earlier will ultimately be Tesla and Westinghouse's Waterloo, and you, along with DC current, will light the country."

Edison laughed.

Why? I didn't know, but I suspected it was sardonic.

"You make it sound simple. It'll be anything but. War is Hell. Yes, I'm confident that I'll ultimately win, but antecedent to that victory, I expect to visit Hell."

---

[436] *Edison vs. Westinghouse: A Shocking Rivalry | History | Smithsonian*, smithsonianmag.com website, 13 Jun. 2018 <https://www.smithsonianmag.com/history/edison-vs-westinghouse-a-shocking-rivalry-102146036/>.

[437] Ibid.

[438] Ibid.

[439] Ibid.

Chapter XXVIII

ONLY A WEEK AFTER THOMAS EDISON HAD SPOKEN TO ME about AC/DC electricity, he and his new bride returned north. The possibility that he might invite me to become a mucker the following winter inspired me to intensify my studies, particularly in the areas of electricity and magnetism. A potential future was in sight. Life was relatively good. I planted two orange trees, expanded my vegetable garden and, at the front of my cabin, added a simple wooden porch, a mere six inches off the ground. I moved my rocker out to the addition.

The balance of the spring was uneventful, except for the second Wednesday in May. The town's lone school, the Fort Myers Academy, succumbed to a blaze. Rumors abounded that some boys, fed up with school, had set the fire, but nothing more than speculation emerged.[440] The summer, as always, was hot and humid. The advent of fall, with daytime highs trending down below ninety, was welcome. September had but one more day. A largemouth bass, nearly a foot long, that I had caught in the morning, had sated me with a great lunch. My physics book in hand, I seated myself in my rocker. Back and forth I swayed, watching an eagle atop a towering slash pine. No sooner than I opened my book, I shut it. An urge seized me. Though years before I had vowed never to renew the activity, an irrepressible impulse took control. I went into the cabin and got a pencil and paper. I returned to my rocker, and using my physics book as a desk, wrote the following letters "L," "D," "G," "A," and "W" in a column down the left side of my paper. I closed my eyes and began rocking. A couple of minutes elapsed, when I wrote the word "garnet" next to the "G." Soon after, I wrote "dollar" next to the "D." Another hiatus, and I scribbled "agate" alongside the "A." Two letters remained. Five, ten, fifteen minutes ticked by. On and on I rocked, until

---

[440] Grismer, Karl H., *The Story of Fort Myers*, op. cit., p.122.

finally something clicked. I jotted "wood" next to the "W." I briefly stared at the freshly written word before crossing it out. Several minutes later, I tentatively wrote "walnut" next to the "W." Only one letter remained. I thought for a while. Lime, the material of a seashell, was the best that crossed my mind. Ambivalent, I got up from my rocker and went into the cabin where I removed the back panel of the cabinet, the one that hid my box of valuables. I took out ten dollars, along with my little cloth sack of stones. I emptied the contents onto the table. The instant they poured forth, a light went on in my brain. I put all the stones back into the bag, except for an agate, a garnet and the sole lapis. I had my "L." With splotches of white all about its surface, the lapis was hardly a valuable, uniform specimen of deep blue.[441]

After storing the bag, I took the agate, garnet and lapis outside. I wrote "lapis" next to the "L" on my paper. I reviewed the entire list, satisfied that I had an acceptable choice for each letter and the individuals they represented: Lucinda, Dad, Grover, Abbey, and the "W" for both Walter and Mr. Wright.

I climbed aboard Cinda, arriving in town a half-hour later. My first stop was Parker and Blount's General Store. Among their wide-ranging inventory, they sold coins of most every date and denomination. Between collectors and folks looking for coins commemorating birth dates, anniversaries and all sorts of events, it was a brilliant strategy for an establishment that handled substantial cash every day. For three dollars I purchased an 1864 Indian Princess Gold Dollar.[442] Parker and Blount made a neat two-dollar profit, while I got a dollar, whose first letter, "D," was symbolic of "Dad," what I called my father. The coin's date, 1864, marked the year he had died. I also bought a beige strip of suede, about 10 inches long and two inches wide.

I had planned to use the shell of a walnut, its "W" to honor Walter and Mr. Wright. The more I thought about the idea, the less I liked it. With its rough-surfaced husk, it was too bulky for my purposes. A small, solid piece of walnut, well sanded and stained, was better suited. Unfortunately, walnut trees only grew as far south as northern Florida.[443] I surveyed the store, looking for a small, walnut trinket. I found nothing. I headed across the street to Hendry's. Not far from the door, I found a barrel full of walking sticks. The proprietor found me one of walnut.

---

[441] *How To Tell If Lapis Lazuli Is Real*, nammu.com website, 27 Apr. 2019 <https://www.nammu.com/eng/how-to-tell-if-lapis-lazuli-is-real/>.

[442] 1864 Large Head Indian Princess Gold Dollar, coinvalues.com, 21 May 2020 <https://coinvalues.com/large-head-indian-princess-gold-dollar/1864>.

[443] *Juglandaceae, The Walnut Family*, University of Florida, SFRC Extension, 28 Apr. 2019 <sfrc.ufl.edu/Extension/ffws/tfjug.htm/#nigra>.

Convinced that its tip neatly trimmed and sanded would meet my needs, I bought the item. Armed with my three purchases, I headed back to my cabin. The stones I had previously removed from my sack covered the remaining three letters, “L,” “G,” and “A” (lapis for Lucinda; garnet for Grover; and agate for Abbey).

As soon as I arrived home, I went to work. I folded the top inch of the suede and sewed it to itself, allowing me an alley through which I threaded a thin cord. I filed, sanded and polished the three stones. I cut off the tip of the walking stick, shaping and sanding it into a tiny cylinder about one-fifth of an inch high and one-half inch in diameter. After drilling a hole through the center of each of the five items, I stained the walnut cylinder. The advent of night, coupled with the need to let the stain dry, forced me to wait for morning to assemble my newest bookmark. As I lay in bed, I tried to come up with a meaningful word using the letters, “L,” “G,” “A,” “D,” and “W.” My plan was to install the items in sequence to symbolically spell out that word. I came up with nothing. Instead, I drifted off to sleep.

The following morning, after a quick breakfast, I tried again, testing all 120 permutations of the five letters. Not one was a word, let alone a meaningful one. Unsuccessful, I put the five mementos onto the cord in the order the persons they represented had come into my life: Dad; Abbey; Grover; Mr. Wright and Walter; and Lucinda. Once I tied the cord, I beheld the bookmark, letting the symbols dangle below. Admittedly, it was bulky. Regardless, I loved it.

I got my physics book, which I took, along with my new bookmark, out to my porch rocker. I slipped the suede portion between random pages near the center of the text. The bookmark worked fine. I leaned back and began to rock. A pang of guilt stirred. Was I wrong to include the agate…to honor Abbey? How would Lucinda feel if she knew about the stone? Was its inclusion an insult to Lucinda’s memory? Consternation swirling, I stared at the bookmark. If the shoe were on the other foot, if I were dead and Lucinda still alive, I would want her to go on whatever way was easiest for her. She would want the same for me. When I had lost my father, when I had arrived at the fort a stranger, Abbey had befriended me and taught me how to read. She had played a critical role, helping me through an extremely difficult time of my life. Like everyone else, her place on the bookmark had been earned. Arguably my analysis was a rationalization. More important, however, it eased my mind.

I held the five symbols in the palm of one hand. Henceforth, whenever I studied, those who had succored and mentored me would be close by. I ran my fingers of my other hand over the five tokens. Each was symbolic. Joined together in a single creation, they reflected something more. I had climbed out of the abyss. I had taken concrete steps to get on with my life.

***

As the New Year approached, anticipation of Edison's return to Fort Myers sparked excitement. But early winter slipped past with no sign of the renowned inventor. Hopes rejuvenated when, in early 1887, a forty-horsepower steam engine and a dynamo were delivered to Seminole Lodge, the name Edison had given to his winter estate.[444] At long last, in March, Edison arrived. Hoping to see him, to become a mucker if he opened a Florida laboratory, more than once I rode Cinda to Fort Myers, walking her back and forth on the road that fronted Edison's home. The strategy failed. Checking in town for information as to when he might be expected in a particular place was no more fruitful.

Shortly after the calendar had declared that spring had officially arrived, word spread that on the last Saturday evening of March, the lights would go on at Edison's estate. The entire town, including me, gathered outside for the big event, one that did not disappoint.[445] Oohs and aahs, akin to reactions common to 4th of July fireworks, filled the air. Never had Fort Myers seen a building so brilliantly lit. Never had the town seen a rhythmical dance of lighted rooms, as switches were flipped on and off.

Gradually, the crowd headed home. I stayed to the last, hoping I might catch a moment with Edison. Just when I was about to give up, fortune shined on me. Edison spotted me standing about halfway between his house and the river. I had endeavored to make myself visible.

Edison came my way. "Mican, it's nice to see you. How have you been?"

"Good, thank you." That he remembered my name was pleasing. "Your home, aglow, is amazing."

"I suspect it's more exciting for the folks here than for me. Having seen cities lit, the novelty has diminished." He gave his house a look before refocusing on me. "I'd love to talk, but…it's been a busy evening."

---

444 Grismer, Karl H., *The Story of Fort Myers*, op. cit., p. 115. (Edison finally opened his Fort Myers laboratory in 1928. It was a botanical laboratory that focused on developing rubber from plants. *Edison and Ford Winter Estates*, Wikipedia, 11 Dec. 2020<https://en.wikipedia.org/wiki/Edison_and_Ford_Winter_Estates>).
445 Ibid.

“I understand.” I tried to hide my disappointment, recognition that my visit with him was ending in the same moment it had begun.

“But if you can come back on Monday…how about at two, I’d like to see you then.”

He could have said four o’clock in the morning on any day, and I would have jumped at the opportunity. “That would be great. I’ll be here at two on Monday.”

“When you do, come right around to the porch.” He gestured at the wide expanse that ran across the rear of his home. “I’ll meet you there.”

Edison no sooner walked away than I started toward the place where Cinda was tethered. Even before I climbed aboard, my feet were seemingly off the ground. I was soaring.

***

Monday could not come fast enough. Riding Cinda, I left home early, arriving near Edison’s home a half-hour before the appointed time. I stayed a few hundred yards away where I gave Cinda a snack and had one myself. When my pocket watch said 1:50, I tethered Cinda to a tree near the border of Edison’s property and slowly continued around to the rear porch. Edison, who was seated there, got up.

“Welcome, Mican.”

I shook the hand he extended. “So nice of you to see me. I hope I’m on time.”

“Relax. You’re early. I was just sitting…contemplating…nothing in particular.” He motioned to the adjacent chair. “Have a seat.”

I sat down alongside him.

“Suppose we get business out of the way first. Then we can talk about whatever. Seem okay?”

“Sounds good to me.” Anything he suggested was fine.

“As things stand, I think I’ll come here next winter and open a lab. If I do, would you like to work here?”

“I’d be honored.”

“Good. That’s taken care of…except how we’ll be in touch.”

“I can stop by. I’m sure I’ll hear about your arrival. Around here it’s big news. Everyone knows.”

“Funny what excites people.” Edison leaned back and chuckled. “So, what should we talk about?” With casual informality, he shrugged. “Pick something. You tell me.”

His congenial demeanor helped relax me; the responsibility of choosing a subject did the opposite. I drew a blank, and, likely, my face showed it.

"Let's do this another way. Suppose I ask you a question, one that nobody can answer, at least with certainty…Is there a God?" Following a brief smile, he said, "What do you think?"

"Well…I have no proof, definitely not the type demanded by the scientific method. And not to beg off, but my answer depends in part on semantics." I swallowed hard. My response bore earmarks that I was avoiding the issue. But falling back on my experience in Mr. Wright's class years before made perfect sense. "My answer is a function of how one defines God. If God represents powers and events in the universe that we don't understand, then I believe in God. On the other hand, if it involves a being that hears and reacts to individual prayers and supplications, I'm skeptical."

"Makes sense." Edison nodded slowly. "But there's a considerable gap between those two scenarios. Where does God fit when it comes to the area in the middle?"

My old friend, but occasional enemy, the Law of the Excluded Middle, hammered my head. Edison's comment rightly suggested that my response had ignored a possible middle ground. What had been a great answer back in my teens, suddenly became incomplete; worse yet, superficial. I said, "Between the two markers, my view is ambiguous. I…I just don't know."

"Fair enough. No one else could answer the question, not authoritatively." Edison gazed thoughtfully into space, staring toward the Caloosahatchee. "'Science proves theories or it rejects them. I have never seen the slightest scientific proof of the religious theories of heaven or hell, of future life for individuals, or of a personal God. I earnestly believe that I am right; I cannot help believing as I do…I cannot accept as final any theory which is not provable. The theories of the theologians cannot be proved. Proof, proof! That is what I always have been after; that is what my mind requires before it can accept a theory as fact…The thing which most impresses me about theology is that it does not seem to be investigating. It seems to be asserting, merely, without actual study.'"[446]

Hearing him voice a view similar to mine was pleasing. Discretion kept me from pointing out that our positions were analogous. Whereas, his lent credence to mine, mine was of little consequence to him. The next time he discussed the subject, the last thing he would do was mention that Mican Reinbow concurred with him. A hiatus in the conversation ensued. Where his thoughts lay, I could not say. Mine

---

[446] Edison Thomas A., Interview in the *NY Times Magazine*, retrieved from *Thomas A. Edison Quotes*, goodreads.com, op. cit.

focused on the coherence with which Edison had expressed his view. More than an inventor and businessman, Edison was a thoughtful and articulate man of letters.

A minute eased past when finally, Edison said, "Do you know the most important rule in my laboratory?"

I yearned for a spark of brilliance, a cannon shot that would hone in on the canon. Sadly, I had no clue. Sitting silent, looking stupid, the diametric opposite of the wisdom I longed to display, was unthinkable. I said, "Determination, stick-to-itiveness, in the face of seeming dead ends."

"Not the answer I was looking for...but a good one. As I've often said, 'The three great essentials to achieve anything worthwhile are, first, hard work; second, stick-to-itiveness; third, common sense.'[447] All too often, people fail only because they give up." He looked me in the eye and said, "'When you have exhausted all possibilities, remember this—you haven't.'"[448] He punctuated his message with a gentle wave of his index finger. "But enough about that. Back to my original question, the most important rule in my lab. Care to hazard another guess?"

Thankful that he had reacted positively to my earlier answer, and certain I could not offer anything better, I said, "No, thank you."

"Fine. I'll tell you...The most important rule is: 'There are no rules here—we're trying to accomplish something here.'"[449]

I made another mental note as the conversation shifted to the mundane. Within a few minutes I was on my way, wondering how long it would be until I would speak to the great man again.

***

In the month that followed, I made weekly trips to town aboard Cinda. Each time, I rode by Edison's estate on the chance that I might see him. Each time, hope yielded to letdown. On April 27, 1887, an item in the Fort Myers Press said: "The dynamo to be used in lighting the town of Fort Myers by electricity arrived one day last week. As Mr. Edison is very busy and his stay short, we have our doubts as to whether he will light Fort Myers by electricity this year...However, the plant will be put in operation in good season next winter and we'll all rejoice."[450]

---

[447] *Thomas A. Edison Quotes (Author of St. Agnes' Stand)*, goodreads.com, 2 Mar. 2019 <https://www.goodreads.com/author/quotes/3091287.Thomas_A._Edison>.
[448] Ibid.
[449] Ibid.
[450] Grismer, Karl H., *The Story of Fort Myers*, op. cit., p. 115.

The future of Fort Myers appeared bright. But being part of huge Monroe County, whose seat was far away in Key West, Fort Myers barely got lip service from the region's political center. A school that had burned and bumpy dirt roads were but two of the issues that had been ignored. Action was demanded lest the town languish. Its highly successful, well-connected cattlemen, Jacob Summerlin, F. A. Hendry and James Hendry, among others, pressed politicians in Tallahassee to carve out a new county based in Fort Myers. In the first week of May 1887, the State Legislature passed a bill creating the new county,[451] one which, upon the motion of F. A. Hendry, was named in honor of Robert E. Lee.[452] Fort Myers had gained control of its destiny.

Temporary quarters for a courthouse were immediately obtained on the second floor of the Hendry General Store, and plans were drawn for a three-story, concrete courthouse building.[453] But the best of plans failed to materialize. Progress came slowly as Fort Myers suffered hard times. Not until December 1894 was a courthouse built, and it was a far cry from the plans drawn seven years before.[454] As for Thomas Edison, though his caretaker maintained Seminole Lodge, the great inventor failed to return to Fort Myers until the next century, on February 27, 1901. So much for the town's great expectations.

So too, for my great expectations. In 1888, I was disappointed. Again in 1889 and 1890, when Edison was still a no-show, I was disappointed. But admittedly, year by year, as hope lessened, the magnitude of my letdown diminished, though not linearly. In my mind the graph was a hyperbola, where my letdown "L," on a scale of ten, was a function of time "t" in years, expressed as follows: $L = 10/t$ for $t \geq 1$. That L would never reach zero reflected that my hope, albeit faint, would still be extant.

A typically mild day in December 1891, two weeks before Christmas, found me sitting on my porch rocking chair, savoring a juicy orange while contemplating principles of physics. On the path I had carved connecting my cabin to the Caloosahatchee, a man approached. Visitors to my cabin were nearly as rare as trains in Fort Myers. (Tracks connecting the town to the world beyond were not completed until 1904.[455]) My first thought, a hope-springs-eternal reaction, was that Edison may have arrived for the winter and sent a messenger to summon

---

451 Ibid. p. 124.
452 *See*, footnote 419, supra, quoting F. A. Hendry, *A History of the Early Days in Fort Myers.*
453 Grismer, Karl H., *The Story of Fort Myers*, op. cit., p. 124, 125.
454 Ibid., p. 125.
455 Ibid., p. 164.

me to his estate. Admittedly it was pie in the sky, but for want of a better explanation, hope stirred.

"Excuse me," said the man, as he drew close. "Are you Mican Reinbow?"

"Yes." My excitement was undeniable.

"I have papers for you." He handed me a two-page document. "You are hereby served with a Writ of Ejectment."

"A what?"

"An application for a court order removing you from these premises. All the details are contained in the papers." The man turned and headed back to the path where he disappeared.

I scanned the papers. They directed me: "…to appear at the Lee County Court in Fort Myers on Monday, the 6th day of January 1892, to show cause why an order should not be granted ejecting me from the premises hereinafter described…" A metes-and-bounds legal description of real property followed. I went back to the beginning and read the papers more slowly. Amidst the legal jargon, I gleaned that the plaintiff, Richard Barkley, claimed a certain 160-acre parcel of land under the Southern Homestead Act of 1866, as amended in 1868; that said parcel encompassed the area where my cabin stood; that I was a trespasser, an illegal squatter; and that I should be compelled to quit and vacate said premises forthwith, and in the event of my failure to do so, be removed by the Sheriff of Lee County.

Verve that had kindled when the process server had approached was long gone. Concern, apprehension bordering on panic, kindled. Was I about to lose my home? Did the Homestead Act—I had heard about it, but didn't know much—entitle someone to take my land? Was Florida's Seminole history, including three wars and their aftermath, about to repeat itself? Would I, a Black Seminole, get a fair shake in the white man's court. I had the better part of a month until I was directed to appear in the proceeding. Common sense said tomorrow was soon enough to find out where I stood. But the claim was too upsetting for me to wait until then. No way would I get a decent night's sleep. I grabbed a quick bite, fed Cinda some oats and rode her to town. I needed to speak with Bill Clay, the only person I could think of who might be able to help me. Clay, himself a homesteader in the area of Twelve-Mile Creek, about nine miles east of town,[456] had a strained relationship with the law. He had set up an illegal still in a shack behind a livery stable after Fort Myers

[456] Ibid., p. 109.

had voted in 1887 to go dry and had closed the town's two saloons, a closure that turned out short lived.[457]

When I arrived in town, I found Clay in the shack. I said, "You have a few minutes, Bill?"

"Yeah, unfortunately I got too much time on my hands." The squirrely guy with small eyes gritted his teeth, a couple of which were missing near the center of his mouth. "Things ain't never gotten right again, not since the bastards shut me down."

"My business has nothing to do with whiskey. I gave that up years ago." Handing him the papers which earlier had been served on me, I said, "A process server brought this little gift a couple of hours ago. To make a long story short, Richard Barkley—he's the petitioner—is suing to eject me from my cabin. He claims he owns the land under the Homestead Act."

"Interesting..." Clay skimmed the document, muttering along the way, "Why can't lawyers talk and write in English?" He spent another minute eyeing the papers. "You aware that I got my property over by Twelve-Mile Creek under the Homestead Act?"

"Yes, and I thought...maybe, you might be able to give me a little guidance, especially given your experience with the powers that be."

Clay shrugged. "I'm not a lawyer, but I'd love to see some of the snakes that shut me down eat crow." He glanced at the papers. "I see that Darby Jenks represents Barkley. You know him?"

"Not really."

"Well, let me tell you. He's a hack who doesn't know marmalade from manure when it comes to the law. For that matter, I doubt he could tell the difference on a slice of bread. Like lots of shysters who hang out a shingle, the dolt never went to school for the practice of law. He didn't even complete an apprenticeship.[458] He's all bluster. Ever since Peter O. Knight, the town's only real attorney, flew the coop to Tampa a couple

---

[457] Ibid., p. 124, 186. Two years after the town went dry, it voted to go wet again. The two saloons were re-opened.

[458] Katcher, Susan, *Legal Training in the United States: A Brief History*, 24 Wisconsin Law Journal 335, retrieved 30 Apr. 2019 <https://hosted.law.wisc.edu/wordpress/wilj/files/2012/02/katcher.pdf> stating at p. 347 that in the 19th century, "apprenticeship continued to be the standard means of legal education..." And at p. 343: "Lincoln himself had written. '[T]he cheapest, quickest and best way' [to become a lawyer was to] read Blackstone's *Commentaries*...get a license, and go to the practice and still keep reading." Katcher notes that as the 19th century wore on, the requirements to practice law became less strict. "The numbers are revealing: compared to 1800, when fourteen out of nineteen jurisdictions had required an apprenticeship, by 1860, only nine of thirty-one jurisdictions required one." (p. 345, 346).

of years ago, Fort Myers hasn't had a legit lawyer.[459] For that matter, the guy who sits on the bench in the so-called courthouse above the general store is anything but a legal genius. But all that could work to your advantage." Clay shot me a sly smile. "Good thing you don't play poker with the local card sharks."

The comment, one I had heard before, evidenced that my puzzlement was transparent.

"Let me explain. If you get yourself a decent argument—even if it's like swiss cheese, with a few holes—you might have a shot to save your place. Arm yourself with some fancy-sounding legal mumbo jumbo. Rehearse it so it sounds convincing, kinda the way a medicine man sells elixir…and you'll have a fightin' chance." He studied me, seemingly making sure I was absorbing the lesson. "Now, here's your ace in the hole. Let 'im know you're prepared to appeal it all the way to Tallahassee. That'll activate Judge Baker's Achilles heel. Most times when his decisions are appealed, they get reversed. Not knowing the ins and outs of the law, he's forced to shoot from the hip. Repeatedly the appellate courts have kicked his ass for errors. A few more of those decisions, suggestin' he's incompetent, which he is, and he might be removed from the bench. Even if he isn't, a few more errors, coupled with criticism from the *Fort Myers Press*, and he's dead meat at the polls. He knows it. So, whenever issues get messy, he tries to bail."

"Bail?"

"He pushes the parties to settle. That way, he can avoid making a decision." Clay chuckled.

I missed his humor.

"Baker thinks he's fooling people when he encourages them to settle. Claims he wants folks on both sides to leave his court happy. It's bull crap. His real motive is self-preservation. The guy's a chicken, afraid that the legal gurus upstairs will stick it up his rear…tag him for the inept clown that he is." Clay looked me in the eye. "I understand you're college educated. You oughta be able to put together sufficient patter to gum up his gavel."

I shrugged. "Don't know. But one thing sure—I'll damn well try." I thanked Clay and left. I unhitched Cinda, but rather than climbing aboard, I walked her slowly, all the time contemplating what Clay had said. I headed down First Street. When I reached Jackson, I turned toward the wharf, armed with a plan. I bought a ticket on the next day's boat to Key West, the Monroe County Seat.

---

[459] Grismer, Karl H., *The Story of Fort Myers*, op. cit., p.126.

***

The following morning, with suitcase in hand and one hundred dollars in my pocket, after arranging board for Cinda at Edgar Jones' stable, I took the boat to Key West. Arriving the next day, I went directly to the site of the Monroe County Courthouse on Whitehead Street, roughly a half mile from the wharf and Fort Zachary Taylor. The stunning judicial building, having opened a few months earlier, was in mint condition. The two-story, red-brick Georgian, reminiscent of photographs I had seen of Independence Hall in Philadelphia, bore a clock tower that rose one hundred feet above the ground.[460] Symmetric, about as wide as tall, its center section included a triangular pediment, beneath which columns rose from the ground portico to the base of the second-story portico, with another set of columns rising to the pediment. It was the antithesis of the Lee County Court, which sat upstairs over a Fort Myers general store. But comparing Lee and Monroe counties was like pitting a small garden against a huge farm. Fort Myers, Lee County's largest town, had a population about one-fiftieth of the more than eighteen thousand who lived in Key West, Monroe's largest city.[461] When it came to law libraries, the difference between Lee and Monroe was no less. Where Lee's book collection was a poor excuse for a joke, Monroe's was reputed to be the finest south of Tallahassee, more than four hundred miles to the north.

Were I not carrying my suitcase, I might have gone directly to the courthouse library. Instead, I went looking for an inexpensive boarding house. Just a few hundred yards away, around the corner on Flemming Street, I got myself a room, far from fancy, for four dollars a week. After checking in and grabbing a quick bite—the next day was soon enough to pick up foodstuffs—armed with two pencils and a pad, I went to the library. In the remaining hour before it closed, with the help of the librarian, I began to acclimate myself to the facility, learning the most efficient method to negotiate the stacks and locate specific cases in lawbooks.

The following morning, I was up early. I bought a variety of non-perishable foods, along with some fruits and vegetables that I took back to my room. After a quick breakfast, I returned to the library, pad and pencils in hand, along with a large supply of wrapped-up beef jerky in

---

[460] *Courthouses of Florida, Monroe County Historic Courthouse,* courthousesofflorida.com, 1 May 2019 <courthousesofflorida.com/courthouse/monroe-county-historic-courthouse/>.

[461] *Key West,* Wikipedia, 1 May 2019 <https://en.wikipedia.org/wiki/Key_West>.

my pocket.[462] I began examining statutes and litigation involving the rights of Native Americans, particularly Seminoles in Florida. For the next three days I focused on the treaties that moved the Seminoles from one place to another. Much of my time was spent copying countless sections from thick tomes. I dug deeply into the 1823 Treaty of Moultrie Creek between the Seminole Sovereign Nation and the United States, pursuant to which the Seminoles ceded twenty-four million acres. The treaty moved the Seminoles to a four-million-acre reservation in the middle of Florida, far from their more desirable coastal lands. It also provided them with compensation, including five thousand dollars for each of the ensuing twenty years.[463] Next I examined the Indian Removal Act, under which President Andrew Jackson had forced the Seminoles out of Florida, moving them west of the Mississippi River.[464]

Throughout my research, I looked for references to Black Seminoles like myself, who had amounted to about one-quarter of the Seminoles in Florida. The Black Seminoles, largely a product of inter-racial marriages between escaped Negro slaves and Seminoles, had generally lived apart from other Seminoles.[465] From all I could glean, the Black Seminoles had not negotiated or signed the Treaty of Moultrie Creek.[466]

For the ensuing two days, I educated myself about treaties generally and due process and what is required to affect the rights of impacted persons. Two more days were filled with research up and down blind alleys. A week after I had arrived in Key West, I hit upon the concept of adverse possession, a legal method to acquire the lands of another by possession. The concept required that a claimant's holding of real estate be actual, open and notorious, hostile to the owner, continuous and exclusive for the required period, twenty years at common law. Apart from the fact that I had only been back in Florida for roughly a decade, I appeared to meet all the prerequisites. My father had built the cabin on land where his father had lived, and we had resided in the structure decades earlier. I had a lot to talk about, and if Clay was right that Darby

---

462 *History of Jerky*, jerky.com website, 1 May 2019 <https://www.jerky.com/pages/history-of-jerky> stating: "Some say Native Americans made the first jerky (buffalo jerky) thousands of years ago, while others say an ancient Inca Tribe called the Quechua made jerky as early as the 1500's [sic]. Whatever the case, the time-tested recipe has been passed from generation to generation."
463 *1822 James Monroe — Treaty of Moultrie Creek*, stateoftheunionhistory.com website, 2 May 2019 <www.stateoftheunionhistory.com/2017/07/1822-james-monroe-treaty-of-moultrie.html>.
464 Ibid.
465 *Seminole, Land Claims,* Wikipedia, 1 May 2019 <https://en.wikipedia.org/wiki/Seminole>.
466 Ibid.

Jenks was anything but a legal wizard, there was an excellent chance he would not know the ins and outs of adverse possession. For that matter, he might not know anything about it.

After two days of copying down information, mostly case citations, names and significant quotations, I packed my things and sailed home to my Fort Myers cabin. For the next two weeks, I devoted every day writing an eighteen-page memorandum laying out my legal arguments. In my neatest penmanship, I made a copy for the judge. Evenings I rehearsed what I would say in court. What at first was a choppy oral presentation evolved into an all-but-memorized exposition. Complete with Clay's tip, my ace in the hole, I was armed and ready for battle.

***

The 6th of January 1892. I arrived in town forty minutes before the appointed time for my court appearance at 10:00 A.M. I climbed the stairs over the general store to the makeshift courtroom. It was deserted. Behind two tables that faced the judge's bench, there were several rows of chairs. Unsure if mine was the only case on the docket or which table was for the respondent, I took a chair in the back. Nervous, I sat alone, silently rehearsing my argument.

A few minutes before ten, Richard Barkley, accompanied by his lawyer, Darby Jenks, entered the courtroom. They seated themselves at the table off to my left. I considered moving forward to the one on the right, but uncertain, I waited. Just moments after the clock behind me struck ten, Judge Baker, a beady-eyed figure whose scruffy beard came to a point, took the bench. Barkley and Jenks jumped from their seats, and I did so as well. We all reseated ourselves once the judge sat down. He looked my way.

"Are you Mican Reinbow?"

"Yes, Your Honor."

The judge motioned me forward and gestured at the open table. "That's yours."

I placed my papers on the table and seated myself.

"Mr. Reinbow, are you representing yourself?"

"Yes, Your Honor."

"Okay, then we can go ahead." Judge Baker turned to the other table. "Mr. Jenks, proceed."

Jenks stood up. "May it please the Court. My client, the petitioner Richard Barkley, is here seeking a Writ of Ejectment against the respondent Mican Reinbow. This is an open and shut case. Mr. Reinbow is illegally and wrongfully occupying a cabin on the lands of the petitioner. Said lands, to wit, 160 acres, were lawfully acquired by the petitioner pursuant to the Southern Homestead Act of 1866. We respectfully request that this Court issue an order directing the defendant to vacate the cabin and said lands, and upon his failure to do so, that the sheriff be directed to remove him."

"Are you seeking removal forthwith?"

"Your Honor, the petitioner has very generously authorized me to allow the respondent thirty days to find another place to live."

Judge Baker turned my way. "Mr. Reinbow, it appears the petitioner has offered you a very reasonable path. Do you wish to follow it?"

Taking a cue from Jenks' earlier action, I stood up. "No, Your Honor. It is my position that the petitioner's claim has no merit."

"Really?" Judge Baker's eyes were wide. "And on what basis do you challenge the petitioner's claim?" His tone, spiced with a trace of incredulity, hinted that he doubted I could substantiate my objection.

"Your Honor, the 160 acres that the petitioner claims are part of a much larger parcel, several million acres that were allegedly acquired by the United States in 1823 as a result of the Treaty of Moultrie that was executed between the Seminole Sovereign Nation and the United States."

"You say allegedly. Are you questioning that treaty, Mr. Reinbow?" Judge Baker's voice resonated with disbelief.

"Yes, Your Honor, to the extent that it purported to take the lands of persons who were not party to the treaty."

"And what parties might that be?"

"Black Seminoles. They were not part of the Seminole Sovereign Nation or its tribes. They lived separate and apart. And I'm sure Your Honor is well aware of the very basic principle of contract law: Parties to an agreement cannot bind non-consenting third parties.[467] Moreover, the Constitution, under the due process clause of the Fifth Amendment, forbids the taking of property of any person without notice and an opportunity to be heard. My father and grandfather, Black Seminoles, were not parties to the treaty. They were not given notice or an opportunity to be heard. That said, principles of contract law and due process preclude the purported taking of their land and the cabin my father built there back in the middle of this century."

"I see," said Judge Baker, his eyes a bit glazed.

"That is only my first point. May I continue?"

Judge Baker nodded.

---

[467] Ibid.

"Even assuming for the sake of argument that the Southern Homestead Act of 1866 was enforceable, and for the reasons already stated, that would be erroneous, I have acquired my cabin and the land on which it sits by adverse possession. My father built it more than forty years ago on lands that had been occupied by his father before him. Our possession, which has been actual, open and notorious, hostile, continuous and exclusive for much more than the twenty-year common-law period, gives me title." Even if Jenks was familiar with the requirements for adverse possession, which was doubtful, as a relative newcomer to town, there was little chance he knew that I had been absent from Fort Myers for a number of years. Loner that I was, living five miles from town, hardly anyone knew that.

"Very interesting." Judge Baker focused on Jenks. "Counselor, what do you say?"

"Uh…may I have a moment to confer with my client?"

"Certainly."

"Excuse me, Your Honor. I have prepared a legal memorandum in support of my arguments." I handed it to Judge Baker.

"Your Honor, I demand a copy," said Jenks.

"I have one here for myself," I said. "I will hand copy another for Mr. Jenks and take it to his office tomorrow, if that's okay?"

"Fine," said Judge Baker. He waited while Jenks whispered back and forth with his client. Once the conference ended, Judge Baker said, "Mr. Jenks, do you wish to reply to the respondent's arguments?"

"They lack merit, Your Honor. My client got his property under an act of the United States Congress."

"I understand," said Judge Baker. "But explain to me how that terminated the respondent's rights."

"Acts of Congress take precedence."

"Excuse me, Your Honor. Mr. Jenks voices a bald-faced conclusion. And he has not addressed my claim of adverse possession."

Still standing, Jenks barked, "So-called adverse possession is an absurd excuse to steal the property of a legitimate owner."

"Apparently, Mr. Jenks dislikes the concept of adverse possession. And well that may be, adverse possession is the law of this jurisdiction and must be applied. Moreover, Mr. Jenks cites no authorities to substantiate any of his contentions. He has failed to address the rights of Black Seminoles, including contractual and due process rights. By contrast, my memorandum of law cites ample cases and authorities demonstrating that my rights persist and that I own my cabin and the area surrounding it. Regardless of the outcome in this court, I am confident that my memorandum of law when presented to an appellate court—and if need be, I intend to pursue this matter to higher courts—will prove me right." I had played my ace in the hole, the one Clay had provided.

"Uh...let's see what we can do to...uh...to resolve this matter," said Judge Baker.

His visible discombobulation intrigued me. I waited for him to play a card.

"Gentlemen, perhaps we can cut the baby in half?"

That Judge Baker was begging a solution buoyed me, but I needed more than a Solomonesque compromise. I said, "I can't live in half a cabin."

"One moment, Your Honor," said Jenks. After conferring with his client, he said, "My client has an extremely magnanimous proposal. He will permit the respondent to remain in his cabin for an entire year."

"Excellent," said Judge Baker. He turned to me. "The petitioner has made you a very generous offer. I urge you to take it."

"No thank you, Your Honor. I would rather have this court and, ultimately, the appellate courts, determine my rights."

"Mr. Reinbow, how do expect to settle this case when you offer the petitioner nothing?" A marginal increase in the volume of Judge Baker's voice hinted at pique.

"Your Honor, with all due respect, I have never sought a settlement. All along, I have been willing to have you examine the authorities, apply the law and render a decision."

A tomblike silence pervaded the courtroom. Perhaps no more than ten seconds elapsed when, having done my homework, I said, "Let me put the matter into perspective. My cabin, garden, and the area I occupy are about 40-yards deep, extending roughly 150 yards to the river. That amounts to approximately 6000 square yards. An acre is equal to 4840 square yards. Put another way, I occupy roughly 1.2 acres of the 160 acres that the petitioner claims. If the courts, appellate included, sustain my argument regarding the claims of Black Seminoles, petitioner stands to lose all his property. Even assuming he has a fifty-fifty chance of winning in court, and I believe the authorities I have cited make his odds far, far less, he stands to lose well over one hundred times as much as he stands to win. It's akin to playing roulette and betting a dollar on black, but getting less than a penny back in profit for a win. Only a fool would make that bet...On second thought, even a fool would decline."

Another silence ensued.

"Your Honor," I said, "may I make a proposal?"

"Please do."

"If the petitioner grants me a 100-year lease on my little 40 × 150-yard plot for one dollar, I will withdraw my objections and recognize his title." I stole a glance at Jenks. He looked incredulous. "Barring that, I'll let the courts decide the matter."

Judge Baker nodded slowly. "Very interesting." He turned to the petitioner's table. "The respondent has made a very intriguing offer. He's giving you what you have asked for in your papers—title."

Judge Baker had to be kidding. I had offered the petitioner a moth-eaten sack of gold...after the gold had been removed. And much like that gold, Judge Baker had shown his true colors: yellow, yellow and yellow! Bill Clay had read the jurist perfectly. He was a politician, short on knowledge and fearful of appellate courts that would expose his incompetence. He was all but begging for a way out.

"Your Honor, may I take a minute to confer with my client?"

"Certainly."

Lawyer and client whispered back and forth. Though I could not pick up on the substance, vituperative moments hinted they were hardly in complete agreement. Several minutes passed. Their confab became totally inaudible whispers.

Finally, Jenks stood up. "The petitioner accepts the respondent's offer. He will grant the respondent his 100-year lease on his plot for one dollar in exchange for recognition of the petitioner's title."

"Mr. Barkley," said Judge Baker. "You heard your attorney, and that's what you want to do?"

"Yes, Your Honor."

"Excellent. Then the matter is settled." Judge Baker sat up tall in a satisfied posture. "Mr. Jenks, you'll draw up the papers, including a stipulation discontinuing this proceeding and the agreed-upon lease, and you'll submit the same to the respondent for signature. If any problems arise, a circumstance I presume you gentlemen will avoid, you can come back here." He looked at the petitioner's table and then at me. "Assuming there is nothing else requiring my consideration, we are adjourned." He banged his gavel.

Pleased with my success, I packed up my papers. I wondered how a knowledgeable appellate court would have reacted to my legal arguments, given the opportunity to weigh them. But my curiosity only went so far. A role of the dice in a field where I lacked expertise paled in comparison to the excellent settlement I had negotiated. I checked an urge to whistle as I headed down the stairs, where I began selecting some peaches from the crates located outside the first-floor general store. Jenks came my way.

"You handled yourself very well in the courtroom. Have to admit, I didn't expect that you'd come armed with all those arguments and papers."

"Appreciate that."

Jenks gazed off into space. "Well, like they say, the exception proves the rule."

I tried unsuccessfully to make sense of his remark. "What rule? What exception?"

He gave me a look. "You need me to spell it out?"

"Apparently."

He shrugged. "Negroes, Seminoles…neither are all that sharp. You being both, you're even more unlikely. But don't get me wrong. You're the exception, the one who proves the rule."

"Really," I said, forcing a sneer.

"Hey, don't get your ass in an uproar. I'm paying you a big compliment."

Sure, a bigoted, left-handed one. I nodded repeatedly, but only for effect. "I see your point. Yeah, the exception proves the rule. Me, a Black Seminole, just got a fair shake in the white man's court. Talk about an exception…Yup, the exception proves the rule." I walked away.

Chapter XXIX

MY YEARS AT THE TAIL END OF THE 19TH CENTURY were among the most nondescript I had yet experienced, not that unremarkable was bad. With my cabin and land in good shape and my 100-year lease duly filed in the Lee County Clerk's Office, I was comfortably established in Southwest Florida. My path crossed that of Richard Barkley no more than a handful of times throughout the period. Exchanges of cordial hellos with virtually no other conversation indicated that our net impact on each other was negligible; and that was how we preferred it, at least I did. Apart from trips to town, on average biweekly, my life was largely solitary. My garden and fruit trees, coupled with lots of fishing and occasional hunting, provided almost all my food. The suede of wild boars, the fur of wolves and bobcats, and snakeskin, all of which I trapped, furnished me with materials I could trade at the general stores and elsewhere.

Employing the Seminole skills my father had taught me, I had fashioned a dugout canoe, much like the one he had helped me make years earlier. Others, some of whom had observed me paddling the Caloosahatchee, had induced me to make them one. The long process demanded patience, but I had the time. By the advent of 1890, requests for canoes had turned my skill into a small business. Using an ax and fire, I hand-hewed the canoes from abundant cypress logs.[468] I buried the logs in mud for about eighteen months, after which I dug them up, allowing them to dry. Cutting, scraping and burning, I worked the dugouts to a uniform thickness. Tapping them with sticks, listening to the pitch of the sound, confirmed they were just right.[469] Each canoe

---

[468] *Florida Memory – Seminole Indian dugout canoe – Everglades, Florida,* floridamemory.com, 18 Aug. 2019 <https://www.floridamemory.com/items/show155403>.
[469] Ibid.

brought me about seventy-five dollars. Rather than needing to dip into my cash reserves, my assets grew year by year.

So too, I continued to improve the simple cabin my father had built. Using wood from scrub pines, I surrounded the cabin and adjoining garden with a split-rail fence, 40 yards on each side. I added a gate at the start of the path to the river. The fence allowed Cinda to roam free rather than wear a tether. I built a hut, posts on the sides and palm leaves nailed to wood for a roof. The simple structure provided her with shade from sun and shelter from heavy rain.

Much like me, Fort Myers saw years that included progress as the 20th century arrived. Where my headway was almost linear, a graph with a slight incremental climb, Fort Myers faced a series of challenges before its upturn was realized. Disappointment following Edison's failure to return after the 1887 lighting of his home heralded a number of difficult years. Expected rail lines, a potential boon for the town, were instead extended to Punta Gorda, 30 miles to the north. The latter became the shipping center of Southwest Florida, leaving Fort Myers to languish.[470] In 1893, a financial panic gripped the nation. Fort Myers suffered the effects, with cattle prices dropping to record lows.[471] On December 29, 1894, record cold, 24 degrees, what in later years was termed the Big Freeze, chilled the hearts of Fort Myers' residents.[472] Little did they realize that the arctic blast, just four days after Christmas, presaged an unexpected Santa Claus, bearing a sack laden with sweet fruit, a combination of oranges and grapefruit. Another freeze in early February, dropping local temperatures to 28 degrees, dipped the thermometer even lower to the north. The hard freeze destroyed the citrus crop throughout most of Florida, but not in the Fort Myers area. Limited supply skyrocketed prices. Fruit of a single tree brought as much as two hundred dollars.[473] Local finances received an unexpected boost. So began a reinvigoration of the town's economy. Construction of the stunning Royal Palm Hotel (originally named the Fort Myers Hotel) altered the image of Fort Myers from a "cow town" to a winter tourist destination.[474] The year saw the town get an electric plant, bringing lights to streets and homes.[475] Cattlemen commenced a building boom.[476]

---

470 Grismer, Karl H., *The Story of Fort Myers*, op. cit., p. 133.
471 Ibid.
472 Ibid., p. 135.
473 Ibid.
474 Ibid., p. 177.
475 Ibid., p.144-146.
476 Ibid., p.148.

Though the growth was nice and my personal life was improving, less auspicious influences were also evolving. A decision of the United States Supreme Court in the case of *Plessy v. Ferguson*[477] dictated that people of color, like me, were destined to suffer the repression of Jim Crow for many more decades. I had followed the case as it had worked its way through the appeals process. It had the potential to end the reactionary trend that had followed Reconstruction. Hope, more than realism, had kept me optimistic. Ultimately, the high court crushed my optimism. The justices ruled that Louisiana's Separate Car Act, which required separate, but equal accommodations for white and non-white passengers, was not violative of the Equal Protection clause of the Fourteenth Amendment; and that states had broad discretion to regulate health, morals and safety under the so-called "police power." The Court upheld the conviction and fine imposed on Plessy, a man of mixed race, for riding in the white-only train car. For those of us of color, the decision was a nail in our coffins. Aspirations for an America in which states could no longer legislate inequality vanished. Separate but equal, a pernicious euphemism for sanctioned discrimination, had become the law of the land. Slavery may have been an outlawed relic, but antebellum intolerance was alive and well. It enjoyed the imprimatur of the United States Supreme Court.

With *Plessy* having cast my second-class citizenship in stone, I felt I had no chance. The bleak picture enticed an alcoholic response. A visit to the Parker-Blount General Store brought the issue to the forefront. Bottles of whiskey lining a back shelf confronted me. I reached out, pawing the narrow neck of one. I lifted the bottle from the shelf. I could all but taste its soporific contents. Self-debate raged. Temptation and rationalization, rather than logic, cajoled me to make the purchase. But was it a solution? The answer was a resounding *no*. Resorting to my prior mind-numbed world, a self-destructive act that would plummet me back into the depths of a woeful abyss, would confer a victory on the bigots. Much as *Plessy* enraged me, I refused to let it destroy me. Nullify it, I couldn't. Outmaneuver it, I could. Living several miles outside of town in my cloistered world, I could maintain my way of life, largely free of its onus. I placed the bottle back onto the shelf. A perverse sense of satisfaction gripped me. My country, its ultimate arbiter, the Supreme Court, had tried to shaft me. I had all but neutralized the impact of its

[477] *163 U.S. 537 (1896)*. In *Plessy*, Justice Harlan, the lone dissenter in a 7-1 decision, predicted that the case would prove as odious as *Dred Scott v. Sanford*. (*Bookmarks'* author's comment: Justice Harlan's prediction proved true. By blessing "separate but equal," *Plessy* legitimized a plethora of state laws that sanctioned racial discrimination, wiping out the advances that had been enacted during Reconstruction.)

evil. It was as if I had won a victory, albeit Pyrrhic. Impose discriminatory rules, those in power could, but control my life, they could not. More important, they had no power to dictate my thoughts, the concepts my mind entertained. I was free to pursue whatever intellectual pursuits I wished. The more complex the concept, the more profound my defiance. Nothing was more complex than the emerging concepts in the world of modern physics. My determination to dig deeply into that most involute realm of science was instant. Knowledge of those principles, far beyond the capacity of the hatemongers who longed to make me second class, would transport me to a plateau high above the bigoted devils.

Shortly before the *Plessy* decision had been handed down in 1896, I had read a brief newspaper clipping about a Dutch physicist, Hendrik Lorentz, who had come up with a series of equations termed, "Contractions." His expressions were a product of the Michelson-Morley research that had determined the speed of light; that it was constant in any reference frame. My only knowledge about the Contractions was that they suggested that mass, length and time might be altered as matter travels close to the speed of light. But that tidbit alone, which challenged fundamental principles of Newtonian mechanics, was sufficient to intrigue me. A more esoteric area of study in any branch of knowledge was impossible to imagine. A compulsion to explore it ignited. Unfortunately, there was no chance that anyone in Fort Myers had any information or materials regarding the Contractions. Consequently, I had to write away to acquire such.

It was 1897 before I finally received anything substantial, a copy of a paper showing the derivation of the Contractions. During the ensuing week, I spent hours every day reading, rereading and analyzing the paper. To the extent that principles of algebra and geometry, including the Pythagorean Theorem, were sufficient to understand the derivations, they were less complex than I had anticipated. That said, they were anything but simple. I struggled to grasp their counterintuitive facets. Performing the derivations on my own was harder yet. But repetition and review gradually enabled me to solidify my understanding.

The three Contractions, were as follows:[478]

---

[478] The Lorentz Contractions as enumerated in this text are expressed using a modern notation, rather than that which Lorentz used. The contractions flow from the principle that the speed of light in a vacuum is constant in any inertial reference frame, as predicted by the Maxwell Equations and the Michelson-Morley experiment. A simple, though far from elegant, derivation for the time contraction formula is as follows: Consider a vehicle with an overhead beam of light in the vehicle's inertial reference frame (at rest relative to the vehicle) shining down at an observer in the vehicle. At all

$$L = L_0\sqrt{1 - \frac{v^2}{c^2}} \qquad T = \frac{T_0}{\sqrt{1-\frac{v^2}{c^2}}} \qquad M = \frac{M_0}{\sqrt{1-\frac{v^2}{c^2}}}$$

where L_0, T_0, and M_0 represent the length, time and mass of matter in an observational reference frame (i.e., a reference frame at rest relative to the matter); *L, T*, and *M* represent the length, time and mass of the same matter in a reference frame moving relative to the observational reference frame; *c*, the speed of light; and *v*, the velocity of the matter relative to the observational reference frame.

Without drifting too far into an abstruse world, in each of the three expressions, the value of the radical can never be more than one (It is

---

times the observer would see the light traveling straight down. Letting T_0 equal the time for the light to go from its source to the observer and "*c*" the speed of light, and using the simple formula "Distance = Rate × Time," the distance the light would travel from its source to the observer in the vehicle would equal "cT_0." Assume the vehicle is traveling in a straight line perpendicular to the beam at a constant velocity "*v*." In time "*T*" the vehicle would travel a distance "*vT*" (again using Rate × Time). For an observer outside the inertial reference frame of the vehicle, owing to the movement of the vehicle, the light ray would appear to travel at an angle, or, more precisely, the hypotenuse of a right triangle whose other two sides, "cT_0" and "*vT*," were established above. Again using Rate × Time, the hypotenuse of the triangle would be "*cT*," the speed of light multiplied by the time the vehicle traveled down the track. Using the Pythagorean Theorem, that the square of the hypotenuse of a right triangle equals the sum of the squares of the other two sides, yields the following equation, which ultimately shows the time "*T*" as measured by the observer outside the vehicle's inertial reference frame vis-à-vis the time "T_0" measured by the observer inside the vehicle's inertial reference frame:

$$c^2T^2 = c^2T_0^2 + v^2T^2$$

$$c^2T^2 - v^2T^2 = c^2T_0^2$$

$$T^2 - \frac{v^2T^2}{c^2} = T_0^2$$

$$T^2(1 - \frac{v^2}{c^2}) = T_0^2$$

$$T^2 = \frac{T_0^2}{1 - \frac{v^2}{c^2}}$$

$$T = \frac{T_0}{\sqrt{1 - \frac{v^2}{c^2}}}$$

By way of example, using a velocity for the vehicle of .98*c* (98% of the speed of light), the contraction formula shows that the time "t" that would be measured by a passenger in the vehicle would be one-fifth of that which would be measured by an observer outside the vehicle's inertial reference frame.

always the square root of a number between 0 and 1). And because c, the speed of light, roughly 186,000 miles per *second*, is so immense, the value of the radical is extremely close to one for all observations in our everyday world. Even at the unthinkable speed of 186,000 miles per *hour*, 1/3600 the speed of light, the value of the radical would be approximately one $\left(\sqrt{1-\frac{(\frac{c}{3600})^2}{c^2}} = \sqrt{1-\frac{1}{3600^2}} = \sqrt{1-\frac{1}{12960000}} = .9999999\right)$. Ergo, at 186,000 miles per hour, the measured length would be $.9999999L_0$. The contraction would be negligible, certainly invisible to the naked eye. The impact on mass and time would likewise be negligible.

Confused, but fascinated, I tried to comprehend the significance of the formulae. Simple mathematics had already demonstrated that because the effect of the Contractions only came into play at velocities approaching the speed of light, for all intents and purposes, the principles of Newtonian mechanics held true in day-to-day world experiences. That, however, still begged the fascinating question: What happens to time and matter when travel approaches the speed of light? Three different conclusions competed. Each had a turn as my favorite. Together they boggled my brain.

The first, what I understood to be the view of Lorentz, commanded the utmost respect. Who was I to argue with the genius who had come up with the equations? Lorentz held the view that "matter (electrons)" moved through a "completely motionless" ether.[479] While he considered the length contraction "a real physical effect," he deemed the time contraction a mathematical device "to simplify the calculation from the resting system to a 'fictitious' moving system."[480] But skeptical as I was that the ether existed, I was reluctant to accept Lorentz's interpretation.

A second possibility was that the effects on length, time and mass, as reflected by the equations, were nothing more than illusions. The convenient explanation appealed to my common sense.[481] But thoughts

---

[479] *Lorentz ether theory explained*, Everything Explained Today website, 5 May 2019 <https://everything.explained.today/Lorentz_ether_theory/>.

[480] Ibid.

[481] Whether length contraction is real or an illusion remains a subject of debate among physicists today. *See*, *Is length contraction only a result related to observation, or a real contraction?* quora.com, 5 May 2019 <https://www.quora.com/Is-length-contraction-only-a-result-related-to-observation-or-a-real-contraction?> where responders voice conflicting views. For example, "The length contraction is not a visual thing; it is not an illusion; it is a real contraction." (Richard Muller, Prof. Physics, UCBerkley, author of *Now—The Physics of Time*). "It's a real effect, in that it has real consequences, but is relative of course." (John Steele,

of the Doppler effect,[482] as it related to sound, dampened my enthusiasm for this simple solution. When one stands alongside a stationary train, its horn emits an unchanging sound. But the horn of a passing train has a higher pitch as it approaches, which grows lower as it passes. To an observer standing on the platform, the frequency of the sound is higher on approach because more sound waves pass each second, owing to the speed of the train being *added* to the normal speed of sound. By way of contrast, to the observer on the platform, the frequency of the sound drops as the train passes and pulls away. Fewer sound waves reach the platform each second because the speed of the sound arriving there is *reduced* by the speed of the train. But someone riding the train would hear a constantly pitched sound. Nevertheless, one could hardly say that the changing pitch heard by the observer on the platform is not real.

The more I thought about it, the more I believed that the results reflected by the Lorentz Contractions were real and that they existed even without an ether. The tantalizing idea that time could pass more slowly and length could contract depending upon reference frame grew more credible. I began playing with the equations, making up hypothetical problems. I had worked through several, when I came up with one that was partly inspired by the Doppler effect for sound. I drew a diagram with two cannons, ten feet apart on a train platform, with a twenty-foot train car racing past at 98% of the speed of light. I imagined that at the instant the center of the train car passed the midpoint between the cannons, the cannons were simultaneously fired. I plugged my hypothetical numbers into Lorentz's length contraction to find out what length an observer, standing midway between the cannons, would measure for "L," the length of the train as it raced past. (At all times, a

---

PhD in General Relativity. But cf. "Length contraction is a highly misunderstood feature of Relativity. Nothing is contracted and when you look at a moving object you can calculate its 'proper length', which is its actual length." (Eli Pasternak, MsEE, BsEE, 28 patents, EM Fields, comm theory, quantum mechanics, relativity). "There is no real contraction. The length of an object never changes in its own rest frame, regardless of how it moves relative to others. The length contraction is apparent, a function of the relative velocity between the observer and the object being observed." (Viktor T. Toth, IT pro, part-time physicist). (*Bookmarks'* author's comment: Without purporting to challenge those with an expertise in modern physics, the foregoing views arguably reflect less conflict than they seemingly suggest. Whether one considers the length contraction "real," is arguably a matter of semantics. If one defines an object's "length" as its rest or proper length, there is no contraction. On the other hand, if one defines its "length" as that which is measured depending upon frame of reference, the contraction is, indeed, real.)

482 The Doppler effect was advanced by Christian Doppler in 1842. *Christian Doppler and the Doppler effect*, AGU Advancing Earth and Space Science, 30 Apr. 2020 <https//:agupubs.onlinelibrary.wiley.com/doi/abs/10.1029/EO065i048p01193>.

passenger on the train, being at rest relative to the train, would measure the length of the train as twenty feet, L_0 .)

$$L = L_0\sqrt{1 - \frac{v^2}{c^2}} \;=\; 20\sqrt{1 - \frac{(.98c)^2}{c^2}} \;=\; 20\sqrt{1 - \frac{.9604c^2}{c^2}} \;=$$

$$20\sqrt{1 - .9604} \;\cong\; 20\sqrt{.04} \;\cong\; 20(.2) \;\cong\; 4 \text{ feet.}$$ [483]

The observer standing between the cannons would measure the train as four feet long. With the cannons ten feet apart, the cannon balls would easily miss either end of the otherwise twenty-foot train. Never in my studies of mathematics and science had I encountered such a stunning result. It blew my mind! I recalculated it three times, confirming its accuracy. I pondered the possibility that it might be a mathematical quirk stemming from the fact that the speed of light was constant. A return to the explanation of illusion was inveigling. But Lorentz had rejected that conclusion. I did so too.

I went outside to my rocking chair to contemplate the oddity. I had been rocking and ruminating for nearly an hour when a bizarre thought exploded! At the instant the cannon balls were fired, a passenger on the train (applying Lorentz's Contraction) would measure the distance between the cannons, which would appear to be flying past, as 2 feet. How could they miss the train, even if it had shrunk to 4 feet? Further complicating the issue, the passenger on the train, being at rest relative to the train, would still measure the train at 20 feet. The anomaly stupefied me.

For the next two days, I repeatedly reexamined the problem. At night, as my brain endeavored to make sense of the incongruous calculations, my sleep was fitful. Equations, explanations and confusion permeated my mind. I longed to discuss it with someone. There was no one in Fort Myers who would have a clue what I was talking about. For that matter, they would deem me daft.

On the third day after I had worked the problem, I was out in my garden picking some tomatoes when a thunderbolt struck! At the instant the cannons were fired, the center of the train would be racing closer to one of the cannons and farther from the other. Analogizing to the

[483] *Bookmarks'* author's comment: The train-and-cannons problem set forth in the text is the identical problem that over a half-century ago inspired my college apartment-mates and myself, when studying modern physics, to make up numerous other hypothetical problems involving the Lorentz Contractions. Fascinated, we continued into the wee hours.

Doppler effect that occurs with sound, applying Lorentz's time contraction,[484] the observer on the train would record a minuscule time gap between the firing of the cannons. That gap explained the anomaly, why the cannon balls missed the train.

I ran inside and, with pencil and paper in hand, began doing calculations using Lorentz's time contraction. They confirmed my conjecture, at least as a matter of mathematics. That said, I was well aware that scientifically, empirically, I had proved nothing. But that was of little moment. I had adopted a theory—in truth, speculation—that I liked. That was enough. Would it be proved valid? I had grave doubts. That didn't bother me either. What did, however, was that answers, determinative ones, would not come for years, perhaps centuries...maybe never. Experiments involving matter traveling close to the speed of light were next to impossible. In the interim, there would be debate whether the principles of Newtonian mechanics go out the window as velocities progress closer to that of light. Of course, most on planet Earth would comfortably reside in their Newtonian world, their concepts of time, length and mass unaffected by velocity.

I once again went out to the porch and the comfort of my rocker. I had added a second, not that there had been a need for it. That's not entirely true. Just as Walter had maintained a seat for Wilma, I now had one for Lucinda. Like Walter, I talked to my spouse. I gave Lucinda's rocker a push. The chair danced back and forth. "I'm trying to do better," I said. "I'm trying to keep my promise...searching for my soul, somewhere in the world of math and physics...It's not easy when half of me is gone. I miss you, Darling." I watched Lucinda's rocker slowly come to a halt owing to friction with the porch floor and the surrounding air. Another time I might have written a differential equation describing the rocker's damped harmonic motion. Instead, I gave the rocker another

---

[484] Though Mican's analogy to the Doppler effect for sound may have been less than perfect, it must be kept in mind that he was brainstorming the problem in 1897, eight years before Einstein propounded his Theory of Relativity in 1905. Unlike the Doppler effect in the case of sound or a moving-boat wave in water, where a medium is involved (air and water respectively), light waves do not require a medium. That said, physics subsequent to Mican's analysis did indeed confirm the Doppler effect in the case of light waves. *See*, *Relativistic Doppler effect*, Wikipedia, 30 Apr. 2020 <https://www.en.wikipedia.org/wiki/Relativistic_Doppler_effect> stating: "The *relativistic Doppler effect* is the change in frequency (and wavelength) of light, caused by the relative motion of the source and the observer (as in the classical Doppler effect), when taking into account effects described by the special theory of relativity. The relativistic Doppler effect is different from the non-relativistic Doppler effect as the equations include the time dilation effect of special relativity and do not involve the medium of propagation as a reference point." (emphasis from original)

push. After watching it for a few seconds, I closed my eyes, imagining Lucinda at my side, swaying blissfully to and fro.

In the days that ensued, I penned a couple of letters to noted physicists, hoping for a reaction to my analysis. My correspondence drew no responses. Perhaps the recipients deemed my ideas absurd. Whatever the future held for the Lorentz Contractions and their bizarre implications, I hoped that the world would accept them graciously. Unfortunately, history dictated otherwise. Heretics who had denied the Earth was the center of the universe had been persecuted.[485]

***

As the 20th century dawned, like many others in Fort Myers, I doubted that Thomas Edison would ever return to Seminole Lodge, his supposed winter home. Even in his absence, his caretaker had maintained the house and property in mint condition, turning it "into a tropical paradise."[486] Fourteen years had elapsed, when shock of shocks, the great man reappeared in 1901. Word spread like current through a circuit, one with manifold parallel and series connections. Several times I walked and rode past his estate, often dawdling, on perchance he would see and engage me in conversation. My efforts went for naught. As spring approached, I mounted the courage to knock at his door. His caretaker informed me that Edison was out for the day. I left a message, one that made it clear I was always available. Nothing came of my effort. Soon enough Edison returned to his northern headquarters. In the winters that ensued, he became a regular winter resident. I hoped he might contact me. No such luck. Several times I rode by his home, endeavoring to be conspicuous. The efforts were futile. I might have knocked had he not ignored my earlier message.

New Year's Day 1907 had recently passed. I had celebrated my 55th birthday. Well, I hadn't actually celebrated, but it had occurred the preceding October 29th, the date selected by the Wrights when they had surprised me with a party years before. I had just finished eating lunch when my attention was drawn to a knock at my cabin door, an occurrence less frequent than my birthdays. I peeked out the front window. The sharp angle necessary to view the visitor made it impossible for me to see who was there. I went to the front door and opened it. I jerked back, my mouth agape. On the porch, before me, stood Thomas Edison.

---

485 *1633, Galileo is convicted of heresy*, history.com, 6 May 2019 <https://www.history.com/this-day-in-history/galileo-is-convicted-of-heresy>.
486 Grismer, Karl H., *The Story of Fort Myers*, op. cit., p. 116.

"I hope I'm not disturbing you."

"Not at all. I…I'm just surprised, but wonderfully so."

"If you're not busy, I'd love to talk a bit."

"It would be a great privilege." I gestured to my left, toward the twin rockers. "We can sit out here, if…if that's okay?"

"Perfect." Edison seated himself in the rocker near the far railing.

As I started to take the adjacent one, I said, "Can I get you an iced tea?" Shortly after Fort Myers had gotten its ice-making plant in 1901,[487] I had built myself an ice box, a large cube with a pair of one-inch layers of palmwood, between which I put three inches of cotton.

"I'd appreciate that. Even with the comfortable temperature, I'm parched."

I made two tall teas, each poured over ample ice. After handing one to Mr. Edison, I seated myself next to him.

"Thank you." He gestured at the land that fronted my cabin. "You have a nice plot. Nicely maintained…a tranquil sanctuary."

"It's a far cry from your estate, but I love it." My eyes and ears took in the familiar setting. Over the years I had done much to improve it, but living there, I had come to take it for granted. The observation was hardly surprising. I had seen amazing photographs of Yosemite, Yellowstone and Niagara Falls to name but a few. For those fortunate enough to visit them, at first sight, no doubt they were jaw dropping. Living adjacent to them, with the passage of time, reactions surely attenuated.

"I had assumed I would return to Fort Myers a whole lot sooner than I did. I also expected to see you much sooner. But as they say, 'the best laid plans of mice and men…'"[488] Edison's voice trailed off and he shrugged. "Gracious as folks have been, I suspect that many were disappointed when I failed to come back in the winter of '88. At the time I never imagined that fourteen years would elapse before I'd see Seminole Lodge again.[489] I built it with the expectation it would be an annual winter retreat." Edison chuckled briefly. "Funny how life fools you. And too, it proves the obvious. Foresight can't compete with hindsight. When I moved my Edison Works from New Jersey up to Schenectady, New York, I had no idea how all-consuming the move

[487] Ibid., p. 158, stating: "The first ice was sold on Wednesday, May 22, 1901. Delivered, it cost a cent a pound; at the factory it was sold for fifty cents a hundred pounds."

[488] Phrases.org, 21 Apr. 2020 <https://www.phrases.com.uk/meanings/the-best-laid-schemes-of-mice-and-men.html>. The phrase originates from Robert Burns' poem *To a Mouse*, 1786. The poem became the basis for the title of the 1937 novel *Of Mice and Men* by John Steinbeck.

[489] Ibid., p. 116.

would be. Looking back, perhaps I should have anticipated it. Growing the Edison Works was the goal. That certainly happened. My company has become the much larger General Electric Company. Along with Willis Whitney and Charles Steinmetz, we've built the world's first industrial research laboratory.[490] Next to it, my old lab in Menlo Park is small potatoes. In the eight short years since our lab opened in Schenectady, it's grown from eight employees to over one hundred, forty percent of whom are scientifically trained researchers.[491] Not to boast, but I believe we're poised for a terrific future. But enough about me and my business. How has life treated you these many years?"

"I can't complain, not that anyone would listen." I gestured at a scrub pine where a crow incessantly cawed. "Even the birds prefer their prattle to my jabber."

"Have you maintained your scientific interests?"

I nodded. "Although I generally hear about breakthroughs well after they occur, I try to keep up. Most days, I spend a couple of hours or so doing that, along with studying."

"Well, if you're interested, we have a few openings on our research team. Most times, students from the local New York colleges, Union and Rensselaer, gobble them up even before we start looking. But lately, between growth, some moving on and whatever, we have several spots."

Unexpected as Edison's visit was, I was unprepared for his proposal. "You realize that I don't have work-related experience."

"Not an issue. As I said, we hire many of our researchers directly out of college.[492] You have lots of independent study beyond your degree. That puts you ahead of many others."

That a man of Edison's stature would consider hiring me was intoxicating, and the high came without a hangover.

"But understand, it'll be no vacation. We pay 'only workmen's wages' for a 6-day, 55-hour workweek.[493] It's the kind of money that one can get anywhere."

Long hours and low pay did not frighten me. What did, however, was frigid winters with ice and snow. My years in South Carolina, far

---

[490] *General Electric Research Laboratory*, Wikipedia, 7 May 2019 <https://en.wikipedia.org/General_Electric_Research_Laboratory>.

[491] Ibid.

[492] *Thomas Edison's 'Muckers,'* thoughtco.com, 24 Jun. 2018 <https://www.thoughtco.thomas-edisons-muckers-4071190>.

[493] Ibid., describing what it was like to work for Edison. "One mucker said that he 'could wither one with his biting sarcasm or ridicule one into extinction.' On the other hand, as electrician, Arthur Kennedy stated, 'The privilege which I had being with this great man for six years was the greatest inspiration of my life.'"

more temperate than the Northeast, indicated I would not fare well in the bitter and extended cold of New York State.

"You wouldn't be the first Negro to work for me. Louis Latimer—perhaps you've heard of him…"

"I know the name, but that's about it."

"He was in my employ for twelve years. The son of an escaped slave,[494] he's an impressive fellow. Before he worked for me, he patented a better design for carbon filaments. After he joined my team, he rose to the status of head draftsman for what was then my Edison General Electric Company.[495] Even though he no longer works for me, he's a member of the Edison Pioneers, a group of my old employees."[496] Edison stared off into space in a moment of apparent reflection. "Some folks think I'm prejudiced, just because most everyone I hire is a traditional, white American. Admittedly, I don't have many Catholics, Jews or Negroes at my plant, but that's just the way things are. Folks naturally prefer to associate with their own. I do as well. On the other hand, race and religion aren't the end all when it comes to talent, scientific and otherwise. Latimer certainly had it. But technically…he wasn't a mucker. He never worked at my Menlo Park or West Orange laboratory."[497] Edison refocused on me. "You would be my first Negro mucker."

"I appreciate the opportunity." His flattering offer felt great, but from the moment he had made it, my decision was clear. "This is where I spent my early years…It's where I belong."

"I understand, but if you change your mind, I'll be here in Fort Myers a while longer before heading back north." Edison sipped his tea and looked around. "I understand why you like it here. For that matter, I'm committed to coming back to Fort Myers every winter. No more staying up north, not when I can enjoy a beautiful subtropical climate. I also like the people here.[498] Though I must admit that I miss having folks around who enjoy confab about the nuts and bolts of inventions and science. You're about the only one with that kind of knowledge…And speaking of science, what in particular has caught your recent fancy?"

---

[494] Ibid.

[495] *African-American Inventors II*, nationalgeographic.org website, 18 Jun. 2018 <https://www.nationalgeographic.org/news/african-american-inventors-19th-century/>.

[496] *Thomas Edison's 'Muckers,'* op. cit.

[497] *African-American Inventors II*, op. cit.

[498] Armbrester, Margaret E., *The Civitan Society,* (Birmingham, Al., Ebsco Media, 1992, p. 34), indicating that Edison was an active member of the Fort Myers Civitan Club and considered "it an honor to be numbered in its ranks."

"The Lorentz Contractions," I said, my response not requiring even a moment's thought.

Edison jerked back. "Heady stuff." He took another sip. "And what do you think of them?"

"They're fascinating. The idea that the length and mass of an object could change or that time could pass differently depending on an object's velocity is mind boggling. It could turn Newton's physics on its head."

Edison gave me a look. "An expert on the Lorentz Contractions, I'm not. But having followed the subject—the ether has long intrigued me—I must take issue with you. From what I've heard, the Contractions may be nothing more than interesting mathematical expressions. But even assuming they have a substantive link to observable science, they won't materially impact the practical applications of Newton's physics. Unless an object travels close to the speed of light, the effects on length and mass and time would be nil. Even at ten thousand miles an hour (Edison began muttering, first inaudibly and then perceptibly)...less than 1/60,000 the velocity of light, the speed would only be a miniscule fraction of that which is required to produce a meaningful effect. Hence, Newton's physics, if not perfect, is a highly accurate measure of what we experience every day. Practical man, inventor that I am, that's sufficient for me."

I gulped. "I...I didn't mean my comment the way it sounded. For that matter, I assume Newton's equations will continue to guide us for many centuries." *Informing the foremost inventor of the day that I gave my blessing to the viability of Newton's physics, one of history's preeminent intellectual achievements, shoved my foot deeper down my throat.* "What I was trying to say is...there may be unexplored realms of physics where Newtonian mechanics won't hold."

"I suppose so."

I was thankful that he had let me off the hook, rather than add an exclamation point to my faux pas.

"As I said, I've been interested in the ether for many years. With the passage of time, my view has shifted. I'm growing more skeptical 'there is any ether with the extraordinary properties ascribed to it. To me it is entirely unnecessary to explain things generally, but it is absolutely necessary to explain the theories of the mathematical brain.'"[499] Edison

---

[499] Letter, dated December 14, 1923, from Thomas A. Edison to Charles Kassel in which Edison, reflecting an evolution of his views over many years, stated: "For years I have read and collected everything I could find time to read relating to the ether of space as created by the mathematical mind to explain physics. The more I read the more I reject their concepts and theories. I cannot think by the use of mathematics, hence am compelled to use other instrumentalities of the brain. The result is that I do

looked me in the eye. "I'm an inventor, not a mathematician. I study the world using the lens of testing and perspiration, rather than equations. You, on the other hand, appear to be the latter. What do you think? Are the Lorentz Contractions a portrait of reality or simply equations resulting from mathematical manipulations?"

I took a deep breath. No way did I want to put my foot back into my mouth. Nor did I want to come across as an arrogant know-it-all, especially on an inscrutable subject plainly beyond my ken. "I don't know. But my guess, and it's nothing more than a speculative guess, is that Lorentz's equations are more than numbers and letters on the page; that they do indeed explain events in our universe. But how the equations apply and what they mean is yet to be figured out. Whatever that may be, it's beyond me."[500]

"Along with perhaps everyone else occupying this planet." Edison chuckled, a guffaw that produced a relaxed lull in our conversation.

My curiosity begged to know what he was thinking. I dared not ask. I said, "Since last we spoke roughly a decade and a half ago, your

---

not believe there is any ether with the extraordinary properties ascribed to it. To me it is entirely unnecessary to explain things generally, but it is absolutely necessary to explain the theories of the mathematical brain." Letter retrieved from raabcollection.com website, 15 Jun. 2019 <https://www.raabcollection.com/thomas-edison-autograph/thomas-edison-signed-sold-agreeing-einstein-edison-states-he-follows-physics>.

[500] Einstein's Special Theory of Relativity, announced in 1905, gave meaning to the Lorentz Contractions. Over the ensuing decade, Einstein advanced his General Theory of Relativity, which took into account the effects of gravity, including the fact that it caused light to bend. Where the Special Theory of Relativity can be examined using the simple mathematics of algebra and geometry, the General Theory demands a working knowledge of not just differential equations but also topology. Wikipedia states: "In mathematics, **topology**…is concerned with the properties of space that are preserved under continuous deformations, such as stretching, twisting, crumpling and bending, but not tearing or gluing." (emphasis from original) *Topology*, Wikipedia, 17 Jun. 2019 <https//en.wikipedia.org/wiki/Topology>. More specifically, General Relativity involves spacetime topology, "the topological structure of spacetime," a physical theory that "models gravitation as a curvature of a four dimensional Lorenzian manifold…" *Spacetime topology*, Wikipedia, 17 Jun. 2019 <https://en.wikipedia.org/wiki/Spacetime_topology>. (*Bookmarks'* author's comment: As a senior mathematics major at Rensselaer Polytechnic Institute, many years ago I took a course in topology. Much of it involved proving a principle was valid for a metric space of any number of dimensions "n," even as n approaches infinity. For me, anything beyond four dimensions (three, plus a coordinate for time) was largely incomprehensible. An infinite number of dimensions bordered on meaningless. Too often I could not prove that which was apparently true, and even when I was successful, the mathematics was so abstract that it left me wondering if my proof might be a product of circular reasoning.)

incandescent light and its progeny have changed the landscape. That must be very satisfying."

He laughed again. "Yes, though the war along the way was far from easy. In some respects, I lost the 'war,' that's with a small 'w,' but fortunately I didn't cut off my nose to spite my face. As a result, I won the 'War,' the one whose 'W' is capitalized."

"Small 'w,' big 'W,' you've lost me."

"Early on, I was confident that DC current would prevail over AC. The development of the AC-powered electric chair, a maniacal device for executions, was AC's coup de gras—no pun intended—at least so I thought. I assumed that fear—it's a great motivator, especially in the political arena—would lead to legislation restricting the use of AC.[501] Back in '88, when AC's high-voltage wires caused a number of deaths,[502] I thought we had AC on the run. But by the early nineties, when the number of electric companies had dropped from about a dozen, so that only Westinghouse, Thomas-Houston and my Edison General Electric remained,[503] the handwriting was on the wall. AC was the future. So, in 1892, I merged with my biggest competitor, Thomas-Houston, combining my lighting patents with its AC patents, giving us control of three-quarters of the country's electrical business.[504] Just because DC lost, that didn't demand that I lose as well. As I've said, I'm pragmatic. I may be an inventor, but I'm also a businessman." He reached for the chain fronting his vest and pulled out his pocket watch. "About time for me to be going. I enjoyed our conversation, as well as the iced tea." He stood up.

I got up too. "The privilege and pleasure were all mine."

He shook my hand. "I look forward to doing this again." He headed off.

As I watched him disappear, my brain raced. That I had just entertained Thomas Edison on my porch was exhilarating. Did I make a

---

[501] *See*, *War of the Currents*, Wikipedia, 21 Mar. 2020 <https://en.wikipedia.org/wiki/War_of_the_currents> regarding Edison's connections to electrical engineer Harold Pitney Brown, a crusader against "dangerous" AC current. "[H]istorians note there grew to be some form of collusion between the Edison company and Brown…Edison Electric seemed to be footing the bill for some of Brown's publications on the dangers of AC. In addition, Thomas Edison himself sent a letter to the city government of Scranton, Pennsylvania recommending Brown as an expert on the dangers of AC. Some of the collusion was exposed in letters stolen from Brown's office and published in August, 1889."

[502] *Thomas Edison,* Wikipedia, 20 Mar. 2020 <https://en.wikipedia.org/wiki/Thomas_Edison>.

[503] Ibid.

[504] Ibid.

mistake passing up the opportunity to join his enterprise in Schenectady? Though a pang of regret stirred, on balance I felt I had made the right decision. I sank back down into my rocker, contemplating the awesome figure with whom I had chatted. He was an indefatigable, inventive genius. But he was also a savvy entrepreneur, a businessman tough enough to play hardball. He struck me as a man of high morals, yet one who could be ruthless. The contradiction, admittedly patent, was unproblematic. Such was the nature of many a man. Principled, yes, often churchgoing, but…

For several minutes I reflected on the ambiguity of human nature before I redirected my attention to Edison. Years earlier, I had wondered whether the great man was a bigot. That he had come to my home and invited me, a Black Seminole, to join his team evidenced the contrary. But as Attorney Jenks, dolt that he was, had noted: Exceptions can prove a rule. The adage was nice, but invoking it, grossly oversimplified a complex question.

The Law of the Excluded Middle, as it often did, popped into my mind. Bigotry was hardly an either-or issue with no middle ground. Years before, I had concluded that it came in gradations, one for which a continuum applied. That begged the question: Where did Thomas Edison lie on that continuum? Compared to the worst of the pre-Emancipation slave owners and the members of the Ku Klux Klan, who still lynched innocent victims, Edison was a prince. That, however, merely meant he was not at the horrible end of the spectrum. That he had hired Latimer and respected him earned Edison additional points. But a token Negro was hardly enough to afford Edison a place at the opposite end of the spectrum. That he included Latimer in his society of Pioneers could not be ignored. I leaned back in my rocker and downed the last of what was melted ice from my earlier iced tea. The several conversations I had shared with Edison were hardly sufficient to judge the man. Still I believed I had a decent perspective. He was a hard-nosed, driven man of huge talent, who, like most, was more comfortable with those with whom he had much in common, be that an interest in business, science, philosophy, religion or whatever. Compassion, equality and other social issues often took a back seat to more pragmatic concerns. When it came to racism, I suspected he lay somewhere in the middle of the spectrum. Harriet Beecher Stowe, he wasn't. Neither was he Andrew Johnson. My best guess, he was a far cry from either.[505] Edison was a complex man, complete with human foibles.

---

[505] In recent years there has been considerable debate about Edison, particularly whether he was a bigot. Articles casting Edison as a villain proliferate the internet. (*See*

A disquieting thought invaded my ruminations. Who was I to judge Thomas Edison? Comparing my accomplishments to his was beyond absurd. What had I achieved? Yes, I had gotten a college education, but what had I done with it? More than three decades clear of my graduation, I had nothing to show for my sheepskin. The admission was painful. But it was not all my fault. The end of Reconstruction, the reemergence of the Democrats and Jim Crow laws had foreclosed opportunities for people of color. Add to that the lynching of Lucinda, and I had ample justification for the course I had chosen. The justifications had merit. They provided reasons for my solitary life. Unfortunately, they were also excuses. They did not preclude me from using my abilities and education to engage in scientific research and improve the state of society.

I got up from my rocker and headed through the woods to the nearby Caloosahatchee. Perhaps I should reconsider Edison's offer. But the idea of exchanging my comfortable life for a full-time job in upstate New York was unappealing. I gazed at the river as it gently meandered toward

---

e.g., *6 beloved scientists who were actually total jerks*, 21 Jun. 2019 <https://www.syfy.com/syfywire/> putting Edison at the top of its list; and *10 Ways Edison Treated Tesla Like a Jerk – Listverse*, 21 Jun. 2019 <https:///listverse.com/2012/06/07/10-ways-edison-treated-tesla-like-a jerk/>; and *Was Thomas Edison anti-Semitic? | Yahoo Answers*, 15 June, 2018 <https://answers.yahoo.com/question/index?qid=20140504111AApnHb9> quoting the Notable Names Data Base to the effect: "Like his friend Henry Ford, Edison was virulently anti-Semitic and blamed the Jews for all of the world's major problems.") But a well-researched article by Lewis Brett Smiler, *Was Thomas Edison anti-Semitic?* (*edison findings*, posted September 21, 2016, retrieved 15 Jun. 2019 <https://edisonpapers.wordpress.com/2016/09/21/was-thomas-edison-anti-semitic/>) concludes in regard to Edison's alleged anti-semitism: "There is no simple answer to this question. The inventor believed in many common Jewish stereotypes, and some of his remarks about Jews can be construed as prejudice. However, Edison also expressed support in their quest for freedom…" Smiler quotes a letter to Bernard Richards, secretary of the American Jewish Congress, in which Edison, in reply to a request for support, said: "I am in favor of a Jewish Congress, as well as any other device that Jews can think of, in order to obtain their rights. I believe the day is not far distant when men will not be persecuted for wanting to go to Heaven in their own way and not in some other people's way." The totality of the evidence suggests that Edison likely harbored and voiced Jewish stereotypes common to his time, but he was not nearly so bigoted as his Fort Myers' next-door neighbor, Henry Ford. A broader examination of Edison leads one to conclude he was neither saint, nor devil. Driven, but at times ruthless and egotistical, his accomplishments were significant. An article entitled, *Thomas Alva Edison, The Accomplishments and life of electrical engineer and entrepreneur Thomas Edison, 1847-1931*, Edison Tech Center, 22 Jun. 2019 <http://edisontechcenter.org/ThomasAlvaEdison.html> states: "Final words of advice: Whether you look up to Thomas Edison or don't like him (and people like him…such as Steve Jobs). [sic] We ask that you please avoid the idiotic simplification of history into the Tesla vs. Edison myth."

the Gulf of Mexico. A great blue heron wading a few yards from the edge of the beach caught my eye. Small as the fowl's brain may have been, he was wise enough never to spend a winter along the frozen Mohawk River in Schenectady, New York. No way was I prepared to make such a commitment. Accepting Mr. Edison's offer seemed impossible. Nevertheless, I felt an urge to explore it.

I picked up a handful of powder-like sand. Making a fist, I rotated my hand, so my thumb was at the top, allowing the grains, as if traveling through the narrow passage of an hourglass, to slip slowly past my pinky, to freely drift according to the whim of gravity and the serendipitous breeze. Such was how Mr. Wright had once described the ease of his unencumbered summer strolls amidst the lakes and streams of the Northeast's uneven terrain. Though he acknowledged that its cruel and icy winters were worse than the South's relentless hot and humid summer days, he contended that June, July and August, be it in the Adirondack, Green, White or Berkshire mountains served up days dwarfing the best the South could offer in any season. Splendid vistas, dotted with streams where crystal-clear water gurgled through mountains and valleys, made the landscape of the deep South seem insipid. Perhaps I needed to see for myself. I could also see what Edison's research laboratory was like; find out what it would be like to work there. The idea was enticing.

Ambling back to my cabin, I returned to my favorite rocker. I closed my eyes. A summer sojourn to New York State was seductive. Stored away behind the secret panel of my cabinet, I had plenteous funds. My parsimonious side preferred to preserve my nest egg. I wanted the best of all worlds. And I could have it. Fort Myers was growing. Construction was rampant. Newspaper advertisements, as well as postings outside the saloons and general stores, showed a need for workers. For three months, April, May and June, I would use my skills to earn the money for a special trip, to spend July in upstate New York. Presumably I would return to my cabin once it was over. If by chance, another alternative caught my fancy, so be it. I was free to do as I pleased. I was ready to explore a new phase of my life. I was excited. Having built a satisfactory life for myself in the cabin of my childhood, unlike other occasions of self-examination, I knew who I was...I was my father's son.

Chapter XXX

AFTER BOARDING CINDA AT EDGAR JONES' PLACE, with my suitcase in hand, I headed to the train depot. More than three months had elapsed since Thomas Edison had paid me a visit. Shortly thereafter, he had headed north. In the interim I had spent twelve weeks working construction, laying bricks and doing carpentry in Fort Myers. Working 58-hour weeks, typical of the time, I had earned sixty-three cents an hour, accumulating a total of $418.48,[506] more than I needed to cover my stay in Schenectady. Whether it might be a single week, a month or even longer, I was uncertain. Depending how much I enjoyed it there, whether I became antsy to get home, would determine the length. Presumably I would seek out Edison while I was there. I might have contacted him in advance, but I had no desire to delay my trip awaiting the back and forth of the mails, especially when a reply was far from guaranteed. I also preferred to keep my options open. I wanted to scout out the area first. If it was not to my liking, I could quietly head home to Fort Myers. Once Edison returned to his laid-back winter home, I could reach out to him there.

The travel time of more than three days, not the fastest available, but not the most expensive either, took me through Richmond, Washington D.C., Philadelphia and New York City. Knowing that I might never have another opportunity to see New York City, rather than continue directly to Schenectady, the terminus of my journey's last leg, I opted to stay in

---

[506] According to a Congressional study, in 1907 bricklayers were averaging from $.50/hour in Buffalo and Milwaukee, the cities with the lowest rates of pay, to $.87½/hour in San Francisco, the highest of twenty-five cities studied; and carpenters were averaging $.37½/hour in Milwaukee, the lowest, to $.62½/hour in San Francisco, New York City and Seattle, the highest. *Wages and Prices of Commodities,* Vol. I, Report of Committee and Views of Minority, 61st Congress, 3rd Session, Sen. Doc. No. 847, retrieved 18 Feb. 2020 from <babel.hathitrust.org/cgi/pt?id=uc1.b3991872&view=1up&seq=9>.

the renowned metropolis overnight. I arrived at Grand Central Station shortly after two o'clock on the afternoon of July 10, 1907. The terminal's size and impressive neo-Renaissance façade awed me, but a frowzy interior, coupled with an accumulation of soot on the exterior walls,[507] stirred mixed feelings. Though electric trains, no longer powered by steam from burning coal, had begun mitigating the production of soot, filth that had poured into the air over the years had scarred the facility. Work was well underway on what would become the new Grand Central Terminal. Inside, a scale-model rendering of the future structure, along with a brochure, suggested the Beaux Arts replacement would be magnificent.[508] Outside, excavated areas, along with ongoing construction, painted a chaotic canvas, one that made it all but inevitable that in the interim between the erstwhile beautiful old structure and the completion of its splendid successor, an unseemly mess would prevail.

After depositing my suitcase in a locker, I headed west on 42nd Street. Less than ten minutes later, as Broadway neared, the New York City I had anticipated, revealed itself. Indeed, it exceeded my expectations. Up ahead, the New York Times headquarters building, from which Times Square had gotten its name, stretched toward the sky. The gothic structure, twice the height of any of its neighbors, drew one's eye to the vertex of what I guesstimated was a thirty-degree angle formed by the intersection of 42nd and Broadway. A plethora of sparkling new theaters screamed of abounding culture. I had been to Columbia and Charleston. Next to New York City, they were pedestrian.

When I was about fifty yards from the New York Times headquarters, essentially a trapezoidal solid, I stopped and gazed upwards in awe. A quick, though admittedly imprecise count suggested it had roughly twenty-five stories.

"Impressive, isn't it?"

The voice of a man just to my right turned my head. I said, "Never seen anything like it. Must be three hundred feet high."

---

[507] *History of Grand Central Terminal*, Wikipedia, 25 Jun. 2019 <https://en.wikipedia.org/wiki/History_of_Grand_Central_Terminal>.

[508] *8 of the Best Beaux Arts Buildings in NYC*, architecturaldigest.com, 25 Jun. 2019 <https://www.architecturaldigest.com/gallery/beaux-arts-buildings-nyc> stating: "After the Baroque era, a spin on classical architecture known as Beaux Arts emerged from Paris in the 1800s. While staying true to the tenets of classicism—symmetry, articulated form, and a common vocabulary—Beaux Arts builders were more interested in decorative flair and monumental grandeur than the perfection of scale and proportion…Huge windows and a clock framed in elegant granite figures make the façade of Grand Central far from just neoclassical—Beaux Arts ornamentation is at work here."

"Three hundred sixty-three,"[509] said the man. "Since it was finished a couple of years ago, this area is the place to be. We think of it as the center of the world. Folks in Paris, with their Eifel Tower, Notre Dame and Arch of Triumph, might disagree, but we can give them a run for their money." The man gestured up and down the intersecting streets. "Before the turn of the century, this area was home to illicit activity…a widespread sex trade.[510] Nowadays, the rich and famous frequent the place. Ever since the Times building went up, this is where people congregate, especially on New Year's Eve. Two hundred thousand came here in 1903 for the fireworks, and already it's a tradition." He pointed toward the tower. "This past January, right at midnight, they lowered a ball, lit with countless electric lights.[511] Spiffiest show I've ever seen." He turned my way. "Where you from?"

"Fort Myers, Florida."

"Heard of it, but don't know where in Florida it is."

"Along the southwest coast."

"Must get unbearably hot there in the summer."

I shrugged. "It's tough, but you get yours in the winter. Can't imagine what it's like to go a week where the thermometer struggles to hit the freezing mark."

"Not good, but a helluva lot better than years back when there was no central heating. Quite a world we've got these days, what with cars, trains, subways, telephones, escalators, typewriters, cameras, vacuum cleaners, power equipment of all kinds and now airplanes…not to forget central heating. Glad I didn't have to live in the olden days, back when the country was founded. Can you imagine if George Washington and Ben Franklin could see the way we live today?"

The thought was intriguing. I said, "For that matter, I'd love to see what the world will be like a hundred years from now, in the early 21st century. If history repeats itself, the rate of change will continue to accelerate." I checked the ridiculous impulse to mention that the second derivative of change as a function of time would be positive. Technically it was not entirely accurate anyway. An era like the Dark Ages would have had a negative second derivative, not to mention the first. The observation demonstrated that the mathematical expression describing

---

[509] *One Times Square*, Wikipedia, 11 May 2021 <https://en.wikipedia.org/wiki/One_Times_Square>.

[510] *Times Square | Location, Description, History, & Facts | Britannica.com*, 25 Jun. 2019 <https://www.britannica.com/topic/Times-Square>.

[511] *20 Things You Didn't Know About Times Square | US City Traveler*, uscitytraveler.com, 26 Jun. 2019 <http://www.uscitytraveler.com/20-things-you-didnt-know-about-times-square/>.

historical development, presumably one with exponents considerably higher than two, was far too complex for casual conversation, not that anyone other than a *gek*, to borrow the vernacular of the early Dutch colonists of New York, would entertain such off-the-wall notions.

The man gestured toward the top of the tower. "Who knows? Maybe by then, we'll all wear motorized suits and fly like doves from rooftop to rooftop." He drew out his pocket watch and glanced at it. "I'd love to stay and gab, but the wife gets cross when I'm late for dinner." Just before he headed off, he added, "Enjoy the rest of your stay in our fair city."

As the Caucasian male walked away, I contemplated what had just transpired. Back home in Fort Myers, white strangers never approached me to make conversation. The possibility that attitudes in the melting pot of New York City might be different crossed my mind. The idea was appealing, but better judgment contravened. Seeing me stare up at the New York Times tower, the man likely suspected that I was a tourist. Proud as he was of his home city—he compared it to Paris—racial disparity could not quell his urge to extol it to an admiring stranger.

I looked around where people were hurrying about. They made no eye contact with those they passed, least of all, me. The man who had approached me, the lone anomaly, proved nothing. As one who relied on the precise logic of mathematics, for me to invoke an exception to prove a rule was absurd. Exceptions were exceptions. They proved nothing, except that a seeming rule lacked universality. What was apparent, the bustling streets of New York City were highly impersonal. Unlike Fort Myers, where folks knew and greeted many of the people they passed, at least those of their own ilk, in New York City, virtually everyone was a stranger. People minded their own business. They ignored those around them.

The elbow of a heavy-set woman, a bull in the Times Square corral, banged my hip as she passed from behind. Rather than begging my pardon, she glared, as if to chide me for being in her way, after which she renewed her charge. Muttering an inaudible epithet, I strolled west on 42nd Street, taking in the theaters, shops and other buildings. Bustling with trolleys, cars and people heading every which way, the area was unlike any place I had ever seen. I turned north at 7th Avenue, following it for several blocks. I continued counterclockwise, completing a quadrilateral that took me back to the Times building. New York City was indeed impressive. But no way would I trade my cabin in a natural Caloosahatchee paradise for the high-rises and cement of metropolitan chaos.

I started to walk back in the direction of Grand Central Station. Just ahead was a staircase leading down into the subway. The half-mile-or-so walk back to the big rail station was easy, but a trip on the crosstown train would be memorable. I climbed down the stairwell into the beautifully tiled-wall chasm. After paying an agent a nickel for a ticket, I wended my way to the area alongside the shuttle's track, where I handed my ticket to the taker at the platform.[512] A minute later, with headlight blazing, the train, about two hundred yards away, roared from the tunnel in my direction. Several cars passed before the shuttle rolled to a stop. Doors slid open. People poured forth, after which those of us waiting climbed in. Most stood. I grabbed a seat. A conductor yelled to stand back from the closing doors. They shut, and seconds later we were on our way, disappearing into the darkness of a tunnel. Less than two minutes later, the train emerged from the darkness and drew to a halt.[513] The doors opened, and everyone climbed out. The quick trip had been fascinating. Missing it would have been a mistake. That said, a daily diet of the cramped novelty was not for me.

I followed the crowd up the stairs of the cavernous maze into Grand Central Station. I fetched my suitcase from its locker. After checking into a small hotel nearby, I found a nice pub with a beautifully carved wooden bar, tin ceiling and lots of fine booths. I seated myself at a narrow one intended for no more than two. My dinner order, corned beef and cabbage, along with a sarsaparilla, arrived shortly. I savored the fine repast, but even more so, the extraordinary afternoon I had spent in the remarkable city. Exactly what awaited me one hundred fifty miles to the north in Schenectady, I was uncertain. Regardless, no way could I have anticipated the surprises I would encounter there.

***

A chamber-of-commerce, mid-July day greeted me as I stepped outside Schenectady's Hotel Foster, where I had registered to stay for a week. The State Street guest house cost me six dollars, an ample savings

---

[512] *NYC Subway History of Fares, Tokens & Cards | LivingIn*, livingin.citihabitats.com, 28 Jun. 2019 <https://livingin.citihabitats.com/nyc-subway-history-the-story-of-fares-tokens-cards/>. When the New York City subway opened in 1904, five cent paper tickets were used. In the 1920s, turnstiles that took nickels came into use. In 1948 when the fare rose to ten cents, turnstiles accepting dimes were added. In 1953 the fare rose to fifteen cents, and tokens were put into use. The tokens went through various iterations until 1992, when the Metrocard was introduced. It remains in use today.

[513] *42nd Street Shuttle*, Wikipedia, 28 Jun. 2019 <https://en.wikipedia.org/wiki/42nd_Street_Shuttle>.

relative to the daily rate of $1.50. My room included hot and cold running water. I saved a little by selecting a room that did not include a bath, requiring me to use the floor's shared facility.[514] I justified the frugal choice, knowing I could always upgrade if I found the option too unpleasant. Having arrived well after dark the evening before and tired from my long journey, I had gone directly to bed without taking time to see anything of the city.

Following a sating breakfast, I headed out to explore Schenectady. The main thoroughfare was as different from Fort Myers as it was from New York City. (My rural home town, which had mushroomed to two thousand,[515] had roughly 1/2500th the nearly five million inhabitants of New York City.[516]) Across the cobblestone street, lined with a pair of trolley tracks and frequented by several cars,[517] well-maintained buildings of three to five stories, each joined to its neighbors, created an impressive zone. Dental moldings along the top facades, along with tall windows, the top rows of which were often Romanesque, sculpted a striking canvas. I stepped off the curb and crossed the street to take in the view from the opposite side. My hotel, the Foster, the tallest building in the area, climbed six stories. Tiny in comparison to the New York Times building, but huge by Fort Myers' standards, the just-completed Foster was faced with glazed white terra cotta and adorned with three-story, fluted Ionic embedded columns, wrapped with garlands.[518] The structure epitomized the Beaux Arts style that was adorning cities everywhere in the late-Victorian era.

I headed west on State Street several blocks to Dock Street, along the Erie Canal, where it paralleled the Mohawk River, a few hundred yards away. To the immediate north, huge locomotive works employing thousands met my eyes. An iron bridge, a short distance to the west,

---

[514] *A.L. Stevens, Schenectady's Rooming House Keeper and Armless Driver*, 22 Jul. 2019 <http://hoxsie.org/2019/06/10/a-1-stevens-schenectadys-rooming-house-keeper-and-armless-driver/>.

[515] *Fort Myers, Florida,* Wikipedia, 1 Jul. 2019 <https://en.wikipedia.org/wiki/Fort_Myers,_Florida> indicating the Fort Myers population was 943 in 1900 and 2,463 in 1910.

[516] *Data and Population - New York City's History From 1870 – 1930,* kelseyburchushistory.weebly.com, 1 Jul. 2019 <https://kelseyburchushistory.weebly.com/data-and-population.html> indicating the New York City population was 3,437,202 in 1900 and 5,620,048 in 1910.

[517] *State Motor Vehicle Registrations, By Years, 1900 - 1995*, 23 Jul. 2019 <https://www.fwha.dot.gov/ohim/summary95/mv200.pdf> indicating there were 140,300 cars registered in the United States in 1907, compared to only 8,000 in 1900.

[518] *Foster Building*, Wikipedia, 1 Jul. 2019 <https://en.wikipedia.org/wiki/Foster_Building>.

spanned the three-quarters of a mile width of the Mohawk River. Several hundred yards to the south was the even larger giant, General Electric Company. Not far from the terminus of Edison Avenue, amidst the large complex, I located the narrow, staple-shaped building that housed the company's laboratory. I approached the entrance where a guard greeted me.

"My name is Mican Reinbow. I met Mr. Edison and spoke with him several times at his winter home in Fort Myers, Florida. I was hoping to see him and his laboratory."

"Mr. Edison is out of town."

"Do you know when he might be expected back?"

"Not any day soon, not that they tell me. Even if they did, I wouldn't blab."

"In Fort Myers Mr. Edison spoke with me about becoming a mucker. Might I see the laboratory?"

The guard eyed me with skepticism. "Only authorized personnel are allowed entrance."

Though I believed the guard, I wondered, given my race, if he would have refused me entrance regardless of the rules. I thanked him for his time and started back north. Whether I would return to the laboratory was uncertain.

As I reached State Street, a trolley, going my way, stopped just ahead. I followed in line behind several others, boarding and paying the fare. I rode the open transport several stops, two or three miles, to upper State Street, where I crossed the street and waited for the trolley heading back the other way. When I reached Nott Terrace, a few hundred yards east of the Foster Hotel, I disembarked, ending what for me had been an amusement-park ride to see the city. I walked north on Nott Terrace for about a half-mile onto the campus of Union College. Not since my days at the University of South Carolina Horseshoe had I seen such an impressive educational setting. Rising high near the center of the campus was a stunning domed building. I circled the structure, counting the sixteen sides of the regular polygon. Numerical propensities irresistible, I muttered, "The sum of the interior angles of an n-sided polygon equals n minus 2 times 180°." Applying the formula, each interior angle of the 16-sided regular polygon was 14 times 180° divided by 16...or 157.5^o, not far from a straight angle. Self-satisfaction and self-deprecation converged. A quick solution to the mathematical challenge was marvelous; the compulsion that drove me to do the calculation, risible. The latter arguably reflected a growing acknowledgement of my eccentricities.

I redirected my focus to the dome with its hundreds of stained-glass windows.[519] Temptation cajoled me to count them, at least one section, which, when multiplied by sixteen, would yield an approximate total, even if each section did not have an identical number. The need to disprove that I was obsessive sent me on my way. I worked my way east across the campus and then along Union Avenue to Wendell Avenue, where I turned north. An impressive array of large homes, many in the four-thousand square-foot range, decorated the street. I continued for about 200 yards when a man on a bicycle turned from a driveway heading along the sidewalk toward me. I stopped and gawked as the Quasimodo-like figure came my way. *Could it be?...Once he drew closer, I knew. It had to be—the renowned tiny man with beard and top hat.*[520]

"Excuse me," he said, coming to a halt and dismounting his humped-over body from his child-size bicycle.

Presumably his message was a polite request that I step aside in order that he could pass. But allowing the rare opportunity to slip away was unthinkable. "Mr. Steinmetz…It's you, Mr. Steinmetz, isn't it?"

Holding his bicycle erect with one hand, with the other, he raised his top hat, using the brim to theatrically scratch his head. "Vy—I beliefe you're right."

The sardonic response left me speechless…and embarrassed.

"Vould you mind makink room so I may pass?"

"I'm sorry." Much as my apologetic words were heartfelt, I yearned to spend a few more moments with the remarkable man. I guessed him to be in his mid-forties, a decade younger than I. "It's such an honor to meet you. I read your solution to the problem of converting direct current to alternating current, the delay which causes motors to overheat."

---

[519] *The Nott Memorial | Union College*, union.edu website, 1 Jul. 2019 <https://www.union.edu/about/history-and-traditions/historic-campus/nott> indicating that with 709 stained glass windows, the Nott Memorial, "one of America's most dramatic High Victorian buildings, is the centerpiece of the Union campus." It is on U.S. National Register of Historic Places.

[520] *Charles Proteus Steinmetz*, Smithsonian.com, 1 Jul. 2019 <https://www.smithsonianmag.com/history/charles-proteus-steinmetz-the-wizard-of-schenectady> stating of Steinmetz: "He stood just four feet tall, his body contorted by a hump in his back and a crooked gait, and his stunted torso gave the illusion that his head, hands and feet were too big…In the early 20th century, Charles Steinmetz could be seen pedaling his bicycle down the streets of Schenectady, New York, in a suit and top hat, or floating down the Mohawk River in a canoe, kneeling over a makeshift desktop, where he passed hours scribbling notes and equations on papers that sometimes blew into the water. With a Blackstone panatela cigar seemingly glued to his lips, Steinmetz cringed as children scurried away upon seeing him—frightened, he believed, by the 'queer, gnome-like figure' with the German accent."

"You read zee Law of Hyshteresis?"[521]

"I did, and may I say, it was elegant."

"Zank you."

Whether his expression of appreciation was sincere or sarcasm denigrating my presumption to pass judgment over his work, I was unsure. I took note that the wee man was even shorter than I had imagined, no more than a few inches over four feet, and the hump in his back, more pronounced.

"So, vat did you learn from readink the Law of Hyshteresis? Vat it says? How it's useful?...Or maybe somezink fery esoteric?"

That he was testing me seemed apparent. Whether he was asking from a mathematical or practical standpoint was less clear. I chose the latter. I said, "It…uh…provided engineers with mathematical models of machines and power lines. That…uh…saved the cost of building and testing many such models."[522]

"Fair enough." He nodded briefly. "Not to put you on zee shpot, but do you know vat the law says, mathematically shpeakink?"

Coming directly from the venerable man, the question on a subject about which I had minimal understanding was intimidating. "Uh…because the magnetization of…uh…magnetic materials like iron lags the changes in a surrounding magnetic field, there's…uh…a loss of energy…in the form of heat…a hysteresis loss. If I…uh…remember correctly, the loss is proportional to the…uh…magnetization in lines of force raised to the power of 1.6. I recall it only as a formula. And to be honest, when I read your paper, I struggled to follow the derivation of that formula."[523]

---

[521] Leonard, Johnathan Norton, *The Life of Charles Steinmetz* (Garden City, NY, Doubleday, Doran & Company, Inc. 1929) p. 168, stating: "Steinmetz was in the class of Newton, Leibnetz, Einstein, and other theorists whose abstract reasonings made it possible for men with less penetrating minds to design practical machines." *And see, Charles Proteus Steinmetz*, Smithsonian.com, op. cit., to the effect: "But he [Steinmetz] was a giant among scientific thinkers, counting Albert Einstein, Nikola Tesla and Thomas Edison as friends, and his contributions to mathematics and electrical engineering made him one of the most beloved and instantly recognizable men of his time."

[522] *Charles Proteus Steinmetz: Genius, Forethinker*, electronicsdesign.com, 17 Jun. 2018 <http://electronicsdesign.com/boards/charles-proteus-steinmetz-genius-forethinker>.

[523] Steinmetz, Charles Proteus, *On the Law of Hysteresis*, edlab.wfiles.com, 2 Jul. 2019 <edlab.wfiles.com/local--files/pioneering-papers/steinmetz_1892.pdf>. *See also, Hysteresis*, Wikipedia, 3 Jul. 2019 <https://en.wikipedia.org/wiki/Hysteresis> indicating more broadly: "Hysteresis is the dependence of the state of a system on its history…Hysteresis can be a dynamic lag between an input and an output that disappears if the input is varied more slowly." Rubber bands and thermostats provide

"Better san vat mosht of my shtudents vould say, eshpecially if I asked sem out of zee blue, razer san zee mornink after zey crammed for an exam." Steinmetz looked me in the eye. "I'm impressed. And zat arouses my curiosity. As Chairman of zee Department of Electrical Engineerink at Union College,[524] I know you are not a member of our faculty. And I can't recall seeink you at GE's research lab. Apart from zee College and zee lab, folks around here who know anysink about hyshteresis are as uncommon as unicorns."

"I assure you, Mr. Steinmetz. I'm not a unicorn." My paltry attempt at humor failed to draw even the hint of a smile. "I…I'm not from Schenectady. I'm just visiting…from Fort Myers, Florida."

Steinmetz looked at me curiously. "You vouldn't by any chance haf met Somas…Mr. Edison sere?"

The question stunned me. "I did, but how…how did you know?"

"He mentioned he had met a Negro-Indian—I believe zee term is Black Seminole—durink his vinter shtays zere. Apparently, science is not zee forte of folks zere. Much as Somas lofs zee area, eshpecially as an escape from zee dreadful Schenectady vinters, it lacks people vith whom he can conduct scientific discussions. You, howefer, are an exception."

That Thomas Edison had mentioned me was flattering. That he enjoyed our exchanges enough to mention them to others, ineffable.

"It seems you haf zee better of me," said Steinmetz. "You know my name, but I don't know yours."

"Mican Reinbow." I shook the hand he extended. "It's an incredible privilege to meet you, Sir. I…I've never…" Angst that I would come across as obsequious, coupled with an inability to find the right words, kept me from voicing a complete thought.

"Zee pleasure is mutual."[525]

---

examples of hysteresis that are easier to understand than electrical hysteresis. If a hanging rubber band is further stretched by repeatedly adding more weights, when the weights are subsequently removed one by one, the rubber band will be a bit longer than before the weight was added. A thermostat set to maintain a temperature of 75 degrees might allow the ambient temperature to drop to 74 degrees before the heat kicks on, and the heat will not shut off until the ambient temperature reaches 76 degrees.

[524] *Charles Proteus Steinmetz*, robinsonlibrary.com, 1 Jul. 2019 <http://www.robinsonlibrary.com/technology/electrical/biography/steinmetz.htm> stating: "Steinmetz retired from General Electric in 1902 to become Chairman of the Department of Electrical Engineering at Union College (in Schenectady), a position he held until 1913."

[525] Ibid. During Steinmetz's twenty-one years at Union College (he continued to teach there after resigning as Chairman of the Electrical Engineering Department), Steinmetz never took any salary and attended all faculty meetings. "When Phi Gamma Delta

I assumed the comment was merely a polite platitude. Regardless, there was no doubt that my pleasure was infinitely greater than his.

"Much as I'd lof to shtand here and chat, a faculty meetink demands I leef." He climbed onto his bicycle. "It's been nice to meet you…"

"Mican," I said, filling in the blank.

"Perhaps durink your shtay, our pazs vill cross again." Steinmetz rode off down Wendell Avenue.

I watched him until he turned west and disappeared. I hoped that we would again meet and, better yet, that our next encounter would be longer.

***

My second and third days in Schenectady saw me take lengthy walks as I explored the progressive, fast-growing city. On the latter, I had circled more than two miles east to the lovely Central Park and returned west on State Street, where I turned south onto Broadway. It was mid-afternoon when, armed with an ample appetite, I headed into a drug store bearing a soda fountain with a half-dozen stools. I seated myself on a stool close to the middle and perused the single-page menu, a selection of carbonated beverages, ice cream treats and several light food items.

"What would you like?" said a teenage boy sporting a white shirt and black bow tie.

"A hot dog and (my eyes scanned the beverage choices)…a vanilla egg cream." I had heard of the fountain drink but had never tasted one. I slowly rotated my stool, taking in the black and white tile floor, tin ceiling, and marble…or maybe granite…counter of the seemingly new and meticulously maintained premises.

About the time my food arrived, a gentleman, perhaps ten years my senior, with a full beard, seated himself on my immediate right. I smeared my hot dog with mustard and bit into it. Using a paper straw, I sipped my vanilla egg cream, a foamed-topped beverage in a narrow V-shaped glass nearly a foot tall.

"You know what's in that?" said the man next to me.

"Eggs, cream and vanilla syrup."

"You belong in the majors."

The stranger's compliment pleased me, although the question about a drink whose ingredients were presumably self-evident required no great genius.

---

needed a new fraternity house he helped raise funds, and also attended fraternity parties and spoke each year at the induction ceremony for new members."

"You're batting .333. One for three produces an excellent average in baseball, but no great mitzvah when you're talking about a drink, one you specifically ordered."

"One for three…what are you talking about?"

"You're right about the vanilla syrup, but as for the eggs and cream, it's no and no."

I gave the man a look, one that would have proved itself a mien of disdain had I taken the time to check it out in the mirror that lined the wall opposite the counter. "You telling me that an egg cream contains no eggs or cream?[526]

He pointed at me. "You're a quick learner."

His patronizing message irked what had been an excellent mood. "So, tell me, what exactly does an egg cream contain?"

"Milk, carbonated water and syrup. And just to set the record straight, I didn't mean to insult you. Outside of New York City, most folks are yet to become familiar with egg creams. I'm originally from Brooklyn. We've been drinking them there for years. I get a kick out of surprising people how they're made."

His explanation eased my pique. I said, "I never would have guessed. Anyway, it tastes mighty good." I took a bigger drink than before.

"I'm Isadore Mirkin."

"Mican Reinbow. Nice to meet you, Mr. Mirkin."

"Mr. Mirkin…that was my father. Please, call me Izzy."

The soda jerk approached Izzy. The heavy-set man with gray beard, large jowls, bald top and sizeable nose ordered a grilled cheese sandwich and carbonated water. He looked back at me. "You work at General Electric?"

I shook my head.

"One of the locomotive plants?"

"Nope."

He muttered under his breath, "0 for 2. That's not even fit for the minors." He grew briefly reflective. "Now that I've bet the chalk and lost twice…" He looked me in the eye. "You into the ponies?"

"Not really, but I think I get your message."

"Not to be nosy…on second thought, I guess it is…If not the GE or the locomotive plants, what's your angle?"

---

[526] *Egg Cream*, Wikipedia, 4 Jul. 2019 <https://en.wikipedia.org/wiki/Egg_Cream> stating: "An egg cream is a cold beverage consisting of milk, carbonated water, and flavored syrup (typically chocolate or vanilla). Despite the name, the drink contains neither eggs nor cream."

"I'm visiting. I'm from Florida...Fort Myers."

"Never been there. For that matter, I've never been further south than Coney Island...Well, that might not be true. I was born in southernmost Russia. Came here just after my first birthday, not that I remember it. But before I get too far afield, tell me: Is Florida really hotter than Hell, like folks say?"

"Never been to Hell, so I'm ill-equipped to make the comparison. Anyway, from what I've seen and heard, it gets nearly as hot here. The big differences are the humidity and how long the heat lasts. Here it comes and goes in a few days. In Florida, once it arrives, it stays for months."

The soda jerk delivered Izzy's food. He bit into his sandwich. "Not the same as what they sell at Coney Island, but not bad either." He pointed at the limited menu. "What I'd really like is a bagel with a schmear and lox, the kind they serve in New York City."[527] He heaved a sigh. "The city is amazing. Can't deny that it has things I miss."

"If that's how you feel, why'd you leave, and for that matter, why don't you go back?"

He finished chewing a bite. "Don't get me wrong. New York has its advantages, but I'll take Schenectady hands down."

"Really...why?"

"Placid streets, the cost of living, lots of green space...folks say hello on the streets, rather than jostle you out of their way...less noise and dirt...civility." Izzy paused. "New York is admittedly more exciting than Schenectady. But my holy book, the Torah, teaches us about both. At the risk of exaggerating, let me put it this way: New York is Sodom; Schenectady, Canaan. Many choose the former. I prefer the latter."

I sank my teeth into my hot dog. Like Izzy, a simple repast was sufficient to sate my appetite. On the other hand, now and then, something different, like an egg cream, was a nice addition to my diet. I said, "You have quite the city here, what with both the home of the railroad and electrical manufacturing industries. Can't imagine there's another place in the world, certainly not the size of Schenectady, that can make such a claim."

---

[527] Adamson, Melitta Weiss and Segan, Francine, *Entertaining from Ancient Rome to the Super Bowl: An Encyclopedia*, (2 volumes, Greenwood Press, Westport, Conn. 2008, p. 94), retrieved from google.com, 5 Jul. 2019 <https://books.google.com/books?id=PPDIx6WWuOQC&source=gbs_navlinks_s> stating, "Around the turn of the century [1900], brunch became a fixture on other American dining scenes. In New York City noshing on a bagel brunch—cream cheese, capers, tomato, red onion, and lox—became the highlight of a social weekend."

"People refer to us as 'the city that lights and hauls the world.'[528] The renowned George Westinghouse, Edison's nemesis—I assume you've heard of him—perfected his airbrake here in Schenectady.[529] But what I really like is that it's progressive. Union College—"

"I walked its beautiful campus my first day here."

"It was the first non-sectarian college in America, founded way back in 1795."[530] People like you, non-Caucasian, and me, Jewish, can attend, albeit, from what I've heard, subject to quotas. My own son went there and on to Albany Medical College, which is part of Union University. I love Schenectady, and I love this country. They've given immigrants like me a chance to provide my family with a better life. Back in Russia, my parents and grandparents endured pogroms. They—"

"Po what?" I said, reacting to the unfamiliar word.

"Pogroms." Izzy spelled the term. "They were anti-Semitic mob attacks, often with the sanction of the government. The mobs pillaged our villages, looted our homes and stores, raped our women and indiscriminately beat and/or murdered us."[531]

I shook my head.

"You don't believe me?" Izzy bore an indignant look.

"No…no. That's not it at all…Just the opposite. I was thinking that your people, the Jews, suffered the same oppression that those of color endured here in the United States."

Izzy pawed his ample beard. "Push comes to shove, I'd have to say that Negroes in America have had it worse than Jews in Russia. At least they didn't make slaves of us there. Even when they stole our property and drove us from our homes and villages, we could usually escape to other countries in Europe or the United States. Horrifically abused, we were, but as long as they didn't kill us, we could leave with our dignity. We weren't chattel."

The distinction he had drawn arguably had merit. But the mere fact that others may have suffered a worse fate did not diminish the evil his people had endured. A bizarre irony struck me. America, among the

---

[528] Nyczepir, Dave, *Smart City Ambitions in the 'City That Lights and Hauls the World,'* routefifty.com, posted October 12, 2016, retrieved 6 Jul. 2019 <https://www.routefifty.com/smart-cities-/2016/10/schenectady-new-york-smart-city/132307/>.

[529] Greene, Nelson, *Charles B. Knox Gelatine Co. Inc. Edition of The Old Mohawk – Turnpike Book*, N. Green (1924, p. 39-71), retrieved from Fulton County NYGenWeb, Herkimer/Montgomery Counties NYGenWeb, 1 Jul. 2019 <http://fulton.nygenweb.net/Turnpike/Turnpike.html>.

[530] Ibid.

[531] *What Were Pogroms*, myjewishlearning.com, 7 Jul. 2019 <https://www.myjewishlearning.com/article/what-were-progoms/>.

havens to which the Jews had fled, had sponsored evil, which this Jewish man deemed even more depraved than that from which the Jews had sought refuge. That the land of the Statue of Liberty, the symbol that welcomed those escaping oppression, could itself oppress, indeed fight a war where one side battled to preserve such evil, made no sense. I said, "I don't get it. How can America, supposedly founded on equality, be on the right side of the fence and the wrong side at the same time?"

Izzy shrugged. "Not really surprising." His tone was as blasé as both his words and manner.

That he had responded to my question, a rhetorical one, was unexpected. Even more surprising was his glibness. I shot him a look. "You gotta be kidding!"

Izzy laid his sandwich down. He looked me in the eye. "Every country, America included, has its share of good and bad people, a multitude of whom are credulous sheep. Narcissistic demagogues, eager to grab power and wealth, lurk. Trumpeting execrable utterances, pointing blame-laden fingers, and appealing to the worst of human predilections, these demagogues lure the sheep to barren wastelands. There the sheep willingly graze on the filthy earth, gobbling up the demagogues' dirt. Those who condemn the crud for what it is, face the wrath of the demagogues' loyal core of vicious sheepdogs...Loyalty is at the core, but it runs only one way. A demagogue's greed and self-interest trumps everything. And as for sheepdogs, they're expendable, be they French Poodles, Belgian Terriers, Tibetan Mastiffs, German Shepherds, Alaskan Huskies, Irish Setters, Russian Toys or whatever. Should they speak a discordant word or merely exhaust their usefulness, they can be thrown to the wolves." Izzy paused, just long enough for a sip of his carbonated beverage.

"Back when my ancestors were in Russia, many did not enjoy the country's economic success. When told their plight was the fault of the Jews, they willingly accepted the explanation, a justification for their own circumstances, sometimes failures." Izzy looked around, as if he were making certain that no one was listening. His voice became little more than a whisper. "As I said, America has many wonderful people, but it has its share of bad people too. Come an economic downturn, the threat of war, whatever, and the demagogues could spur anti-Semitism here. I have it good in America. I'm so blessed. But I also know that the wonderful, secure life my family and I enjoy could evaporate as fast as a puddle under a blazing summer sun. At any time, in any place, the demagogues, masters of scapegoating, lying in wait, can strike. Education, buttressed by free speech and a free press, is imperative if the demagogues are to be kept at bay."

I took a drink of my egg cream. Even more so, I imbibed Izzy's wisdom. A minute before I had asked him a baffling question, a sphinxlike anomaly, seemingly as unsolvable as Fermat's Last Theorem. An answer was unexpected. But not only had Izzy addressed the matter, he had done so with articulation as incisive as the most elegant of mathematical proofs. If that weren't enough, he had applied the resulting principle to the future. It was like Steinmetz and Edison rolled into one, abstract analysis producing a rule, coupled with a practical application vis-à-vis the future. Unfortunately, the product, possible discrimination and persecution at any time, was unappealing. It was akin to phosphorous, valuable, but volatile, capable of spontaneously bursting into flames at room temperature.[532] Impressed as I was, I wanted to confirm my understanding of his message. An example involving the United States, the country we both knew, would work best. I said, "So, what you're saying is that given adverse circumstances, a bad economy, war or a pandemic, many of the white Anglo-Saxon Protestants who founded and rule this country wouldn't hesitate to scapegoat folks like you and me."

Izzy's thick eyebrows furrowed. "That's probably true, but I believe you're painting the landscape with much too broad a brush. Sure, the waspish elements include demagogues, as well as many who are happy to follow them. But there are also courageous men and women like Abraham Lincoln, Samuel Hopkins and Harriet Beecher Stowe who fought for equality for your people, and King Boleslav of Poland—"[533]

"King who?"

"King Boleslav. I assume you've never heard of him. As the world emerged from the Dark Ages and moved into the Renaissance, King Boleslav came to power in Poland. At that time, the country, which had become Christian in the 11th century, had been carrying out the oppressive policies of Rome.[534] King Boleslav 'invited the Jews, granting them unprecedented rights and privileges.'[535] Life was good for the Jews until the middle of the 17th century, when Bogdan Chmienicki, a Ukrainian Cossack, still considered a hero by many in Kiev, led a

---

532 "White phosphorous is highly reactive, and spontaneously ignites at about 30^oC [86^oF] in moist air. It is usually stored under water, to prevent exposure to air." *Burning Phosphorous*, angelo.edu, 7 Jul. 2019 <https://www.angelo.edu/faculty/kboudrea/demos/burning_phosphorous/burning_phosphorous.htm>.

533 *The Jews of Poland – Gazeta Warszawska*, gazetawarszawska.net, 8 Jul. 2019 <https://www.gazetawarszawska.net/pugnae/2737-the-jews-of-poland>.

534 Ibid.

535 Ibid.

murderous rebellion whose genocide included the murder of 100,000 Jews.[536] And so it is, in every era, in every place, one can find those worthy of sainthood, individuals like King Boleslav, but also the most brutal hatemongers, *mamzers* as we say in Yiddish, like Chmienicki. And too, there are always many less famous people who fight oppression, but others who promote it. In between are the countless sheep, satisfied to accept the wind, whatever way it blows, and do that which is best for them."

Izzy paused before consuming the last bite of his sandwich. Rather than finishing my hot dog, I digested his comments.

"What I'm trying to say is that people, whatever their faith, whatever their race or whatever their nationality, should not be judged by such aspects. Each individual should be measured by what is in his heart, his rectitude, and what he does unto others. On the street I hear people refer to other ethnicities as micks and wops and spics. They call the Poles, cement heads. Men from my own congregation, the Hamilton Street Shul (he gestured toward the front window, in an easterly direction) are a perfect example. Most are kosher, observe the Sabbath faithfully and fast on Yom Kippur. But their mouths reflect what is in their hearts. Mention a menial task, and they're quick to urge that it should be left for a Schwartze." Izzy eyed me apologetically. "It's a Yiddish word, a demeaning one, for a black person. They may not be Chmienicki, but they are the sheep, often worse, who willingly look the other way or even cheer when Chmienicki and those like him oppress." Izzy shook his head. "And because they're my friends, rarely do I call them on it. I tell myself that I'm not nearly as bad as they. That may be true. But that's hardly a satisfactory response." A beleaguered sigh accompanied Izzy's lowering head.

A discomforting disquiet ensued. I wanted to tell him he should not blame himself, but I doubted that was what he wanted to hear, not when he had stepped back and objectively appraised his own conduct. I took hold of my hot dog and consumed the last of it. I thought of the fine people who had crossed my path over the years: Lucinda, Grover, Mr. Wright, Walter, Abbey and, most recently, Izzy. They were of differing races, sexes and religions. But as Izzy had stressed, such attributes were not the measure of a human being. People could be good regardless of color, sex, ethnicity or how they prayed to God, if they did at all. But just as surely, all races, both sexes, every ethnicity, the disciples of every

---

[536] Ibid., stating, "Chmienicki was one of the biggest anti-Semites in human history, on par with Hitler. His aim was genocide and his forces murdered an estimated 100,000 Jews in the most horrendous ways."

religion, and atheists as well, had been the face of evil, even its justification.

A minute passed when Izzy said, "I apologize."

His words of compunction dumbfounded me. "For what?"

"Putting you through a harangue...sermonizing...It's my worst habit. Sarah—she's my wife—tells me so regularly...and she's right."

I patted Izzy on the back, conscious how atypical the spontaneous reaction was for me. "You have absolutely no reason to apologize. A distaste for injustice is hardly a sin. And for that matter, I enjoyed your excellent insights."

"Thank you. You're too kind...Would you...uh...like to come for Shabbat dinner at my home tomorrow night?"

The invitation flummoxed me. "You...you're asking me, a stranger, to join your family for dinner?"

"It won't be my family. My children are long since grown with homes and families of their own. It will just be my wife Sarah and me. She's always happy to have guests on Friday evening. And as to you being a stranger (Izzy gestured at our empty plates and shook his head)...we just ate lunch together. Thirty minutes ago, you were a stranger. Not anymore. But even if you were, all the more reason to invite you. Torah teaches, 'You shall also love the stranger, for you were strangers in the land of Egypt.'[537]...So, you'll come?"

"I would love to."

"I must tell you that we don't eat until sundown. It comes late this time of year. That's when we light the candles."

"That's fine. I look forward to it."

"Wonderful. We look forward to having you." Izzy got up from his stool. "Oh, I almost forgot. You'll need to know where we live. It's 818 Hamilton Street." He pointed out the big front window of the drug store. "Over there, a couple doors down, that's Hamilton Street. Follow it up the hill for a little less than a half-mile and you'll come to 818. Ours is the upper flat." Izzy got up from his seat. "We'll see you there tomorrow evening, say 7:30." Just before he headed out the door, he put a dime tip on the counter and called to the soda jerk. "I'll deduct thirty-five cents from Mort's bill at the butcher shop."

I finished the last of my egg cream. I eyed the empty glass. Pride inhibited the temptation to order another. But no one in Schenectady knew me. "Another vanilla egg cream, please," I said. A minute later, the soda jerk brought me a second foamed-topped beverage. I sipped the

[537] Deuteronomy, 10:19.

tall delight, making sure to savor every mouthful. Schenectady was a charming place.

***

Having allowed myself plenty of time, so as not to be late, but not wanting to arrive early, I dawdled as I reached the 800-block of Hamilton Street. My pocket watch read 8:28. A minute later, I reached number 818. I rang the bell to the second-floor flat. Following the sound of footsteps, the door opened.

"Welcome," said Izzy. "Come on upstairs." He led the way to the top, where we entered an open door. To my right, toward the front of the flat, was a living room, and to my left, a dining room with a table bearing a white cloth, set with fine china and two silver candlesticks in the center.

I handed Izzy a box of chocolates and a bouquet of flowers.

"Thank you, but you needn't have." He laid the gifts aside. "Let me take your jacket. July is too warm for such attire."

I had worn my suit but was happy to rid myself of the jacket.

Izzy guided me into the dining room. "This is my wife, Sarah," he said, as a petite, gray-haired woman, barely five feet, in her sixties, entered from the kitchen.

"Mican Reinbow." I shook the hand she extended. "Thank you for inviting me."

"The pleasure is ours," said Sarah. "Shabbat is so much nicer with company."

Izzy pointed to the candy and flowers. "Mican brought us these."

"Oh, so kind of you. The flowers are beautiful." Sarah put them into a vase that she placed onto the table between the two candlesticks. She struck a match and lit the two white tapers, reciting a Hebrew blessing at the same time.

Izzy gestured me to a chair on one side of the table. Sarah seated herself at the end nearest the entryway to the kitchen, while Izzy took a crystal decanter from an adjacent credenza. "Will you join me in a glass of schnapps?"

"Yes, thanks," I said reflexively, though I had no knowledge of the term, apart from the fact that it was alcoholic.

Izzy laid a highball glass in front of me. "It's a peach brandy. Made it myself. It's a bit less fiery than the popular gin-based schnapps."

Izzy raised the glass he had poured for himself. "To good health, peace and our welcome visitor."

"And to both of you...with many thanks for your kind hospitality." I took a sip. The potent spirits, likely more than fifty proof, tasted good…too good. As a reformed alcoholic, who, over the preceding two decades had not imbibed, the beverage's appeal unnerved me. I knew all too well that imprudent indulgence could induce inauspicious implications.

"Izzy tells me you're visiting from Florida. How do you like our city?"

"Impressive. Well planned, lovely neighborhoods…it's a bastion of modern America, at the forefront of science and technology. Truly a progressive place."

Izzy chuckled.

"Did I say something funny?"

"Well, not funny…but ironic."

That my compliments to Schenectady could be deemed ironic was hard to comprehend. "How so?"

"Well…" Izzy sat motionless.

I sensed his pause involved judgment, more about whether to respond than its content.

Izzy fondled his glass of schnapps. "If I get carried away, stop me…please." He took a deep breath. "As cities go, Schenectady is indeed progressive. I often make that very point, well-aware that Jews, like Sarah and me, have it very good here. Still we're aware that this is a waspish place. Certain clubs and organizations exclude us. We're barred from most resorts in Lake George and Lake Placid.[538] When our children were in elementary school, they began their day with the Lord's Prayer. Jobs at GE and ALCO are open to all, but up against a Protestant with qualifications equal or anywhere close, we're sure to lose out. Catholics lose out as well, though their shots are better than ours. It's not all virulent bigotry. Much of it is indirect. People lean toward others who are similar, be that in religion, race, views, appearance, associations, you name it." Izzy stroked his beard. "This tangled mass fits in well at the shul…not so well with organizations like the Elks[539] or the Odd

---

[538] *Lake George | Adirondack Activism: John Apperson's Story*, 11 Jul. 2019 <https://adirondackactivism.com/lake-george/> stating: "For the '*Great and Gracious*' who owned estates on Millionaire's Row, Lake George was an exclusive playground. Like the Lake Placid Club, where Jews and consumptives were barred from membership, the Lake George Club and the Lake George Association had strict membership requirements. Most of the club members were not particularly concerned about preserving the natural undeveloped scenery for generations to follow."

[539] Bolton, Brian, *Why Do Elks Clubs Have a Religious Test* (December, 2000), 11 Jul. 2019 <https://ffrf.org/about/getting-acquainted/item/17259-why-do-elks-clubs-have-a-religious-test> indicating that the Elks Club's exclusion of non-believers ("skeptics, rationalists, humanists, agnostics, atheists, and nontheists") continues into the 21st century.

Fellows.[540] They don't welcome folks like you and me. And that's important, because relationships that often lead to jobs and other opportunities are established at those organizations. Their strict—"

A telling look from Sarah had clipped her husband's tongue. She put a bowl in front of me. "It's matzoh ball soup." She set a bowl in front of Izzy and one at her place. "Please, start. Don't let it get cold."

Following Izzy's lead, I tasted a spoonful. "It's delicious." With my spoon I lopped off a piece of one of two large matzoh balls. "So light and fluffy…absolutely luscious."

As Sarah reseated herself, a smile lit her face.

"Sarah makes the best matzoh balls." Izzy eyed his wife affectionately.

A telling moment of quiet, one hinting at a home with mutual respect and affection, ensued.

"If I may be so bold to ask," said Izzy, "have you experienced prejudice living in Florida?"

"Yes, but less in Fort Myers than when I lived in South Carolina. My wife Lucinda—she was Negro, where I'm a Black Seminole—was a social activist, fighting for civil rights for both Negroes and women. She…she was lynched by two Ku Klux Clan members." My words grew soft. The indelible image of her lifeless body, as it lay prone hours after the hanging, stirred buried emotions. Tears welled up in my eyes.

"I…I'm sorry…so sorry," said Izzy.

"Thank you," I said. "For centuries your people…the Jews have endured as bad."

"We have," said Sarah. "But our immediate families, both Izzy's and mine, were spared the horror that was visited upon you, the murder of your wife." Sarah heaved a sigh. "That it could happen in this country is hard to imagine."

"Is it?" said Izzy. "No matter the time, no matter the place, the hatemongers are present. Their numbers may vary, but they're always there. As I said yesterday, add a devious demagogue, and the vilest of forces become the norm." Izzy chortled.

Sarah gave her husband another look. "What you said was hardly funny."

"My laugh was sardonic, an acknowledgement that the tormentors foment their hate under the pretense of noble purposes…often in the

---

540 IOOF History - Iron Links Lodge No. 5, mariettaoddfellows.org, 11 Jul. 2019 <https://www.mariettaoddfellows.org/ioof-history.html> indicating it was not until 1971 that the Independent Organization of Odd Fellows removed the white-only clause from its constitution.

name of religion and God." Izzy turned my way. "No better examples than the treatment of your wife and your people. That's not to—"

"Izzy, you're preaching," said Sarah. "Mican is our guest…not a postulate in your would-be philosophy institution." She heaved a sigh as she turned my way. "Izzy loves to lecture."

"I find him interesting. He makes me think."

"Kind of you to say," said Sarah, "but you shouldn't have to endure such—"

"No, really. His insights intrigue me."

Izzy pushed out his chest. "There, you see, Sarah. Someone appreciates my…pontificating." A self-deprecating shrug, accompanied by a sheepish grin, punctuated his words. He ate some soup before continuing. "As I was about to say before the interruption, I know little of the Christain Bible, but I'm familiar with the notorious scriptures that folks used to justify slavery. Ephesians, 6:5, tells slaves to obey their 'masters with fear and trembling;' and Titus, 2:9, directs 'slaves to be submissive to their masters.'[541] And that's how it was, Mican, when the nation repeatedly removed your people, the Indians, from their native lands. Americans asserted that God had ordained that it was the nation's *manifest destiny* to expand the United States."[542]

As I digested Izzy's remarks, a thought I had entertained the day before raced through my head. This Jewish man, born in Russia, who spoke with no accent, was surprisingly egalitarian, articulate and wise.

"From the look on your face," said Izzy, "I can tell that I got carried away…just like yesterday."

"That's Izzy," said Sarah. "He loves his soapbox."

"No…no, that's not what I was thinking," I said. "I was reflecting on his thought-provoking comments."

"See, Sarah." Izzy's theatric smirk was so broad that his eyes squinted.

Sarah rolled her eyes. She circled to the far end of the table and patted her husband's balding pate before heading into the kitchen.

---

[541] *How the Bible was used to justify slavery, abolitionism—CNN Belief Blog*, cnn.com, 12 Jul. 2019 http://religionblogs.com/2011/04/12/how-the-bible-was-used-to-justify-slavery-abolitionism/>.

[542] *Manifest Destiny and Indian Removal*, Smithsonian American Art Museum website, 12 Jul. 2019 <americanexperience.si.edu/wp-content/uploads/2015/02/Manifest-Destiny-and-Indian-Removal.pdf> stating: "The self-serving concept of manifest destiny, the belief that the expansion of the United States was divinely ordained, justifiable, and inevitable, was used to rationalize the removal of American Indians from their native homelands."

Their words in a vacuum might have suggested tension, but the full scope of their antics was palpable affection.

"I hope that nothing I've said has offended you," said Izzy. "Many deem politics, religion and the like, a no-no with company." Izzy leaned over and whispered. "Don't tell Sarah, but I know my zeal gets the best of me."

I ran my index finger over my mouth. "My lips are sealed." I reached for my glass of schnapps. Discretion suggested that my lips should remain sealed for another reason. I took a drink. I felt very relaxed. "Earlier you spoke about people showing bias against those who are different. Though I was aware of the point, the extent to which it occurs escaped me."

Izzy's eyes widened. "Living in the South, you obviously saw it. Indeed, at its worst, given what happened to your wife."

"To be sure. But I failed to recognize the degree to which bias-spawned distinctions may have affected my life, especially my childhood. My mother, Negro, died when I was a toddler. My father, a Seminole Indian, was killed when I was only twelve. As Black Seminoles, not surprisingly, whites disdained us. Negroes and Seminoles, while less standoffish, were far from welcoming. But living in the isolation of the woods, prejudice affected me less than most people of color. In some respects, I was blind to it. That my parents sheltered me did not, however, imply it did not exist."

Izzy nodded. "It's everywhere. I see it in my own congregation, the Hamilton Street Shul. We're orthodox. About fifteen years ago, another Synagogue on North College Street, Congregation Shaarai Shamayam, shifted to a more liberal form of Judaism, a reform ritual.[543] Much of their service is in English, and they have forsaken many of our orthodox traditions. Some at my shul look down on them, even refer to them as 'goyim,' a not-so-endearing term for those who are not Jewish." Izzy shook his head. "I hate it. I don't know why people need to denigrate those who are different...You see it even among children. The boy or girl who is different—he or she might be smaller, smarter, look different or whatever—gets bullied. Our Torah, the Christian Bible, the Koran...they all teach kindness...yet people are mean...I don't get it.

[543] *Our History – Gates of Heaven,* cgoh.org, 12 Jul. 2019 <https://cgoh.org/our-history/>. Congregation Gates of Heaven is the oldest Jewish Congregation in Schenectady, New York. Originally orthodox, it turned toward a more liberal form of Judaism in 1892, and in 1920 officially changed its name to Gates of Heaven, the English translation of Shaarai Shamayim. (*Bookmarks'* author's comment: Growing up in Schenectady, my family belonged to both the Hamilton Street Synagogue and Gates of Heaven, but worshipped at the latter.)

Perhaps it makes them feel better, more important, if they put someone else down." Izzy lifted his glass and, after eyeing it pensively, took a drink.

I took a drink as well, the last of the tumbler's contents. I felt the effects of the alcohol.

Sarah returned from the kitchen with a tray of brisket, its seductive aroma announcing that it would please the most demanding tastes. As Izzy dished me an ample portion, Sarah fetched two side dishes, a potato knish and an unusual carrot-based mixture. She completed my gold-trimmed, ivory-hued plate with a mound of each. From my other side, Izzy refilled my glass with schnapps. Had he offered the liquor before he poured, discretion would have led me to decline.

"Please start," said Sarah. "Otherwise, it will get cold."

I hesitated, preferring to wait until her plate was filled, but once Izzy took a bite, I dug my fork into the brisket. The instant the tender, oven-roasted beef, flavored with a caramelized onion sauce, touched my tongue, I shut my eyes and basked. I slowly chewed the mouthful, savoring its heavenly taste. I said, "Your brisket is amazing, far beyond delicious."

Sarah smiled. "I'm glad you like it."

Following another bite of brisket, I tried the carrot-based mixture. It was luscious, though not the equal of the brisket. That was all but impossible. I said, "The carrots are wonderful."

"It's a tzimmis," said Sarah. "Roasted carrots, sweetened with prunes and honey."

I turned to Izzy. "You're a lucky man. Sarah is a fantastic cook."

Izzy put his hand next to his mouth and pretended to whisper. "I know, but don't tell her. She'll get a swelled head and, worse yet, make me do more chores."

"More?" said Sarah.

"I mow the lawn and…" Izzy shrugged. "Well, what can you expect when I work over sixty hours in the butcher shop."

"He does work hard, but as to the lawn, it's not all that large, and we alternate with the family downstairs. And put a hammer in his hand, and *oy vey ist mir…*"

Conversation lapsed into occasional small talk as we enjoyed the delicious meal. In between bites, I imbibed the schnapps, my sips as guilt provoking as tasty. Once our plates, including seconds, were empty, Sarah cleared the table. A minute later, she returned with a delectable strawberry shortcake. She dished me a huge portion. Decanter in hand, Izzy leaned over from my other side, ready to refill my glass.

"I better pass," I said, just before he poured. "Your schnapps is excellent, but I've exceeded my limit." The two glasses were the first I had consumed since my inebriated days in South Carolina. I took a taste of my shortcake, moistened with berries and their sugar-sweetened juice. "Scrumptious…absolutely scrumptious."

"Glad you like it," said Sarah. "If we hadn't eaten meat, I would have topped the shortcake with whipped cream. Being kosher, we don't mix milk with meat." She dug her fork into the dessert, but before taking a bite, she halted and said, "Perhaps you would like to join us for services at the Synagogue tomorrow morning?"

"Sarah!" said Izzy. "We're not evangelicals, recruiting others to Judaism. I'm sure Mican does not want to watch us daven, all in Hebrew, for three long hours."

With no plans for the day and having never seen a Jewish service, I said, "I would welcome the chance to join you."

"Did you hear that, Izzy?" said Sarah.

He looked my way. "You sure? You're not saying it, just to be polite?"

"No, I'd consider it a privilege…uh…so long as I'd be welcome."

"You will. Not to brag, but in our schul, I'm a *macher*, though certainly not the biggest. If you're with me, you're fine. Sure, some may harbor unkind thoughts. You find them everywhere. But that's their problem…Our services start at 9:00 sharp. We have a new synagogue. It just opened in April, only a block or so away, right here on Hamilton Street."[544]

"I noticed it on my way here, coming up the hill."

"Suppose we meet out front at 8:45. Okay?"

"I'll be there."

Once we finished dessert, we moved to the living room. Seated in an easy chair across from Sarah and Izzy, who were on the couch, I grew increasingly comfortable. The lovely couple, affable, kind and unpretentious, had been strangers to me only a day earlier. Already they felt like more than acquaintances. I looked forward to joining my newfound friends the following day.

---

[544] *Beth Israel and Orthodox Congregations*, schenectadyhist.wordpress.com, 14 Jul. 2019 <read://schenectadyhist.wordpress.com/tag/Schenectady/>.

Chapter XXXI

NOT WANTING TO KEEP IZZY AND SARAH WAITING, Saturday morning, I arrived at the Synagogue several minutes early. Shortly thereafter, they approached, greeting me amiably. Izzy led the way up the cement stairs into the small synagogue. Rows of pews, each covered with a padded cushion, faced an elevated altar. At the front, facing one another, on either side of the altar, were two pews. Izzy pointed at them. "Our biggest *machers*, our most important elders, occupy those two front pews."

Several people appeared to give me a look. Whether it was my imagination is hard to say. Regardless, I was less than comfortable.

Sarah went up a staircase to one of two side balconies, each of which ran most of the building's length from front to back.

"Our shul is orthodox," said Izzy. "Women pray separated from the men, who occupy the main floor. It's tradition."

"Interesting." Curiosity wheedled me to inquire how Izzy felt about the tradition. Discretion blocked the question from crossing my lips.

"Schenectady's reformed congregation, largely composed of Jews who are eager to assimilate themselves in America, does not follow many of our traditions from Europe. Their men and women sit together and few keep kosher."

Curiosity kindled again. This time, I unbridled it, rationalizing that the issue was less delicate. "How do you feel about that?"

"Let's get our seats, and then I'll answer." Izzy led the way to the far end of a pew several rows from the front. Once we were seated, with me on the end, he said, "I have mixed emotions. When you've lived with traditions for more than sixty years, it's hard to change. But change is good…I think." He chuckled. "That's a dithering answer. But…I guess that's where I'm at. Not long ago, I had to deal with the issue. The Russian Jews—that's Sarah's and my ancestry—broke off and formed a new congregation, Agudas Achim. Most everyone here is of Hungarian descent. Because we live in this neighborhood, we opted to stay with this Shul.[545] I like praying with my neighbors, but I miss the traditions that my parents brought from Russia." He shrugged. "I've got mixed emotions but...that's life. You rarely get a full cup." He stared off into space. "Given that I was able to make a choice, my cup is definitely more than half full. That's what you get in a free country...I love America."

As more congregants filed in, Izzy introduced me to several. The Rabbi and Cantor ascended the altar, and the service commenced. Initially the Rabbi spoke in what I believe was Yiddish, given that it sounded like German, not that I understood the language. The congregants opened their prayer books and, beginning at what I considered the back, commenced praying in Hebrew. People continued to file in. At times the Rabbi recited, and at others, the Cantor chanted. In between, the congregants seemingly mumbled prayers at breakneck speed, sometimes turning eight or ten pages in a minute. I had no idea what was transpiring. I repeatedly checked what page Izzy was on, flipping the pages in my prayer book accordingly, not that I could read a word. The first fifteen minutes of the service intrigued me. Intent though the supplicants appeared, their pace, coupled with what often sounded like a drone, suggested the recitations might be mindless, rather than thoughtful.

On and on...and on...the praying continued. Numerous congregants arrived long after the start of the service. Others got up and went outside, returning a while later. I would have been happy if Izzy had chosen to make us among them. My mind grew increasingly distracted. My eyes occasionally closed. I welcomed the numerous times that we stood up and sat again. The tiny bit of exercise helped me avoid nodding off. I looked around, watching men in the row in front of me. Each appeared to be fully immersed in his praying. As best I could judge, they enjoyed it. How?—was hard for me to imagine. But if not, why would they return week after week, subjecting themselves to torture? I told myself that if I knew Hebrew, my reaction would be different. The argument was unconvincing.

I began making up numerical mind games to pass the time. I calculated how many days it would take a centipede crawling at thirty inches per minute to travel the 1400 miles from Schenectady to Fort Myers. With no pencil and paper, I lost track of my calculations and had to begin anew. Where ordinarily that would have been frustrating, I welcomed the confusion; anything to eat up more time. I made up more problems: a calculation of the approximate number of words in the

---

545 Ibid.

prayer book; the number of bricks it would take to build a structure the size of the synagogue; and how many one-foot-square tiles it would take to cover the surface of the Earth. That my calculations involved estimates that may have been grossly inaccurate and that I may have made numerical errors was fine. Killing time, not accuracy, was my goal.

At long last the service came to an end. “Shabbat shalom,” said Izzy, reaching out and shaking my hand.

“Shabbat shalom,” I said, having heard the phrase years earlier in Savannah.

“Sitting through it was hard for you, wasn’t it?”

“It was fine.” My white lie was no more convincing than my earlier logic that I would enjoy the service if I knew Hebrew.

“I tried to warn you when Sarah extended the invitation. Several years ago I sat through a Catholic mass in Latin. I have a notion what this was like for you, not that the Catholic service was nearly this long.”

“It wasn’t—” I cut myself off. Another unconvincing white lie would do me no good. “Well, now I can say that I have observed a Jewish service.”

“That you can,” said Izzy. “On a brighter note, now we adjourn to the basement for our *Kiddush*.”

The possibility that the praying was about to resume was hardly a brighter note. My face apparently reflected my thought.

“Before I strike fear into your heart, let me explain. The *Kiddush* is where we grab a nosh and socialize. C’mon, let’s go downstairs.”

I followed Izzy into the basement. The women, who had already gathered there, were laying out a variety of foodstuffs on two long tables. Izzy introduced me as he exchanged greetings with other men. They paid me little attention. Whether they were snubbing me or anxious to eat was difficult to discern. Perhaps, both. Izzy grabbed two mini-cups of wine from one of the tables.

“Before eating, we have to say the blessing over the wine.” He handed me a cup. “Don’t drink it yet. First we have to recite the prayer.”

The last thing I needed was alcohol. Less than twenty-four hours before, I had consumed two drinks in one sitting for the first time in more than two decades. Adding another first, alcoholic beverages on consecutive days, was a debacle waiting to happen.

The Cantor led everyone in chanting a brief Hebrew blessing, one they called the *Kiddush*, after which the men all called out, *L’Chaim*, and imbibed.

I raised the cup to my lips, barely allowing them to be moistened by the vessel’s purple liquid.

The Cantor chanted another blessing, *HaMotzi*, over a large challah bread, two feet long, bearing a golden brown, rippled crust. He made the first cut into the loaf, after which another man continued to carve. Amidst a growing din, the men surged to the spread of food: bagels, lox, white fish, capers and cream cheese. On the other side of the table, the women did likewise. I hung back until Izzy encouraged me to move forward. I laid my cup of wine on the table and made myself a small sandwich, folding a large slice of challah, coated with cream cheese, around two small slices of lox. With my sandwich on a little plate, I stepped back from the table, allowing others access. My cup of wine remained on the table, abandoned.

Once we finished eating, a tasty repast at that, we headed outside where Sarah joined us.

"What did you think of the service?" said Sarah.

"What do you think he thought?" said Izzy. "Having to endure hours of incomprehensible—"

"Let Mican speak for himself."

I would have been happy to let Izzy speak for me, but he had been silenced. "It…it was interesting and…uh…different." The euphemisms poorly masked the truth. It had been an unintelligible bout with mind-numbing tedium.

"Sorry we put you through it," said Izzy.

"Oh, it wasn't all that bad." My denial echoed…resoundingly. It was pregnant with admission, enough so, that Sarah allowed Izzy the last word, a look that said, *I told you so.*

A blue canopy reigning high above greeted us as we descended the stairs that led from the synagogue's front entrance.

"We're going to the library," said Izzy. "It's what we do every Saturday after services. We're not allowed to work or cook or even operate a light switch until sundown when the Sabbath ends. We walk, read, think…things like that. Some view it as a burden, but I revel in it. It forces me to relax. Without the stricture, I'd be at the butcher shop, eleven or so hours, the way I am Monday through Friday, slaving away—excuse my hyperbolic use of the shameful term. I'm also grateful for the Christian blue laws. I get Sunday off as well, though admittedly on Sunday I do chores like mowing the lawn, tending to our little garden and…whatever." Izzy hesitated. "Don't feel obliged…but if you'd like, you're welcome to accompany us to the library."

Sarah threw up her hands in what was plainly a melodramatic display. "You give me a hard time because I invite Mican to services. At least that was something new. He can go to a library anytime."

"Well…since I have no plans, and I like libraries, I'd love to go."

"See," said Izzy, punctuating the word with a smirk, a loving one nonetheless.

"You're sure, Mican?" said Sarah, seemingly ignoring her husband.

"No, really. I would love to go."

Sarah turned to Izzy. "Gosh, that's twice you were right." She turned to me. "That ups his batting average to roughly .085. He'd better stick to butchering, because the Yankees sure don't need players with those numbers.

That Sarah, like her husband, apparently had an interest in baseball surprised me, not that there was a reason for my presupposing otherwise. On second thought, there was, my ignorance-based bias. I had assumed that Orthodox Jews, especially their women, with their unusual religious traditions, didn't appreciate frolic and sports, including baseball.

"I think you'll like our library," said Izzy. "It was built just four years ago.[546] It's a beautiful structure, bigger than one might expect in a city of our size. We're proud of it, as well as our school system. Folks here care about education." Izzy pointed. "The library is about a mile north of here, approximately a twenty-minute walk…if that's okay?"

"Fine," I said, happy to stroll through more of the city's lovely tree-lined streets.

Izzy led the way. He said, "Today in shul, I prayed that you enjoy *nachas*—that's Hebrew for satisfaction and pleasure. Good people like you deserve good things."

"Thank you. But if anyone deserves…*nachas*—did I say that right?"

Izzy nodded.

"It's you and Sarah, with all the kindness you've shown me."

"It's our privilege," said Sarah. "We love the chance to get to know people from other cultures. It's not easy, even though we have a melting pot, a mixture of Italians, Polish, Irish, to name a few, as well as people of different religions. Most everyone tends to be clannish. They gravitate to their own. All too often they distrust those who are different. I see it in our own Jewish community. God forbid their children should marry a non-Jew. It's a *shanda*…a disgrace. Some even disown their children." Staring off into space, Sarah shook her head. "How can a parent disown

---

[546] *Schenectady Public Library — Hoxsie*, hoxsie.org, 9 Jul. 2019 <http://hoxsie.org/2017/08/22/schenectady-public-library/> stating: "The building…was completed in 1903 at a cost of $55,000, greatly aided, as so many city libraries were, by the Andrew Carnegie Foundation, which donated $50,000, and by Union College, which offered the land on the northeast corner of its pasture. General Electric donated $15,000, and the City Council appropriated $5,000 annually for light, heat and general maintenance."

a child?" She heaved a beleaguered sigh. "And for of all reasons, loving someone."

"Sarah's ahead of her time," said Izzy. "And for that matter, like me, she was happy when our children married Jewish. It's nice to go to their homes and see the Jewish traditions carried on. But in the great scheme of things, it's far more important that they chose spouses who are good people...kind, caring and honest. Sadly, many Jewish parents prefer that their children marry a mean-spirited Jew, rather than a kind-hearted gentile. Hypocrisy, along with pride, supersedes the happiness of their children. A few in our synagogue still arrange marriages. I love my traditions, but not all vestiges from the old country are good. Unfortunately, some not so sound, persist."

"I hear what you're saying." My response was knee-jerk, rather than weighed. Sarah and Izzy's comments had laid bare a bias of my own. My earlier surprise that Izzy was articulate, knowledgeable and spoke with no accent had been predicated upon stereotypes, not facts. A man who had arrived in America shortly after his first birthday, attended American schools and visited the library regularly was likely to be well-spoken and accent-free. That he was an Orthodox Jew of Russian descent did not imply otherwise. Izzy and Sarah were every bit American as I. How often I had been offended by people who assumed that a Black Seminole, such as myself, could not be educated and display an excellent command of the language. That I would invoke another's race, religion or ethnicity to arrive at an analogous, haughty presumption was reprehensible. Fortunately, my indiscretion, though undeniable, was apparent only to me.

As we turned onto Seward Place, passing along the westerly side of the Union College campus, Sarah said, "Mican, you are the first Indian, Black Seminole or otherwise, with whom I have ever spent any time. I am thankful for the chance. Like Izzy, I too love America. But we in this country owe apologies to those who bear the scars of our past. No people merit such apologies more than Negroes and Indians. You fit into both categories. You have ancestors who were indigenous. You also have ancestors who were brought to this country involuntarily, in chains, as chattel. Most of us, from the Pilgrims to the countless European transplants of the 19th century, came as immigrants seeking a better life. Rather than slamming our doors on new immigrants, we should offer them sanctuary. We should repay the largess that we enjoy. You, on other hand, owe no such debt."

Having always faced the challenge of second-class citizenship, it was the first time anyone had ever suggested that I was part of a special class, arguably entitled to distinct recognition.

"Sarah's point is well taken," said Izzy. "The Indians, such as yourself, occupied this country long before Columbus set foot in the New World. These lands were wrongfully taken from them."

I shrugged. "Isn't that the way it's been throughout history. Nations have repeatedly pursued conquests and engaged in economic exploitation and imperialism. No sooner do they accomplish their misdeeds than they rewrite history, often pretending their conduct was a noble cause."

"That's exactly as I see it," said Izzy. "I've often made the point to others. They generally agree, at least until I link it to our own country. Once I mention the Indians and Manifest Destiny, the annexation of Hawaii, the Mexican American War, and, more recently, the acquisition of the Philippines, Guam and Puerto Rico following the Spanish American War,[547] they become indignant. They argue that we were defending our interests or otherwise justified...Don't get me wrong. As I've previously said, I'm thrilled to be an American, to live in this wonderful country, but as blessed as we are, we need to look into the mirror and judge ourselves objectively. Egypt, Greece and Rome all did great things. They built empires that lasted centuries. They had remarkable intellectual, social and economic achievements, but along the way, each embraced slavery, assaulted and plundered other societies and

---

[547] *American Imperialism*, Wikipedia, 19 Jul. 2019 <https://en.wikipedia.org/wiki/American_imperialism> stating: "The US is generally agreed to have had a policy of formal imperialism in the late 19th century...A national drive for territorial acquisition across the continent was popularized in the 19th century as the ideology of Manifest Destiny. It came to be realized with the Mexican-American War of 1846, which resulted in the annexation of 525,000 square miles of Mexican territory, stretching to the Pacific Ocean...The Indian Wars against the indigenous population began in the British era. Their escalation under the federal republic allowed the US to dominate North America and carve out the 48 continental states. This is now understood to be an explicitly colonial process, as the Native American nations were usually recognized as sovereign entities prior to annexation. Their sovereignty was systematically undermined by US state policy (usually involving unequal or broken treaties) and white settler-colonialism. The climax of this process was the California genocide...[Theodore] Roosevelt claimed that he rejected imperialism, but he embraced the near-identical doctrine of expansionism...Roosevelt was so committed to dominating Spain's former colonies that he proclaimed his own corollary to the Monroe Doctrine as justification, although his ambitions extended even further, into the Far East...Industry and trade are two of the most prevalent motivations of imperialism. American intervention in both Latin America and Hawaii resulted in multiple industrial investments, including the popular industry of Dole bananas. If the United States was able to annex a territory, in turn they were granted access to the trade and capital of those territories. In 1898, Senator Albert Beveridge proclaimed...'Fate has written our policy for us; the trade of the world must and shall be ours.'"

perpetrated atrocities.[548] One could argue that the propensity to do evil is an inherent facet of human nature. I believe otherwise. I want our country to be better. But to do so, objectivity is a prerequisite."

Sarah shot Izzy a look.

"What's the matter, Dear? Don't tell me you disagree."

"No. But that's not the point. You're back on your soapbox, and of all people, you're preaching to Mican, an Indian and a Negro, one who has endured the repercussions of America's worst indiscretions."

A sheepish expression painted Izzy's face. "Uh, sorry. I got carried away…again."

"Izzy means well," said Sarah, "but now and then…well, what can I say?" She turned to her husband. "Last night, after Mican left, you mentioned that you needed to clarify your pontifications about Protestant Americans. Rather than adding more pontifications, now might be a good time for that clarification."

Izzy swallowed hard. "The other day, when I criticized white Anglo-Saxon Protestants for their treatment of people of other religions, races and from other countries, I didn't mean to single them out. I was merely using them as an illustration because they happen to be the dominant group here in America. But their conduct is common to dominant groups everywhere. More important, singling them out makes me guilty of the very discrimination I was condemning. Many white Anglo-Saxon Protestants were abolitionists. They fought for racial equality. Others advocated for the rights of women. They fostered policies that enabled people like me to come to this country. The bottom line is that every person is entitled to be judged according to his or her individual merit. Every…"

"Dear, you've made your point!" Sarah winked at her husband.

---

[548] *PELOPONNESIAN WAR (431 B.C. TO 404 B.C.). THUCYDIDES AND THE END OF CLASSICAL GREECE*, factsanddetails.com, 19 Jul. 2019 <http://factsanddetails.com/world/cat56/sub366/item2039.html> stating: "The Peloponnesian War was one of the bloodiest and cruelest wars in ancient history. Greeks for [sic] Athens and Sparta committed horrible atrocities against one another and refused to tolerate neutrality by the other Greek city states. Children were murdered in their classrooms by mercenaries; civilians were murdered and enslaved en masse; worshippers were burned at the altar where the[y] prayed and the dead were left to rot in the battlefields." *Slavery & Sexual Exploitation: Why The Romans Were an Appalling Civilisation* [sic], sabotagetimes.com, 20 Jul. 2019 <https://sabotagetimes.com/life/slavery-sexual-exploitation-why-the-romans-were-an-appalling-civilisation> stating: "The glory of Rome was founded on blood. The Republic's – and, later, Empire's – massive economy and rapid territorial expansion were both funded primarily by plunder." *See also*, *Top 10 Worst Moments in Human History – Listverse*, listverse.com, 20 Jul. 2019 <https://listverse.com/2012/03/02/top-10-worst-moments-in-human-history/> listing the Crusades as number one.

Izzy looked my way. "Sorry, I—"

"Don't apologize. You hate injustice. That's hardly grounds for regrets."

"Thanks," said Izzy. He pointed. "Straight ahead. That's our new public library. What do you think?"

"Impressive." The large, off-white, two story stone structure was much larger than I had anticipated. Set back on a small hill, it was more typical of what one might have expected for a courthouse or a new high school.

"It's in the Beaux Arts style," said Izzy.

"So, I see. I love the center section with its engaged columns[549] and Greek pediment at the top. The symmetry of the tall Romanesque windows and dental molding all the way around give it character."

Izzy was wide eyed. "You know more about our library than we do. You an architect by any chance?"

"No, though I had a good friend, back during my days in Savannah and St. Augustine, who loved the subject and often pointed out the architectural aspects of buildings." My comment triggered a momentary notion, how long it had been since I had thought about Noah. "As for my knowledge of Beaux Arts, it's merely by chance. Just before coming to Schenectady, I stopped in New York City. A scale model of the new Grand Central Terminal they're building, along with a pamphlet, clued me in. Walking the streets of New York, I saw more examples. Had you shown me your library a week ago, I would have known next to nothing."

"You should have kept that a secret," said Sarah. "Even so, we're impressed."

Izzy led the way inside the main hall. We circled the area before climbing a stone staircase to the second floor.

"It's not merely an impressive building. There are so many books."

"Isn't that what you expect to find in a library?" said Sarah.

"Yes, but…" The absurdity of my comment a moment earlier gave me pause. "But so many thousands in a city of this size—it's unexpected."

"I was teasing. I knew what you meant." Sarah smiled.

That she felt comfortable enough to rib me good-naturedly was welcome. It reinforced my observation from the prior evening about the rapidity with which our relationship had progressed. It also reinforced

---

[549] An engaged, applied or attached column is a column that is attached to a building such that it only protrudes as a half-column. Unlike a pilaster, which is rectangular, a column is rounded. *All About Pilasters in Architecture,* thoughtco.com, 20 Jul. 2019 <https://www.thoughtco.com/what-is-a-pilaster-engaged-column/4045117>.

the fact that I had stereotyped orthodox Jews. Knowing almost nothing about them, except that they followed strict religious rules, I had erroneously presumed they were somber, with little sense of humor.

"We're going back to the main floor," said Izzy. "Every week I read twenty pages from the encyclopedia. It replaces the college education I couldn't afford when I graduated high school. Sarah likes to read fiction, especially the classics. To each his…or her own."

"Novels," said Sarah, "are a nice escape from the everyday world, not that the latter is bad. Drifting into imaginative places, the kinds that kids enjoy, is fun."

I eyed the many rows of shelved books. "I think I'll wander around up here for a while."

Izzy and Sarah headed downstairs. I meandered through the second-floor stacks. I randomly stopped, pulling a book from a shelf, merely because its spine was attractively trimmed. Fort Myers had a cute little library, but it was nothing by comparison. Not since my days at the University of South Carolina, more than thirty years before, had I seen such an extensive library. Even the fine collection at the Key West Courthouse fell short. Schenectady was no New York City, but in its own way, very impressive. Cutting edge industry, a research laboratory, a well-maintained business district, complemented by a fine college, excellent library and public education system, all of which was interwoven with lovely homes on tree-lined streets, combined to form a delightful community. Sublime or idyllic, certainly not; but extraordinary, indeed. Save for the winters, I could imagine myself spending much more time in the uncommon place. That said, I loved my tropical-paradise environs south of Fort Myers. Small though my home was, with the many improvements I had made over the years, it was a far cry from the simple cabin of my childhood. I had no thoughts of abandoning my home. But original ambivalence whether my stay might be nearer to a week or a month had been resolved. It would be much closer to the latter. There was much to see and do in Schenectady, and with the Schenectady Railway Company operating trolleys to nearby Albany, Troy and Saratoga, I could visit those other nearby cities. I was especially interested in Saratoga with its legendary healing mineral springs, and, more important, its racetrack, where wealthy Americans, as well as Europeans, gathered, as they had done each summer since the middle of the War of Secession, to view and place bets on thoroughbred races.[550]

I wandered among the shelves looking for a book or two that I could read at night in my hotel room or while relaxing in a park on a sunny afternoon. In the fiction area, I selected Anton Chekhov's *Cherry Orchard*, and in the non-fiction section, I chose John Stuart Mill's *On Liberty*. I took my selections to a librarian behind the main desk on the first floor.

"Excuse me, Ma'am. I'm visiting Schenectady from Florida for a few weeks, and I was wondering, might I take these books out of the library?"

"You certainly can." The woman handed me an index card,[551] along with a pencil. "Just put your name, date of birth, home address and the address where you're staying in Schenectady on this card."

I filled out the card as she had instructed and handed it back to her.

Her head jerked back and her eyes went wide. She stared at me. Her face bore a bewildered expression. "I'll be right back." She went to a private section far behind the main desk.

Baffled by her bizarre behavior, I became antsy. Did her reaction relate to my race? Did she think I was a criminal, the kind whose photograph and name appeared on the wall of a post office? I considered leaving. But she had my personal information, written in my own hand. Ambivalent and confused, I waited.

A minute later she returned. Without saying a word, atop the two books I had chosen, she laid a bookmark. Crafted of birchbark with a red heart and bearing a turquoise in the shape of a hexagonal solid, attached by a leather cord, it was unmistakable. I glanced at the woman and back at the bookmark, as my mind endeavored to digest the evidence. I refocused on the woman. With stunned disbelief all but choking off my voice, I whispered, "Abbey…Abbey, is that you?"

She nodded.

Studying her, or more precisely gawking, I observed the resemblance to my childhood sweetheart. Slim and shapely, she appeared younger than her age, middle fifties, like me. Her once blond

---

[550] *History of Saratoga Race Course, One of the Oldest Race Tracks in America*, saratogatrack.com, 23 Jul. 2019 <https://www.saratogaracetrack.com/about/history-saratoga-race-course/>.

[551] The index card was invented by Carl Linnaeus, referred to as "the father of taxonomy," the science of classifying organisms. *Index Card - Wikipedia*, Wikipedia, 24 Jul. 2019 <https://en.wikipedia.org/wiki/Index_card> stating: "Card catalogs as currently known arose in the 19th century, and Melvil Dewey standardized the index cards used in library card catalogs in the 1870s."

hair had turned to shiny silver, but her blue eyes were as lovely as ever. Still apparent were the high cheekbones and turned-up nose adorning the heart-shaped face that I recalled. Characteristics of my childhood sweetheart were manifest, but in all probability, had I passed her on the street, even spoken to her, without the benefit of a telling clue, like the bookmark, no way would I have recognized her. The oddity that our paths would intersect crossed my mind. But maybe it was not so odd. This was the area to which her family had moved when Fort Myers had shut down at the end of the war. I said, “It’s wonderful to see you.”

“Wonderful to see you too.” She smiled.

I gestured at the bookmark. “I can’t believe you still have it.”

“I would never part with it, though it is a bit worn. The birchbark has darkened, and the edges are frayed, but that’s because I use it all the time.”

“You’re a librarian?”

“And you must be a detective.” She winked.

I relished the good-natured jab. “The decades have done nothing to dull your sense of humor.”

Her eyes narrowed, as she seemingly analyzed my comeback. “For the sake of politeness, I’ll take that as a compliment. But don’t you dare think me a gudgeon for doing so.”

I shrugged. “No risk of me doing that…not when I don’t even know the word.”

“That’s okay. You were the numbers whiz kid. Matter of fact, I’ve never met anyone quicker.”

“You remember when you taught me to read?”

She nodded. “It was easy. It was also a pleasure. You were an excellent student, not to mention that I had a crush on you.”

“The feeling was mutual, as you well know…By any chance, do you remember the last time we were together?”

“You must be kidding. No woman forgets her first kisses.”

“You recall—”

She motioned about ten feet to my right where another patron was apparently waiting to be helped. “I’ve got to get back to work.” She checked out my books and handed them to me.

“Might we talk a bit once the library closes?”

“Provided you’re willing to wait till four. That’s when we close on Saturdays.”

“That would be fine.”

She headed off to help the waiting patron.

I glanced at the big clock on the wall behind the desk. It was several minutes after two. Less than two hours to kill.

I searched out Izzy and Sarah to thank them, let them know that I had met a childhood friend and that I intended to stay at the library until closing. I seated myself at a table on the main floor and began to read *The Cherry Orchard*. Mill's *On Liberty* was far too deep. It turned out that even a child's book would have been more than I could handle. My mind remained transfixed on Abbey. Perhaps I could invite her to dinner. But what if she was married? No way would she accept my invitation. I hadn't noticed whether she was wearing a wedding ring, and the table where I sat was too distant to tell, especially with her behind the main desk.

The minutes slowly ticked. Boredom set in as I constantly checked the clock. It was as if the library were moving past me at more than ninety percent of the speed of light such that the time dilation predicted by Albert Einstein's Theory of Special Relativity, a recent outgrowth of the Lorentz Contractions, was evident. The thought of the scientific theory, brought to mind one of its core postulations, $E = mc^2$. The elegant expression, tiny though it was, voiced amazing principles: energy and matter are interchangeable; a meager amount of matter is equivalent to a humungous quantity of energy; and the relationship between the two quantities, energy and mass, is proportional to the square of the speed of light. The musing triggered a recollection of a view Professor Hopkins had expressed in my calculus class years earlier at the University of South Carolina. He had called the equal sign the most powerful word in any language. At the time I deemed the claim intriguing, not that I was convinced. But Einstein's equation, the quintessential example of Professor Hopkins' contention, pressed me to reconsider the matter. The simple expression manifested the power of the equal sign. Professor Hopkins may have been an insufferable bigot, but his point bore more credence than I had originally afforded it. My concession, however, was not without irony. The word *equal*, evidence of its power, appeared in no more noteworthy site than the Declaration of Independence, the document's pronouncement, "All men are created equal." Professor Hopkins may have recognized the power of the word *equal*, but respect it, he did not. Intolerance was his calling card. The observation, coupled with continued ruminations about Einstein's brilliant proposition, shifted my brain into high gear. Ennui associated with my wait for Abbey evaporated. Time seemingly accelerated, and before I knew it, the four o'clock hour arrived.

Abbey came my way. "I'll meet you outside. I have to make certain that everyone is out of the library before locking up."

I went outside and waited not far from the front door. About five minutes later, Abbey came through the portal, which she locked behind her. As she approached, I stole a glance at her left hand. There was no ring.

"Would you like to join me for an early dinner?"

"Dinner?"

Her interrogatory inflection, coupled with ensuing hesitation, elevated the odds of an unfavorable reply.

"Well…for old times' sake…why not?"

"Great…Since I'm unfamiliar with the area, perhaps you could suggest a place."

"If you don't mind walking—it will give us some time to build up an appetite—the restaurant in the Vendome Hotel is nice. It's about a mile from here, in the four-hundred block of State Street."

"Yes, I've passed by it. I'm staying nearby, at the Foster Hotel."

We started on our way, heading south on Seward Place.

"What brings you to Schenectady?"

"Having never been north of South Carolina, I thought it might be nice to see the Northeast. I met Thomas Edison in Fort Myers and—"

"Wow! You met Thomas Edison? That's impressive."

"Not really. As you may know, he winters in Fort Myers. That's where I live. He's very friendly, and with our population only about two thousand, lots of folks there get to meet him. But anyway, he told me a little about Schenectady, and it, including his laboratory, seemed like an interesting place to visit."

"Have you been in Fort Myers ever since the War of Secession ended?"

I shook my head. "No, I've moved around. First to Savannah and then—"

"Now that you mention it, I recall, that was where you were going when they shut the fort down, when my family came here. You went with…uh…I don't remember his name, the nice Negro stableman."

"Grover."

"Ah, yes, Grover. He helped you make my bookmark. Right?"

"You've got a great memory, not that it's a shocker. You were always very smart."

"You were nobody's fool." She gestured at the two books I held at my side. "And I'm glad to see you're still reading."

"Thanks to you."

"It was my pleasure. I loved spending time with you. As for my parents, they were not so keen about it."

"I recall that all too well. How are they?"

Abbey sighed. "They both passed. My dad died about…seven years ago, and my mom, just last year, shortly before her seventy-sixth birthday."

"I'm sorry." I might have said more, but the unexpected news left me ill-equipped. Regardless, I suspected that Abbey might prefer a few moments of quiet reflection.

For several hundred yards, we continued in silence. Melodic voices of songbirds filled my ears as we strolled the sidewalks of neatly maintained streets beneath the shading canopies of elms and maples and others I couldn't identify. More than anything, I basked in the tranquility, savoring the pleasure of Abbey's company.

As we passed a bright white wooden fence, fronted by lavender, purple and pink flowers, Abbey gestured at the array and said, "I love their 'heavenly, sweet-spicy scent.'[552]…You know what they are?"

"Not really, but their fragrance is wonderful."

"They're sweet peas. Do you have them in Fort Myers?"

I shrugged. "When it comes to flowers, not many I recognize…But I know that we turn at the corner up ahead. That's State Street. Right?"

"Exactly…and the Vendome is just a couple of blocks down the hill."

We turned west onto State, downhill past a tiny park that divided an extra-broad portion of the thoroughfare and proceeded to the restaurant. Just inside the entryway, a fashionably attired maître d' stood behind a lectern.

"A table for two, please," I said.

The maître d' gave me a look, one that I instantly translated.

"Miss Abbey, it's a pleasure to see you," said the maître d'. "Been a while. Not like the days when your father, the major, and your mother were frequent visitors. Follow me." He led the way to a table in a back corner. He helped Abbey into her chair and handed us each a menu before leaving.

Once I seated myself, I said, "Your father was a major?"

"Yes, after we moved up here, he was promoted, first to captain and then major."

I looked around the establishment. Early as it was, only a couple of tables were occupied, both near the front. The half-dozen patrons were all white. I said, "I have the feeling the maître d' might not have seated us were I with someone other than you."

Abbey heaved a sigh.

---

552 *19 Fragrant Flower and Shrub Favorites for Your Garden*, gardenerspath.com, 28 Jul. 2019 <https://gardenerspath.com/plants/flowers/fragrant-favorites/>.

"That was hardly a denial."

"The world still isn't the way it should be…not that I need to tell you. It's…it's…what can I say? We both know it." She shook her head.

"What does that mean?"

"Do I have to say it in so many words?"

Rather than respond, I waited.

"It's been more than forty years since my parents forbade me to see you. For that matter, they're probably turning over in their graves right now."

I looked her in the eye. "Would you rather we leave? We could grab sandwiches at the deli and eat them on a bench in the park. Or for that matter, if this whole idea of dinner was bad, one that makes you uncomfortable, we can skip it." My chivalrous offer reverberated, its echoes warning that it was an invitation to nix a wonderful evening.

"No, all the more reason for us to stay."

Whether Abbey was making a political statement or voicing a desire to spend the evening with me, I couldn't say. Though I preferred the latter, the former was acceptable. It was enough for us to have dinner together.

A Negro gentleman, likely in his forties, poured us some water.

Once he left, I said, "At least our waiter should be fine serving us."

Abbey rolled her eyes. "He's only a bus boy. All the waiters here are white."

"Oh…" I said.

She looked me in the eye. "You okay?"

"Absolutely. I asked you to dinner. I'm thrilled you accepted. And nothing on my part will change that."

"Nothing on my part either."

I reveled in her response. "I guess we should check the menu, unless you already know and can make a recommendation."

"If past experience holds true, the sirloin steak will be excellent."

"Sounds good to me."

Moments later our waiter approached. Once we passed on drinks, he took our order and left. Unlike the maître d', he was pleasantly civil. The eventuality buoyed me with the possibility the balance of our meal would be free of further discomfiture.

I said, "Earlier we talked about Fort Myers and me. Tell me what you've been doing these many years."

"Okay, but afterwards you'll have to fill in more details about yourself." Abbey sipped her water. "There's not a lot to tell. Once we moved here, I went to the local public schools. After high school came Vassar."

"Vassar…that's impressive."

As if I hadn't made the comment, Abbey, with familiar modesty, disregarded it.

"After graduating, I took a job as a librarian, and that's what I've been doing ever since."

"No marriage or children?" Qualms about impertinence failed to quell my curiosity.

She shook her head. "I lived at home with my parents until they passed away. Not very exciting, but it's been a good life. They left me quite comfortable. For that matter, my mom, before she died, repeatedly encouraged me to give up my job and, as she put it, 'relax.'"

"So, why didn't you?"

"I love the library. You know I love books. Anyway, what would I do all day if I didn't work?"

"Read."

"Fourteen hours a day?...I enjoy being with people." She reached for her water, but before taking a drink, said, "I've filled you in on my life. Now it's your turn."

"It's a long story. I'm not sure you—"

"I've got time, and if it's too long, I'll let you know."

I told her about my education in Savannah and the Wrights. I made no mention of Sarah Jones. I related my time in St. Augustine, the foreman who falsely accused me while working on construction of the hotel, and my time building homes and working on the lighthouse. Our waiter brought our food. I reached the point when I applied to the University of South Carolina.

Abbey's fork, laden with a piece of steak, stopped inches from her mouth. "You applied to the University of South Carolina?"

"Yes, and I was accepted."

Her eyes ballooned.

"Believe it or not, for several years during Reconstruction the student population of the University of South Carolina was predominantly Negro."

"Really?" She spoke the word with a full mouth.

"It was only a few years. Once Reconstruction ended, the university closed. It reopened around 1880 as an all-white school."

"Did you graduate before the school closed?"

"I did, with concentrations in mathematics and physics."

"Impressive."

I chewed a mouthful of baked potato, an accompaniment to our steaks. Self-debate whether to mention Lucinda was quickly resolved. A mere hour with Abbey had bridged the half-century gap. I felt remarkably comfortable. "I met my wife, Lucinda, at the University of South Carolina."

"What did she study there?"

If Abbey had a reaction to the fact that I had been married, she did not show it. "Her concentrations were also in math and physics. She was extremely bright."

"Did you say *was*?"

I nodded slowly. "She was an activist…fighting for racial equality and women's rights. A pair of Ku Klux Klanners lynched her."

Abbey laid her fork down. Voice soft, she said, "I'm so sorry."

"Even including our courtship, we…we only had a few years together." My voice cracking, I had all I could do to complete the sentence. The ghastly image of her lifeless body after it had been taken to the AME Baptist Church reemerged from my memory bank. A tear dripped onto my cheek.

Abbey sat motionless, likely at a loss for words.

Self-debate raged again. I took a couple of bites. Finally, I said, "After Lucinda died, I languished in a wretched void. For a number of years, I turned to the bottle. It numbed me, not that it altered reality."

"No one could blame you. Losing someone you love is always hard, but the way you did, it's…it's unspeakable."

"Thank you," I said, conscious that her heartfelt words helped. I realized that scars of Lucinda's loss, far from erased, covered wounds never properly healed.

For several minutes we dined in silence, finishing our entrees. To label it a pall would be hyperbolic, but the mood was somber. We finished our entrees and, after declining anything further, I paid our bill. Abbey surprised me when she offered to share the cost, but like any proud man of the day, no way would I consider it. We headed outside.

"My home is about a fifteen-minute walk from here, on Park Avenue, not far from the college. Since your hotel is just up the street, no need for you to accompany me."

"On the contrary, my dear, chivalry demands." I bowed, doffing an imaginary hat. Quite apart from decorum, my desire to spend more time with Abbey prompted my offer.

Abbey gestured to the northeast. "It's this way."

I considered taking her hand. Not sure how she would react, I avoided the risk. An irony struck me. The nervousness I felt when courting Abbey when we were kids at Fort Myers was back. In the years since Lucinda had died, with my hermit's life, I had not courted a woman. Confidence acquired over several years during my younger days was ancient history.

We worked our way north, where we turned west, following Union Street until we reached Park Avenue. Turning north again, as we moved into what was a fine residential area, we passed about a half-dozen houses, some one-family, but others, two.

"This is it," said Abbey. She gestured at a well-maintained, one-family, red and gray wood Victorian, a two-story, plus an attic, with porches fronting both the first and second floor.

Invoking my construction experience, as well as my numerical propensities, I guesstimated it to be roughly twenty-five feet wide and forty feet deep, about one-thousand square feet per floor. "Very nice."

We climbed the several stairs onto the porch.

"I had a lovely evening," said Abbey.

"Me too."

She unlocked the door and stepped inside. "I'm so glad we had a chance to catch up after all these years." She appeared ready to close the door.

"Would you…uh…like to get together…go to Central Park or something…tomorrow?"

"Well, on Sunday I always go to church…but if you'd like to join me, you're welcome."

I gestured at myself. "Do folks in your congregation welcome people like me…you know, those who aren't white?"

"Some do…and some don't. But that's their problem. I went through that with my parents nearly a half-century ago. I vowed back then if there was ever a next time, I would not be cowed. So, if you're willing, the invitation is open."

"I'd love to."

"You sure…even before you know what kind of congregation I belong to?"

I shrugged. "This morning I went to services at an orthodox Jewish synagogue with this lovely Jewish couple I met. It was all in Hebrew. I didn't understand a word. If I can do that, I can handle anything."

"Okay, but just for the record, I'm Presbyterian."

"Gee, that's not far from Baptist, what I was, sorta, back when…" My voice trailed off. Referencing Lucinda again was too difficult. "What time should I come for you?"

"Sunday services are at ten. Our church is about a mile west of here at 209 Union Street—that's the street we just came from. Your hotel, the Foster, is south of the church. It makes no sense for you to come here first. Suppose I meet you outside the church about twenty minutes before the service?"

"I'll be there."

Abbey looked me in the eye. “You sure you want to spend another day praying?”

“C’mon, as a stranger in the city, I don’t have anything else to do.” The insipid response reverberated in my ears. “I didn’t mean that the way it sounded.”

Abbey rolled her eyes.

“Really. I would love to spend more time with you.”

Abbey smiled, just before she closed the door.

Chapter XXXII

SUNDAY MORNING, I ARRIVED AT THE FIRST PRESBYTERIAN CHURCH about ten minutes before the appointed time. Rather than wait directly in front, I located myself adjacent to the sidewalk, beneath a shady ash on the approach to the church property. That way I was certain to see Abbey as she drew near. Minutes later she came my way.

"Good morning," I said.

"Been waiting long?"

I shook my head. "I like your outfit." Abbey was decked out in a fashionable turquoise hobble skirt.[553] Atop her head, she wore a red hat with a feather. "You look lovely."

"Thank you." She blushed, her high cheekbones a complement to her feathered bonnet. She led the way up the street, so we stood directly in front of the church. The Sun, angling in from the eastern sky, lit the front of the white-trimmed, red-brick structure, turning it into a picture postcard.

"It's a beautiful church."[554]

"Our congregation is proud of it. There are hundreds of its ilk, all around the world. They're generally modeled after London's Saint

---

[553] Goenka, Kanupriya, *Why did the Hobble skirt become popular?,* medium.com, 31 Jul. 2019 <https://medium.com/@kanupriya.goenka/why-did-the-hobble-skirt-become-popular-e86dbdd880>. In the first decade of the 1900s, even as women began demanding more rights and more comfortable fashion, the constricting hobble skirt came into vogue. "Popular between 1905 and 1910, the hobble skirt was so tight at the ankles that the woman wearing it could only walk in very short steps."

[554] For a photograph of the church, *see, First Presbyterian Church (Schenectady, New York)*, Wikipedia, 23 Mar. 2020 <https://en.wikipedia,org/wiki/First_Presbyterian_Church_(Schenectady,_New_York)>

Martin-in-the-Fields, which was completed in 1726.[555] Ours, begun nearly one hundred years later, is a copy of the Ransom Court Presbyterian Church in Philadelphia.[556] Like St. Martin, we have a hexagonal steeple. But unlike Saint Martin with its classical Greek pentagonal front, ours only has a dwarf, Greek-style portico.[557] And we're red-brick Georgian, not the classical Greek stone of St. Martin. We're fancier than some you find across America, but simpler than others." For several seconds, Abbey appeared to study the house of worship, seemingly admiring its familiar details. "Shall we go in?" she said.

We headed up the tree-lined walkway to the front entrance. Even as I looked straight ahead, stares directed our way were palpable. We passed through the open doors.

"For years my family and I have sat in the fourth pew." Abbey guided us there.

Though I might have chosen the back row, wherever she said was fine. We had no sooner seated ourselves in the middle of the bench than a couple passing up the center aisle paused to wish Abbey a good Sabbath. Another woman tapped her on the shoulder with a warm greeting before circling forward on the far-left side. Moments later, a frumpy woman, about seventy, in the row ahead of us, turned our way. She breathed a huffy murmur before looking forward again.

I whispered, "Did you see what that woman just did?"

Abbey nodded, after which she chuckled.

"You find that funny?"

"Yes and no…That's Elvira Hotchkins. She's a busy body, the biggest gossip in the entire congregation."

"She's judging us, isn't she?" I said, continuing to keep my voice low.

"Unfortunately, yes. And no doubt she'll repeatedly communicate her disapproval." Abbey emitted a beleaguered sigh. "God—and please excuse my invoking the Lord's name, especially here in church—if Elvira had her way, New York, like most states, would have an anti-

---

[555] Loth, Calder, *Saint Martin-in-the-Fields and the American Protestant Church*, sacredarchitecture.org, 29 Jul. 2019 <http://www.sacredarchitecture.org/articles/soaring_steeple_and_classical_portico/>.
[556] *First Presbyterian Church*, 1stpreschurchschdy.org, 29 Jul. 2019 <1stpreschurchschdy.org/index.php/about-us/our-history>.
[557] Ibid.

miscegenation statute.[558] I've heard her rail about the abomination, to use her word, of mixing the races."

"I apologize. I've put you in a terrible spot."

"Don't you dare apologize. You've done nothing wrong. For that matter, if anyone did, it is I."

"You?"

"Yes, I invited you here knowing some would object; that a few would even revile us. You, on the other hand, are an innocent victim."

I shook my head. "Not so innocent. I anticipated the issue. But eager to come, I ignored the matter."

"Well…then perhaps we're even. Regardless, neither of us did anything wrong. Bigotry is the problem of the bigots, not ours."

Abbey's reaction dispelled any guilt I might have harbored. Her response was no shock. She was the fair-minded person I knew in my Fort Myers childhood.

"If I were to guess," said Abbey, "and it would be a wild stab, a fair number of our congregants, though admittedly a decided minority, accept interracial couples."

"Nice to know…I think."

"Why the qualification?"

"What you said leaves open the likelihood that the vast majority disapproves. That's hardly reassuring."

"Agreed…but what can I say?" Abbey looked around. "We have here a congregation that happens to be Presbyterian. But like so many other groups, it's made up of a variety of people. Some are kind. Some are backbiters. Some have huge egos. Most, I believe, are honest, but a few, given the opportunity, would steal their grandmothers' gold teeth. It's what you get with any population, a little of this and a little of that." Abbey shrugged. "No group, be it religious, racial, ethnic or whatever, has a corner on truth or righteousness. And for that matter, none has a corner on hate." She rocked her head back and groaned. "I might better leave the sermons for the Reverend."

---

[558] In *Loving v. Virginia*, 388 US 1 (1967), the United States Supreme Court struck down Virginia's 1924 Racial Integrity Act as violative of the Equal Protection and Due Process clauses of the United States Constitution. Mildred Loving, a person of color, and Richard Loving, white, had been sentenced to a year in prison for marrying one another in violation of Virginia's law criminalizing marriages between whites and people of color. *See*, *marriage_miscegenationlaws_map.jpeg,* aclu.org, 2 Aug. 2019 <https://www.aclu.org/sites/default/files/images/racial/justice/marriage_miscegenationlaws_map.jpeg> showing that sixteen states had anti-miscegenation laws when *Loving* was decided and that another fifteen states had such laws in the 1940s.

“Not so.” My reaction was even stronger than my words. Odds were that no homily delivered from the lectern that day would be more profound. Abbey’s views bore similarity to those voiced by Izzy. The reflection prompted a question. With virtually all religions endorsing the moral principles that Abbey and Izzy had voiced, why wasn’t the world more equitable? Abbey and Izzy had already furnished the answer. Every religion included a variety of people, many of whom were mean-spirited and/or hypocrites.

Coming up the center aisle, a man and a woman, accompanied by a small boy, caught my eye. The boy ran his hand over the corner of every pew he passed. The man smacked him on the back of the head, admonishing him sternly. Good chance the man was a mean-spirited hypocrite.

Another question popped into my head. I turned to Abbey. “Your congregation is Presbyterian. Is that the same as Congregationalist?”

“Presbyterians and Congregationalists, as well as Episcopalians, are all Protestants and share similar Christian theology and values. But they’re separate, the greatest difference resting in their polity.”

“Polity?”

“The form of government of a social organization…in this case, a church. Presbyterians are led by ministers and elders. In Congregationalism, each congregation is independent. Episcopalians are governed by bishops.”[559]

I would have continued to explore the subject, but the voice of the minister commencing the service contained me. In English and much shorter than the orthodox Jewish service I had endured the day before, it was far more bearable. As soon as the final amen was sounded, with Abbey’s encouragement, we bolted for the door.

Once outside, she said, “Would you like to come to my house for Sunday afternoon dinner. We could walk for a while first, given that it’s still early.”

“I’d like that, especially along a route that includes nice sites.”

“We could go via Jackson’s Garden. It’s located at the north end of the college campus.”

“Lead the way.”

We ambled east on Union Street, turning north through the iron gates of Union College. After roughly a mile, about twenty-five minutes owing

---

559 *Difference between “Presbyterian” and “Congregationalist”? | Christian Forums*, christianforums.com, 30 Jul. 2019 <https://www.christianforums.com/threads/difference-between-presbyterian-and-congregationalist.771678/>.

to our leisurely pace, we passed through another ornate iron gate, arriving at Jackson's Garden.

"This is it," said Abbey. "I come here often. In the summer when sunset is late, I sit on one of the numerous benches and read a book. In the fall I sometimes take the long way home, so I can pass through. "What do you think?"

"Beautiful…so peaceful."

"That's why I love it." Abbey gestured at a tall tree, one that from a distance resembled a maple. "That's a ginkgo biloba tree, one of two here in the garden. In the fall their leaves turn dazzling yellow. They can live a thousand years and have been around since the dinosaurs.[560] The ginkgo you're looking at was planted by Isaac Jackson, a mathematician. He created the garden way back in 1830. It was the first such garden on any college campus, roughly seven decades ahead of Yale's Marsh Botanical Garden and the gardens at Princeton."[561]

We continued alongside a brook across a bridge, past blossoms of different colors.

"My favorite flowers," said Abbey, "are the scilla with their blanket of purple bells that come out in May and the huge peonies, pink and magenta, that appear in June."[562]

That Abbey had maintained simple tastes, including an appreciation of nature, did not surprise me. A wooden bench adjacent to the creek drew my attention. "Shall we sit a bit?"

"I always do, either to read or just to luxuriate."

We eased down. Nearby, a red-headed woodpecker rapped its beak against the trunk of an oak. The creek's gurgle nearly drowned out the beat of the feathered fowl. The scent of pine, commingled with fragrant flowers, filled the air. I closed my eyes, connecting to a time four decades earlier, when I was alone with Abbey at my favorite spot along the Caloosahatchee. The tenderness of our parting kiss was palpable. Halfway between the past and present, I opened my eyes just long enough to catch a glimpse of her hand resting on the slats. I placed mine atop hers, adding a soft caress. Her hand rotated, such that I held it in mine. My heart raced, much as it had years before. We were in our fifties,

---

[560] *Ginkgo Trees | Buy at Nature Hills Nursery*, naturehills.com, 2 Aug. 2019 <https://www.naturehills.com/ginkgo-biloba-trees>.

[561] *Jackson's Garden a peaceful retreat at Union College | The Daily Gazette*, dailygazette.com, 2 Aug. 2019 <https://www.dailygazette.com/article/2015/05/10/jackson's-garden-peaceful-retreat-union-college>.

[562] Ibid.

but we were children making our first innocent foray into the world of love. With senses heightened, we sat silent, savoring our Eden.

Minutes, glorious minutes, slipped by. Amidst the paradise, words, an unwelcome intrusion, were superfluous. Rapture begged nothing more. But alas, idyll was fleeting. A growing clop invaded our reverie. Opening my eyes, I observed a finely garbed couple, considerably our senior, walking across the very bridge that had led us to Eden. The heels of their shoes pounding the slatted span beat annoyingly. Where Mozart, Beethoven or Bach might have added welcome music, the dissonant percussion despoiled our world. Out of the corner of my eye, I watched the couple turn from the end of the bridge onto the path that passed our bench. I wondered if and how they might react to us, an interracial couple.

"Beautiful day in such a magnificent garden," said the woman. She smiled warmly.

"It is indeed," said Abbey.

"Enjoy the day," said the man.

"You too," I said, as the couple went on their way.

"See that," Abbey whispered. "Not everyone is judgmental."

That Abbey had read my mind was a given. She knew it as well as I. I said, "But unfortunately, the world also has its Simon Legrees. And speaking of him, my favorite book—it still enjoys the prime position on my bookshelf—is *Uncle Tom's Cabin.* You'll never guess who gave it to me."

"Oh, probably some young hussy who was looking to run your life." Abbey took hold of the small pendant watch that hung from her neck. "It's nearing twelve. I don't know about you, but I'm famished. Time we head to my house, where I'll serve you that dinner I promised."

***

Sunday afternoon with Abbey was wonderful. Following a delectable dinner, we rehashed memories of times together at Fort Myers. Each reminded the other of experiences, many at the little schoolhouse, that the other had forgotten. I told her how I had moved back to the cabin of my childhood, fixed it up and how I traded furs and earned an adequate income making and selling dugout canoes. We were like a couple of kids in more ways than one. Thirty years removed from Lucinda's death, a relationship with a woman, courting, was foreign to me. As for Abbey, never married, the time that had lapsed since she had shared a relationship with a man was...perhaps as long as mine. It was not that I didn't want to make a move, but inertia...unease...whatever...I didn't. I reasoned that by taking my time, not pressing Abbey, I could get a better sense of whether she wanted romance. The cogent argument, well thought out, was in truth a product of apprehension, decades devoid of intimacy.

I would have suggested that we spend Monday together, but she had to work at the library. I was pleased when she accepted my invitation to come for her at day's end, at which time I would take her for dinner. That meant my daytime hours would be free. As I prepared to retire for the night, I debated how to spend those hours. An attempt to contact Edison was the obvious possibility. When I had left Fort Myers, I had presumed it would be an integral part of my visit to Schenectady. But now that I was there, something greater than Edison and science had come into my life—Abbey. Not since my days with Lucinda had I experienced such excitement. Nothing was going to interfere, Edison included. Even so, I did not want to burn bridges. Concerned that Edison would take offense if I showed up at his door only to again refuse an offer to work in his laboratory, I decided to defer contact with him until he returned to his Fort Myers winter home. That still left the early hours of the coming day free. Before retiring on Sunday night, I decided how I would spend them.

***

Up almost with the Sun, following an early breakfast, I headed north to the area of Wendell Avenue. Folks had told me that with students on summer recess, Charles Steinmetz regularly went to his office on the Union College campus. Having already verified that his reputation for approachability was well-deserved, I hoped for another chance to speak with him. To suggest that I intended to stalk him would be degrading, but the truth be known, my plan was tantamount to stalking. Well before eight, I began strolling the portion of Wendell Avenue from Rugby Road to Avon Road, about four hundred yards, between which, on my left as I walked north, was the huge, multi-gabled, brick home of Charles Steinmetz. Set on about two acres, about two hundred feet from the sidewalk, the structure bore the style of a Dutch manor.[563]

Up and down the street I walked, frequently pausing beneath the canopy of trees adjoining the sidewalk. From time to time I stopped and pretended to examine their bark. Now and then I crossed over to the

---

[563] *Site of the Home of Charles Proteus Steinmetz Historical Marker*, HMdb.org, The Historical Marker Database, 4 Aug. 2019 <hhtp://www.hmdb.org/marker.asp?marker=50131> containing a photograph of the home of Charles P. Steinmetz from the collection of the Edison Tech Center with credit to Howard C Ohlhous. Steinmetz's home is no longer there.

opposite side of the street. Over the better part of an hour, I made about a dozen passes. One watching me might have suspected that I was casing the area. Finally, the unique gentleman emerged.

"Excuse me," he called out.

I looked around. With no one else in sight, he had to be talking to me. "Yes," I said.

"Can I help you?" He walked in my direction.

"Oh, it's you, Mr. Steinmetz," I said, feigning surprise.

As he drew near, he said, "Vile eatink my breakfast, I noticed you out zee vindow, goink up and down zee shtreet. I recognized you as zee man I met vile ridink my bicycle a few days back. I'm sorry. I forgot your name."

"Mican."

"Mican...Mican." He repeated my name softly, as if committing it to memory. "Are you lookink for somesing, Mican?"

That he had seen me going back and forth discombobulated me. For want of an excuse, I confessed. "I was hoping I might have another chance to speak with you."

"Vy didn't you rink zee doorbell?"

"I...I didn't want to be presumptuous...intrude."

"Vell, if you're game, you can join me in my canoe on zee Mohawk, once I grab my top hat, cigars and pad."[564]

"I'd love to."

"Good. Jusht vait here."

A minute later he returned, wearing a top hat that matched his dark suit and tie. "Ve'll valk down to zee river. Zat's vere I keep my canoe."

He led the way, and I followed. We went a short distance, after which we worked our way generally west toward the river, though I hardly noticed the route as I focused on Steinmetz.

"So, tell me. Vy did you vant to see me?"

The question was simple; yet I found it difficult. "I...I've heard people speak of you...and, as I said the first time we spoke, I...I read a bit about your work with hysteresis...You're..." The glowing adjectives that came to mind were too unctuous to utter.

"...a schort, funny lookink gnome, zee kind people come to see at zee carnifal side schow."

---

[564] Ibid., stating: "At Schenectady Steinmetz built a campsite...on the Mohawk River. During the summer he would work in his canoe, paddling up and down the river. Boards would be placed from gunwale to gunwale to serve as a desk, and he would kneel on a cushion in the canoe doing mathematical calculations. He enjoyed inviting guests to the camp...As host he enjoyed doing the cooking, but refused to do dishes, which became the guests' chore."

"No…no. That's not what I meant at all." I felt not half his size.

"Relax. I know vat you meant. I vas only teasink…And sank you." Steinmetz smiled.

His words eased my embarrassment. I marveled at how he invoked self-deprecation as a device to mitigate my discomfort. Ironically, his brilliance, coupled with an engaging personality, so overshadowed his deformed body and diminutive size that taken in total, he was a giant.

When we reached the river, Steinmetz gestured at one of several canoes. "Zat's mine, second from zee left." Once we lowered it to the shore's edge, he said, "Choose your poison, bow or shtern."

Except when I was a youngster, when my father would take the stern and I, the bow, most of my canoeing had been solo and, naturally, from the stern. I said, "The stern works for me."

We climbed in, pushed off and turned east on the river. We had only gone a short distance when Steinmetz said, "Zis isn't your firsht regatta. You'fe done zis before."

"I've been canoeing as far back as I can remember. As one who is half-Seminole, it's inherent to my heritage."

Steinmetz pulled a big, black panatela from the handkerchief pocket of his suit coat. He slipped it into his mouth between his black mustache and beard and lit it. With an adroitness evidencing years of practice, keeping two hands on his paddle, he spoke while manipulating the stogie in the corner of his mouth. "I lof it on zee rifer, communink vith nature. 'Shpiritual power is a force vich hishtory clearly teaches has been zee greatesht force in zee defelopment of men…Someday people vill learn zat material sinks do not brink happiness, and are of little use in makink people creatif and powerful.'"[565]

A small, steam-powered boat approached. I stroked on the left, directing the canoe more to the right. Steinmetz's words echoed in my head, juxtaposed with an image of his huge home. "So, you don't care about money?"

He glanced back over his shoulder. "'Money is a shtupid measure of achiefment, but unfortunately it is zee only unifersal measure ve haf.'"[566]

[565] *Top 20 Quotes by Charles Proteus Steinmetz | A-Z Quotes*, azquotes.com, 2 Aug. 2019 <https://www.azquotes.com/author/25739-Charles_Proteus_Steinmetz>. (Note: Quotations of Charles Steinmetz, when used in the dialogue of *Bookmarks'* text, as referred to in this footnote and the ensuing six footnotes, have been written in a voice that reflects Steinmetz's German accent. That German accent was added using the methodology contained in *How to Type and Talk With a German Accent,* Instructables.com, 22 Mar. 2020 <https://instructables.com/id/How-to-Type-and-Talk-With-a-German-Accent/>).

[566] Ibid.

His response made sense, but in the context of his words about material things, it seemed odd. I feared that the brilliant man might have mocked me. "Did I ask a foolish question?"

He drew his paddle from the water and turned my way, much more demonstratively than before. "Absolutely not. 'Sere are no foolish queshtions, and no man becomes a fool until he has shtopped askink queshtions.'"[567]

I shifted my paddle to the right side as I digested his comment.

"Since I haf no desire to become a fool," said Steinmetz, "let me ask you a queshtion: Do you believe sere is a God?"

Not knowing his views on the subject, the inquiry unnerved me. "I...I just don't know. I guess you could say I'm agnostic. What do you think, Sir?"

"You're askink me, a scientisht?"

"Yes," I said, not because his profession was an element of my question, but to avoid being argumentative.

"Vell...'In zee realm of science, all attempts to find any efidence of supernatural beinks, of metaphysical concepts, as God, immortality, infinity, etc., haf zus far failed, and if ve are honest, ve musht confess zat in science sere exishts no God, no immortality, no soul or mind, as dishtinct from zee body.'"[568] Steinmetz chuckled. With his paddle, he made a couple of easy strokes. "But ven it comes to God, the exishtence of an all-knowink and all-powerful deity, I haf no more proof san zee next person. Yet on subjects on vich I haf no shpecial expertise, people are more apt to listen to me...'[Z]ee American people are villink to listen to anyone who has attained prominence. Zee main fact is zat ve'fe heard a man's name a great many times; zat makes us ready to accept vatever he says.'"[569]

Paradoxically, his humility, suggesting that his views on subjects outside of science or mathematics were not entitled to extra weight arguably earned them greater credibility. I pulled my paddle, full thrust, twice on the left and then twice on the right. The canoe, responding to Newton's "Third Law of Motion" (For every action, there is an equal and opposite reaction), surged forward. "This is a great river," I said.

"It is indeed. It inshpires me. Zat's vy I come here to vork." Puffing his panatela, he paddled several strokes before looking back my way.

---

567 *Charles Proteus Steinmetz – Wikiquote*, wikiquote.com, 3 Aug. 2019 <https://www/wikiquote.org/wiki/Charles_Proteus_Steinmetz>.

568 *Top 20 Quotes by Charles Proteus Steinmetz,* op. cit.

569 *Charles Proteus Steinmetz – Wikiquote*, op. cit.

"Vater is amazink. It's key to life…Out here, it's a source of inshpiration and recreation. And I believe it vill change zee vay ve lif in zee future."

I suspected that Steinmetz's underlying message was escaping me. I might have kept my ignorance to myself, but given what he had said earlier about questions and fools, I was emboldened. "Change the future? What do you mean?"

"Sink about it. Electricity is changink our vorld. 'Electricity is doink for zee dishtribution of energy vat zee railroads haf done for zee dishtribution of materials.'"[570]

And? Showing my ignorance would have been one thing. Insulting the scientific genius, another. No way was I about to voice the one-word question. Unfortunately, he looked back over his shoulder where my face apparently did the very act my tongue eschewed.

"You don't see—or maybe you doubt—zee link in my reasonink?"

"Only the former," I said sheepishly.

Steinmetz rested the tip of his paddle on the floor of the canoe. He lifted one leg over his seat, turning so his entire torso faced me.

I sensed that he was about to convey something of great import.

"For centuries a majority of zee vorld's population, residink significant dishtances from zee Equator, haf frozen durink zee vinter. Central heatink syshtems, powered by energy, haf enabled people to enjoy a comfortable enfironment. Of course, most in zee vorld lack central heatink. Zee demand for it, for all kinds of sinks powered by electricity, vill grow by leaps and bounds. '[Z]ee electricity generated by vater power is zee only sink zat is goink to keep future generations from freezink. Now ve use coal venefer ve produce electric power by shteam engine, but sere vill be a time ven sere vill be no more coal to use. Zat time is not in zee fery dishtant future…Oil is too insiknificant in its afailable supply to come into much consideration.'"[571]

---

570 *Top 20 Quotes by Charles Proteus Steinmetz,* op. cit.

571 Ibid. (*Bookmarks'* author's comment: This quotation from Steinmetz exemplifies that even the greatest of geniuses are hard pressed to predict the future. More than a century later, the world is still wrestling with the best source(s) of energy to power the future. Water, along with fossil fuels, solar and nuclear energy, has been part of the solution. In the 1970s the United States faced oil embargoes. Discovery of domestic reserves far greater than past estimates mitigated the problem, providing a bridge to the future. But ongoing damage to the environment complicated the issue. Predicting how energy issues will ultimately be resolved is a crapshoot. At this juncture one might, however, contend that whatever the outcome, Steinmetz's belief that water would be key has been proven wrong. Not so fast. While this author would not attempt to foretell the future, with oceans occupying roughly two-thirds of the Earth's surface, water, H_2O, though a longshot, could, with a fundamental scientific breakthrough, provide virtually boundless energy. The development of an efficient controlled fusion process

Steinmetz's analysis was intriguing, not that I had a substantive reaction to it. I was thankful he couldn't read my mind. Silently I celebrated the fact that my home was in Fort Myers where winter temperatures were pleasantly balmy and the issue of bitter cold of no consequence.

For the ensuing two hours we paddled and drifted, conversed and contemplated, and, owing to Steinmetz's influence, soaked in all that the river and its surrounding environs bestowed. When we finally returned to our starting point and pulled the canoe from the water, we wended our way back in the direction of his house. As we passed the Union campus, he said, "I need to shpend some time in zee library, so zis is ver I leaf you. Sank you for the pleasure of your company today."

"Thank *you*," I said, finding it hard to believe that he had expressed appreciation to me. "I had a wonderful time. It was an extraordinary experience, one I won't forget."

"I'm glad ve could do it." Panatela extending from the corner of his mouth, he headed off.

I continued slowly, watching him out of the corner of my eye until an ivy-covered building obscured him from view. A check of my pocket watch confirmed that I had hours to kill before Abbey would get off from work. I headed west to see more of Schenectady, areas yet unexplored. Along the way, a hot dog purchased from a street vendor fed an appetite built while paddling the Mohawk. Delicious as the meaty delight was, it paled in comparison to the banquet I had savored on the river.

***

Shortly after four, having cleaned myself up at the Foster, I began negotiating my way toward the Schenectady County Public Library. En route I stopped at a corner grocery where I picked up some sliced roast beef, two rye rolls, swiss cheese, dill pickles, a bunch of grapes, a small jar of mustard, along with a disposable wooden spreading stick, a pair of

---

(the merger of four hydrogen nuclei to form a helium atom, the ongoing energy process of the Sun), would accomplish this. *See*, Pillington, Mark, *Cold Fusion | Science | The Guardian*, theguardian.com, posted April 9, 2003, retrieved 7 Aug. 2019 <https://www.theguardian.com/science/2003/apr/10/farout> detailing that two chemistry professors from Utah, in 1989, announced that they had achieved "nuclear fusion – normally produced by the intense heat and pressure inside stars – in a glass jar, at room temperature…As the University of Utah's press release stated, the pair may have discovered an 'inexhaustible source of energy,' - the Holy Grail of physics." The experiment did not prove out. Nevertheless, one should not preclude the possibility that one day, fusion reactors, fueled by hydrogen from water, will supplant fossil fuels.)

giant macaroons and several of the recently minted paper plates.[572] I considered a separate stop to buy a bottle of Virginia Dare white wine, but judgment led me to instead supplement my purchases with two bottles of Hires Root Beer.[573]

I took a slightly circuitous route, killing just enough time that I arrived at the library shortly before five. Abbey was working behind the front desk.

"Once we let the last patrons out, I'll meet you on the front stairs."

I went outside. Minutes later Abbey joined me.

I held up my bag of goodies. "Where should we dine?"

"Jackson's Garden is the most convenient."

I gave a thumbs up, and we were on our way, arriving at the familiar site minutes afterward. We found a picnic table not far from the brook, where I unpacked the food.

"Very nice spread," said Abbey.

I gestured at the root beer. "I…I hope you're a fan of soda. I considered a bottle of Virginia Dare but thought better of it." I hesitated, swallowing hard. *Was I about to stab myself in the back?* "As I told you, years ago, after my wife Lucinda died, I…I got hooked on whiskey." I eyed Abbey closely, watching for a reaction. "I've been sober for about a quarter century. Almost never imbibe. The…uh…less, the better."

"Root beer is a favorite of mine," she said, punctuating her words with a warm smile.

I breathed a sigh of relief. Hindsight, much more sagacious than hope, had vindicated the risk of forthright disclosure.

A gourmet feast in the most elegant hall would not have surpassed our simple picnic. Even at moments when conversation grew sparse, a momentary glance, the meeting of our eyes, silently uttered volumes replete with the sweetest prose. We guzzled our root beer straight from the bottle. I laughed. Abbey guffawed as well. Soon, we were both roaring.

"What's so funny?" I said.

---

[572] Donohoe, Ashley, *Paper Plate Facts | Bizfluent*, bizfluent.com, updated February 3, 2020, retrieved 27 Mar. 2020 <https://bizfluent.com/about-5385120-paper-plate.html>. Paper plates were invented in New Hampshire by Martin Keyes in the early 1900s, who established a company in 1903 to make "pie plates out of molded pulp."

[573] Bellis, Mary, *The History of Root Beer and Inventor Charles Hires*, thoughtco.com, updated July 7, 2019, retrieved 7 Aug. 2019 <https://www.thoughtco.com/history-of-root-beer-1992386> stating: "Hires introduced his version of root beer to the public at the 1876 Philadelphia Centennial exhibition. Hires' Root Beer was a hit. In 1893 the Hires family first sold and distributed bottled root beer."

"No idea. You tell me." Her laughter rendered her words barely intelligible.

I shrugged.

We laughed even harder. Tears streamed from our eyes.

I tried to recall the last time I had laughed so wildly...so wonderfully. If ever, it must have been when I was a child, before my father had been taken from me. The somber recollection restored my more typical sober mien. I said, "You'll never guess with whom I spent a chunk of today."

"Charles Steinmetz."

"Who told you?"

"No one. I'm clairvoyant."

"Sure...and I'm Attila the Hun."

Abbey nodded. "That explains your nasty disposition."

"C'mon, tell me—how did you know that I was with Steinmetz?"

"A lucky guess."

Groaning loudly, I threw up my hands.

"Really," she said. "And for that matter, it was almost predictable, once you posed the question. I know how impressed you were with him. No one is more recognizable, and his reputation for accessibility is well-known. He hangs out with the students at one of Union's fraternities, invites all sorts of people to his camp and converses with strangers on the streets."

Though the explanation confirmed what I had observed and heard, it was disillusioning. My self-satisfaction, owing to his willingness to spend time with me, diminished. Regardless, I could forever claim that I had toured the Mohawk River with the great Charles Proteus Steinmetz. No one could take that away.

Abbey and I savored the balance of our meal. Our mood was one of unmitigated ease. The tension that so often accompanied courting was absent. Well...not entirely. Sexual tension was unmistakable. Her laugh at my most insipid attempts at humor, the come-hither smiles that each of us displayed and, most of all, the gazes we exchanged, looking deeply into each other's eyes, smoldered with carnal yearnings begging to be requited.

Our appetites...for food...all but sated, we devoured the macaroons, topping them off with the remains of our root beer.

I noted a curious expression on Abbey's face. "Whatcha thinking?" I said.

She smiled but remained silent, her mien more sphinxlike than when first I had asked the question. Finally, she said, "I was recalling my first kiss...the wonderful moments we shared behind the storehouse at Fort

Myers." She looked me in the eye. "I vaguely referenced it the other day, not that I thought you would remember it."

"You can't be serious. How could I forget it? In case you don't remember, it was my first kiss too."

"So I recall, but we were just kids…and you, a boy."

"Brilliant observation." I dragged out the words to be sure she caught my sarcasm. "What's that got to do with it?"

"Give me a break. Girls remember romance. Boys, on the other hand…" Eye contact, like her voice, trailed off.

"What about boys?" I said, unwilling to let her off easily.

"If you need an explanation, I'll tell you. Boys keep score, how much they get from a girl, how far they get."

I gave her a look. "I take it you've studied this?"

"Not using the scientific method, if that's what you're driving at, but in case you've forgotten, I'm a librarian. I've read hundreds and hundreds of books. The pattern is clear."

"C'mon, you're talking about fiction."

"Fiction, maybe, but based upon life."

"Well, whatever your books may say, anecdotally, I can assure you that my experience does not fit your mold."

"Aha, the exception proves the rule." Abbey winked.

Before I could organize my attack on the all-too-familiar banality, Abbey continued. "Just kidding. I'm glad…very glad you remember our first kiss." She stretched her arm out across the picnic table.

I took her hand in mine, conjuring the image of the marvelous scene from our youth. The possibility that we might recapture it, add a fuller sequel, excited me. I might have tried to kiss Abbey had the picnic table dividing us not been too broad, too restricting.

Conversation, countless details of how we had spent the intervening years, flowed as deftly as the waters of the nearby brook that meandered through Jackson's Garden. So too did time. The Sun dipped behind the western horizon.

"It's nearly dark," said Abbey. "We should be going."

Once we cleaned up the remains of our picnic, hand in hand, we strolled toward her Park Avenue home, arriving there roughly a half-hour later.

Abbey gestured at the sky. The few clouds that had floated above earlier in the day had dissipated, leaving in their wake starlit heavens. "Gosh, that's as many stars as I've ever seen."

In the total darkness that surrounded my isolated Fort Myers home, I had seen more. But the difference was not worthy of mention. "I think you're right." I pointed at the northern sky. "There's the Big Dipper."

Abbey positioned herself, so she could sight along the line created by my arm.

"See, the seven stars, four making the ladle and three more completing the bent handle."

"Yes…and for that matter, once you spot it, it's hard to miss."

We continued to gaze at the Heavens.

"You think anyone else is out there…somewhere?" she said.

"I do."

She studied me. "That's not the answer I expected from a man of science, not without evidence."

"Well, you asked for my opinion, and I gave you my best guess. While I have no proof, statistically it makes sense. There are more than one hundred billion galaxies, on average containing several hundred billion stars.[574] Multiply that out and you have an astronomical number of stars. No pun intended. Uh…on second thought, it was."

Abbey moaned.

"Anyway, with all those stars, each one like our Sun, the logic of statistical probabilities leads me to believe that lots of them have planets, like Earth, that can support life."

"That's not what the Bible says."

"Perhaps…not that I believe the Bible should be taken literally…But let's assume that God created everything, as the Bible suggests. Why create this incredibly vast universe and only put life on a single planet, leaving the other trillions and trillions of solar systems utterly barren?"

Abbey gazed back up at the Heavens. "I see your point." Still looking skyward, she said, "You think we'll ever come in contact with someone or something from another solar system?"

I shook my head.

"Why not?" Her tone suggested my response surprised her.

"It's a simple matter of distance. Alpha Centauri, the nearest star to Earth, except for the Sun, is over four light years away.[575] Getting from here to there is a virtual impossibility. Yes, we now have airplanes, and likely, they will be much more sophisticated in the future. Assuming we build airplanes or other space vehicles that can escape Earth's gravity, do you have any idea how long it would take to get to Alpha Centauri?"

---

[574] *How Many Stars are There in the Universe – Universe Today*, universetoday.com, 10 Aug. 2019 <https://www.universetoday.com/102630/how-many-stars-are-there-in-the-universe/>.

[575] *How Far is the Closest Star | The Sun's Nearest Neighbor*, skyandtelescope.com, 10 Aug. 2019 <https://www.skyandtelescope.com/astronomy-resources/far-closest-star/> indicating that Alpha Centauri is three stars bound together by gravity, the closest of which is the faint star Proxima Centauri, which is 4.24 light years from Earth.

Abbey shrugged.

"Well, let's assume that in the future we build space vehicles that can travel 186,000 miles per hour."

"That's crazy."

"I know, but I'm making the assumption to demonstrate my point. The speed of light is 186,000 miles per second. There are 3600 seconds in an hour, 60 times 60…which means light travels 3600 times as fast as our hypothetical super-speed vehicle. Since light takes more than four years to travel from Alpha Centauri to Earth, it would take our vehicle, incredibly fast as we imagined it, more than 4 times 3600, or more than 14,400 years."

Abbey laughed.

"What's so funny?"

"Everyone on the vehicle would be dead almost two hundred times over."

"On the other hand," I said, my mind engaging in wild self-debate, "if time dilation, as reflected in the Lorentz Contractions and Einstein's recent Theory of Relativity, is made part of the equation, and assuming we could travel very close to the speed of light…a crazy assumption by itself…then people might be able to get there."

Abbey eyed me like I was nuts. "Thanks a heap. Just when I understood everything you had said, you add Relativity to the discussion. I've heard of the esoteric term, but I have no idea what it is or means. And for that matter, almost nobody on this planet does."

"Sorry, I was just thinking out loud, mulling bizarre nothings…But on a less obscure level, there is a way we might make contact with life in other solar systems."

"I'm all ears." Abbey's sarcastic tone and expression contradicted her words.

"Now that we have wireless telegraphy—the wireless telegraph that Marconi invented a little more than a decade ago[576]—perhaps we could send a signal to life in another solar system, or vice versa, using the electromagnetic waves that are implemented in wireless telegraphy. They travel at the speed of light. A message sent from Earth to Alpha Centauri would only take a little over four years."

"You think that would work?"

"Not really."

Abbey shot me a look.

---

[576] *Wireless Telegraphy*, Wikipedia, 10 Aug. 2019 <https://en.wikipedia.org/wiki/Wireless_telegraphy>.

"Sorry, I was only throwing out the idea as a remote possibility. Unfortunately, it's replete with problems. Assuming there are stars with planets supporting life does not imply that satellites of Alpha Centauri fit the bill. The stars with life may be millions or billions of light years away, not just four. Even if they're much closer, how do we find them? How do we direct our signal and get it all the way there? Even if it gets there, who will understand it, let alone pick it up in the first place?" I heaved a sigh. "As I said before, I believe intelligent life exists beyond Earth; unfortunately, I doubt we'll ever make contact."

Abbey and I both turned our gaze back to the sky. Perhaps a half-minute of silence elapsed before she said, "Well, whoever or whatever may be out there in the infinite Heavens, one thing is sure—it's magnificent."

I nodded to her well-taken point.

Our gazes met. Eyes, filled with alluring glow, voiced emotions, drawing us forward. Electricity abounding, we inched closer. Moments later, our lips met…tenderly at first…and then more passionately, as our arms wrapped themselves around each other. A tight embrace, a fiery kiss sustained itself for at least a minute.

Still embraced, when finally our heads drew back, though only inches, Abbey whispered, "Out here on the street, people can see us. Perhaps we best go inside."

The quiescent street appeared deserted apart from us. Making the point, one that would have inhibited the realization of her suggestion, was daft. "Let's go."

Abbey led the way onto the porch where she unlocked the portal. We stepped inside. The door barely closed, we enveloped one another more passionately than before. With our lips locked in enraptured unity, my hand traveled back and forth across her back. It drifted down and slithered around her waist, straying upward so it pressed against the base of her ample breast. Abbey inhaled deeply just as I slid my hand, fully spread, so it cupped the entirety of her glorious contour. Her nipple, pressed against the surface of her blouse, titillated the center of my palm. My fingers caressed her majestic mountain. I began to undo the buttons of her blouse.

Abbey leaned back ever so slightly, putting her hand on the back of mine.

I feared she would put a halt to my passion.

She whispered, "Come with me. We'll be more comfortable." With her fingers draped over the back of my hand, she drew me to the staircase.

We wended our way to a second-floor bedroom, decidedly Victorian, draped in purple and pink, bedecked with two Tiffany lamps, a gold-trimmed dresser and chest, and a canopy bed of carved mahogany. An irony, albeit brief, struck me. Time, four decades, had erased the risk that young lovers face. The possibility of a new life, what a twisted Victorian society labeled a bastard, had evaporated over the intervening years. Puritanical dictates no longer ruled our lives. Societal strictures proscribing not merely our intimacy but also our entire relationship had been eradicated. Love first seeded in the distant ashes of the War of Secession was free to blossom.

With chains unfettered, Abbey and I complemented the innocent kisses of our youth with the passion of adulthood. Lust ignited outside beneath countless orbs flamed with the intensity of those heavenly bodies above. Love, pleasure-filled love, contradicted the well-reasoned science I had enunciated earlier. Abbey and I achieved the impossible—a voyage to the stars.

***

Tuesday morning, Abbey and I slept in. She had arranged in advance to take the day off from the library. It was nine o'clock before we seated ourselves at her kitchen table. She had made a wonderful breakfast of orange juice, blueberry buckwheat pancakes, scrambled eggs, sausage and fresh-brewed coffee. We were about halfway through our meal when she said, "Where are we?"

"Park Avenue, Schenectady, New York."

Abbey furrowed her brow. "C'mon, that's not what I meant, and you know it."

In my defense, I was uncertain exactly what she had intended. Arguing the point seemed futile because I knew her question was more substantive than an inane inquiry as to our physical location. "I hear you, but can you be a bit more specific?"

She laid her fork down and looked me in the eye. "Last night...what was it? What does it mean?"

"Uh...I don't know." Much as I disliked my answer, for the moment, I did not have a better one.

"Was it just a one-time night of passion?"

"I hope not."

Abbey smiled, but in a manner that communicated foxiness. "What does that mean?"

"Just what I said."

"So, you talking about several nights while you're here in Schenectady, and then adieu? Or you referring to a real relationship? And before you answer, understand, I'm not pressing you in any way. If you prefer one night or a few, so be it. Whatever the outcome, I'll cherish what we have."

Abbey's directness was surprisingly welcome. In the back of my mind, the issue had stirred, but I had failed to address it. Chivalry, as well as my conscience, demanded that I be up front. I said, "Having lost you years ago to the arbitrary rules of society, I don't want that outcome to repeat itself. But..."

"But what?"

I sighed plaintively. "I live in Fort Myers, you in Schenectady, fourteen hundred miles apart. How do we bridge that gap?"

"I don't know...unless you'd like to become a Schenectadian?"

"Not really. Would you like to live in Fort Myers?" I asked the question rhetorically, certain Abbey was not eager to move.

"No thanks."

We refocused on our food, though speaking for myself, it was not with the same enthusiasm as before. It wasn't that I was looking for a commitment, and I assumed the same could be said for Abbey. But what was disappointing was the likelihood that our relationship was doomed from the start. I said, "Does this mean that at most we have a fling, one that has no long-term prospects?"

"I don't know, but..."

I waited patiently, yearning for Abbey to add a ray of hope. When it didn't come, I echoed her response from a minute earlier. I said, "But what?"

"Perhaps we were never destined to be together."

As a scientist and one who placed little stock in destiny, the response was unsatisfactory. If I were honest, my objection had less to do with fate than it did with its predicate, that our relationship had no chance.

"I have my home here in Schenectady, and you have yours in the Fort Myers' woods. Both of us love the home we have, its locale. Neither of us wants to give that up. That's not a great formula for a relationship."

"A long distance one, perhaps?" I had barely completed the suggestion than I shook my head. Living fourteen hundred miles apart, several days by train, was hardly a relationship.

"Seems you've answered your own question," said Abbey. With her fork she cut a bite of her pancake and chewed the morsel. "I have to admit that as I've grown older, my distaste for the winters, their bone-chilling winds, has magnified. Sledding and ice skating no longer have the appeal of bygone days. And the novelty of pristine snow is too quickly replaced by icy sidewalks, rut-begotten roads and grungy black slush. The warmth of Fort Myers' winters, the kind I enjoyed when my family was stationed there, would be nice."

Might her musing be the ray of hope I had sought earlier?

"But don't get me wrong," said Abbey. "No way would I abandon Schenectady." She looked me in the eye.

I sensed what she was thinking, at least I thought I did. "I have to admit that Schenectady is lovely in the summer, much more comfortable than Florida's oppressive months of heat and humidity. And too, the change of seasons—I experienced it during my years in South Carolina—is pleasant." What a minute earlier had looked like a stone wall was morphing into a tunnel with a seeming source of light emanating from the end.

"But before we get ahead of ourselves," said Abbey, "there's a problem, one that might be without solution."

"Problem...what do you mean?" I voiced the question, not that I wanted an answer.

"Let me guess, Florida, a deep southern state, unlike New York, has an anti-miscegenation statute. Right?"

"Yes, but..." The idea that third parties would block our relationship, the way Abbey's parents had done more than two score earlier, was outrageous. A way to circumvent the roadblock, sound or not, was begged. I said, "My cabin is off in the woods, five miles south of Fort Myers. I doubt the powers that be would bother us as long as we didn't flaunt our relationship."

"Just what do you mean by...*flaunt*?"

I weighed the word, trying to decipher exactly what I had intended. "If, for example, we seated ourselves in the church on First Street—that's Fort Myers' main thoroughfare—in the pew next to the Wigmeiers—they're very hoity-toity—we could expect trouble. On the other hand, if we minded our own business, I doubt there'd be a problem."

"What could we expect in other public places?"

I pictured the stunning Royal Palm Hotel, with its numerous gables and magnificent row of palms, whose splendor, stretching down Royal Palm Avenue, had earned Fort Myers the moniker "City of Palms."[577] What would it be like if Abbey and I seated ourselves on the hotel's enormous porch, even at the far end, away from the main entrance? Wishful thinking told me most would let us be. A few would give us a put-off look. Some would simply ignore us. Those were the best-case

[577] Grismer, Karl H., *The Story of Fort Myers*, op. cit., p. 145, 181.

scenarios. Doubtless, others would turn the matter into a cause célèbre. Much as I wished I could tell Abbey that Fort Myers would be a welcoming place, it was impossible. She deserved better, an honest answer. "Life for us in Fort Myers wouldn't be all roses." My forthright words plunged a dagger into my heart.

"That's kind of what I expected."

I studied her expression. "If I read you correctly, you're saying it won't work."

Abbey sat motionless for several seconds. "No, that's not what I'm saying." She stared off into space. After a moment of pensive contemplation, she continued. "When we were children, unable to assert our independence, others, my parents to be specific, deprived us of the opportunity to be together. They were good parents. But that said, I'd be hard pressed to name anything they did that I resented more. They claimed it was for my own good. At the time, though skeptical, I yielded to their mature experience, not to mention parental authority. As I grew older, I became more certain of their motivation. They could not bear what to them was shameful, a daughter courted by a boy of color. Their bigotry deprived me of that which should be sacrosanct, the right to choose whom one loves. But not all the blame rests with my parents." Abbey heaved a sigh. "I bear my share."

"You? How so?"

"I could have defied my parents. I could have met with you secretly."

"But with your parents resolute, that would have been incredibly hard."

Abbey nodded. "True, but not impossible." With face reflective, for a moment she remained still. "More important, my failure to flout my parents was influenced by my own ambivalence about our racial disparity. Initially, I was fine with it. But once my parents objected, I had second thoughts. Their influence was enough to counteract my desire to ignore their ultimatum. Not until the time came for us to leave Fort Myers did I realize my mistake, that I had been a fool. That's why I sought you out just before we headed north." Lips pursed, Abbey shook her head. "Of all the decisions I've made over the years, heeding my parents' directive regarding our relationship is the one I rue most. Over the years I've often thought about it. The past couple days I did so again. I know where I stand. No way will I duplicate my error. What others think is irrelevant. I have long since become a free-thinking adult. At this stage of life, well into my fifties, no one can dictate to me, not on this issue. Whom I love is my decision." She looked me in the eye. "You agree?"

"Absolutely…but what about your job at the library?" I no sooner uttered the words than I kicked myself. Was my goal to keep adding boulders until the light emanating at the tunnel's end vanished?

Abbey laughed. "That's not an issue. I can work part-time or volunteer or…not at all. As I told you, my parents provided for me. For that matter, I've provided for myself."

Breathing a sigh of relief, I thought before I opened my mouth, making certain not to dump another load of rocks. "If you're willing to spend part of the year in Fort Myers, I'd be happy to spend part in Schenectady. On second thought, just to be with you, I'm willing to spend time in Schenectady, regardless whether you come to Fort Myers."

"Well, as I said before, I'd love to escape the Northeast winters."

It crossed my mind that with our separate homes, we could enjoy seven or eight or whatever number of months together, with each of us spending the balance of the year in our familiar environs. That was a possibility…but I suspected we would find a way to spend the entire year together, perhaps six months in each place. I took a bite of my pancake, savoring the sweet flavor of blueberries and maple syrup. "Abbey Parker, your pancakes are delicious…Oh, and by the way…I love you."

"I love you too…It's been that way ever since I inscribed it in the book I gave you…let's see (Abbey mumbled briefly under her breath)…forty-two years ago."

"As I told you, I still have the book, *Uncle Tom's Cabin*. I cherish it."

A sparkle lighting her eyes, she said, "I'd love to borrow it. It's been eons since I've read it."

"They must have copies here in the Schenectady Public Library."

"I assure you, they're not nearly as good, plus I have the perfect bookmark to line the pages. Like their owners, book and bookmark have been apart far too long."

"Unfortunately," I said, "the book is in Fort Myers. So, you'll have to come to Florida to read it."

"Not if you bring it here."

"Maybe you'd like to read it twice…both in Florida and here."

Abbey leaned over and pecked me on the lips. "That would be perfect."

I took another bite of my pancake. That pan-fried batter could taste so incredible defied logic. But I had no interest in logic. I basked in the euphoria of life's greatest gift…love.

***

The day before my weeklong reservation at the Foster Hotel ended, I moved in with Abbey. It soon became apparent that my return to Fort Myers was weeks, perhaps months, away. I telephoned Edgar Jones and arranged for the continued boarding of Cinda. Life was a party, akin to the wonderful summer that Lucinda and I had enjoyed the year we were wed. Using the skills I had developed building houses, as well as the St. Augustine Lighthouse, I put Abbey's home into tiptop shape, not that it was in disrepair. Abbey and I picnicked in Jackson Gardens and Central Park. We rode the trolley to Saratoga and Albany. More than once we rented a rowboat and fished the Mohawk. I discovered that Sarah and Izzy had gotten to know Abbey over the many years that they had visited the library after Shabbat services. We invited the lovely couple to Abbey's house for dinner, and they returned the kindness at their home.

I considered returning to Edison's laboratory on the chance that I might see him. Preferring to spend my time with Abbey, and not wanting to again refuse a potential offer to become a mucker, I decided to wait until winter to contact him.

In mid-November, Abbey quit her job at the library, and we traveled to my Fort Myers home for the winter. She adapted to my Florida environs as easily as I had to hers in Schenectady. Her preference for warm winters was immediate. More important, each of us valued the other's companionship and love, the opportunity to be together.

Several weeks following our arrival in Fort Myers, with devilish propensities stirring, I modified Abbey's bookmark. After returning it to the pages of her favorite book, *Uncle Tom's Cabin*, which she was rereading, I hid both bookmark and book.

It was mid-afternoon when Abbey rushed out to the porch where I was working on an equation. "Mican, have you seen *Uncle Tom's Cabin*? I…I've looked everywhere."

Though I knew what she meant, I said, "No, I've never been to Kentucky. But anyway, the story and the cabin are fictional. Right?"

Abbey rolled her eyes. "I'm not referring to the structure. I can't find Volume I and my bookmark."

"Uh…let me see." I scratched my head in dramatic display. "I think I might have seen it." I went inside and, after fetching both book and bookmark, returned to the porch. Eager for an enthusiastic reaction, I handed them to Abbey.

Her lips pursed. She shook her head repeatedly. "Absolutely not!" She looked me in the eye. "How dare you alter my most prized possession?" She pulled the bookmark out from between the pages and began removing the item, a diamond ring, that I had added to its tether.

Crestfallen, I said, "You don't like it?"

"Not on my bookmark!"

"I…I…" Disappointment rendered me unable to find the right words.

Abbey eyed the ring. "As I said, no way does it stay on my bookmark…As for the fourth finger of my left hand, that's another matter." A smile, indeed a smirk, supplanted what had been a pouty face. She said, "I love it. It's beautiful. And yes, I would be thrilled to marry you."

Joy…ineffable joy exploded as I took Abbey in my arms and kissed her.

***

Abbey and I had recently celebrated a joyous Christmas and New Year's Eve. We had wed in a private ceremony before a justice of the peace. Life was wonderful. Abbey had begun working several hours, three days per week, as a volunteer in Fort Myers' tiny library. I was busy creating mathematical models, endeavoring to solve the equations they generated. It was a typical January day, sunny with temperatures in the seventies, when I arrived aboard Cinda at Edison's winter estate. Though he had come to town several weeks before, I had waited until the holidays were over to visit his home. After tying Cinda to a palm, I rang the front doorbell. His caretaker, whom I had gotten to know years earlier when I had helped build the house, answered the door.

"Mican…it's been a long time. Nice to see you."

"You too. Place looks great, as always." I gestured at the surroundings. "Uh…you think I might arrange to see Mr. Edison…at his convenience, of course."

"Just so happens he's out back on his favorite bench overlooking the river. Circle around, and I'm sure he'll welcome you."

I wended my way to the rear, where Edison, shaded by a sprawling mysore fig tree, was seated facing the river. As I approached the great man from behind, I said, "Mr. Edison."

Perhaps only half-awake, he lurched, taking a moment to grab his bearings. "Mican…what a pleasant surprise." He slid to his right and patted the middle of the bench. "Please, come join me. I was communing with nature, allowing my mind to drift…like the waters that amble by."

I sat down next to him.

"How have you been?"

"Good," I said. "And you?"

"Sterling." He spread his arms. "How else could one be amidst these glorious surroundings, not that I need to tell you who knows the area better than I." He looked me in the eye. "I'm glad you came. Just the other day, I told Mina that I have to pay you a visit."

His comment brought a smile to my face.

"Perhaps you've reconsidered my offer and would like to come work in my research laboratory?"

I shook my head abashedly. "My path crossed with my childhood sweetheart. We were recently married."

"That's wonderful. I'm happy for you...I imagine she's from this area. If I recall correctly, you spent your early years here."

"Actually, she's from Schenectady. She has a home there."

"Really...then why not become a mucker? You can have the best of all worlds, both love and science...and, for that matter, nature."

"I already do."

"Someone else, perhaps one of my competitors, another research lab, gobble you up first?"

I shook my head. "I've been doing research...analysis and writing on my own."

"About what, if I may ask. And I'll certainly understand should you decline. With my many patents, secrecy on the front end is familiar."

"No, it's nothing like that. My work is very different from the pragmatic world of your laboratory. It requires nothing more than a pen and paper...and one's brain. I'm playing with equations. Spinning hypotheses and seeing what might reside on the far side of an equal sign. I'm playing with the Lorentz Contractions. I'm exploring the world of modern physics...relativity and the like. It's fascinating. I've sent some letters to mathematicians and physicists, even some in Europe. Whether they'll reply is another matter. In the meantime, I've begun a paper, a manuscript. The working title is 'Beyond Newtonian Physics.' Don't know if it'll ever see the light of day; regardless, I'm savoring my work. Add the love that came into my life, and my cup is full."

Edison smiled. "You're a very rich man, Mican."

Coming from the wealthy inventor and businessman, the words were a great compliment. I said, "I really enjoy our conversations. If it's okay, I'd love to visit you here occasionally."

"On one condition."

More often than not, conditions irked me, but in exchange for the opportunity to spend time with Edison, flexibility was easy. "Tell me what."

"That I can come to your place now and then."

Rather than a burden, the condition was a welcome bonus. "Anytime," I said.

"Like mine, your home is a tranquil retreat in the world of nature." Edison gestured behind us in the direction of his house. "Your manual skills, something on display at both our properties, has to bring you great satisfaction…And that reminds me, I wanted to ask if you would make me a dugout canoe. I've seen your handiwork. I'd pay you, of course…in advance."

"Well, I'll make you one…on one condition."

His brow furrowed. "What's the condition?"

"That you don't pay. That it be my gift to you."

"But…" Edison gazed out at the Caloosahatchee and murmured just loud enough to be audible. "When someone does something nice for you, be gracious. Don't deprive your benefactor of the pleasure." He looked back my way. "You drive a tough bargain…but fair enough."

"Thanks," I said, knowing that my condition was contrary to the astute businessman's preference.

"God…it's glorious here, isn't it?"

I nodded, directing my focus to the beautifully treed grounds, manicured lawn and gardens, and the inexorable flow of the Caloosahatchee.

Conversation, as it had on other occasions, ebbed. Amidst the serenity, we were each left to our own ruminations. Where in the past such a hiatus had me speculating about Edison's thoughts, I zeroed in on my own. A familiar question stirred. *Who am I?* Over the years, I had addressed the issue numerous times, responding with a wealth of disparate answers. A new one flashed into my brain. Despite its complexity, its logic satisfied my mathematical and scientific nature. I knew who I was. I was Mican Reinbow, a Black Seminole, the sum total of that which I was at birth and everything I had experienced thereafter: my childhood days in a Fort Myers cabin and War of Secession fort; my years in Savannah, St. Augustine and Columbia; and most recently, the decades in Fort Myers.

A discordant thought, one that paradoxically undermined the very logic I had just countenanced, popped into my head. Perhaps I was not the sum of all my experiences. Might I be the product? Excellent mathematician that I was, I should have been able to address the incongruity. But the answer escaped me. So too, did a means to calculate the answer. The history of my life experiences became a hodgepodge that lacked a common denominator or other mathematical device to integrate its many units. Ergo, I didn't know who I was. Another time, an earlier year, the anomaly of simultaneously knowing, but not knowing, would have racked my brain. But sitting on the halcyon bank of the Caloosahatchee, I was at peace. Whoever I was, I was comfortable in my skin. Free of worries, I had a home and security. I had mathematical and scientific interests that challenged my mind and made use of my many years of accumulated knowledge. For most, such abstruse matters would have been the font of ennui. For me, they were fascinating diversions, a source of unceasing gratification. As for the unsolved problem of my identity, a singular factor, one that saw emotions supersede reason, squelched my otherwise persistent compulsion to demand a definitive answer. I had something far more valuable. I had a wonderful, loving partner with whom I could share my days and nights…indeed, the entirety of my life. I had Abbey.

www.ingramcontent.com/pod-product-compliance
Lightning Source LLC
Chambersburg PA
CBHW031227090426
42742CB00007B/109

* 9 7 8 1 6 3 8 6 8 0 2 6 0 *